The Limits of Universal Rule

All major continental empires proclaimed their desire to rule "the entire world," investing considerable human and material resources in expanding their territory. Each, however, eventually had to stop expansion and come to terms with a shift to defensive strategy. This volume explores the factors that facilitated Eurasian empires' expansion and contraction: from ideology to ecology, economic and military considerations to changing composition of the imperial elites. Built around a common set of questions, a team of leading specialists systematically compare a broad set of Eurasian empires – from Achaemenid Iran, the Romans, Qin and Han China, via the Caliphate, the Byzantines and the Mongols to the Ottomans, Safavids, Mughals, Russians, and Ming and Qing China. The result is a state-of-the art analysis of the major imperial enterprises in Eurasian history from antiquity to the early modern that discerns both commonalities and differences in the empires' spatial trajectories.

Yuri Pines is Michael W. Lipson Professor in Chinese Studies at the Hebrew University of Jerusalem.

Michal Biran is Max and Sophie Maydans Foundation Professor in the Humanities at the Hebrew University of Jerusalem.

Jörg Rüpke is Fellow in Religious Studies and Vice-Director of the Max Weber Centre at Erfurt, Germany.

The Limits of Universal Rule

Eurasian Empires Compared

Edited by

Yuri Pines
Hebrew University of Jerusalem

Michal Biran
Hebrew University of Jerusalem

Jörg Rüpke
University of Erfurt

CAMBRIDGE
UNIVERSITY PRESS

University Printing House, Cambridge CB2 8BS, United Kingdom

One Liberty Plaza, 20th Floor, New York, NY 10006, USA

477 Williamstown Road, Port Melbourne, VIC 3207, Australia

314–321, 3rd Floor, Plot 3, Splendor Forum, Jasola District Centre, New Delhi – 110025, India

79 Anson Road, #06–04/06, Singapore 079906

Cambridge University Press is part of the University of Cambridge.

It furthers the University's mission by disseminating knowledge in the pursuit of education, learning, and research at the highest international levels of excellence.

www.cambridge.org
Information on this title: www.cambridge.org/9781108488631
DOI: 10.1017/9781108771061

© Cambridge University Press 2021

First published 2021

A catalogue record for this publication is available from the British Library.

ISBN 978-1-108-48863-1 Hardback

Contents

List of Maps   *page* vii
List of Figures   ix
List of Contributors   x
List of Abbreviations   xi
Preface   xiii

Introduction: Empires and Their Space   1
YURI PINES WITH MICHAL BIRAN AND JÖRG RÜPKE

1. From the Mediterranean to the Indus Valley: Modalities and
   Limitations of the Achaemenid Imperial Space   49
   PIERRE BRIANT

2. Limits of All-Under-Heaven: Ideology and Praxis of "Great
   Unity" in Early Chinese Empire   79
   YURI PINES

3. The Roman Empire   111
   WOLFGANG SPICKERMANN

4. The Medieval Roman Empire of the East as a Spatial Phenomenon
   (300–1204 CE)   141
   JOHANNES PREISER-KAPELLER

5. Early Islamic Imperial Space   180
   A. C. S. PEACOCK

6. The Mongol Imperial Space: From Universalism to Glocalization   220
   MICHAL BIRAN

7. The Territories and Boundaries of Empires: Ottoman, Safavid
   and Mughal   257
   STEPHEN F. DALE

8. Delimiting the Realm Under the Ming Dynasty   284
   DAVID M. ROBINSON

9. The Expansion of the Qing Empire Before 1800   316
MATTHEW W. MOSCA

10. All Under the Tsar: Russia's Eurasian Trajectory   342
JANE BURBANK

Index   376

Maps

0.1	Major Eurasian empires, *c*.1 CE	*page* 11
0.2	Major Eurasian empires, *c*.750 CE	13
0.3	Major Eurasian empires, *c*.1700 CE	16
1.1	The Achaemenid Empire	50
1.2	The Zagros area	61
2.1	Shang and Western Zhou	81
2.2	The Warring States world, *c*.350 BCE	84
2.3	The Qin Empire	95
2.4	Early Han Dynasty, *c*.195 BCE	98
2.5	The Han Empire after Emperor Wu's campaigns	100
3.1	Rome, 2nd century BCE	120
3.2	Roman Empire, *c*.44 BCE	124
3.3	Roman Empire under Trajan, 117 CE	129
4.1	Approximate borders of the Byzantine Empire, *c*.1045 and *c*.1118 CE	143
4.2	Network model of the connections between provinces of the Byzantine Empire due to activities of the *genikoi kommerkiarioi* (economic administrators), 673–728 CE	152
4.3	Mobilisation of Byzantine troops for the expedition against Crete, 911 CE	153
4.4	The Byzantine Empire, *c*.600 CE, in a global perspective	156
4.5	The Byzantine Empire, the Abbasid Caliphate and the Carolingian Empire, *c*.840 CE	159
5.1	The rise of the Caliphate, 632–750	184
5.2	The Abbasid Caliphate, *c*.800	195
5.3	The Islamic world, *c*.950	197
5.4	The Islamic world, *c*.1050	200
6.1	Mongol Eurasia, 1206–1368	221
6.2	The campaigns of Chinggis Khan (r. 1206–27)	226
6.3	Conquests of the United Empire, 1206–59	233
6.4	"The Mongol Commonwealth": The Four Uluses, after 1260	238

6.5	The map of integrated regions and terrains and historical countries and capitals	242
7.1	The Ottoman, Safavid, and Mughal Empires	258
8.1	Ming dynasty, *c.*1443	291
8.2	Ming dynasty, *c.*1582	304
8.3	The Seldon Map	309
9.1	Qing territorial expansion, to 1820	325
10.1	Kievan Rus', around 1200	343
10.2	Kievan Rus' and Volga Bulgar in Western Eurasia, *c.*1100	346
10.3	The Golden Horde and Russian principalities, 14th century	350
10.4	Moscow and Kazan, around 1500	352
10.5	Expansion of Moscow, 1300–25	355
10.6	Imperial Russia's expansion, 1613–14	360
10.7	USSR, 1989	367
10.8	The Russian Federation and its neighbors	370

Figures

4.1 Estimates on the territorial extent of the Byzantine Empire, 395–1400 CE *page* 142

4.2a Ethno-geographic origins of eighty-five families of the 'military aristocracy' of Byzantium, 11th–12th centuries 150

4.2b Ethno-geographic origins of fifty-one families of the 'civil aristocracy' of Byzantium, 11th–12th centuries 150

5.1 Al-Muqaddasi, *Ahsan al-Taqasim fi Ma'rifat al-Aqalim.* Depiction of the road network of Arabia 206

5.2 Ibn Hawqal's *Kitab Surat al-Ard*, map of Sistan 207

5.3 Al-Istakhri, *Kitab al-Masalik wa'l-Mamalik* (Persian translation), map of Khurasan 208

5.4 Ibn Hawqal, *Kitab Surat al-Ard*, map of the world 210

5.5 Ibn Hawqal, *Kitab Surat al-Ard*, map of the world 211

5.6 Ibn Hawqal, *Kitab Surat al-Ard*, map of Iraq 212

5.7 Mahmud Kashghari, *Diwan Lughat al-Turk*, map of the world 214

Contributors

Professor Michal Biran, Hebrew University of Jerusalem

Professor Emeritus Pierre Briant, Collège de France, Paris

Professor Emerita Jane Burbank, New York University

Professor Emeritus Stephen F. Dale, The Ohio State University

Professor Matthew W. Mosca, University of Washington

Professor A. C. S. Peacock, University of St Andrews, UK

Professor Yuri Pines, Hebrew University of Jerusalem

Dr. Johannes Preiser-Kapeller, Institute for Medieval Research/Division of Byzantine Research, Austrian Academy of Sciences

Professor David M. Robinson, Colgate University

Professor Jörg Rüpke, Max Weber Centre for Advanced Cultural and Social Studies of the University of Erfurt

Professor Wolfgang Spickermann, University of Graz

Abbreviations

BHAch I, II	Pierre Briant, *Bulletin d'Histoire Achéménide*, I (1997), II (2001)
CIL	*Corpus Inscriptionum Latinarum*
DB, DNa, DPd, DPe, DPh, DSab, DZe	Royal inscriptions of Darius the Great (522-486 B. C.) found at Behistoun (*DB*), at Nash-i Rustam (*DNa*), at Persepolis (*DPd, DPe, DPh*), à Suse (*DSa*) and at Suez in Egypt (*DZe*)
HPE	Pierre Briant, *History of the Persian Empire* (1996)
ILS	*Inscriptiones Latinae Selectae*
KCP	Pierre Briant, *Kings, Countries and Peoples* (2017)
NN	Unedited Persepolis tablets.
PF	Richard T. Hallock, *Persepolis Fortification Tablets* (1969)
PFa	Richard T. Hallock, "Selected Fortification Texts," (1978)
PT	George G. Cameron, *Persepolis Treasury Tablets* (1948)
SPQR	Senatus Populusque Romanus
TADAE	Bezalel Porten and Ada Yardeni, *Textbook of Aramaic Documents from Ancient Egypt*. 4 vols. (1992–9)
TIB	Tabula Imperii Byzantini

Preface

Max Müller (1823–1900), the German professor of religion at Oxford, had famously stated that "He who knows one [religion], knows none." Whether or not this dictum applies to studies of imperial histories is debatable; but what is undeniable is that a growing number of historians – including the editors and contributors to this volume, as well as many colleagues involved in parallel projects worldwide – believe that adding a comparative perspective to the study of "their" empire will enrich them immensely. It is with this understanding in mind that we inaugurate herewith the first volume of what we hope will become a series of studies that compare functioning patterns of major imperial formations in Eurasia.

Two of the co-editors (Biran and Pines) had the fortune to participate in several cross-disciplinary workshops initiated by the late Professor S. N. Eisenstadt (1923–2010). It is the intellectual breadth of our teacher that inspired us to undertake this project and it is to Professor Eisenstadt that we want to dedicate this volume.

This volume would never have been possible without enthusiastic collaboration of our contributors and the other participants at the Erfurt 2015 conference, from which this volume derives, as well as the dedicated research assistance, particularly of Dr. Ishayahu Landa. We thank them all and hope for new rounds of fruitful collaboration.

We are also extremely grateful to the Alexander von Humboldt Foundation, the generous support of which (via Michal Biran's Anneliese Maier Research Award) enabled us to launch our project and convene its first two conferences. In addition, in preparing this volume we were supported by the Israel Science Foundation (grants 240/15 and 568/19) and the Michael William Lipson Chair in Chinese Studies (Yuri Pines), and the European Research Council under the European Union's Seventh Framework Programme (FP/2007–13) through ERC Grant Agreements n. 312397 (Michal Biran) and n. 295555 (Jörg Rüpke).

Introduction
Empires and Their Space[*]

Yuri Pines with Michal Biran and Jörg Rüpke

NEBUCHADNEZZAR: Where are you from?

ANGEL: From there, beyond Lebanon.

NEBUCHADNEZZAR: As established by the great king Nebuchadnezzar, the universe ends beyond Lebanon. This view is shared by all the geographers and astronomers.

ANGEL (LOOKING AT HIS MAP): Beyond Lebanon there are still some villages: Athens, Sparta, Carthage, Moscow, Peking. Do you see? (*shows king the map*).

NEBUCHADNEZZAR (ASIDE): I shall also have the Geographer Royal hanged. (*To the Angel*): The great king Nebuchadnezzar will conquer these villages too.

(Friedrich Dürrenmatt, *An Angel Comes to Babylon*, 1953)

This is a book about Eurasian empires and their spatial dimensions. What were the factors that prompted their expansion and caused some of their leaders to embark on ever more costly wars on the increasingly remote frontiers? And, conversely, what were the factors that limited this expansion? How did the builders and custodians of major empires conceive of their space? And what measures did they take to integrate this vast space into a coherent political entity? To what extent were imperial expansion and contraction influenced by common factors – from ecology to ideology, from military and economic considerations to the nature of the ruling elite? How did these distinct factors influence the trajectories of individual empires?

This book is envisioned as the first in a series of focused studies of the common problems faced by the major Eurasian empires throughout history. We start our discussion by outlining the rationale of our project. Then we present our working definition of the term "empire" and briefly outline three waves of empire formation in Eurasia, introducing therewith the empires on which our project – including the current volume – focuses. The largest part of this introduction is devoted to the analysis of ideological, ecological, military, economic, political, and administrative considerations that prompted the imperial

[*] This research by Yuri Pines was supported by the Israel Science Foundation (grant no. 568/19) and by the Michael William Lipson Chair in Chinese Studies. Pines is indebted to co-editors (especially Michal Biran, who revised the work twice), to the volume contributors and to many other colleagues, particularly Johann Arnason for their critical comments and suggestions.

1

expansion and contraction. In a nutshell, we believe that so many causes – domestic and foreign, subjective and objective – influenced the trajectories of individual empires that it is all but impossible to come out with an "one-size-fits-all" explanation of the empires' spatial dimensions. What is possible is to outline the relative weight of each of these factors and to analyze commonalities and differences in how empires dealt with spatial challenges.

1   Introducing Comparative Imperiology

To understand the background for our endeavor, it will be useful to briefly revisit the changing attitudes to the word "empire" in political discourse at large and in academic circles in particular during the last century. Recall that at the turn of the 20th century, most of the world was ruled by political entities that proudly identified themselves as "empires." Among the major powers of that age, only France and the United States called themselves republics. Lesser colonial powers – Belgium, Holland, Italy, Portugal, and the then recently battered Spain – were headed by kings. Other great Western powers – Britain, Germany, Russia, and Austria-Hungary – defined themselves as empires. Among the non-conquered parts of Asia and Africa, imperial titles (or their equivalents) were borne by the rulers of China, Japan, Korea, Annam (Vietnam), the Ottoman Empire, and Ethiopia. To be sure, some of these "emperors" were not awe-inspiring rulers: think of the puppet emperor of Annam, ruling a French protectorate, or the short-lived "Great Korean Empire" (1897–1910), en route to being fully annexed by Japan. Yet the very fact that these leaders sought an imperial title testifies to the enormous prestige of the words "emperor" and "empire" at that time.

This prestige, however, turned out to be short-lived. Few empires survived the vicissitudes of World War I, and even fewer remained intact after World War II. Since the abolition of the short-lived Central African Empire (1976–9), only the Japanese head of the state continues to maintain the title of emperor, but "empire" is absent from the official self-designation of Japan. This is not surprising. Already half a century ago, an author of one study of imperial formations noticed: "Empire has become an ugly word" (Hazard 1965: 1; cf. Garnsey and Whittaker 1978: 1). Being associated primarily with the predatory imperialism of the 19th and 20th centuries, the idea of empire was denounced by liberals and Marxists alike. It was correlated with enslavement, denial of freedom, and "unnatural" subjugation to a supreme authority (Wesson 1967).[1] Needless to say, this intellectual atmosphere did not encourage systematic studies of past empires.

---

[1] This enmity toward the idea of empire, and the view that it is "unnatural" in distinction to the nation-state, can be traced back to Johann Gottfried von Herder (1744–1803). For him and other late 18th-century critics of the imperial idea, and their failure to influence the 19th-century European political thought, see Muthu 2009.

It is against this backdrop that we can understand the immense audacity of S. N. Eisenstadt, who in the early 1960s undertook a bold project of outlining a political typology of the major imperial formations in human history (Eisenstadt 1963). Back then, few if any scholars followed his lead. Throughout the rest of the 20th century, discussions of empires were overwhelmingly focused on the immediate context of the modern-age imperialism and its historical roots (for a notable exception, see Mann 1986). In the meantime, the rapidly accumulating knowledge of the historical peculiarities of each of the major empires of the past has challenged the very possibility that a single scholar – even as brilliant as Eisenstadt – might create an analytical framework able to satisfy critical historians.[2] This may have further discouraged the continuation of Eisenstadt's project.[3]

And then, after a very long lull in interest in empire, the pendulum started swinging back. Since the beginning of the 21st century, and especially in the last decade, the number of publications related to empires as distinct political formations has increased exponentially. Dozens of collected volumes and monographs have appeared, and the pace of publication has accelerated. These volumes differ greatly in their emphasis. Some introduce different case studies of imperial formations worldwide (e.g., Alcock et al. 2001; Münkler 2007; Gehler and Rollinger 2014), while others are more focused spatially or temporally (e.g., Morris and Scheidel 2009; Cline and Graham 2011; Düring and Stek 2018). Some offer a systematic comparison between a few paradigmatic empires, notably the Roman and Chinese Empires (Mutschler and Mittag 2008; Scheidel 2009; Scheidel 2015), while others try to re-chart world history from a distinctive "imperial" perspective (e.g., Burbank and Cooper 2010; Reinhard 2015a). Some focus on empires as promoters of commercial and cultural interaction (Kim et al. 2017; Di Cosmo and Maas 2018), others explore their administrative systems (Crooks and Parsons 2016a), their policies of cultural integration (Lavan et al. 2016a), their cultural arsenal (Bang and Kolodziejczyk 2012), and the like. One cannot but be impressed by the immense richness of these recent studies.

There are many reasons for the renewed interest in the imperial formations of the past among historians, sociologists, and more recently political scientists. Some are related to immediate political contingencies. What appeared at the beginning of the 21st century as the unstoppable rise of US unilateralism and militarism aroused stormy debates about the relevance of past imperial projects

---

[2] Eisenstadt himself may have realized this difficulty. In his comparative study of urbanization (Eisenstadt and Shachar 1987), he opted at least for a co-author.

[3] Note that whereas Eisenstadt's impact on historians remained limited, his book had a larger impact on sociologists. The imperial visions, elites, and strategies that he discovered were the main themes that ultimately led to the civilizational turn of the 1970s and a radical break with structural-functionalism (Johann Arnason, personal communication, 2018).

to the current US trajectory. Social scientists and historians alike participated in subsequent heated exchanges (see, e.g., Mann 2003; Ferguson 2004; Pomper 2005; Calhoun et al. 2006; Münkler 2007; Pitts 2010; Kagan 2010; McCoy 2012; Blanken 2012, and many others). This is an understandable and common phenomenon of what in China is called "using the past to serve the present."[4] For social scientists, analyzing early empires through the prism of modern politics may well be advantageous, but for historians there is a major pitfall: contemporary concerns may dictate a selective reading of the past and the glossing over of important phenomena that are irrelevant to current questions. Worse, some scholars may be prone to dismiss previous imperial experiences just in order to reject the dangers of modern imperialism (e.g., Parsons 2010).

Yet immediate contingency aside, other developments in recent decades have brought about the resurrection of interest in empires. The most notable was the weakening of the erstwhile paradigm of the progressive shift from empires to "natural" nation-states. The erosion of certain aspects of nation-state sovereignty in the rapidly globalizing world, most notably the formation of the European Union, caused many scholars to critically rethink the centrality of nation-states in world history. Parallel to that, the bloody conflicts of the 1990s with their element of ethnic cleansing (e.g., in the former Yugoslavia and Rwanda) further undermined the nation-state appeal. It is against this backdrop that historians turned to imperial examples, absolving the word "empire" from its previous pejorative connotations (Burbank and Cooper 2010; Lavan et al. 2016b). Other scholars questioned the empire/nation-state dichotomy, arguing that at least in some cases empires acted not as an antithesis but as direct precursor to nation-states (Kumar 2010; Berger and Miller 2015; cf. Malešević 2017). As explorations of the imperial trajectories of the past advanced, scholars were able "to shed ourselves of the nineteenth-century baggage which tended to present the great agrarian empires as avatars of stagnation" (Bang and Bayly 2011b, 8). The road to open-minded exploration of the past empires had been cleared.[5]

It is these later trends that inform our project. We want to address Eurasian empires by focusing on their own dynamics: neither through modern, nor through post-modern (Negri and Hardt 2000) lenses; neither as an antecedent to nation-states, nor as a foil to current superpowers or transnational organizations. Empires are fascinating in their own right: owing to their past prestige,

---

[4] For instance, much of research on early empires in the 19th-century United Kingdom was intrinsically linked with the contemporaneous imperial project (see Bayly 2011). Historically, astute empire builders worldwide were keen students of past precedents (for one example, see Elliott 2005).
[5] For a good example of changing attitudes toward empires, see a highly positive account of the imperial enterprise in Yuval N. Harari's popular *Sapiens: A Brief History of Humankind* (Harari 2015, 188–208).

their lasting cultural impact, their remarkable successes, and also to their failures and the historical lessons that can be learned from these. A systematic comparative analysis of major imperial formations in the past will contribute, so we hope, not just to the nascent field of "comparative imperiology," but also to broader studies of Eurasian and global history.

Our project, of which the current volume is the first publication, is aimed to further develop "comparative imperiology" by proposing systematic analyses of certain aspects of empire-building. We want to single out common problems faced by major imperial polities and to investigate how different empires in various parts of the world and in distinct periods of imperial formation tackled those problems. Rather than producing a single volume that would try to amalgamate the entire imperial experience across time and space, we aim at a series of publications with well defined sets of questions addressed by all the contributors. The current volume, which deals with the questions of imperial space and its perceptions, is the first step in this direction.

2   What Is an Empire?

One of the trickiest questions for authors and editors of comparative studies of empires is the definition of empire. The long history of the term "empire" and of its derivative and related terms (Latin *imperium, imperator,* or modern "imperialism") creates inevitable terminological confusion (see, e.g., Reynolds 2006). Not a few theorists reject the possibility of producing an adequate definition at the current stage of our knowledge. For instance, Johann Arnason (2015, 494) plainly states: "Given the enormous variety of imperial regimes, and the unsatisfactory state of comparative research, we cannot begin with a general definition of empire as a category." This is a fair assessment (and a fair criticism of comparative research), but it cannot serve as a starting point for a comparative volume. After all, without producing at least a temporary working definition of what an empire is we cannot proceed toward selecting case studies for a comparative endeavor. Although not all of the comparative volumes start with the discussion of what an empire is, several authors and editors did provide useful answers. For instance, Burbank and Cooper proposed:

Empires are large political units, expansionist or with a memory of power extended over space, polities that maintain distinction and hierarchy as they incorporate new peoples. (Burbank and Cooper 2010, 8)

Burbank and Cooper contrast the empire with the nation-state, which "proclaims the commonality of its people" and "tends to homogenize those inside its borders and exclude those who do not belong." The problem of this juxtaposition, however, is that nation-states are a relatively recent phenomenon, and it is not clear how to apply the distinction between empires and smaller-scale states in pre-modern periods. This may lead to some questionable conclusions, such as the one reached by Reinhard (2015b, 15): "in the period 1350–1750, there are only 'empires' throughout the world."

One of the most sophisticated recent discussions of empires and states is that by Goldstone and Haldon (2009). They concluded that empire is:

A territory . . . ruled from a distinct organizational center . . . with clear ideological and political sway over varied elites, who in turn exercise power over a population in which a majority have neither access nor influence over positions of imperial power. (Goldstone and Haldon 2009, 18–19)

Goldstone and Haldon's construct is surely more impressive than a minimalistic definition according to which certain states were empires "because they identified themselves as empires" (Kagan 2010, 9). However, it still poses an immediate problem, well identified by Goldstone and Haldon themselves: it turns an empire into "the typical formation by which large territorial states were ruled for most of human history." Once again, the definition becomes so inclusive as to undermine the possibility of meaningful discussions of imperial peculiarity.[6]

The inclusiveness of the above definitions is mirrored in a great variety of recent volumes that discuss imperial formations (e.g., Alcock et al. 2001; Reinhard 2015b; and even, despite their attempts to narrow the definition of empires, Bang and Bayly 2011a). This inclusiveness is understandable and even laudable as an antidote to the narrow Eurocentric discussions that dominated studies of empires until the relatively recent past (of which Doyle 1978 is a paradigmatic example). However, eagerness to recognize a great variety of pre-modern and early modern polities as "empires" creates a new set of methodological problems. Sheldon Pollock complained:

The term [empire] has become so elastic that scholars can speak, without qualification, of a Swedish or a Maratha empire in the seventeenth century, a Tibetan or a Wari empire a millennium earlier. (Pollock 2006, 177)

Pollock's complaint is understandable. At times, it seems that the number of polities that can be qualified as "empire" is almost limitless. Should, for instance, the Athenian *thalassokratia* count as an empire?[7] Or regional regimes

---

[6] In distinction from most other analyses of the term empire, Münkler (2007, 9) proposes to start with a temporal rather than spatial definition. He qualifies as empires polities that "have gone through at least one cycle of rise and decline and had begun a new one." It is an interesting interpretation, but not necessarily useful in determining the distinctions between empires and other large polities. Besides, even a short-lived empire – such as Qin (221–207 BCE) in China or that of Alexander the Great – could have a tremendous long-term impact.

[7] For an excellent discussion which tends to answer negatively, see Morris 2009; cf. Smarczyk 2007.

on Chinese soil during the periods of political fragmentation, even when they controlled just a single province far away from the traditional loci of imperial authority (Schafer 1954)? Or sub-Saharan Ghana (7th–11th centuries) (Tymowski 2011)? Or the "Angevin empire" (1154–1204) (Gillingham 2016)? Or the "kinetic empire" of the Comanches in the 19th century (Hämäläinen 2008)? The answers to each of these questions may well be positive.[8] But there is an obvious danger that by trying to cast our net as widely as possible, we weaken our ability to identify distinctive imperial cultural and political repertoire. Therefore, as the first step it would be advisable to focus only on major imperial polities, the qualification of which as empires is less controversial. Having properly understood their patterns of functioning, we may then utilize these understandings for analyzing other imperial and quasi-imperial cases.

This need to narrow the definition of empire was noticed recently by Bang and Bayly, who proposed a concept of "world empires":

We have emphasized those that could credibly be called world-empires; in other words, vast empires that dominated their wider worlds and were able to absorb many of their competitors and reduce them either to taxpaying provinces or tributary client kingdoms. Their rulers saw themselves as universal emperors, claiming supremacy over all other monarchs. (Bang and Bayly 2011b, 6–7)

We consider Bang and Bayly's narrower definition as a step in the right direction. In what follows we shall confine ourselves to what they define as "world empires." Two of their points – the universalistic pretensions of the empire's leaders and their ability to dominate their wider world – fit well with each of the case studies discussed in this volume. Moreover, as we shall argue below, it is precisely the avowed desire to attain "universal" rule – at the very least within the empire's macro-region – that distinguished the empires from other expansive territorial states or European colonial powers. Without at least a pretension to maintain superiority over its neighbors, an empire loses its most essential imperial feature.

This understanding explains why we have opted to leave European colonial powers out of this volume. (The only exception is Russia, which, as Burbank [Chapter 10] demonstrates in this volume, was primarily indebted to the Mongolian, or in Burbank's definition, "Eurasian" mode of empire-building.) Europe did not lack individual emperors who tried to dominate the entire continent (and not just their overseas colonies): Charles V (1500–58) (Tracy 2002) and most notably Napoleon (Woolf 1991) come immediately to mind. Yet they were exceptions, not the rule. For most of the time, European colonial empires could satisfy themselves with a status of equality with other major continental powers, or, at most, strive for the *primus inter pares* type of

---

[8] For the most extreme example of inclusive approach, see the recently published *Encyclopedia of Empire* with over 400 entries (MacKenzie 2016).

dominance (as was observable in the case of Great Britain). This normative acceptance of equality with neighboring states distinguishes European colonial empires from their Eurasian predecessors. Hence, for the time being, we prefer not to discuss these case studies and focus on the empires with less equivocal universalistic claims.

3   Eurasian Empires: Spatial and Temporal Distinctions

Our exploration of "world empires" is limited to the Eurasian continent (including North African regions that were ruled from time to time by Eurasian empires). This spatial focus is not fortuitous. Eurasia comprises no less than five macro-regions – namely, Europe, the Near East, the Indian subcontinent, the steppe belt of Inner Asia, and continental East Asia – that are useful for the comparative study of empires. The macro-regions as defined here are primarily a heuristic construct: namely, vast areas within which human interaction (and the resultant cultural cohesiveness) is usually higher than with the outlying areas. The boundaries of the macro-regions are defined primarily by topography and ecology, especially in the case of the Indian subcontinent and East Asia, in which mountain ranges and deserts separate the agriculturally productive heartland from other macro-regions. In the case of Europe and the Middle East, topography is less inhibitive of intensive contacts and the borders of the areas to the north and to the east of the Mediterranean are less clearly defined. This said, for most of human history, these areas were sufficiently politically and culturally distinct to merit treating them as two separate macro-regions. As for the Inner Asian steppe belt, it is distinguished from other Eurasian areas less by topography and more by a peculiar climate and soil quality that make most of this huge region less productive agriculturally but exceptionally fit for pastoral nomadism. Nomadic mobility and the lack of natural barriers between the steppe and other macro-regions allowed the steppe empires to penetrate other macro-regions (and even to rule parts of them) more easily than was possible in other cases. These penetrations and borrowings from sedentary neighbors notwithstanding, the nomads continuously maintained their distinctive political culture (Biran, Chapter 6, this volume), which allows one to speak of the steppe belt as a specific macro-region.

These five Eurasian macro-regions were selected for this study because of the exceptional importance of imperial formations in their history.[9] First, each had an imperial experience of over twenty centuries. Second, major empires established in each macro-region had a profound impact on the political, social,

---

[9] To be sure, other parts of the Eurasian continent, such as Southeast Asia, also had their own imperial or quasi-imperial experiments, but, arguably, these were usually shorter and less consequential for their macro-region's history. Hence, these areas are not discussed in our volume.

and cultural history of their respective realms. Third, and importantly for our endeavor, these major empires are usually well documented (through transmitted texts, paleographic sources, and material evidence, or at least through the accounts of their neighbors, biased as they may be), which allows meaningful reconstruction of their distinct trajectories and their political and cultural repertoire. Moreover, although our study does not focus on modern and current politics (except for the final part of Burbank's Chapter 10), it is worth noticing that the imperial past continues to influence the present-day dwellers of each of these macro-regions in myriad ways.

Speaking of macro-regions is furthermore heuristically convenient because most (but not all) of the empires self-styled as "universal" were focused primarily on ascertaining their direct or indirect control over their macro-region, while accepting – openly or tacitly – that areas beyond their immediate realm could neither be fully incorporated nor even meaningfully subjugated. It should be immediately emphasized here that the Eurasian macro-regions were by no means isolated from each other. Some exceptionally powerful imperial polities – from the Achaemenids to the Romans, the Caliphate, and, most notably, the Mongols – were able to transcend, even if briefly, their macro-regional boundaries. More importantly, the rise of the earliest empires in the three western and two eastern regions was an inter-connected process (see below). Moreover, aspects of the imperial repertoire could travel across Eurasia (sometimes even from one edge to another). We should not err by over-emphasizing macro-regional exclusivity. This said, the basic political trajectory of imperial (and non-imperial) formations in each of the macro-regions was usually more indebted to the region's indigenous political culture than to outside influences.

Speaking in macro-historical terms, it may be useful to discern three periods in Eurasian imperial history. The first, spanning the middle of the 1st millennium BCE to the first centuries of the Common Era (but with much earlier antecedents in Mesopotamia), can be called the age of early or "first-wave" empires. In Mesopotamia, the first quasi-imperial polities had already appeared by the end of the 3rd millennium BCE, and by the end of the 2nd millennium BCE territorial expansion had become a regular feature of governance, especially in the case of Assyria (c.1300–609 BCE). This expansion radically intensified in the last century and a half of the so-called Neo-Assyrian Empire and its successor, the Neo-Babylonian Empire (609–539 BCE). The latter was taken over by the Achaemenids (539–333 BCE), who dramatically expanded the territory under their control, becoming, arguably, the first "world empire" in Eurasian history (Briant, Chapter 1, this volume). The Achaemenid realm spanned the entire area between the Indian subcontinent and Europe. Their imperial enterprise (inherited and briefly reenacted with even more grandeur by Alexander the Great [356–323 BCE], "the last of the Achaemenids" [Briant 2002: 876]) had profound influence on both fringes of the Near East. In the east, it may have contributed to the formation and functioning of the Maurya Empire (late 4th to early 2nd centuries BCE), the first imperial entity on the Indian subcontinent (Pollock 2005). In the West, through Alexander's intermediary, it contributed first to the Hellenistic empires (Strootman 2014), and ultimately to the Roman Empire, the single most successful continental imperial enterprise on European soil (Spickermann, Chapter 3, this volume).

Independent of these developments, a parallel process of imperial formation started on the opposite edge of Eurasia. Early dynastic entities in continental East Asia, the Shang (*c*.1600–1046 BCE), and Zhou (*c*.1046–255 BCE), were not empires but contained the seeds of the future imperial repertoire much like early Mesopotamian quasi-imperial entities. The disintegration of the Zhou polity brought about a prolonged period of intense inter-state competition, during which the ideal of political unification of "All-under-Heaven" as the only means for ensuring lasting peace came into being. The Qin unification (221–207 BCE) was the realization – albeit violent and much maligned in later generations – of this common ideal. The Qin model, modified under its heir, the Han dynasty (206/202 BCE–220 CE) became the foundation of subsequent Chinese imperial regimes (Pines, Chapter 2, this volume). Parallel to the Qin unification, the formation of the first nomadic empire – that of the Xiongnu – took place. This empire was preceded by a long period of political experimentation among earlier nomadic polities and the fashioning of a nomadic culture that stretched across the Eurasian Steppe (Khazanov 2015), but the scope and relative stability of the Xiongnu empire were novel in the steppe. The simultaneous appearance of East Asian and Inner Asian empires was not accidental, although the precise nature of the relations between the two processes is still debated (Barfield 1989 vs. Di Cosmo 2002) (Map 0.1).

These first-wave empires played an exceptional role in the subsequent history of their respective macro-regions. They were a source of inspiration for future empire builders. Their political repertoire and its associated cultural symbols were utilized and reinterpreted by numerous political entities within their macro-region and beyond. Their memories lived for centuries and in some cases for millennia to come; their cultural impact is perceptible well into our days. These were also among the most innovative and audacious imperial polities in human history. Aside from synthesizing, adapting, and modifying institutions and practices borrowed from their predecessors and from subjugated contemporaries, these empires had to develop new modes of rulership and a new cultural repertoire to deal with their extraordinary broad space. Having no clear imperial precedents in their respective macro-regions, the leaders of these early empires were most prone to improvise, to develop novel methods of governance, and also to stretch the limits of territorial expansion, as discussed in section 4.

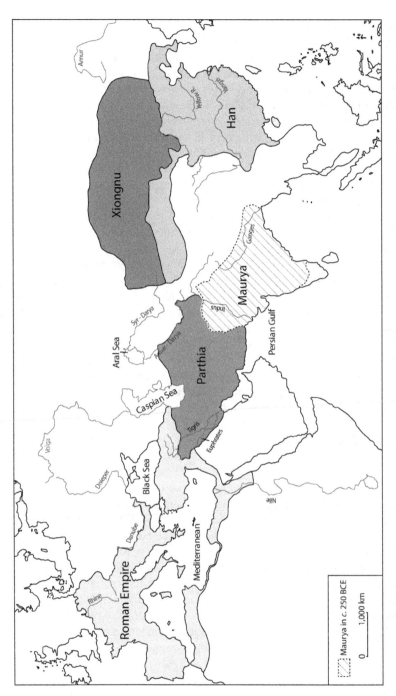

Map 0.1 Major Eurasian empires, c.1 CE. Produced on the basis of the "Interactive World History Atlas since 3000 BC" (http://geacron.com/home-en/?sid=GeaCron44764).

Eventually, these early empires entered into their distinctive systemic crises, causing major setbacks to the imperial rule throughout the continent. The crisis first erupted in the Indian subcontinent, where the Maurya empire did not long outlive its most illustrious ruler, Aśoka (r. *c*.268–232 BCE) (Thapar 1961). In Europe and the steppes, the empires survived for much longer, but in both cases the demise of the Xiongnu and the Roman empires caused a prolonged lull in empire-building. Elsewhere (the Near East and East Asia), the rupture was less dramatic, and the imperial system remained largely intact. Yet even the largest empires formed in the second quarter of the 1st millennium CE – such as the Roman Empire of the East (Byzantine Empire) (330–1204; Preiser-Kapeller, Chapter 4, this volume), Sasanian Iran (224–651), some of the Chinese post-Han dynasties, most notably Northern Wei (386–534), as well as the Indian Gupta Empire (fourth-sixth centuries) and the Rouran Khaganate (402–555) in the Mongolian steppes – invariably failed fully to restore the grandeur of their predecessors, especially in spatial terms.

By the 6th and 7th centuries CE we witness the formation of more successful imperial regimes across the continent. Sui (581–618) and Tang (618–907, prosperous until 755) in China, the Turkic Khaganate (552–630/659 and 682–744) in the steppes, and most notably the Arab Caliphate (632–1258, with its peak in the first two centuries) in the Near East and beyond – all succeeded in matching or even outdoing their predecessors in terms of territorial expansion, domestic stability, and dazzling prosperity (Map 0.2). Most of these "second-wave" empires – with the notable exception of the Caliphate – tended to present themselves as restorers of past imperial glory in their macro-region, and were less committed to driving outward into the unknown. Nonetheless, territorially speaking, two of these empires (the Turks and Tang) succeeded, even if briefly, in expanding beyond the limits of the Xiongnu and Han, respectively, thereby becoming an additional and more attractive source of inspiration to future imperial entities in their realm and beyond.

The second age of imperial prosperity did not encompass all of the macro-regions discussed here. In the post-Gupta Indian subcontinent several expansive territorial polities emerged, but these were markedly smaller than either the Maurya or the Gupta empires. In Europe, the successors of the Roman Empire – the Carolingians (800–88) and later the Holy Roman Empire in the West (inasmuch as the latter qualifies as an "empire" at all, which is debatable),[10] and the badly battered Byzantine Roman Empire in the East – remained unable to reenact Roman successes, and in the West were not even able to ensure domestic stability for more than a generation or two. Ultimately, in the history of both India and Europe major continental empires became an exception rather than the rule.

[10] For a short take on this long-debated question, see Scales 2018.

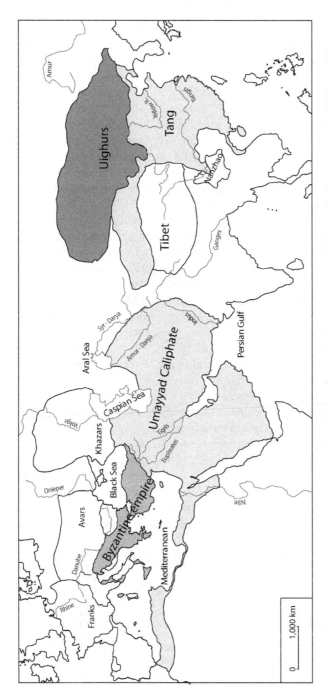

Map 0.2 Major Eurasian empires, c.750 CE. Produced on the basis of the "Interactive World History Atlas since 3000 BC" (http://geacron.com/home-en/?sid=GeaCron44764).

In the mid-9th century major empires in Eastern and Western Eurasia entered a new period of prolonged crisis. The Abbasid Caliphate weakened by domestic struggles disintegrated after 861 into what can be called the Muslim Commonwealth: the caliphs preserved their nominal authority over much (but not all) of this commonwealth, but were stripped of a large part of their political power (Bonner 2010; Kennedy 2010; cf. Peacock, Chapter 5, this volume). In the steppe, the extinction of the politically highly successful Uighur Khaganate (744–840) left a power vacuum that was not filled in for centuries to come (Drompp 1999). And in China, the partial resurrection of the Tang dynasty in the early 9th century came to an end with a series of popular rebellions from which the Tang had never recovered, eventually collapsing in 907 (Peterson 1979; Somers 1979).[11]

The 9th century crises had severe repercussions on imperial polities. Throughout Eurasia, the multi-polar systems ("commonwealths"; see more section 4.2) replaced the previous situation in which a single major locus of gravity existed in every macro-region. This multi-polarity was true even in the East Asian subcontinent (Rossabi 1983), where the ideological aversion to political fragmentation was the greatest (Pines 2012: 11–43).[12] Empires formed in the 10th century and later were more modest in their ambitions than their predecessors, and in certain macro-regions, notably the steppe, no empire rose to power for several centuries. Had this situation continued, one may speculate that even the discourse of universality and imperial inclusiveness would have eventually died out. However, this discourse – and the accompanying praxis of an expansionist empire – was resurrected on an unprecedented scale with the advent of the Mongol Empire (13th–14th centuries).

Mongol rule was unique in Eurasian history. For the first and last time, three of the five imperial macro-regions (and precisely the three where the "second-wave" empires were most successful, namely, East Asia, Inner Asia, and much of the Near East) were controlled by a single ruling house (Biran, this volume and Map 6.1, p. 221). The Mongols' century and a half or so of effective control (1206–1368) reshaped the political, social, and cultural dynamics of these regions for centuries to come (Biran 2007, this volume). No single imperial polity, with

---

[11] The crises that struck major Eurasian empires in the middle of the 9th century (to which one may add the disintegration of the Tibetan Empire in 842 and, on the other edge of Europe, of the Carolingians after 840) were not related to each other. In East Asia, however, they may have been exacerbated due to the severe 9th-century drought (Di Cosmo et al. 2018).

[12] It should be mentioned here that multi-polarity existed in East Asia much earlier: e.g., during the first decades of the Han dynasty, which had to acquiesce to the bi-polar contest with the Xiongnu (Pines, Chapter 2, this volume) and during the lengthy period following the collapse of the Han dynasty in 220 CE. It remained visible even in the period of the Tang dynasty's ostensibly unilateral hegemony (Wang Zhenping 2013). What differed in the 10th to 13th centuries is that the main Chinese dynasty, the Song, had to accept what Wang Gungwu (1983) aptly names "the rhetoric of a lesser empire," undermining therewith its own legitimacy. For the impact of this dramatic change of mind on Song's self-perception, see Tackett 2017.

the major exception of Britain at the apex of its imperial expansion in the 19th century, could rival the Mongol impact throughout the Eurasian continent.

One of the many aspects of the Mongol impact was the reinvigoration of empire-building across Eurasia. The new continental empires that emerged between the 14th and 17th centuries were all indebted to the Mongols, even though this debt was not always readily acknowledged. These "third-wave" or post-Mongol empires include Russia (Burbank, this volume), Chinese Ming (1368–1644, Robinson, Chapter 8 this volume), Manchu Qing (1636/1644–1912, Mosca, Chapter 9 this volume), and the Islamic empires of the Timurids, the Ottomans, the Safavids and the Mughals (for the last three, see Dale, Chapter 7 this volume; Map 0.3). Oddly, the weakest post-Mongol empires were those established in the steppe regions, particularly in Mongolia itself, where the Chinggisid charisma was not enough to overcome either the steppe's centrifugal forces, or the rivalry of the post-Mongol sedentary empires. Ironically, the post-nomadic empires that built on the Mongol experience while combining it with the rich resources and improved technology of the sedentary population – Russia and the Qing China – succeeded in eventually subjugating the descendants of Chinggis Khan (Perdue 2005; Allsen 2015; Biran, this volume).

Our volume aims to provide a sample of major imperial cases from each of the regions and periods under discussion. We first introduce three major first-wave empires (the Achaemenids, Qin-Han China and the Roman Empire). The second-wave empires are represented by the Roman (Byzantine) Empire of the East and the Caliphate. Finally, the Mongol and post-Mongol empires merited five contributions, covering the Mongols themselves, the Muslim empires in Near East and South Asia (the Ottomans, the Safavids, and the Mughals), Ming and Qing China, and the Russian Empire. The result, we hope, is a fair and balanced presentation of major case studies. Below we shall outline the major parameters of our discussion.

4   Universalism and Its Limits

The avowed desire to rule "the four corners of the universe" may be considered the hallmark of imperial political culture worldwide. Actually, it is so old as to predate the creation of the empires *senso strictu*, being associated with the earliest quasi-imperial formations mentioned above. The rulers of Akkad (2334–2193 BCE), founded by Sargon, took the titles "king of the universe, king of the four regions of the world." This "early instance of universalistic discourse" (Strootman 2014: 40)[13] was echoed regularly by all powerful

---

[13] Strootman associates the earliest instance of this discourse with the Sumerian king Shulgi (r. *c.*2029–1982 BCE), but the precedents can go back already to Sargon and to his singularly important successor, Naram-Sin (r. *c.*2211–2175 BCE), who was the first to call himself "king of the four quarters of the universe" (Van De Mieroop 2016, 73).

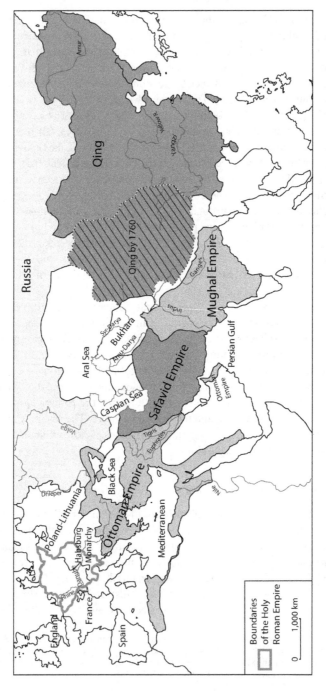

Map 0.3 Major Eurasian empires, *c*.1700 CE. Produced on the basis of the "Interactive World History Atlas since 3000 BC" (ht tp://geacron.com/home-en/?sid=GeaCron44764).

rulers in the ancient Near East. Egyptian pharaohs referred to themselves as rulers of "all that sun encircles," "kings of kings," and so forth, allowing Morkot (2001, 227) to conclude that Egypt should be qualified as an empire. This discourse – usually augmented with territorial expansion – remained the *sine qua non* of an imperial self-presentation thereafter.[14] Assyrian kings boasted of ruling the "universe"; China's emperors claimed to control "All-under-Heaven"; Romans proudly spoke of possession of *orbis terrarum*. From the Assyrian "lord of lords, king of kings" and Persian "king of kings" to the Mughal Jahangir ("Conqueror of the World," r. 1605–27) and Shah Jahan ("King of the World," r. 1628–58), rulers of powerful empires overwhelmingly tended to present themselves as rulers of the entire world.

Imperial self-presentation and representation, their discourse of unity and its symbolic manifestations have been explored in many recent studies, most notably by Bang and Kolodziejczyk (2012). Our goal in the present volume is to go beyond the level of presentation and investigate how the ideas of universal rule were actualized (if at all) in imperial praxis. To do so, our contributors tried to address a common set of questions:

> What prompted the imperial expansion?
> Which factors limited expansion?
> How were the territories under the empire's control incorporated?
> And how are these actual achievements and failures related to the presentation of the imperial space?

By answering these questions, we hope to understand the peculiarities of the creation of the empires' space, and the relation between the imperial ideology with its multi-faceted symbolic manifestations and actual spatial dimensions.

4.1   Ideology

The first and most easily observable impetus for an empire's expansion is its universalist ideology noted above. Here, however, a historian faces a trap. Abundant pronouncements in favor of universal rule may as often conceal weakness and retrenchment as they reflect assertiveness and expansionism. They can inspire aggressiveness, or be used as post-factum justification of expansion that had little to do with ideology. And the "universe" due to be conquered can be of quite limited proportions.

First, let us remind ourselves that geographical dimensions of the "world" as envisioned by various empire-builders could differ tremendously. Strootman (2014, 40) explains, following Mario Liverani (1979), that in ancient

---

[14] For a perceptive discussion of the Near Eastern discourse of universal control and the tension between universalistic claims and the reality on the ground, see Liverani 2001, 23–8ff.

Mesopotamia, the "universe" referred just to a limited civilized space surrounded by chaos. The king controlled the civilized core and only gradually expanded his power into the chaotic periphery. This observation is fully applicable to Bronze Age China. Back then, the term "All-under-Heaven" could refer to a very limited space, not even the Zhou realm as a whole but just the royal domain, that is, areas under the direct control of Zhou kings (Pines 2002, 101–4). The spatial horizons of later Iron Age empires were incomparably broader. Yet even for these, the "universe" normally remained confined to their macro-region. As we shall demonstrate below, topography, ecological conditions, and the problem of maintainability of distant lands – all could limit the expansion of any empire, however loudly its universalistic pretensions were proclaimed.

Second, not only the space of the "universe" could be very limited; the monarch's control over it could be illusionary at best. The language of universal rule, inherited from early empires, was spoken for millennia throughout Eurasia by many rulers who had not the slightest chance of establishing a vast empire, and who employed the symbols of universality just to maintain their domestic prestige. Think for instance of Southeast Asia that "over the course of at least fifteen hundred years, was dotted with universal monarchs, each represented, in the declamations of his cult, as the core and pivot of the universe, yet each quite aware that he was emphatically not alone in such representation" (Geertz 1981, 125). Or think of the carefully orchestrated pageantry of an ecumenical empire, rooted as it is in the Roman past, but performed by the Catholic Church in the early 21st century (Bang and Bayly 2011b, 1–5). In these cases, the symbolic language of universal dominance has very little to do with actual political control. To paraphrase Alexander Martynov (1987, 29), this is no more than a "yardstick" of the erstwhile utopia of universal rule. Elsewhere, the hollowness of the monarchs' universalistic pretensions was less obvious, but was still well observable from their grudging acquiescence to the existence of powerful neighbors in what once was their own imperial space. See, for instance, the case of the Safavids, discussed by Dale in this volume, or the aforementioned Song (960–1279) dynasty in China (Wang Gungwu 1983).

Third, even in the most successful expansionist empires we should not postulate the primacy of ideology as the prime mover of expansion. Quite often, the idea of universal rule (which was frequently conceived of as sanctioned by the divine authority) developed in tandem with the actual expansion rather than preceded it. For instance, in the well-documented Roman case, the idea of universal control evolved gradually in the 1st century BCE, peaking under Augustus (r. 27 BCE–14 CE), that is fully two centuries after the beginning of robust expansion (Spickermann, this volume). In the case of the Caliphate, the concept of dividing the world into *dār al-Islām* (the "abode of Islam"), and *dār al-ḥarb* (the "abode of war") – the major ideological justification for the ongoing expansion – actually gained prominence long *after* the actual expansion peaked under the Umayyads (660–750).[15] In the Mongol case as well, the idea of truly universal control evolved only in the wake of their unprecedented successes. During the enthronement of Chinggis Khan in 1206, his mandate was limited to controlling "the people of the felt walled tents," i.e., the steppe dwellers (Biran, this volume).

That said, at times ideology could matter a lot. This is most notable in cases of expansion into territories that carried symbolic significance as markers of universal rule. In many early Eurasian empires the ocean (sea) was considered the limit of the universe, and reaching the sea shores, or, better, crossing the sea and subjugating distant islands was the hallmark of territorial success. Robert Rollinger (2013) has shown how Assyrian rulers, eager to outdo their illustrious predecessor, Sargon of Akkad, invested considerable resources in expanding toward the sea shores, be it by absorbing the Phoenician island city of Tyre, or, later, by expanding into the sea itself, e.g., by occupying Cyprus in the middle of the "Upper Sea" (Mediterranean) or Bahrain in the "Lower Sea" (Persian Gulf). The symbolism of reaching (or, better, crossing) the sea was reenacted by the Achaemenid rulers, such as Darius I (r. 522–486 BCE), whose campaign against Scythians "from across the sea" involved the symbolic bridging of the Bosporus (Haubold 2012), and later by Alexander the Great who sought to reach the Indian Ocean (Romm 1992, 25–6, 137–9). Roman leaders and emperors, starting with Julius Caeasar (d. 42 BCE), sought to reach and cross the Ocean, either by expanding into Britain (Braund 1996, 94ff.) or by advancing in other directions (Mattern, 1999, 59ff.).[16] On the opposite side of Eurasia, the First Emperor of Qin (emp. 221–210 BCE) marked his unprecedented achievement of unifying "All-under-Heaven" by touring the newly conquered territories, specifically by going to the sea shores, and even (exceptionally for Chinese emperors) sailing into the sea and killing there a "huge fish" (a whale?) (Watson 1993, 62).[17] More than a millennium later, the ultimate world conqueror, Chinggis Khan, opted for a title meaning "Oceanic Khan." Chinggis Khan's grandson, Qubilai Qa'an (r. 1260–94), tried – unsuccessfully – to demonstrate the universal reach of the Mongol armies by sending naval expeditions to Java

---

[15] As the recent volume of Calasso and Lancioni (2017) suggests, the *dār al-Islām* and *dār al-ḥarb* antinomy developed relatively late (9th to 10th centuries), and it had multiple meanings, not necessarily mandating the expansionist Holy War. To be sure, the religious ideology of fighting the unbelievers did serve to justify military campaigns under the Umayyads (Peacock, this volume), but it may be significant that the sophisticated ideological justifications of *jihad* appear only under the subsequent and much less expansionist Abbasid dynasty (see, e.g., Denaro 2017).

[16] Mattern shows that many of these attempts to reach the "ocean" were based on misidentification of its location.

[17] Unbeknown to the first emperor, a millennium earlier it was the Assyrian king Tiglath-pileser I (1114–1076 BCE) who prided himself of killing "a *nāḥiru*, which is called a sea-horse" in the middle of the sea (Rollinger 2013, 98–9).

and Japan. For sure, in each of the above cases the expansionist policies had a variety of different motivations, but the desire to manifest one's achievements by reaching the limits of earth and "conquering" the ocean was arguably among the major drivers for this persistent push toward the sea shores.

The quest for universal rule could influence the course of the imperial expansion on yet a deeper level: in certain circumstances, it could become the defining factor behind the shaping of the imperial space. Perhaps the most notable case is that of the Chinese Empire, which was to a certain extent "envisioned" even if not necessarily "pre-planned" in the centuries preceding the actual imperial unification. In particular, the idea that political fragmentation means ongoing bloodshed and that unification of All-under-Heaven – referring at the very minimum to the "civilized" agricultural core of the East Asian subcontinent – is the only way to peace and prosperity became the cornerstone of Chinese political culture long before the empire actualized (Pines, this volume). From the Warring States period (453–221 BCE) on, political fragmentation was perceived as coequal with permanent war: it was a zero-sum game from which only one winner could emerge. The determination of competing regimes during periods of fragmentation to attain political unity became a self-fulfilling prophecy as it precluded the long-term peaceful coexistence of rival emperors. Thus, after longer or shorter periods of division, a unified empire in China's core territories invariably re-emerged (Pines 2012, 11–43).

Elsewhere the dictum of annihilation of alternative loci of power in the given macro-region could similarly become a potent political force. Rolf Stoorman (2014, 43) retells an anecdote about Alexander the Great. When, in 331 BCE, Darius III offered Alexander huge territorial concessions and enormous payment in exchange for peace, Alexander "told the envoys that the earth could not preserve its plan and order if there were two suns, nor could the inhabited world remain calm and free from war so long as two kings shared the rule" (Diodorus 17.54). We cannot ascertain the veracity of the anecdote, but there is little doubt that the idea of singularity and universality of the "king of kings" adopted by Alexander from his Persian foes served him well. Even if not necessarily the primary reason for his quest to annex the Achaemenid realm in its entirety, this ideological orientation certainly played an important role in determining Alexander's course of action.

The example of Alexander is indicative of another dimension of the ideological impetus for the empire's expansion, namely reenacting the glory of its major predecessor(s). It was the size of the Persian realm that dictated Alexander's course of conquests (Briant, this volume). Later, the Hellenistic empires sought to reenact Alexander's (and earlier Achaemenid) success within more-or-less the same territorial framework. Like their predecessors, they adopted the language of universal rule. From time to time they tried to subjugate each other and reunify the realm, albeit with little success (Stoorman

2014). Much later, the Sasanian kings of Iran may have been inspired by Achaemenid precedent as well, although the evidence is not conclusive.[18] What is not doubted is that the Sasanians' major rivals, the Byzantine emperors, focused their concern on the protection or restoration of the territories of the "divinely protected Roman Empire" (Preiser-Kapeller, this volume). In the steppe, the idea of the unity of the "felt tents' dwellers" was strongly pronounced ever since the Xiongnu; it was reinforced by the Turks (Golden 1982), and became the cornerstone of the Mongol expansion. It was only the Mongols' unprecedented success that extended their universal aspirations even further to include both steppe and sown, namely the whole world (Biran, this volume).

It should be noticed that "restorationist" ideology could at time hinder rather than promote territorial expansion. The Byzantine Empire is a good example. Even when the situation was favorable for expansion beyond the areas of the Roman *imperium*, that is, into Russian territories after the Rus' had accepted Orthodox Christianity, such an attempt was not undertaken.[19] The post-Mongol empires from the Near East to India had also accepted, even if grudgingly, the territorial divisions among them dating back to earlier imperial formations in their respective realms (Dale, this volume). Nor did the Abbasid Caliphate endeavor to expand beyond the areas incorporated by its Umayyad predecessors (actually it lost control over considerable parts of the former Umayyad realm). Similarly, the Qing dynasty (which was robustly expanding to the west and to the north) was cautious not to commit itself to direct control over mainland Southeast Asia, because these areas remained outside the sphere of rule of its predecessor, the Ming (Mosca, this volume).

4.2   Religion

Speaking of ideologies that justified or mandated territorial expansion, we should address the religious factor. Most empires boasted divine support of their rulers – from Aššur and Ahura Mazda to Jupiter, to the Turco-Mongol Tengri, Chinese *tian* (Heaven), and beyond. But it would be a leap of faith to consider these claims as the initial reasons for imperial expansion. It is more plausible to consider the religious reasoning as coeval with actual expansion: military success can engender belief in divine support, which, after having been

---

[18] Whether or not early Sasanian kings sought to restore Achaemenid glory – as argued in some of the Roman sources – is contestable. See Yar-Shater 1971 vs. Shahbazi 2001. For the immense complexity of the alleged "Achaemenid revival" under the Sasanians and earlier under the Arsacids (rulers of Parthia), see Shayegan 2011.

[19] The Byzantine rulers' willingness to acquiesce to the existence of the parallel empire in the East (the Sasanians and then the Caliphate) derived from their military inability to subjugate eastern rivals, but the legitimacy of this ideology may have also derived from the fact that the Romans – even at the apex of their power – had never tried to expand to the east of Mesopotamia. See more in Preiser-Kapeller, this volume.

internalized, may push for further expansion, as, for instance, was the case of the Mongols (Biran, this volume). A more interesting case to consider in this regard is that of the major proselytizing religions of Eurasia: Buddhism, Christianity, and Islam. Each experienced periods of endorsement by major empires, and Islam was actually the creator of one of the most illustrious imperial regimes worldwide. But what was the role of these religions in the expansion of their respective empires?

Somewhat counter-intuitively, the answer would be that religions were not the prime mover of imperial expansion even in the case of the most pious emperors. One good example would be that of Aśoka, the single most renowned Buddhist monarch. Aśoka's conversion to Buddhism was to a certain extent a rejection of his own violent past. He had famously proclaimed that conquering others should be done not by force but through the power of *dharma* (religious law), the promulgation of which worldwide was conceived as the emperor's mission. Yet, as noticed by Patrick Olivelle (2018), "the ideology of *dharma* that Aśoka was propagating had a different and broader intent than the propagation of the Buddhist religion." For Aśoka, maintaining domestic balance among the adherents of different creeds (Buddhists, Hindus, Jains) in the Indian subcontinent seems to have been by far more important than unilateral promotion of Buddhism.

Aśoka's reign did introduce the Indian idea of a universal king (*cakravartin*; Scharfe 1989, 51–5) into Buddhism (Strong 1983), but this notion did not evolve into a lasting pattern of proselytizing Buddhist empires. Powerful emperors, such as Emperor Wen of the Sui dynasty in China (r. 581–604) could borrow the *cakravartin* image, and gain the Buddhist clergy's support for their expansionist endeavor (Wright 1957: 93–104). However, these cases were rare and exceptional. The Buddhist establishment's occasional support of aggressive emperors did not evolve into a firm symbiosis (Lai 2010). The expansion of Buddhism throughout eastern Eurasia depended less on imperial backing and more on private initiatives by the missionaries.

This observation, *mutatis mutandis* is true for Christianity and Islam as well. Garth Fowden (1993) analyzed the emerging forms of "imperial monotheism," showing the paradoxical relations between proselytizing monotheistic religions and the imperial order ever since the conversion of Constantine the Great (r. 306–37) . Although the power of the new, revelation-based religion generated unprecedented expansive energies, the "one God – one empire – one emperor" schema promulgated by Constantine's biographer, Eusebius (260–339) (Fowden 1993, 94) did not work well. The persistent tensions between orthodoxy and heresy, intrinsic to monotheist religions, eventually weakened Roman imperial rule. The Christian Roman Empire was transformed into a commonwealth, or, more precisely, two commonwealths, the Byzantine-Orthodox (for which see also Preiser-Kapeller, this volume) and the Latin. In both cases the decentralized commonwealth system proved more viable than the unified proselytizing empire.[20]

The case of Islam is the clearest example of convergence between the missionary monotheistic creed and the expansionist empire; yet once again the trajectory was much more complex than the "one God – one empire – one emperor" scheme would suggest. Actually, in the first decades of the caliphate a strong tension existed between the universal religion under the banners of which the caliphate was founded and the narrower ethnic Arab-centered nature of the imperial institution under both the righteous caliphs (632–660) and the Umayyads (660–750) (Robinson 2010; Cobb 2010; Peacock, this volume). Fowden suggests that the eventual acceleration of the pace of conversion, especially under the Abbasids, allowed the reassertion of suppressed local identities and created "an atmosphere in which the political disintegration of the Abbasid Empire seemed less unthinkable" (Fowden 1993, 163). Whether this explanation is correct or not cannot be dealt with here; what is undeniable is that the Muslim empire followed the same path as its Christian rivals, namely the dissolution into a "Muslim commonwealth," most of which first existed under nominal Abbasid superiority (see also Kennedy 2016). Eventually, preaching Islam became a personal mission (later institutionalized primarily through Sufi orders) rather than an undertaking initiated by a Muslim state or by a certain "church" leader. For sure, in both Christianity and Islam, aggression against infidels frequently received religious blessing, and members of religious communities could be at the forefront of territorial expansion. But in both cases, the ecumenical religion survived and developed without much need of an ecumenical empire.[21]

4.3   Natural Boundaries?

Moving from the ideological software of empires to the hardware factors that determined their spatial dimensions, we should start with the idea of "natural boundaries." The idea that boundaries between empires or states are determined (or at least should be determined) by natural features, such as waterways, mountains, and so forth, has a long pedigree (e.g., Finch 1844). Whereas this idea has been justifiably criticized both due to its factual inaccuracy and because it could be utilized to serve questionable political and ideological agendas (Fall 2010), it should not be dismissed outright. Terrain, climate, and ecological conditions do all have an impact on the imperial space.

[20] See also Hglin 1982 for the case of unsuccessful attempts to reunify the empire and the church in the Christian west. For the complex trajectory of the Byzantine case and the tensions between the empire and the church there, see Geanakoplos 1965; Dagron 2003; Preiser-Kapeller 2018.
[21] This statement certainly does not mean to deny the importance of religion's piggybacking on a powerful empire to facilitate its expansion: this was for instance the case for the Ottoman Empire, as well as for European colonial empires. This topic requires further study.

Of terrestrial features, oceans served as the clearest natural boundaries of Eurasian empires up until the onset of the maritime empires in the 15th and 16th centuries. Inland seas (such as the Mediterranean) and rivers were less important as boundaries, since more often than not they could serve as a means of communication rather than separation (e.g., Parker 2002, 373). In distinction, mountain ranges did play the role of natural barriers. For instance, the Himalaya or Pamir ranges posed such formidable obstacles to different armies as to make them almost impenetrable.[22] These ranges served as natural limits for the expansion of South and East Asian empires. Even lower mountain ranges could play a similar role. The Assyrians and Arabs' difficulty in crossing the Taurus Mountains in eastern Anatolia (Parker 2002, and Peacock, this volume); the Zagros Mountains serving as a protective barrier of the Iranian plateau in the face of invaders from the west, or the Sulaiman Mountains being a natural boundary between Iran and India-based empires (Dale, this volume) are the most notable examples.

That said, recall that logistical difficulties involved in crossing mountain ranges could be overcome by a committed imperial regime if ideological, strategic, or economic considerations prompted it to invest sufficient resources in surmounting natural barriers. Sichuan province in China provides a good example. Its agriculturally rich interior is conveniently surrounded by mountain ranges which make access to this territory from the north or the east (i.e., from China's heartland) notoriously difficult. The region's topography made it particularly suitable for establishing an independent regime, and such regimes indeed prospered there (most notably prior to the 4th century BCE, and in the 3rd, 4th, and 10th centuries CE). And yet Sichuan-based kingdoms and self-proclaimed empires were invariably overrun – often at great cost – by China's imperial unifiers, who would never tolerate the existence of an independent locus of power within the Chinese world (see Section 4.1). Mountain ranges could postpone the assault but not prevent it. Similarly, the Taurus, Zagros, Sulaiman and other mountain ranges were surmounted whenever powerful imperial leaders, committed to the task of further expansion, invested sufficient resources in the assault.

Mountain ranges aside, another major factor that determined the space configuration of most (but not all) empires, was ecology. In an insightful study, Turchin, Adams, and Hall noticed that empires mostly expand into regions of the same biomes (Turchin et al. 2006). A biome is a major type of ecological community such as grassland, desert, or temperate seasonal forest.

---

[22] Among rare instances of armies crossing these formidable ranges, one can mention the Tang dynasty's expedition under general Gao Xianzhi to Gilgit (modern Pakistan) in 747 CE to save the Tang protectorate there from the Tibetan aggression, or the successful Qing expedition into Katmandu valley (Nepal) in 1792 CE to protect Tibet from the Gurkha invasion. The very rarity of such expeditions buttresses their exceptionality.

Since biomes are determined primarily by similarities in climate and soil, they tend to extend along lines of latitude (i.e., along an East–West axis) rather than along lines of longitude (a North–South axis). The same pattern of East–West orientation characterizes major continental empires. Putting aside some quibbles concerning the data utilized by these scholars, there is no doubt that empirically they are right (as the maps – however problematic – employed in our volume, including the current chapter, testify).

In particular, ecology played a crucial role in distinguishing the steppe as a special imperial macro-region (see also below). It was the peculiarity of the steppes' soil and climate that protected the steppe empires from their sedentary neighbors. For the latter, incursions into the steppe were nightmarishly expensive and unsustainable in the long term, as had become obvious already under the Han dynasty in China (Pines, this volume). The steppe warriors actually faced a similar challenge once they tried to penetrate to the south of the ecological borders of the steppe, i.e., to the areas in which mounted archers lost their military advantage (Peacock and Biran, this volume). In these cases, ecology could become a major determinant of the empire's spatial configuration.

Military and administrative considerations alike encouraged most empires to stay within the familiar biome. Expanding into a different biome required an imperial army to accustom itself to war in a terrain that was unsuitable to its original modes of warfare. Even more challenging was the task of permanent incorporation of territories whose mode of production differed dramatically from that to which the empire-builders were used to at their homeland. And yet these difficulties aside, a powerful and resolute empire could overcome ecological constraints if the price was found worthwhile. The Mongol conquest of Southern Song, which required advance well into the areas of subtropical forests (Biran, this volume) is a good example. Several China-based empires are another notable exception. As noted by Turchin et al. (2006, 225), these empires were remarkably able to overcome the biome's constraints, advancing into the Mongolian steppe, into the alpine biome (Tibet), or into the tropical rain forest area of Vietnam. Owing to the successful incorporation of some of these areas (albeit not Vietnam), China became the most climatically heterogeneous continental empire worldwide (McNeill 1998). It should be noted, however, that the most robust expansion of "Chinese" empire was actually achieved under the dynasties that were either themselves established by nomads or semi-nomads (Yuan and Qing; Biran and Mosca, this volume), or at least were culturally close to the nomads (Tang; Chen Sanping 1996). The nomads' success in these cases derived from their remarkable ability to appropriate and mobilize not just the material but also the cultural resources of their sedentary neighbors. This adaptability stands behind the most successful imperial enterprise which transcended the ecological constraints of expansion more than any other – the Mongol Empire (Biran, this volume).[23]

4.4   Military Factors

Military factors are among the most significant determinants of imperial space. To begin with, the very birth of most if not all empires started with robust military expansion. Yet once the "imperial threshold" (establishing clear hegemony in a given macro-region) was reached, the empires behaved differently. In some cases, aggressive expansion continued for generations, whereas in others empires shifted focus to the consolidation of their space, even if this required retrenchment. Among multiple factors that influenced both trajectories, military considerations occupy pride of place. Two points in particular should be considered in this context: first, is the degree of imperial elites' belligerence; and, second, are the strategic considerations behind expansion and retrenchment.

In the popular imagination, empires are depicted as intrinsically belligerent (being associated with predatory imperialism), and in many – albeit not all – cases this association is undoubtedly correct. Successful wars have bolstered a leadership's prestige throughout much of known human history. In certain political cultures, most notably the steppe, military success was essential for ensuring the legitimacy of the ruler and the ruling clan (Biran, this volume). In these cultures, military activism was a norm rather just a response to external circumstances. As revealed in the autobiography of the founder of the Mughal dynasty, Babur (1483–1530), "kingdom-seizing" was normative behavior for "any self-respecting descendant of Temür" (Timur or Tamerlane, 1336–1405) (Dale, this volume). This belligerence was not exceptional to the nomads. In Republican Rome, the "chiefly military system of values, which was not only binding for the elites but also for large parts of the Roman citizenry and therefore a key to success, formed the basis of massive Roman expansion" (Spickermann, this volume). Individual commanders' search for prestige associated with victorious campaigns bolstered the extraordinary expansion of the Umayyad space (Peacock, this volume). In some cases, belligerence could be even constructed into society from above. In the pre-imperial state of Qin, for instance, the system of ranks of merit that made success on the battlefield the primary channel of individual social, economic, and political advancement

---

[23] Speaking of ecology, one should mention the related issue of climate changes as a possible trigger of the empires' formation or disintegration. This topic, which became very popular recently (see, e.g., Ellenblum 2012; Brooke 2014; Li et al. 2019, q.v. for further references), is not addressed here because of two reasons. First, studies of the history of climate changes are still relatively new and climate-related explanations of the empires' dynamics are still much contested (see, e.g., Peacock and Biran, this volume). Second, and most importantly, climate changes are more relevant to the empires' temporal rather than spatial dimensions, and hence do not belong to the framework of the present volume.

brought about a profound militarization of the society and turned Qin, "the state organized for war" (Lewis 2007, 30), into a formidable expansionist machine (Pines, this volume).

Yet the elite's commitment to military aggrandizement, important as it was for imperial expansion, was not a permanent feature of the empire's life. In Rome, sociopolitical changes under the principate resulted in a less belligerent society and gradual cessation of expansionist zeal. In China, changes in the elite's composition under the Han dynasty brought about the sidelining of combative military-based elite members by others, who were more civilian-oriented and less prone to benefit from robust military action (Pines, this volume; cf. Tse 2018; for parallels with the Ming dynasty, see Robinson, this volume). This tendency is observable, albeit less clearly, even in the Mongol Empire, particularly in the Yuan dynasty in China, although the details of the process there still require better understanding.

Going back to the early empires or would-be empires, it is worth noticing that elite belligerence as such did not necessarily result in empire-building. For the nomads, in particular, successful raids were sufficient to demonstrate the leadership's charisma; permanent occupation of the enemy's territory was not their first choice. The same can be said of Roman magistrates or Qin generals, who strived for successful campaigns but were not necessarily committed toward full annexation of the enemy's territory. The latter option could be an outcome of peculiar power configurations on the ground. For instance, the conquest of a neighboring territory could be considered a preemptive measure against future aggression. The Roman case is a good demonstration of expansion as a means of self-preservation. Without accepting the Roman view that every war launched by Rome was *bellum iustum* (just war), one should admit that many of the Roman wars could be indeed justified as either defensive or preemptive strikes against equally predatory polities. In the Mongol case, a potential threat to Chinggis Khan's status as the sole leader of the Mongolian tribes stood behind many of the Mongols' early campaigns – such as their wars against the Jurchen Jin (1115–1234) or the Naiman leader, Güchülüg (d. 1218) (Biran 2007). Russian expansion into the steppes was also prompted by rivalry with the Kazan Khanate, which was a coequal player "in a larger game for control in the same space" (Burbank, this volume).

This brings us to the contentious issue of the role of strategic considerations behind imperial expansion or cessation thereof. These considerations were highlighted in an influential – and highly controversial – study by Edward Luttwak, who argued that the Romans' imperial space under the principate was shaped by the empire's "grand strategy." This strategy aimed "to provide security for the civilization without prejudicing the vitality of its economic base and without compromising the stability of an evolving political order" (Luttwak 1976, 1). Luttwak identifies consistent policies in different periods of the principate's history, aimed at determining protectable borders and defending them in the least costly way. Whereas Luttwak's neat theoretical explanation was criticized by historians who noticed its empirical flaws (cf. Mattern 1999, 81–122; Kagan 2006), overall the idea of a "grand strategy" cannot be easily dismissed. Without doubt, major empires often had long-term strategic goals that determined their military actions. For instance, for Chinese empires from the Qin and Han to the Ming and Qing, the primary strategic goal was stabilizing the volatile northern frontier (Pines, Robinson, and Mosca, this volume). For the Mongols under Chinggis Khan and his immediate descendants, the need to prevent the emergence of a rival locus of power in the steppe and, later, annihilation of "competing rulers with universal claims, such as the Abbasid Caliph and the Jin and Song emperors" (Biran, this volume) was equally important. The question is: What was the impact of these strategic considerations on the shaping of the imperial space?

The answer to this question is not simple. Even when the "grand strategic" goals are easily discernible in an empire's policy, these goals more often than not could be realized in a variety of ways, the territorial impact of which differed dramatically. Take for instance the case of the Chinese empires. The common goal of securing the northern frontier could be achieved by highly divergent policies – from appeasing the nomads, to establishing client nomadic polities, instigating inter- and intra-tribal conflicts among the rivals (*yi yi zhi yi* [ruling the aliens through aliens], a Chinese variant of the Roman *divide et impera* [divide and rule] principle), launching preemptive attacks into the steppe, or, conversely, strengthening the defending line of the Great Wall and adopting purely defensive policy (Pines and Robinson, this volume). Policies fluctuated due to a variety of ever changing factors: shifts in the balance of power between China and its nomadic neighbors and among different factions in Chinese imperial courts, individual preferences of certain emperors, and sometimes sheer contingencies (such as succession crises in nomadic polities). Only exceptionally, most notably under the Qing, can we discern the empire's leaders' lasting commitment to absorbing the Mongol territories, in addition to the areas that were ideologically (Tibet) or economically (southern Xinjiang) important for the Mongols into "a carefully-regulated and constantly-monitored part of the realm" (Mosca, this volume). However, as Mosca shows, the ultimate annexation of these territories was still as much a result of contingencies and individual decisions by resolute emperors as it was a product of strategic imperatives (see also Dai Yingcong 2009; Perdue 2005; Millward 1998). In the final account, the evidence does not suggest a direct impact of the empire's strategic considerations on the contours of its space.

Strategic imperatives could not only prompt expansion but also cause its halt or even bring about territorial contraction. Logistical factors, for instance, were of crucial importance for limiting the scope of imperial military operations and putting an end to expansion (Preiser-Kapeller, this volume). The strategic vulnerability of the outlying territories could cause their abandonment in the aftermath of successful conquest and even after a relatively lengthy period of control, especially when the empire was threatened on two or more fronts. China's imperial rulers, for instance, were ready to give up the outlying Western Regions (today's Xinjiang and at times even parts of Gansu) whenever domestic turmoil or external threat elsewhere weakened the empire's core and made these territories indefensible. This retrenchment happened in the 1st and 2nd centuries CE (Tse 2018), then in the mid-8th century CE, and almost recurred in the 19th century CE when one of the most powerful officials, Li Hongzhang (1823–1901), urged retreating from the Western Regions and focusing on coastal defense instead).[24] The Ottomans' abandonment of Tabriz (Dale, this volume) and the Romans' decision to give up expansion beyond the Rhine River may be attributed to the same logic.

4.5   Costs and Benefits of Expansion

Aside from ideological, ecological, and strategic factors, the contours of the imperial space were influenced by economic considerations. The very emergence of empires was often a by-product of predatory expansion, which was a common feature of powerful political entities from the beginning of recorded human history. For the Assyrians, Romans, Macedonians, the rulers of the pre-imperial state of Qin, as well as for countless other would-be imperial leaders, expansion meant first of all enrichment. Areas of high agricultural productivity, foci of major trade routes, territories rich in mineral and human resources – all were naturally attractive to the empire-builders. For instance, Egypt with its extraordinary fertility was a coveted prize for Near Eastern and European empires from the Achaemenids and Romans to the Ottomans, France, and Britain. The incorporation of such a rich area could easily offset the costs of its conquest.

The conquest itself was, however, a relatively cheap enterprise in comparison to the costs of permanent incorporation of the subjugated area into the empire. Even establishing a minimal level of control over the conquered space required considerable resources. Let us focus on the costs of just one essential necessity of any empire: maintaining a system of communication between the center and the outlying areas. This "nerve system" of any expansive polity came into existence, not incidentally, with the formation of the earliest major imperial entity, the Neo-Assyrian Empire of the mid-9th century BCE. Karen Radner notes that the Neo-Assyrian Empire "must be seen as a turning point in

---

[24] Chu 1966. Calls to discontinue the costly engagement in the southwestern part of Xinjiang (the Tarim basin) were made long before Li Hongzhang, in the 1820s, in the aftermath of local turmoil and the deterioration of the military situation in the region. See Millward 1998: 225–31.

the history of communications. It saw the creation and implementation of an innovative, and very expensive, long-distance high-speed information network designed for the exclusive needs of the state" (Radner 2014a, 6, with more in Radner 2014b). This system of communications was in turn inherited and expanded by the Achaemenids (Briant, this volume; Kuhrt 2014). Similar systems were employed by any major imperial regime elsewhere – from the Mauryas (Thapar 1961), to the Romans (Spickermann, this volume; Corcoran 2014), to Qin and Han (e.g., Barbieri-Low and Yates 2015, 729–37), to the Caliphate (Peacock, this volume; Silverstein 2007), to the Mongols (Biran, this volume; Allsen 2011), and so forth. A well-developed system of communications became the major means through which the empires tried to overcome the "tyranny of distance."

The effectiveness of the imperial postal systems astonished observers beginning with Herodotus and Xenophon (Radner 2014a, 1). In some cases, a good relay system could produce truly amazing results. Take for instance the Mongol Empire, in which authorized travelers were able to cover about 350–400 km a day (Biran, this volume). Even in the early Chinese empires the mandatory speed of a foot courier, who had to cover $c.83$ km in twenty-four hours (Barbieri-Low and Yates 2015, 740–41), is very impressive. The improved connectivity not only contributed to the empire's administrative cohesiveness but also brought about manifold economic and cultural benefits (Korolkov 2020, 428–555). But let us pause and think of the costs. An effective system of communications required construction and maintenance of roads, bridges, and waterways, establishment of relay stations and provision of lodgings for those on official duties. The empire had to manage an army of couriers, and to supply them with horses, camels, or mules, with chariots and boats. The costs of all these could become exorbitant (see examples in Radner 2014c).[25] When these investments were made in agriculturally productive and densely populated areas with abundant human resources, the benefits could eventually offset the costs. Yet once an empire expanded into sparsely populated areas with difficult terrain, maintenance of an effective communication system would become prohibitively expensive. Generally speaking, providing efficient control over these areas meant a permanent drain on the empire's resources, and the farther these areas were removed from the imperial center the more severe this drain became.

What was the impact of these "cost–benefit" calculations on shaping the imperial space? Can we discern instances of stopping territorial expansion (or even opting for territorial contraction) primarily for economic reasons? The

---

[25] Hou Xudong (2016) shows how even a minor item such as providing lodging for officials on duty in government-run hostels along the routes of communication could incur unbearable expenses.

answer is somewhat equivocal. On the one hand, it is clear that economic factors were secondary to ideological or strategic ones in determining imperial territorial extent. A powerful empire could opt to invest considerably in controlling (or trying to acquire) areas that were economically profitless, but were symbolically or politically important. For instance, the Romans held "with ferocious tenacity" Britain, which "was neither a military threat nor economically lucrative," because "as the ancient sources tell us, once conquered, it could not have been let go without disgrace" (Mattern 1999, 160–1). The Mughal attempt to reconquer Samarqand in 1645, more than a century after the city was lost forever to the Timurids, was likewise prompted neither by economic nor even by strategic considerations but primarily by the ongoing nostalgia for the "hereditary kingdom of [their] ancestors" (Dale, this volume). In distinction, Qing's incorporation of Xinjiang and particularly of Tibet, however costly and profitless, derived primarily from strategic considerations insofar as it was deemed helpful in solidifying the empire's control over its Mongolian subjects (Mosca, this volume). In these and myriad similar cases, the economic liabilities of the conquest were not a primary factor in determining the empire's expansion.

This said, thinking of the empires' longue durée, one can discover a latent tendency to confine expansion primarily to the economically profitable areas. Usually, having acquired rich territories, empires became less bellicose. The Roman case is a good example. Late Republican Rome was clearly a predatory polity. Military success was an important, at times the major source of enrichment for individual citizens and for Rome as a whole. Aside from immediate gains such as obtaining booty, slaves, land for colonization, lucrative positions for Roman tax farmers, and the like, one should consider the major benefit of empire-building for the city of Rome as a whole: creating a system of permanent exploitation of the provinces so as to allow a free supply of wheat to Rome's citizens (Spickermann, this volume; Hopkins 2009). However, having acquired the richest areas in the immediate reach of the Roman armies, Augustus (63 BCE–14 CE) himself reportedly called for restraint, reminding that further expansion would be as risky as "fishing with a golden hook, the loss of which, if it were carried off, could not be made good by any catch" (Suetonius, *Augustus*, 25).[26] A century after Augustus, writing shortly after Roman expansion peaked under Trajan (r. 98–117 CE), Appian (*c*.95–*c*.165 CE) opined:

Possessing the best part of the earth and sea they [the Roman emperors] have, on the whole, aimed to preserve their empire by the exercise of prudence, rather than to extend their sway indefinitely over poverty-stricken and profitless tribes of barbarians. (Appian, *The Foreign Wars*, Preface, 7)

[26] Whether or not Augustus really planned to stop further expansion is a contentious issue; see Grüll 2017, 23–7 for further details.

This transition from predatory expansion toward self-restraint characterizes many other empires. Of these, China presents the best example. The founding Qin dynasty had absorbed most of the agriculturally productive territories in East Asia. Expanding beyond these territories (which are roughly coterminous with what is often dubbed "China proper") was less economically advantageous. This explains why this additional expansion caused considerable resentment within the educated elite already at its early stages under the Han dynasty (Pines, this volume), and why it was discontinued altogether under certain later dynasties, such as the Ming after the third generation of its emperors (Robinson, this volume). The same logic may explain the empire-building patterns in the Indian subcontinent as well. Having incorporated the economically most productive areas within their reach, the Maurya and their later emulators were prone to consider "the horizon" to which the royal power was to be extended as just "the horizon of subcontinental space" (Pollock 2006, 181; see more in Dale, this volume).

In marked distinction from China and India, steppe empires were located in an economically disadvantageous area. For them, the conquest of productive agricultural areas to the south of the steppe belt could be an attractive choice. Nonetheless, the nomads were not very keen on expanding southwards. Aside from the ecological difficulties of making war in hot and humid areas and aside from the perennial demographic disadvantage vis-à-vis sedentary polities, a reason that normally inhibited their conquest was the realization that the challenging task of running a sedentary empire and supervising an agricultural economy could offset the benefits of the conquest. Coffers could be more easily filled through the periodic plunder of sedentary areas. Moreover, military intimidation of sedentary neighbors could either ensure access to lucrative trade, or, better, solicit payments of tribute from agriculturalists to the steppe rulers (Barfield 1989; cf. Di Cosmo 2002). Normally, the nomads were pushed to permanent conquest of sedentary areas only due to political contingency. It was only with Chinggis Khan that this pattern was decisively discontinued and the idea of the world empire that combines both steppe and sown came into existence (Biran, this volume).

4.6   Integrating Imperial Space

A final factor that should be considered here in the context of shaping imperial spatial dimensions is the nature and degree of the control empires had over their space. In a nutshell, the more the empire expanded, the more difficult it was to maintain the imperial center's effective control over outlying territories. In due time, many empires succumbed to collapse under their own weight. The dissolution of the Roman Empire into Western and Eastern halves is probably the best known example, but it is not an exception. A similar trajectory characterizes the Turkic Khaganate, which dissolved within a few decades into Western and Eastern Khaganates (Sinor 1990; Drompp 2018); the Abbasid Caliphate, in which outlying provinces became first autonomous and then de facto independent polities from the 9th century (Peacock, this volume); and the Mongol Empire, which dissolved after 1260 into four successor states (Biran this volume). Yet going beyond these initial observations can we discern a deeper impact of the ways by which the empire-builders and custodians tried to integrate their heterogeneous space on the empire's actual dimensions?

In the previous sub-section we mentioned that control over imperial space started with facilitating internal connectivity. Parallel to this, the imperial rulers had to place adequate military forces in the newly conquered territories to ensure domestic order and frontier security. In the next stage, most empires sought to establish a viable revenue-collection system, which required the introduction of at least a rudimentary administration staff to the new lands. Then, assertive leaders could move from ensuring "the trinity of security, finance, justice" (Whitby 2016) to a more substantial incorporation of their territories, including the social and cultural integration of at least a part of the empire's subjects alongside a variety of "civilizing projects" (e.g., Mosca, this volume). Each of these steps, if followed, could have far-reaching ramifications not only for the degree of the empire's control over the areas under its sway but more broadly for the configuration of the imperial space in general.

It is often assumed that empires were satisfied with a relatively low degree of control over their subjects. In a recent brief discussion of the contrasts between traditional empires and modern states, Clifford Ando summarized a widespread view according to which "modern states seek to extend metropolitan norms uniformly throughout their territory and down through their population," whereas empires acted along different parameters:

Ancient empires largely conceived themselves as aggregates of subordinate populations and developed sophisticated normative resources by which to describe and explain themselves as internally heterogeneous. In modern judgment, the ambitions of rule among such states [i.e., empires] were narrowly extractive, and this could be accomplished by delivering local control into the hands of parties and institutions who were granted considerable autonomy. (Ando 2018, 175–6)

Ando shows in his article that the reality was more complex than this common perception. The indirect rule practiced by the Roman Republic during its quasi-imperial period and then by the Roman Empire under the principate actually allowed the Romans to penetrate "far more fully into the fabric of local social and economic conduct than they had heretofore been seen to do." The Romans succeeded in mobilizing local institutions in the subjugated areas "in the service of overall intensification of governmentality" (Ando 2018, 179). But let us put aside the Roman case and go back to Ando's depiction of the supposedly normative conduct of "ancient empires." Is it true that the default choice of imperial leaders was exercising indirect rule over their subjects and confining themselves to "narrowly extractive" goals? And, if indirect rule was indeed the primary choice, what are the implications of this understanding on our perception of the imperial space?

The answer to the first of these questions is, again, equivocal. On the one hand, most of the empires discussed in our volume clearly preferred to employ indirect rule over some of their subjects, relegating considerable authority to local elites much in accord with Ando's depiction. On the other hand, there were some notable exceptions, of which the Qin Empire in China is the most remarkable. The reforms that propelled the pre-imperial state of Qin to a position of prominence in continental East Asia focused precisely on the elimination of autonomous loci of power and the formation of a powerful centralized bureaucratic state that penetrated society to its foundation, much like the modern European states. Once "All-under-Heaven" was unified, this model of the centralized territorial state was imposed – with varying degrees of success – on all the subjugated areas (Pines, this volume). Qin became arguably the most profoundly centralized and bureaucratized of all the early (and not just early) empires worldwide.[27] Yet Qin's trajectory exemplifies what Crooks and Parsons (2016b, 28) define as "the Goldilocks paradox": "You can't have an empire without a bureaucracy, but too much bureaucracy and you won't keep your empire for very long." The spiraling costs of maintaining a huge administrative apparatus aimed at full extraction of material and human resources from the populace backfired. Qin's hyperactive administrative machine contributed to the population's discontent and to the resultant popular rebellions that toppled the dynasty just fourteen years after its establishment (Shelach 2014; Pines, this volume).

Several other empires adopted an entirely different model of rule, which is much closer to the one presented by Ando. This model is represented most vividly in the case of the Achaemenid Empire. Briant (this volume) summarizes:

Insofar as their decisions and activities did not oppose the requirements of the imperial power, various local authorities (kings of the Phoenician cities, heads of Egyptian and Babylonian sanctuaries, governments of Greek cities, etc.) preserved their sphere of influence. Influence would be preserved if obligations (e.g., taxes, supply of troops, ships, and so forth) remained fulfilled.

A similar system of indirect control was practiced, at least initially, by many other empires, most notably the Roman (Ando 2018; Spickermann, this

---

[27] The Maurya Empire in Thapar's (1961) account appears as no less bureaucratized than the Qin. The problem of this account, though, is Thapar's frequent resort to Kauṭilya's *Arthaśāstra* as reflective of the practices of the Mauryan Empire. Later research cast doubt on this connection: it is likely that the *Arthaśāstra* was penned much later than the Maurya age, i.e. not before c.50–125 CE (see Olivelle 2013).

volume). This system allowed considerable autonomy to local elites under the overall supervision of the imperial super-elite, such as the Persian dominant "ethno-class" (Briant, this volume), or the senatorial or equestrian classes in Rome. The super-elite – which could maintain its exceptional political role even once more direct control over localities was established – provided a core of satraps, governors, and tax farmers, who served as the glue for the empire's heterogeneous space. As the primary beneficiaries of the empire's existence, members of the imperial super-elite generally remained loyal to the empire's interests.

Indirect rule had the clear advantage of minimizing frictions between the imperial rulers and their subjects. It also permitted a significant degree of cultural flexibility, allowing subordinate groups to maintain "their culture, language, and religion as well as their elites" (Lavan et al. 2016b, 18). However, this policy had several distinct disadvantages. First, owing to lax supervision, it commonly allowed native elites to retain the lion's share of local revenues in their hands. Second, it could become politically dangerous. In territories with a relatively strong degree of domestic cohesiveness – such as Babylon under the Assyrians and the Achaemenids, Egypt under the Achaemenids, or Judea under the Romans – revolts and secession led by indigenous elites (or by counter-elites, as in the case of Judea) were a permanent threat. Third, whereas the imperial super-elite remained faithful to the empire as such, it was usually the major challenger of individual emperors, taking an active part in coups and counter-coups. All these explain why many empires preferred at a certain point to shift toward a more direct bureaucratic rule, which was more effective, reliable, and also diluted the power of the super-elite.

The trajectory of imperial bureaucratization differed considerably. In the Roman case, for instance, establishing direct rule over newly acquired territories was a very long process. The first provinces under Rome's direct control were established in the aftermath of the First Punic War (264–241 BCE), but for centuries thereafter, as mentioned above, Rome was satisfied with the maintenance of only superficial control over most of the subjugated population, delegating as much power as possible to native elites. The empire's shift toward comprehensive bureaucratization came in the aftermath of the 3rd-century CE crisis. The need to enhance local resource extraction in order to face a variety of military challenges, as well as the emperors' desire to weaken the once-powerful senatorial super-elite brought about profound overhaul of the empire's system of government, which became incomparably more bureaucratic than under the principate (Whitby 2016). In China, in distinction, in the aftermath of Qin's collapse the shift was toward a looser control. Putting aside the details of manifold cycles of decentralization and renewed centralization, we may summarize that Qin's excessive assertiveness remained an exception rather than the rule. Although the Qin bureaucratic model was never discarded – at least in the territories of China proper – beneath the veneer of the fully bureaucratized empire much leeway was given to local elites.[28] In the meantime, on the outskirts of the empire different types of indirect rule were maintained, as will be discussed below.

Throughout their history most empires experimented with different combinations of direct and indirect control over their subjects. One of the most common solutions was establishing direct control over core territories (or territories of exceptional economic and military importance), while allowing more lax control in outlying or otherwise marginal areas. The division between the core and peripheral areas was not uniform (Qin and Russia [Burbank, this volume] are notable exceptions), but in most cases it became the default choice. This means that the imperial periphery was normally ruled less tightly than the core areas. Yet this observation allows us to move to the second question asked above: Should we treat the areas under loose (and often purely nominal or even entirely fictional) control of the imperial center as parts of the empire's space?

Think of the Ottoman example, for instance. Karen Barkey (2016) depicts the complexity of the empire's internal structure, which included areas under direct rule, outer areas under indirect control, where, however, the tendency was toward bureaucratization and assimilation of local elites as "genuine Ottoman provincial officials" (Barkey 2016, 119); and yet less assimilated areas at the empire's fringes. For instance, in the areas affected by the Saffavid–Ottoman struggle (on which see Dale, this volume), Ottoman rule was based on "intense negotiating, trading of incentives and threats of military intervention." As a result, local chieftains "felt the weight of Ottoman control only lightly and felt independent and empowered to maintain rivalry between states [i.e., between the Ottomans and the Safavids]" (Barkey 2016, 121). The question is: Should we consider the areas with such a low density of imperial rule as belonging to the empire at all? This is not an idly asked question. When the Ottoman Empire started disintegrating amid the crisis of the 18th and 19th centuries, its leaders tried to reassess the nature of its lax to non-existent control over nominal parts of the empire by employing the novel concept of "suzerainty" rather than "sovereignty." Some of the territories under the Ottoman "suzerainty" (and even some under its nominal "sovereignty") were already fully independent or subjugated by other imperialist powers (Fujinami 2019). When did the Ottoman control over them become a fiction? Or was it a fiction throughout?

To demonstrate the difficulty in providing an answer, let us turn once again to an example of Chinese Empire. The Han dynasty's expansion beyond the areas

---

[28] For the fluctuation of the empire's relations with these elites, see Pines 2012, 104–33. For tensions surrounding these relations (especially the struggle between the elites and the court over the distribution of revenues), see, e.g., Miller 2009.

of China proper prompted organization of the outlying space in a way that would preserve the fiction of the emperor's universal rule, without however, necessitating direct incorporation of distant lands. The result was the so-called "tribute system" (Pines, this volume). To maintain relations with the Han court, foreign leaders had to pose as the emperor's subjects and present a token tribute as a symbol of their subservient status. The problem was that whereas the Han did distinguish between "internal" and "external" subjects, the tribute obliga-tions of the two groups (i.e., surviving internal princedoms and foreign polities) were often conceptualized along the same lines. This ideologically motivated lack of clear differentiation between the domestic and foreign realms remained characteristic of most Chinese imperial polities. Take, for instance, the Ming and Qing dynasties discussed by Robinson and Mosca in this volume. Their rulers often adopted similar means of interaction with a great variety of distinct political entities – from minor indigenous leaders of ethnic enclaves within China proper (the so-called *tusi*), to peripheral dependencies (like Tibet), to neighboring polities who formally acknowledged their nominal dependence (i.e., Vietnam and Korea), to completely independent outsiders unilaterally regarded as tributaries (i.e., European powers). Which of these should be considered part of China's imperial space?

This question is confusing not only for modern observers. It seems that for the imperial Chinese literati the issue of whether or not the outlying dependencies belonged to the empire's space was confusing as well. Take for instance, the official dynastic history of the Ming, composed almost a century after its fall, that is, in the heyday of the Qing reign. As is common in Chinese dynastic histories, the last chapters of the so-called "arrayed biographies" section are dedicated to non-Chinese political entities. The grouping of these entities into different chapters reflects the compilers' view of these entities' position within the Chinese world order. The Ming history divides these polities into three groups. The first are indigenous leaders within China proper (*tusi*). The second are "foreign states," which include both Ming dependencies (such as Korea and Vietnam) as well as all other known foreign states that maintained only minimal relations with the Ming (e.g., France and Holland). The third group is defined as "Western Regions" and it comprises polities in Tibet, Qinghai, and modern Xinjiang, as well as further west into modern Uzbekistan and even Iran. It seems that the compilers were not entirely sure how to treat these areas, some of which were controlled by the early Ming, then escaped the dynastic control, and later were in the process of absorption into the Qing (Robinson and Mosca, this volume). Unable to decide whether these territories are "internal" or "exter-nal" to the Chinese Empire, the authors opted for a neutral geographic category.

The difficulty of defining the precise contours of the imperial space is not peculiar to China, of course. Many, if not most, empires contained areas, the position of which within the imperial space was contestable. Briant (this volume) discusses areas in the Zagros Mountains and Asia Minor that were nominally under the control of the Achaemenid "king of kings" or his satraps, but the position of which within or outside the imperial space depended "on a balance of power, which sometimes required expeditions at the conclusion of which the king or satrap reasserted his authority through official treaty." In the later Abbasid Caliphate, the gap between the caliph's nominal authority (i.e., his naming in the Friday sermon [*khutba*] and inscribing the coins with his names [*sikka*]) and his real power (i.e., to appoint and supervise local officials) could be huge (Kennedy 2016, 129ff., and more in Peacock, this volume). In this and hundreds of other instances, it is not always easy to determine with certainty which of the areas of the empire's nominal or symbolic control should be treated as part of the imperial space.

5   Summary: The Imperial Space – Image and Reality

The difficulty in distinguishing between the outer and internal realm, as demonstrated by the above examples, suffices to caution us against an attempt to simplify a history of the empires into a neat scheme that would explain the trajectories of their expansion and contraction. Such a scheme, as presented in the studies by Rein Taagepera (1978a; 1978b; 1979; 1997) is problematic not only because of Taagepera's countless historical flaws but primarily because the very method of calculating imperial space as if the empires were contiguous political entities on a par with modern states is fundamentally flawed. Whereas the maps presented in the atlases utilized by Taagepera, as well as the maps prepared for this volume, maintain the heuristic convenience of painting imperial territory in a uniform shade, it should be remembered that this is a convention rather than an accurate depiction of reality (Smith 2005). Tabulating the empires' size on the basis of these maps and then making far-reaching conclusions about their dimensions and long-term trajectories as advocated by Taagepera is untenable.

Our goal in this introduction and this volume is not to substitute Taagepera's scheme with another one-size-fits-all explanation of imperial spatial growth and its cessation. Instead, we wish to summarize our findings by revisiting major factors that influenced the expansion and contraction of imperial space surveyed above and by clarifying why, as historians, we feel that no neat explanation of the changing spatial dimensions will ever be attainable.

Expansionism can be considered the foundational feature of empires (a non-expansionist polity would never become an empire in the first place!). Expansionism was fueled by an avowed desire to attain "universal" rule (a desire that was often conceived as a realization of an empire's divine mission), even if in practice "universal rule" normally meant dominating the empire's macro-region only. In addition, conquest of new territories could bring about a variety of social, political, and economic benefits for the imperial elites (and at times even for the lower strata as well), which further fueled the empire's expansionism. Besides, acquiring territories could be conceived of as a defensive measure aimed to secure the empire from its equally predatory neighbors or as strategic necessity. All these factors combined contributed decisively to the empires' spatial growth.

This growth, however, could not continue forever. Reaching inhibitive terrain (oceans, high mountain ranges) or mere ecological constraints could put an end to the expansion of most (albeit not all) empires. Logistical difficulties or vulnerability of outlying territories could cause cessation of expansionist campaigns and even abandonment of recently conquered territories. The exorbitant costs of maintaining control over expanding space and the related administrative difficulties could further constrain territorial expansion. Besides, once the imperial elites became less reliant on military success for social advancement and economic well-being, they started losing their belligerence and expansionist zeal. At a certain point the imperial leaders had to find ways to retain their symbolic quest for universal supremacy without veering into the direction of over-extension that would threaten domestic stability. Maintaining this delicate balance was a tough task.

The interaction between these multiple factors explains the huge divergence in imperial spatial trajectories. Add to these yet more factors that could influence the empires' dimensions – from the ever changing balance of power between the empire and its external enemies, to shifts in the composition of domestic elites, to the degree of local resistance to the imperial control, to the individual agency of emperors and leading statesmen. Clearly, no neat scheme would ever be able to take all these into account. The contours of the imperial space were shaped through a complex interaction between objective and subjective factors, were influenced by a variety of ideological, military, economic, political, and ecological considerations, and were at times determined by mere contingency. Therefore, whereas major continental empires faced a common set of problems and challenges and often employed similar means of dealing with these challenges, the outcomes differed too much to allow the drawing of a uniform bottom line.

It is against this backdrop that we can understand the complex nature of representing the imperial space. Imperial propaganda (directed at either foreign or domestic audiences), artistic and literary representations of an empire's dimensions, maps and travelogues, historical texts and administrative manuals, imperial pageantry and religious exegesis – these and many other means were utilized to reflect empires' real and imagined spaces. Some representations were descriptive and some prescriptive, some focused on the present, while other were more concerned with the past or the future. Yet behind this plethora of images, one can discern the persistent tension between the ideal and the real, between lofty goals and the quotidian difficulties to attain these goals, between the commitment to *imperium sine fine* and the need to establish its *limes*.

The short dialogue from the brilliant cynical comedy by Friedrich Dürrenmatt with which we opened this introduction is a good expression of this tension between the presentation and actualization of an empire's space. The chapters in this volume focus on the latter as the necessary precondition for understanding the former. The successes and failures of the empires discussed, their remarkable territorial expansion and their inability to expand beyond a certain threshold, their difficulty in coming to terms with their own spatial limits, and their creative ways of overcoming these difficulties – all these open the door to understanding some of the core issues behind imperial political trajectories. Other aspects of imperial dynamics shall be addressed in future volumes.

Bibliography

Alcock, Susan E., with Terence N. D'Altroy, Kathleen D. Morrison, and Carla M. Sinopoli. 2001. *Empires: Perspective from Archaeology and History.* Cambridge: Cambridge University Press.

Allsen, Thomas T. 2011. "Imperial Posts, West, East and North: A Review Article," *Archivum Eurasiae Medii Aevi* 17(1): 237–76.

Allsen, Thomas T. 2015. "Eurasia after the Mongols." In *The Cambridge World History. Volume 6, The Construction of a Global World, 1400–1800 CE, Part 1: Foundations*, ed. Jerry Bentley, Sanjay Subrahmanyam, and Merry E. Wiesner-Hanks, 159–81. Cambridge: Cambridge University Press.

Ando, Clifford. 2018. "Empire as State: The Roman Case." In: *State Formations: Global Histories and Cultures of Statehood*, ed. John L. Brooke, Julia G. Strauss, and Greg Anderson, 175–89. Cambridge: Cambridge University Press.

Arnason, Johann P. 2015. "State formation and empire building." In *The Cambridge World History. Volume 5, Expanding Webs of Exchange and Conflict, 500CE–1500CE*, ed. Benjamin Kedar and Merry E. Wiesner-Hanks, 483–512. Cambridge: Cambridge University Press.

Bang, Peter Fibiger and Christopher A. Bayly, eds. 2011a. *Tributary Empires in Global History.* New York: Palgrave Macmillan.

Bang, Peter Fibiger and Christopher A. Bayly, 2011b. "Tributary Empires – Towards a Global and Comparative History." In: *Tributary Empires in Global History*, ed. Bang and Bayly, 1–17. New York: Palgrave Macmillan.

Bang, Peter Fibiger and Dariusz Kolodziejczyk, eds. 2012. *Universal Empire: A Comparative Approach to Imperial Culture and Representation in Eurasian History.* Cambridge: Cambridge University Press.

Barbieri-Low, Anthony J. and Robin D.S. Yates. 2015. *Law, State, and Society in Early Imperial China: A study with Critical Edition and Translation of the Legal Texts from Zhangjiashan Tomb no. 247.* Leiden: Brill.

Barfield, Thomas. 1989. *The Perilous Frontier: Nomadic Empires and China.* Oxford: Basil Blackwell.

Barkey, Karen. 2016. "The Ottoman Empire (1299–1923): The Bureuacratization of the Patrimonial Authority." In: *Empires and Bureaucracy in World History: From Late Antiquity to the Twentieth Century*, ed. Peter Crooks and Timothy H. Parsons, 129–46. Cambridge: Cambridge University Press.

Bayly, Christopher A. 2011. "Religion, Liberalism and Empires: British Historians and their Indian Critics in the Nineteenth Century." In: *Tributary Empires in Global History*, ed. Peter Fibiger Bang and Christopher A. Bayly, 21–47. New York: Palgrave Macmillan.

Berger, Stefan and Alexei Miller 2015. "Introduction: Building Nations In and With Empires – A Reassessment." In *Nationalizing Empires*, ed. Stefan Berger and Alexei Miller, 1–30. Budapest: Central European University Press.

Biran, Michal. 2007. *Chinggis Khan*. Oxford: Oneworld.

Blanken, Leo J. 2012. *Rational Empires: Institutional Incentives and Imperial Expansion*. Chicago: The University of Chicago Press.

Bonner, Michael. 2010. "The waning of empire, 861–945." In *The New Cambridge History of Islam*, ed. Chase Robinson, 305–59. Cambridge: Cambridge University Press.

Braund, David. 1996. *Ruling Roman Britain. Kings, Queens, Governors and Emperors from Julius Caesar to Agricola*. New York: Routledge.

Briant, Pierre. 2002. *From Cyrus to Alexander: A History of the Persian Empire*, trans. Peter D. Daniels. Winona Lake, IN: Eisenbrauns.

Brooke, John L. 2014. *Climate Change and the Course of Global History: A Rough Journey*. Cambridge: Cambridge University Press.

Burbank, Jane and Frederick Cooper. 2010. *The Empires in World History: Power and the Politics of Difference*. Princeton, NJ: Princeton University Press.

Calasso, Giovanna and Giuliano Lancioni, eds. 2017. *Dār al-islām, dār al-ḥarb: Territories, People, Identities*. Leiden: Brill.

Calhoun, Craig, Frederick Cooper, and Kevin W. Moore, eds. 2006. *Lessons of Empire: Imperial Histories and American Power*. New York: New Press.

Chen Sanping, 1996. "Succession Struggle and the Ethnic Identity of the Tang Imperial House," *Journal of the Royal Asiatic Society* (Third Series) 6(3): 379–405.

Cline, Eric H. and Mark W. Graham. 2011. *Ancient Empires: From Mesopotamia to the Rise of Islam*. Cambridge: Cambridge University Press.

Chu Wen-djang. 1966. *The Moslem Rebellion in Northwest China, 1862–1878: A Study of Government Minority Policy*. Paris: The Hague.

Cobb, Paul. 2010. "The Empire in Syria, 705–763." In *The New Cambridge History of Islam*, ed. Chase Robinson, 226–68. Cambridge: Cambridge University Press.

Corcoran, Simon. 2014. "State Correspondence in the Roman Empire: Imperial Communication from Augustus to Justinian." In: *State Correspondence in the Ancient World: From New Kingdom to the Roman Empire*, ed. Karen Radner, 172–209. Oxford: Oxford University Press.

Crooks, Peter and Timothy H. Parsons. 2016a. *Empires and Bureaucracy in World History: From Late Antiquity to the Twentieth Century*. Cambridge: Cambridge University Press.

Crooks, Peter and Timothy H. Parsons. 2016b. "Empires, Bureaucracy, and the Paradox of Power." In: *Empires and Bureaucracy in World History: From Late Antiquity to the Twentieth Century*, ed. Crooks and Parsons, 3–28. Cambridge: Cambridge University Press.

Dagron, Gilbert. 2003. *Emperor and Priest: The Imperial Office in Byzantium*, trans. Jean Birrell. Cambridge: Cambridge University Press.

Dai, Yingcong. 2009. *The Sichuan Frontier and Tibet: Imperial Strategy in the Early Qing*. Seattle, WA: University of Washington Press.

Doyle, Michael W. 1986. *Empires*. Ithaca, NY: Cornell University Press.

Denaro, Roberta. 2017. "Naming the Enemy's Land: Definitions of *dār al-ḥarb* in Ibn al-Mubārak's *Kitāb al-Jihād*." In: *Dār al-islām, dār al-ḥarb: Territories, People, Identities*, ed. Giovanna Calasso and Giuliano Lancioni, 93–107. Leiden: Brill.

Di Cosmo, Nicola. 2002. *Ancient China and Its Enemies: The Rise of Nomadic Power in East Asian History*. Cambridge: Cambridge University Press.

Di Cosmo, Nicola and Michael Maas. 2018. *Empires and Exchanges in Eurasian Late Antiquity: Rome, China, Iran, and the Steppe, ca. 250–750*. Cambridge: Cambridge University Press.

Di Cosmo, Nicola, Amy Hessl, Caroline Leland, Oyunsanaa Byambasuren, Hanqin Tian, Baatarbileg Nachin, Neil Pederson, Laia Andreu-Hayles, and Edward R. Cook. 2018. "Environmental Stress and Steppe Nomads: Rethinking the History of the Uyghur Empire (744–840) with Paleoclimate Data." *Journal of Interdisciplinary History* 48(4): 439–63.

Drompp, Michael R. 1999. "Breaking the Orkhon Tradition: Kirghiz Adherence to the Yenisei Region after AD 840," *Journal of the American Oriental Society* 119(3): 390–403.

Drompp, Michael R. 2018. "The Kök Türk Empires." *Oxford Research Encyclopedia: Asian History*. DOI:10.1093/acrefore/9780190277727.013.52.

Düring, Bleda S., and Tesse D. Stek, eds. 2018. *The Archaeology of Imperial Landscapes: A Comparative Study of Empires in the Ancient Near East and Mediterranean World*. Cambridge: Cambridge University Press.

Eisenstadt, Shmuel N. 1963. *The Political System of Empires*. London: Free Press of Glencoe.

Eisenstadt, Shmuel N. and Arie Shachar. 1987. *Society, Culture, and Urbanization*. Newbury Park, CA: SAGE Publications.

Ellenblum, Ronnie. 2012. *Collapse of the Eastern Mediterranean: Climate Change and the Decline of the East, 950–1072*. Cambridge: Cambridge University Press.

Elliott, Mark C. 2005. "Whose Empire Shall It Be? Manchu Figurations of Historical Process in the Early Seventeenth Century." In: *Time, Temporality, and Imperial Transition: East Asia from Ming to Qing*, ed. Lynn A. Struve, 31–72. Honolulu, HI: University of Hawaii Press.

Fall, Juliet J. 2010. "Artificial States? On the Enduring Geographical Myth of Natural Borders." *Political Geography* 29: 140–7.

Ferguson, Niall. 2004. *Colossus: The Rise and Fall of the American Empire*. London: Penguin.

Finch, John. 1844. *The Natural Boundaries of Empires: And a New View of Colonization*. London: Longman.

Fowden, Garth. 1993. *Empire to Commonwealth: Consequences of Monotheism in Late Antiquity*. Princeton, NJ: Princeton University Press.

Fowden, Garth. 2012. "Pseudo-Aristotelian Politics and Theology in Universal Islam." In: *Universal Empire: A Comparative Approach to Imperial Culture and Representation in Eurasian History*, ed. Peter Fibiger Bang and Dariusz Kolodziejczyk, 130–48. Cambridge: Cambridge University Press.

Fujinami Nobuyoshi. 2019. "Between Sovereignty and Suzerainty: History of the Ottoman Privileged Provinces." In: *A World History of Suzerainty: A Modern History of East and West Asia and Translated Concepts*, ed. Okamoto Tadashi, 41–60. Tokyo: Toyo Bunko.

Garnsey, Peter D. A. and C. R. Whittaker. 1978. *Imperialism in the Ancient World.* Cambridge: Cambridge University Press.

Geanakoplos, Deno J. 1965. "Church and State in the Byzantine Empire: A Reconsideration of the Problem of Caesaropapism." *Church History* 34(4): 381–403.

Geertz, Clifford. 1981. *Negara: The Theatre State in 19th Century Bali.* Princeton, NJ: Princeton University Press.

Gehler, Michael and Robert Rollinger, eds. 2014. *Imperien und Reiche in der Weltgeschichte. Epochenübergreifende und globalhistorische Vergleiche. Teil 1: Imperien des Altertums, Mittelalterliche und frühneuzeitliche Imperien.* Wiesbaden: Harrassowitz.

Gillingham, John. 2016. "Bureaucracy, the English State and the Crisis of the Angevin Empire, 1199–1205." In *Empires and Bureaucracy in World History: From Late Antiquity to the Twentieth Century*, ed. Peter Crooks and Timothy H. Parsons, 197–220. Cambridge: Cambridge University Press.

Golden, Peter B. 1982. "Imperial Ideology and the Sources of Political Unity amongst the pre-Činggisid Nomads of Western Eurasia." *Archivum Eurasiae Medii Aevi* 2: 37–77.

Goldstone, Jack A. and John F. Haldon. 2009. "Ancient States, Empires and Exploitation: Problems and Perspectives." In *The Dynamics of Ancient Empires: State Power from Assyria to Byzantium*, ed. Ian Morris and Walter Scheidel, 3–29. Oxford: Oxford University Press.

Grüll, Tibor, 2017. "The Idea of World Empire in Ancient Rome." *Specimina Nova Universitatis Quinqueecclesiensis* 24: 7–57.

Hämäläinen, Pekka. 2008. *The Comanche Empire.* New Haven, CT: Yale University Press.

Harari, Yuval N. 2015. *Sapiens: A Brief History of Humankind.* New York: Harper Collins.

Haubold, Johannes. 2012. "The Achaemenid Empire and the Sea." *Mediterranean Historical Review* 27(1): 5–24.

Hazard, Leland, 1965. "New World Factors and Old Empire." In: *Empire Revisited*, by Leland Hazard with contributions by Bernard Brodie, 1–20. Homewood, IL: Irwin.

Hglin, Thomas O. 1982. "The Idea of Empire: Conditions for Integration and Disintegration in Europe." *Publius* 12(3): 11–42.

Hopkins, Keith. 2009. "The Political Economy of the Roman Empire." In: *Dynamics of Ancient Empires: State Power from Assyria to Byzantium*, ed. Walter Scheidel and Ian Morris, 178–204. Oxford: Oxford University Press.

Hou Xudong. 2016. "The Helpless Emperor: The Expenditure on Official Hostel System and Its Institutional Change in the Late Former Han China." *World History Studies* 3(2): 1–23.

Kagan, Kimberley. 2006. "Redefining Roman Grand Strategy." *The Journal of Military History* 70(2): 333–62.

Kagan, Kimberly, ed. 2010. *The Imperial Moment*. Cambridge, MA: Harvard University Press.

Kennedy, Hugh. 2010. "The Late ʿAbbāsid pattern, 945–1050." In *The New Cambridge History of Islam*, ed. Chase Robinson, 360–94. Cambridge: Cambridge University Press.

Kennedy, Hugh. 2016. *Caliphate: The History of an Idea*. New York: Basic books.

Khazanov, Anatoly M. 2015. "The Schitians and their Neighbors." In *Nomads as Agents of Cultural Change: The Mongols and Their Eurasian Predecessors*, ed. Reuven Amitai and Michal Biran, 32–49. Honolulu, HI: University of Hawaii Press.

Kim, Hyun Jin, Frederik Juliaan Vervaet, and Selim Ferruh Adalı. 2017. *Eurasian Empires in Antiquity and the Early Middle Ages Contact and Exchange between the Graeco-Roman World, Inner Asia and China*. Cambridge: Cambridge University Press.

Korolkov, Maxim. 2020. "Empire-Building and Market-Making at the Qin Frontier: Imperial Expansion and Economic Change, 221–207 BCE." PhD dissertation, Columbia University, New York.

Kuhrt, Amélie. 2014. "State Communications in the Persian Empire." In: *State Correspondence in the Ancient World: From New Kingdom to the Roman Empire*, ed. Karen Radner, 112–40. Oxford: Oxford University Press.

Kumar, Krishan. 2010. "Nation-states as Empires, Empires as Nation-states: Two Principles, One Practice?" *Theory and Society* 39(2): 119–43.

Lavan, Myles, Richard E. Payne, and John Weisweiler. 2016a. *Cosmopolitanism and Empire: Universal Rulers, Local Elites, and Cultural Integration in the Ancient Near East and Mediterranean*. New York: Oxford University Press.

Lavan, Myles, Richard E. Payne, and John Weisweiler. 2016b. "Cosmopolitan Politics: The Assimilation and Subordination of Elite Cultures." In: *Cosmopolitanism and Empire: Universal Rulers, Local Elites, and Cultural Integration in the Ancient Near East and Mediterranean*, ed. Myles Lavan et al., 1–28. New York: Oxford University Press.

Lewis, Mark E. 2007. *The Early Chinese Empires: Qin and Han*. Cambridge, MA: Harvard University Press.

Li Yali, Gideon Shelach, and Ronnie Ellenblum. 2019. "Short-Term Climatic Catastrophes and the Collapse of the Liao Dynasty (907–1125): Textual Evidence." *Journal of Interdisciplinary History* 49(4): 591–610.

Liverani, Mario. 1979. "The Ideology of the Assyrian Empire," in *Power and Propaganda: A Symposium on Ancient Empires*, ed. Mogens T. Larsen, 297–317. Copenhagen: Akademisk forlag.

Liverani, Mario. 2001. *International Relations in the Ancient Near East, 1600–1100 BC*. Houndmills: Palgrave.

Luttwak, Edward. 1976. *Grand Strategy of the Roman Empire from the First Century A.D. to the Third*. Baltimore, MD: Johns Hopkins University Press.

Malešević, Siniša. 2017. "Empires and Nation-States: Beyond the Dichotomy." *Thesis Eleven* 20: 1–8.

Mann, Michael. 1986. *The Sources of Social Power. Volume I: A History of Power from the Beginning to A.D. 1760*. Cambridge: Cambridge University Press.

Mann, Michael. 2003. *Incoherent Empire*. London and New York: Verso.

Martynov, Aleksandr S. 1987. "Конфуцианская утопия в древности и средневековье." In: *Китайские социальные утопии*, ed. Lev P. Deliusin and L. N. Borokh, 10–57. Moscow: Nauka.

Mattern, Susan P. 1999. *Rome and the Enemy: Imperial Strategy in the Principate*. Berkeley, CA: University of California Press.

MacKenzie, John M., ed. 2016. *The Encyclopedia of Empire*. Chichester: Wiley-Blackwell.

McCoy, Alfred W., Josep M. Fradera, and Stephen Jacobson. 2012. *Endless Empire: Spain's Retreat, Europe's Eclipse, America's Decline*. Madison, WI: Wisconsin University Press.

McNeill, John R. "China's Environmental History in World Perspective." In *Sediments of Time: Environment and Society in Chinese History*, ed. Mark Elvin and LiuTs'ui-jung, 31–49. Cambridge: Cambridge University Press, 1998.

Miller, Harry. 2009. *State versus Gentry in Late Ming Dynasty China, 1572–1644*. New York: Palgrave Macmillan.

Millward, James. 1998. *Beyond the Pass: Economy, Ethnicity, and Empire in Qing Central Asia, 1759–1864*. Stanford, CA: Stanford University Press.

Morris, Ian and Walter Scheidel, eds. 2009. *The Dynamics of Ancient Empires: State Power from Assyria to Byzantium*. Oxford: Oxford University Press.

Morkot, Robert. 2001. "Egypt and Nubia." In: *Empires: Perspective from Archaeology and History*, ed. Susan E Alcock, Terence N. D'Altroy, Kathleen D. Morrison, Carla M. Sinopoli, 227–51. Cambridge: Cambridge University Press.

Morris, Ian. 2009. "The Great Athenian State." In *The Dynamics of Ancient Empires: State Power from Assyria to Byzantium*, ed. Ian Morris and Walter Scheidel, 99–178. Oxford: Oxford University Press.

Münkler, Herfried. 2007. *Empires: The Logic of World Domination from Ancient Rome to the United States*. Cambridge: Polity.

Muthu, Sankar. 2009. *Enlightenment against Empire*. Princeton NJ: Princeton University Press.

Mutschler, Fritz-Heiner, and Achim Mittag, eds. 2008. *Conceiving the Empire: China and Rome Compared*. Oxford: Oxford University Press.

Negri, Antonio and Michael Hardt 2000. *Empire*. Cambridge, MA: Harvard University Press.

Olivelle, Patrick. 2013. *King, Governance, and Law in Ancient India: Kauṭilya's Arthaśāstra*. Oxford: Oxford University Press.

Olivelle, Patrick. 2018. "Imperial Ideology and Religious Pluralism in The Aśokan Inscriptional Corpus." Paper presented at the workshop "Empires and Religions," Berlin, March 1–3.

Parker, Bradley J. 2002. "At the Edge of Empire: Conceptualizing Assyria's Anatolian Frontier ca. 700 BC." *Journal of Anthropological Archaeology* 21: 371–95.

Parsons, Timothy H. 2010. *The Rule of Empires: Those Who Built Them, Those Who Endured Them, and Why They Always Fall*. Oxford: Oxford University Press.

Perdue, Peter C. 2005. *China Marches West: The Qing Conquest of Central Eurasia*. Cambridge, MA: The Belknap Press of Harvard University Press.

Peterson, Charles A., 1979. "Court and Province in Mid- and Late T'ang." In: *The Cambridge History of China. Volume 3, Sui and T'ang China, 589–906 AD, Part One*, ed. Denis C. Twitchett, 464–560. Cambridge: Cambridge University Press.

Preiser-Kapeller, Johannes. 2018. "A Christian Roman Empire? Byzantium between imperial monotheism and religious multiplicity, 4th–9th century CE." Paper presented at the workshop "Empires and Religions," Berlin, March 1–3.

Pines, Yuri. 2002. "Changing Views of *tianxia* in Pre-imperial Discourse." *Oriens Extremus* 43(1/2): 101–16.

Pines, Yuri. 2012. *The Everlasting Empire: The Political Culture of Ancient China and Its Imperial Legacy.* Princeton, NJ: Princeton University Press.

Pitts, Jennifer. 2010. "Political Theory of Empire and Imperialism." *Annual Review of Political Science* 13: 211–235.

Pollock, Sheldon. 2005. "Axialism and Empire." In: *Axial Civilization and World History*, ed. Johann P. Arnason, Shmuel N. Eisenstadt, and Björn Wittrock, 387–450. Leiden: Brill.

Pollock, Sheldon. 2006. "Empire and Imitation." In: *Lessons of Empire*, ed. Craig Calhoun, Frederick Cooper, and Kevin Moore, 175–88. New York: New Press.

Pomper, Philip. 2005. "The History and Theory of Empires." *History and Theory* 44 (4): 1–27.

Radner, Karen. 2014a. "Introduction: Long-Distance Communication and the Cohesion of Early Empires." In: *State Correspondence in the Ancient World: From New Kingdom to the Roman Empire*, ed. Karen Radner, 1–9. Oxford: Oxford University Press.

Radner, Karen. 2014b. "An Imperial Communication Network: The State Correspondence of the Neo-Assyrian Empire." In: *State Correspondence in the Ancient World: From New Kingdom to the Roman Empire*, ed. Karen Radner, 64–93. Oxford: Oxford University Press.

Radner, Karen, ed. 2014c. *State Correspondence in the Ancient World: From New Kingdom to the Roman Empire.* Oxford: Oxford University Press.

Reinhard, Wolfgang, ed. 2015a. *Empires and Encounters: 1350–1750.* Cambridge, MA: The Belknap Press of Harvard University Press.

Reinhard, Wolfgang. 2015b. "Introduction." In: *Empires and Encounters: 1350–1750*, ed. by Wolfgang Reinhard, 1–52. Cambridge, MA: The Belknap Press of Harvard University Press.

Reynolds, Susan. 2006. "Empires: a Problem of Comparative History." *Historical Research* 79(204): 151–65.

Robinson, Chase. 2010. "The Rise of Islam, 600–705." In: *The New Cambridge History of Islam*, ed. Chase Robinson, 171–225. Cambridge: Cambridge University Press.

Rollinger, Robert. 2013. "The View from East to West: World View and Perception of Space in the Neo-Assyrian Empire." In: *Aneignung und Abgrenzung. Wechselnde Perspektiven auf die Antithese von 'Ost' und 'West' in der griechischen Antike*, ed. Nicolas Zenzen, Tonio Hölscher, and Kai Trampedach, 93–134. Heidelberg: Antike Verlag.

Romm, James S. 1992. *The Edges of the Earth in Ancient Thought: Geography, Exploration, and Fiction.* Princeton, NJ: Princeton University Press.

Rossabi, Morris. 1983. *China among Equals: The Middle Kingdom and its Neighbors, 10th–14th Centuries.* Berkeley, CA: University of California Press.

Scales, Len. 2018. "Eschatology and the Medieval Western Empire." Paper presented at the workshop "Empires and Religions," Berlin, March 1–3.

Schafer, Edward H. 1954. *The Empire of Min: A South China Kingdom of the Tenth Century.* Rutland, VT: Tuttle.

Scharfe, Hartmut. 1989. *The State in Indian Tradition.* Leiden: Brill.

Scheidel, Walter, ed. 2009. *Rome and China: Comparative Perspectives on Ancient World Empires*. Oxford: Oxford University Press.

Scheidel, Walter, ed. 2015. *State Power in Ancient China and Rome*. Oxford Studies in Early Empires. Oxford: Oxford University Press.

Shahbazi, Alireza Shapour. 2001. "Early Sasanians' Claim to Achaemenid Heritage." *Journal of Ancient Persian History* 1(1): 61–73.

Shayegan, M. Rahim. 2011. *Arsacids and Sasanians: Political Ideology in Post-Hellenistic and Late Antique Persia*. Cambridge: Cambridge University Press.

Shelach, Gideon. 2014. "Collapse or Transformation? Anthropological and Archaeological Perspectives on the Fall of Qin." In: *Birth of an Empire: The State of Qin revisited*, ed. Yuri Pines, Lothar von Falkenhausen, Gideon Shelach and Robin D.S. Yates, 113–40. Berkeley, CA: University of California Press.

Silverstein, Adam J. 2007. *Postal Systems in the Pre-Modern Islamic World*. Cambridge: Cambridge University Press.

Sinor, Denis. 1990. "The Establishment and Dissolution of the Türk Empire." In *The Cambridge History of Early Inner Asia*, ed. Denis Sinor, 285–316. Cambridge: Cambridge University Press.

Smarczyk, Bernhard. 2007. "Religion und Herrschaft: Der Delisch-Attische Seebund." *Saeculum* 58(2): 205–28.

Smith, Monica. 2005. "Networks, Territories, and the Cartography of Ancient States." *Annals of the Association of American Geographers* 95(4): 832–49.

Snyder, Jack. 1991. *Myths of Empire: Domestic Politics and International Ambition*. Ithaca, NY: Cornell University Press.

Somers, Robert M. 1979. "The End of the T'ang." In: *The Cambridge History of China. Volume 3, Sui and T'ang China, 589–906 AD, Part One*, ed. Denis C. Twitchett, 682–789. Cambridge: Cambridge University Press.

Strong, John S. 1983. *The Legend of King Aśoka. A Study and Translation of the Aśokāvadāna*. Princeton, NJ: Princeton University Press.

Strootman, Rolf. 2014. "Hellenistic Imperialism and the Ideal of World Unity." In: *The City in the Classical and Post-Classical World: Changing Contexts of Power and Identity*, ed. Claudia Rapp and H. A. Drake, 38–61. Cambridge: Cambridge University Press.

Taagepera, Rein. 1978a. "Size and Duration of Empires: Systematics of Size." *Social Science Research* 7: 108–27.

Taagepera, Rein. 1987b. "Size and Duration of Empires: Growth-Decline Curves, 3000 to 600 BC." *Social Science Research* 7: 180–96.

Taagepera, Rein. 1979. "Size and Duration of Empires: Growth-Decline Curves, 600 B. C. to 600 A.D." *Social Science History* 3: 115–38.

Taagepera, Rein. 1997. "Expansion and Contraction Patterns of Large Polities: Context for Russia." *International Studies Quarterly* 41: 475–504.

Tackett, Nicolas. 2017. *The Origins of the Chinese Nation: Song China and the Forging of an East Asian World Order*. Cambridge: Cambridge University Press.

Thapar, Romila. 1961. *Aśoka and the Decline of the Mauryas*. Oxford: Oxford University Press.

Tracy, James D. 2002. *Emperor Charles V, Impresario of War: Campaign Strategy, International Finance, and Domestic Politics*. Cambridge: Cambridge University Press.

Tse, Wicky W.K. 2018. *The Collapse of China's Later Han Dynasty, 25–220 CE: The Northwest Borderlands and the Edge of Empire*. London: Routledge.

Turchin, Peter, Jonathan M. Adams, and Thomas D. Hall. 2006. "East-West Orientation of Historical Empires and Modern States." *Journal of World-Systems Research* 12(2): 218–29.

Tymowski, Michal. 2011. "Early Imperial Formations in Africa and the Segmentation of Power." In: *Tributary Empires in Global History*, ed. Peter Fibiger Bang and Christopher A. Bayly, 108–19. New York: Palgrave Macmillan.

Van De Mieroop, Marc. 2016. *A History of the Ancient Near East ca. 3000–323 BC*, 3rd edn. Chichester: Wiley Blackwell.

Wang Gungwu. 1983. "The Rhetoric of a Lesser Empire: Early Sung Relations with Its Neighbors." In *China Among Equals: The Middle Kingdom and Its Neighbors, 10th–14th Centuries*, ed. Morris Rossabi, 47–65. Berkeley, CA: University of California Press.

Wang Zhenping. 2013. *Tang China in Multi-Polar Asia: A History of Diplomacy and War*. Honolulu, HI: University of Hawai'i Press.

Watson, Burton, trans. 1993. *Records of the Grand Historian. Vol. 3: Qin Dynasty*. Hong Kong: Chinese University of Hong Kong.

Wesson, Robert G. 1967. *The Imperial Order*. Berkeley, CA: University of California Press.

Whitby, Michael. 2016. "The Late Roman Empire Was before All Things a Bureaucratic State." In: *Empires and Bureaucracy in World History: From Late Antiquity to the Twentieth Century*, ed. Peter Crooks and Timothy H. Parsons, 129–46. Cambridge: Cambridge University Press.

Woolf, Stuart. 1991. *Napoleon's Integration of Europe*. London: Longman.

Wright, Arthur. 1957. "Sui Ideology." In: *Chinese Thought and Institutions*, ed. John K. Fairbank, 71–104. Chicago, IL: University of Chicago Press.

Yar-Shater, Ehsan. 1971. "Were the Sasanians Heirs to the Achaemenids?" In *La Persia nel Medioevo, Atti del Convegno Internazionale (Roma, 31 Marzo–5 Aprile 1970)*, 517–31. Rome: Accademia Nazionale dei Lincei.

1   From the Mediterranean to the Indus Valley: Modalities and Limitations of the Achaemenid Imperial Space

Pierre Briant

1.1   Preliminary Remarks: Power and Control

The Achaemenid Empire founded by Cyrus the Great (550–530 BCE),[1] expanded by his successors, Cambyses (530–522) and most importantly Darius the Great (522–486), was conquered by Alexander the Great between 334 and 323. After the wars between the successors of the Macedonian conqueror, also known as the Diadochi, the empire imploded into several competing kingdoms (the Hellenistic kingdoms). From a geopolitical global perspective, the establishment of the empire of the Great Kings put an end to a very long period of territorial divisions among several kingdoms and empires, such as those existing around 550 (Pharaonic Egypt, the Lydian Kingdom in Asia Minor, the neo-Babylonian kingdom in Mesopotamia and in the Fertile Crescent, the Median kingdom in the surroundings of Hamadan/Ecbatana, etc.). The Achaemenid historical phase represents thus a singular moment in the *longue durée*: it is the first and last time in history that these peoples and countries were united within a unitary state structure for more than two centuries. This would later be called the Persian-Achaemenid Empire, in line with the name of the reigning dynasty (Map 1.1).

To the great surprise of his contemporaries, Alexander the Great succeeded in seizing the empire following four major battles. One of which, the Battle of Gaugamela in October 331, made possible the consequent capturing of the large royal residences situated in the Babylonian and Elamite plains (Babylon, Susa) as well as those situated on the Persian (Persepolis, Pasargadae) and Median plateau (Ecbatana). Since antiquity, Alexander's victory traditionally served as a proof to the weakness of state control in the Achaemenid region and an indication of its irremediable decadence. In line with the fourth-century Plato and Xenophon views, this decadence is proposed as starting with the death of Cyrus in 530.[2] In modern Europe, one of the most popular thesis was to

---

[1] Hereafter all dates are before common era (BCE) unless indicated otherwise.
[2] See Briant 2002b, where the texts are quoted and commented.

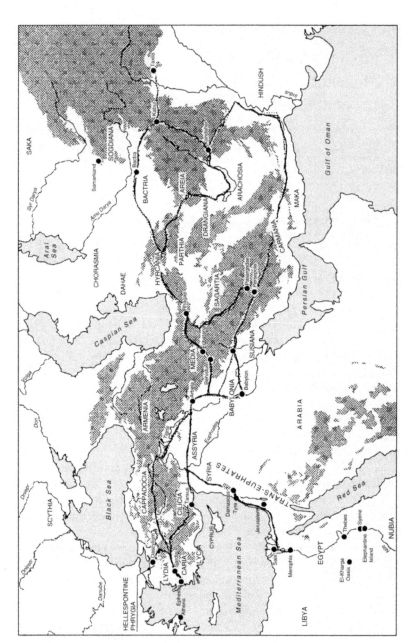

Map 1.1 The Achaemenid Empire. Copyright Achemenet, Paris.

condemn together the Achaemenid and the Ottoman Empires: both were depicted as "despotic," but also as extremely fragile structures. Notwithstanding their arrogant claims, the despotic rulers of these polities were said to be unable to fully control the territories under their nominal rule. Put to the challenge of an exterior shock, both polities "collapsed under their own weight."[3]

Generally, the abovementioned thesis is nowadays considered too simplistic and is by and large dismissed. Nonetheless, the victorious crossing of the empire's western borders in 334 by Macedonian armies, followed by the fall of the royal residences in 331–330, poses substantial questions about the nature of the Achaemenid rule. How did the Achaemenids conceive the control of their imperial space? What were the governance techniques that enabled the empire to remain intact for more than two centuries? The difficulty in answering these questions is aggravated by the evident absence, under the Achaemenid Empire, of either dissemination of the Persian language or the emergence of archeologically identifiable "Achaemenid civilization," which could have assisted in bringing together the various peoples of the empire. This explains why in 1980 a British archaeologist, the late Roger Moorey, made the following observation:

Material traces of the two hundred years of Persian rule in the Near East are still generally elusive. In many regions of their far-flung empire, this period is amongst the least known archaeologically. . . . As rulers, they [the Achaemenids] seem primarily to have lived in enclaves or in military strongholds, widely scattered, but linked by a highly efficient communication system and by the strongly centralized administration it served and fostered.[4]

The formulations create an image of an empire comprised of territories most of which were not under the effective control of the conquerors, who were reduced to living in "enclaves." In 1990, Heleen Sancisi-Weerdenburg, summed up the impasse in the debates at that time in a provocative title "The Quest for an Elusive Empire," and attempted to define an approach that would not confront the "archeological" and "historical" visions. This also explains why, in the first lines of my 1996 synthesis (Briant 2002a, 1), I raised a programmatic question in an interrogative and provocative manner: "Was there ever an Achaemenid Empire?" Lastly, in 2003, Remy Boucharlat and myself once again used a similar formulation when organizing a colloquium on the archaeology of the Achaemenid Empire.[5]

During the last twenty-five years, the discoveries and publications have increased to such an extent that a territory, which, in evidence available in 1990 appeared not to be covered by a tightly knit administrative network,

---

[3] On this theme, see Briant 2010; 2017a, 318–39.
[4] See citation, references and commentaries in Briant 1987 and KCP, 48–9.
[5] See Briant and Boucharlat 2005, 17–25.

presents in 2017 a very different image.[6] In this context, the research done on the Elamite tablets of Persepolis is of paramount importance.[7] A good example is that of Central Asia since the arrival on the antiquity market (in 2000) of Aramaic documents on leather from Afghanistan (Naveh and Shaked 2012), and also the publication of fragments of Elamite tablets found in Old Kandahar (Fischer and Stolper 2015). Renowned as a largely autonomous area in the empire of the Great Kings, this vast territory was under the control of satraps.[8] Despite maintaining a significant degree of autonomy, these satraps were under the supervision of Persepolis and employed Aramaic scribes whose vocabulary and formulations were similar to those used by other Aramaic scribes, for example, in Achaemenid Egypt. Meanwhile, the publication of the 460 demotic ostraca discovered in the Ayn Manawîr oasis in western Egypt is likewise very telling. These ostraca that mention the regnal years of the Great Kings from the fifth century show that at the other end of the empire, this Egyptian village was well included in the empire's space.[9] In particular, the question is whether the existence of underground water channels in that oasis indicates the extension towards Egypt of an Iranian technique (attested on the Persian plateau during the Achaemenid period) as part of an active development policy of the Achaemenid central government.[10] There are other examples, including the findings of archaeological excavations from the Bactria-Sogdiana area, the Caucasus and Western Minor Asia, and the great royal residences, all of which considerably expand the available documentation.[11] In this regard, it is also important to consider the iconographic documentation bearing witness to

[6] Besides BHAch I (1997) and II (2001), Briant 1999, a collection of commented documents of Kuhrt (2007), and conference proceedings published in the series *Transeuphratène* (Paris), *Persika* (Paris) and *Classica et Orientalia* (Wiesbaden), see my bibliographical reviews in Briant 2016a; 2017b, 1–39. See also www.achemenet.com, where numerous publications of documents may be found, and since 2001, specialized articles published in the online publication ARTA: www.achemenet.com/en/table/?/on-line-publications/arta/tableau-des-articles.

[7] Selectively published by Cameron 1949 and by Hallock (1969, 1978), the Persepolis tablets are currently being exhaustively published by a team led by M. W. Stolper in Chicago: see, for example Briant, Henkelman, Stolper 2008, 16–25 and passim; Jacobs, Henkelman, and Stolper 2017 (in particular Stolper 2017 and Henkelman 2017). In principal, the chronological arc of the tablets is limited (see HPE, 422–424), yet we understand today that the setup of this system dates before the establishment of Persepolis by Darius. This system was maintained throughout the entire Achaemenid history.

[8] The satrap is the head of one of the (around twenty-five) imperial administrative units (called satrapies): see section 1.4.

[9] *Ostraka* published on www.achemenet.com/en/tree/?/textual-sources/texts-by-languages-and-scripts/hieroglyphic-and-demotic-egyptian/ostraca-from-ain-manawir#set, with all necessary references.

[10] See Briant 2001 and 2002c, with edits in KCP, 16–17. I also reflected (2017d, §1.3) on possible relationships between the village micro-history and imperial history. Concerning the underground channels of irrigation in Achaemenid Egypt, the debate continues (cf. Agut and Moreno-Garcia 2016, 638, and Boucharlat 2017, particularly pp. 291–2).

[11] See Briant-Boucharlat 2005; Khatchadourian 2016.

the imprint of Persian themes in the provinces – a documentation provoking diverging political interpretations.[12]

Owing to the persistent ambiguity of the available documentation, the question of the Persian imperial presence posed above should still be born in mind, even though today it must be phrased differently (e.g., Colburn 2017). It is time to renounce the debate between a "centralist" thesis – based on the implicit postulate that antiquity state-building can be analyzed through concepts and ideas that came into being very late and exclusively in Europe – and an "autonomist" thesis that reduces the imperial authority to the network of the great royal roads. A distinction must be made between "control" and "authority." Local authorities (sanctuaries, kings, peoples, cities) did not necessarily come into conflict with imperial control. On the contrary, the recognition of local authorities was one of the modes of exercising imperial authority in the provinces. Insofar as their decisions and activities did not oppose the requirements of the imperial power, various local authorities (kings of the Phoenician cities, heads of Egyptian and Babylonian sanctuaries, governments of Greek cities, etc.) preserved their sphere of influence. Influence would be preserved if obligations (e.g., taxes, supply of troops, ships, and so forth) remained fulfilled. Among many others, one wonderfully eloquent document – the famous trilingual inscription of Xanthos – allows us to analyze the entanglement of powers and responsibilities, those exerted by the satrap (Pixodaros) and those exercised by the city of Xanthos: "Royal power and satrapal authority oversee the maintenance of peace and prosperity in their states, by acknowledging the customs, languages and institutions of local communities whose continued existence and functioning they favored."[13]

1.2   Imperial Space Limited by Its Borders

Through text and images, the Great Kings have frequently exalted their power over their diverse territories and peoples. Following his victories in 522–520 over the nine "liar-kings," who were depicted as displayed before him, bound to each other, in a defeated position, Darius had the text of his exploits engraved on the cliff of Media's Behistun:[14]

I am Darius, the Great King, King of kings, king in Persia, king of peoples/countries (*dayava*) ... These are the peoples/ countries who obey me ... In all, twenty-three, ... they were my faithful subjects.

These peoples are regularly enumerated in the inscriptions of Darius and his successors. They are carved on the royal tombs (in the form of the throne

---

[12] See review in Briant 2015.
[13] See KCP, 99–127 (with several updates, pp. 7–8); citation, p. 122.
[14] The translations of the royal inscriptions are borrowed from Kuhrt 2007, 141–57 and 476–505.

bearers), on the stairs of the Persepolis *apadana*[15] (as delegations carrying tributes/gifts of the most remarkable products from their regions) or even on the base of the statue of Darius discovered in Susa but carved in Egypt. On the folds of the statue itself, Darius is adorned with the following titles: "I am Darius, Great King, King of kings, King of countries, King on this great earth." Furthermore, Darius proclaims that in the future those who gaze at the statue would "know that the Persian man holds Egypt." Another example is that of the foundation charters of the palace of Susa in which Darius flatters himself that he could have used materials and artisans from the entire empire. For example, the gold arrived from Lydia and Bactria, the lapis-lazuli from Sogdiana and Chorasmia, the ivory from Nubia, India and Arachosia, etc. The number and order of the people and countries might have varied but the message remained the same: the message of immense territorial power, symbolized by the seizure of the material and human wealth of each country submitted to the Great King. Beyond this ideal unity, the royal declarations do not fail to highlight the ecological and cultural diversity of the empire. This is well illustrated in the trilingual inscription of Persepolis:

Over this wide earth, there are many lands: Persia, Media and the other lands of other tongues, of mountains and plains, from this side of the sea to that side of the sea, from this side of the desert to that side of the desert. (HPE, 172–81)

Beyond these repetitive declarations that are more ideological than administrative,[16] the royal inscriptions provide information on one concrete reality, namely the existence of imperial boundaries. Let us start with a sentence from Darius's inscription, which was engraved on four plates of gold and silver deposited in pairs at the northeast and southwest corners of the Persepolis *apadana* (DPh): "This [is] the kingdom which I hold, from the Saka who are beyond Sogdiana, from there as far as Kush, from the Indus as far as Sardis." This text alone makes one doubt that the Achaemenids had ever aspired to universal domination, except by implicitly assimilating imperial space and the universe.[17] Their empire is immense and of infinite variety, but it is limited to the four cardinal points.

---

[15] Known through royal inscriptions, the term *apadana* is usually translated or rather understood as audience-hall.

[16] The list of lands (*dahyava*) inspired multiple analyses: See for example Herrenschmidt (2014).

[17] Cf. HPE, 179: "What Darius calls the land (*bûmi*) – what the Greeks call *arkhè* [territorial dominion] and what we ourselves call Empire – is notionally merged with the frontiers of the known world: the Empire represents the totality of lands and peoples." This is precisely the reality expressed by Dino who writes (*ap.* Plutarch, *Alex.* 36.4): "The Persian kings had water fetched from the Nile and the Danube, which they laid up in their treasuries as a sort of testimony of their power (*arkhè*) and universal empire (*to kyreuein hapantôn*)." The borders of the empire are also evoked in other classical texts (Herodotus, Xenophon, etc.) yet under vague formulations (HPE, 179).

1. Towards the west, the imperial lands are bordered by the eastern Mediterranean. Equipped with an acropolis, a garrison and a treasury, the city of Sardis can be considered the center of the imperial domination in western Asia Minor, at least symbolically, due to its status as the capital of the ancient Lydian kingdom, which the Persian empire replaced.[18]

2. Towards the south, the land of Kush (Nubia) is theoretically included in the list of lands under Achaemenid control but in reality the border was situated at the level of the second Nile cataract in Elephantine (Agut and Moreno-Garcia 2016, 634). There, a powerful garrison, composed of troops from all over the empire, was stationed.[19] Moreover, when, in 332, after the conquest of Egypt, Alexander had to choose a place to imprison rebels, he sent them to Elephantine.[20] In general, border zones were sites of banishment, whether located in southern Egypt, Bactria-Sogdiana or the islands of the Persian Gulf.[21]

3. To the north, Darius evokes the Sakas, also called the Scythians of Asia in the Greek sources. Cyrus had already waged war against them, and Darius himself led an army against them in 520, as shown by the late addition of their king, Shunkha, on the cliff of Behistun. On this frontier, facing the Scythian population, the information once again stems from the accounts of Macedonian military operations near the Syr-Darya (Jaxartes). The region had seven fortified towns, which Alexander and his lieutenants had to reduce one by one: "Cyropolis, the largest of all had a rampart higher than the other cities since it had been built by Cyrus" (Arrian IV.2.2; 3.1–4). Strabo (XI.11.4) refers to the city as Cyra and describes it as the "furthest from the foundations of Cyrus, a city situated on the Jaxartes and marking the limit of the Persian empire." The available narratives thus give the image of a boundary reinforced by a series of fortresses. According to Arrian (IV.1.3), the city that Alexander wanted to found in this region "would be well placed for any eventual invasion of Scythia and as a defense bastion (*prophylakè*) of the country against the raids of the barbarians dwelling on the other side of the river." Faithful to a stereotyped representation of the perils posed by the "nomad," the Greek expression highlights, in a clearly exaggerated way, a state of structural and permanent hostility between the empire and the Scythian confederations. Everything suggests that during the Achaemenid period, the cultural and commercial relations between the two were significant. It is probable that some Sakas/Scythian peoples were the subjects of the

---

[18] The expression used by Plutarch, *Alex.*17.1 (Sardis: "the barbarian empire's rampart on the sea front [*to proskema tès epi talassèi tôn barbarôn hègemonias*]") gives an account of the city's defensive capacities in facing an attacking army. The voluntary surrender of Mithrenes to Alexander completely annulled this. (See discussion in the text, section 1.7.)

[19] The organization of the garrison of Syene-Elephantine is well-known thanks to Aramaic documentation: see HPE, 417–18, 448–51, 472–3, etc. Despite their age, the books of Porten (1968) and Grelot (1972) remain invaluable references.

[20] Arrian, *Anabasis* III.2.7.   [21] See Briant 1984, 97.

Great King and were to send the military contingents demanded by the satrap. Moreover, the various Scythian peoples are present among the peoples enumerated in the royal inscriptions and are represented in the imperial iconography at Persepolis, at Naqsh-i Rustam and on the statue of Darius. But, undoubtedly, a recognized frontier existed between the two sides.[22]

4. From west to east, says Darius in his inscription of Persepolis, the empire extends from "Sardis to the Indus." We know that in the Achaemenid period, there were two great provincial units to the east, Gandhara and the Indus. The Indus was undoubtedly one of the frontiers of the empire (HPE, 754–7). Alexander's forceful halt on the banks of the Hyphasis River (Beas) seems to indicate that, among the five rivers of Punjab, the Hyphasis marks the eastern border of the province of Gandhara (see Briant 2010b, 38 and n. 29). The erection of altars on the river frontiers indicates that Alexander was conscious of having reached the edge of the Achaemenid world.[23] From Sardis to the Indus, from Elephantine to the Scythians of Central Asia, his victorious march enabled him to take over the borders of the empire of Darius.

1.3   A Center Without Capital

According to Herodotus (III.197), alone of all the peoples, the Persians were not subject to tribute. If the tablets of Persepolis qualify such an affirmation (HPE, 397–99), the royal inscriptions serve as a testimony to the eminent and privileged place of Persia proper (*Parsa*; the Fārs). "Great King, King of Kings, King of countries containing all kinds of men, King in this great earth far and wide," Darius defined himself also by his lineage and family links ("Son of Hystaspes, an Achaemenian") as well as his ethnic origin ("a Persian, son of a Persian, an Aryan having Aryan lineage" [DNa]). The Persians were frequently designated as conquerors:

These are the countries which I got in my possession along with the Persian people [DPe].
    The spear of a Persian man has gone far. A Persian man has delivered battle far indeed from Persia [DNa].
    I am a Persian; from Persia I seized Egypt [DZe].
    The Persian man/warrior (*martiya*) conquered Egypt [DSab].

In his prayers, Darius regularly called for the protection of Ahuramazda over Persia and "her good horses and good warriors." In addition, Darius asked

---

[22] On this point, see Briant 1982, 181–234; HPE, 1026; for the cultural exchanges between Bactria-Sogdiana and the world of steppes, see Francfort 2013.

[23] See Liverani (1990, 59–65) on older examples of erections of steles "at the extreme and opposite points of the world, [which] affirm even more completely the universal control." Lastly, Seleucids imitated Alexander's moves on the Iaxartes (Kosmin 2014, 61–63).

Ahuramazda to protect his people and realm from three evils: "an [hostile] army, famine and Lie (*drauga*)." Thus, protection from the dangers of a foreign invasion, the troubles following a weak harvest or internal dissent (DPd). Lastly, we also find: "May Ahuramazda protect from harm, and my royal house, and this land" (DNa), etc.

The close alliance between the dynasty and the clans of the Persian nobility also reflects the privileged position of Persia at the heart of the empire. It also underscores the quasi-hegemonic role of the Persians at the core of the ruling class that administered and controlled the empire. This group remained largely loyal to Darius III when facing Alexander.[24] Persia was also, among the countries subjected to the Great King, designated by Darius and his successors as the cradle of the Persian nation and culture. It is in this land that Cyrus erected the city of Pasargadae (where his tomb is located). It is also where Darius built Persepolis, as well as inaugurated the cliff near Naqsh-i Rustam as the location for the royal tombs before Artaxerxes II and III ordered to carve out their own respective tombs above the Persepolis platform.

The Great King had many residences in which he stayed during the year. Besides Pasargadae (site of the royal investiture according to Plutarch) and Persepolis, the Great King and his royal court resided periodically in Susa (entirely remodeled by Darius the Great and his successors), in Babylon (also partly remodeled to accommodate the court) and, finally, in Media's Ecbatana. In each of these residences, palaces were built according to the same plans, and figurative representations elaborated on the same model.[25] Even though the royal residences were not empty in the absence of the king, the real center of the empire remained the location graced by the king's presence, be it Persia, Elam, Babylonia, Media, or any provincial residences to which his travels or military expeditions between Sardis and Bactria or between Babylon and Memphis would lead him. If one desires to identify a center of the empire, one must think of a "multipolar center" organized on a Persepolis–Susa–Babylon–Ecbatana quadrilateral (Map 1.1), sometimes extended as far as Sardis, Memphis or Bactria when the Great King led his armies in conquest or reconquest.

Classical writers frequently evoked the Persian custom of periodical migrations of the royal court, which they attributed to seasonal periodicity (HPE, 183–95).[26] From this point of view, the Achaemenid monarchy may be conceived as a type of territorial power well attested over the ages. One thinks, for

[24] What I typically refer to as the "ruling ethno-class"; see HPE, chapter 8, "The King's men" and chapter 17.2: "The great King and the Persian aristocracy." Updated in KCP, 4–5.

[25] For example, we know that under the form of a painted fresco, a replica of the Persepolis carved "Frieze of tributaries and donors" existed in Susa: Cf. Boucharlat 2013 and fig. 434–5.

[26] A close examination of the Persepolis tablets hints to this point (Tuplin 1998) yet does not question the itinerancy of the Achaemenid court. Quite the contrary, the Elamite archives generously supply the documents pertaining to the movements of the court (Henkelman 2010). These are equally attested by Babylonian sources (Waerzeggers 2010, 800–4).

example, of the Carolingian royalty, of which R. McKitterick (2011, 146, 168) recently claimed that "it is not merely the ceremonial circumambulation of the royal progress to take symbolic possession of the kingdom, but actually a mean of ruling. . . . Charlemagne's solution to the problem of royal control of his realm was thus a combination of itinerancy and stability with a complex network of officials empowered to conduct business on his behalf, so that the king himself . . . was 'like a great railway junction shunting personnel all over the kingdom'". Unfortunately, we do not possess precise information for the movement of the Persian Great Kings, but there is no doubt that on these occasions peoples and cities laid on luxury and magnificence to greet the Great King with dignity.[27] Similarly, every satrap was compelled to greet the Great King at the borders of his territory.[28] For his part, the Great King was displaying his political and financial power, by exchanging valuable gifts and taking on-spot decisions aimed to strengthen his authority.

For this reason, in the Achaemenid case similar to the Carolingian kingdom, the term "capital" should be avoided.[29] Contrary to what Greek authors suggest, Susa was not the capital of the Great King and the term should not to be used either for Pasargadae, Persepolis or Ecbatana. The Great King had no capital. During periodical movements of the royal court, the royal tent served as the ultimate (mobile) center of the empire. From this itinerant locus of power, the king remained in contact with the senior administrators left in the large royal residences, while using the services of his accompanying scribes (Briant 2014).

Nonetheless, beyond the seductive semantics of an itinerant power, we must remain cautious regarding the consequences of this mobility that remained of a limited scope against the backdrop of the immensity of the imperial space. The comparison to the Carolingian monarchy is suggestive, but it should not be carried too far. In quite a comparable manner, one should not ascribe too a great importance to the travels of the Seleucid kings across their empire: These do recall the Achaemenid traditions, but they also take on specific characteristics (Kosmin 2014, 142–80). On this point I share the reservations made by Capdetrey (2015, 663): "The Seleucid 'system of circulation' made sense and was effective only if, in the absence of the king and his court, the taxes were collected, the borders remained more or less protected and the local arbitrations were rendered and applied by the royal agents. These continued to be applied even though the king did not step foot in the region for a decade or two. In other

---

[27] See as a comparison the greetings reserved to Alexander by the Persian and Babylonian authorities (HPE, 189–90).

[28] See Arrian VI.29.2 and Quintus Curtius X.1.24.

[29] On the latter see Brühl (1967, 198 and 200): "Let us be warned against the inconsiderate and uncritical use of the term 'capital' in scientific literature, [as] 'itinerant monarchy' and the idea of 'capital' are mutually excluding."

words, the Seleucid power could not rely solely on a simple and irregular epiphany of the king and his court."

If we restrict the analysis to the quadrilateral of the four large Achaemenid royal residences, we immediately discover that the presence of the king and his court could not have been conceived without the activity of the satrapal administrations of Susa, Babylon and Ecbatana, if only because the presence of several thousand extra people implies additional levies on food and labor on cities and sanctuaries, and an extended use of stocks held in the royal stores (Henkelman 2010). To this we should add the enormous requisitions made for the construction and maintenance of the royal palaces and princely residences available to the king and the members of the court.[30] And what about the tremendous levies made beforehand among the peoples and cities forced to ruin themselves in order to welcome the royal caravan and army? (HPE, 402–3). Conversely, there were many peoples and cities that never had the pleasure, or misfortune, to welcome the royal procession into their midst. In other words, the mobility of the royal court was an element of territorial control, but it was certainly not sufficient to ensure its permanence and solidity.

1.4   External and Internal Borders

In principle, all peoples situated within the borders of the empire were subjects of the king without any limitations or exceptions. All were under the authority and supervision of the satraps, who were the personal representatives of the Great King in the various lands of the empire.[31] To enforce the imperial order, the satraps had at their disposal a civil and fiscal administration as well as armed forces and garrisons.[32] The maintenance of order, therefore, presupposed the satraps maintained absolute loyalty to the Great King, which was not the case in general. That said, it is inappropriate to construe the revolts of the satraps as the structural cause for the empire's fragility. Moreover, even within the borders of the empire, several peoples had established specific relationships with the Great King, which some observers willfully interpret as an abandonment of imperial sovereignty over a certain territory. This interpretation then serves to prove the weakness of imperial control, which is deemed incapable of maintaining order even in the regions adjacent to the heart of the empire.

---

[30] See e.g. Briant 2013, 12–13 (Babylonia and Susa); Waerzeggers 2010, 805–9 (Susa); Tolini 2001 and 2013 (Babylonia).

[31] The number of satrapies (approximately twenty-five) varied throughout the history of the Achaemenid empire.

[32] On the powers of satraps, see HPE, 338–47, and Klinkott 2005; for provincial administrations see the excellent research by Tuplin 1987a (see pp. 113–37: "geographical divisions"; 145–7: "Satrapies and Provinces"); on the garrisons see Tuplin 1987b (Asia Minor) and HPE, 374–6.

Of all the peoples systemically branded as "brigands" by classical sources, the best known example is that of the peoples of Zagros (Uxians and Cossaeans in particular, yet others as well)[33] (Map 1.2). Their situation and status can be studied by accounts of Alexander's passage through the Uxians' territory during his march between Susa and Persepolis, at the end of the year 331; Alexander's visit of the Cossaeans in 324; and Antigone's attempts several years later to cross through Cossaean territory. One of the characteristics attributed to these people is that they demanded a certain payment when the Great King crossed their territory, going from Ecbatana to Babylon (Cossaeans) or from Susa to Persepolis (Uxians). Reading Arrian (III.17.1): in contrast to another group of Uxians, "who inhabited the plains and obeyed the Persian satrap and now surrendered to Alexander, the Uxian hill men, as they were called, were not subject to Persia. And now they sent a message to Alexander that they would only permit him to take the route towards Persia with his army if they received what they used to receive from the Persian king on his passage."

These texts are built upon a series of depreciative Greek stereotypes of the lifestyle of populations qualified indistinctively as "nomads." These stereotypes prevented ancient observers from seeing the Cossaeans or Uxians as fully constituted societies. This is well demonstrated in Arrian's (III.17.6) abrupt statement: "The Uxians had neither money nor arable land." In fact, neither the Cossaeans or the Uxians sustained themselves through banditry and gathering, even if they could revert to these in times of peril (e.g., when Alexander attacked the Uxians in the middle of winter). They devoted themselves to valley bottom cultivation and mostly to herding in a localized semi-nomadic framework. This is well demonstrated by the amount and composition of the tribute that Alexander demanded from the Uxians: "The tribute assessed was a hundred horses every year, with five hundred transport animals, and thirty thousand from their flocks and herds." The misunderstanding of ancient authors stems also from their desire to systemically set up a contrast between the weakness of the Great Kings and the sturdiness of Alexander, who refused to pay the agreed sum. A few years later, facing the same Cossaeans, Antigonus dismissed the advice of one of his lieutenants, namely "to buy the passage with money, he considered it cowardliness to purchase through a treaty or tribute the permission to pass freely" (Diodorus XIX.19.2–8). Consequently, what had been long labeled a "ransom" was taken as evidence of weakness of the Great Kings incapable of controlling the roads used by the itinerant court.

Once duly decrypted and contextualized, the information derived from classical sources is quite different from the interpretation given to them.

---

[33] I present comprehensive research in Briant 1976, Briant 1982b: 57–112; summarized in HPE, 727–33.

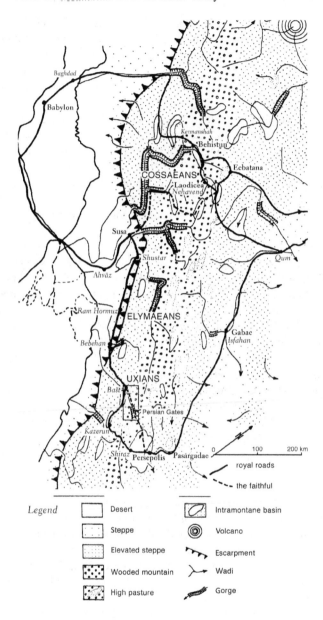

Map 1.2 The Zagros area. Produced by Pierre Briant.

Neither the Cossaeans nor the Uxians strictly controlled the main roads used by the royal caravan when traveling between the royal residences. On the contrary, the king had to make a detour to meet the Cossaean and Uxian leaders. The relations between the central government and these peoples were managed through an annual exchange of gifts and counter-gifts during a carefully codified ceremony. Neither the Cossaeans nor the Uxians were strictly speaking external to the empire. Nor should they be regarded as internal enemies whom the central authorities had to monitor militarily. Moreover, both peoples provided military contingents to the royal army. This relatively flexible relationship allowed the establishment of what may be called a "peripheral integration." This integration may have facilitated the regular exchanges of goods (herds) with the royal economy of Persepolis.[34]

The relationship with other peoples could be much more troublesome. One is struck, for example, by the numerous expeditions led by the Great Kings against the Cadusians in Media's Zagros.[35] While the context remains unknown, it seems that this people were divided between two kings, both recognized by the imperial power. According to Plutarch (*Art.* 24.6,9), the war led by Artaxerxes II ended with the conclusion of a formal agreement with each of those two kings in the form of a "peace and alliance treaty (*philia kai symmakhia*)." This type of treaty was also established with the Scythians of Central Asia who in 332/1 are presented as "allies (*symmakhoi*)," just like the Cadusians (Arrian III.19.3). To a certain extent, the relations between the imperial power and these petty kings and princes can be compared to those that, through the treaties of loyalty (*ādū/ādē*), linked the local authorities to the Neo-Assyrian and Neo-Babylonian kings, or to those regimenting the rights and duties of client kings within the framework of the Roman imperial domination. Imperial sovereignty was established on a balance of power, which sometimes required expeditions at the conclusion of which the king or satrap reasserted his authority through official treaty.

In Asia Minor, too, the existence of kinglets is well documented. This is the case with Paphlagonia, situated in northwestern Asia Minor, whose kings were under the supervision of the satrap of Daskyleion (HPE, 642–3, 698–9). In spite of Xenophon's insistence on the periodical disturbances caused to the Persians by the Mysians, Pisidians, Lycaonians or even the indigenous people of Armenia, their territories were not beyond the empire. They were closely watched by the satrap's troops. Often referred to as "non-subjects" by Greek authors, these people regularly provided specialized military contingents (cavaliers, slingers) to the imperial forces (HPE, 641–2; 697–9; 730–1;

---

[34] For more on this read the well-informed suggestions in Henkelman 2005, 159–65 and 2011; see also Bahadori 2017 and more particularly Balatti 2017.

[35] Ancient texts and analyses in HPE, 613–14, 732–3, 766–8.

765–8; 793–5). The permanence of indigenous political structures (royalty) does not imply that these peoples were fully independent. One of the most interesting examples is that of Mausolus, who continued to claim the title of "King of Caria"; yet from the empire's perspective he officially was the Achaemenid satrap of Caria, fully responsible to the Great King.[36]

1.5   From One Edge of the Empire to the Other[37]

Despite the existence of provincial governments with troops and garrisons and notwithstanding the multiple agreements with kinglets and other local leaders, the immensity of the imperial space remained problematic: How to ensure that orders of the imperial government would be received and applied throughout the empire? Greek observers tended to focus on the difficulties involved in bringing together military contingents from across the empire in the case of an invasion led by an enemy from within (revolt of Cyrus the Younger against Artaxerxes II) or by an external enemy (Alexander against Darius). Others claimed that on the contrary, the capacity of a Great King to disseminate orders swiftly, given the effectiveness of the road and mail systems, made it possible "to remedy the immensity of the empire."[38] We also know the famous passage where Herodotus depicted the route and organization of the royal road and its relays (*stathmoi*), which, from Sardis to Susa, included inns, stopovers and guard posts (V.52–54). Contrary to what has long been postulated, the road linking Sardis to Susa was not the only "royal road (*odos basilikè*)." In a work unfortunately lost, Ctesias "enumerated the relays (*stathmoi*), days of travel and parasangs from Ephesus to Bactria and India."[39] Besides, the Greek military narratives offer information on the distances and durations of these journeys: twenty-two days from Babylon to Susa; approximately thirty days between Susa and Persepolis; twenty days between Susa and Ecbatana (nine days for the same journey if using the direct and difficult route through Cossaean land).[40]

On this point, the analysis of the tablets of Persepolis brings incomparable details. Within the archives of the tablets of the Persepolis fortifications (PFT), Richard Hallock (1969) identified several series that were individualized by their functions, one of which (the Q series) refers to the movement of people

---

[36] See HPE, 667–70; 767–8; 1032, in which I link the example of Caria's king-satrap to the one known during the Neo-Assyrian era according to the inscriptions of Tell Fekheriye, in which the local dynast is qualified both as a *mlk* (king) and *saknu* (governor).

[37] On the roads and communications in the Achaemenid empire, see Briant 1991 (KCP, 359–75); Graf 1994; HPE, 357–74 and 927–9 (with references); BHAch I, 78–81 and II, 125–7; Kuhrt 2007, 730–62 and 2014b; Briant 2012 and KCP, 18–21; Colburn 2013.

[38] See Xenophon, *Cyr.* 8.6.17 and Herodotus VIII.98.

[39] Ctesias F33 (76). The parasang is a historical Persian unit measuring itinerant distance. It is difficult to evaluate out of context; according to most estimates it was roughly 5 km.

[40] Diodorus XIX.19.2; 19.8; 55.2.

and livestock along these roads.[41] The tablets show very clearly that all the lands of the empire are the starting and ending point of travelers, from Sardis to Bactria, passing through Babylon, Persepolis, Ecbatana and even Kandahar;[42] Lebanon is also mentioned once (NN 1609). Taking the particular example of the movements recorded towards Susa[43] or from Susa:[44] Out of sixty-two cases (thirty-nine towards Susa, twenty-three from Susa), one can notice in particular the lands of eastern Iran, such as Bactria[45] (2), Kerman (13), Hindus (18), Arachosia (4), Gandhara (2), Makkan (1), Aria (2), Drangiana (1) and Sagartia (1). Moreover, there are many mentions of travel towards Media.[46]

Who could make use of the royal roads and their logistical facilities? The principle is simple: in order to travel on the royal roads and thus to have access to the relay stations and depots, the group leader had to obtain a sealed authorization (*halmi*) prior to his departure. Once presented to the relevant authorities, he could obtain food rations at each station in accordance with the terms and quantities specified in the travel document. The authorization could be issued in the name of the king or in the name of the high administrator of Persepolis (Parnaka, for example).[47] It was more regularly issued by the satrap in charge of the territory of departure. Among hundreds of others, one example illustrates the mode of writing and shows that animals also received rations (PF 1397):

[1-7]29 [BAR of] flour, supplied by Mirizza, Karabba the Indian, sent forth from the king [to] India, received for rations, [for] 1 day [in] the third month, 24th year. [8-9] He himself received 2 QA. [9-11]180 "people" (passengers?) received each 1½ QA. [11-12]50 boys received each 1 QA. [12-13]3 horses consumed each 3 QA. [14-15]3 mules consumed each 2 QA. [15-16]He carried a sealed document of the king.[48]

Another interesting example is a voyage in 495 of a certain Dauma and thirty-five other persons under his command from Sardis to Persepolis. Dauma had obtained an authorization (*halmi*) that had been issued by Irdapirna, also known as Arthaphernes, the satrap of Sardis (PF 1404). Another tablet also referred to Sardis. It reads:

---

[41] The tablets mentioning the rations for the animals in movement along the routes constitute a series labeled S3 by Hallock ("travel rations for animals").

[42] Fragments of Elamite tablets found in the fortifications of old Kandahar and analyzed by Fischer and Stolper 2015.

[43] PF 1287, 1289, 1318, 1351, 1358, 1377, 1399, 1436, 1439, 1529, 1552, 1555, 1953[34], 2050, 2051, 2056; PFa 4; NN 317, 431, 809, 881, 901, 946, 1044, 1081[74], 1081[81]–[82], 1264, 1571, 1580, 1585, 1621, 1713, 1898, 1939, 2040[4]–[6], 2062, 2139, 2323.

[44] PF 1332, 1348, 1361, 1383, 1385, 1398, 1440, 1484, 1540, 1550, 1556, 2057; PFa 17; NN 615, 765, 844, 946, 1458, 2095, 2096, 2383, 2503, 2383. See Briant 2013.

[45] For mentions of Bactria and Bactrians in the archives of Persepolis, see Henkelman 2018.

[46] See Henkelman 2008b, 310–12.

[47] Possibly a parent of Darius, Parnaka was the director of the administration in Persia proper, perhaps holding the title of satrap.

[48] 1 BAR = *c*.10 liters; 1 QA = slightly less than 1 liter.

7 marriš (ca. 70 liters) beer Datiya received as rations. [4–5] He carried a sealed document of the king. [5–9]He went forth from Sardis (Išparda) [via] express service (*pirradaziš*), went to the king [at] [10–13] 11th month, year 27. [13] [At] Hidali (NN-809).

As D. Lewis (1980) had shown, Datiya is no other than Datis, sent by Darius on an inspection tour in western Asia Minor at the time of the Ionian revolt. The very high beer ration (roughly 70 liters) received here at a station located on the edge of Persia (Hidali), illustrates the fact that the volume of rations was calculated according to the status of power and prestige. Among the beneficiaries are the high-ranking court figures (princes and princesses), including the king, whose itinerancy paved the way to special preparations in the relevant stopover stations. This is evident from an Elamite tablet found in Susa stating: "64 marriš (of) ghee/clarified butter, supplied by Maštetinna, was dispensed on behalf/before of the king, at Susa and 5 villages (*humanuš*), in the twenty-second year."[49] Again, this is only a piece of a well-documented record (the J texts of Hallock) on the logistical preparations in the course of the king's movements, including those within Fārs outside the seasonal migrations.[50] The king's table had to be served by certain immutable rules: only slight variations are observable from one place of residence to another.[51]

As store managers knew that they are accountable,[52] the tablets certify that the rations were delivered according to the *halmi*, but they do not quote *halmi* directly. However, a parchment document written in Aramaic and found in Egypt demonstrates what a *halmi* is. It is a letter that the satrap of Egypt, Aršama (then in Babylonia), entrusted to his steward Nehtihôr, whom he sent back to Egypt. The letter is addressed to seven officials overseeing stations along the road, among which one easily recognizes Arbela and Damascus. They are given the power to distribute flour, beer and wine in precisely defined quantities according to the status of the travelers. The horses are not forgotten, as they receive fodder. The obligations of the travelers are strictly defined. They are forbidden to take advantage of the system unduly: "Give them this ration, each official in turn, according to the route which is from province to province until he reaches Egypt. And if he be in one place more than one day then for those days do not give them extra rations" (Briant 2012, 193–5, q.v. for further references).

The Q series report on numerous movements of groups, frequently very large ones, of *kurtaš*, a term referring to workers from across the empire, frequently

---

[49] See Briant 2013, 13 with references.
[50] The file was fully edited and analyzed in detail by Henkelman 2010.
[51] See the fascinating text by Polyaenus, Strat. IV.3.32 (HPE, 286–9; Amigues 2003; Henkelman 2010, 684–9). Polyaenus points out that during all halts of the court between Susa and Babylon, the wine supplied is half grape wine and half palm wine. Certain produce, such as carthamus grains and saffron, are only distributed when the court is in Media (Ecbatana).
[52] For more on the accounting practices of the royal administration see Fischer and Stolper 2015 and Stolper 2017.

working in construction sites (Persepolis, Susa, Tamukkan, etc.), in agriculture as well as in workshops. For example, groups of *kurtaš* moved between Persepolis and Susa: 100 Lycians (PF 1566), 108 Capadoccians (PF 1577), 26 Thracians (PF 1575) and 124 Babylonians (NN 2133). The *kurtaš* were also enumerated by their specialties such as 416 stonemasons (NN 2426). In another tablet (PF 1557), a group of 547 Egyptians was moved between Persepolis and Tamukkan followed by a group of 690 Egyptian *kurtaš*-masons (NN 0480). Tamukkan, the location of another royal residence on the Persian Gulf (close to Bushir), was also the site of the arrival of 150 Skudrian female *kurtaš* from Media, 980 Lycian *kurtaš*, 980 Cappadocian *kurtaš*, 74 Bactrians and workers sent from Babylonia's Sippar (Henkelman 2008b, 305–10, q.v. for further references).

Among the men of the central and provincial administrations circulating the roads, we may notice the *pirradaziš*, whom Hallock identified as "fast messengers."[53] The same qualifier *pirradaziš* may also refer to horses used in the express service ("express [horse]").[54] The *pirradaziš* travelled alone or in small groups (two or three) and were almost exclusively sent directly by or to the king. They were sometimes sent for a journey between Persepolis and Susa (PF 1335), or for a distant destination such as Sardis (PF 1321). The existence of this specific class of messengers and horses dedicated to a rapid service sheds light on well-known passages from Xenophon and Herodotus, who were deeply impressed by the contrast between the immensity of the imperial space and the rapidity in which orders were conveyed from one corner of the empire to the other.[55] The tablets also evoke other characters involved in the road and mail services such as the "elite guides" (*barrišdama*) and the "caravan leaders" (*karabattiš*).[56] Lastly, there were also servicemen responsible for the opening and maintenance of roads.[57]

If we synthesize the information from the Persepolis documentation, the Aramaic records (between Egypt and Bactria), the Babylonian documentation and the accounts of the Greek military expeditions (in particular that of Alexander), a certain pattern of administrative practices across the empire emerges. The existence of archives from Sardis to Bactria is the clearest illustration of this.[58] Not only were all the regions of the empire linked by a network of royal roads, which kept them in constant contact with the center,

---

[53] PF 300, 1285, 1319, 1320, 1321, 1329, 1334–5, 2052.   [54] PF 1672, 1700, 2061, 2062.

[55] Texts cited and analyzed in HPE, 369–71; see Colburn's 2013 reflections on pp. 41–9.

[56] See Hallock 1969, 42 (with observations by the author pertaining to the hypothetical characteristics of translations).

[57] See Henkelman 2017, 63–79; on the continuities between the Achaemenid system of surveying roads and the specialists in Alexander's army (the so-called *bematistai*), see also Briant 2016b, 264–8 and mainly Kegerreis 2017.

[58] See HPE, 422–71; Briant 2009a; and now Fischer and Stolper 2015 (Kandahar), and revised by Henkelman 2017, with my comments (Briant 2017d, 833–6, 841–2).

but also the maintenance of such an impressive network presupposed the existence of an enormous administrative mechanism capable of managing stores across thousands of kilometers. Every year, from Sardis to Bactra, the heads of stores had to make a report of all the inputs and outputs. The reports were then meticulously audited by accountants in Persepolis. Local authorities had to monitor the stocks.[59] The recently published Aramaic documentation from Bactria elucidates the sophistication of the satrapal administration, which was strongly influenced by the administration known from the Persepolitan sources (Briant 2009a, 148–51). All this presupposes the existence of a gigantic centralized imperial logistics.[60] Persepolitan sources also clearly show that the control of the empire's peoples did not stem merely from the rhetoric of royal declarations. The levying of workers (*kurtaš*) in all regions and their movement from one site to another on the basis of simple administrative decisions show that the power of the empire owed much to the conscription of soldiers and workers as well as other forms of taxation. No region in the empire was exempt from this.

1.6   The Land and the Sea

Documentation regarding maritime space and imperial control is infinitely less abundant. Yet, since the 17th and 18th centuries CE, a postulate has circulated widely in historical literature, namely that Persians have never been interested in maritime activity. Some even claimed that they were thalassophobic. Thomas Kelly (1992: 7) claimed they were like the Assyrians: "Both were essentially land-locked people who had no real experience with the sea prior to their respective conquest of the Phoenician cities along the east coast of the Mediterranean." Kelly continues by claiming that if, under the reign of Cambyses and Darius, the Persians exerted control over the Mediterranean thanks to Phoenician warships, this hegemony quickly dissipated following defeats at Salamis and Mycale in 480/479. A similar thesis was proposed by B. Revere in 1957. One can trace its origin to a report delivered to Colbert in 1667 by Bishop Huet, who published it in 1716; it was also presented by Montesquieu in his *Spirit of Laws* in 1748 and 1757 (Briant 2017a, 135–49; 164–8).

Concerning the alleged thalassophobia of the Persians, it should be noted that this thesis was drawn up on the basis of an abusive reduction of the Achaemenid maritime space in the Mediterranean, which was almost

---

[59] See the very illuminating anecdote transmitted in the *Oeconomica* of Pseudo-Aristoteles (2.2.38) and located in the last years of Alexander in Babylonia: "Antimenes bade the governors of the provinces to replenish, in accordance with the law of the country, the magazines along the royal highways. Whenever an army passed through the country or any other body of men unaccompanied by the king, he sent an officer to sell them the contents of the magazines." See Briant 2012, 188.

[60] See also section 1.7 below.

exclusively conceptualized through the prism of the relations between the Achaemenid Empire and the Greek cities, particularly Athens. It should not be forgotten that the empire included in its midst several maritime spaces, which the Great Kings repeatedly mentioned in their inscriptions as territories under their control.[61] Darius presented his power from "this side of the Bitter River and the far side of the Bitter River" (*DPg*, Bab. 2).[62] Besides the shores of the Mediterranean, the northern borders reached the Black Sea, the Marmara Sea, the Caspian Sea and the Aral Sea;[63] to the west and the south, the empire comprised the Red Sea and the Persian Gulf. Darius ensured the maritime link between the Mediterranean and the Red Sea by digging the canal (a precursor of the Suez Canal), thereby creating another link between Egypt and Persia.[64]

The fact that the Persians called upon the Phoenicians shows that, in this area as in others, they knew how to capitalize on the specialties of each of the subjugated peoples. However, this does not prove that they themselves were inexperienced in the maritime domain. The existence of sailors is mentioned, for instance, in several tablets from the Persepolis Fortification Archive,[65] and a "ship-commander" is mentioned in one of the Persepolis Treasury Tablets.[66] Furthermore, an Aramaic document found in Egypt demonstrates that the Persian-Iranian technical vocabulary of shipbuilding was highly developed and specialized.[67] Another Aramaic document from Egypt provides essential information on the control of merchant ships.[68] This is the now famous Customs Accounts document, in which the Achaemenid administration is seen to control all the boats from Phoenicia and Asia Minor, when they approached to the border port of Thônis in the delta. A thorough inventory check was carried out and tariffs were levied on entry and exit according to strict standards.[69] The royal stores' export of wheat from the ports of Asia Minor was also controlled in part by the satraps (KCP, chapter 19).

---

[61] See more on this in the form of the important reflections by Haubold 2012, situating the Achaemenid Empire in the lineage of their Middle Eastern predecessors.

[62] On the so-called *Babylonian World Map*, the earth "is surrounded by a circular body of water called the ocean or, literally, the 'Bitter River'" (Haubold 2012, 8).

[63] It is possible that the Aral Sea is referred to in the Behistun inscriptions, in which Darius congratulates himself for subjugating "the Sakas from beyond the sea" (DB §74).

[64] On this point, see Klotz 2015 who against a widely-accepted interpretation and through a reexamination of the "canal steles" concluded that Darius "sought to ensure a steady flow of tribute and other precious materials from Egypt to Persia, by all routes possible."

[65] See e.g. tablet NN 2261, ll. 4–8, cited by Henkelman 2008b, 310. Two hundred and fifty nine "boatmen" were sent from Persepolis to Media (these may refer to the river navigation: HPE, 378–84).

[66] PT 008. Referring to Bakabada, identified by Cameron (1948, 95) with Megabates known by Greek sources for being *navarkhos* in Xerxes's navy. We may also compare to the title of *Mithradata* in the Aramaic document listed as such: **nav-pati* (naval commander) – a term which is identical in its construction to the Greek *navarkhos*.

[67] TADAE 1, pp. 99–101, with commentaries by Grelot 1972, 283–95; see also HPE, 449–51.

[68] See KCP, chapter 18, and updates on pp. 19–20.

[69] The levying on boats is also known in Lycia and Babylonia.

Unquestionably, the thalassophobia thesis was developed particularly with regard to the policies attributed to the Persians in the Persian Gulf. According to ancient authors (Arrian and Strabo), Alexander decided in 325 to destroy river fortifications (*katarraktai*) which the Persians, supposedly inexperienced in naval warfare and fearful of a maritime invasion, erected across the Tigris and Euphrates. Such a presentation postulates that the Persians were incapable of defending even the heart of their empire since, not only were the Great Kings to pay "tolls" to the Uxians and Cossaeans when moving from one residence to another (see section 1.4), but they were forced also to take refuge behind fortifications on the side of the Persian Gulf. It is unnecessary to repeat here in detail the arguments which, in my opinion, invalidate the recurrent thesis of Persian maritime ineptitude, based as it is on the postulate of a profound transformation of a "despotic and decadent" Achaemenid Empire under the "progress" brought by the Macedonian conquest.[70] Suffice it to mention two points. First, the *katarraktai* on the Tigris River were not permanent military fortifications but light dams constructed at the time of the dry season for irrigation purposes and dismantled during the rainy season.[71] Second, there is no reason to suppose that the Persians had abandoned the Persian Gulf to pirates: the (too few) available clues suggest that the Persian presence in the Gulf remained relatively solid, even during the advance of Alexander's naval fleet.[72]

1.7   The Downfall of an Empire

In principle, all precautions were taken to maintain the integrity of the empire and its borders by protecting it from an exterior threat. Yet, as we know, between spring 334 and autumn–winter of 331/330, Alexander successfully conquered Asia Minor, the Syrian-Phoenician coast and Egypt, as well as seized control of the large royal residences of Babylonia, Susa, Persepolis and Pasargadae. Later on, between 330 and 324, Alexander conquered the satrapies of eastern Iran and the Indus valley before returning to Babylonia via the Persian Gulf, Pasargadae and Persepolis, coming to rest in Ecbatana. Naturally, the Persian defeat raised questions and doubts on the reality and effectiveness of the control of the imperial space. Without being able to answer it in all the details, I shall bring forward several reflective elements within the framework of a survey of the external and internal borders of the imperial space.

[70] See Briant 2002b; 2009b; 2010a; 2016b, 206–85; 2017a, 305–39; KCP, 429–610.

[71] I frequently dealt with this question and retraced in detail its historiography in a study the main conclusions of which are translated in KCP, chapter 28 ("The *katarraktai* of the Tigris: Irrigation-works, commerce and shipping in Elam and Babylonia from Darius to Alexander"). See also a summary in Briant 2010b, 89–93.

[72] See HPE, 758–62, 1028–9, KCP, 600–5; Potts 2010; Henkelman 2017 §1.1–3; §2.3.3 (citing a Babylonian tablet [YOS 3, 10], attesting the use of a maritime route linking southern Babylonia to Tamukkan, situated to the north of the Persian coast of the Persian Gulf).

In contrast to a popular thesis, the attested satrapal revolts never truly endangered the solidity of the empire.[73] The most dangerous revolt affecting the empire's center, without, however, reaching the royal residences, was the revolt of Cyrus the Younger and it was of a dynastic nature. Namely, it was not intended to destroy the empire but to replace the Great King (Artaxerxes) by his brother (Cyrus). If, strategically speaking, it prefigures the offensive carried out by Alexander from Asia Minor, it nonetheless failed. Despite the insistence of the ancient authors (all devoted to the memory of Cyrus) on emphasizing the king's difficulties in gathering all available contingents "due to the remoteness of these regions (the Iranian Plateau and India),"[74] Artaxerxes managed to mobilize a considerable force to face his brother.

The greatest danger came from the revolts of the conquered nations.[75] Darius I struggled during the years 522–520 having to suppress revolts that spread throughout the empire, from the Syr-Darya to the Nile Valley. These revolts also enflamed the lands of the center such as Media, Babylonia, Elam and even Persia itself. That said, the leaders of these revolts never attempted to join forces to face Darius.[76] The manifestation of so many revolts erupting at the same time from one end of the empire to the other did not recurred in the empire's history. Putting aside occasionally volatile relations with certain peoples of Anatolia, mostly resolved by periodic strikes by the satraps in charge of these territories, and the Ionian revolt against Darius (HPE, 146–156), two main lands posed enduring problems to the Achaemenid Empire: Babylonia and even more Egypt. After the revolts of 522–521, Babylonia revolted again, twice in the early years of Xerxes; these revolts were brief, though. Similarly, to the acts taken by his father during the 521–520 revolts, Xerxes took the necessary measures to nip the ferments of insubordination in the bud.[77] Babylonia does not seem to have caused any further disturbances. Egypt, however, posed incomparably more acute problems. Not only did an indigenous king revolt in 522/521 but the history of the Nile was punctuated by successive revolts, until under ill-known circumstances, Egypt regained its full independence in 404 under indigenous pharaohs.[78] Reconquered by Artaxerxes III in 343/342, it revolted again under the reign of Pharaoh Khabbabash. The consequent takeover by the Persians lasted only a few

---

[73] For more on the satrapal revolts against Artaxerxes II see HPE, 656–73, and conclusions, pp. 674–5.

[74] Diodorus XIV.22.2 (see above section 1.6); on the revolt of Cyrus, see HPE, 615–30 (p. 627 on the preparations of Artaxerxes).

[75] On the precautions and military measures taken by the Achaemenid authorities, see the compilation of cases and sources in Tuplin 2014.

[76] See analysis in HPE, 107–26, 898–901; Kuhrt 2007, 140–58.

[77] On the revolts of 521, see Beaulieu 2014; on the revolts against Xerxes and the takeover by the Great king, see Waerzeggers 2003/4 et Kuhrt 2014a.

[78] On our ignorance, see HPE, 619–20, 987.

years since in 332 Alexander conquered it without any real opposition from the Persian forces.[79]

Despite the fragility of the Persian position in Egypt, it is clear that in 334 the Achaemenid Empire extended from Sardis to the Indus and from the Syr-Darya to Aswan, in a spatial configuration that was almost unchanged since 480. Moreover, between 334 and 331, the Great King managed on several occasions to assemble imposing military forces levied among all the peoples of the empire, and he had at his disposal, in the Mediterranean, naval forces far superior to the fleet of Alexander. We cannot therefore say that the empire crumbled under the weight of its own weaknesses. Darius was defeated, first, because Alexander excelled on the battlefield (the reasons are still explored, but some of which undoubtedly relate to the tactical superiority of Alexander and his army). The second reason for the initial defeats was that (for reasons that still escape us[80]) Darius's general staff failed to prepare a systematic defense of the Mediterranean coast. Should that have been done, the defenders would have perhaps prevented Alexander from unloading his troops. Besides, although it was carried out consistently until the aftermath of the Battle of Issos, the defense of the Mediterranean front was very soon weakened considerably by the surrender without battle of the commander of Sardis (Mithrénès) to Alexander.[81]

Moreover, the successive defeats in Issos (November 333) and Gaugamela (October 331) ceded to the Macedonian enemy the vital infrastructure of the territories behind the battlefields. This infrastructure allowed the conquerors to overcome the challenge posed to the invader of supplying its military on a daily basis. According to Donald Engels, the author of the sole book dedicated to the military logistics of Alexander's army (published back in 1978): "the terrain of the Persian empire was in a real sense the Persian king's most formidable weapon. Its extensive deserts, salt wastelands, barren, impenetrable mountain ranges, rivers of salt water, severe climatic extremes, and the often vast distances between cultivated inhabited regions were immense obstacle to any invading army" (p. 121). Without denying the existence of these obstacles and challenges (which also faced the army of the Great King), I believe, on the contrary, that the existence of multiple stores and stocks[82] in the satrapies and

---

[79] I studied the Egyptian revolts in HPE, to which I am referring the reader; see also the recent Agut and Moreno-Garcia 2016, 653–81.

[80] On this, see HPE, 818–23; 1042–3.

[81] While still isolated at that point in time (HPE, 842–4), the recruitment of a member of the Persian aristocracy raises questions about the existence of man-to-man agreements prior to Alexander's arrival. About Alexander's preexisting knowledge of the Achaemenid imperial inner-workings, see KCP, 499–504, 519–20, 573–82.

[82] Stores of food stuff, weaponry and other types of supplies: see e.g. Xenophon, *Anab.* III.4. 1 (bow and lead cords used in preparing slings).

on the routes of the great royal roads was an important advantage to Alexander. Alexander thus used the resources of the Achaemenid imperial logistics against itself: it was the imperial machinery[83] that offered the invader all the resources he needed.

Thus, far from illustrating the structural fragility of the Achaemenid Empire, the Macedonian conquest, on the contrary, eloquently underscores the superior administrative, technical and military management of the imperial space. It was paradoxically the organizational strength of Darius's empire that Alexander built upon to defeat him. The route of the invasion is essentially identical with that of the great royal roads known from the Persepolis tablets. As his armies progressed, Alexander retraced the Achaemenid borders and reconstituted the imperial space, which was no different from the one held by Darius III until his assassination in July 330. We may now comprehend the politics of Alexander who relentlessly recruited existing administrative cadres and gathered around him the Persian-Iranian nobility. Whatever the indisputable ferments of change brought about by the conquest, Alexander's empire, in 323, was the direct heir of the empire previously held by Darius III.[84]

Bibliography

Agut, Damien and Juan Carlos Moreno-Garcia. 2016. *De Narmer à Dioclétien: 3150 av. J.C.-284 ap. J.C. L'Égypte des pharaons*, Paris: Belin.

Amigues, Suzanne. 2003. "Pour la table du Grand Roi," *Journal des Savants* 1: 3–59.

Bahadori, Ali. 2017. "Achaemenid Empire, tribal confederations of Southwestern Persia and seven families." *Iranian Studies* 50(2): 173–97.

Balatti, Silvia. 2017. *Mountain Peoples in the Ancient Near East*. Wiesbaden: Harrassowitz.

Beaulieu, Paul-Alain. 2014. "An episode in the reign of the Babylonian pretender Nebuchadnezzar IV." In: *Extraction and Control. Studies in Honor of Matthew W. Stolper*, ed. Michael Kozuh et al., 17–25. Chicago, IL: The Oriental Institute of the University of Chicago.

Boucharlat, Rémy. 2013. "Other works of Darius and his successors." In: *The Palace of Darius at Susa. The Great Royal Residence of Achaemenid Persia*, ed. Jean Perrot, 359–403. London: I.B. Tauris & Co.

Boucharlat, Rémy, 2017, "*Qanāt* and *Falaj*: polycentric and multi-period innovations. Iran and the United Arab Emirates as case studies." In *Underground Aqueduc Handbook*, ed. Andreas M. Angelikis, Eustathios Chiotis, Saeid Eslamian and Herbert Weingartner, 280–301. New York: CRC Press.

---

[83] See Briant 2018. The recently published Aramaic documents of Bactria showcase that the Persepolitan system (magazines, distributions, goods and supplies, etc.) was well-organized at the time of Alexander's arrival. Furthermore, it survived the Achaemenid defeat (Briant 2009a, 148–51).

[84] Only thus may I present Alexander as the "last of the Achaemenids" (while adding that he was also "the first of a long dynasty of Hellenistic kings"): see updates in KCP, 21–9.

Briant, Pierre. 1976. "Brigandage, conquête et dissidence en Asie achéménide et hellénistique," *Dialogues d'histoire ancienne* 2: 163–259.

Briant, Pierre. 1982. *États et pasteurs au Moyen-Orient ancien*. Paris: Édition de la Maison des sciences de l'homme.

Briant, Pierre. 1984. *L'Asie centrale et les royaumes moyen-orientaux du premier millénaire av. n.è.*, Paris: Editions Recherche sur le Civilisations.

Briant, Pierre. 1987. "Pouvoir central et polycentrisme culturel dans l'Empire achéménide (Quelques réflexions et suggestions)." In: *Achaemenid History I: Sources, Structures and Synthesis*, ed. Heleen Sancisi-Weerdenburg, 1–31. Leiden: Nederlands Instituut voor het Nabije Oosten. Translated as "Central Power and Cultural Polycentrism in the Achaemenid Empire: some observations and suggestions." In Briant 2017b, 43–76.

Briant, Pierre. 1991. "De Sardes à Suse." In: *Achaemenid History VI: Asia Minor and Egypt: Old Cultures in a New Empire*, ed. Heleen Sancisi-Weerdenburg and Amelie Kuhrt, 67–82. Leiden: Nederlands Instituut voor het Nabije Oosten. Translated as "From Sardis to Susa." In Briant 2017b, 359–74.

Briant, Pierre. 1999. "L'histoire de l'empire achéménide aujourd'hui: l'historien et ses documents." In: *Annales HSS* 54(5): 1127–36.

Briant, Pierre. 2001. "Polybe X.28 et les qanāts: le témoignage et ses limites." In *Irrigation et drainage dans l'Antiquité. Qanāts et canalisations souterraines au Proche-Orient, en Égypte et en Grèce*, ed. Pierre Briant, 15–40. Paris: Thotm Éditions (Persika 2).

Briant, Pierre. 2002a. *From Cyrus to Alexander: A History of the Persian Empire*. Trans. Peter D. Daniels. Winona Lake, IN: Eisenbrauns.

Briant, Pierre. 2002b. "History and ideology: the Greeks and Persian decadence." In: *Greeks and Barbarians*, ed. Thomas Harrison, 193–210. Edinburgh: Taylor & Francis.

Briant, Pierre. 2002c. "L'État, la terre et l'eau entre Nil et Syr-Darya: Remarques introductives." *Annales. Histoire, Sciences Sociales* 57(3): 517–29.

Briant, Pierre. 2009a. "The Empire of Darius III in perspective." In: *Alexander the Great: A New History*, ed. Waldemar Heckel and Lawrence A. Tritle, 141–70. Oxford: John Wiley & Sons

Briant, Pierre. 2009b. "Alexander and the Persian Empire, between 'decline' and 'renovation.'" In: *Alexander the Great: A New History*, ed. Waldemar Heckel and Lawrence A. Tritle, 171–88. Oxford: John Wiley & Sons.

Briant, Pierre. 2010a. "The theme of 'Persian Decadence' in eighteenth-century European historiography: remarks on the genesis of a myth." In: *The World of Achaemenid Persia: History, Art and Society in Iran and The Ancient Near East*, ed. John Curtis & St. John Simpson, 3–15. London: I.B. Tauris.

Briant, Pierre. 2010b. *Alexander the Great and His Empire: A Short Introduction*. Trans. Amélie Kuhrt. Princeton, NJ: Princeton University Press.

Briant, Pierre. 2012. "From the Indus to the Mediterranean: the administrative organization and logistics of the great roads of the Achaemenid Empire." In: *Highways, Byways and Road Systems in the Pre-Modern World*, ed. Susa E. Alcock, John Bodel and Richard T. Talbert, 185–201. Chichester: Wiley-Blackwell.

Briant, Pierre. 2013, "Susa and Elam in the Achaemenid Empire." In: *The Palace of Darius at Susa: The Great Royal residence of Achaemenid Persia*, ed. Jean Perrot, 3–25. London: I.B. Tauris.

Briant, Pierre. 2014. "Les tablettes de bois du Grand roi (Note sur les communications officielles dans un royaume itinérant)." In: *Extraction and Control. Studies in Honor of Matthew W. Stolper*, ed. M. Kozuh et al., 37–40. Chicago, IL: Oriental Institute of the University of Chicago.

Briant, Pierre. 2015. "À propos de l'"empreinte achéménide' (*Achaemenid impact*) en Anatolie. (Notes de lecture)." In: *Zwischen Satrapen und Dynasten. Kleinasien im 4. Jahrhundert v.Chr*, ed. Engelbert Winter and Klaus Zimmermann, 175–93. Bonn: R. Habelt.

Briant, Pierre. 2016a. "The Achaemenid Empire." In: *The World around the Old Testament. The People and Places of the Ancient Near East*, ed. Brent A. Strawn and Bill T. Arnold, 379–415. Ada, MI: Baker Academic.

Briant, Pierre. 2016b. *Alexandre. Exégèse des lieux communs*. Paris: Gallimard.

Briant, Pierre. 2017a. *The First European: A History of Alexander in the Age of Empire*. Trans. Nicholas Elliott. Cambridge, MA: Harvard University Press.

Briant, Pierre. 2017b. *Kings, Countries and Peoples: Selected Studies on the Achaemenid Empire*. Trans. Amélie Kuhrt. Stuttgart: Franz Steiner Verlag.

Briant, Pierre. 2017c. "De Samarkand à Sardes *via* Persépolis dans les traces des Grands rois et d'Alexandre (Concluding remarks)." In: *Die Verwaltung im Achämenidenreich – Imperiale Muster und Strukturen / Administration in the Achaemenid Empire* ed. Bruno Jacobs, Wouter F. M. Henkelman and Matthew W. Stolper, 827–55, Wiesbaden: Harrassowitz.

Briant, Pierre. 2018. "L'approvisionnement de l'armée macédonienne: Alexandre le Grand et l'organisation logistique de l'empire achéménide." In: *L'Orient est son jardin. Hommages à Rémy Boucharlat* (Acta Iranica 58), ed. Sébastien Gondet and Ernie Haerinck, 55–70. Leuven: Peeters.

Briant, Pierre and Rémy Boucharlat, eds. 2005. *L'archéologie de l'empire achéménide : nouvelles recherches*, ed. (Persika 6). Paris: De Boccard.

Briant, Pierre and Francis Joannès, eds. 2006. *La transition entre l'empire achéménide et les royaumes hellénistiques (vers 350–300 av. J.C.)*. (Persika 9). Paris: De Boccard.

Briant, Pierre, Wouter F. M Henkelman, and Matthew W. Stolper, eds. 2008. *L'archive des Fortifications de Persépolis. État des questions et perspectives de recherche*. (Persika 12). Paris: De Boccard.

Briant, Pierre and Michel Chauveau, eds. 2009. *Organisation des pouvoirs et contacts culturels dans les pays de l'empire achéménide*, (Persika 14). Paris De Boccard.

Brühl, Carl-Richard. 1967. "Remarques sur les notions de 'capitale' et de 'résidence' pendant le Haut Moyen Âge." *Journal des Savants* 4: 193–213.

Cameron, George C. 1948. *Persepolis Treasury Tablets*. Chicago, IL: The University of Chicago Press.

Capdetrey, Laurent. 2015. "Le royaume séleucide à l'épreuve du *Spatial Turn*." *Topoi* 20: 557–65.

Colburn, Henry P. 2013. "Connectivity and Communication in the Achaemenid Empire." *Journal of the Economic and Social History of the Orient* 56: 29–52.

Colburn, Henry P. 2017. "Globalization and the study of the Achaemenid Persian Empire." In: *The Routledge Handbook of Archaeology and Globalization*, ed. Tamar Hodos, 871–84. London: Routledge.

Fischer, Michael T. and Matthew W. Stolper.2015. "Achaemenid Elamite administrative Texts 3: Fragments from Old Kandahar, Afghanistan." ARTA 2015.001: 1–27 htt p://www.achemenet.com/pdf/arta/ARTA_2015.001-Fisher-Stolper.pdf.

Francfort, Henri Paul. 2013. *L'art oublié de la Bactriane aux époque achéménide et hellénistique*. (Persika 17). Paris: De Boccard

Graf, David F. 1994. "The Persian royal road system." *Achaemenid History* 8: 167–89.

Grelot, Pierre. 1972. *Documents araméens d'Égypte*. Paris: Éd. du Cerf.

Hallock, Richard T. 1969. *Persepolis Fortification Tablets*. Chicago, IL: The University of Chicago Press.

Hallock, Richard T. 1978. "Selected Fortification Texts." *Cahiers de la Délégation archéologique française en Iran* 8: 109–36.

Haubold, Johannes. 2012. "The Achaemenid Empire and the Sea." *Mediterranean Historical Review* 27(1): 4–23.

Henkelman, Wouter F. M. 2005. "Animal sacrifice and 'external' exchange in the Persepolis Fortification tablets." In: *Approaching the Babylonian Economy: Approaching the Babylonian Economy*, ed. Heather D. Baker and Michael Jursa, 137–65. (Alter Orient und Altes Testament 30). Münster: Ugarit Verlag.

Henkelman, Wouter F. M. 2008a. *The Other Gods Who Are: Studies in Elamite-Iranian Acculturation Based on the Persepolis Fortification Texts*. Leiden: Nederlands Instituut voor het Nabije Oosten.

Henkelman, Wouter F. M. 2008b. "From Gabae to Taoce: The Geography of the Central Administrative Province." In: *L'archive des Fortifications de Persépolis. État des questions et perspectives de recherches*, ed. Pierre Briant, Wouter F.M. Henkelman and Matthew W. Stolper, 303–16. (Persika 12). Paris: De Boccard.

Henkelman, Wouter F.M. 2010. "'Consumed Before the King.' The Table of Darius, that of Irdabama and Irtaštuna, and that of His Satrap, Karkiš." In: *Der Achämenidenhof / The Achaemenid Court*, ed. Bruno Jacobs and Robert Rollinger, 666–775. (Classica et Orientalia 2). Wiesbaden: Harrassowitz.

Henkelman, Wouter F.M. 2011. "Of Tapyroi and tablets, states and tribes: the historical geography of pastoralism in the Achaemenid heartland in Greek and Elamite sources." *Bulletin of the Institute of Classical Studies* 54(2): 1–16.

Henkelman, Wouter F.M. 2017. "Imperial signature and imperial paradigm: Achaemenid administrative structure and system across and beyond the Iranian plateau." In: *Die Verwaltung im Achämenidenreich – Imperiale Muster und Strukturen / Administration in the Achaemenid Empire– Tracing the Imperial Signature*, ed. Bruno Jacobs and Wouter F.M. Henkelman, 45–256. Wiesbaden: Harrassowitz.

Henkelman, Wouter F.M. 2018. "Bactrians in Persepolis – Persians in Bactria." In: *A Millennium of History: the Iron Age in Southern Central Asia (2nd and 1st Millennia B.C.)* (Archäologie In Iran und Turan 17 = Mémoires de la Délégation Archéologique Française en Afghanistan 35), ed. Johanna Lhuillier and Nikolaus Boroffka, 223–255. Berlin: Dietrica Reimer Verlag.

Henkelman, Wouter F.M. and Margaretha L. Folmer. 2016. "Your tally is full! On wooden credit records in and after the Achaemenid Empire." In: *Silver, Money and Credit. A Tribute to Robartus J. Van der Spek on the Occasion of his 65th Birthday*, ed. Kristin Kleber and Reinhard Pirngruber, 133–239. Leiden: Nederlands Instituut voor het Nabije Oosten.

Herrenschmidt, Clarisse. 2014. "Designation of the empire and its political concepts of Darius I according to old Persian records." In: *Excavating an Empire. Achaemenid Persia in Longue Durée*, ed. Touraj Daryaee, Ali Mousavi and Khodadad Rezakhani, 12–36. Costa Mesa, CA: Mazda Publishers.

Jacobs, Bruno, Wouter F. M. Henkelman and Matthew W. Stolper, eds. 2017.*Die Verwaltung im Achämenidenreich – Imperiale Muster und Strukturen / Administration in the Achaemenid Empire*. Wiesbaden: Harrassowitz.

Kegerreis, Christopher, 2017, "Setting a royal pace: Achaemenid kingship and the origin of Alexander the Great's *Bematistai*." *Ancient History Bulletin* 31(1–2): 39–64.

Kelly, Thomas. 1992. "The Assyrians, the Persians and the sea." *Mediterranean Historical Review* 7: 5–28.

Klinkott, Hilmar. 2005. *Der Satrap: Ein achaimenedischer Amsträger und seine Handlungsspielräume*, Frankfurt am Main: Verlag Antike.

Klotz, David. 2015. "Darius I and the Sabaeans: Ancient Partners in Red Sea Navigation." *Journal of Near Eastern Studies* 74(2): 1–14.

Kosmin, Paul J. 2014. *The Land of the Elephant Kings: Space, Territory and Ideology in the Seleucid Empire*. Cambridge, MA: Harvard University Press.

Khatchadourian, Lori. 2016. *Imperial Matter. Ancient Persia and the Archaeology of Empires*. Oakland, CA: University of California Press.

Kuhrt, Amélie. 2007. *The Persian Empire: A Corpus of Sources from the Achaemenid Period*. London: Routledge.

Kuhrt, Amélie. 2014a. "Reassessing the Reign of Xerxes in the Light of New Evidence." In: *Extraction and Control. Studies in Honor of Matthew W. Stolper* (Studies in Ancient Oriental Civilization 68), ed. Michael Kozuh et al., 163–69. Chicago, IL: The Oriental Institute of the University of Chicago.

Kuhrt, Amélie. 2014b. "State communication in the Achaemenid Empire." In: *State Correspondence in the Ancient World: From New Kingdom Egypt to the Roman Empire*, ed. K. Radner, 112–40. (Oxford studies in early empires). Oxford: Oxford University Press.

Lewis, David Malcolm. 1980. "Datis the Mede." *Journal of Hellenic Studies* 100: 194–5.

Liverani, Mario. 1990. *Prestige and Interest. International Relations in the Near East ca. 1600–1100 BC*. Padova: Sargon.

McKitterick, Rosamond. 2011. "A king on the move: the place of an itinerant court in Charlemagne's government." In: *Royal Courts in Dynastic States and Empires:*

A Global Perspective (Rulers & Elites: Comparative Studies in Governance 1), ed. J. Jeroen Duindam and Metin Kunt, 145–69. Leiden: Brill.

Naveh, Joseph and Shaul Shaked. 2012. *Aramaic Documents from Ancient Bactria (Fourth Century BCE) From the Khalili Collections.* London: The Khalili Family Trust.

Porten, Bezalel. 1968. *Archives from Elephantine: The Life of an Ancient Jewish Military Colony.* Berkeley, CA: University of California Press.

Porten, Bezalel and Ada Yardeni. 1992–1999. *Textbook of Aramaic Documents from Ancient Egypt.* 4 vols. Jerusalem: The Hebrew University of Jerusalem.

Potts, Daniel T. 2010. "Achaemenid interests in the Persian Gulf." In: *The World of Achaemenid Persia: History, Art and Society in Iran and the Ancient Near East: Proceedings of a Conference at the British Museum 29th September–1st October 2005*, ed. John Curtis and St. John Simpson, 523–33. London: I.B. Tauris.

Revere, Robert B. 1957. "'No man's coast': ports of trade in the eastern Mediterranean." In: *Trade and Market in the Early Empires: Economies in History and Theory*, ed. Karl Polanyi, Conrad M. Arensberg and Harry W. Pearson, 38–63. Glencoe, IL: The Free Press.

Sancisi-Weerdenburg, Heleen. 1990. "The quest for an elusive empire." In: *Centre and Periphery: Proceedings of the Groningen 1986 Achaemenid History Workshop*, ed. Amélie Kuhrt, 263–74. Leiden: Nederlands Instituut voor het Nabije Oosten.

Stolper, Matthew W. 2017. "Investigating irregularities at Persepolis." In: *Die Verwaltung Im Achaemenidenreich: Imperiale Muster und Strukturen / Administration in the Achaemenid Empire – Tracing the Imperial Signature*, ed. Bruno Jacobs, Wouter F. M. Henkelman and Matthew W. Stolper, 741–822, Wiesbaden: Harrassowitz.

Tolini, Gauthier. 2009. "Les repas du Grand Roi en Babylonie: Cambyse et le palais d'Abanu." In: *Et il y eut un esprit dans l'homme: Jean Bottéro et la Mésopotamie*, ed. Xavier Faivre, Brigitte Lion and Cécile Michel, 237–54. Paris: De Boccard.

Tolini, Gauthier. 2013, "Les ressources de la Babylonie et l'approvisionnement de la Table de Darius le Grand." In: *Le banquet du monarque dans le monde antique*, ed. Catherine Grandjean, Christophe Hugoniot and Brigitte Lion, 145–62. Rennes: Presses universitaires de Rennes.

Tuplin, Christopher. 1987a. "The administration of the Achaemenid Empire." In *Coinage and Administration in the Athenian and Persian Empire: the Ninth Oxford Symposium on Coinage and Monetary History*, ed. Ian Carradice, 109–66. Oxford: BAR.

Tuplin, Christopher. 1987b. "Xenophon and the garrisons of the Achaemenid Empire." *Archäologische Mitteilungen aus Iran* 20: 167–245.

Tuplin, Christopher. 1998. "The seasonal migration of Achaemenid kings: a report on old and new evidence." In: *Studies in Persian History: Essays in Memory of David M. Lewis*, ed. Maria Brosius and Amélie Kuhrt, 63–114. Leiden: Nederlands Instituut voor het Nabije Oosten.

Tuplin, Christopher. 2014. "From Arshama to Alexander. Reflections on Persian responses to attack." In: *From Source to History. Studies on Ancient Near Eastern Worlds and Beyond: dedicated to Giovanni Battista Lanfranchi on the*

Occasion of his 65th Birthday on June 23, 2014, ed. Salvatore Gaspa, et al., 669–96. Münster: Ugarit-Verlag.

Waerzeggers, Caroline. 2003/2004. "The Babylonian Revolts against Xerxes and the 'End of Archives.'" *Archiv für Orientforschung* 50: 150–78.

Waerzeggers, Caroline. 2010. "Babylonians in Susa: the travels of Babylonian businessmen to Susa reconsidered." In: *Der Achämenidenhof*, ed. Bruno Jacobs and Robert Rollinger, 777–813. Wiesbaden: Harrassowitz.

2   Limits of All-Under-Heaven: Ideology and Praxis of "Great Unity" in Early Chinese Empire[*]

Yuri Pines

One of the most challenging tasks in studying the functioning of empires is the need to distinguish between the imperial discourse and the imperial praxis. On the level of discourse, there are many similarities among major imperial formations worldwide. For instance, boasting of territorial expansion, employing the language of inclusiveness and universality, or promising lasting peace and orderly rule to the empire's subjects may be considered a common denominator of the imperial propaganda. Yet the realities on the ground can differ tremendously. The same rhetoric of expansion and universal superiority can reflect the empire's real awesomeness, but also can be employed to conceal its perennial weaknesses; it can be utilized by an expansionist and militarist empire, but also by the one concerned with defense only. This is especially true in the case of China, where remarkable cultural continuity provided the imperial statesmen with the common repertoire of ideas, ideals, symbols, and legitimation devices, which could be employed under highly distinct circumstances. At times, lofty pronouncements appear so divorced from the realities on the ground that a student may feel tempted to dismiss them as nothing but a meaningless brouhaha.

Yet discourse of inclusiveness and universality in China and elsewhere was not just a smokescreen used to conceal a dynasty's weakness. It was also a powerful political force in its own right. Firmly entrenched values, perceptions, and ideals could at times direct the ruling elite toward a certain course of action that was hazardous from military, economic, or sociopolitical points of view, but which was required to bolster the dynasty's legitimacy at home and abroad. Moreover, the declared commitment to certain ideals – such as the dictum to preserve political unity in "All-under-Heaven" (*tianxia*) – could occasionally preclude alternative courses of action and limit the dynasty's

[*] This research was supported by the Israel Science Foundation (grant No. 568/19) and by the Michael William Lipson Chair in Chinese Studies.

79

policy choices. Analyzing the interaction between the imperial discourse and the actual policies adopted in response to different circumstances is one of the most promising avenues in China's imperial history research.

In an earlier study, I have explored the ways in which the ideal of "Great Unity" shaped political, military, and administrative dynamics in China both under the unifying dynasties and during the periods of disunion (Pines 2012, 11–43). In this chapter I want to focus on the impact of this ideal on China's territoriality, especially under the early imperial dynasties, Qin (221–207 BCE) and Han (206/202 BCE–220 CE). I shall analyze pre-imperial antecedents of the idea of unified rule, the formation of pro-unification discourse amid political disintegration of the Warring States era (Zhanguo, 453–221 BCE), the interplay between universalistic and particularistic visions of unity, and, finally, the ways in which these pre-imperial ideas influenced dynastic leaders' policy choices in the aftermath of imperial unification. I shall conclude by outlining tensions between the ideological commitment to the idea of universal rule and the manifold factors – ecological, military, economical, and cultural – which limited the empire's expansion.

2.1   Origins: The Primeval Unity of the Zhou House

The archaeological discoveries of recent decades have revolutionized our understanding of China's past. A previously widespread uncritical acceptance of Chinese political mythology, which postulated the existence of a single legitimate locus of power on China's soil since the very inception of civilization, gave way to a polycentric perspective. It is now widely accepted that multiple Neolithic and Bronze Age cultures interacted for millennia in the basins of the Yellow and Yangzi Rivers, and beyond, none of them obviously superior to the others (Shelach 2015). Even the first historical royal dynasty, the Shang (c.1600–1046 BCE), might have enjoyed only a relative cultural, military, and political superiority over its neighbors, but by no means ruled the territories beyond its immediate sphere of influence in the middle Yellow River valley (Keightley 1999).

The overthrow of the Shang by the Zhou dynasty (c.1046–255 BCE) became an important turning point. The victorious Zhou leaders utilized their success to rapidly expand the territory under their direct and indirect control, establishing a military and civilian presence beyond their original Wei River valley locus to the middle and low Yellow River basin, and even further to the south, to the Huai and Han Rivers area (Map 2.1). Notably, in contrast to the conquest of the Shang and the immediate crushing of the pro-Shang rebellion which were accompanied by considerable violence, the subsequent expansion of the Zhou rule, including the establishment of new settlements ruled by royal kin and allies, the relocation of the subjugated Shang population, and the imposition of the Zhou elite over the

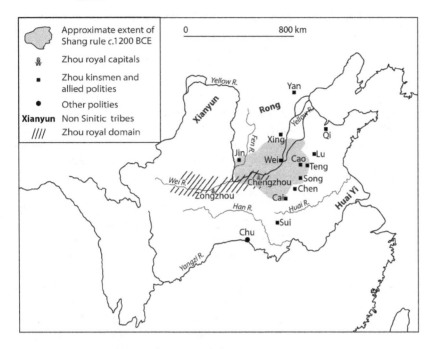

Map 2.1 Shang and Western Zhou.

indigenous inhabitants of the eastern parts of the realm, appear to have been accomplished relatively smoothly (Li Feng 2006). Probably, the successful extermination of the Shang bolstered the new dynasty's prestige and prevented the formation of an effective opposition.

Having accomplished their immediate expansion, the Zhou rulers shifted decisively from military to civilian modes of rule. The dynasty's major asset was its religious legitimation. The Zhou kings succeeded in positioning themselves as exclusive mediators between the supreme deity, Heaven, and the people below; and in their capacity as "Sons of Heaven" (*tianzi*) they continued to enjoy obvious superiority over their allies and subordinates, the regional lords (*zhuhou*). Currently available textual and paleographic evidence suggest that even the leaders of non-Zhou polities, who appropriated the royal title, dared not proclaim themselves "Sons of Heaven," recognizing thereby the ostensible supremeness of the Zhou kings.[1] The combination of religious superiority, kinship ties to most of regional lords, as well as ongoing cultural

---

[1] For instance, in an inscription on the Guai Bo-*gui* vessel, the author, a leader of a non-Zhou polity, refers to his father as "king" but reserves the designation "Son of Heaven" for the Zhou monarch (see Li Feng 2006, 183–5).

prestige of the Zhou royalty, allowed the dynasty to maintain its rule in the Yellow River basin for almost three centuries, even after marked decline in its military, economic, and political prowess.

In retrospect, the Western Zhou period (*c*.1046–771 BCE) was re-imagined as an age of unity and order. This positive image notwithstanding, the eventual trajectory of the dynasty was less impressive. Within a century or so it started losing territories to external competitors or to erstwhile allies-turned-foes; and its ability to monitor subordinate regional lords declined as well. In 771 BCE, the dynasty was delivered a dreadful blow by the coalition of dissenting nobles and foreign invaders. Although the Zhou house survived in the crippled eastern part of its domain for five more centuries, its ability to exercise effective rule within the Chinese oecumene had drastically declined.[2]

It is difficult to assess to what extent the early Zhou kings developed the universalistic claims with which they were associated in retrospect. On the one hand, the exclusivity of their position as Sons of Heaven, as well as their clear superiority over neighboring polities might have encouraged the development of universalistic pretensions; on the other hand, these pretensions appear incomparably milder than in the case of later imperial polities. Zhou's territorial expansion peaked early in its history, and the readiness to resort to arms in order to project the dynasty's rule over the "barbarians of the four quarters" remained very limited.[3] The Zhou rulers continued to employ the Shang terminology of "the four quarters" (*si fang* 四方), which implied their centrality but not necessarily the inclusivity of their rule.[4] They clearly distinguished between the internal dependencies, which the kings could "inspect," and the external foes, who could be invaded or fought against, but who were not expected to be subordinate to the Zhou (Pines 2008, 70–1). The very notion of "All-under-Heaven," so central to the later universalistic discourse, remained underdeveloped in the early centuries of the Zhou. Even when this term is – very rarely – employed, it is unclear whether it refers to the entire known world (as was the case later), or only to the area under the Son of Heaven's direct control (Pines 2002b, 102). All these suggest a less inclusive and universalistic polity than the later texts want us to believe. When we add to this the kings' limited ability to monitor the activities of their nominal underlings, the regional lords, we may conclude that the Zhou were *not* an empire on a par with later Chinese imperial polities. They were a powerful primeval polity, which supplied the future empire-builders with certain symbolic capital,

---

[2] For new data regarding these dramatic events, see Chen and Pines 2018.

[3] The fiasco of the Zhou attempt to subjugate the southern polity of Chu in *c*. 957 BCE marked the end of Zhou's southward expansion, and to a large extent the end of its territorial expansion in general (Li Feng 2006, 93ff.).

[4] For a different view of the Zhou concept of *si fang*, see Wang 2000, 67–73. I believe that Wang's interpretation reflects a much later, markedly post-Western Zhou perspective.

but which fell short of establishing effective control even over its dependencies, not to say over outer territories.

2.2   Fragmentation and Integration in the Zhou World

In the aftermath of the collapse of the Western Zhou in 771 BCE, the political situation within the Chinese world had profoundly changed. The Zhou kings remained symbolically important, but lost the ability to dictate their will over regional lords, whose territories became independent polities in their own right. These polities were henceforth engaged in vibrant diplomatic and military activities: they concluded alliances, waged wars, and annexed weaker neighbors. The Sons of Heaven became hapless spectators of internecine struggles, in which they could occasionally intervene but the outcome of which they could not determine. The Zhou oecumene began disintegrating. The centrifugal tendencies were to a certain extent counterbalanced by the ongoing cultural unity of the aristocrats from rival polities, who routinely intermarried, continued to maintain common written and ritual culture, and adhered to common rules of diplomatic intercourse and to chivalry codes on the battlefield. These cultural factors, however, could not compensate for the absence of an effective political center, which could rein in aggravating interstate conflicts.

Throughout the Springs-and-Autumns period (Chunqiu, 770–453 BCE) various attempts were made to stabilize the multi-state order. At times a degree of stability could be temporarily achieved under the aegis of a powerful overlord, who would nominally act as an executor of the Son of Heaven's will to bolster his own legitimacy. At times two rival alliances competed for power; and twice (in 546 and 541 BCE) the beleaguered parties even initiated multi-state conferences to attain universal peace; but all was in vain (Pines 2002a, 105–35). On the ruins of the multi-state order of the Springs-and-Autumns period a new age of the war of all against all emerged, giving, in retrospect, the subsequent period its ominous name: the age of the Warring States (Map 2.2).

The centrifugal process of the Springs-and-Autumns period eclipsed not just the Zhou oecumene at large, but also most of its component polities. These polities were torn apart by rival aristocratic lineages that amassed sufficient political, military, and economic power to challenge their lords. By the 6th century BCE most political entities throughout the Zhou world had become entangled in a web of debilitating power struggles between powerful nobles and the lords, among aristocratic lineages, and among rival branches within some of these lineages, in addition to endless wars with foreign powers. In 453 BCE, the crisis reached its nadir, as one of the richest and militarily most successful states of the Springs-and-Autumns period, Jin, disintegrated and was divided among three major ministerial lineages. The entire sociopolitical system designed by the Zhou founders and their successors was on the verge of collapse.

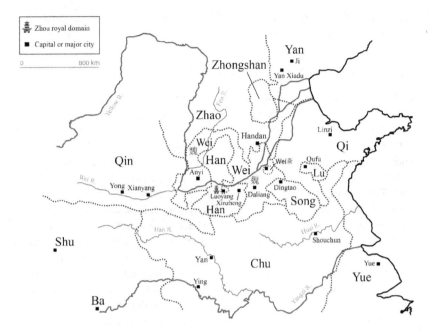

Map 2.2 The Warring States world, *c.*350 BCE.

It is under these conditions that the seeds of radical change and of subsequent reintegration were sown. Incidentally, the "scheming ministers" who tore apart the state of Jin were the first to experiment with new administrative policies aimed at curbing the forces of disintegration within their domains. In due time these policies brought about administrative centralization, restoration of the ruler's effective control over his ministers, and eventual replacement of the hereditary aristocracy with a new broad elite of *shi*, "men-of-service," who owed their position to individual skills rather than pedigree. These profound political and social changes evolved in tandem with economic reforms, prompted by the "iron revolution," which allowed the creation of proactive agro-managerial state, and with parallel advances in military technologies, which brought about the replacement of aristocratic chariot-based armies with mass infantry armies staffed by peasant conscripts. A new highly central-ized bureaucratic state was born. This state replaced the loose aristocratic polities of the Springs-and-Autumns era and laid the foundation for the future tightly integrated imperial regime.[5]

---

[5] See Lewis 1999 for the overall survey of the Warring States-period reforms; Wagner 1993 for the iron revolution; Pines 2009, 115–35 for the rise of the *shi*.

In the context of our discussion, what matters most is the territorial integration of the newly formed Warring State. This integration was a natural byproduct of the state's need to control all of its material and human resources. All the arable lands, which in the central Yellow River basin accounted for 60 percent and more of the state's territory (*Book of Lord Shang* 6.2), had to be measured, recorded, allocated to peasants, and taxed. All the inhabitants had to be registered to ensure efficient taxation, conscription, and general surveillance. In the densely populated agricultural heartlands of China, a non-demarcated land could not be tolerated. A well known anecdote of a war triggered by two women's rivalry over the right to collect the leaves of mulberry trees in a disputed borderland area (*Shiji* 31, 1426) may not be true, but it does reflect the importance of clear demarcation between rival polities. Not only arable lands mattered: a state had to control its "mountains, forests, marshes, swamps, valleys and dales" from which benefits could be extorted (*Book of Lord Shang* 6.2). Every piece of land had to be identified as either "ours" or "theirs."

The territorial integration of individual states eventually contributed toward the future integration of the entire realm, but in the short term, it also aggravated centrifugal forces by increasing separation among rival polities. The separation was promulgated through administrative regulations, which monitored movements of population and merchandise into neighboring polities; through legal distinctions between the native and foreign population; and, most visibly, through long protective walls which distinguished between the "inner" and "outer" realms. These walls were defensive in their nature, but they had far-reaching symbolic significance, changing not only the physical but also the mental landscape. The land outside the walls became a dangerous *terra incognita*, venturing into which was considered a most inauspicious event, which required a special exorcist ritual, similar to the ritual performed upon leaving one's native settlement.[6]

The combined result of these developments was somewhat equivocal: whereas individual states became better integrated, the Zhou world became even more fragmented. To the erstwhile political and military contest among rival polities one may add an increasing sense of cultural alienation. The ongoing divergence in the material and, to a lesser extent, written culture of the major states is well documented by material, paleographic, and textual evidence. The decline of the aristocratic elite of the Springs-and-Autumns period meant partial abandonment of the Zhou ritual culture, which once served as a common cultural denominator of the upper classes throughout the Zhou

---

[6] For inauspiciousness of departure from a native state, see Qin "Almanacs" ("*Ri shu*") in *Qin jiandu* 2, 392–3 (slips 145 and 144); for exorcist rituals, see Hu 1998. For an example of monitoring cross-state trade, see Falkenhausen 2005. For an example of legal distinction between natives and foreigners, see, e.g., a Qin legal regulation from the Shuihudi Tomb 11 hoard in *Qin jiandu* 1, 250 (slips 177–8). For the early walls, see Pines 2018b.

world. The new elite, some of whose members had risen from the lower social strata, was more diversified culturally than its predecessors. This diversification is particularly evident in the changing image of powerful "peripheral" states, Qin in the northwest (Pines 2004; Pines et al. 2014) and Chu in the south (Cook and Major 1999). Both originally were members of the Zhou oecumene; but by the 4th and 3rd centuries BCE they were treated as cultural strangers. Cultural separation followed the lines of political fragmentation, indicating that centuries of division might well have resulted in the complete disintegration of the Zhou world into distinct quasi-national entities.

This process of internal consolidation of large territorial states, and their political and cultural separation from the neighbors, unmistakably recalls similar developments in early modern Europe, where, as is well known, these resulted in the formation of nation-states. In China, however, the development trajectory was markedly different. The potential transformation of the competing Warring States into full-fledged separate entities never materialized. Instead, these polities were submerged by the unified empire in 221 BCE, becoming thereafter a focus of ethnographic curiosity rather than of political separatism.[7] To understand why and how this happened we should turn now to the realm of thought.

2.3   "Stability Is in Unity"

The Warring States period is one of the most fascinating ages in China's long history: the age of bloody struggles and devastating wars, but also of rapid economic growth and profound social transformation, of technological breakthroughs and of radical innovations in economy, warfare, and administrative techniques. This was the most creative age in China's intellectual history: the age of bold departures and remarkable ideological pluralism, which was unhindered by either political or religious orthodoxies. Thinkers of the so-called Hundred Schools of Thought competed for the rulers' patronage, moving from one court to another in search of better employment. They proposed distinct remedies to social, political, economic, and military maladies, their views ranging from harsh authoritarianism to anarchistic individualism, from support of a laissez-faire economy to advocacy of state monopolies, from blatant militarism to radical pacifism. Yet this immense pluralism notwithstanding, the competing thinkers held core beliefs in common. Among these, the commitment to the universal benefit of All-under-Heaven – eventually through political unification – stands as one of the most remarkable features of the Warring States-period intellectual discourse. An individual state never appears as the ultimate beneficiary of the thinkers' proposals, but, if at all, as a springboard for attaining the highest aim of resolving "universal" problems.

---

[7] See Lewis 2006, 189–244 and the review in Pines 2005b, 181–7.

This remarkable universalism ostensibly stands at odds with the dominant tendency of the Warring States-period states to strengthen their sociopolitical cohesiveness. The contradiction reflects a major difference between the lives of members of the educated elite, or at least its highest segment, and those of the rest of the populace. In an age when most states tried to prevent emigration, intellectually active elite members, the so-called *shi* ("men-of-service" or "intellectuals") were free to cross boundaries in search of better careers. Any known thinker of that age served more than one court; and this very flexibility of movement through the interstate "market of talent" broadened their horizons, causing their concerns to transcend the confines of individual polities. Eventually, this breadth of horizons became associated with high elite status, whereas localism – local customs and identities – was viewed as characteristic of culturally impaired commoners (Lewis 2006, 192–212). Lacking the intellectuals' endorsement, the local identities of the Warring States never developed into a politically meaningful factor, as happened elsewhere, for example, in modern Europe.

The proclaimed universalism of the Warring States-period intellectuals had immediate political implications. Attaining peace in All-under-Heaven became the major goal of conflicting policy proposals. In an age of escalating warfare, of endless bloodshed and inherent lack of stability, in an age when every state routinely tried to undermine domestic order in rival polities, it was all too clear that the internal problems of an individual state would never be resolved unless the entire oecumene was settled (*Lüshi chunqiu* 13.7 and 26.2). And, insofar as diplomatic means of stabilizing All-under-Heaven were inadequate, political unification became the only feasible way out of unending disorder. Therefore, the quest for unity became a peculiar intellectual consensus of the thinkers of the Warring States period, legitimating the universal empire long before it came into being.

I shall not discuss here in detail the pro-unification discourse of the Warring States period, as I have done it elsewhere (Pines 2000). Suffice it to summarize the major aspects of this discourse. Most immediately, one cannot but be impressed by a great variety of arguments put forward by competing thinkers to bolster the idea of political unification as singularly legitimate. Some, as Confucius (Kongzi, 551–479 BCE) connected it to the putative legacy of the early Zhou sage kings (*Lunyu* 16.2). Other, like Confucius's great rival, Mozi (*c*.460–390 BCE), traced it back to the very origins of organized society (*Mozi* III.11 ["Shang tong shang"]). Other, like the authors of an immensely influential text, the *Laozi* (*c*.4th century BCE), sought metaphysical justifications for political unity: the singularity of the monarch on earth should parallel the singularity of Heaven, Earth and, most importantly, of the cosmic Way (Dao) (*Laozi* 25). Yet the most compelling rationale for unification was provided by one of Confucius's most eminent followers, Mengzi (aka Mencius, *c*.380–304

BCE). When asked by a regional ruler "how to stabilize All-under-Heaven," Mengzi plainly replied: "Stability is in unity" (*Mengzi* 1.6).

Mengzi's reply reflects the consensus of the competing thinkers. The texts from the second half of the Warring States period seem no longer to be preoccupied with justifications for the future unification, since the need to unify the entire subcelestial realm became the unquestionable common desideratum. Henceforth, the debates revolved primarily not about why the world should be unified, but about how the unity should be achieved. Many thinkers hoped that this could be done through non-violent means. Mengzi, for instance, ridiculed those who wanted to subjugate All-under-Heaven militarily as daydreamers who "look for fish by climbing a tree" (*Mengzi* 1.7); elsewhere he stated that only he who has "no proclivity to kill, will be able to unify" the world (*Mengzi* 1.6). However, laudable as it was, Mengzi's and like-minded thinkers' vision of peaceful unification under a morally upright sovereign was impractical. Mengzi himself lamented that the True Monarch – the ultimate unifier – comes once in five hundred years, and his coming is long overdue (*Mengzi* 4.13). Yet there were other thinkers who preferred not to wait for a savior but to hasten unification practically. The most notorious – and most successful of these – Shang Yang (d. 338 BCE), plainly stated that the True Monarch is the one who commits himself to resolute war, in which he will subjugate his rivals and bring about the long-desired peace and tranquillity (*Book of Lord Shang* 7.2). The difference in means between Mengzi and Shang Yang could not be greater, but the bottom line remained all the same: "Stability is in unity."

Aside from explicit calls for unity, the philosophical discourse of the Warring States period facilitated future imperial unification in a variety of other ways. For instance, the political mythology of that age backdated the notion of unity to the remote past, implying thereby that political fragmentation is an aberration and not an acceptable state of affairs (Pines 2008; 2010). Ritual compendia postulated the existence of a universal sociopolitical pyramid headed by the Son of Heaven as the singularly appropriate arrangement, de-legitimating thereby the current situation of competing *loci* of authority. The very language of political discourse, with its repeated postulates of the superiority of universality to particularity (Lewis 2006) was conducive to the goal of unification. Yet perhaps the most interesting aspect of pro-unification discourse is not in what was said but in what the thinkers did not say. That not a single individual or text is known ever to have endorsed a goal of a regional state's independence is most remarkable. Even in the texts unearthed from the supposedly culturally distinctive state of Chu we find a clear commitment to the "universal" perspective, which postulates the superiority of "All-under-Heaven" over its component parts (Pines 2018a). Thus, denied ideological legitimacy, separate polities became intrinsically unsustainable in the long term.

2.4   Limits of *Tianxia* Before the Unification

The absolute priority of the ideal of political unity in pre-imperial ideological discourse is undeniable; now it is time to ask what were the limits of "All-under -Heaven"? Did it include the Zhou oecumene alone, namely the areas of shared elite culture (written language, mortuary rites, ritual gradations), or did it encompass the "barbarian" periphery as well? Was the vision of unity truly universal, or was it of more limited nature, something which may be defined, somewhat anachronistically, as "the unity of China"?

The answer is equivocal. On the one hand, an exclusive view is duly present in a variety of texts that emphasize the gap between the cultured Chinese and the "barbarian" periphery. This emphasis is particularly strong in the texts related to the Springs-and-Autumns period, when China's Central States (*zhongguo*) faced a series of incursions from neighboring ethnic groups. The latter are resultantly depicted as insufficiently human, as "wolves and jackals who cannot be satiated" (*Zuozhuan*, Min 1.2). Although these harsh pronouncements about the "barbarians" impaired humanity represent only one strand of pre-imperial discourse, and are qualified by many statements that emphasize the mutability of the aliens and the possibility of their eventual acculturation (Pines 2005a), the emphasis on "Sino-barbarian" dichotomy in a variety of early texts cannot be easily dismissed. This dichotomous view was conducive to the emergence of a spatial outlook that placed the aliens outside the pale of civilization, on the fringes of *tianxia* and beyond the immediate concern of the Son of Heaven.

The Sino-centric spatial view is represented in several ritual texts, of which the "Yu gong" ("The Tribute of Yu") chapter of the *Canon of Documents* is singularly representative. This text, which was probably composed in the middle Warring States period, narrates the merits of the legendary demiurge Yu. Having subdued the flood, Yu arranged the world into Nine Provinces (*jiu zhou*). The Nine Provinces (the precise location and names of which vary from one text to another) are fundamentally congruent with the territories of China proper, i.e., with the Zhou civilization. This terrestrial organization implies that the entire known world is a complete and closed system, organized in a three-by-three grid, which cannot be meaningfully altered (Dorofeeva-Lichtman 2009). The immutability of this scheme becomes even clearer from a parallel "field-allocation" (*fen ye*) astrological system, which divides the sky into nine partitions associated with each of the Provinces below. As noticed by Paul R. Goldin this association meant that "no tenth region [to the Nine Provinces] could ever have been added. There would simply have been no tenth part of the sky to identify with it" (Goldin 2015, 44). The Nine Provinces scheme (the origins of which may well precede the Warring States period) is purely Sino-centric, as it glosses over the areas associated with alien ethnic groups. If the

Nine Provinces are coterminous with the *tianxia* (and this is a big "if," since both terms are normally separated in the majority of texts),[8] they represent a vision of a spatially limited subcelestial realm.

The Nine Provinces system displays little interest in the alien periphery; but the latter is more prominent in a parallel system of Five (or Nine) Zones. An early account of this system is attached to the account of the Nine Provinces in the "Tribute of Yu," but the correlation between the two schemes remains unclear (*Shangshu* 3, 202–6). Having accomplished the Nine Provinces, Yu is said to have subdivided the earth into five concentric zones of five hundred *li* (approximately 200 km) breadth each. The zones start with the royal domain, for the dwellers of which different types of tribute obligations are defined; then come the zone of regional lords, the "pacified zone," the "zone of restraint," and the "zone of wilderness." The third zone is the last inhabited by Chinese; it is subdivided into the domain of "civilized learning" and that of "military defense." The two outer zones are inhabited by alien ethnicities and by Chinese criminals who undergo different types of banishment.

The Five Zones scheme, which is repeated with certain variations in several other pre-imperial texts (Dorofeeva-Lichtman 2009, 606–7), may be a later addition to the much more elaborate system of Nine Provinces. It might have been designed deliberately to incorporate the aliens into a universal design centered around the Son of Heaven. Yet alien areas remain only indirectly subordinate to the Son of Heaven in this system. In the "Tribute of Yu" version they are not supposed to submit tribute, and their contact with the civilized world is limited to the acceptance of the banished Chinese criminals. The same marginality characterizes later elaborations of the Five Zone scheme, such as the Nine Zone division in the *Rites of Zhou* (*Zhouli* 33, 863–4 ["Xiaguan-Sima"]). Spatial dimensions of concentric zones could be expanded, but the principle of separation between the civilized realm under the direct control of the Son of Heaven and the "realms of wilderness" inhabited by the aliens remained intact.

The above views present All-under-Heaven as fundamentally coequal to the Chinese Central States and their immediate periphery. They epitomize a conservative and particularistic vision, which is related, even if not directly, to the legacy of the Western Zhou. In this vision, the Son of Heaven's superiority remains effective only in the immediate vicinity of his domain, and diminishes gradually, vanishing in the "realm of wilderness." Yet this vision, which gained much influence in the imperial period, was not necessarily shared by the majority of the Warring States-period thinkers. On the contrary, a great variety of the texts from that period advocate the truly universal unification in which

---

[8] The only text in which the both terms are consistently used coterminously is the *Rites of Zhou* (*Zhouli*), a very peculiar text composed either in the late Warring States or the early imperial period (Elman and Kern 2010). For different variants of the Nine Provinces model and for the provinces' location, see Dorofeeva-Lichtman 2009.

the dividing lines between Chinese and the aliens are blurred, and the Son of Heaven exercises effective rule over the entire subcelestial realm.

Universalistic worldview has manifold manifestations in the Warring States-period texts. Some justify universalism by attributing it to ancient paragons. For instance, Mozi, himself a cultural relativist, who dismissed pejorative views of the aliens as an unjustifiable bias (Pines 2005a, 75–7), was keen to emphasize how encompassing the rule of early paragons was. In his discussion of "universal love" or "care for everyone" (*jian'ai*), Mozi extolled the demiurge Yu and the Zhou dynastic founders for benefiting aliens and Chinese alike in their activities (*Mozi* IV.15 ["Jian'ai zhong"]). Clearly, for Mozi the universality of love/care meant to encompass all the people under Heaven, not just the residents of the Central States. A slightly later text, a recently discovered manuscript, *Rong Cheng shi* (Mr. Rong Cheng) (composed *c.*300 BCE), uses a different angle in emphasizing the universality of the paragons' rule:

[The people] from beyond the four seas arrived as guests, and those from within the four seas were corrected. Birds and beasts came to court; fish and turtles submitted [tribute]. (Pines 2010, 507)

Here the universality reaches its apex: even the beasts and birds are incorporated into the all-encompassing framework of the ancient monarchs' control. Undoubtedly, this framework should include the alien periphery as well. By associating universality with the sage-monarchs of antiquity, the authors employed the common means of "using the past to serve the present." Namely, if the ancient paragons' rule was truly universal, so should be the rule of the future unifier. Yet other thinkers disagreed. They criticized the former monarchs for failing to achieve comprehensive and lasting unity, and demanded of the future unifier to surpass his predecessors rather than merely emulating them. This view, which caused much indignation to the Confucian philosopher, Xunzi (d. after 238 BCE),[9] became particularly important in the immediate aftermath of the imperial unification of 221 BCE (see section 2.5).

Other thinkers avoided the difficulty of discussing the failures of former sage-monarchs; instead they insisted that universal rule reflected the paragons' intentions rather than deeds. This approach is most clearly pronounced in the *Gongyang zhuan*, a *c.*300 BCE commentary on the canonical text *Springs-and-Autumns Annals* (*Chunqiu*) (Gentz 2015). The *Gongyang* commentary combines very strong emphasis on "Sino-barbarian" dichotomy with an equally unequivocal support for the ultimate incorporation of the "barbarians" within the unified realm of the Son of Heaven. The text reiterates that "nothing is external" to the Son of Heaven, and that the true goal of his activity is the

---

[9] *Xunzi* XII.18, 328–329 ("Zheng lun"). See more in Pines 2008, 83–4.

comprehensive unification of the entire subcelestial realm. A position of an "external subject" by an alien leader is just a temporary aberration:

The *Annals* (*Chunqiu*) considers its state (Lu) as internal, and All the Xia ("Chinese") as external, it considers All the Xia as internal, and the Yi and Di ("barbarians") as external. – [But] the True Monarch wants to unify All-under-Heaven, so why talk of internal and external? – This means that he must begin with those who are near. (*Gongyang zhuan*, Cheng 15, 417)

The ultimate goal of the True Monarch, the would-be unifier, is the unification of all the lands under Heaven so that nothing remains external to his rule. Below we shall see how this view could contribute toward expansionist policies of early emperors. But before we turn to the actualization of the unification ideal, it is time to pause and ask: What were the sources of the optimism of pre-imperial thinkers with regard to the truly comprehensive unification? Did not they expect insurmountable difficulties in attaining this goal?

I think that this optimism reflects two peculiarities of pre-imperial Chinese thought: the thinkers' good historical and limited geographic knowledge. History provided multiple examples of erstwhile "barbarians" who became fully assimilated into a broader Chinese culture. During the Warring States period in particular, the Sinitic states expanded into peripheral areas inhabited by alien ethnic groups, and while this expansion was not necessarily peaceful, nor did it encounter prolonged resistance by the local populations. The successful incorporation of such areas as Sichuan Basin, Liaodong peninsula, or southern reaches of the Yangzi basin into the Zhou world proved the feasibility of assimilating the aliens. A similar conclusion could be drawn from an equally successful assimilation of multiple alien ethnicities, who inhabited enclaves within and among the Sinitic states during the Springs-and-Autumns period but who vanished from subsequent historical accounts. Moreover, even powerful polities established by non-Sinitic ethnic groups, such as the southeastern Wu and Yue during the Springs-and-Autumns period (Falkenhausen 1999, 525–42), or northern Zhongshan during the Warring States period (Wu 2017) became eventually absorbed into the written and ritual culture of the Central States, losing much of their "otherness" in the process. The resultant expansion of the Zhou civilization was conducive to the optimistic belief that the entire known world should eventually become "a single family" (*Xunzi*, "Wang zhi" V.9, 161).

Another possible reason for the thinkers' universalistic optimism is their relatively meager knowledge of the outside world. China never was hermetically isolated from civilizations in central, southern, and western Eurasia, as can be demonstrated by technological transfer and import of prestige goods from afar already during the Bronze Age (*c.*1500–400 BCE; see Shelach 2015, 257–62). Yet China's contacts with the outside world remained too limited to inform the elites of the existence of faraway loci of sedentary civilization.

Wherever pre-imperial texts mention the outside world, they invariably refer to the areas in the immediate vicinity of China proper;[10] even the steppe nomads do not merit particular attention. All this was to change in the aftermath of the imperial unification of 221 BCE. In the meanwhile, an optimistic expectation of comprehensive unification of the entire human habitat was still possible.

2.5   Reaching the Limits: Qin Unification

The year 221 BCE marks a momentous beginning in China's history. After a series of brilliant and bloody campaigns, the king of the northwestern state of Qin succeeded in eliminating or subjugating each of the six "hero-states" that comprised the rest of the Warring States world. The aspirations of generations of thinkers were finally realized: the entire subcelestial realm was unified. Proud of his unprecedented achievement the king of Qin adopted a new title of "emperor" (*huangdi* 皇帝, literally "the august thearch"). This was the start of a new, imperial era in Chinese history, the era which was to last for 2,132 years, until the last bearer of an imperial title, Puyi 溥儀, abdicated on February 12, 1912, in favor of the newly proclaimed Chinese Republic.

The court debates that preceded the adoption of the imperial title by the king of Qin reflect something of the mind-set of the new imperial leaders. The courtiers explained to the king why he should adopt a new and theretofore unheard-of title:

In antiquity, the lands of the Five [legendary] Thearchs were one thousand *li* squared [ca. 160,000 km^2], beyond which was the zone of regional lords and that of the aliens. The lords sometimes attended the court and sometimes did not, and the Son of Heaven was unable to regulate this. Now, your Majesty has raised a righteous army, punishing the savage criminals, has pacified and stabilized All-under-Heaven, turning the territory between the seas into commanderies and counties; and laws and ordinances have a single source. From antiquity it has never been so; the Five Thearchs could not reach this! (*Shiji* 6, 236; Watson 1993, 43)

Hubris aside, this statement encapsulates two major differences between the newly emergent Qin model of a "real" empire and an earlier model of a powerful quasi-universal polity associated with the Zhou dynasty and with the age of the legendary paragons of the past. First, the Qin rule is perceived as effective and highly centralized ("laws and ordinances have a single source"). In effect, this means the expansion of the Warring States-period model of a centralized territorial state to encompass the entire known world. This was not an empty declaration. From the newly available archeological and paleo-graphic materials, of which the Imperial Qin archive from Qianling County

---

[10] For a good example, see the depiction of outside peoples in *Lüshi chunqiu*, a major compendium composed on the eve of the imperial unification (*Lüshi chunqiu* 20.1).

(modern Liye) in the mountains of northwestern Hunan is most notable, we learn of amazing effectiveness and profoundness of Qin's incorporation of these remote corners of its new realm: unifying weights and measures, laws and administrative regulations, script and administrative vocabulary; conducting meticulous population census; registering land and other natural resources; imposing government control over tiny hamlets; tracing fugitive debtors; monitoring local officials down to the tiniest monetary transaction[11] – all epitomize the ability of the Qin government apparatus to reach, paraphrasing Hobsbawm (2000, 80) "down to the humblest inhabitant of the least of its villages." As such, Qin differed fundamentally from the loose entity of the Western Zhou type. The empire was an effectively unified territorial state. For sure, the effectiveness of Qin's rule on the ground may have been hindered by large distances from the imperial center, by insufficiency of administrative personnel, and by local resistance (Korolkov 2020); but at the very least the desideratum – and often the practice – was of a centralized and fully bureaucratized polity whose officials wielded real and not just symbolic power.

The second distinction between Qin and its predecessors emphasized in the above memorandum is the territorial scope of Qin's rule. Qin courtiers derided the particularistic visions of rule as embedded in the Five Zones system; and they ignored the Nine Provinces scheme altogether. Instead, they emphasized that Qin governs All-under-Heaven in its broadest meaning, that is, it rules the entire known world. This inclusiveness is fully visible in a series of inscriptions on the steles, which the First Emperor (r. 221–207 BCE) erected on sacred mountains in the newly acquired territories of his realm (Kern 2000). One of these inscriptions, that on the Langye 瑯邪 stele (219 BCE), merits citation:

> Within the six combined [directions],
> This is the land of the August Thearch:
> To the west it ranges to the flowing sands,
> To the south it completely takes in where the doors face north.
> To the east it enfolds the Eastern Sea,
> To the north, it goes beyond Daxia.
> Wherever human traces reach,
> There is none who does not declare himself [the August Thearch's] subject.
> His merits surpass those of the [legendary] Five Thearchs,
> His favor extends to oxen and horses.   (*Shiji* 6, 245; Kern 2000, 32–3)

The rule of the First Emperor as presented here includes all the known human habitat: from the sea in the east to the deserts of the west, from northern steppes to the areas to the south of the Tropic of Cancer, where people allegedly "opened

---

[11] For Liye documents and the degree of Qin's rule in the Liye area, see, e.g., Yates 2012/13; Sanft 2015. For the magnitude of Qin's impact on the remotest corners of the new realm, see also Feinman et al. 2010.

their door north to face the sun" (Kern 2000, 33n76). Not only the entire humankind, but even "oxen and horses" are encompassed by the emperor's munificence. The idea of a comprehensive unification promulgated by pre-imperial thinkers reaches here its apex. However, at the second glance we can discern certain tension behind this propaganda: whereas geography provides convenient limits for the expansion in three cardinal directions (provided that Qin did not want to advance south of the Tropic of Cancer), the northern part of the realm is ambiguously depicted as "beyond Daxia," possibly referring to the areas beyond the northern loop of the Yellow River (Ordos) (Map 2.3).

This implicit tension over the empire's limits reflects tough policy choices that faced the First Emperor. Having annexed the territories of each of the rival states,

Map 2.3 The Qin Empire.

down to their remotest periphery, Qin was now facing the unknown: the possibility to expand further southward to the lands of those whose "doors face north," and northward into the steppe. Politically speaking, all the enemies worthy of concern were subjugated; and, as a later observer noticed, "this was the moment to preserve authority, stabilize achievements, and found the lasting peace" (*Shiji* 6, 283). Yet the Qin emperor was not satisfied. Ruling over "the state organized for war" (Lewis 2007, 30), he was prone to attain an even higher glory of the truly universal unifier. Another series of highly successful campaigns followed, allowing Qin to incorporate territories far to the south (current Guangdong, Guangxi, and North Vietnam), and simultaneously move northward, into the steppe, the realm of the Xiongnu tribes. New territories were duly integrated into the empire, with additional commanderies and counties established (Map 2.3).

Qin campaigns can be seen as manifestation of its ruler's ongoing commitment to the idea of universal unity. Surely, they were audacious: recall that shortly before the Qin unification, a leading thinker, Han Fei (d. 233 BCE) noted that the southeastern areas of Yue are not coveted by the Warring States leaders because, despite their wealth, they are too difficult to control (*Han Feizi* IV.11 ["Gu fen"]). The Qin emperor had dismissed these fears, committing huge armies to expand to the far south, and he was successful, indeed. However, in the northern direction the expansion was not as easy. It was there that amid military successes, seeds of fundamental change were sown.

Qin's incursion into the steppe initiated a chain reaction, which eventually contributed toward the formation of a new political entity, the Xiongnu Empire, the first of the mighty nomad polities in Eastern Eurasia and the centuries-long rival of the Chinese Empire (Di Cosmo 2002). The entrance of the pastoral nomads into Chinese politics changed the rules of the game: militarily, socially, economically, and culturally, they proved to be a challenge with which only few Chinese monarchs knew how to deal. This was a long-term development; but the impact of the encounter with the Xiongnu could be felt almost immediately in the aftermath of Qin's successful campaign. In 214/213 BCE, the First Emperor ordered the construction of a new protective wall, the early version of the "Great Wall of China." By doing so, he tacitly dispensed with the idea of comprehensive universality proclaimed in Langye (and other) inscriptions just a few years earlier. Evidently, the difficulties of waging war in the inhospitable steppe terrain convinced the emperor to put a limit to his state's expansion.

The erection of the new Great Wall, just years after its numerous predecessors, the walls that separated one Chinese state from another, were demolished on the First Emperor's orders, marks, in my view, a turn away from universalism toward particularism: the idea of a spatially limited empire (cf. Hsing 2011). That this turn occurred under a dynasty with such a remarkably universalistic outlook as the Qin is singularly significant. It was the encounter with the nomads that challenged the inclusive worldview of the empire's custodians

(Goldin 2011). New geographic and cultural realities necessitated profound reassessment of the erstwhile optimism of pre-imperial thinkers. The Qin dynasty was too short-lived to cope systematically with the new situation. It was up to its heir, the Han dynasty, to redefine profoundly the nature of the imperial polity and its territorial scope.

2.6   The Han Empire: Between Contraction and Expansion

The Han dynasty was established in the aftermath of prolonged civil wars that accompanied the fall of Qin, the wars that had radically weakened the empire for generations to come. Facing a plethora of domestic and external pressures, early Han leaders adopted the policy of appeasement. Internally, they allowed renewed formation of autonomous princedoms in the eastern half of the empire; externally, they acquiesced to the secession of manifold areas formerly under Qin's control in the south, southwest and northeast. Yet the most consequential setback was in the Han relations with the newly formed Xiongnu Empire. An attempt by the Han founder, Liu Bang (d. 195 BCE) to repel the Xiongnu assault into the Han territories ended in a fiasco: the emperor was besieged and barely escaped capture. It was the first time that the nomads demonstrated their formidable military prowess. The Xiongnu reoccupied much of the borderlands between the steppe and the sown, which were conquered by the Qin. They did not, however, try to occupy Han's agricultural heartland. Their goal was extracting Han's resources but not supplanting the dynasty. They were a menace, but not an existential threat.

The battered Han dynasty was quick to adapt itself to the new powerful neighbor. In the aftermath of Liu Bang's failure, Han recognized the Xiongnu as a "fraternal" or "rival" (*diguo*) state, that is, as Han's equal, and established with them relations based on the "harmony of the kin" (*heqin*). Practically this meant granting the Xiongnu leader, the *chanyu*, a Han princess, maintaining diplomatic equality, and subsidizing the Xiongnu with lavish Han "gifts," which were supposed to deter the nomads from renewed attacks. Alas, the "harmony of the kin" relations never became harmonious: in the next decades the Xiongnu repeatedly invaded Han lands, necessitating renegotiation of previous agreements on ever more favorable terms for the Xiongnu (Di Cosmo 2002, 190–227).

The early Han was a much smaller empire than the Qin (Map 2.4); it was militarily and economically weaker, and had to resort to diplomacy rather than war in settling relations with its neighbors, including not only the Xiongnu, but, notably, the state of Nan Yue, which seceded from the Han in the far south. Yet these setbacks notwithstanding, the Han statesmen did not abandon their universalistic posture. To the contrary, even those thinkers, such as Jia Yi (200–168 BCE) or Lu Jia (d. 178 BCE), who were highly critical of Qin's senseless expansionism and excessive reliance on the military, repeatedly proclaimed adherence to the empire's universality. Jia Yi explained:

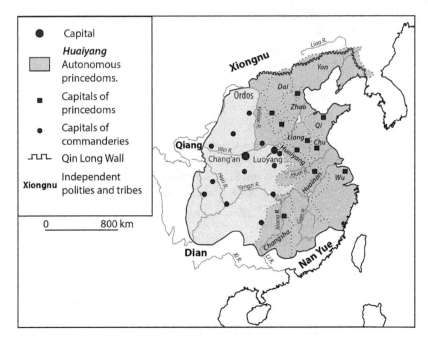

Map 2.4 Early Han Dynasty, *c.*195 BCE. Adapted from the *Cambridge History of China*, Vol. 1, *The Ch'in and Han Dynasties*, p. 125.

The correct meaning of the past [titles]: when to the east, west, south, and north, wherever chariots and boats have an access, wherever human traces reach, there is none who does not declare himself subject – only then one can speak of a Son of Heaven ... Nowadays, the designations are most beautiful, but the real power does not reach beyond the Great Wall. These [the Xiongnu] are not just non-submissive, but are also greatly irreverent. (*Xinshu* 3, 131 ["Wei bu xin"])

Jia Yi was not a warmonger, but he was deeply concerned with the impaired legitimacy of the Han emperors due to their acceptance of the Xiongnu's equal standing. For him this meant incomplete unification of the realm: an aberration that should be corrected or else the Han's imperial title will become fraudulent. This sentiment was shared by many imperial statesmen, and it explains Han's change of course under Emperor Wu (r. 141–87 BCE). Although prior to his ascendancy the Xiongnu incursions decreased (*Hanshu* 64A, 3765), the emperor was adamant: Han had to resort to arms in order to eliminate once and forever the Xiongnu menace.

By the time of Emperor Wu's ascendancy, the domestic situation of the Han had stabilized, and the empire was incomparably more powerful economically and militarily than sixty years before, during Liu Bang's inglorious campaign. Emperor Wu's decision to denounce peace relations with the Xiongnu and deliver them a blow might have been a well-calculated gamble, but the results were unpredictable. The eighty-year war that started in 135 BCE brought about a radical change in Han's geopolitical situation. Initially, the Han armies scored a series of great victories, which resulted in the empire's tremendous expansion not only northward into the steppes but also westward into the oases of the Gansu Corridor, which became a vital artery for Han's move into the theretofore barely known Western Regions. The Han discovery of sedentary civilizations in what is now Xinjiang and further west into Central Asia was one of the most spectacular outcomes of the epochal struggle with the Xiongnu, and the start of the celebrated Silk Road trade. It also expanded greatly Han's geographic horizons and eventually necessitated adjustment of its relations with the outer world.

Emperor Wu's northward expansion had a clear strategic motivation: to deprive the Xiongnu of the territories precariously close to the Han heartland, to cut off their major areas of agricultural supplies (such as the "Western Regions") and to preclude the Xiongnu alliances with other ethnic groups, such as the Qiang. Yet strategic considerations aside, we can discern an equally strong ideological impetus behind Emperor Wu's campaigns: to expand the empire anew to the areas previously occupied by the Qin and even beyond. Hence, parallel to wars with the Xiongnu, the Han resumed expansion into each of the cardinal directions.

Emperor Wu's campaigns were greatly successful. Within slightly more than twenty years, he succeeded in doubling the territories under Han's control (Map 2.5). Dozens of new commanderies and counties were established from Hainan Island in the south to the Ordos in the north, from Yunnan in the southwest to Korea in the northeast, from the southeastern coast to the northwestern deserts. Hundreds of thousands of paupers and convicted criminals were sent to the newly acquired lands to organize agricultural settlements, which allowed full incorporation of the new territories (Yü 1986). Once again it appeared that a universal empire is coming into being. The dictum of the *Gongyang* commentary (which, not incidentally, became the singularly important canonical text under Emperor Wu) that "nothing is external to the Son of Heaven" seemed to be close to actualization.[12] Some of Emperor Wu's courtiers even adopted an arrogant imperialistic discourse, which remained a rarity in Chinese history, arguing that the emperor's urgent task is to encompass the outlying barbarians within a moral universe radiating from the Son of Heaven (Dai 2001, 154).

---

[12] It should be mentioned here that despite the possible service of the *Gongyang* ideology to the policy of territorial expansion, several leading *Gongyang* exegetes were among the bitter opponents of this policy under Emperor Wu (Gentz 2015).

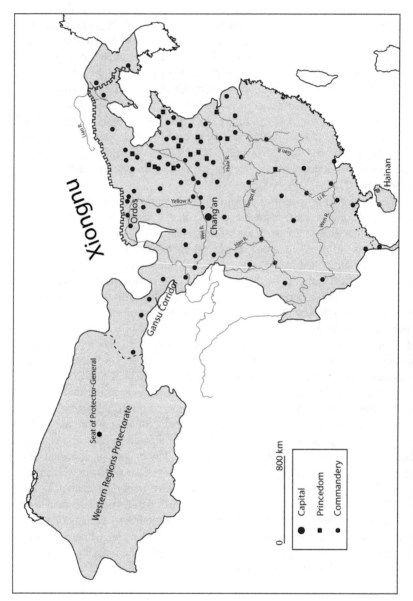

Map 2.5 The Han Empire after Emperor Wu's campaigns.

Yet impressive as they were, Emperor Wu's spectacular victories turned to be an extremely costly affair. Aside from direct military expenses, the Han dynasty had to stretch its resources to provide subsidies to the surrendered Xiongnu chiefs, to reward meritorious soldiers and generals, to support resettlement of farmers in the new areas, to provide administrative infrastructure to the newly incorporated territories, and so forth. Even such a minor issue as maintaining hostels for the officials travelling across the empire on their business could cause exorbitant expenditures in a new extra-large empire (Hou 2016). To cover the rising costs, the government had to increase its revenues, which meant, among other things, competing for profits with local elites who were the major beneficiaries of the previous laissez-faire policies. Not surprisingly, these elites formed a powerful opposition to the policy of further territorial expansion.

The resurrection of powerful local elites was one of the most consequential developments in the Han (and subsequent imperial) history (Cui 2003). Under Emperor Wu, these elites suffered from the state's renewed assault on their profits. They were compensated to a certain extent by opening the ways for their representatives into the government apparatus. Soon enough, some of these newcomers became a formidable opposition to the government's expansionist policies. Their dissatisfaction with Emperor Wu's legacy became fully visible shortly after his death, during the so-called Salt and Iron Debates of 81 BCE (Polnarov 2018) and intensified thereafter (Loewe 1986, 179–98). The opposition considered Emperor Wu's robust campaigns as the ultimate cause of socioeconomic disasters. The real outcome of the territorial expansion was "the people being impoverished," "bandits and criminals rising side-by-side," and "orphans howling on the roads" (*Hanshu* 72, 3077 and 64, 2833). Soon enough, the opposition scored its first success: the southernmost commanderies on Hainan were abandoned in 46 BCE.

Putting aside for the time being the complex question of the opposition's motives for assaulting the government's policies, we should acknowledge that at least on one point it was right: economically speaking further expansion of the Chinese Empire was no longer profitable. Most arable lands in East Asia were already under China's control during the Qin dynasty, and although some of the lands in the new territories could be reclaimed for agriculture, the costs were huge while the profits thin. Only a tiny segment of the military and civilian elite did benefit from the military victories, but the vast majority of the population and the elite did not. Actually, rather than benefiting from the new territories, the country's core areas had to subsidize these newly acquired lands. Considered from this angle, further expansion of the empire's territory was no longer attractive.

Politically speaking, the expansion also had to be limited. Whereas many of the campaigns under Emperor Wu aimed to annex enemy territory and incorporate it into the empire, gradually the goal shifted. It became patently clear to the empire's leaders that neither in the vastness of the newly discovered Western Regions, nor in the depth of the steppe would it be possible to establish direct control over the local population. Henceforth, the northern and western campaigns became focused not on direct expansion but on attaining the foreign leaders' recognition of their status as "outer subjects" (*wai chen*) in accordance with the Five Zones spatial arrangement (Yü 1986, 379–83). The status of outer subjects was inferior to China's Son of Heaven, as buttressed in the similarities between their ritual obligations – such as delivering local products as tribute – and those of "internal subjects," that is, heads of internal princedoms and marquisates. Yet the so-called tribute system, within which the relations with "outer subjects" were maintained, was flexible enough: at times it allowed a degree of real control over the Han dependencies (e.g., through requiring periodic visits to the Han court, sending a local dignitary [usually the crown prince] as a hostage, or accommodating Han officials and military personnel), but it could also be maintained on a purely symbolic level of diplomatic intercourse or trade disguised as tribute (Yü 1986, 416). In any case, by adopting this system as the primary means of dealing with alien polities, the Han court gave up the desire of fully integrating them into the imperial polity, reverting to the means ridiculed by the Qin courtiers a century earlier: "The lords sometimes attended the court and sometimes did not, and the Son of Heaven was unable to regulate this."[13]

Of all the alien groups, the Xiongnu were the most stubborn in opposing the Han demands to submit as outer subjects. And when they finally did it – in the wake of fratricidal dynastic conflict between the candidates to the *chanyu* throne – they were lavishly rewarded by the Han Emperor Xuan (r. 74–49 BCE). Yet Xiongnu acceptance of the Han superiority proved an ephemeral victory. First, it caused deep cleavage between the pro-Han and anti-Han factions of the Xiongnu, necessitating ongoing and costly Han support for their protégés, the Southern Xiongnu. Second, even the pro-Han Xiongnu could under certain circumstances turn into China's formidable enemies, as happened to *chanyu* Yu (r. 18–46 CE). Third, even when military success was achieved, such as smashing the anti-Han Northern Xiongnu in 92 CE, the respite did not come: new enemies appeared in the steppe to fill in the void left by the Xiongnu, and their menace could not be fully eliminated (de

---

[13] Han made several attempts to solidify its rule over the Western Regions by establishing an office of protector-general, maintaining rudimentary military presence, and even establishing agricultural colonies deep into modern Xinjiang; yet all these measures were temporary, and were adopted primarily in response to the Xiongnu's attempts to secure their dominance in Central Asia. Whenever the Xiongnu pressure declined, Han interest in the Western Regions declined as well (Yü 1986, 405–21).

Crespigny 1984). In short, the indirect rule proved to be of limited value politically, even if satisfying on the symbolic level.

It can be asserted that insofar as the Han had something akin to "grand strategy" – namely, weakening the Xiongnu confederation and preventing re-emergence of a new powerful entity to the north of the Great Wall – this strategy was not translated into consistent policies. Many means were tried – starting with appeasement, through deep incursions into the steppe and into the adjacent areas of the Xiongnu real and potential dependencies, through establishment of a client Xiongnu polity (or several client polities), and the like. As generations passed, it became increasingly clear to many members of the Han elite, especially the Latter Han (25–220 CE) elite that the steppe predicament could not be adequately dealt with. This frustration is fully observable in the comments of the eminent Han historian, Ban Gu (32–92 CE). Ban Gu summarized his account of the ebbs and flows in Han's relations with the Xiongnu with a lengthy personal digression, in which he dismissed both the ideas of military commanders, eager to combat the Xiongnu, and of civilian officials who hoped to acculturate the enemy. Instead, he proposed the third course – that of segregation.

Their [the aliens'] lands cannot be tilled for living; their people cannot be treated as subjects; therefore they must be regarded as external and not internal, as strangers and not as relatives. The cultivation through proper government does not reach these people, proper calendar cannot be given to their lands; when they arrive, we must block and repel them; when they leave we must make preparations and be on guard against them. When they admire rules of propriety and submit tribute, we should accept it in accordance with the rules of ritual yielding; we should not sever the loose rein and leave for them the minute details. This is the constant Way applied by the sage kings to repel the savages.[14]

Ban Gu is unequivocal: the ecological division between the external and internal realm makes any attempt to incorporate the former or even to establish firm control over it unfeasible. The savage inhabitants of the outer lands would never become part of the cultivated Central States, and should not be enticed to do so. The separation is eternal and should be maintained forever; the connections between the two realms should be limited to an absolute minimum. This was, as Ban Gu readily admitted, a minority view in his time; but this was not a negligible minority. Actually, by Ban Gu's time a subtle but visible change occurred in the composition of Han's ruling elite. The power of the military declined, and the literati-dominated court felt strong aversion toward excessive military activism. Not incidentally, it was during the Latter Han that proposals were made to abandon the entire northwestern areas so as to put an end to the conflict there with the Qiang tribes (de Crespigny 1984; Tse 2018). These

---

[14] *Hanshu* 94, 3833–4.

voices were not heeded ultimately, but they are yet another manifestation of the change in the mood at the Han court. The days of robust expansion were over.

The three factors combined – a lack of effective military solution to the steppe problem, aggravating economic costs of assertive foreign policy, and changes in the elite composition in the Latter Han – explain the proliferation of particularistic and exclusivist vision of All-under-Heaven as seen in Ban Gu's words. Centuries of experimentation with different types of territorial expansion taught the empire's leaders a lesson: a smaller empire may be more viable than an ostensibly universal one.

2.7   Epilogue: Universalism Versus Particularism Revisited

The dictum of political unity of All-under-Heaven emerged in China as a response to the aggravating domestic crisis and the war of all against all, which started after the end of the Western Zhou in 771 BCE and accelerated in the subsequent centuries. The emergence of this quest for unity coincided with the formation of a territorially integrated Warring State and with relatively smooth expansion of the rival Sinitic polities into outlying alien periphery. As a result, unity was envisioned by many as comprehensive both territorially and administratively: a single centralized and uniformly ruled state in the entire known area of human habitat. The Qin unification of 221 BCE can be considered as the singularly important attempt to actualize this dream. However, Qin were also the first to compromise the ideal of universality. By erecting the Great Wall in 214/213 BCE the Qin rulers had tacitly recognized that they reached the ecological limit of unifiable All-under-Heaven.

In the aftermath of the short-lived Qin unification and after another round of successful military campaigns under Emperor Wu of the Han, the Chinese leaders realized that further expansion into outlying territories was neither feasible militarily, nor justifiable economically. From a purely economic point of view it was reasonable to limit the empire to the lands of China proper (mostly coinciding with the Qin Empire), as was the case, for instance, in the Song (960–1279) and Ming (1368–1644) dynasties (notwithstanding differences in their territorial layout). However, a "lesser empire" was problematic both ideologically and strategically. An ideological commitment to the universalist vision of the empire, going back as it was to the legacy of the classical era, could not be easily dismissed. More significantly, the accumulated historical experience proved that a militarily passive empire would sooner or later encounter formidable enemies at its frontiers, most notably at the northern frontiers along which a series of powerful nomadic and semi-nomadic entities emerged, threatening the peace of China proper. This strategic consideration encouraged the empire's leaders to adopt from time to time activist military and diplomatic policies, which often led to territorial expansion and incorporation of peripheral regions into the empire (see Robinson [Chapter 8] and Mosca [Chapter 9], this volume). The tension between economic and military rationale, on the one hand, and ideological dictums cum strategic considerations, on the other, determined much of the empire's spatial trajectory during the two millennia of its existence.

Dividing "All-under-Heaven" into inner and outer realms was often employed as a neat solution to the above tension: it allowed maintaining the empire's superiority beyond its ecological limits at a relatively low cost. The so-called tribute system was flexible enough to maintain the semblance of the Son of Heaven's universal singularity without overstretching the empire's military and economic resources. In practical terms, though, this system was of limited value. Symbolic superiority could not be maintained for long without adequate military and economic backing, which again required overstretching the empire's resources. Worse, tribute relations could be maintained with ease only with militarily insignificant polities in the west, east, and south, but not with the northern nomads. Those remained submissive only in times of relative weakness; whenever an opportunity occurred, their leaders would try to redefine the relations with the Chinese emperors striving for equality with or even superiority over their sedentary neighbors. Ban Gu's ideal of segregation behind the Great Wall never worked well.

To complicate the matters, the boundaries between the "inner" and the "outer" constantly fluctuated, reflecting the shifting balance of power between China and its neighbors, and the changing demographic and cultural composition of the extensive frontiers of China proper. At times, such as during the peak of territorial expansion under the Tang dynasty (618–907 CE), the "inner" realm could include the steppe nomads; intermediate areas under military rule were established, expanding well into Central Asia; and the even broader "outer" realm was defined as an area of "loose rein" (*jimi*), where the superiority of the Chinese monarch remained primarily symbolic (Pan 1997; cf. Skaff 2012; Wang 2013). At times of weakness, the designation "outer" could be applied not only to border areas once under Chinese control, but even – scandalously – to the Chinese heartland itself, the Yellow River valley, ruled by the Jurchens since 1127 CE (Goncharov 1986). Regions once rendered "outer" could be firmly reincorporated into China proper, as happened to the Gansu and Yunnan provinces under the Ming dynasty (Robinson, this volume), while other areas could move in the opposite direction, as happened to North Vietnam (Annam), once an imperial province, which turned into an "outer subject."

Ironically, it was primarily under the alien dynasties, established by the nomadic and semi-nomadic conquerors of China proper that the ecological and cultural limitations on the empire's expansion could be meaningfully overcome. The conquerors' ability to incorporate peripheral regions within the territory of the empire proper bolstered their prestige and their legitimacy (see Biran [Chapter 6] and Mosca, this volume). The Manchu Yongzheng Emperor (r. 1723–35) of the Qing dynasty (1636/1644–1912) had proudly proclaimed:

Unity of the Central Lands [China proper] began with Qin; unity beyond the border passes began with [the Mongol] Yuan [1271–1368], and peaked under our dynasty. Never before were Chinese and foreigners one family and the country so expansive as under our dynasty! (Cited in Liu 2000, 19)

These words, pronounced in the midst of bitter polemics with a dissenting Chinese subject over the legitimacy of Manchu rule,[15] are revealing. The Yongzheng Emperor was not a warmonger; actually at the beginning of his career he contemplated withdrawal from some of the territories acquired under his father, the Kangxi Emperor (r. 1661–1722) , most notably Tibet (Dai Yingcong 2009: 92–100). Yet he might have apprehended that the remarkable territorial expansion of the Qing and their incorporation of the alien periphery into the empire proper would be hailed by many Chinese subjects as a hallmark of Qing's success. These sentiments were echoed by the Yongzheng's son, the Qianlong Emperor (r. 1736–95), who appealed to the "greatness of All-under-Heaven" to silent critical voices of those advisers, who feared that the Qing ongoing expansion would overstretch its human and material resources.[16] Insofar as the emperors' expectations that appeals to universality would be a convincing argument in domestic debates were correct (and we have no reasons to assume otherwise), they indicate that a latent desire for attaining truly universal unification remained intact – or was reproduced – a full two millennia after the First Emperor) ordered the construction of the Great Wall, which was supposed to set limits to "All-under -Heaven."

Bibliography

The Book of Lord Shang: Apologetics of State Power in Early China. 2017. Trans. and ed. Yuri Pines. New York: Columbia University Press.
Boshu Laozi jiaozhu 帛書老子校注. 1996. Compiled and annotated by Gao Ming 高明. Beijing: Zhonghua shuju.
Chen Minzhen and Yuri Pines. 2018. "Where Is King Ping? The History and Historiography of the Zhou Dynasty's Eastward Relocation." *Asia Major* (Third Series) 31(1): 1–27.

---

[15] For the context of the controversy that spurred the emperor's statement, see Spence 2001, 116–34.

[16] For the Qianlong Emperor's polemic with his critics, see Millward 1998, 20–43, especially pp. 38–40. Millward illustrates there how in the process of the Qing territorial expansion the borders between "internal" and "external" realms were continuously redrawn. For more about the Qing expansion policy, see Perdue 2005; Dai Yingcong 2009.

Chunqiu Gongyang zhuan yizhu 春秋公羊傳譯注. 2011. Annotated by Liu Shangci 劉尚慈. Beijing Zhonghua shuju.

Chunqiu Zuozhuan zhu 春秋左傳注. 1990. Annotated by Yang Bojun 楊伯峻. Beijing: Zhonghua shuju.

Cook, Constance A. and John S. Major, eds. 1999. *Defining Chu*. Honolulu, HI: University of Hawai'i Press.

Cui Xiangdong 崔向東. 2003. *Handai haozu yanjiu* 漢代豪族研究. Wuhan: Chongwen shuju.

Dai Liuzhu 戴留柱. 2001. "'Wang zhe wu wai' he 'Huayi zhi fang': Qin Han shiqi bianjiang sixiang lunlue" "王者無外"和"華夷之防" – – 秦漢時期邊疆思論略. In: *Qin Han shi luncong* 秦漢史論從, ed. Zhongguo QinHan shi yanjiu hui 中國秦漢史研究會, Vol. 8, 149–60. Kunming: Yunnan daxue chubanshe.

Dai Yingcong. 2009. *The Sichuan Frontier and Tibet: Imperial Strategy in the Early Qing*. Seattle, WA: University of Washington Press.

De Crespigny, Rafe. 1984. *Northern Frontier: The Policies and Strategy of the Later Han Empire*. Canberra: Australian National University Press.

Di Cosmo, Nicola. 2002. *Ancient China and Its Enemies: The Rise of Nomadic Power in East Asian History*. Cambridge: Cambridge University Press.

Dorofeeva-Lichtman, Vera. 2009. "Ritual Practices for Constructing Terrestrial Space (Warring States-Early Han)." In: *Early Chinese Religion, Part One: Shang through Han (1250 BC-220 AD)*, ed. John Lagerwey and Marc Kalinowski, Vol. 1, 595–644. Leiden: Brill.

Elman, Benjamin A. and Martin Kern, eds. 2010. *Statecraft and Classical Learning: The* Rituals of Zhou *in East Asian History*. Leiden: Brill.

Falkenhausen, Lothar von, 1999. "The Waning of the Bronze Age: Material Culture and Social Developments 770–481 B.C." In: *The Cambridge History of Ancient China*, ed. Michael Loewe and Edward L. Shaughnessy, 450–544. Cambridge: Cambridge University Press.

Falkenhausen, Lothar von. 2005. "The E Jun Qi Metal Tallies: Inscribed Texts and Ritual Contexts." In *Text and Ritual in Early China*, ed. Martin Kern, 79–123. Seattle, WA: University of Washington Press.

Feinman, Gary M., Linda M. Nicholas, and Fang Hui, 2010. "The Imprint of China's First Emperor on the Distant Realm of Eastern Shandong," *Proceedings of the National Academy of Sciences* 107(11): 4,851–6.

Gentz, Joachim. 2015. "Long Live The King! The Ideology of Power between Ritual and Morality in the Gongyang zhuan 公羊傳." In *Ideology of Power and Power of Ideology in Early China*, ed. Yuri Pines, Paul R. Goldin, and Martin Kern, 69–117. Leiden: Brill.

Goldin, Paul R. 2011. "Steppe Nomads as a Philosophical Problem in Classical China." In *Mapping Mongolia: Situating Mongolia in the World from Geologic Time to the Present*, ed. Paula L. W. Sabloff, 220–46. Philadelphia, PA: University of Pennsylvania Museum of Archaeology and Anthropology.

Goldin, Paul R. 2015. "Representations of Regional Diversity during the Eastern Zhou Dynasty." In *Ideology of Power and Power of Ideology in Early China*, ed. Yuri Pines, Paul R. Goldin, and Martin Kern, 31–48. Leiden: Brill.

Goncharov, S.N. 1986. Китайская Средневековая Дипломатия: Отношения между Империями Цзинь и Сун, 1,127–42. Moscow: Nauka.

Gongyang zhuan. See *Chunqiu Gongyang zhuan*.

Han Feizi jijie 韓非子集解. 1998. Compiled by Wang Xianshen 王先慎 (1859–1922), collated by Zhong Zhe 鍾哲. Beijing: Zhonghua shuju.

Hanshu 漢書. 1997. By Ban Gu 班固 (32–92) et al. Annotated by Yan Shigu 顏師古 (581–645). Beijing: Zhonghua shuju.

Hou Xudong. 2016. "The Helpless Emperor: The Expenditure on Official Hostel System and Its Institutional Change in the Late Former Han China." *World History Studies* 3(2): 1–23.

Hsing I-tien (Xing Yitian 邢義田). 2011. "Cong gudai tianxiaguan kan Qin Han changcheng de xiangzheng yiyi" 從古代天下觀看秦漢長城的象徵意義. In Hsing I-tien, *Tianxia yi jia: huangquan, guanliao yu shehui* 天下一家－－皇權、官僚與社會, 84–135. Beijing: Zhonghua shuju.

Hu Wenhui 胡文輝. 1998. "Qin jian 'Ri shu – chu bang men' xin zheng" 秦簡《日書 － 出邦門》新證, *Wenbo* 文博1: 91–4.

Keightley, David N. 1999. "The Shang: China's First Historical Dynasty." In: *The Cambridge History of Ancient China*, ed. Michael Loewe and Edward L. Shaughnessy, 232–91. Cambridge: Cambridge University Press.

Kern, Martin. 2000. *The Stele Inscriptions of Ch'in Shih-huang: Text and Ritual in Early Chinese Imperial Representation*. New Haven, CT: American Oriental Society.

Korolkov, Maxim. 2020. "Empire-Building and Market-Making at the Qin Frontier: Imperial Expansion and Economic Change, 221–207 BCE." PhD dissertation, Columbia University, New York.

Laozi . See *Boshu Laozi*

Lewis, Mark E. 1999. "Warring States: Political History." In *The Cambridge History of Ancient China: From the Origins of Civilization to 221 B.C.*, ed. Michael Loewe and Edward L. Shaughnessy, 587–650. Cambridge: Cambridge University Press.

Lewis, Mark E. 2006. *The Construction of Space in Early China*. Albany, NY: State University of New York Press.

Lewis, Mark E. 2007. *The Early Chinese Empires: Qin and Han*. Cambridge, MA: Harvard University Press.

Li Feng. 2006. *Landscape and Power in Early China: The Crisis and Fall of the Western Zhou, 1045–771 BC*. Cambridge: Cambridge University Press.

Liu Zehua 劉澤華. 2000. *Zhongguo de Wangquanzhuyi* 中國的王權主義. Shanghai: Renmin chubanshe.

Loewe, Michael. 1986. "The Former Han Dynasty." In *The Cambridge History of China*, vol. 1, *The Ch'in and Han Empires, 221 BC–AD 220*, ed. Denis C. Twitchett and John K. Fairbank, 103–222. Cambridge: Cambridge University Press.

Lunyu yizhu 論語譯注. 1992. Annotated by Yang Bojun 楊伯峻. Beijing: Zhonghua shuju.

Lüshi chunqiu jiaoshi 呂氏春秋校釋. 1995. Compiled and annotated by Chen Qiyou 陳奇猷. Shanghai: Xuelin.

Mengzi yizhu 孟子譯注. 1992. Annotated by Yang Bojun 楊伯峻. Beijing: Zhonghua shuju.

Millward, James, A. 1998. *Beyond the Pass: Economy, Ethnicity, and Empire in Qing Central Asia, 1759–1864*. Stanford, CA: Stanford University Press.

Mozi jiaozhu 墨子校注. 1994. Compiled and annotated by Wu Yujiang 吳毓江 (1898–1977). Beijing: Zhonghua shuju.

Pan Yihong. 1997. *Son of Heaven and Heavenly Qaghan: Sui-Tang China and its Neighbors*. Bellingham, WA: Center for East Asian Studies, Western Washington University, 1997

Perdue, Peter C. 2005. *China Marches West: The Qing Conquest of Central Eurasia*. Cambridge, MA: Belknap Press of Harvard University Press.

Pines, Yuri. 2000. "'The One That Pervades the All' in Ancient Chinese Political thought: The Origins of 'The Great Unity' Paradigm." *T'oung Pao* 86(4–5): 280–324.

Pines, Yuri. 2002a. *Foundations of Confucian Thought: Intellectual Life in the Chunqiu Period, 722–453 B.C.E.* Honolulu, HI: University of Hawai`i Press.

Pines, Yuri. 2002b. "Changing Views of *tianxia* in Pre-imperial Discourse." *Oriens Extremus* 43(1/2): 101–16.

Pines, Yuri. 2004. "The Question of Interpretation: Qin History in Light of New Epigraphic Sources." *Early China* 29: 1–44.

Pines, Yuri. 2005a. "Beasts or Humans: Pre-imperial Origins of Sino-Barbarian Dichotomy." In *Mongols, Turks, and Others: Eurasian Nomads and the Sedentary World*, ed. Reuven Amitai and Michal Biran, 59–102. Leiden: Brill.

Pines, Yuri. 2005b. "Bodies, Lineages, Citizens, and Regions: A Review of Mark Edward Lewis' *The Construction of Space in Early China*." *Early China* 30: 155–88.

Pines, Yuri. 2008. "Imagining the Empire? Concepts of 'Primeval Unity' in Pre-imperial Historiographic Tradition." In: *Conceiving the Empire: China and Rome Compared*, ed. Fritz-Heiner Mutschler and Achim Mittag, 67–90. Oxford: Oxford University Press.

Pines, Yuri. 2009. *Envisioning Eternal Empire: Chinese Political Thought of the Warring States Era*. Honolulu, HI: University of Hawai'i Press.

Pines, Yuri. 2010. "Political Mythology and Dynastic Legitimacy in the *Rong Cheng shi* Manuscript." *Bulletin of the School of Oriental and African Studies* 73(3): 503–529.

Pines, Yuri. 2012. *The Everlasting Empire: The Political Culture of Ancient China and Its Imperial Legacy*. Princeton, NJ: Princeton University Press.

Pines, Yuri. 2018a. "Chu Identity as Seen from Its Manuscripts: A Reevaluation." *Journal of Chinese History* 2(1): 1–26.

Pines, Yuri. 2018b. "The Earliest 'Great Wall'? Long Wall of Qi Revisited." *Journal of the American Oriental Society* 138(4): 743–62.

Pines, Yuri with Lothar von Falkenhausen, Gideon Shelach, and Robin D.S. Yates. 2014. "General Introduction: Qin History Revisited." In: *Birth of an Empire: The State of Qin revisited*, ed. Yuri Pines, Lothar von Falkenhausen, Gideon Shelach, and Robin D.S. Yates, 1–36. Berkeley, CA: University of California Press.

Polnarov, Anatoly. 2018. "Looking Beyond Dichotomies: Hidden Diversity of Voices in the *Yantielun* 鹽鐵論." *T'oung Pao* 104: 465–495.

Qin jiandu heji shiwen zhushi xiuding ben 秦簡牘合集釋文注釋修訂本. 2016. Ed. Chen Wei 陳偉. Wuhan: Jing Chu wenku bianzuan chuban weiyuanhui and Wuhan Daxue chubanshe. 4 vols.

Sanft, Charles. 2015. "Population Records from Liye: Ideology in Practice." In: *Ideology of Power and Power of Ideology in Early China*, ed. Yuri Pines, Paul R. Goldin, and Martin Kern, 249–69. Leiden: Brill.

Shangshu jin guwen zhushu 尚書今古文注疏. 1998 (1815). Compiled by Sun Xingyan 孫星衍 (1753–1818), proof-read by Sheng Dongling 盛冬鈴 and Chen Kang 陳抗. Beijing: Zhonghua shuju.

Shelach-Lavi, Gideon. 2015. *The Archeology of Early China: From Prehistory to the Han Dynasty.* Cambridge: Cambridge University Press.

Shiji 史記. 1997. By Sima Qian 司馬遷 (*c.*145–*c.*85 BCE) et al. Annotated by Zhang Shoujie 張守節, Sima Zhen 司馬貞, and Pei Yin 裴駰. Beijing: Zhonghua shuju.

Shuihudi Qinmu zhujian 睡虎地秦墓竹簡. (1990) 2001. Ed. Shuihudi Qinmu zhujian zhengli xiaozu 睡虎地秦墓竹簡整理小組. Beijing: Wenwu chubanshe.

Skaff, Jonathan K. 2012. *Sui-Tang China and its Turko-Mongol Neighbors. Culture, Power, and Connections, 580–800.* Oxford: Oxford University Press.

Spence, Jonathan D. 2001. *Treason by the Book.* New York: Viking, 2001.

Tse, Wicky W.K. 2018. *The Collapse of China's Later Han Dynasty, 25–220 CE: The Northwest Borderlands and the Edge of Empire.* London: Routledge.

Wagner, Donald B. 1993. *Iron and Steel in Ancient China.* Leiden: Brill.

Wang Aihe. 2000. *Cosmology and Political Culture in Early China.* Cambridge: Cambridge University Press.

Wang Zhenping. 2013. *Tang China in Multi-Polar Asia: A History of Diplomacy and War.* Honolulu: University of Hawai'i Press.

Wu Xiaolong. 2017. *Material Culture, Power, and Identity in Ancient China.* Cambridge: Cambridge University Press.

Xinshu jiaozhu 新書校注. 2000. Composed by Jia Yi 賈誼 (201–168 BCE). Ed. Yan Zhenyi 閻振益 and Zhong Xia 鍾夏. Beijing: Zhonghua shuju.

Xunzi jijie 荀子集解. 1992. Annotated by Wang Xianqian 王先謙 (1842–1917). Ed. Shen Xiaohuan 沈嘯寰 and Wang Xingxian 王星賢. Beijing: Zhonghua shuju.

Yates, Robin D.S. 2012/13. "The Qin Slips and Boards from Well No. 1, Liye, Hunan: A Brief Introduction to the Qin Qianling County Archives." *Early China* 35–6: 291–330.

Yü Ying-shih. 1986. "Han Foreign Relations." In: *Cambridge History of China.* Volume 1, *The Ch'in and Han Empires, 221 B.C.–A.D.220,* ed. Denis C. Twitchett and Michael Loewe, 377–462. Cambridge: Cambridge University Press.

Zhouli zhushu 周禮注疏. (1815) 1991. Annotated by Zheng Xuan 鄭玄 (127–200) and Jia Gongyan 賈公彥 (7th century). In *Shisan jing zhushu fu jiaokanji* 十三經注疏附校勘記, compiled by Ruan Yuan 阮元 (1764–1849), vol. 1, 631–940. Beijing: Zhonghua shuju.

Zuozhuan. See *Chunqiu Zuozhuan zhu* 1990.

3   The Roman Empire

Wolfgang Spickermann

In his *Aeneid* (6, 851–3), the Roman poet Virgil, a contemporary of the first Emperor Augustus, lets Anchises, Aeneas's father, say:

Tu regere imperio populos, Romane, memento – haec tibi erunt artes – pacique imponere morem, parcere subiectis et debellare superbos.

You, Roman, remember to rule people by command (these were arts to you), and impose the custom to peace, to spare the subjected and to vanquish the proud!

The influence of Virgil's Rome conception cannot be underestimated, as it assigns to the town on the Tiber River the divinely legitimised task of gaining domination of all known people, neither limited in time nor in its geographical dimensions and, at the same time, stylises Rome as a guarantor of peace and security (Mančić 2015, 44). While the poet was looking back upon a long period of military expansion during the Republican period, he also saw with Emperor Augustus (30 BCE–14 CE) the beginning of the Imperial period, which seemed to bring peace and security to the inhabitants of almost the whole world after the most atrocious civil wars. It cannot be denied that the Roman Empire rose to become one of the most successful and lasting empires in world history. Hence, the poet Tibull's *Roma aeterna* idea can still be felt in today's Western world (Carmen 2,5,23 sq.: *Romulus aeternae nondum formaverat urbis moenia*; 'Not yet Romulus had formed the walls of the eternal city'). The English historian David J. Mattingly comments most aptly upon the almost nostalgic veneration of Rome in the occident when he says, 'Rome certainly stands up to this sort of scrutiny as an extraordinary example of a preindustrial superstate' (Mattingly 2011, 3n1).

The steady territorial expansion during the Roman Republic and, after the violent civil wars, the long period of peace within the empire, which encompassed the major part of the world known at the time, created a huge economic and cultural area with Rome remaining its political centre until the foundation of Constantinople in 330 CE. The military monarchy and Roman citizenship constituted a common bond, which held this area together. Like most Romans, Caesar and Cicero, the best documented witnesses of the waning republic, believed in the legitimacy of their conquests, as they had been warring for their own and their allies' security. They were convinced that victory entitled them to rule the conquered and, of course, to profit from this right by pillaging and exacting tributes (Brunt 1978, 161). This conviction in connection with a constant willingness to wage wars and to serve in the armed forces can be detected in all strata of the Roman Empire. The historian Livy summarises Roman belief in certain victory as follows: 'No human force could resist Roman might' (Livy 1,16,7), to which Greg Woolf notes, 'Sometimes it feels as if empire was written into Roman DNA' (Woolf 2012, 13).

This chapter defines the term 'empire' in the Roman context (3.1), and then outlines the expansion of the Roman Empire during the Republican period (3.2). It goes on to discuss the consequences of this expansion, the subsequent installation of a military monarchy (*principate*) and the Roman boundaries during that time (3.3), the Roman Empire as a legal, cultural and economic area (3.4), and, finally, as a conclusion the underlying factors behind the growth of the spatial dimensions of the Roman Empire (3.5).

3.1   Roman Imperialism

Since the 19th century all debates about Roman imperialism have focused largely on the different interpretations of the term *imperium*, 'empire', its underlying claims to power and, more specifically, the various methods of exerting influence on other territories and communities, which could eventually lead to their subjugation and integration into an empire. The resulting network of control mechanisms enabled dominating communities to encroach upon the sovereignty of other political entities. In the 19th century, the ancient empires gained centre stage in debates about imperialism, which were downright booming at the beginning of the 20th century, influenced as they were by Marxist ideas. The expansion of the Roman Empire, in particular its multi-ethnic character and its principle *divide et impera* became the paradigms of ancient 'imperialism' per se. The proverbial *Pax Romana* referred to the domains of the *Senatus Populusque Romanus* (SPQR), in which the Romans pacified conquered territories through the principle of power sharing with local elites and monopolised foreign policy.

Rome was the first local power in the Mediterranean region that can effect-ively be considered a global empire. The question is whether the expansion of Rome was the result of a long-term strategy or it emerged from ad hoc responses to the need to maintain the status quo and to safeguard its possessions. This question was considered by ancient authors who either stressed the 'fortuitous-ness' of Rome's rise to a global power (Cicero) or ascribed its expansion to a long-term strategy (Greek authors, such as Polybius). This discussion resumed much later in classical studies. Theodor Mommsen (d. 1903), for example, emphasised the 'accidental' expansion of the Roman Empire and recognised

Rome's right to defend its interests with all available means (theory of defensive imperialism; according to Mommsen1856, esp. 757–9). This theory experienced some contradiction in contemporary and later research (good overview: Bleicken 2004, 168–75). According to this school of thought, the highly developed Greek culture had been distinctly disadvantaged over the superior Roman political system in this regard.

Today, empires are not regarded solely in a negative way. From a historical point of view, it has to be conceded that in many parts of the world they guaranteed continuity and stability. The case of the Roman Empire makes this sufficiently clear. It also has to be noted that, almost as a rule, ancient Mediterranean empires saw themselves as peacekeeping powers, which generally led them to take certain actions to protect themselves and their allies. Roman's strive to establish *Pax Romana* should be analysed in this Mediterranean context.

3.2   Rise to World Power: the Republican Period

Armin and Peter Eich (2005) have established a direct connection between Roman imperialism, in particular, the bellicose and violent period of expansion during the late Roman Republic, and the emergence of a community that grew with its challenges. However, they largely neglect the impact of the enormous military success on the social and economic structure of the Roman polity. Culturally as well, the impact of the conquered on the conquerors was huge, at least insofar as Greek culture is concerned. In the 2nd century CE, at latest, disciples of Greek education, the so-called *pepaideumenoi*, regarded Athens and not Rome as the cultural capital of the empire (Lucian, Nigrinus 15). Yet not even the greatest admirers of Greece would foster any doubts that Rome was the political *caput mundi* and, moreover, that the city of Rome became an idea that embraced the whole empire. Aelius Aristides expressed this sentiment most aptly in his Roman Oration, which he gave in 143 CE: 'What a city is for its frontiers and territories, this city is for the whole world. After all, it is selected as the general capital for the entire empire. You could say that all those who live in surrounding areas or – constitutionally – in a different country come together around one and the same fortress' (Oratio 61).

In its early days, the city on the Tiber River, with its seven hills, had apparently been just a loose assembly of individual settlements, which seemed to join forces in the area of today's forum after the swampland had been drained. The traditional founding date of 753 BCE is habitually associated with Romulus as Rome's legendary founder. Owing to the fact that literary sources are lacking and historiography does not set in before the Second Punic War (218–201 BCE), not much is known about the early years of this settlement. Yet it can be said that it was situated at an important river crossing. The community was primarily inhabited by peasants of Latin and Etruscan origin. The traditional seven kings of the early years and their institutional and political reforms remain legendary and are barely tangible. Rome's real story started with the Republican period, the beginning of which is traditionally dated 509 BCE but is more likely to have been some generations later. The heads of the aristocratic (patrician) clans (*gentes*) and their clientele seemed to have agreed on the establishment of a periodically changing form of leadership (*praetor*) as a replacement of permanent kingship. In addition, a council of elders consisting of clan leaders appears to have been in existence since the ancient Roman kingdom. This, however, did not change the fact that clan leaders were at liberty to organise their own military enterprises against neighbours as warlords. For instance, in the Battle of the Cremera against the Etruscan city of Veii (477 BCE), almost all male members of the Roman gens Fabii lost their lives (Livy 2.48–50).

Just like in Greece, modification of fighting techniques from aristocratic cavalry charge and single combat to phalanx formation and combat in the battle line, which required enlisting ever-larger groups of men who had to provide their own equipment, led to the political emancipation of the heavily armed foot soldier. In Roman history, this process is associated with the so-called Conflict of the Orders, which started with the secession of the plebeians, commoners not belonging to any patrician clan, to the Sacred Hill (*mons sacer*) in 494 BCE and was settled in 287 BCE with the Lex Hortensia. This law provided that all bills passed by the Plebeian Council (*Concilia plebis*) were binding for the entire community. The political significance of the army and the high regard for military strength, which eventually led through the rise of a medium-sized soldier-peasant community to a hegemonic power first in Latium then in the whole of Italy and ultimately in the entire Mediterranean world, became apparent from the very outset. Jeremy Armstrong (2016) recently emphasised the shift from individual warfare of single groups (*gentes*) to collective warfare of the whole *res publica*. Life as a Roman peasant involved not only working a farmstead but also serving as a soldier and hence participating in the assembly (of arms-bearing men).

In the formation of the Roman institutions, it is most fascinating to observe that, on the one hand, the assembly of arms-bearing men developed into an assembly of citizens whose members were organised according to their wealth into elective bodies. Their main task was to make decisions on war and peace and to elect the highest-ranking magistrates with military power. On the other hand, the plebeians were able to bring forth their own magistrates (plebeian tribunes, *aediles*) and assemblies (*concilia plebis*), which survived the Republican period and were held in high esteem due to their political flexibility. These institutions convey vividly the struggle of independent soldier-peasants, who were able to provide their own equipment, to gain political acknowledgement. An increase of military power was achieved through further steps towards internal political consolidation (see Bleicken 2008, 242–9). The Greek historian Polybius (*c*.200–*c*.120 BCE), who spent some time in Rome as a hostage and witnessed the final destruction of Carthage in 146 BCE, described the institutions of the Roman state as a form of mixed government, being the ideal mixture of monarchy (consulship), aristocracy (senate) and democracy (people's assembly) (6.11.10–18; see Nippel 1980).

From a modern point of view, the *res publica Romana* was a political entity ruled by an aristocracy of patrician and plebeian senatorial elite families, which had an exclusive character and called themselves nobility. Their economic wealth was based on huge landholdings and their benchmark – and this is crucial – was a consulship combined with military success. As a result, the leading aristocrats competed unremittingly for the highest magisterial offices, particularly the consulship, since the holders of this office were invested with so-called *imperium*, the power to command the military. This competitive system pressurised each holder of *imperium* into waging as many wars as possible. Apart from hauling back home the spoils of war, parts of which had to be consecrated to the gods, the most worthy and most visible ambition of every military commander was to complete a successful campaign with the rite of triumph, which had to be granted by the senate. In Rome, the triumph was celebrated in the presence of all citizens. The exhibition of military force, the display of the spoils of war and the parade of the victorious commander in a chariot were a blatant manifestation of victory and not peace. Thus, a triumph constituted a much sought-after opportunity to permanently increase one's own and one's family's reputation within the nobility (see Itgenshorst 2005).

Two factors were crucial for the stability of this system. First, each successful magistrate and military commander had to resume his private life and return to the senate upon the expiry of his term of office. This means that none was able to rise above his peers through success and achievements. Second, every political act was connected with a religious act. The gods had to be compensated, as their benevolence was considered as key factor for prosperity. Polybius regarded the Roman religion, in fact, as a major basis for Roman superiority because in regarding the public religion in a very serious way the common people were kept under control of the priest and magistrates (6.56.6–15).

This chiefly military system of values, which was not only binding for the elites but also for large parts of the Roman citizenry and therefore a key to success, formed the basis of massive Roman expansion (Rüpke 1995). A first significant step was Rome's assuming a leading role in the Latin League. This confederation of thirty Latin towns emerged from the First Roman-Latin War, traditionally dated 493 BCE (*foedus Cassianum*) but which, according to modern scholarship, might have been fought a whole century later. Another important milestone was the war against the Etruscan rival Veii about 20 km northwest of Rome (405–396 BCE). The war ended with the complete destruction of Veii and the incorporation of its territory. Consequently, Roman territory almost doubled from 822 km^2 to 1,500 km^2 and the Roman general M. Furius Camillus was able to celebrate several triumphs. Ultimately, Veii's defeat presaged Rome's way to superpower (see Bleicken 2008, 190).

The total destruction of an enemy, however, and the annexation of its territory remained a rare case. Subsequently, a system was developed, which heavily contributed to Rome's success due to its flexibility and originality: a system of alliances and the establishment of colonies for Roman citizens. Temporarily, however, Rome suffered considerable setbacks when the Celts invaded Roman territory from the north and threatened to conquer the city of Rome itself: *vae victis!* (389–386 BCE). However, when the Romans together with the Latins managed to drive them back, a period of renewed expansion began. Conquered adversaries were forced to conclude a treaty (*foedus*) with Rome, which granted them internal autonomy but obliged them to contribute troops to the Roman army without giving them a vote in the Roman people's assembly (*civitas sine suffragio*). This fate fell to the conquered Etruscan city of Caere and almost all cities that had been subjugated during the Second Roman-Latin War (340–338 BCE). These cities were called *municipia*, a term derived from *munera capere* as their citizens had the same obligations towards Rome as Roman citizens. The method of binding once independent communities to Rome turned out to be successful, particularly as Rome managed to isolate these communities in terms of their foreign and military policy. Treaties were highly customised and only applicable between Rome and the respective municipality. Two types of leagues (*foedera*) were used: the *foedera aequa*, a treaty on equal terms, and the *foedera iniqua*, which contained a majesty-clause in order to secure the higher interests of the Roman people. Three different kinds of communities emerged from this system: the *civitates liberae ac foederatae*, which were friends of and on equal terms with the Roman people, the *civitates sine suffragio* and, finally, the so-called *dediticii*, subjugated people who were denied any rights because of their resistance.

It was, in particular, the need to control the seaways and the affiliated Italian trade routes that induced the Romans to establish on the coasts fortified towns for Roman settlers as another instrument to secure their rule. The settlers could keep Roman citizenship and would receive a plot of land by lot. As a rule, only a comparatively small number of colonists (typically 300 families) was set up in these *Coloniae civium Romanorum*. In later times, colonies were also established further inland and furnished with a greater number of settlers. The first colony of Roman citizens was Ostia Antica, which, according to tradition, had already been founded during the monarchy. Mutina and Parma followed somewhat later and after the Latin War, Antium became a colony and a naval base. These colonies represented Rome in miniature outside the actual capital. They secured strategic routes and put down riots in subjugated regions. This enabled Rome to control the area permanently through militias without deploying occupation troops. Besides, colonies presented an important driving force in economy and trade and spread Roman culture. During the expansion towards the south and further inland, Rome established colonies under Latin right. Their inhabitants were only granted full Roman citizenship when they returned to Rome. Within the competitive system of the leading noble families, allied towns (*socii*) and colonies tried to gain influence over Roman politics through senatorial patrons in order to, for example, obtain privileges.

Rome rose to become a leading central power in Italy after the Latin League had been dissolved and its territory, as well as large parts of Etruria, had been brought under control. Rome promptly turned towards the south against the Oscan tribes of the Apennine (Samnites), which were subjugated after some drawbacks in probably two wars (the first from 343 to 341 BCE may be legendary) between 326 and 290 BCE. A change in military strategy and armament eventually smoothed the path to success.[1] The systematic establishment of colonies in Samnite and Lucani territory also contributed towards their complete subjugation. In the north, the Romans were able to achieve a great victory against the Sabines and Etruscans and their Celtic allies in the Battle of Lake Vadimo (283 BCE). Consequently, Rome rose to the status of superpower within Italy. However, Rome's new position antagonised the powerful Greek towns in Southern Italy, above all the city of Tarentum, which summoned military assistance from the homeland. The "condottiere" Pyrrhus, King of Epirus, was able to defeat the Romans in 280 and 279 BCE in two battles but suffered such heavy losses (Pyrrhic victories) that he had to return to Epirus in 272 BCE without resounding results. The Roman system of alliances had finally proved its worth, at least to a large extent as only the Samnites and the Lucani had defected. The Romans punished them by terminating the Samnite alliance and erecting new colonies. Around 240 BCE, Rome had over twenty-eight colonies, and by around 180 BCE, Roman colonies had increased to more than thirty-five, most of which had been established in the territory of the former Samnite alliance.

As soon as the superpower Rome exercised control over major parts of Italy, it came into conflict with other superpowers. The rivalry among the leading noble families played a crucial role in this process. To live up to the standards of military success new fields of action had to be invented continuously and these were eventually found in the dispute with the North African maritime power of

---

[1] In the mountainous area, the Romans were forced to give up phalanx combat, which proved to be rather inflexible, and fought with smaller, independently operating units (maniples). The lance, the main weapon until this point, was replaced by the short sword (*gladius*) and the javelin (*pilum*). This combat technique, which was based on a strong and flexible infantry and did not rely so much on cavalry, turned out to be superior.

Carthage. In 264 BCE, Rome answered a call for assistance from Campanian mercenaries (Mamertines) in Sicily who had been expelled from the region only a couple of years before. This led, in due course, to a confrontation with Carthage, which was operating in Western Sicily, despite the fact that several treaties of amity had been concluded in the past, including an agreement to provide support in the war against Pyrrhus. The so-called First Punic War (264–241 BCE) resulted in the utter defeat of Carthage, which had to pay reparations, withdraw from Sicily and later from Sardinia and Corsica, whereas Rome, as successor, rose to become a maritime power. The city-state of Rome now possessed overseas territories, which caused some problems in terms of administration. Again, the Romans were able to display their flexibility, which was their greatest strength. Sicily, Sardinia and Corsica were not accepted in the alliance system but administrated within the scope of a Roman magistrate (*provincia*). In 227 BCE, they were subjected as exclusive domains to a *praetor*, while taxes and duties were leased to Roman tax farmers (*publicani*).

The First Punic War broadened the Roman horizon considerably. As a result, Rome campaigned twice in Illyria to secure Adriatic trade and at the same time conquered Celtic territories in Upper Italy, including Mediolanum, modern-day Milan (225–222 BCE). Carthage, in turn, focused after its defeat on southeastern Spain and managed to conquer large parts of the Iberian Peninsula, with its rich gold and silver deposits. It concluded a treaty with Rome in 227–225 BCE, which stipulated that the River Iberus, which was not to be crossed with ill intention, would serve a boundary between the two spheres of interest (Polybius 2.13.7). Whether the name 'Iberus', which is mentioned in this treaty, denotes today's river Ebro is still strongly debated in modern scholarship, as the Ebro is situated far to the north whereas the town of Sagunto, whose conquest by the Carthaginian general Hannibal triggered the Second Punic War, is located much further to the south (Matijević 2015). The ensuing Second Punic War (218–202 BCE) began with Hannibal's spectacular crossing of the Alps and pushed Rome to the brink of destruction. The Romans suffered a whole series of defeats through Hannibal's superior military skills, particularly in Cannae (216 BCE), where the Roman army was annihilated. However, Hannibal refrained from attacking the city of Rome itself and Rome's ill fate turned when the Roman dictator Q. Fabius Maximus Cunctator ('the lingerer') deployed a defensive strategy. Moreover, most allies and colonies displayed a remarkable loyalty towards Rome, only a few, such as Capua, defected. In contrast, Hannibal did not receive sufficient support from Carthage. P. Scipio Africanus was able to conquer Carthaginian Spain and Hannibal was forced to retreat to North Africa, where he lost the decisive battle of Zama (202 BCE). Rome then imposed a humiliating peace agreement on Carthage, which provided that it had to surrender all territories outside of Africa, give up almost its entire war fleet and pay reparations for a period of fifty years. In addition, Carthage was forced into allying with Rome and was therefore not allowed to raise an army outside Africa, while in Africa any military action required Rome's prior consent.

Meanwhile, the Romans took possession of Carthaginian territories in Spain (see Map 3.1). They subjugated native tribes and established the provinces of Hispania Citerior and Ulterior in 197 BCE. However, armed conflicts with Iberian and Lusitanian tribes continued until 133 BCE. In Northern Italy, the conquest of former Celtic territories progressed and the Celtic tribes were pushed further back.

After the victory over Carthage, the significance of the rising Western power of the Roman Republic surpassed all other Mediterranean powers that had emerged from the empire of Alexander the Great. It goes without saying that they, too, instantly clashed with Rome. Macedonia, in particular, but also the Seleucid Empire had sided with Carthage and opposed Rome. In 200 BCE, they took advantage of weaknesses displayed by Ptolemaic Egypt, Rome's ally, in order to annex its territories in the Aegean. Two Macedonian Wars against Philip V and his son Perseus followed (200–179 and 171–168 BCE, see Map 3.1). Titus Quinctius Flaminius eventually proclaimed the freedom of the Greek states, which had been occupied by Macedonia, and at the end of the day, the Macedonian Empire was destroyed and divided into four client states. It was during these wars that Polybius was taken to Rome as a hostage. The peace agreement considerably limited the influence of the Seleucid Empire, whose sphere of interest was already menaced by the Kingdom of Pergamum, Rome's closest ally in Asia Minor.

In 146 BCE, an uprising in Macedonia and Greece caused the destruction of Corinth by consul L. Mummius and the establishment of Macedonia as a Roman colony. Meanwhile, Carthage had regained so much of its former wealth that it was able to pay the reparations in one go and resume its former significance as a commercial power. This aroused the suspicions of influential Roman politicians, including Cato the Elder, who, after having visited the town, regularly demanded that Carthage had to be destroyed. When the Carthaginians started to take active action against the constant harassment of Masinissa, king of Numidia and a Roman ally, they also provided a convenient *casus belli*. In the ensuing Third Punic War (149–146 BCE), P. Cornelius Scipio once and for all razed the city of Carthage to the ground and Rome's greatest rival ceased to exist. The Carthaginian territory formed the basis of the Roman province *Africa proconsularis*, which was established later. The city of Carthage was not re-built at first. C. Gracchus and Caesar failed in their attempts to re-settle it. In 29 BCE, however, Augustus finally succeeded in re-establishing the town, which was later made the capital of the province.

Yet again, Rome, the new world power, had to cope with administrative difficulties. In the long run, it was not possible to create praetorships for every overseas colony, as this office was subjected to the regulations of annual

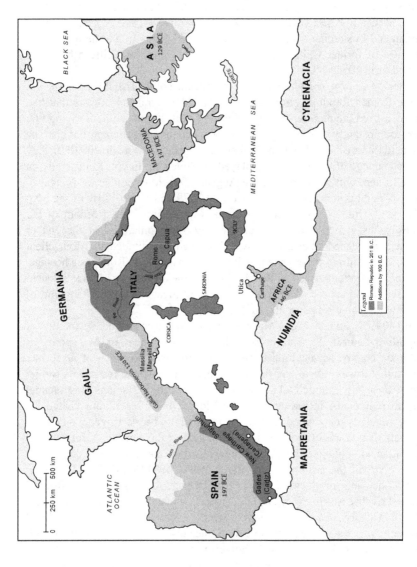

Map 3.1 Rome, 2nd century BCE. Adapted from http://www.emersonkent.com/map_archive/roman_republic_2nd_century_bc.htm.

magistracies. To solve this problem the system of prolongation of office outside the city of Rome *(prorogatio)* was introduced. It allowed the creation of governorships for former praetors and consuls who were then able to administrate their provinces as propraetors or proconsuls ('instead of consuls') with full authority for a longer period than just one year. In Rome, however, they did not have any authority. Their power ceased entirely when they crossed the city limits. Upon returning to Rome, they turned into private citizens who could even be prosecuted before the so-called extortion court for exploiting the provinces for personal gain. Cicero's orations against Verres, the governor of Sicily, are the most famous example.

Rome's territorial gains did not always arise from violent war. Occasionally, the Romans managed to extend their empire without shedding blood. In 133 BCE, Attalus III, the last king of Pergamum, died without an heir and bequeathed his kingdom to Rome. After having quelled various uprisings, the Romans were finally able to accept the inheritance in 129 BCE and establish the province of Asia, which included large parts of Asia Minor.

Rome's steady rise to leading world power was accompanied by numerous conflicts and uprisings in the provinces. Until the monopolisation of military victory by the emperors, this offered the senatorial elites enormous opportunities for personal gain and increase in prestige. In addition, a new elite of entrepreneurs emerged. As tax farmers and big-style merchants, they were able to climb the social ladder and formed the equestrian rank *(equites)*, the lower of the two aristocratic classes, ranking below the senators. This system, however, entirely failed the rural middle class. Many soldiers had to serve overseas and were therefore forced to neglect their farms. Migration into the cities had dire consequences. A lower class of urban poor emerged that was able to exert considerable social and political pressure (see Brunt 1971; Will 1991). The brothers Tiberius and Gaius Sempronius Gracchus benefited from this situation when both tried to implement social reforms in opposition to the senate through the plebeian assembly. These reforms stipulated that large landowners surrendered state-owned land, which was, in turn, distributed to small peasants. Although both brothers were eventually assassinated (133 and 121 BCE), they added a new dimension to the disputes among Rome's political elites. Broadly speaking, two different political factions can be distinguished: the *populares* – those who favoured the cause of the plebeians through the people's assembly; and the *optimates* – those who were represented by the senate.

In the long run, the Gracchean reforms caused the professionalisation of the armed forces, which had so far been composed of non-professional fighters. Owing to the reforms of Gaius Marius, the so-called *capite censi*, landless Roman citizens, were accepted in the legions and provided with weapons by the state. Marius also initiated a tactical change in combat technique, in the course of which the thirty maniples of a legion (*c*.6,000 men) were re-organised into ten cohorts. This led to the development of military clients, as generals were not only obliged to surrender parts of the spoils to soldiers, but also had to furnish them with a plot of land when they retired after having served for sixteen years. In turn, Marius could count on the soldiers' allegiance in elections and political disputes. The result was a professional army of volunteers with a uniform period of service. Yet the veterans turned into a dangerous domestic factor, depending on to which former or current general they were committed. The egalitarian rule of the aristocracy was reduced to absurdity as those generals upon whom important commands had been conferred were able to rely upon the support of their soldiers even after a campaign had been completed, thus surpassing their peers in social standing and political influence. Successful generals, such as Marius, Sulla, Pompey and Caesar, were no longer willing to yield their command and to become simple senators when the time came.

At that point, the Roman Empire had to cope with a serious external threat for the first time in many years. The Germanic tribes of the Cimbri, Teutones and the Ambrones invaded Italy and Gaul from the north. In 113 BCE and 105 BCE, they were able to defeat the Roman armies at Noreia and Arausio. Gaius Marius, who had already been campaigning successfully in North Africa, had managed to rout the Germanic tribes in 101 BCE and become elected consul every year despite the non-iteration statute. As Marius favoured the *populares,* he soon clashed with the *optimates* and Sulla, who became the latter's most prominent representative. Several other conflicts challenged Rome's power but did not even come close to toppling the empire. These conflicts included the Social War over Roman citizenship, to which the Marian military reforms may have contributed. The war was carried on relentlessly from 91–88 BCE and ended with the conferral of Roman citizenship to all Italian allies. The three so-called Mithridatic Wars in Greece and Asia Minor (88–63 BCE) and Sulla's two marches on Rome (88 and 82 BCE), which broke a taboo and led to an atrocious civil war, Sulla's installation as permanent dictator, and the eradication of his political opponents, also rank among the major conflicts of the period. These disturbances interrupted the wars in the East but did not seriously jeopardise Rome's hegemony. The system of indirect rule through client kings, which had been established, for example, in Asia Minor and Judaea, proved to be stable and effective, thus facilitating control over the empire's periphery.

Sulla's reforms to the benefit of the senate increased domestic stability, but after his retirement (79 BCE) and death (78 BCE), these reforms were in part repealed by his successors who represented the *populares*. In the waning Roman Republic, the leading aristocrats were solely concerned with increasing their personal power and influence at the expense of the community. As in earlier times this required a military command. However, opportunities to prove themselves were ample: various uprisings had to be put down, such as the insurrection of Quintus Sertorius in Spain (83–72 BCE), in southern Italy

Spartacus had to be fought in the Servile War (73–71 BCE), and war had to be waged against Mithridates of Pontus in the Third Mithridatic War (73–63 BCE), a task which was carried out by Lucullus and Pompey. The latter re-organised the eastern provinces and established the province of Syria on the remains of the former Seleucid Empire. As a result, the Roman Empire became a direct neighbour of the Parthian Empire, which had been able to conquer primarily the eastern parts of the former Seleucid Empire, including Mesopotamia. Military clashes between Rome and Parthia, particularly over Armenia, occurred frequently. One of the best known events is Rome's defeat in the battle of Carrhae (53 BCE), in which 25,000 Roman soldiers as well as their general Licinius Crassus lost their lives; a further 10,000 men were barely able to reach Syria. The Roman scholar Pliny the Elder reports that after the battle of Carrhae, 10,000 Roman captives were brought to the city of Margiana where they were forced to build the town wall (*Naturalis Historia* 6.18).[2]

The co-existence of two large empires in the *oecumene* known at the time challenged the theory of the successiveness of empires that figures most prominently in the Book of Daniel (Nebuchadnezzar's dream: 2.31–45; and Daniel's Vision of the Beasts: 7.1–27). This is the reason why the histori-ographer Pompeius Trogus, a contemporary and officer of Caesar who's Philippic Histories are preserved only in excerpts by the later author Justin, refers to an overlordship that only one empire could hold. Trogus saw in the return of the lost military standards by the Parthian king Phraates to Imperator Augustus, who, of course, had exploited the event exhaustively for propagand-istic purposes, a clear manifestation of Rome's overlordship (Justin 42.5, see van Wickevoort Crommelin 1993, 222–4; for the long run of the 'two empires' topos, see Preiser-Capeller (Chapter 4, this volume, pp. 158–161).

The final stages of the Roman Republic were dominated by civil wars between the most powerful members of the nobility. In 60 BCE, Licinius Crassus, Pompey the Great and C. Julius Caesar allied in order to pursue their personal ambitions (triumvirate). After the expiry of his consulship, Caesar became proconsul and managed to conquer in a violent war from 58 to 51 BCE all of Gaul except for those parts in southern Gaul that had already been integrated into the empire as provinces. The Romans now ruled the entire area between the (today) French Atlantic coast, the River Rhine, the English Channel and the Pyrenees. This was an enormous territorial expansion. At the same time, he made the Roman claim to an *Imperium sine fine* 'Empire without frontiers' more than

---

[2] A Chinese report narrates that, in 36 BCE, approximately 100 men under the command of Zhizhi defended the palisade fortifications by deploying a 'fish scales formation' in the battle against the Han forces. In scholarship, these men are sometimes identified as the captured Roman legionaries who were transferred to the east. This, however, cannot be proven, even if some of today's inhabitants of the town of Liqian would still like to believe that their lineage goes way back to these Roman soldiers: see Manthe 2014.

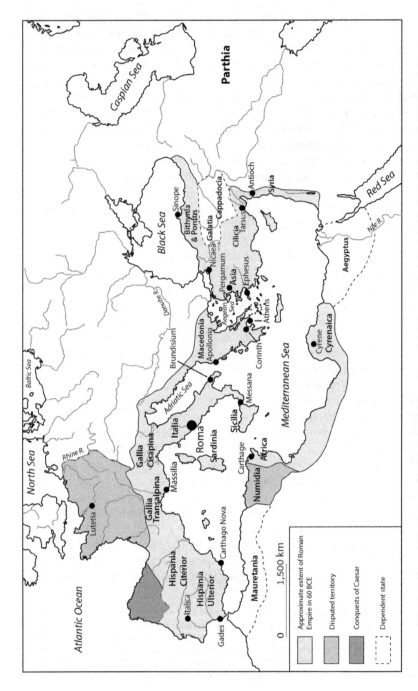

Map 3.2 Roman Empire, *c*.44 BCE. Adapted from https://i.pinimg.com/originals/cd/1e/30/cd1e304725a68d12da6056
cae755cc17.jpg.

clear by symbolically crossing over to Britannia (54/53 BCE) and crossing the River Rhine (55 and 53 BCE), even though he himself had defined the latter as the boundary of the Roman Empire (see Map 3.2).

Caesar commanded a huge military clientele, thus being the most powerful man in the entire Roman Empire. This, however, led inevitably to a confrontation with his former ally, the successful general Pompey, and his faction. The ensuing civil wars (49–30 BCE) resulted in the defeat of Pompey and his supporters and precipitated the establishment of a monarchy when Caesar became dictator in perpetuity almost in the same manner as Sulla before him. This was followed by Caesar's assassination by leading senators on 15 March 44 BCE and violent clashes among Caesar's murderers, Octavian, Caesar's posthumously adopted son and sole heir, and Caesar's former political cronies Mark Antony and M. Aemilius Lepidus, who had initially taken over the government as new triumviri. After the defeat of Caesar's assassins at Philippi in 42 BCE, war broke out between Octavian, who had assumed the name C. Julius Caesar and had deified his adoptive father in order to be able to call himself son of the divine (*divi filius*), and Mark Antony, who had allied with the Egyptian queen Cleopatra VII and even married her. In 30 BCE, Octavian emerged as victor from this power struggle. He turned Egypt, the last remaining Hellenistic kingdom, into a Roman province, which was administrated by Octavian personally (he was represented by a prefect of equestrian rank). As a result, the whole Mediterranean belonged to the Roman Empire, which henceforth ruled the major parts of the oecumene.

In summary, the city of Rome, originally an Etruscan foundation on a Tiber crossing, over a period of 500 years was able to build an empire, which included first Italy, then large parts of the western and finally the eastern Mediterranean. At the end of this process of expansion, Rome was a global power but with the constitution and the institutions of a city republic ruled by an aristocratic elite. However, the consensus of a division of political power between the leading families was counteracted by the enormous growth of the empire, as victorious generals and their soldier clientele claimed more and more power and resources for themselves. Finally, the enormous military success led to the downfall of the republican system and to the establishment of a military monarchy. Nevertheless, the republican ideals and values of a senatorial elite continued to influence political and social action of the empire.

3.3   Consequences of the Expansion: the Imperial Period

After the civil war, the senate eventually accepted the de facto authority of a single man. A senatorial decree granted Octavian extraordinary powers and gave him the name Augustus, which had, until then, been reserved for the divine (27 BCE). Octavian skilfully managed to convert the republic into a military monarchy, the so-called principate, without abolishing the traditional institutions and changing the political organisation visibly. Augustus continued to pass laws through the senate, and magistrates were still elected, even if he reserved for himself the right to nominate and veto candidates in more crucial cases. The institution of dictatorship, which his adoptive father had held, had been abolished after Caesar's assassination and was never re-introduced. A standing army, which depended on the emperor (*Princeps*) as its sole patron and funder, was now of utmost importance for the empire. This, however, involved the emergence of a professionalised body of officers through an institutionalised military career. The legions offered young Romans the oppor-tunity to climb the social ladder, as they were usually granted a plot of land after twenty years' service, and provincials who served in one of the numerous auxiliary and special units were able to acquire Roman citizenship for themselves and their offspring. These new agents replaced the individual expansionist motivation of republican nobles aiming at office, military leadership and booty.

The expansionist ideology had to be catered for by the emperor, but it was served primarily by propaganda, coinage and the celebration of victory in the centre. Real expansion slowed down and the focus shifted from extending to consolidating the empire. Augustus stylised himself as restorer of peace, which he demonstrated propagandistically by closing the gates of the Temple of Janus and the erection of the Altar of Augustan Peace (*Ara Pacis*). The belligerent consuls from the ranks of senatorial nobility now belonged to the past. Since any orders issued by the senatorial elite were subject to the emperor's supreme command (*auspicia*), only the emperor or members of his family were hence-forth allowed to celebrate a triumph after military victories. The soldiers had to swear allegiance to the emperor, as he was now their sole patron and their only general. The army as such also lost some of its expansionist zeal, yet it remained the major force behind the empire's consolidation. In particular, throughout the whole period of the Roman principate period, until about 250 CE, it played the major role in the process of Romanisation, specifically by spreading the imperial cult throughout the empire. This cult, which evolved on the basis of the modified Hellenistic traditions, became an important common bond that held the different parts of the realm together (see, e.g., Garnsey and Saller 1987, 164).

Augustus's new order precipitated many changes. The administration of the provinces was re-organised and a number of magnificent edifices were erected in Rome, the capital and centre of the oecumene. The Deeds of the Divine Augustus, a funerary inscription engraved upon bronze tablets and originally placed in front of Augustus's mausoleum, contain thirty-five body paragraphs in which Augustus mentions numerous roads, water supply systems, public edifices and particular temples that he had erected anew or re-built. The account of his deeds was spread throughout the empire and major parts of the original text have been preserved in a bilingual version discovered on a temple to Augustus in

Ancyra (Ankara). Economy and culture thrived in the Roman Empire. It was in particular the literature, with Virgil, Ovid, Horace and the historiographer Livy as its most important exponents, which was actively supported by the emperor, and it consequently flourished. Scholarship refers to this time as the Augustan formative period (see Galinsky 1996, 363–70).

Augustan foreign policy focused on pacifying and reorganising the provinces, particularly Spain, Illyria and Gaul. As already mentioned above, Rome concluded a peace with the Parthian Empire, which was 'compelled . . . to seek the friendship of the Roman people' (Augustus, Res Gestae 29) so that in the end all former major centres of conflict had been appeased to a large extent. 'Augustan art and poetry is full of images of world conquest, and the submission of India, Britain and northern Scythia was confidently predicted' (Woolf 2012, 167). This claim to world domination, which is particularly vividly expressed in the Virgil quotation cited right at the beginning of this chapter, could not be implemented, as this would have overstretched the resources of the huge empire. Most notably, Rome's claim to Germania had to be abandoned in 9 CE when the Roman army was defeated by a coalition of Germanic tribes including well-trained Roman auxiliary forces, thereby losing three legions in the so-called 'battle of the Teutoburg Forest'. Only the Alpine region and the Raeti could be subjugated permanently through the campaigns of Augustus' stepsons Drusus and Tiberius. Possible plans to establish a province of Germania as far as the Elbe River came to a standstill upon the banks of the River Rhine. Uprisings in the Danube region and their violent suppression also revealed that the empire had reached the limits of its capacity. Nevertheless, the claim to world domination was never really given up.

The idea resurfaced repeatedly during the entire Imperial period, despite the fact that Tiberius (14–37 CE), Augustus' successor, displayed sound judgement by commanding his stepson Germanicus to abort his mission to re-conquer Germania after years of successes and failures. All the same, the empire's territory continued to expand. Under Emperor Claudius, large parts of Britain were conquered. An inscription (CIL VI 31537a-d, Rome) attests to the fact that the emperor celebrated the event by extending the *pomerium*, the religious boundary around the city of Rome. Rome remained the *caput mundi*, the capital of the world. In accordance with tradition of earlier emperors of the Julio-Claudian dynasty, Claudius refrained from conferring upon himself honorific titles referring to his victories and instead named his son Britannicus, similar to emperors of other dynasties who assumed names that visibly advertised their glorious military triumphs. Emperor Domitian, for example, conferred upon himself the title Germanicus after his victory over the Chatti (83 CE). Under Emperor Trajan (98–117 CE), the empire expanded again quite considerably. After two violent wars (101–7 CE), the province of Dacia was established on the territory of present-day Romania to the arch of the Carpathian Mountains.

The important moments of the Dacian Wars are depicted most vividly on the famous Trajan's Column in Rome. In addition, Trajan managed to turn the Nabataean kingdom into the province of Arabia (106 CE). In 115 CE, he conquered the Parthian capital Ctesiphon and set up the province of Mesopotamia. In the end, Trajan held the titles Germanicus, Dacicus and Parthicus. Under Trajan's rule, the Roman Empire attained its maximum territorial extent (see Map 3.3), stretching as far as Britain in the north and to the 24th parallel in southern Egypt, from Gibraltar in the west to the Persian Gulf in the east.

The *optimus princeps* Trajan was committed to the idea of being a world conqueror, even though he must have been aware of the fact that he did not have the resources to control the conquered Parthian territories permanently, as Rome's campaigns were almost certainly not profitable enough to cover the expenses. It is therefore hardly surprising that Trajan's immediate successor, Emperor Hadrian (117–38 CE), had to relinquish these territories. Under the rule of Hadrian, a profound paradigm shift occurred. Although the idea of world domination never completely disappeared, Hadrian may have decided silently to consolidate the boundaries of the empire instead of expanding them even further. In Britannia, Hadrian's Wall was erected to keep out the Caledonian tribes and the fortifications of the so-called Limes Mauretaniae and the Upper Germanic and Rhaetian Limes were improved. The construction of the latter, which included territories east of the Rhine River, had probably already begun under Trajan and had been more like a customs boundary than an actual border defence. Hadrian was incidentally the only emperor who actually toured most of the Roman provinces. The building of Hadrian's wall was for defensive measures rather than any further increase of territory. This would not change until the late Roman Empire. Therefore, instead of expanding, Hadrian optimised the defence of the empire and its management, reforming the central administration and its headquarters at the emperor's court in Rome. Within the administration, the equestrian rank gained even greater importance.

Antonius Pius (138–61 CE), Hadrian's successor, deviated slightly from the principle that called for the preservation of the acquired when he pushed the Limes Britannicus further north to the Firth of Forth after an uprising. In the long run, however, it was not possible to maintain this position. Between 155 and 160 CE the Upper Germanic Limes was moved several kilometres further east, but only to straighten its course.

Roman border defence was organised by armed forces that were stationed in camps erected at regular intervals along the border. Rivers, particularly the rivers Rhine and Danube, connected these camps and were used for transporting goods and soldiers, as naval engineering was sufficiently advanced to contrive this (see Aßkamp/Schäfer 2008). As a rule, small auxiliary units were positioned in the immediate vicinity of the border while the legions were stationed in the

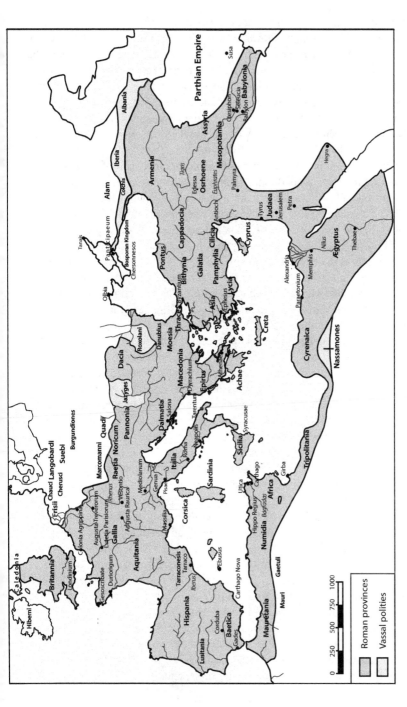

Map 3.3 Roman Empire under Trajan, 117 CE. Produced on the basis of https://en.wikipedia.org/wiki/File:Roman_Empire_Trajan_117AD .png prepared by Tataryn.

backcountry at important traffic junctions (roads and rivers). The largest naval units were based in Misenum, Forum Iulii and Ravenna. Before 270 CE, the city of Rome had not been surrounded by a fortification wall and during the Republican period, no military units had been stationed in the city. Augustus was the first to install an elite unit, the so-called praetorians, for his own protection. Two prefects of equestrian rank commanded the praetorians, the only line troops in the whole of Italy. It is quite remarkable that the interior of the empire had been virtually stripped of armed forces, as they had all been moved to the border provinces where, with Egypt being the only exception to this rule, they were commanded by senatorial governors on behalf of the emperor.

The succeeding emperors did not attempt to expand Roman territory, as they were busy enough with subduing uprisings and defending the borders. The victorious campaign against Parthia, which was conducted by Marcus Aurelius (161–80 CE) and his co-emperor Lucius Verus (161–9 CE), secured the eastern border of Syria. The following wars against the Germanic Marcomanni precipitated the improvement of the Danube frontier and the establishment of Marcomannia and Sarmatia as new provinces seemed finally to have been within reach. The column of Marcus Aurelius in Rome is the most famous monument to commemorate this war. The emperor died during his last campaign and was succeeded by his youthful son Commodus (180–92 CE), who, lacking the resources as well as the prospects of success, concluded a peace with the Marcomanni. However, the concept of world domination was still alive. The fact that Commodus' peace was widely resented despite his triumph over the Germanic tribes in 180 CE reveals this more than clearly (Herodian 1.6; Historia Augusta, Commodus 3). The Marcomannic Wars demonstrated that the limes system ceased to work as soon as the borders were threatened simultaneously at more than one place. Since the entire army was scattered over the Roman provinces, it was only possible to amass armed forces strategically in one spot by withdrawing troops from those parts of the empire that were not as threatened.

Commodus' assassination precipitated a return to civil war, which ended upon the accession of the North African Severans, the last imperial dynasty (193–235 CE), who put a special focus on defending the borders along the rivers Danube and Rhine and in Syria, which had developed into an ongoing problem. As the remuneration of the soldiers was raised despite climate deterioration and depreciation of currency, some areas of the empire enjoyed an economic boom. However, the external pressure increased steadily. Although the emperors conferred upon themselves ever more honorific titles, which referred to their victories, and even added the epithet Maximus to their names, permanent military success failed to materialise. Worse still, in 233 CE, the Germanic tribe of the Alemanni surmounted the limes and launched raids deep into Roman territory before they could be driven back. In the east, the Sasanian Empire succeeded the Parthian Empire and, from 230 CE onwards, its ruler Shapur I managed to defeat the Roman forces repeatedly. The decline of the Roman Empire began, at the latest, with the soldier-emperors (235–84 CE). This period, in which more than sixty emperors ruled successively and occasionally simultaneously, was marked by endless crises and civil wars. The empire gradually lost territory and separate states emerged, for example in Gaul and Palmyra. In 260 CE, the Romans had to vacate the limes and retreat behind the River Rhine. They also abandoned large parts of Dacia, withdrawing to the Danube River where they found better defences.

With the installation of a tetrarchy (284–305 CE), Diocletian changed the empire fundamentally. The city of Rome lost its position as the political centre of the empire. A period of stability set in, allowing the empire, which would soon become Christian, to persist. However, the former world power, particularly its western part, was gradually shrinking. Rome never abandoned its claim to the lost areas. In the west, however, the future belonged to the Germanic kingdoms, which gradually emerged on former Roman territory, whereas in the east a new centre was created. Constantinople became the new capital of the Eastern Roman Empire after the city had been re-founded in 330 CE. Until its conquest by Ottoman troops, the Eastern Roman Empire remained in a nearly perpetual state of war with its neighbours (Preiser-Kapeller, this volume).

3.4 The Roman Empire as a Legal, Economic and Cultural Area

Roman citizenship was the empire's most important common bond. Its acquisition entailed the privilege of being able to enrol in one of the subdivisions of the Roman citizenry (*tribus*) and, consequently, the right to vote in assemblies during the Republican period and, for members of the elite, the right to run for office. Even more importantly, Roman citizens enjoyed tax privileges, the right to landownership, the right to appeal to assemblies in felony cases and, in the city of Rome, the right to receive food rations. Once citizenship had been attained, the offspring of a valid marriage (*conubium*) would inherit these rights. A citizen's duties included service in the militia, observance of the gods and, if any, levies payable to the community. During the Republican period, Roman citizenship was dealt out very sparingly. This changed after the above-mentioned Social War when citizenship was offered to all Italic people. On a basic level, however, every Roman was able to pass on his citizenship by, for example, freeing slaves. These slaves would then assume the gentile name of their former master. While freed slaves were still subject to legal restrictions, their children enjoyed the full rights of a Roman citizen if they had been fathered after their father's manumission in a valid marriage. In the Imperial period, the emperor granted Roman citizenship to larger groups from outside Italy either by establishing colonies of Roman citizens or by awarding it for special merits. In cities subject to Latin right, the members of the city senate (*ordo*) regularly received Roman citizenship. The so-called *decurions* formed the urban upper class and were responsible for the administration and maintenance of the empire's territorial towns. Michael Rostovtzeff (1971, 190) refers to them, as 'the importance of the city *bourgeoisie* cannot be exaggerated'. For him they practically ruled the empire. Under Tiberius, at latest, the right to vote and the obligation to serve in the military had lost their importance. Yet tax privileges, legal privileges and the right to appeal to the emperor were still sought-after. The Apostle Paul's trial before Festus (Acts 25.11) is probably the most famous example of the latter. Generally speaking, Roman citizenship turned into a status symbol (Hopkins 2009, 181).

The Roman army of the Imperial period, which consisted of volunteers, offered those who already had Roman citizenship the opportunity to enlist and, maybe, climb the social ladder. Others could acquire citizenship and the right to enter a valid marriage after serving in an auxiliary unit for 25 years. Numerous military diplomas preserved on bronze tablets as copies from the *tribus* scrolls in Rome corroborate this fact. Children born during military service were usually not regarded as legal. This provision was not rescinded until the Severian dynasty in 197 CE.

The Roman Empire was based on indirect rule exerted via many, mostly small cities, reaching well into their respective hinterlands (see Revell 2009). The city of Rome ruled an oecumene, which consisted to a large extent of cities and their surroundings. Attempts were made to restrict administration to a minimum. Subjugated cities were usually permitted self-governance. As mentioned above, in the Republican period, cities and later whole territories were tied to Rome through treaties of alliance, which provided that they were not allowed to ally among each other. During the Imperial period, the provincial cities were granted a wide range of differing privileges. The governor's seat marked a province's principal town. This, however, did not mean that these towns had the legal status of a Roman town. Nonetheless, the cities under Roman law (colonies and municipia) were responsible for first instance jurisdiction in general, proceedings under local law against non-Romans, and the collection of taxes. The city senate was jointly liable for the due payment of proceeds to Rome. Unlike imperial offices, civil service positions were not remunerated. Similar to senators, aspirants to such posts were required to possess certain minimum financial resources, as they were expected to render outstanding services to the town by donating large sums of money. If a town managed to produce a prominent representative of equestrian or even senatorial rank, this man would frequently assume the role of the town's patron, representing it in Rome. Its lean bureaucracy in the government centre marked this system, as Rome had transferred administrative tasks to local institutions, which could be held liable (see Hopkins 2009, 183–4). The governors took care of superior jurisdiction, tax collection through procurators, and supervision of provincial towns and their institutions and, last but not least, the police and military forces.

The letters by Pliny the Younger testify eloquently to his activities as governor of Bithynia. The bases of this system were the largely self-governing cities and their hinterland in the provinces with their own peregrine or Roman legal systems.

In 212 CE, the Constitutio Antoniniana, preserved on Papyrus Gissensis 40, granted Roman citizenship to all free inhabitants of the empire. This can very well be regarded as a clear breach from tradition. Consequently, the distinction between Romans and provincial subjects (*peregrini*) disappeared. The Roman world was now divided into distinguished (*honestiores*) and less distinguished inhabitants (*humiliores*). The new law also had consequences for the military forces. Less affluent men from the provinces could no longer obtain citizenship through military service in auxiliary units. So, the distinction between legions and auxiliary forces also gradually became obsolete.[3]

The empire's enormous territorial extent opened up an equally enormous economic area. The professional exploitation of waterways for transporting goods and people, as well as the improvement of the road network stimulated economic exchange. Routes through the Mediterranean Sea in particular, but also through the Atlantic were used systematically for economic purposes. In this manner, the supply of goods could be secured throughout the empire.[4] The Mediterranean Sea was ideal for distributing goods and adjusting imbalances in supply, which contributed considerably towards lasting stability within the empire. However, both republican and imperial policy prioritised the city of Rome in terms of the supply of food, particularly grain, in order to sustain the urban population and avoid riots in the immediate vicinity of the rulers. The emperors sorely felt dependent on the mood of the capital's inhabitants and tried to compensate for denying political participation by donating food and organising lavish distractions. The poet Juvenal refers to this as 'bread and circuses' (*panem et circenses:* Satires 10, 81). With its about 1 million inhabitants in the Imperial period, Rome was the largest city of the empire. The city's population consisted primarily of free Italian landowners, slaves and freed slaves from all over the Mediterranean, free craftsmen and merchants.

It is amazing that landownership remained the most important criterion for the assessment of wealth throughout the Roman period. This can be ascribed to the fact that, since 180 BCE (*lex Claudia*), senators were forbidden to participate in large-scale maritime trade. They had to invest their fortune in land instead, while non-senatorial members of their kinship group should engage in maritime trade. This would explain why coins were not introduced before the war against King Pyrrhus around 275 BCE. Livy narrates that in the early days before silver coins were minted, the senators had to pay their war tax with heavy copper discs, which

[3] For various aspects concerning this issue, see Ando 2016.
[4] For a recent study with new and surprising results concerning Roman maritime trade see Warnking 2015.

had to be transported in carts (4, 60, 6). Nevertheless, the use of coinage quickly gained acceptance in trade and became even more important later when soldiers were paid with coins. The authority to mint coins rested in the hands of the senate and was later transferred to the emperors, who standardised the currency and used coins extensively for propaganda purposes. In principle, the face value of coins was supposed to equal their content in precious metal. The numerous crises of the Imperial period, however, caused a steady decline in precious metal purity (see Scheidel 2009).

The huge latifundia of the senatorial landowners were chiefly situated in Italy. They were farmed by slaves who had been captured in war or taken by pirates, with the island of Delos being the main hub of the slave trade. In the Imperial period, the proportion of slaves working in the manufacturing sector and in agriculture, in particular, decreased steadily, while the number of small tenant farmers increased. The emperor was the largest landowner in the whole empire. A special imperial administrative body was specifically created for the task managed his personal assets. Mines were not only frequently operated using slaves but also with wage labourers. Social advancement was basically only open to household slaves with specialist knowledge who were able to earn money and buy their freedom. Affluent freedmen are frequently documented in inscriptions. Petronius's *Satyricon*, which was written during the reign of Emperor Nero (54–68 CE), renders a satirical exaggeration of the wealthy freedman, a prototype of the *nouveau riche*, in Trimalchio's banquet. Slaves freed by the emperor could gain considerable political influence. The more power the empire gained during the last centuries BCE, the more tasks in the administration and organisation of the empire's public and private revenues were transferred to slaves and private people (Woolf 2012, 86). A kind of social-climber mentality developed, which contributed fundamentally towards internal cohesion and, consequently, towards the lasting success of the empire.

Owing to the reliable infrastructure, it was possible to disseminate throughout the empire the results of scientific and literary production, centred, of course, in Rome, but also in Athens, Alexandria and various towns in Asia Minor. Greek philosophy, Greek and Roman literature and historiography, and particularly scientific and technical knowhow was adopted by imperial and local elites. The latter included not only military technology but also urban construction and water management. The advanced technological level, which proliferated in almost all areas ruled by the Romans, in Europe could not be reached again before the Early modern period.

The Greek historian Polybius, who lived in Rome from 167 to 151 BCE, was a great admirer of the Romans, regarding their religion as the basis of their superiority as they had managed to integrate 'superstitions' into the public cult (Polybius 6.56.12–15). Rome's deities were addressed throughout the entire empire even without any policy to export them; they assimilated local gods or were equated with indigenous deities. Rome, in turn, turned into a hub city, disseminating provincial deities throughout the realm. With a small number of exceptions, Rome did not develop an exclusive caste of priests, as every magistrate had to fulfil sacral duties. Strict separation between religion and politics was therefore impossible. It was of utmost importance to achieve a balanced relation with the gods. For this reason, every important political decision was preceded by augury or other rituals. Jupiter, the city's prime god, made a career as 'public deity' across the whole empire and was integrated into local pantheons by equating him with the supreme deities on site. The imperial cult was spread by the military in the provinces, thus constituting another common bond between Rome and its provinces.

3.5 A World Power: The Development of the Spatial Dimensions of the Roman Empire

In the preamble of his *Deeds*, the first Emperor Augustus notes that he had submitted the globe to Roman dominion. This, of course, was mere propaganda, as he knew quite well that he was at odds with the truth. He then goes on to describe the areas, which had been brought under Roman rule during his reign – areas where no Roman had gone before (*Res gestae* 26). The globe as a symbol of world domination appears on Augustus' coins and monuments and was also used by later emperors. Augustus reformed the Roman priesthood and religious cults, erected temples and had himself venerated as son of the divine (*divi filius*) and later as a deity. As a monarch, a function that he did not want to assume officially, he could pride himself on being a religious reformer. While he made his reign appear outwardly republican, he stylised himself as a divine ruler of the world, a mediator between heaven and earth. The propagandistic iconographic pro-gramme of the Temple of Mars Ultor and its forum, erected by Augustus in 2 BCE, the year he becomes *pater patriae*, depicts the emergence of Rome as world power from the foundation of Rome to the Republican period, eventually converging on Emperor Augustus himself as the new Romulus and reorganiser of the city of Rome and the territories subjugated by it. Rome was the 'Centre of the World' and its *princeps*, the father of the country (*pater patriae*), represented it. His successors based their reigns on this idea.

As I have shown in section 2.2 of this chapter, Rome's expansion from a city-state to a major power in Italy, then in the western Mediterranean and finally in the Greco-Hellenistic East was a long process that reached its apogee in the first century BCE, giving rise to Rome's distinctive imperial ideology formulated during the Augustan age. This ideology of Rome's 'manifest destiny' to dominate the world exercised considerable impact on the Roman emperors well into the end of the second century CE. In the long term, however, although the ideology of the conquest did not fade completely, it had to be discontinued due to the combination of military and economic factors. Hadrian's retrenchment, discussed above derived in all likelihood from his understanding that the empire 'had temporarily exceeded the size that its legionary establishment could protect' (Kagan 2006: 360). The burden of supporting manifold legions was too high, and the prospects of financing them through new conquests too slim (Mattern 1999: 123–161). Add to this internal difficulties caused by military units who were often eager to raise their generals to emperors, which further hindered additional expansion. Eventually, the empire became more and more defensive and was primarily concerned to defend its own territory, until it definitively began to shrink during the civil wars of the so-called soldier-emperors (235–84 CE).

The tremendous success of over 500 years of policy of conquest is more than extraordinary. It was initially fuelled by the ambition of Roman aristocratic magistrates who wanted to excel as generals to celebrate triumphs. It succeeded due to the establishment of a well-woven network of diverging alliance systems in Italy, augmented by fortified colonies in subjugated areas. Domestically speaking, this system backfired when the glorious generals started refusing to retire their temporally limited supreme commands and tried to extend their positions at the expense of the *res publica* with the help of their client-soldiers. This resulted in a period of civil wars that ended with the installation of a military monarchy and a regular army. Under the new system the impetus for ongoing expansionist campaigns did not disappear entirely but might have lessened in comparison to the earlier age of the ambitious magistrates. This political change may be an additional explanation for the gradual cessation of the expansionist momentum under the principate.

My chapter has not attempted to answer the question frequently raised by historians of the Roman Empire: whether or not it had a 'grand strategy' and if it had, how this 'grand strategy' determined the territorial scope of the empire.[5] During the period of the most robust expansion of Roman rule, from the late third century BCE to the Augustan era, it is difficult to speak of uniform strategy. Rome's wars were a by-product of multiple coexisting factors, ranking from predatory imperialism to the need to defend itself and its allies against other predators, from the magistrates' quest for glory to the generals' need to boost the morale of their armies and acquire political backing from the soldiers. Similarly, under the principate multiple factors influenced the empire's expanding or contracting borders – from the desire of certain emperors to immortalise themselves by crossing the ocean, the symbolic limit of *orbis terrarum* (Mattern 1999: 169–71), to the need to maintain the armies within the eco-

---

[5] For the classical study of the Roman alleged 'grand strategy' under the principate, see Luttwak 1976; for a pointed criticism of Luttwak (and an interesting, yet only rudimentary attempt to outline an alternative approach towards the 'grand strategy' question), see Kagan 2006.

logically sustainable areas (Whittaker 1994 and 2004), to the degree of pressure from the empire's enemies and recalcitrant subjects. Rather than presenting a one-size-fits-all explanation to the empire's territorial extent, I preferred therefore to follow the historical narrative that outlines multiple factors that influenced the empire's size at every given moment.

At least until the second half of the 3rd century CE, the city of Rome remained the *caput mundi*, the centre of various territorial, political, religious and cultural systems. The image of an eternal, golden, sacred Rome as the head of the *oecumene* and home of the empire remained virulent until the Middle Ages and was transported to the farthest corners of the empire in various ways. So, Roman traditions and festivals can be found from Hadrian's Wall in Britain to the Euphrates River (Cancik 2006). At least from the 3rd century CE on, a lengthy process of transition began that affected the entire empire. At the end, Rome was no longer its political and cultural centre and had merely a symbolic significance. The Roman Empire was now structurally different from what Augustus had created, while it had lost its character as a state of conquest long time ago (Woolf 2012, 247). Its subsequent history is the subject of Chapter 4 by Johannes Preiser-Kapeller in this volume.

Setbacks and complexities aside, it should be reminded that Rome was the first Mediterranean power that can effectively be considered a global empire. Contrary to the empire of Alexander the Great, the Roman Empire managed to hold huge territories together and to implement a uniform organisation. Similar to China under the Han dynasty and the Achaemenid and Parthian Empires, the Roman Empire was marked by an economy based on agriculture, differentiated social hierarchies, advanced technology based on iron and a high level of literacy. The perfectly organised and well-equipped military, which outclassed all its enemies for a long time, was Rome's driving force. Its success justified Rome's claim to world domination – an empire *sine fine*!

Bibliography

Ando, Clifford, ed. 2016. *Citizenship and Empire in Europe 200–1900. The Antonine Constitution after 1800 years*. Stuttgart: Franz Steiner Verlag.

Armstrong, Jeremy. 2016. *War and Society in Early Rome*. Cambridge: Cambridge University Press.

Aßkamp, Rudolf and Christoph Schäfer, eds. 2008. *Projekt Römerschiff. Nachbau und Erprobung für die Ausstellung 'Imperium Konflikt Mythos 2000 Jahre Varusschlacht'*. Hamburg: Koehler.

Beard, Mary, John North and S. R. F. Price. 2013. *Religions of Rome*, 15th edn. Cambridge: Cambridge University Press.

Bleicken, Jochen. 2004. *Geschichte der Römischen Republik*. Oldenbourg Grundriss der Geschichte 2. 6. Auflage. München: Oldenbourg.

Bleicken, Jochen. 2008. *Die Verfassung der Römischen Republik. Grundlagen und Entwicklung*. 8. Auflage. Paderborn: F. Schöningh.

Brunt, Peter A. 1971. *Social Conflicts in the Roman Republic*. London: Chatto and Windus.

Brunt, Peter A. 1978. 'Laus imperii'. In: *Imperialism in the Ancient World*, ed. Peter Garnsey and C. R. Whittaker, 159–91. Cambridge: Cambridge University Press.

Cancik, Hubert 2006. 'Caput mundi. Rom im Diskurs "Zentralität"'. In: HubertCancik, Alfred Schäfer and Wolfgang Spickermann, eds., *Zentralität und Religion. Zur Formierung urbaner Zentren im Imperium Romanum*. Tübingen: Mohr Siebeck 2006, 9–20.

Cornell, Tim J. 1995. *The Beginnings of Rome. Italy and Rome from the Bronze Age to the Punic Wars (c. 1000–264 BC)*. London: Routledge.

Edwards, Iorwerth E. S., Cyril J. Gadd, and Nicholas G. L. Hammond, eds. 2008. *The Cambridge Ancient History. Vol. 1. Part 1, Prolegomena and Prehistory*. Cambridge: Cambridge University Press.

Eich, Armin and Peter Eich. 2005. 'War and State-Building in Roman Republican Times'. *Scripta Classica Israelica* 24: 1–33.

Galinsky, Karl. 1998. *Augustan Culture. An Interpretive Introduction*. Princeton, NJ: Princeton University Press.

Garnsey, Peter and Richard Saller. 1987. *The Roman Empire. Economy, Society and Culture*. London: Duckworth.

Garnsey, Peter and C. R. Whittaker, eds. 1978. *Imperialism in the Ancient World*. Cambridge: Cambridge University Press.

Goldsworthy, Adrian Keith. 1996. *The Roman Army at War. 100 BC–AD 200*. Oxford: Clarendon Press.

Hopkins, Keith. 2009. 'The Political Economy of the Roman Empire'. In: *Dynamics of Ancient Empires: State Power from Assyria to Byzantium*, ed. Walter Scheidel and Ian Morris, 178–204. Oxford: Oxford University Press.

Itgenshorst, Tanja. 2005. *Tota illa pompa. Der Triumph in der römischen Republik*. Göttingen: Vandenhoeck & Ruprecht.

Kagan, Kimberley. 2006. 'Redefining Roman Grand Strategy'. *The Journal of Military History* 70(2): 333–62.

Luttwak, Edward. 1976. *Grand Strategy of the Roman Empire from the First Century A. D. to the Third*. Baltimore, MD: Johns Hopkins University Press.

Mančić, Emilia. 2015. 'Von der Aeneis bis zu den Nationalepen. Gründungs- und Begründungsnarrative im imperialen und nationalen Kontext'. In: *Narrative im (post)imperialen Kontext. Literarische Identitätsbildung als Potential im regionalen Spannungsfeld zwischen Habsburg und Hoher Pforte in Zentral- und Südosteuropa*, ed. Matthias Schmidt, 37–48. Tübingen: Francke Verlag.

Manthe, Ulrich. 2014. 'Soldaten der Crassus-Armee in China?'. *Gynnasium* 121: 477–92.

Matijević, Krešimir. 2015. 'Der Ebrovertrag und die Verantwortlichkeit für den 2. Punischen Krieg'. *Gymnasium* 122: 435–56.

Mattern, Susan P. 1999. *Rome and the Enemy: Imperial Strategy in the Principate*. Berkeley, CA: University of California Press.

Mattingly, David J. 2011. *Imperialism, Power, and Identity. Experiencing the Roman Empire*. Princeton, NJ: Princeton University Press.

Mommsen, Theodor. 1856: *Römische Geschichte*. Vol. 1. 2. Auflage, Berlin: Weidmann.

Nippel, Wilfried. 1980. *Mischverfassungstheorie und Verfassungsrealität in Antike und früher Neuzeit*. Stuttgart: Klett-Cotta (Geschichte und Gesellschaft: Bochumer Historische Studien, Bd. 21).

Revell, Louise. 2009. *Roman Imperialism and Local Identities*. Cambridge: Cambridge University Press.

Rostovtzeff, Michael I. 1971. *The Social and Economic History of the Roman Empire*. Unter Mitarbeit von Edition revised by P. M. Fraser. 2. Aufl. 2 Bände. Oxford: Clarendon Press.

Rüpke, Jörg. 1995. 'Wege zum Töten, Wege zum Ruhm: Krieg in der römischen Republik'. In: *Töten im Krieg*, ed. Heinrich von Stietencron and Jörg Rüpke, 213–40. Freiburg im Breisgau: K. Alber.

Rüpke, Jörg and Richard Gordon. 2007. *Religion of the Romans*. Cambridge: Polity Press.

Scheidel, Walter. 2009. *Rome and China. Comparative Perspectives on Ancient World Empires*. Oxford: Oxford University Press.

Scheidel, Walter, ed. 2015. *State Power in Ancient China and Rome*. Oxford: Oxford University Press.

Scheidel, Walter. 2015. 'The Monetary Systems of the Han and Roman Empires'. In: *State Power in Ancient China and Rome*, ed. Walter Scheidel, 137–207. Oxford: Oxford University Press.

Scheidel, Walter and Ian Morris, eds. 2009. *Dynamics of Ancient Empires: State Power from Assyria to Byzantium*. Oxford: Oxford University Press.

Schmidt, Matthias, ed. 2015. *Narrative im (post)imperialen Kontext. Literarische Identitätsbildung als Potential im regionalen Spannungsfeld zwischen Habsburg und Hoher Pforte in Zentral- und Südosteuropa*. Tübingen: Francke Verlag.

Schulz, Raimund. 1997. *Herrschaft und Regierung. Roms Regiment in den Provinzen in der Zeit der Republik*. Paderborn: Schöningh.

Stietencron, Heinrich von and Jörg Rüpke, eds. 1995. *Töten im Krieg*. Freiburg im Breisgau: K. Alber.

Syme, Ronald. 1939. *The Roman Revolution*. Oxford: Clarendon Press.

van Wickevoort Crommelin, Bernard Raymond. 1993. *Die Universalgeschichte des Pompeius Trogus. Herculea audacia orbem terrarum adgressus*. Hagen: Verl.- und Buchhandlsges.

Walbank, Frank William et al., eds. 1989–2005. *The Cambridge ancient history, vols. 7-12*, 2nd edn. Cambridge: Cambridge University Press.

Warnking, Pascal. 2015. *Der römische Seehandel in seiner Blütezeit. Rahmenbedingungen, Seerouten, Wirtschaftlichkeit*. Rahden/Westf.: VML, Verlag Marie Leidorf GmbH (Pharos, Band 36).

Welles, C. Bradford. 1934. *Royal Correspondence of the Hellenistic Age: a study in Greek epigraphy*. New Haven, CT: Yale University Press.

Whittaker, C. R. 1994. *Frontiers of the Roman Empire: A Social and Economic Study.* Baltimore, MD: Johns Hopkins University Press.

Whittaker, C. R. 2004. *Rome and Its Frontiers: The Dynamics of Empire.* London: Routledge.

Will, Wolfgang. 1991. *Der römische Mob. Soziale Konflikte in der späten Republik.* Darmstadt: Wiss. Buchges.

Woolf, Greg. 2012. *Rome. An Empire's story.* Oxford: Oxford University Press.

4 The Medieval Roman Empire of the East as a Spatial Phenomenon (300–1204 CE)

Johannes Preiser-Kapeller

This chapter analyses the medieval Roman Empire of the East, commonly known as the 'Byzantine Empire',[1] as a spatial phenomenon in the Eastern Mediterranean and beyond. A particular focus of members of the Vienna School of Byzantine Studies, entire books have been written about this subject; the fundamental long-term project *Tabula imperii Byzantini* (devoted to the historical geography of Byzantium) being a prime example.[2] In this chapter, I discuss some general principles of spatial organisation and perception as can be reconstructed from Byzantine sources as well as the definition and dynamics of frontiers between competing imperial formations in early medieval western Eurasia. The chronological focus is 330–1204[3]; from the inauguration of Constantinople as new capital of the Roman Empire to the Fourth Crusade. After that time, the permanent political fragmentation of the former core sphere of the Byzantine Empire provided a very different spatial framework.[4]

4.1 The Perception and Organisation of Space

4.1.1 Borders and Territories

When estimates of the territorial extent of the medieval Roman Empire are plotted on a graph, a clear downwards trend is evident (Fig. 4.1), seemingly in accord with the image of Byzantium's history as a long and painful decline from the height of the Imperium Romanum as established by Edward Gibbon (1737–94).[5] The

---

[1] On the terms 'Roman' and 'Byzantine' see esp. Stouraitis 2014, 175–220. Throughout the chapter, I use both terms.
[2] Koder 2001; Hunger and Koder 1976–2020 (http://tib.oeaw.ac.at/). A very insightful analysis of the spatial dimensions of Byzantine history is also provided in Whittow 1996, esp. 15–37 on the strategic geography of the Near East.
[3] All dates are CE unless indicated otherwise.
[4] See Prinzing 1992, 129–83; Laiou 2006, 42–53; Preiser-Kapeller 2012a, 69–127.
[5] Gerland 1934; Hunger 1966; Angelov online.

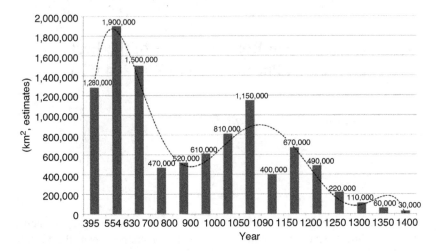

Fig. 4.1 Estimates on the territorial extent of the Byzantine Empire, with a linear trend line, 395–1400 CE. Graph: Johannes Preiser-Kapeller.

Byzantine Empire faced severe crises and dramatic loss of territories in the 7th and 11th centuries (especially to Arab and later Turkish conquest).[6] Periods of territorial expansion were mostly 'reconquista' of former provinces of the empire and therefore, within the imperial ideological framework, always 'bella iusta' for the protection or restoration of the territories of the 'divinely protected Roman Empire'.[7]

Despite the territorial loses, there remained in the 11th century a notion of the (considerable) territorial complex of the medieval Roman Empire in the Eastern Mediterranean ranging from the Danube to the Nile and from the Adriatic Sea to the Euphrates- Emperor Alexios I Komnenos (1081–1118), who restored Byzantine power after its near-collapse in the aftermath of the Battle of Manzikert in 1071 (and the temporary loss of nearly all of Asia Minor), is lauded for the reconstruction of the extent of the empire between the Adriatic Sea in the west and the Euphrates and Tigris Rivers in the east in the historiographical work of his daughter Anna Komnene (Map 4.1); he even would have restored the empire's entire former glory, says Anna, if circumstances had not hindered him. Similar pretensions we find in a treaty between Emperor Alexios I, and the city of Pisa from the year 1111, in which the Pisans

---

[6] For an overview see Brubaker and Haldon 2011; Angold 1997.
[7] See Stouraitis 2009 and Stouraitis 2012, esp. 239–240. On 'just wars' and other elements of imperial thinking see also Hardt and Negri 2000, esp. 7–21.

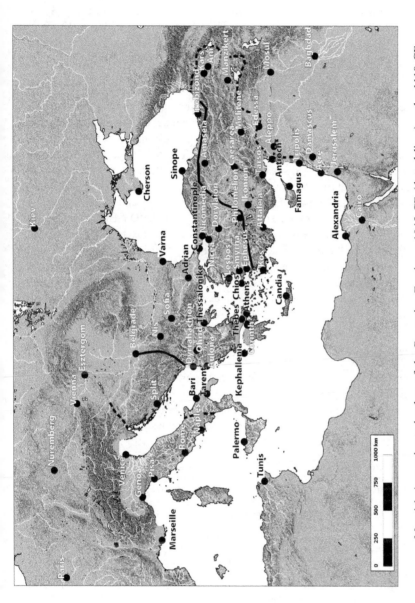

Map 4.1 Approximate borders of the Byzantine Empire, c.1045 CE (dotted lines) and c.1118 CE (continuous lines). Map by Johannes Preiser-Kapeller.

promise never to support an attack on the Byzantine Empire neither within its current nor its future extent; these 'potential' imperial territories include the entire Balkans (starting from Croatia and Dalmatia), Asia Minor, Syria, Palestine and even Egypt, with Alexandria. Such notions of the 'legitimate' extent of the empire and furthermore claims to a universal rule over the oecumene during most of Byzantine history did not match with the actual range of imperial authority and resources.[8]

In many cases, the borders of the empire were neither very secure nor well-defined. The late Roman Empire in the East tried to maintain 'natural' borders between it and the 'barbarians' along the course of the Lower Danube. However, this frontier proved to be the most porous one between the 4th and 7th centuries CE.[9] Later, other topographical features served as approximate frontier and defence zones, such as the Balkan Mountains facing the Bulgarian Khanate or the Taurus Mountains facing the Arab Caliphate.[10] We also encounter attempts to mark (and control) frontiers in the landscape in the absence of such topographic features. One example is the so-called 'Old Bulgarian boundary wall' (now known by its Turkish name, *Erkesija*), most probably erected in the aftermath of the Byzantine–Bulgarian treaty of 815/16, which determined the border between the two empires after a long period of war. In this case, the Bulgarians secured their frontier against the Byzantines over a distance of more than 130 km from the Black Sea coast to the River Maritza with a series of earth walls and ditches.[11]

4.1.2   Mental Maps and Spatial Organisation

In general, the 'maps in the minds' of ancient and medieval authors, their approaches to putting objects in spatial relation to each other, have little connection to modern-day scaled maps.[12] Research on 'mental maps' has illustrated that humans used non-cartographic modes of the imagination and depiction of space for the 'collection, organisation, storing, recalling, and

---

[8]   Anna Komnene VI 11,3: 193, 7–24; Dölger and Wirth 1995, no. 1255; Lilie 2004, 46; Stouraitis 2012, 250–6; Fögen 1993, 49–50; Koder 2002, esp. 20–1 (on the limits of the Roman Oecumene) and 27–31. On the scale and limits of the state's resources see esp. Hendy 1985. For similar concepts in the Ottoman Empire with regard to the Danube frontier for instance see Panaite 2000, 77–9 and 84–6.

[9]   See Curta 2001; Curta 2006, esp. 53–69.   [10]   Angelov, Batsaki and Bazzaz 2013, 4.

[11]   Soustal 1991, 261–2; Whittow 1996, 278. Most of the Erkesija was still visible until the end of the 19th century and was delineated in the maps of a modern project of imperial organisation of space, the 'Franzisco-Josephinische Landesaufnahme' of the Austrian-Hungarian Monarchy (1869–87). For a general overview of such fortification systems in ancient and medieval Eurasia see Spring 2015, 154–5, also on the Erkesija wall and the possible constructions of parts of it already after the Byzantine–Bulgarian treaty of 716. See also Lorge 2008, 59–74; Tackett 2008, 99–138.

[12]   Brodersen 2003, 33–5.

manipulation of information about the spatial environment'. In ancient texts and 'maps' (such as the *Tabula Peutingeriana*, a medieval copy of a late Roman map) we mostly encounter 'topological' representations of the relative position of localities, connected through routes, not their absolute position in space as indicated by coordinates as in modern-day cartography. Points (landmarks) and routes (paths) are essential elements of these spatial concepts, which also could be combined into relatively complex spatial relational systems in order to convey knowledge about the land and how to travel between places.[13] Central to the survey, description or depiction of spaces was the definition and naming of landmarks, which stood out due to their visibility and significance; landmarks could be larger cities, but also sites of religious relevance, for instance. With the indication and naming of such landmarks, 'map drawing and naming of physical features' became 'an act of appropriation', of integrating space within one's cultural framework.[14]

A second important element of 'mental mapping' is the indication of routes, depicted as chains of landmarks; if one followed them in the indicated order, one was on the 'right track'. Thereby the topological structure, the relative position of points to each other was documented. As 'people are supposed to be sensitive to the costs of overcoming distance', sometimes the duration of a journey from one point to the next was indicated. Such information was transmitted in texts (*itineraria*, *periploi*) or in diagrams (such as the *Tabula Peutingeriana* or late medieval portolans). This was the pre-dominant form of the description of spaces until the early modern period: a sequence of landmarks, which were also described, along a route, while spaces between them were seldom characterised in greater detail. Space thus was appropriated as a sum of landmarks, of significant points, whose sequence for a specific purpose was defined in texts and images.[15]

With similar concepts in mind, Byzantine authors also depicted their empire; the 6th century *Synekdemos* of Hierokles from the reign of Emperor Justinian is a register of 923 cities, arranged in the 64 provinces they had been assigned to during the administrative re-organisation under the Emperors Diocletian and Constantine I at the turn of the 4th century CE.[16] An even more impressive example is the *Notitia dignitatum* from the early 5th century CE, a hierarchical

---

[13] Downs and Stea 1977, esp. 6–28 (for the citations); Gould and White 1986, esp. 1–30; Brodersen 2003, 33–5, 44–8, 191; Talbert 2010; see also Strässle 2006, 127–34, for the military strategic implications of such a mode of perception of space.

[14] Downs and Stea 1977, 41–7, 108–19; Gould and White 1986, 12–13; Woodward 1987, esp. 330–5; Brodersen 2003, 111–26.

[15] Downs and Stea 1977, 47–55, 77, 119–44 (for the citations); Campbell 1987, esp. 376–8, 439–46; Ramin 1994, 37, 50–2; Brodersen 2003, 54–8, 94, 165–80; Landwehr 2008, 111, 116–17, 121.

[16] Hierokles. See also http://soltdm.com/sources/mss/hierocl/hierocles.htm. On the spatial organisation of the Empire in the East from the 4th to the 6th centuries see esp. Drakoulis 2010.

list of all civil and military officials for the (then still existing) Western and Eastern halves of the Imperium Romanum. The *Notitia dignitatum* also detailed the provinces and cities each official was responsible for and the units and garrisons each military commander had under their command (both depicted with accompanying graphical visualisations).[17] Similarly, Byzantine officials in the 9th and 10th centuries compiled hierarchical lists (in Greek called *taktikon* from *taxis* – order, arrangement) of the contemporary functionaries, with their respective (geographical) areas of responsibility (and their court rank).[18]

The spatial organisation of the Church, since the 4th century, was likewise based on the late Roman imperial administrative divisions, with a hierarchy of patriarchs (since the 5th century, numbering five: in Rome, Constantinople, Alexandria, Antioch and Jerusalem), metropolitans (for every province) and bishops (for every city). This ecclesiastical hierarchy was understood as mirroring the celestial one and written down in lists (equally called *taxis*) registering the metropolitan sees according to their rank, and below each metropolitan see its suffragan bishoprics, according to their rank within the metropolitan province. Thus, ecclesiastical space was equally organised in lists of landmarks (episcopal sees), which were connected through 'routes' between levels of administrative hierarchy one had to follow in juridicial procedures as in case of an appellation.[19]

4.1.3   Socio-spatial Arrangements Within and Beyond Byzantium

Both the imperial *taktika* of the 9th and 10th centuries and the ecclesiastical lists were more about social relations than geographical connections. They were mainly used to document differences of rank among state and church dignitaries in official encounters at the imperial court or in ecclesiastic assemblies. These differences had a twofold spatial dimension: first, the position of rank allocated to a dignitary partly depended on the relative (strategic, economic or religious) significance of the province or city in his area of responsibility within the framework of the empire or the church. Second, this rank became manifest in the relative spatial proximity of the dignitary to the emperor in court ceremonies or to the patriarch during liturgy.[20] In contrast to the ideal of the stability of the imperial and ecclesiastical order of the world (and maybe also in contrast to the modern image of 'Byzantine' stagnation[21]) the existence of several of these lists (four imperial *taktika* from the years 842 (or 812/813), 899, 934/944 and 971/

---

[17] *Notitia dignitatum*. See also http://members.iinet.net.au/~igmaier/notitia.htm.
[18] *Listes de préséance*.
[19] Notitiae episcopatuum; Selb 1981, 58–9, 118–34, 192–203; Selb 1989, 189–90, 198–200, 211–19, 227–35; Preiser-Kapeller 2008, IX-X, XII-XVIII (with sources).
[20] See Treitinger 1956; Oikonomides 1997, 199–215.   [21] See Said 1978; Angelov online.

975; 21 lists of bishoprics between the 7th and 15th centuries) indicates the dynamics of these socio-spatial arrangements. And even at the time of their compilation these lists were not set in stone; the actual influence and hierarchical position of officials depended on the politics of respective emperors and the strength of their networks of patronage and support.[22]

To a certain degree, within the general ideological framework of imperial domination of the known and habitable world (in Greek *oikoumene*) the relations between the empire and neighbouring polities were also perceived along these lines.[23] Franz Dölger and other scholars have established the notion of a 'family of kings' centred on the Roman/Byzantine emperor as head of the oecumene and *pater familias* of the (lesser) princes of various peoples and regions, whose rank within the world order was expressed in graded termini of kinship with the emperor (son (*teknon*), [younger] brother (*adelphos*) or friend (*philos*), the later terminus for non-Christian rulers).[24] Constellations of fictitious kinship relations had been used since early antiquity (at least since the 14th century BCE, as documented in the Amarna Letters) to symbolise the precedence among rulers; Roman emperors and the Great Kings of Persia (the only neighbouring monarch considered on (more or less) equal 'imperial' level with the emperor in Rome or Constantinople), for example, called each other brothers (see also below).[25] Dölger mainly derived his concept of a 'family of kings' as being something like a foreign-policy 'doctrine' from a list of addressees of the emperor integrated by Constantine VII Porphyrogennetos (913–59) in his compilation on the ceremonies at the imperial court. But this list of addressees is similar to the imperial and ecclesiastical *taktika*; a snap-shot of an attempt at 'book-keeping' the customs of the imperial chancellery at a specific time under specific geo-political circumstances.[26] More stable than actual hierarchies were the underlying principles of socio-spatial arrangements: again, the degree of fictitious kinship allocated to a prince very much depended on the relative significance of his realm in the imperial politics at a specific time (in the list of Constantine VII the highest-ranking 'sons' of the emperor were the most powerful Christian rulers nearest to the imperial borders: the Emperor of Bulgaria, the King of Greater Armenia and the Prince of the Alans in the north-western Caucasus). The rank of these rulers became equally manifest in the relative spatial proximity of their representatives to the emperor in court

---

[22] Listes de préséance; Notitiae episcopatuum; Treitinger 1956.

[23] For a general overview see Shepard 2006, 15–55.

[24] Dölger 1976, 34–69; see also Ostrogorsky 1936, 41–61; Beihammer 2004, esp. 166–7.

[25] Dignas and Winter 2007, 148–9, with n. 149; see Avruch 2000, 154–64; Jönsson 2000, 191–204 (on the Amarna Letters); Schmalzbauer 2004, 408–19; Koder 2002, 15–34.

[26] De Ceremoniis, II 48: 686–92. See also Martin-Hisard 2000; Preiser-Kapeller 2013; Kresten 1993; Beihammer 2004, 166–7.

ceremonies, as Liutprand of Cremona as ambassador of the western Emperor Otto I (936/962–73) had to learn when the envoys of the Bulgarian emperor were allotted places at the table nearer to Emperor Nikephoros II Phokas (963–969) than he was.[27]

The dynamic social framework of spatial arrangements becomes equally visible in another work of Emperor Constantine VII, the so-called 'De administrando imperio', where the 'primary focus is on peoples rather than territories, or peoples as the identifiers of the territories they occupy' (thus following ancient traditions of geography often equalling ethnography[28]). Furthermore, the 'De administrando imperio' serves as advice to his son and successor (Romanos II, 959–63) on which 'nations are useful and dangerous to the empire, and how to use them against each other', thus how to establish and maintain social relations with these peoples and their rulers and how to manipulate them for the benefit of the empire. As Paul Magdalino has analysed, the emphasis on the 'potential for imperial intervention and domination' also very much determined the selection of people and regions described in 'De administrando imperio'. Therefore, for the Balkans one can find longer passages on the Serbs and the Croatians, but little on the much more important and powerful (and therefore less susceptible to Byzantine intervention) Bulgarians. The same holds true for the relatively long chapters on the 'smaller' Armenian princedoms at the eastern frontier in contrast to the still threatening Islamic polities in Iraq, Syria and Egypt. This selective perspective of 'De administrando imperio' has even led some scholars to the assumption that the Byzantine Empire in the time of Constantine VII Porphyrogennetos had renounced the Roman imperial agenda of dominion over the entire habitable world in favour of a 'limited oecumene', especially with regard to the former Roman territories of the Western Mediterranean (which equally feature little in the text). But 'De administrando imperio' should be read (together with other strategic 'handbooks' of the time) more as a another piece of evidence of the pragmatic and dynamic handling of current political and geo-spatial conditions by Byzantine imperial politics, which at least theoretically did not negate the traditional concept of an *imperium sine fine*.[29] When circumstances changed in the second half of the 10th century, for instance, the emperors mobilised enormous military and diplomatic resources to 're-integrate' the (temporarily competing) empire of the Bulgarians into the *Basileia ton Rhomaion*.[30]

---

[27] Liutprand of Cremona, Legatio XVIII–XIX: 185–6. For an English translation: http://legacy .fordham.edu/halsall/source/liudprand1.asp.

[28] De administrando imperii. See Müller 1972/1982.

[29] Kutaba-Deliboria 1993; Magdalino 2013, 23–42; Angelov 2013, 45; Koder 2002 (also on the debate on a 'limited oecumene'); Lounghis 1995, 117–28. For the citation see Virgil, Aeneid I, 278–9.

[30] See Strässle 2006; Shepard 2006, 20–1, also on the ideological implications of the conquest of the Bulgarian Empire.

4.1.4   Authorities, Networks and Peripheries

The spatial extent and the strength of imperial power thus very much depended on the range, quality and quantity of the social networks established, maintained and modified between the imperial centre (the emperor, his entourage and the central administrative apparatus) and the holders of power at the 'periphery' (and from the Byzantine point of view, this periphery started immediately beyond the city walls of Constantinople) across the oecumene.[31] The actual presence and authority of the imperial regime depended on regional socio-economic frameworks as well as topographies and ecologies, and on imperial decisions and strategies regarding how and how much power could or should be exerted. Furthermore, it depended on the basis of a cost–benefit analysis, for example, whether it was worth the effort to try to forcibly integrate independently minded transhumant groups in remote, unproductive and at the same time un-controllable mountain or semi-desert areas (which Byzantium had on both its frontiers in the Near East as well as in core regions within the Balkans or in Anatolia), into the full framework of imperial taxation and administration.[32] And even within the administrative system, various and sometimes competing networks were at work.[33] Yet, such networks were not only limiting imperial power; on the contrast, ties of patronage, spiritual kinship or authority based on religion or ideology could also range far beyond imperial borders. Taking a comparative case, Jonathan Karam Skaff has highlighted that 'patrons, clients, and allies of various ethnicities could engage in informal, mutually acceptable, reciprocal relationships because there were widely shared values and expectations regarding political networking . . . it offered the utilitarian advantage of extending an . . . emperor's power to spaces within a large multi-ethnic empire that were beyond the reach of bureaucratic control'.[34] Through these networks elites from within and beyond the imperial borders were also mobilised for imperial service; statistics on ethno-geographic origins of elite families in the 11th/12th centuries highlight a predominance of individuals from outside the core regions and even from beyond the borders of the empire (especially the Caucasus) in the military, while civil elites were mostly recruited from the core areas and Constantinople itself (do we find similar patterns in other empires?) (Fig. 4.2a and 4.2b).[35]

---

[31] See also Barkey 2008, 9–10, for such a concept of empire.

[32] For such considerations in imperial Rome see James 2011, 144–5; Harris 2016, 114–50. See also Neville 2004 for medieval Byzantium. For the imperial politics towards the inhabitants of the mountainous region of Isauria in south-eastern Asia Minor see for instance Feld 2005. For the Balkans see Stephenson 2000. In general, on such cost–benefit analyses with regard to further imperial expansion see also Menzel 2015, 43 and 63; Münkler 2007. For a definition of core regions of the Byzantine Empire see Koder 2001, 13–19.

[33] Brubaker and Haldon 2011, 724. For a comparative entanglement of administration, spatial organisation and networks in Song China see Mostern 2011, esp. 4–7.

[34] Skaff 2012, 75 and 104.   [35] Kazhdan and Ronchey 1999, 333–338.

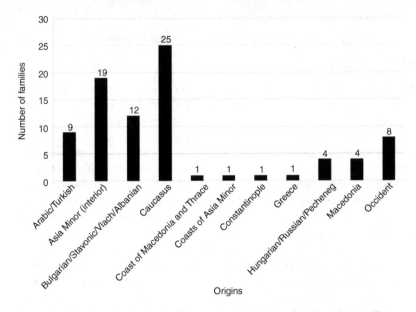

Fig. 4.2a Ethno-geographic origins of eighty-five families of the 'military aristocracy' of Byzantium, 11th–12th centuries. Data: Kazhdan, Alexander and Silvia Ronchey. 1999. *L'aristocrazia bizantina dal principio dell'XI alla fine del XII secolo*. Palermo: Sellerio editore Palermo, 1999. Graph: Johannes Preiser-Kapeller.

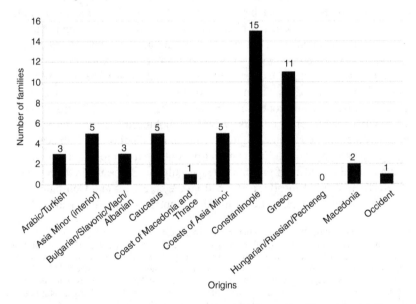

Fig. 4.2b Ethno-geographic origins of fifty-one families of the 'civil aristocracy' of Byzantium, 11th–12th centuries. Data: Kazhdan, Alexander and Silvia Ronchey. 1999. *L'aristocrazia bizantina dal principio dell'XI alla fine del XII secolo*. Palermo: Sellerio editore Palermo, 1999. Graph: Johannes Preiser-Kapeller.

Patterns of service in the army or administration implied wide-ranging mobility in many provinces across the Mediterranean (Map 4.2). Thereby, imperial formations brought about encounters of elites of various ethnic, religious, linguistic and regional backgrounds and worked as 'regimes of entanglements'.[36] Conversely, depending on the scale of the engagement of the imperial centre, elite groups had (more or less) room to negotiate the actual quantity and quality of their integration into the imperial project.[37]

4.1.5   Logistics and Limits of 'Hard Power'

The logistics of empire were another central aspect of spatial organisation in Byzantium, especially with regard to the 'measurement and evaluation of landed resources, the planning and execution of defensive and offensive warfare, the management of communications and supplies, the dispatch and reception of embassies, the gathering of foreign intelligence, the deployment of administrative personnel in the provinces and the frontier areas, and the referral of decisions from the periphery to the center'.[38] Particularly essential were the organisation and maintenance of those lifelines for the 'particular flow of resources and population directed by the imperial center' on which its success and survival depended (what Sam White has called the 'imperial ecology').[39] In this regard the medieval Roman Empire demonstrated a remarkable resilience; even in times of severe crisis, Constantinople was able to mobilise new resources and to establish new lifelines for its purposes. After the loss of Egypt and Syria to the Arabs in the 7th century, for instance, Western Asia Minor (Bithynia, Paphlagonia and the provinces towards the Aegean) as well as North Africa and Sicily stepped in as sources of grain and other supplies for Constantinople (see also Map 4.2).[40] The economic and demographic growth of its territories in south-eastern Europe (especially in Greece) enabled the empire to survive the loss of many of its former core provinces in Asia Minor to the Seljuks and other Turkish groups after a period of internal crisis and the Battle of Manzikert in 1071.[41]

---

[36] For this concept see Schuppert 2014, 28–9: 'As a regime of entanglements can be conceived network structures in which certain structural and habitual circumstances – principles, rules, standards and mutual expectations – allow for the establishment of long-term linkages. In addition to religious and missionary societies also imperial formations (Roman Empire, Ottoman Empire, Mughal Empire) are examples of regimes of entanglements where religions and ethnicities, as well as certain functionaries interact.'

[37] See also Maier 2007, 21–31.   [38] Magdalino 2013, 25.

[39] For the concept of imperial ecology and an analysis of the circuits of the imperial metabolism centred on Constantinople in the Ottoman period see White 2011, esp. 16–51 (17 for the citation).

[40] Howard-Johnston 1995, 136–137; Brubaker and Haldon 2011, 563. On Sicily see Vaccaro 2013, 34–69. On the significance of the regions of Western Asia Minor see also Whittow 1996, 31–33.

[41] Preiser-Kapeller 2015b.

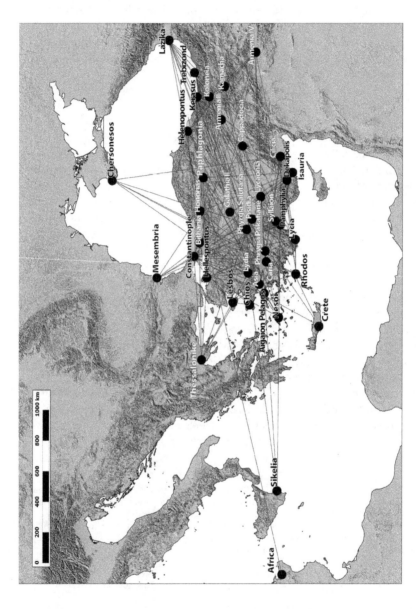

Map 4.2 Network model of the connections between provinces of the Byzantine Empire due to activities of the *genikoi kommerkiarioi* (economic administrators), 673–728 CE. Map by Johannes Preiser-Kapeller.

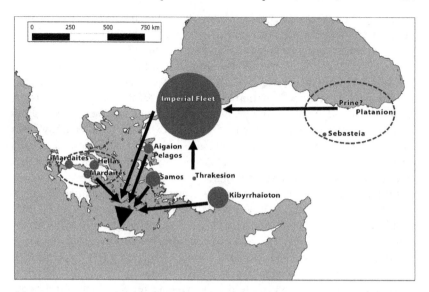

Map 4.3 Mobilisation of Byzantine troops for the expedition against Crete, 911 CE. Map by Johannes Preiser-Kapeller.

We can re-construct to a certain degree the workings of this system in the 10th century, when Byzantium's armies were increasingly successful, on the basis of two relatively detailed lists of the manpower and resources mobilised for two expeditions against the Arab-ruled island of Crete in the years 911 and 949 (both ultimately a failure); these texts were integrated into Constantine VII's Book of Ceremonies (ch. 44 and 45 of book II). For the first campaign in 911, a total of 47,127 soldiers and seamen and more than 130 ships were mobilised, mostly from the central troops and fleet in Constantinople (including 700 Rus mercenaries), but also from the provinces on both sides of the Aegean and even from north-eastern Anatolia (especially Armenian mercenaries), from where they were transported to the capital over the Black Sea. In addition, an enormous volume of weapons, goods and supplies was prepared in various provinces adjacent to the theatre of war in Western Asia Minor and Greece (Map 4.3).[42] Logistics were facilitated by the usage of maritime transport; despite the immense costs of fleet building and maintenance, the potential range of maritime military expeditions across the Mediterranean was generally larger than for terrestrial campaigns (on average, fleets could cover a distance of 100 km per day; still, larger operations demanded regular landfalls to take on supplies,

---

[42] Haldon 2000, esp. 210 and 247–252. See also Haldon 1997, 111–151.

especially of drinking water); this mobility allowed for the re-conquest of central areas of the Western Mediterranean in the reign of Justinian I (527–65), for instance, or maritime expeditions to Egypt still in the 12th century.[43]

We also have official documents from the 10th century, especially for campaigns in Asia Minor, for expeditions on land, where Byzantium was heir to the road system of the Imperium Romanum. In order to facilitate provision, troops mobilised at various points, marched separately and met the core army of the emperor at previously prepared, often permanently installed army bases (*aplekton*); at these bases supplies were also collected and prepared following advance orders from Constantinople. According to the sources, such camps were installed at least in a distance of 400 km between each other, since troops could be expected to carry with them (on pack animals) supplies for up to twenty days and to march on average 20 km a day (as we also know from Roman and modern-day manuals on the infantry). John Haldon has calculated that for a period of three weeks an army of 15,000 men (a considerable force in the 10th century) needed at least 290,000 kg of supplies. The preparation of such large amounts of supplies was certainly a challenge within the provinces of the empire, especially in less fertile and passable regions, such as in Eastern Anatolia.[44] These calculations confirm the range of military operations beyond the borders and supply bases of the empire and are also confirmed by similar analyses for the Ottoman Empire. Its military arm in the 16th and 17th centuries ranged from Constantinople to the Carpathian basin in the west (distance Istanbul–Budapest 1,073 km) and to north-western Iran in the east (distance Istanbul–Tabriz 1,522 km), but normally not much beyond, similar to Byzantium in the 6th and 7th centuries.[45] Also the recent calculations of Walter Scheidel and his team of the Orbis-project on the costs in terms of time and money for transport both on sea and on land in the Roman Empire confirm these numbers; in their model, Alexandria in Egypt was 'nearer' to the imperial centre (1,088 km as the bird flies) from a logistical point of view than places 300 km inland from Constantinople in the Balkans or in Anatolia.[46] Accordingly, Alexandria was regarded as located within the 'natural' borders of the empire even in the 12th century (see above) more than 400 years after its loss to the Arabs.

---

[43] Haldon 2000, 301; Pryor 1992; Pryor and Jeffreys 2006, esp. 7–122 on the 'operational context' of maritime warfare up to 1204; Decker 2013, 180–191. For the main sea routes of the Byzantine Empire see Koder 2001, 70–73; Kislinger 2010.

[44] See also Haldon 2006; Strässle 2006, 141–3, 336–50. On the road system and its development in Byzantine times see Koder 2001, 65–70.

[45] Murphey 1999, esp. 20–5 and 65–103; see also Luttwak 2009; Decker 2013, 98–103. See also Whittow 1996, 317, on the campaigns of John Kurkuas in Armenia in 927 and 928 which led him up to 500 km from the nearest imperial territory.

[46] Scheidel 2014.

4.2 The Definition of Imperial Spheres and Frontiers Between Empires

4.2.1 The 'Christian Oecumene' and 'Byzantine Commonwealths'

Beyond the limits of its 'hard' power, the 'appeal' of Byzantium reached widely via diplomatic and also commercial activities and the diffusion of objects communicating imperial glory (silk garments or gold coins with the image of the emperor, for instance) across entire Afro-Eurasia (Map 4.4).[47] In the empire's more immediate neighbourhood this potential was closely connected with the emperor's role as God-installed patron of the universal Christian church as established since Constantine the Great.[48] This 'Christian oecumene' expanded from the 4th to the 6th centuries into Armenia, Georgia, Caucasian Albania, Axum (modern-day Ethiopia) or Nubia, often with active support from the empire (Map 4.4).[49] Yet this universality was challenged especially during the 5th to 7th centuries, when the debate on the relationship between divine and human nature in Jesus Christ led to the emergence of ecclesiastical communities distinct from the imperial 'orthodox' mainstream especially in the richest provinces in the east (Syria, Egypt) and in Armenia. But in contrast to the texts of various zealots on both sides, we have ample evidence that even after the loss of all these territories to the Arabs in the 7th century, Christians beyond the frontiers of the empire were still referring to the emperor in Constantinople as most important Christian ruler on earth. The communities still in dogmatic agreement with the Byzantine Church were even called the followers of the emperor (or 'king' = Arabic *malik*; the 'Melkites'). Garth Fowden (in a development of earlier concepts of Dimiter Obolensky, see below) proposed to call this 'group of politically discrete but related' communities and polities (from Axum in East Africa to the Caucasus) with a 'shared culture and history' a 'Commonwealth', in which Byzantium served as model of a Christian polity and as attractor and propagator of Christian learning; this includes elements of 'soft power', which could compensate for a lack of 'hard power' (in terms of military or economic muscle). But while Fowden marks the end of this 'First Byzantine Commonwealth' with the Arab conquests of the 7th century, the appeal of the Christian Roman Empire beyond the new borders in

---

[47] See for instance Canepa 2010b, 121–54; Cutler 2001, 247–78; Daim 2001, 143–88; Jacoby 2004, 197–240; Walker 2012; Preiser-Kapeller 2018. On the prestige connected to the quality of the Byzantine gold coins ('nomisma') up to the 11th century, when a severe debasement occurred see Hendy 1985, esp. 506–10; Morrison 2002, esp. 931–3; Caplanis 2003, 768–801.

[48] See Dagron 2003; Höfert 2015.

[49] See for instance Seland 2012, 72–86; Signes Codoñer 2014, 116–63, also on the significance of the emergence of 'Christian' alphabets and Christian literatures among the peoples in this sphere.

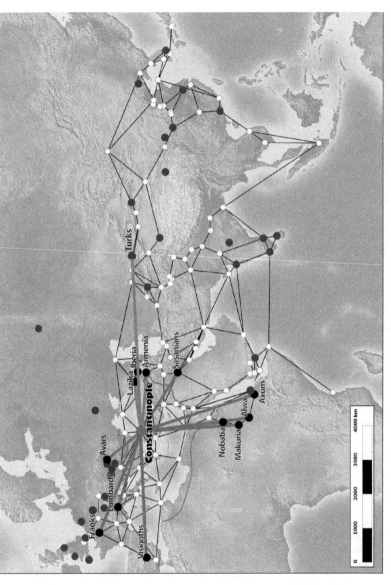

Map 4.4 The Byzantine Empire, c.600 CE (borders: regular grey lines), in a global perspective: in black letters addressees of diplomatic embassies in the second half of the 6th century CE (also indicated with bold grey lines); black dots: selected find spots of objects of Byzantine provenience, 5th–6th centuries CE; black lines: important long distance routes between cities (white dots) across Afro-Eurasia. Map by Johannes Preiser-Kapeller.

the Near East may allow us to claim its continued existence, although Byzantium lost its political hegemony within this sphere.[50]

Imperial politics and missionary work led to the establishment of other groups of Christian people of Byzantine tradition especially in the Slavic world of south-eastern and eastern Europe from the 9th century onwards. Despite all political conflicts (such as that between Byzantium and Bulgaria, for instance) they maintained strong spiritual and ideological connections to the political and ecclesiastical centre in Constantinople. D. Obolensky has called this new emerging sphere of impact and influence the 'Byzantine Commonwealth', which in Fowden's interpretation would be the 'Second'.[51] In any case, in later centuries the reference to these peoples and territories under the spiritual (and partly also still political) guidance of emperor and patriarch served as a proof for the 'ecumenical' importance of the imperial person (in compensation for the shrinking territorial extent of full imperial power) also in the confrontation with the papacy and the renewed Roman Empire in the west. 'Soft power' thus had replaced 'hard power', although the almost total lack of the latter affected also the efficiency of the former (as the often cited example of the removal of the name of the Byzantine emperor from commemoration in the liturgy by Great Prince Vasilij I of Moscow in 1393, when the fall of Constantinople to the Ottomans loomed, illustrates). Finally, from this circle of Byzantium's sphere of influence would also emerge an empire somehow considering itself the legitimate successor of the Christian New Rome: the Russian tsardom.[52]

After the deposition of the last Roman emperor, Romulus Augustulus, in Italy in 476 CE by the Germanic general Odoacer, also the western territories of the Imperium Romanum theoretically fell under the authority of the remaining emperor in Constantinople; this was formally acknowledged by Odoacer himself and other rulers of the emerging new kingdoms.[53] With the 're-conquest' under Emperor Justinian in the 530s–550s, Italy, North Africa and southern Spain came under actual control of the empire once more. Although large parts of Italy were lost to the Lombards soon after Justinian's death (565) and North Africa in its entirety to the Arabs in the late 7th century, Byzantium's presence

[50] For an overview see Wood 2015, 23–50; Papaconstantinou 2008, esp. 143 ('for most of the conquered Christians still the legitimate political entity, the centre out there with which they had not entirely severed their mental bonds'). For the concepts of Commonwealth see Fowden 1994; Signes Codoñer 2014, 116–63; Shepard 2006. On the significance of 'soft power' and concepts of hegemony see Menzel 2015, 51–4, 58–9.

[51] Obolensky 2000; Shepard 2006, 17–28 (speaking about Byzantium's 'First Circle'); Fowden 1994; Signes Codoñer 2014.

[52] Shepard 2006; Preiser-Kapeller 2013. On the affair of the commemoration of the emperor in Moscow see Miklosisch and Müller II, 191, no. 447; Darrouzès 1979, no. 2931; Meyendorff 1989, 254–257. On the actual complexity of the development of imperial concepts in Moscow see Ostrowski 1999, and Ostrowski 2004, 170–179.

[53] Lounghis 1980; Shepard 2006, 40–53.

in Italy (Ravenna, Rome, Naples, Sicily and Venice) remained strong. Equally, until the 8th century the emperor remained the highest-ranking political point of reference both for the pope in Rome and the Christian kings of the west (a further 'Byzantine Commonwealth', maybe).[54] Only with the loss of Ravenna and control of Rome in the mid-8th century and the rise of Frankish power under the Carolingians, Byzantium's position in the west was significantly weakened and finally challenged in an unprecedented way with the coronation of Charlemagne as Emperor of the Romans by Pope Leo III in 800 (Map 4.5).[55] Constantinople sometimes (and pragmatically) was prepared to accept the use of the imperial title as personal rank attribute by Charlemagne and succeeding 'emperors' in the west on the basis of their significant power as rulers over several peoples (as later in the case of Simeon of Bulgaria (893–927)).[56] However, it was beyond the pale to accept them as 'Emperor of the Romans' at an equal level to the emperor in Constantinople and with the same share in the management of the Christian oecumene.[57] Relying on the same Roman–Christian traditions,[58] the ideological conflict between the Roman emperors in Constantinople and their counterparts in the 'Holy Roman Empire' of the west simmered until the very end of Byzantium (and even beyond).[59] It was even more intensified when disputes over jurisdictional spheres (in southern Italy and south-eastern and Central Europe) as well as dogmatic issues between the papacy and the Byzantine Church led to an increasing alienation, culminating in the so-called 'Schism of 1054' (which had less definite character for the contemporaries than for later commentators) and especially in the conquest of Constantinople in 1204 by the army of the Fourth Crusade.[60]

4.2.2   'The Two Eyes of the Earth': Diplomacy and Confrontation Between Rome and Persia

In contrast to the non-recognition of the 're-vitalised' empire in the west, we have several examples that at least some members of the Roman/Byzantine elites were prepared to perceive their imperial rivals to the east as empires on an (more or less) equal footing. Already in the 1st century CE, Tacitus referred to the Iranian Empire of the Parthians as second 'maximum imperium' and

[54] Noble 1984; Ekonomou 2007; Gantner 2014.
[55] Norden 1903; Classen 1985; Fried 2014, 462–95 and 508–16, also on Charlemagne's exchange of embassies with the Caliphate.
[56] Nerlich 1999.   [57] De administrando imperii c. 26, lns. 5–8: 108–9; Nerlich 1999.
[58] See Folz 1953; Goetz 1991, 851–3.
[59] Lilie 1985, 219–43; Kresten 1993. On the continuation of these disputes into the Ottoman period see for instance Köhbach 1992, 223–34.
[60] Bayer 2002; Chadwick 2003; Kolbaba 2000; Shepard 2006, 49–53; Shepard 1988. See also Hunger 1987; Kislinger 2008; Koder 1987, 191–201.

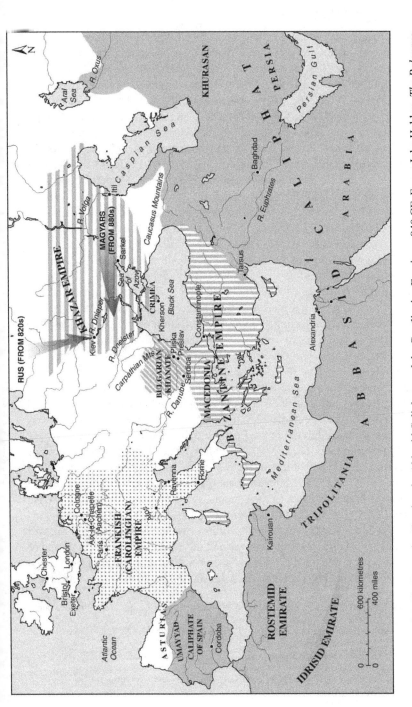

Map 4.5 The Byzantine Empire, the Abbasid Caliphate and the Carolingian Empire, c.840 CE. From: John Haldon, *The Palgrave Atlas of Byzantine History*. Basingstoke: Palgrave Macmillan 2005; free download [open access] from: https://teamweb.uni-mainz.de/fb07/kartenprojekt/SitePages/Homepage.aspx.

Flavius Josephus wrote about the 'two greatest dominions under the sun'.[61] Later authors developed this into a model of of these two empires' special responsibility for the maintenance of the order of the world. The 6th-century author Petros Patrikios has a Persian ambassador on the occasion of the Roman–Persian peace negotiations in 299 say: 'It is obvious for all mankind that the Roman and the Persian Empires are just like two lamps; and it is necessary that, like eyes, the one is brightened by the light of the other and that they do not angrily strive for each other's destruction.'[62] Theophylaktos Simokattes (7th century) transmits the following passage from a letter of the Sasanian Great King Xusrō II to Emperor Maurikios (dated to the year 589): 'God saw to it that the whole world would be lit up from above and from the beginning by two eyes, namely by the most powerful Roman Empire and by the wisest rulers of the Persian state. For by these greatest powers the disobedient and bellicose nations are winnowed, and man's way of life is well ordered and always guided.' And the Great King's ambassadors added: 'For one power alone is not able to shoulder the immense burden of taking care of the organisation of the universe and one man's pulse is not able to steer everything created under the sun.'[63] Interestingly enough, both authors put these ideas into the mouths of representatives of the Persian Empire, as if it were more acceptable to hear such potentially disturbing thoughts about a co-existence of the two empires from outside the empires themselves.

Furthermore, until the late Byzantine period, the emperors formally did not conclude treaties on equal footing, but only granted privileges to groups and individuals who had petitioned for it.[64] Yet de facto, we encounter various agreements between the empire and Persia and formal peace treaties after longer periods of war in 299, 363, 532, 562, 591 and 629 CE. In these cases, envoys of both parties tried to define the respective spheres of influence, especially with regard to points of strategic relevance and the suzerainty over 'lesser' polities in between the two empires (such as Armenia, Iberia (Eastern Georgia) or Lazika (Western Georgia)), but not in the form of a clearly demarcated borderline.[65] Again, the focus was on landmarks and places which allowed for control over surrounding territories and especially also of the movements of resources and of people to be imposed; an agreement of the year 408/9 CE, for instance, limited trade at the Roman–Persian border to Artaxata (the capital of Persian Armenia)

---

[61] For the limits of Roman expansion towards the Parthian and later Sasanian realm see also James 2011, 141–3 and 204–11; Isaac 2000; Harris 2016, 114–33, 143–7.

[62] Peter the Patrician, fragment 13–14 (trans. Dignas and Winter 2007, 122–3). On these concepts see now esp. Canepa 2010a.

[63] Theophylact Simocatta iv.11.2–4 and iv.13.7 (trans. Dignas and Winter 2007, 238–9).

[64] Treitinger 1956, 211–12; Laiou 2002, esp. 358.

[65] Güterbock 1906; Dodgeon and Lieu 1991, 133–4; Greatrex and Lieu 2002, 1–9, 21–30, 96–7, 131–4, 174–5 and 226–8; Dignas and Winter 2007, 118–51.

as well as to the cities of Nisibis and Kallinikon (in Mesopotamia).[66] But actually the border between the two empires was often quite permeable. The ideal of co-existence also implicated (especially Persian) requests for mutual support in the establishment and maintenance of fortified frontiers towards the 'the disobedient and bellicose nations' in the Caucasus region, which would have been in the interest of both polities (and the world order they had to sustain).[67]

4.2.3 The Emergence of a New Frontier Between Empires: Byzantium and the Caliphate

In the long term, the ideal of co-operation between the two empires proved not very potent: after a period of détente in the 5th century, Byzantine–Persian warfare intensified again in the 6th century and culminated in two long wars (570–91 and 602–28) which left both empires significantly weakened. In their aftermath, the emerging Islamic Arab Caliphate between 632 and 651 was able to deprive the Byzantine Empire of its richest provinces in Syria and Egypt and to conquer the Sasanian Empire in its entirety (Map 4.5). While Arab forces conquered Syria and Palestine within a few years, they could not permanently occupy the Byzantine territories to the north of the Taurus Mountains (above 3,000 m) in Asia Minor. During the second half of the 7th century, the Byzantine empire re-located its remaining field armies into these provinces, where they were able to establish an increasingly effective system of fortifications and defence.[68] These limits to Arab expansion were also grounded in topographical and ecological differences; the interior of Anatolia is character-ised by a continental climate with hot and arid summers and cold winters, which proved an obstacle for permanent Arab occupation. As Amr ibn Bahr al-Jahiz (d. 868) recorded, the camels that the Arab troops used as their most important pack animals suffered from the cold in the 'land of the Romans' and died, in contrast to other breeds of camels from Anatolia and later imported by the Turks from Central Asia in the 11th century.[69]

---

[66] Codex Justinianus 4, 63, 4 (ed. Krueger); Dignas and Winter 2007, 204–7. For similar percep-tions of inter-imperial frontiers in China see Tackett 2008.

[67] In his book 'On the buildings', the 6th-century historian Procopius describes the usual perme-ability of the Roman-Persian border in Armenia: Proc., De aed. III, 3, 3, 9–12 (ed. Dewing); trans. Dignas and Winter 2007, 208. For the shared interest in the protection of the Caucasus frontier see Dignas and Winter 2007, 188–195; Greatrex and Lieu 2002, 56–59.

[68] Lilie 1976; Whittow 1996, 175–81 (especially also on strategy and tactics); Brubaker and Haldon 2011, 551–4; Izdebski 2013; Asa Eger 2015, esp. 257–63 on the economic resources of the Byzantine borderlands; Stouraitis 2012, 256–8, on the broader strategic considerations of the imperial centre in this period.

[69] Bulliet 1990, 231–4; Bulliet 2009. On the logistics of Arab armies see also Kennedy 2001, 85–8, 104–7. For considerations on limits to Steppe warfare in the more humid areas of Central Europe, the Balkans or Asia Minor (due to effects on the effectivity of composite bows and archery) see Bowlus 2006, 27–36.

Along the Byzantine–Arab frontier in the 7th and 8th centuries there emerged a zone of deserted and weakly populated 'no-man's-land', which should have impeded the advance of larger armies, especially of the Arabs towards Byzantine territory.[70] The Arabs did not succeed in permanent conquest beyond this zone, neither under the Caliphate of the Umayyads (661–750), which twice attempted to capture Constantinople, nor under the succeeding dynasty of the Abbasids (from 750 onwards), whose most prominent members campaigned in person against the Romans.[71] Yet until the 10th century, at least on a small scale, warfare across these frontier – called *al-thugūr* (the 'openings' or 'rifts' after the passes over the Taurus Mountains) in Arabic and *akra* (the 'tops', the 'extreme borders') in Byzantine sources – was almost permanent, with annual raids from frontier bases (*ribat*) by troops of the caliphate, augmented with voluntary fighters in the name of Allah, into the Byzantine territories.[72] In the emerging classical Islamic law, a permanent peace with a non-Muslim polity was not envisaged; but temporary truces in the interest of the *umma* (the Islamic community of believers) were possible.[73] Such short-term agreements served to organise the exchanges of captives, which took place regularly between the 8th and 10th centuries at the River Lamos in Cilicia, where sometimes several thousands of people crossed the frontier in either direction.[74] Furthermore, there was frequent diplomatic exchange between Constantinople and Damascus, later Baghdad, dealing with the payments of tribute or the exchange of presents or craftsmen. And, as between Byzantium and Persia, elaborate and competing ceremonials for the reception of and communication with envoys of the other imperial power developed.[75] We find rarely details on territorial delimitations of spheres of influence as negotiated between the Romans and Persians. Under the specific circumstances of interior unrest in the Caliphate, in 686/7 Emperor Justinian II and Caliph Abd al-Malik agreed upon a division of the revenues of Armenia, Iberia (Eastern Georgia) and Cyprus; however Justinian II breached the treaty shortly afterwards with a campaign into the Caucasus region and the deportation of population from Cyprus, which for a longer period had the special status of a 'condominium' or 'middle ground' between the two empires.[76] On

---

[70] A Syrian Chronicle from the year 775 describes the formation of this zone on the occasion of an Arab assault in 716/17: Chronicon ad annum Christi 1234, 156–7; Palmer, Brock and Hoyland 1993, 62.

[71] See also El-Cheikh 2004, 91–2.

[72] Haldon and Kennedy 1980, 79–116; Asa Eger 2015, esp. 246–3 on the Byzantine side of the borderlands.

[73] Bonner 2004; Panaite 2000; Rohe 2009, 147–53.   [74] Campagnolo-Pothitou 1995.

[75] Kaplony 1996; Walker 2012; Beihammer 2004, esp. 173–89; El-Cheikh 2004, 83–111, 152–62; Shepard 2006, 30–5.

[76] Dölger, Müller, Preiser-Kapeller and Riehle 2009, no. 253a; Beihammer 2000, no. 295. On Cyprus see now Zavagno 2013.

other occasions (similar to Roman–Persian treaties), specific fortresses in the frontier regions are mentioned as objects of exchange or destruction.[77]

4.2.4 Co-existence or Annihilation – Ideas and Practices Between Competing Imperial Monotheisms[78]

Byzantine power, benefiting from the fragmentation of political power in the caliphate (whose universal power over the Islamic *umma* was also replaced by something like an 'Islamic Commonwealth'[79]), re-expanded into Cilicia, northern Syria and Mesopotamia, and Cyprus in the second half of the 10th century (see Map 4.1).[80] When the immediate threat of annihilation had disappeared, the older notions of co-existence between the two empires were reanimated; using metaphors very similar to the authors of the 6th and 7th centuries, Patriarch Nikolaos I Mystikos of Constantinople in 913/14 wrote to the Abbasid Caliph al-Muqtadir in Baghdad: 'I mean, that there are two lordships, that of the Saracens and that of the Romans, which stand above all lordship on earth, and shine out like the two mighty beacons in the firmament. They ought, for this very reason alone, to be in contact and brotherhood and not, because we differ in our lives and habits and religion, remain alien in all ways to each other.'[81] And equally following the practice of diplomatic exchange between Rome and Persia, Patriarch Nikolaos I called the emperor and the caliph 'brothers superior to and preferred above their brethren, and entrusted with the administration of the greatest rules and authorities'.[82] In the addresses to foreign potentates collected in the 'Book of Ceremonies' at a slightly later time, however, we find metaphors of kinship applied exclusively to rulers of Christian belief, while Muslim potentates are only called 'friends' of the emperor.[83] Yet beyond the immediate Christian oecumene, 'a Sasanian "King of kings" (or an Arab "Caliph of the Prophet Mohammed" and "Commander of the Believers" of Islam) could be acknowledged and respected by a Roman emperor as a much honoured equal, and this status was not 'a threat to the universal claims of the world power Rome'[84] as was another self-styled emperor of the Romans in the west. There was no

---

[77] See Dölger, Müller, Preiser-Kapeller and Riehle 2009, no. 368b (a. 806), 425 (a. 831), 430 (a. 833), 434–5 (a. 838). See also Asa Eger 2015.
[78] For this term see Höfert 2015.   [79] Fowden 1994.
[80] See Felix 1981; McGeer 1995; Krsmanović 2008; Miotto 2008. For the ideological background and legitimation of this 'Reconquista' see Stouraitis 2012, 263–4.
[81] Nicholas I, Letter I: 2, lines 16–21 and 3 (trans.); Beihammer 2004, 164–5. From the Arab literature one gets the impression that some Caliphs considered themselves the heirs and replacement of all world empires such as Rome, Persia, the Turkic Khaganate, China or India, see El-Cheikh 2004, 85–86.
[82] Nicholas I, Letter I: 2, lines 14–15 and 3 (trans.); Shepard 2006, 33.
[83] Beihammer 2004 170–1. See also Beihammer 2002, 1–34.
[84] Dignas and Winter 2007, 241; see also Papaconstantinou 2005, 167–81.

room for a 'third eye of the earth', especially not within the Christian oecumene (Map 4.5).[85]

Besides the re-appearing concept of co-existence between the two empires, however, also ideas of mutual annihilation were still present. The empire of the Romans received 'a unique place in Islamic demonology, and its conquest was considered a final step towards a realisation of the promise given to the Prophet Muhammad that all mankind would be integrated into the *umma* of the Islam'.[86] Also the Christian empire expected a unification of humanity under the sign of the cross; the empire was equated with the chosen people, Constantinople became not only the New Rome, but since the beginning of the 6th century also the New Jerusalem.[87] Within the Byzantine *Reichseschatologie*, as Podskalsky has called it, the Roman Empire was normally identified with the *katechon*, 'the withholding power' from the second Letter to the Thessalonians (2 Thess 2, 7); accordingly, the Imperium Romanum would be the only empire which would exist until the Last Judgement. As it became clear that for the time being Constantinople and the empire would not fall into the hands of the Muslims, this interpretation again became popular, as can be seen in the Apocalypse of Pseudo-Methodius, composed in Syriac in the last decade of the 7th century. Here the apocalyptic interpretation of the empire was combined with the hope that a Roman emperor from the west ('the King of the Greeks') would defeat the Muslims and liberate the Christians of the east.[88]

When Roman armies actually were on advance in the east again, Emperor Nikephoros II Phokas in 966/7 in a letter threatened the Abbasid Caliph in Baghdad not only to re-conquer all former Roman territories in Syria and Egypt, but also to capture Baghdad and to devastate the Arab peninsula including Mecca up to Yemen in order to 'propagate everywhere the religion of the cross'. The authenticity of this text is controversial, but if the emperor sent a message along these lines, he maybe was reflecting these earlier apocalyptic expectations (in a time, when the year 1000 after the birth of Christ was near).[89]

---

[85] See Fried 2014, 462–95 and 508–16, on Charlemagne's exchange of embassies with the Caliphate, which may hint at an attempt of compete with Constantinople for the position of the 'Christian' eye of the earth, see also McCormick 2011.

[86] El-Cheikh 2004, 60–71; Shepard 2006, 31 (for the citation); Papaconstantinou 2008, 141–2.

[87] See Dagron 2003, 4 and 97; Magdalino 2003, esp. 243 and 255, also on the 'apocalyptic' relevance of Constantinople. See also Külzer 2000, 51–76.

[88] Pseudo-Methodius. See in general Podskalsky 1972, esp. 4–76; Reinink 2002, esp. 82–3; On the Ps.-Methodius apocalypse see: Möhring 2000, 58–92 (also on the circumstances of the genesis of the Ps.-Methodius apocalypse); Magdalino 2003, 240 and 253; Brandes 2007, 72–3, 81; Hoyland 1997, 263–67, 294–99; Heilo 2016.

[89] Dölger, Müller and Beihammer 2003, no. 707i. See also El-Cheikh 2004, 173–178, also for Arab reactions; Magdalino 2003; Stouraitis 2012, 241. See also Whittow 1996, 356–357, for a similar propagandistic letter of Nikephoros II Phokas' successor John I Tzimiskes sent to the

Yet despite phantasies of annihilation, Nikephoros II Phokas (often depicted as a grim crusader and as an exception of the usual Byzantine refusal of any notion of 'holy war')[90] followed more pragmatic traditions of politics when circumstances made it necessary: around the same time in 967, a Byzantine fleet was defeated by an Arab one near Sicily. In order to stabilise the front there, the emperor had to sue for a peace treaty with the (Shiite-Ismailite) Fatimid Caliph al-Mu'izz (whose claim on the caliphate denied the rights of the Sunni Abbasid Caliph in Baghdad), who at that time ruled over North Africa. With his embassy, Nikephoros II sent a sword, which allegedly had been owned by the Prophet Mohammed, thus suggesting that he was prepared to acknowledge the supreme leadership of al-Mu'izz over the Islamic *umma* – and providing an advantageous entry for his envoys at the Fatimid court.[91]

The Fatimids became even more important neighbours when in 969 their troops conquered Egypt and they re-located their residence to the Nile, where Cairo was founded as new imperial capital. In their further advance towards the east, Fatimid troops also clashed with Byzantine ones in Syria, but despite several conflicts a détente was established (also since the Fatimids were more interested in eliminating the competing Abbasid Caliphate in Baghdad). Again, the Byzantines were prepared to accept the superiority of the Fatimid claim within the Islamic oecumene in symbolic terms; in a peace treaty in 988 it was stipulated that in the mosque in Constantinople the name of the Fatimid caliph (al-'Azīz, 975–96) should be mentioned during the Friday prayer instead of the name of the Abbasid caliph (as had been the case until then). The existence of this mosque (whose beginnings can be traced back to the aftermath of the Arab siege of 717/18) within the capital of the Christian empire was based on the principle of reciprocity, as became evident when the Fatimid Caliph al-Hākim, (996–1021) in 1009 decreed the destruction of several churches, among these the Church of the Holy Sepulchre in Jerusalem, and several measures against the Christian (and Jewish) communities. In return, the mosque in Constantinople was closed down. Only in 1027, when a new treaty was closed between the successor of al-Hākim, az-Zāhir, and Emperor Constantine VIII (1025–8), the mosque was re-opened in return for the reconstruction of the Church of the Holy Sepulchre and the permission for those Christian who compulsory had converted to Islam to return to their former faith.[92]

Armenian King Ašot III which aimed at a mobilisation of the Christian rulers of the Near East for warfare against the Muslims.

[90] See Stouraitis 2012, 241–50, who comes to the conclusion: 'The notion of a "holy war" against infidel enemies for the promotion of religion remained a rival idea with the Byzantine imperial state's ruling ideology, the resonance of which was rather marginal and confined to small groups or individuals in certain periods.'

[91] Dölger, Müller and Beihammer 2003, no. 501 a. See Beihammer 2004, 185.

[92] Reinert 1998, 125–50; Anderson 2009, 86–113; El-Cheikh 2004, 64.

166   *Johannes Preiser-Kapeller*

The Friday prayer in Constantinople continued in the name of the Fatimid caliph until 1055/6, when the Seljuqs captured Baghdad and destroyed the geo-political equilibrium between Byzantium and the Fatimids to the disadvantage of both established powers and thus initiated a period of much higher fragmentation of the former imperial spheres both in the Byzantine and the Islamic world.[93] But until that time, a co-existence between the imperial monotheisms of the 'abode of Islam' and the 'Christian oecumene' as well as between mosques and churches in the imperial centres was possible both in ideological and practical terms without doing (too much) damage to claims of universal rule in the respective spheres.

4.3   Conclusions and Comparative Questions

Elites in Constantinople considered their state as an uninterrupted Roman Empire. Nonetheless, the geo-political and socio-economic challenges of the 6th to 8th centuries necessitated a considerable reconfiguration of core elements of the imperial framework. Among these was a considerable reduction of the territorial extent of the empire shortly after the campaigns of Emperor Justinian I had suggested the possibility of a complete restoration of the Roman oecumene around the entire Mediterranean. The spatial dynamics of Byzantium were mostly not characterised by expansion, but by preservation, contraction and maybe eventual re-conquest (see Fig. 4.1).[94] In general one can observe:

that the political discourse of the notional limits of the broader Roman Oecumene ...
was not intended to provide real political limits and aims, but rather to function as an
ethically and politically legitimizing point of reference of the ruling élite's ... geopolit-
ically realistic aims within the framework of the continuation of the Roman imperial
culture. These realistic aims were constrained and defined through domestic and foreign
socio-political conditions as well as practical-strategic aspects (space, time, resources)
which made the waging of continuous warfare for the re-conquest of the whole former
Roman world practically impossible.[95]

Accordingly, scholarship considers Justinian's campaigns for conquest in the western Mediterranean an unwise overloading of the empire's resources, and similar verdicts have been made with regard to Emperor Manuel I Komnenos' attempts to regain territory in Italy in the 12th century. Thus, even within the

---

[93] Preiser-Kapeller 2012b, 26–47, also for the later development of the mosque; Dölger and Wirth 1995, no. 823b; Shepard 2006, 37–8.
[94] On the concept of 'Augustan threshold', which expansionist empire have to pass in order to establish an equilibrium between further expansion and interior stabilisation see Doyle 1984, 93–5; Menzel 2015, 43; Münkler 2007.
[95] Stouraitis 2012, 250–6, esp. 255 for the citation.

'traditional' limits of the Roman oecumene, there was potential for an 'imperial overstretch'.[96]

An evaluation of the possibilities and feasibility of an empire's spatial development requires an analysis of its resource basis and the logistical, ecological as well as ideological limits to its administrative and military apparatus. Therefore, it could be profitable to analyse how imperial elites and imperial systems acting against a similar or almost identical spatial or ecological background faired in comparison with Byzantium (the Roman Empire, the Ottoman Empire[97]), or to compare Byzantium with those empires that shared borders with and interacted and competed with it (Sasanian Persia, the Umayyad, Abbasid and Fatimid Caliphates), but also with imperial formations of different spatial and ecological dynamics such as the 'kinetic' empires[98] of the steppes. The concept of 'imperial ecology' (see above) invites for further comparisons basically with all empires facing the challenge to maintain the essential flows of resources and manpower, also under changing environmental and geo-political conditions.[99]

Comparisons are also possible with regard to the significance of various qualities of power, be it 'hard' (military, economic) or 'soft' (cultural, religious), for the spatial extent of imperial authority and impact; this includes an analysis of the structure, range and resilience of imperial networks both within and beyond the imperial borders.[100] More specifically again, one could compare the structure and dynamics of spheres maybe similar to the 'Byzantine commonwealth' (the Chinese imperial sphere in East Asia, for instance) and their role for the resilience of empires and imperial pretensions even in the absence of equivalent 'hard' power.[101]

The case of the medieval Roman Empire of the East thus illustrates the equal significance of frontiers and networks for the spatial manifestation of empire and invites to augment topographies with 'connectographies' (see Maps 4.2, 4.3 and 4.4) between places and people within and across imperial frontiers; of special interest are the 'middle grounds' between two (or more) empires, which served as areas of mutual provocation and inspiration for the development and adaption

---

[96] On this concept see Kennedy 1987; see also Menzel 2015, 63; Münkler 2007. For the Byzantine campaigns in Italy in the 12th century see Magdalino 1993, 53–66; Hendy 1985, 222 (the costs for one unsuccessful campaign against the Normans in 1155/1156 amounted to 2,160,000 hyperpyra = 30,000 pounds of gold).

[97] See also section 4.1.5 on logistics and the limits of 'hard power' for some considerations along these lines.

[98] See Hämäläinen 2013, 81–90.

[99] See in addition to studies already cited: Morris and Scheidel 2009; Mutschler and Mittag 2009; Scheidel 2009; Bang 2008 (for a comparison of the Roman Empire and the Mughals in India); Elvin 2004; Brook 2010.

[100] See for instance Preiser-Kapeller 2012a/b/c, 2015a; Barkey 2008; Gramsch 2013; Tackett 2014.

[101] See Kang 2010; Adshead 2004.

of concepts of imperial universal rule.[102] Within such a framework, empires cannot be understood in isolation, but only in connection and comparison.

Acknowledgements

This study was undertaken within the framework of the project 'Moving Byzantium: Mobility, Microstructures and Personal Agency' (Z 288 Wittgenstein-Preis; PI: C. Rapp; http://rapp.univie.ac.at/) at the Institute for Medieval Research/ Division for Byzantine Research of the Austrian Academy of Sciences.

Bibliography

Primary Sources

Anna Komnene: *Annae Comnenae Alexias* (Corpus fontium historiae Byzantinae 40), ed. Diether R. Reinsch and Athanasios Kambylis. Berlin: De Gruyter 2001.

Chronicon ad annum Christi 1234: Jean-Baptiste Chabot, *Anonymi auctoris chronicon ad annum Christi 1234 pertinens* (Corpus Scriptorum Christianorum Orientalium 109). Louvain: Peeters 1937 (Reprint 1965).

Codex Justinianus: *Codex Justinianus*, ed. Paul Krueger. Berlin: Weidmann 1888.

De administrando imperii: *Constantine Porphyrogenitus, De administrando imperii*, ed. by Gyula Moravcsik, trad. Romilly J. H. Jenkins (Corpus Fontium Historiae Byzantinae 1). Washington, DC: Dumbarton Oaks Research Library 1967.

De Ceremoniis: *Constantine Porphyrogennetos, The Book of Ceremonies* in 2 volumes trans. by Anne Moffatt – Maxeme Tall, with the Greek edition of the Corpus Scriptorium Historiae Byzantinae (Bonn, 1829). Canberra: Byzantina Australiensia 2012.

Hierokles: Ernest Honigmann, *Le Synecdèmos d'Hiéroclès et l'opuscule géographique de Georges de Chypre*. Brussels: Éditions de l'institut de philologie et d'histoire orientales et slaves 1939.

Listes de préséance: Nicolas Oikonomides, *Les listes de préséance byzantines des IXe et Xe siècles*. Paris: Éditions du Centre National de la Recherche Scientifique 1972.

Liutprand of Cremona: *Liutprandi Episcopi Cremonensis Opera*, ed. Joseph Becker. Hannover – Leipzig 1915: Buchhandlung Hahn (reprint 1993).

Miklosisch and Müller: Franz Miklosich and Joseph Müller, *Acta patriarchatus Constantinopolitani MCCCXV–MCCCCII e codicibus manu scriptis Bibliothecae Palatinae Vindobonesis* (Acta et diplomata grae-ca medii aevi sacra et profana I and II). 2 Vols. Vienna 1860 and 1862 (Reprint Aalen: Scientia Verlag 1968).

Nicholas I, *Letters: Nicholas I Patriarch of Constantinople, Letters*, ed. and trans. Romilly J. H. Jenkins – Leendert G. Westerink (Corpus Fontium Historiae Byzantinae VI). Washington, DC: Dumbarton Oaks Research Library 1973.

---

[102] See Khanna 2016 for the concept of 'connectography', and White 1991 as well as Preiser-Kapeller 2015a for the 'middle ground'.

Notitia Dignitatum: Concepción Neira Faleira, *La Notitia dignitatum. Nueva edición crítica y comentario histórico*. Madrid: Consejo Superior De Investigaciones Cientificas 2005.

Notitiae episcopatuum: Jean Darrouzès, Notitiae episcopatuum Ecclesiae Constantinopolitanae: texte critique, introduction et notes. Paris: Peeters 1981.

Palmer, Andrew, Sebastian Brock and Robert Hoyland. 1993. *The Seventh Century in the West-Syrian Chronicles*, intro., trans. and annotated by Andrew Palmer. Including two seventh-century Syriac Apocalyptic Texts, intro., trans. and annotated by Sebastian Brock with added Annotation and an historical Introduction by Robert Hoyland. Liverpool: Liverpool University Press.

Procop, De aed.: Procopius, ed. by H. B. Dewing. 7 vols. Cambridge, MA: Harvard University Press, 1914–1940.

Pseudo-Methodius: *Pseudo-Methodius, An Alexandrian World Chronicle*, ed. and transl Benjamin Garstadt (Dumbarton Oaks Medieval Library 14). Cambridge, MA: Harvard University Press, 2012.

References

Adshead, Samuel Adrian M. 2004. *T'ang China. The Rise of the East in World History.* Houndsmill: Palgrave Macmillan.

Anderson, Glaire D. 2009. 'Islamic spaces and diplomacy in Constantinople (tenth to thirteenth centuries CE)'. *Medieval Encounters. Jewish, Christian and Muslim Culture in Confluence and Dialogue* 15: 86–113.

Angelov, Dimiter G. online: *The Making of Byzantinism*: http://www.hks.harvard.edu /kokkalis/GSW1/GSW1/01%20Angelov.pdf.

Angelov, Dimiter. 2013. 'Asia and Europe Commonly called East and West: Constantinople and Geographical Imagination in Byzantium'. In: *Imperial Geographies in Byzantine and Ottoman Space*, ed. Sahar Bazzaz, Yota Batsaki and Dimiter Angelov, 43–68. (Hellenic Studies Series 56). Cambridge, MA: Harvard University Press.

Angelov, Dimiter, Yota Batsaki and Sahar Bazzaz. 2013. 'Introduction. Imperial Geographies in Byzantine and Ottoman Space'. In: *Imperial Geographies in Byzantine and Ottoman Space*, ed. Sahar Bazzaz, Yota Batsaki and Dimiter Angelov, 1–21. (Hellenic Studies Series 56). Cambridge, MA: Harvard University Press.

Angold, Michael. 1997. *The Byzantine Empire 1025–1204*. London: Longman.

Asa Eger, A. 2015. *The Islamic-Byzantine Frontier. Interaction and Exchange among Muslim and Christian Communities*. London: I.B. Tauris.

Avruch, Kevin. 2000. 'Reciprocity, Equality, and Status-Anxiety in the Amarna Letters'. In: *Amarna Diplomacy. The Beginnings of International Relations*, ed. Raymond Cohen and Raymond Westbrook, 154–64. Baltimore, MD: The Johns Hopkins University Press.

Bang, Peter Fibiger. 2008. *The Roman Bazaar A Comparative Study of Trade and Markets in a Tributary Empire*. Cambridge: Cambridge University Press.

Barkey, Karen. 2008. *Empire of Difference: The Ottomans in Comparative Perspective*. Cambridge: Cambridge University Press.

Bayer, Axel. 2002. *Spaltung der Christenheit: das sogenannte Morgenländische Schisma von 1054*. Cologne: Böhlau Verlag.

170   *Johannes Preiser-Kapeller*

Beihammer, Alexander Daniel. 2000. *Nachrichten zum byzantinischen Urkundenwesen in arabischen Quellen (565 bis 811)* (Poikila byzantina 17). Bonn: Habelt Verlag.

Beihammer, Alexander Daniel. 2002. 'Reiner Christlicher König – Pistos en Christō Basileus'. *Byzantinische Zeitschrift* 95: 1–34.

Beihammer, Alexander Daniel. 2004. 'Die Kraft der Zeichen: symbolische Kommunikation in der byzantinischen-arabischen Diplomatie des 10. und 11. Jahrhunderts'. *Jahrbuch der Österreichischen Byzantinistik* 54: 159–89.

Bonner, Michael. 2004. *Arab-Byzantine Relations in Early Islamic Times* (The Formation of the Classical Islamic World 8). Aldershot: Routledge.

Bowlus, Charles R. 2006. *The Battle of Lechfeld and its Aftermath, August 955. The End of the Age of Migrations in the Latin West*. Aldershot: Routledge.

Brandes, Wolfram. 2007. 'Die Belagerung Konstantinopels 717/718 als apokalyptisches Ereignis. Zu einer Interpolation im griechischen Text der Pseudo-Methodios-Apokalypse'. In: *Byzantina Mediterranea. Festschrift für Johannes Koder zum 65. Geburtstag*, ed. Klaus Belke, Ewald Kislinger, Andreas Külzer and Maria A. Stassinopoulou, 65–91. Vienna: Böhlau Verlag.

Brodersen, Kai. 2003. *Terra Cognita. Studien zur römischen Raumerfassung* (Spudasmata 59). Hildesheim: Olms.

Brook, Timothy. 2010. *The Troubled Empire. China in the Yuan and Ming Dynasties*. Cambridge, MA: Harvard University Press.

Brubaker, Leslie and John Haldon. 2011. *Byzantium in the Iconoclast Era c.680–850: a history*. Cambridge: Cambridge University Press.

Bulliet, Richard W. 1990. *The Camel and the Wheel*. New York: Morningside Books.

Bulliet, Richard W. 2009. *Cotton, Climate, and Camels. A Moment in World History*. New York: Columbia University Press.

Campagnolo-Pothitou, Maria. 1995. 'Les échanges de prisonniers entre Byzance et l'Islam aux IXe et Xe siècles'. *Journal of Oriental and African Studies* 7: 1–56.

Campbell, Tony. 1987. 'Portolan Charts from the Late Thirteenth Century to 1500'. In: *The History of Cartography, Volume 1: Cartography in Prehistoric, Ancient, and Medieval Europe and the Mediterranean*, ed. J. B. Harley and David Woodward, 371–463. Chicago, IL: University of Chicago Press.

Canepa, Matthew P. 2010a. *Two Eyes of the Earth: Art and Ritual of Kingship between Rome and Sasanian Iran*. Berkeley, CA: University of California.

Canepa, Matthew P. 2010b. 'Distant Displays of Power. Understanding Cross-Cultural Interaction among the Elites of Rome, Sasanian Iran, and Sui-Tang China'. *Ars Orientalis* 38: 121–54.

Caplanis, Costas. 2003. 'The Debasement of the "Dollar of the Middle Ages"'. *The Journal of Economic History* 63(3): 768–801.

Chadwick, Henry. 2003. *East and West: The Making of a Rift in the Church. From Apostolic Times until the Council of Florence* (Oxford History of the Christian Church). Oxford: Oxford University Press.

Classen, Peter. 1985. *Karl der Große, das Papsttum und Byzanz. Die Begründung des karolingischen Kaisertums*. Nach dem Handexemplar des Verfassers, ed. Horst Fuhrmann and Claudia Märtl (Beiträge zur Geschichte und Quellenkunde des Mittelalters 9). Sigmaringen: Jan Thorbecke Verlag.

Curta, Florin. 2001. *The Making of the Slavs: History and Archaeology of the Lower Danube Region, c.500–700* (Cambridge Studies in Medieval Life and Thought). Cambridge: Cambridge University Press.

Curta, Florin. 2006. *Southeastern Europe in the Middle Ages 500–1250* (Cambridge Medieval Textbooks). Cambridge: Cambridge University Press.

Cutler, Anthony. 2001. 'Gifts and Gift Exchange as Aspects of the Byzantine, Arab, and Related Economies'. *Dumbarton Oaks Papers* 55: 247–78.

Dagron, Gilbert. 2003. *Emperor and Priest. The Imperial Office in Byzantium.* Cambridge: Cambridge University Press.

Daim, Falko. 2001. 'Byzantine Belts and Avar Birds. Diplomacy, Trade and Cultural Transfer in the Eighth Century'. In: *The Transformation of Frontiers: From Late Antiquity to the Carolingians*, ed. Walter Pohl, Ian Wood and Helmut Reimitz, 143–88. Leiden: Brill.

Darrouzès, Jean. 1979. *Les regestes des actes du patriarcat de Constantinople, I/6.* Paris: Institut français d'études byzantines.

Decker, Michael J. 2013. *The Byzantine Art of War.* Yardley: Westholme Publishers.

Dignas, Beater and Engelbert Winter. 2007. *Rome and Persia in Late Antiquity: Neighbours and Rivals.* Cambridge: Cambridge University Press.

Dodgeon, Michael H. and Samuel N. C. 1991. *The Roman Eastern Frontier and the Persian Wars AD 226–363.* London: Routledge.

Dölger, Franz. 1976. 'Die "Familie der Könige" im Mittelalter'. In: *Byzanz und die europäische Staatenwelt*, ed. Franz Dölger, 34–69. Darmstadt: Wissenschaftlich Buchgesellschaft.

Dölger, Franz and Peter Wirth. 1995. *Regesten der Kaiserurkunden des oströmischen Reiches, 2. Teil. Regesten von 1025–1204.* Munich: C.H. Beck.

Dölger, Franz, Andreas Müller and Alexander D. Beihammer. 2003. *Regesten der Kaiserurkunden des oströmischen Reiches, 1. Teil, 2. Halbband. Regesten von 867–1025.* Munich: C.H. Beck.

Dölger, Franz, Andreas Müller, Johannes Preiser-Kapeller and Alexander Riehle. 2009. *Regesten der Kaiserurkunden des oströmischen Reiches, 1. Teil, 1. Halbband. Regesten von 565–867.* Munich: C.H. Beck.

Downs, Roger M. and David Stea. 1977. *Maps in Minds. Reflections on Cognitive Mapping.* New York: Joanna Cotler Books.

Doyle, Michael W. 1984. *Empires.* Ithaca, NY: Cornell University Press.

Drakoulis, Demetrios P. 2010. *E periphereiake organose ton oikismon tes Anatolikes Romaïkes Autokratorias kata ten proime Byzantine period (4os-6os aionas)*, 2 vols Thessalonike: Kentro Byzantinon Ereunon.

Ekonomou, Andrew J. 2007. *Byzantine Rome and the Greek Popes: Eastern Influences on Rome and the Papacy from Gregory the Great to Zacharias, A.D. 590–752.* Lanham, MD: Lexington Books.

El-Cheikh, Nadia Maria 2004. *Byzantium viewed by the Arabs* (Harvard Middle Eastern Monographs 36). Cambridge, MA: Harvard University Press.

Elvin, Mark. 2004. *The Retreat of the Elephants. An Environmental History of China.* New Haven, CT: Yale University Press.

Feld, Karl. 2005. *Barbarische Bürger. Die Isaurier und das Römische Reich.* Berlin: De Gruyter.

Felix, Wolfgang. 1981. *Byzanz und die islamische Welt im früheren 11. Jahrhundert* (Byzantina Vindobonensia 14). Vienna: Verlag der österreichischen Akademie der Wissenschaften.

Fögen, Marie Theres. 1993. 'Das politische Denken der Byzantiner'. In: *Pipers Handbuch der politischen Ideen, Vol. 2: Mittelalter,* ed. Iring Fetscher and Herfried Münkler, 41–86. Munich: Piper.

Folz, Robert. 1953. *L'idée d'empire en occident du Ve au XIVe siècle.* Paris: Aubier.

Fowden, Garth. 1994. *Empire to Commonwealth: Consequences of Monotheism in Late Antiquity.* Princeton, NJ: Princeton University Press.

Fried, Johannes. 2014. *Karl der Große. Gewalt und Glaube.* Munich: C.H. Beck.

Gantner, Clemens. 2014. *Freunde Roms und Völker der Finsternis. Die Konstruktion von Anderen im päpstlichen Rom des 8. und 9. Jahrhunderts.* Vienna: Böhlau Verlag.

Gerland, Ernst. 1934. *Das Studium der Byzantinischen Geschichte vom Humanismus bis zur Jetztzeit* (Texte und Forschungen zur byzantinisch-neugriechischen Philologie. Zwanglose Beihefte zu den Byzantinisch-Neugriechischen Jahrbüchern 12). Athens: Chronika.

Goetz. Hans-Werner. 1991. 'Art. Kaiser, Kaisertum, I. Westen'. In: *Lexikon des Mittelalters* 5, 851–3. Munich : Metzler Verlag.

Gould, Peter and Rodney White. 1986. *Mental Maps.* London: HarperCollins.

Gramsch, Robert. 2013. *Das Reich als Netzwerk der Fürsten. Politische Strukturen unter dem Doppelkönigtum Friedrichs II. und Heinrichs (VII.) 1225–1235.* Ostfildern: Thorbecke.

Greatrex, Geoffrey and Samuel N. C. Lieu. 2002. *The Roman Eastern Frontier and the Persian Wars. Part II: A.D. 363–630. A Narrative Sourcebook.* London: Routledge.

Güterbock, Karl. 1906. *Byzanz und Persien in ihren diplomatisch-völkerrechtlichen Beziehungen im Zeitalter Justinians. Ein Beitrag zur Geschichte des Völkerrechts.* Berlin: J. Guttentag, Verlagsbuchhandlung.

Haldon, John F. 1997. 'The Organisation and Support of an Expeditionary Force: Manpower and Logistics in the Middle Byzantine Period'. In: *Byzantium at War*, ed. Nikos Oikonomides, 111–51. Athens: National Hellenic Research Foundation.

Haldon, John F. 2000. 'Theory and Practice in Tenth-century Military Administration. Chapters II, 44 and 45 of the Book of Ceremonies'. *Travaux et Mémoires* 13: 201–352.

Haldon, John F. (ed.). 2006. *General Issues in the Study of Medieval Logistics. Sources, Problems and Methodologies.* Leiden: Brill.

Haldon, John F. and Hugh Kennedy. 1980. 'The Arab-Byzantine Frontier in the Eighth and Ninth Centuries. Military, Organisation and Society in the Borderlands'. *Zbornik Radova Vizantološkog Instituta* 19: 79–116.

Hämäläinen, Pekka. 2013. 'What's in a Concept? The Kinetic Empire of the Comanches'. *History and Theory* 52(1), 81–90.

Hardt, Michael and Antonio Negri. 2000. *Empire.* Cambridge, MA: Harvard University Press.

Harris, William V. 2016. *Roman Power. A Thousand Years of Empire.* Cambridge: Cambridge University Press.

Heilo, Olof. 2016. *Eastern Rome and the Rise of Islam: History and Prophecy.* Abingdon: Routledge.

Hendy, Michael F. 1985. *Studies in the Byzantine Monetary Economy c.300–1450*. Cambridge: Cambridge University Press.

Höfert, Almut. 2015. *Kaisertum und Kalifat. Der imperiale Monotheismus im Früh- und Hochmittelalter*. Frankfurt: Campus Verlag.

Howard-Johnston, James. 1995. 'The Siege of Constantinople in 626'. In: *Constantinople and its Hinterland. Papers from the 27th Spring Symposium of Byzantine Studies*, eds. Cyril Mango and Gilbert Dagron, 131–42. Aldershot: Routledge.

Hoyland, Robert. 1997. *Seeing Islam As Others Saw It: A Survey and Evaluation of Christian, Jewish and Zoroastrian Writings on Early Islam*. Princeton, NJ: The Darwin Press.

Hunger, Herbert. 1966. Byzanz im europäischen Geschichtsdenken des 20. Jahrhunderts. *Jahrbuch der österreichischen byzantinischen Gesellschaft* 15: 49–60.

Hunger, Herbert. 1987. *Graecus perfidus – Italos itamos. Il senso dell'alterità nei rapporti greco-romani ed italo-bizantini*. Rome: Unione Internazionale degli Instituti di Archeologia.

Hunger, Herbert and Johannes Koder (eds.). 1976-2020. *Tabula Imperii Byzantini* (TIB). Vienna: Verlag der Österreichischen Akademie der Wissenschaften.

Isaac, Benjamin H. 2000. *The Limits of Empire: the Roman Army in the East*. Oxford: Clarendon Press.

Izdebski, Adam. 2013. 'A Rural Economy in Transition. Asia Minor from Late Antiquity into the Early Middle Ages'. *Journal of Juristic Papyrology* Supplement vol. 18.

Jacoby, David. 2004. 'Silk Economics and Cross-Cultural Artistic Interaction: Byzantium, the Muslim World, and the Christian West'. *Dumbarton Oaks Papers* 58: 197–240.

James, Simon. 2011. *Rome and the Sword. How Warriors and Weapons Shaped Roman History*. London: Thames & Hudson.

Jönsson, Christer. 2000. 'Diplomatic Signaling in the Amarna-Letters'. In: *Amarna Diplomacy. The Beginnings of International Relations*, ed. Raymond Cohen and Raymond Westbrook, 191–204. Baltimore, MD: The Johns Hopkins University Press.

Kang, David C. 2010. *East Asia before the West. Five Centuries of Trade and Tribute*. New York: Columbia University Press.

Kaplony, Andreas. 1996. *Konstantinopel und Damaskus. Gesandtschaften und Verträge zwischen Kaisern und Kalifen 639–750. Untersuchungen zum Gewohnheits-Völkerrecht und zur interkulturellen Diplomatie* (Islamkundliche Untersuchungen 208). Berlin: Klaus-Schwarz-Verlag.

Kazhdan, Alexander and Silvia Ronchey. 1999. *L'aristocrazia bizantina dal principio dell'XI alla fine del XII secolo*. Palermo: Sellerio editore Palermo.

Kennedy, Paul. 1987. *The Rise and Fall of the Great Powers: Economic Change and Military Conflict from 1500 to 2000*. New York: Random House.

Kennedy, Hugh. 2001. *The Armies of the Caliphs. Military and Society in the Early Islamic State*. London: Routledge.

Khanna, Parag. 2016. *Connectography: Mapping the Global Network Revolution*. London: Random House.

Kislinger, Ewald. 2008. 'Von Drachen und anderem wilden Getier. Fremdenfeindlichkeit in Byzanz?'. In: *Laetae segetes iterum*, ed. Irena Radová, 389–404. Brno: Masaryk University Press.

Kislinger, Ewald. 2010. 'Verkehrsrouten zur See im byzantinischen Raum'. In *Handelsgüter und Verkehrswege. Aspekte der Warenversorgung im östlichen*

174   *Johannes Preiser-Kapeller*

Mittelmeerraum (4. bis 5. Jahrhundert) (Veröffentlichungen zur Byzanzforschung 18), ed. Ewald Kislinger, Johannes Koder and Andreas Külzer, 149–74. Vienna: Verlag der Österreichischen Akademie der Wissenschaften.

Koder, Johannes 1987. 'Zum Bild des "Westens" bei den Byzantinern in der frühen Komnenenzeit'. In: *Deus qui mutat tempora. Menschen und Institutionen im Wandel des Mittelalters*, ed. Ernst-D. Hehl, Hubertus Seibert and Franz Staab, 191–201. Sigmaringen: Jan Thorbecke Verlag.

Koder, Johannes. 2001. *Der Lebensraum der Byzantiner. Historisch-geographischer Abriß ihres mittelalterlichen Staates im östlichen Mittelmeerraum* (Byzantinische Geschichtsschreiber Ergänzungsband 1). Nachdruck mit bibliographischen Nachträgen. Vienna: Fassbaender.

Koder, Johannes. 2002. 'Die räumlichen Vorstellungen der Byzantiner von der Ökumene (4.–12. Jahrhundert)'. *Anzeiger der phil.-hist. Klasse der Österreichischen Akademie der Wissenschaften* 137: 15–34.

Köhbach, Markus. 1992. 'Çasar oder Imperator? – Zur Titulatur der römischen Kaiser durch die Osmanen nach dem Vertrag von Zsitvatorok (1606)'. *Wiener Zeitschrift für die Kunde des Morgenlandes* 82: 223–34.

Kolbaba, Tia M. 2000. *The Byzantine Lists – Errors of the Latins* (Illinois Medieval Studies). Urbana, IL: University of Illinois Press.

Kresten, Otto. 1993. 'Der "Anredestreit" zwischen Manuel I. Komnenos und Friedrich I. Barbarossa nach der Schlacht von Myriokephalon'. *Römisch-Historische Mitteilungen* 34/35: 65–110.

Krsmanović, Bojana. 2008. *The Byzantine Province in Change (on the Threshold between the 10th and 11th Century)*. Athens: National Hellenic Research Foundation.

Külzer, Andreas 2000. 'Konstantinopel in der apokalyptischen Literatur der Byzantiner'. *Jahrbuch der Österreichischen Byzantinistik* 50: 51–76.

Kutaba-Deliboria, Barbara. 1993. *O geographikos kosmos Konstantinou tou Porphyrogennetou*, 2 vols. Athens: Parousia.

Laiou, Angeliki. 2002. 'The Emperor's Word: Chrysobulls, Oaths and Synallagmatic Relations in Byzantium (11th–12th c.)'. *Travaux et Mémoires* 14 (= Mélanges Gilbert Dagron), 347–62.

Laiou, Angeliki. 2006. 'Byzantium and the Neighboring Powers: Small-state Policies and Complexities'. In: *Byzantium: Faith and Power (1261–1557). Perspectives on Late Byzantine Art and Culture*, ed. Sarah T. Brooks, 42–53. New Haven, CT: Yale University Press.

Landwehr, Achim. 2008. *Historische Diskursanalyse*. Frankfurt: Campus Verlag.

Lilie, Ralph-Johannes. 1976. *Die byzantinische Reaktion auf die Ausbreitung der Araber. Studien zur Strukturwandlung des byzantinischen Staates im 7. und 8. Jhd.* (Miscellanea Byzantina Monacensia 22). Munich: Institut für Byzantinistik und Neugriechische Philologie der Universität München.

Lilie, Ralph-Johannes. 1985. 'Das "Zweikaiserproblem" und sein Einfluß auf die Außenpolitik der Komnenen'. *Byzantinische Forschungen* 9: 219–43.

Lilie, Ralph-Johannes. 2004. *Byzanz und die Kreuzzüge*. Berlin: Kohlhammer.

Lorge, Peter. 2008. 'The Great Ditch of China and the Song-Liao Border'. In: *Battlefronts Real and Imagined. War, Border, and Identity in the Chinese Middle Period*, ed. Don J. Wyatt, 59–74. New York: Palgrave Macmillan.

Lounghis, Telemachos C. 1980. *Les ambassades byzantines en Occident depuis la fondation des états barbares jusqu' aux Croisades (407–1096)*. Athens: Typographe.

Lounghis, Telemachos G. 1995. 'Die byzantinische Ideologie der "begrenzten Ökumene" und die römische Frage im ausgehenden 10. Jahrhundert'. *Byzantinoslavica* 56: 117–28.

Luttwak, Edward N. 2009. *The Grand Strategy of the Byzantine Empire*. Cambridge, MA: Harvard University Press.

Magdalino, Paul. 1993. *The Empire of Manuel I Komnenos, 1143–1180*. Cambridge: Cambridge University Press.

Magdalino, Paul. 2003. 'The Year 1000 in Byzantium'. In: *Byzantium in the Year 1000* (The Medieval Mediterranean. Peoples, Economies and Cultures 400–1500, Vol. 45), ed. Paul Magdalino, 233–70. Leiden: Brill.

Magdalino, Paul. 2013. 'Constantine VII and the Historical Geography of Empire'. In: *Imperial Geographies in Byzantine and Ottoman Space* (Hellenic Studies Series 56), ed. Sahar Bazzaz, Yota Batsaki and Dimiter Angelov, 23–42. Cambridge, MA: Harvard University Press.

Maier, Charles S. 2007. 'America among Empires? Imperial Analogues and Imperial Syndrome'. *GHI Bulletin* 41: 21–31.

Martin-Hisard, Bernadette. 2000. 'Constantinople et les archontes caucasiens dans le Livre de cérémonies, II, 48'. *Travaux et Mémoires* 13: 359–530.

McGeer, Eric. 1995. *Sowing the Dragon's Teeth: Byzantine Warfare in the Tenth Century*. Washington, DC: Dumbarton Oaks Research Library.

Menzel, Ulrich. 2015. *Die Ordnung der Welt. Imperium oder Hegemonie in der Hierarchie der Staatenwelt*. Berlin: Suhrkamp Verlag.

Meyendorff, John. 1989. *Byzantium and the Rise of Russia. A Study of Byzantino-Russian Relations in the Fourteenth Century*. New York: Cambridge University Press.

McCormick, Michael 2011. *Charlemagne's Survey of the Holy Land. Wealth, Personnel, and Buildings of a Mediterranean Church between Antiquity and the Middle Ages*. Washington, DC: Dumbarton Oaks Research Library.

Miotto, Marco. 2008. *O antagonismos Byzantiou kai Chaliphatou ton Phatimidon sten Engys Anatole kai e drase ton italikon poleon sten perioche kate ton 10o kai ton 11o aiona*. Thessaloniki: Kentro Byzantinon Ereunon.

Möhring, Hannes. 2000. *Der Weltkaiser der Endzeit. Entstehung, Wandel und Wirkung einer tausendjährigen Weissagung* (Mittelalter-Forschung 3). Stuttgart: Jan Thorbecke Verlag.

Morris, Ian and Walter Scheidel (eds.). 2009. *The Dynamics of Ancient Empires. State Power from Assyria to Byzantium*. Oxford: Oxford University Press.

Morrison, Cécile. 2002: 'Byzantine Money: Its Production and Circulation'. In: *The Economic History of Byzantium*, ed. Angeliki E. Laiou, 909–66. Washington, DC: Dumbarton Oaks Research Library.

Mostern, Ruth. 2011. *'Dividing the Realm in Order to Govern'. The Spatial Organisation of the Song State (960–1276 CE)*. Cambridge, MA: Harvard University Press.

Müller, Klaus E. 1972/1980: *Geschichte der antiken Ethnographie und ethnologischen Theoriebildung von den Anfängen bis auf die byzantinischen Historiographen* (Studien zur Kulturkunde 29). Vols. I–II. Wiesbaden: Steiner.

Münkler, Herfried. 2007. *Empires: The Logic of World Domination from Ancient Rome to the United States*. Cambridge: Polity Press.

Murphey, Rhoads. 1999. *Ottoman Warfare 1500–1700*. New Brunswick, NJ: Routledge.

Mutschler, Fritz-Heiner and Achim Mittag (eds.). 2009. *Conceiving the Empire: China and Rome Compared*. Oxford: Oxford University Press.

Nerlich, Daniel. 1999. *Diplomatische Gesandtschaften zwischen Ost- und Westkaisern 756–1002*. Bern: Peter Lang.

Neville, Leonora. 2004. *Authority in Byzantine Provincial Society, 950–1100*. Cambridge: Cambridge University Press.

Noble, Thomas F. X. 1984. *The Republic of St. Peter: The Birth of the Papal State, 680–825*. Philadelphia, PA: University of Pennsylvania Press.

Norden, Walter. 1903. *Das Papsttum und Byzanz. Die Trennung der beiden Mächte und das Problem der Wiedervereinigung bis zum Untergang des byzantinischen Reichs*. Berlin: B. Behr.

Obolensky, Dimitri. 2000. *The Byzantine Commonwealth. Eastern Europe 500–1453*. London: Sphere Books.

Oikonomides, Nikos. 1997. 'Title and Income at the Byzantine Court'. In: *Byzantine Court Culture from 829 to 1204*, ed. Henry Maguire, 199–215. Washington, DC: Dumbarton Oaks Research Library.

Ostrogorsky, Georg. 1936. 'Die byzantinische Staatenhierarchie'. *Seminarium Kondakovianum* 8: 41–61.

Ostrowski, Donald. 1999. *Muscovy and the Mongols. Cross-Cultural Influences on the Steppe Frontier, 1304–1589*. Cambridge: Cambridge University Press.

Ostrowski, Donald. 2004. '"Moscow the Third Rome" as Historical Ghost'. In: *Byzantium: Faith and Power (1261–1557)*, ed. Helen C. Evans, 170–79. New Haven, CT: Metropolitan Museum of Art.

Panaite, Viorel. 2000. *The Ottoman Law of War and Peace. The Ottoman Empire and Tribute Payers*. New York: East European Monographs.

Papaconstantinou, Arietta. 2005. 'Confrontation, interaction, and the formation of the early Islamic Oikumene'. *Revue des études byzantines* 63: 167–81.

Papaconstantinou, Arietta. 2008. 'Between Umma and Dhimma. The Christians in the Middle East under the Umayyads'. *Annales islamologiques* 42: 127–56.

Podskalsky, Gerhard. 1972. *Byzantinische Reichseschatologie. Die Periodisierung der Weltgeschichte in den vier Großreichen (Daniel 2 und 7) und dem Tausendjährigen Friedensreich (Apok. 20). Eine motivgeschichtliche Untersuchung*. Munich: Fink.

Preiser-Kapeller, Johannes. 2008. *Der Episkopat im späten Byzanz. Ein Verzeichnis der Metropoliten und Bischöfe des Patriarchats von Konstantinopel in der Zeit von 1204 bis 1453*. Saarbrücken: VDM Verlag.

Preiser-Kapeller, Johannes. 2012a: 'Complex Historical Dynamics of Crisis: the Case of Byzantium'. In: *Krise und Transformation*, ed. Sigrid Jalkotzy-Deger and Arnold Suppan, 69–127. Vienna: Verlag der Österreichischen Akademie der Wissenschaften.

Preiser-Kapeller, Johannes. 2012b. 'Großkönig, Kaiser und Kalif – Byzanz im Geflecht der Staatenwelt des Nahen Ostens, 300–1204'. *Historicum. Zeitschrift für Geschichte* (Linz), 26–47.

Preiser-Kapeller, Johannes. 2012c. 'Networks of Border Zones – Multiplex Relations of Power, Religion and Economy in South-eastern Europe, 1250–1453 CE'. In: *Proceedings of the 39th Annual Conference of Computer Applications and Quantitative Methods in Archaeology, 'Revive the Past' (CAA) in Beijing, China*, ed. Philip Verhagen, 381–93. Amsterdam: Pallas Publications.

Preiser-Kapeller, Johannes. 2013. 'Eine "Familie der Könige"? Anrede und Bezeichnung von sowie Verhandlungen mit ausländischen Machthabern in den Urkunden des Patriarchatsregisters von Konstantinopel im 14. Jh'. In: *The Register of the Patriarchate of Constantinople. A central source to the History and Church in Late Byzantium*, ed. Christian Gastgeber, Ekaterini Mitsiou and Johannes Preiser-Kapeller, 253–85. Vienna: Verlag der Österreichischen Akademie der Wissenschaften.

Preiser-Kapeller, Johannes. 2015a. 'Liquid Frontiers. A Relational Analysis of Maritime Asia Minor as Religious Contact Zone in the 13th–15th Centuries'. In: *Islam and Christianity in Medieval Anatolia*, ed. A.C.S. Peacock, Bruno de Nicola and Sara Nur Yıldız, 117–46. Aldershot: Ashgate.

Preiser-Kapeller, Johannes. 2015b. 'A Collapse of the Eastern Mediterranean? New Results and Theories on the Interplay between Climate and Societies in Byzantium and the Near East, ca. 1000–1200 AD'. *Jahrbuch der Österreichischen Byzantinistik* 65: 195–242.

Preiser-Kapeller, Johannes. 2018. *Jenseits von Rom und Karl dem Großen. Aspekte der globalen Verflechtung in der langen Spätantike, 300–800 n. Chr.* (Expansion – Interaktion – Akkulturation. Globalhistorische Skizzen 32). Vienna: Mandelbaum Verlag.

Prinzing, Günter. 1992. 'Das Byzantinische Kaisertum im Umbruch – zwischen regionaler Aufspaltung und erneuter Zentrierung in den Jahren 1204–1282'. *In Legitimation und Funktion des Herrschers: vom ägyptischen Pharao zum neuzeitlichen Diktator.* (Schriften der Mainzer Philosophischen Fakultätsgesellschaft 13), ed. Rolf Gundlach and Hermann Weber, 129–83. Stuttgart: Franz Steiner Verlag.

Pryor, John H. 1992. *Geography, Technology, and War: Studies in the Maritime History of the Mediterranean, 649–1571.* Cambridge: Cambridge University Press.

Pryor, John H. and Elizabeth M. Jeffreys. 2006. *The Age of the Dromon. The Byzantine Navy, ca 500–1204.* Leiden: Brill.

Ramin, Andreas. 1994. *Symbolische Raumorientierung und kulturelle Identität. Leitlinien der Entwicklung in erzählenden Texten vom Mittelalter bis zur Neuzeit.* Munich: Iudicium.

Reinert, Stephen W. 1998. 'The Muslim Presence in Constantinople, 9th-15th Centuries: Some Preliminary Observations'. In: *Studies on the Internal Diaspora of the Byzantine Empire*, ed. Helene Ahrweiler and Angeliki E. Laiou, 125–50. Washington, DC: Dumbarton Oaks Research Library.

Reinink, Gerrit J. 2002. 'Heraclius, the New Alexander. Apocalyptic Prophecies during the Reign of Heraclius'. In: *The Reign of Heraclius (610–641): Crisis and Confrontation* (Groningen Studies in Cultural Change 2), ed. Gerrit J. Reinink and Bernard H. Stolte, 81–94. Leuven: Peeters Publishers.

Rohe, Mathias. 2009. *Das islamische Recht. Geschichte und Gegenwart.* Munich: C.H. Beck.

178   *Johannes Preiser-Kapeller*

Said, Edward. 1978. *Orientalism. Western Conceptions of the Orient*. London: Penguin Books.

Scheidel, Walter. 2009. *Rome and China: Comparative Perspectives on Ancient World Empires* (Oxford Studies in Early Empires). Oxford: Oxford University Press.

Scheidel, Walter. 2014. 'The Shape of the Roman World: Modelling Imperial Connectivity'. *Journal of Roman Archaeology* 27: 7–32.

Schmalzbauer, Gudrun. 2004. 'Überlegungen zur Idee der Oikumene in Byzanz'. In: *Wiener Byzantinistik und Neogräzistik*, ed. Wolfram Hörandner, Johannes Koder and Maria A. Stassinopoulou, 408–19. Vienna: Verlag der Österreichischen Akademie der Wissenschaften.

Schuppert, Gunnar Folke. 2014. *Verflochtene Staatlichkeit. Globalisierung als Governance-Geschichte*. Frankfurt am Main: Campus Verlag.

Seland, Eivind Heldaas. 2012. 'Trade and Christianity in the Indian Ocean during Late Antiquity'. *Journal of Late Antiquity* 5(1): 72–86.

Selb, Walter.1981. *Orientalisches Kirchenrecht, Band I: Die Geschichte des Kirchenrechts der Nestorianer (von den Anfängen bis zur Mongolenzeit)*. Vienna: Verlag der Österreichischen Akademie der Wissenschaften.

Selb, Walter. 1989. *Orientalisches Kirchenrecht, Band II: Die Geschichte des Kirchenrechts der Westsyrer (von den Anfängen bis zur Mongolenzeit)*. Vienna: Verlag der Österreichischen Akademie der Wissenschaften.

Shepard, Jonathan. 1988. 'Aspects of Byzantine Attitudes and Policy towards the West in the Tenth and Eleventh Century'. In: *Byzantium and the West, c.850–c.1200: Proceedings of the XVIIIth Spring Symposium of Byzantine Studies* (Byzantinische Forschungen 13), ed. James Howard-Johnston, 67–118. Amsterdam: Verlag Adolf M. Hakkert.

Shepard, Jonathan. 2006. 'Byzantium's Overlapping Circles'. In: *Proceedings of the 21st International Congress of Byzantine Studies, London, 21–26 August, 2006*, ed. Elizabeth Jeffreys, 15–55. Aldershot: Ashgate.

Signes Codoñer, Juan. 2014. 'New Alphabets for the Christian Nations: Frontier Strategies in the Byzantine Commonwealth between the 4th and 10th centuries'. In: *New Perspectives on the Late Roman Eastern Empire*, ed. Ana de Francisco Heredero, David Hernández de la Fuente and Susana Torres Prieto, 116–63. Newcastle upon Tyne: Cambridge Scholars Publishing.

Skaff, Jonathan K. 2012. *Sui-Tang China and its Turko-Mongol Neighbors. Culture, power, and connections, 580–800*. Oxford: Oxford University Press.

Soustal, Peter. 1991. *Thrakien (Thrake, Rhodope und Haimimontos)* (Tabula Imperii Byzantini 6). Vienna: Verlag der Österreichischen Akademie der Wissenschaften.

Spring, Peter. 2015. *Great Walls and Linear Barriers*. Barnsley: Pen and Sword.

Stephenson, Paul. 2000. *Byzantium's Balkan Frontier. A Political Study of the Northern Balkans, 900–1204*. Cambridge: Cambridge University Press.

Stouraitis, Ioannis. 2009. *Krieg und Frieden in der politischen und ideologischen Wahrnehmung in Byzanz, 7.–11. Jahrhundert* (Byzantinische Geschichtsschreiber, Ergänzungsband 4). Vienna: Fassbaender Verlag.

Stouraitis, Ioannis. 2012. '"Just War" and "Holy War" in the Middle Ages. Rethinking Theory through the Byzantine Case-Study'. *Jahrbuch der Österreichischen Byzantinistik* 62: 227–64.

Stouraitis, Ioannis. 2014. 'Roman Identity in Byzantium: a Critical Approach'. *Byzantinische Zeitschrift* 107/1: 175–220.

Strässle, Paul M. 2006. *Krieg und Kriegführung in Byzanz. Die Kriege Kaiser Basileios' II. gegen die Bulgaren (976–1019)*. Cologne: Böhlau Verlag.

Tackett, Nicolas. 2008. 'The Great Wall and the Conceptualization of the Border under the Northern Song'. *Journal of Song-Yuan Studies* 38: 99–138.

Tackett, Nicolas. 2014. *The Destruction of the Medieval Chinese Aristocracy*. Cambridge, MA: Harvard University Press.

Talbert, Richard J. A. 2010. *Rome's World. The Peutinger Map Reconsidered*. Cambridge: Cambridge University Press.

Treitinger, Otto. 1956. *Die oströmische Kaiser- und Reichsidee nach ihrer Gestaltung im höfischen Zeremoniell*. Reprint. Darmstadt: Wissenschaftliche Buchgesellschaft.

Vaccaro, Emanuele. 2013. 'Sicily in the Eighth and Ninth Centuries AD: A Case of Persisting Economic Complexity'. *Al-Masaq* 25(1): 34–69.

Walker, Alicia. 2012. *The Emperor and the World. Exotic Elements and the Imaging of Middle Byzantine Imperial Power, Ninth to Thirteenth Centuries CE*. Cambridge: Cambridge University Press.

White, Richard. 1991. *The Middle Ground. Indians, Empires, and Republics in the Great Lakes Region, 1650–1815*. Cambridge: Cambridge University Press.

White, Sam. 2011. *The Climate of Rebellion in the Early Modern Ottoman Empire* (Studies in Environment and History). Cambridge: Cambridge University Press.

Whittow, Mark. 1996. *The Making of Byzantium, 600–1025*. Berkeley, CA: University of California Press.

Wood, Philip. 2015. 'Christians in the Middle East, 600–1000: Conquest, Competition and Conversion'. In: *Islam and Christianity in Medieval Anatolia*, ed. A. C. S. Peacock, Bruno De Nicola and Sara Nur Yıldız, 23–50. Aldershot: Ashgate.

Woodward, David. 1987. 'Medieval Mappaemundi'. In: *The History of Cartography, Volume 1: Cartography in Prehistoric, Ancient, and Medieval Europe and the Mediterranean*, ed. J. B. Harley and David Woodward, 286–370. Chicago, IL: Chicago University Press.

Zavagno, Luca. 2013. 'Two Hegemonies, One Island: Cyprus as a "Middle Ground": between the Byzantines and the Arabs (650–850 A.D.)'. *Reti Medievali Rivista* 14 (2): 3–32.

5   Early Islamic Imperial Space[*]

A. C. S. Peacock

Within a century of the hijra (migration) of the Prophet Muhammad from Mecca to Medina in 622, the event taken as the start of the Muslim calendar and sowing the seeds for the establishment of the first Islamic state, Arab armies had conquered a vast territory stretching from Spain in the west to the Pamir mountains in Central Asia, and had begun the penetration of India. The formation of this empire profoundly reshaped the geopolitical environment of Eurasia, permanently depriving Byzantium of some its richest territories, destroying the Sasanian Empire which dominated Iran and the Middle East, and turning Spain into a Muslim-ruled space (a process it would take some seven hundred years to reverse definitively). However, just as the Islamic state reached its fullest extent, at least matching the Roman Empire at its height in terms of expanse and population (Kennedy 2007, 363), it started to disintegrate internally, in particular owing to the dissatisfaction of Muslims in recently conquered peripheral regions. The Umayyad Caliphate, under which the bulk of these conquests were undertaken, was overthrown by the Abbasids (750–1258), who drew their support largely from Muslim converts in Khurasan (eastern Iran and Central Asia), but the Abbasids were unable to maintain the unitary empire of earlier times. In Spain, survivors of the Umayyads established their own realm, which they eventually proclaimed to be a caliphate, and gradually even wealthy provinces closer to the Abbasid capital of Baghdad, such as Egypt, established a de facto independence under their governors. Similarly, in Central Asia and Iran governors, though nominally loyal to the Abbasids, formed their own dynasties by the 9th century, among them the ethnically Iranian Tahirids, Saffarids and Samanids. The rise of Shiism as a political force resulted in the emergence of a further rival caliphate, that of the Fatimids in North Africa, Egypt and Yemen, who established their base in Cairo in 969. At the same time, these centrifugal forces provided a further

[*] I am very grateful for the comments of Timothy Greenwood, Andrew Marsham, Eduardo Moreno Manzano and the editors during the composition of this chapter. I am also grateful to acknowledge the Türkiye Yazma Eserler Kurumu Başkanlığı for granting permission to reproduce images of manuscripts from Istanbul libraries.

impetus for the expansion of the Islamic world. In particular, the Turkish dynasties that came to dominate Central Asia and the Middle East in the 11th century, the Qarakhanids, Ghaznavids, and Seljuqs, played a crucial role in expanding the territories of the Islamic world towards China, India and Anatolia respectively.

In classical Islamic thought, as it evolved by the late 8th century, the world was divided into the realms subject to Muslim law, the *dar al-Islam*, and the non-Muslim 'abode of war' (*dar al-harb*), which in principle should ultimately be incorporated into the *dar al-Islam* through jihad (Albrecht 2016). Despite, or perhaps because of, the acute political fragmentation that started to emerge in this period, Muslims continued to conceive the *dar al-Islam* as a unitary whole, a vast region united by a common religious culture in which political boundaries did not impede travel and communication. To describe this as an imperial space is perhaps anachronistic even at the height of Umayyad and Abbasid rule, for classical Arabic contains no equivalent for the word 'empire'. Indeed, in the opinion of some jurists, the *dar al-Islam* was defined by territories where Muslims could live under Islamic law rather than simply the exercise of Islamic political sovereignty.[1] Rather than territorial expanse, Arabic political terminology (which was borrowed into Persian and Turkish) stressed the personal nature of rule using the term *dawla*, which originally indicated a turn of fate, but came to mean 'dynasty'. Terms like *khilafa* (caliphate), *mulk* (kingship) and *sultan* indicated the position and authority of the ruler, but not the territories subject to him (Kristó-Nagy 2016, 60). Perhaps the closest equivalent of the imperial vision was the caliphal claim to represent 'God's command' (*amr allah*) on earth, with its evident echoes of the Roman idea of *imperium*, which may have influenced the development of the Islamic concept (Marsham 2018, 26). Indeed, notwithstanding the absence of specific lexical equivalents to the term empire in the classical languages of the Islamic world, there is evidence that Muslim rulers and dynasties often perceived themselves to be the heirs to imperial traditions of late antiquity, as we will discuss further below. For this reason, I shall employ the term empire. In this chapter, I shall seek to establish the factors that limited and defined the early Islamic empires' territorial extent, down to the end of the 11th century, and ideological as well as the practical factors that encouraged expansion. I shall also consider the interplay between the ambitions of the caliphal

---

[1] Thus, in the opinion of some Muslim jurists, notably of the Hanafi school of law, areas subject to non-Muslim rule but which had a Muslim population that could live under Islamic law and was contiguous to other Muslim-ruled territories could be considered *dar al-Islam* (see Albrecht 2016). In practice, such a situation was limited to a few border locations such as the frontier with Byzantium, and of course in the view of such jurists the re-incorporation of such territories into Islamic political sovereignty was desirable, if not inevitable. Other schools of law, such as the Malikis who predominated in North Africa and Spain, insisted that Islamic political sovereignty was a prerequisite for a territory being considered part of the *dar al-Islam*.

centres, and those of local governors and actors in the establishment of the *dar al-Islam*, and how this space was imagined and represented in the geographical works that proliferate from the 9th century onwards.

5.1   The Emergence of the Islamic Empire, 622–750

Reconstructing the emergence of the Islamic Empire is fraught with difficulties. Although we have an abundance of Arabic sources that purport to relate in painstaking detail every campaign organised by the Prophet and his successors, these accounts, of which the most famous is the *Futuh al-Buldan* ('Conquest of Lands') by al-Baladhuri (d. 892) were all written down at a much later date, largely in the 9th to 10th centuries in Iraq. For such authors, the conquests needed little explanation; rather they showed God's favour to Muhammad and his community, which enabled them to seize such vast territories against overwhelming odds. Conversely, the non-Muslim sources, written largely by Christian authors in the lands conquered or attacked by the Arabs (very few written sources indeed survive from Sasanian Iran), offer only patchy snapshots of the conquests as perceived by their victims, and can offer little insight into the ideological motivation of the invaders (Hoyland 1997). Indeed, with good reason has it been questioned whether it is even legitimate to describe the early conquests as either Arab or Islamic. Arab identity was in the process of formation, and it is far from clear that the founders of the empire saw themselves as 'Arab', a term which may have had negative connotations in the conquest period (Athamina 1987, 11–13; however, see Hoyland 2014, 26 and in detail Webb 2016). Even the term Muslim or Islamic may not be appropriate (Donner 2018, 5–19). There is some evidence that suggests that the early Muslim community described itself as *mu'minun*, 'believers', and this term could in the early period also encompass Christians and Jews; certainly the term Islam appears rather rarely in our few contemporary documents. The first leaders of the community after Muhammad's death in 632 styled themselves *amir al-mu'minin* ('Commander of the Believers'), the title caliph (*khalifat allah*, God's deputy) only coming into use occasionally in literary contexts from the 650s, and spreading into more widespread use by the end of the 7th century, but even then only sporadically (Marsham 2018).

Thus, while in this chapter for the sake of comprehensibility I shall not eschew the terms Arab and Muslim, it must be born in mind when discussing the early to mid-7th century they may represent a later back projection of identity. Moreover, it is far from certain to what extent Muhammad had envisaged the new religion as universal, and whether his ambitions extended much beyond Arabia (Hoyland 2014, 37–8). In his own lifetime the most distant raid he conducted reached into modern Jordan, at least according to our later Arabic sources, while most of Arabia was probably still unsubdued. Muslim tradition records the letters he composed summoning to Islam the great rulers of the age, the Byzantine emperor and the Sasanian shah among them, although these are certainly fabrications of a later generation. Similarly, later tradition puts into Muhammad's mouth claims such as 'I have been ordered [by God] to fight people until they say "there is no god but God"; if they say that, they preserve their lives and their wealth inviolate, and they account for themselves to God' (al-Waqidi 2004, 2: 470). Such traditions clearly reflect Qur'anic ideas of the importance of engaging in holy war, as expressed for example in Q. 9: 111 'God has bought from the believers their selves and their possessions against the gift of Paradise; they fight in the way of God; they kill, and are killed; that is a promise binding upon God.'[2] In reality there is little evidence of forced conversion of subjugated peoples. Indeed, quite the opposite is the case (at least outside Arabia), for the Umayyad dynasty was eventually undone by its refusal to accommodate local converts.

That does not mean the early conquests were devoid of religious content. In fact, the key concept in the early Islamic period seems to have been that of hijra – of migration from one place to another, just as the Prophet had done in 622. Even Christian sources frequently refer to the invaders as *muhajirun*, those who make the hijra, and the concept was seen as a religious duty akin to waging holy war (jihad), which also brought financial rewards for those who participated in it (Crone 1994; Athamina 1987, 8–10). One imperative behind the conquests was the desire of the believers to perform the religious duty of hijra before the imminent last day. While initially the believers emulated Muhammad in migrating first from Mecca to Medina and then back again, in subsequent years men serving in the military performed hijra to the newly conquered territories outside Arabia, in particular the new garrison-cities (*amsar*) in Iraq and Egypt where they lived separated from the local population. Thus the concept of hijra remained potent under Muhammad's successors, the so-called Rashidun ('Rightly-guided') caliphs, namely Abu Bakr (d. 634), 'Umar (d. 644), 'Uthman (d. 656) and 'Ali b. Abi Talib (d. 661), who headed the community for the first thirty years after Muhammad's death in 632, and beyond.

Despite severe tensions within the early Muslim community over the legitimate succession to Muhammad, the Rashidun caliphs, based in Medina, saw a dramatic expansion in their territories. The first area to fall outside Arabia was Syria in 634–6, which was rapidly followed by conquests in Iraq, the political heartland of the Sasanian Empire, around 636–9, followed by Egypt in 639–40 (Map 5.1).[3] Yet it seems the conquering armies were rather unimpressive, both

---

[2] Translation from Arberry 1955.
[3] The sources are often rather contradictory about some of the precise dates, especially those for the conquest of Iraq; nonetheless, the broad pattern of consolidation of Muslim control by the end of the 630s seems clear, even if there were on occasion subsequent revolts, e.g. in Egypt. For the dates see Donner 1981; Kennedy 2007.

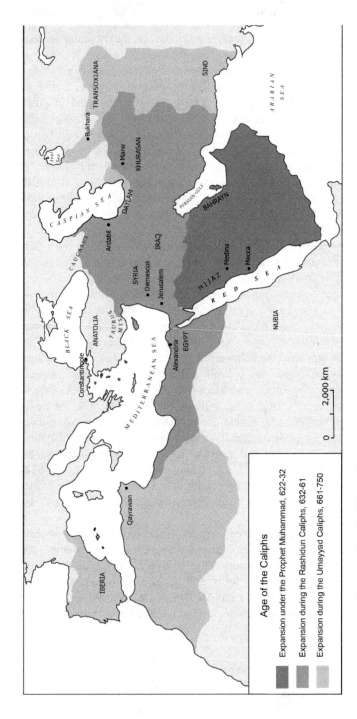

Map 5.1 The rise of the Caliphate, 632–750.

in terms of numbers and technological prowess (Kennedy 2001, 3–4; Sijpesteijn 2013, 53). The reasons for the Arab success must be sought not in their overwhelming military supremacy, but rather in the superior Arab morale, the ideological impetus for expansion provided by the new faith (cf. Donner 1981), and in the structural causes that had weakened existing empires from the mid-6th century onwards. The plague had blighted large parts of the Byzantine Middle East since 540, causing long-term decline in population, and there is evidence of severe climate change possibly resulting in crop failures and thereby contributing both to depopulation and a reduction in tax revenues. Alongside this picture of economic depression, warfare between the Byzantine and Sasanian Empires intensified, which presented a major financial challenge to Byzantium, and both empires also suffered from attacks of steppe peoples, the Avars and the Turks (Hoyland 2014, 29–30; Haldon 2016, 231–2, 251–2; Preiser-Kappeler 2018, 226–33). The Arab advance thus coincided with a more general crisis that debilitated the two major powers of western Eurasia. It is clear that there were numerous other groups, some of them Arab, operating before and during the lifetime of Muhammad but not associated with his venture, who sought to take advantage of the more general political collapse in the region by encroaching on Sasanian and Byzantine territory (Hoyland 2014, 56–7). Even in the late 620s, sources record the presence of Arab auxiliaries serving in the armies of both Byzantium and the Sasanians, assisting the Byzantine advance against Persia, on the one hand, and serving on the Sasanians' Caucasian frontier against the rival Khazar Empire, on the other (Whitby and Whitby 1989: 185; Dowsett 1961: 105).

The Hijaz may have been to some degree sheltered from the economic depression of the 6th to 7th centuries by the numerous gold mines located there (Heck 1999), and it is perhaps worth approaching sources that emphasise the poverty and barbarity of the invaders with a measure of scepticism. Similarly, the old thesis that Arab expansion was impelled by population pressure in the Hijaz has rightly been criticised (Donner 1981, 3–8; Donner 1995, 341–3). In fact, Arab success was doubtless assisted by the alliances they formed with local groups. Significant elements of the local population, espe-cially in Egypt where non-Chalcedonian versions of Christianity prevailed,[4] were alienated by religious differences from their masters in Constantinople and actively assisted the conquerors (Kennedy 2007, 148–9, 351–2; Sijpesteijn 2013, 54–8). Other groups agreed to be recruited into the service of the invaders in return for peace terms, as happened with the Jarajima, a group from the mountains of North Syria that had formerly been in Byzantine service. They

---

[4] Non-Chalcedonian churches, prevalent in Byzantium's Middle Eastern territories, rejected the conclusions of the Council of Chalcedon in 451 regarding the nature of Christ which was accepted by the empire's official Orthodox Church.

were given a treaty by the Muslims exempting them from the *jizya* and allowing them a share of the spoils of battle in return for military assistance (al-Baladhuri 1987, 217; cf. Kennedy 2007, 131–2). In North Africa, despite their initial resistance, which caused the Arab advance to falter over the later 7th century, the Berbers were converted to Islam, and in fact became the predominant element in the Muslim armies that went on to conquer Spain. In Iran and Central Asia, conversion and intermarriage gave rise to a Persian-speaking Muslim population.

It is questionable to what extent the conquests were centrally directed by the *amir al-mu'minin* in Medina. 'Umar is said to have been furious when he learned of the general 'Amr b. al-'As's advance on Egypt, the conquest of which was presented to him as a fait accompli (al-Baladhuri 1987, 298; see also Donner 1995, 347–500). 'Uthman is said to have been 'undecided' about whether North Africa (Ifriqiya) should be raided, even though it seems the attacks had already started (al-Baladhuri 1987, 317, *mutawaqqifan 'an ghaz-wiha*). Similarly, the conquest of the Iranian province of Fars is represented as a deliberate act of disobedience to 'Umar by the local Arab governor of al-Bahrayn (Daryaee 2002, 8–9). On other occasions the *amirs al-mu'minin* are represented as taking a more decisive role, appointing generals and governors (Donner 1995, 353–4; Kennedy 2001, 4), and, clearly, we must be cautious as to the picture presented by our later Arabic sources. In many instances these are evidently grinding axes with regard to the nature of the conquests, for this had significant financial implications for later generations: who had conquered a territory, and under what circumstances, whether peacefully (*sulhan*) or by force (*'anwatan*) determined the revenues to which Arab settlers were entitled, and indeed the legality of subsequent property transactions (Donner 1995, 351–2; Kennedy 2001, 3; Antrim 2012, 56–8). Yet it seems unlikely that an overall strategy directed the conquests in more remote areas, and in the tense religio-political environment of the early Islamic community, the *amir al-mu'minin* would have had reasons to be sceptical as to the motives and loyalties of those who fought in distant lands far beyond their effective control. Nonetheless, even if he could not and did not direct the details of tactics on the *dar al-Islam*'s frontiers, he may have given a general policy direction to his commanders, who seemed to have formed a cohesive social group hailing largely from the same Hijazi background as the *amir al-mu'minin*, and therefore probably understood what was expected of them even in the absence of explicit instructions (Donner 1995, 358–9).

The internal divisions within the early Muslim community over the rightful succession to Muhammad ultimately resulted, after a bloody civil war in 656–61, in the emergence of the Umayyad dynasty, distant relatives of the Prophet and former leaders of his tribe of Quraysh. With the accession of the governor of Syria, the Umayyad Mu'awiya, as *amir al-mu'minin* in 661, the centre of power shifted from the Hijaz, to Damascus, where the Umayyads had their base. Initially the Umayyad Empire was effectively divided into two halves for administrative purposes, with separate (and non-interchangeable) coinages adhering to the old Byzantine system and the Greek language in Greater Syria, the heart of the empire, and the Sasanian system and Pahlavi in Iran (Treadwell 2009). The Umayyad period witnessed an increased centralisation of power, with garrison towns established at far-flung parts of the empire such as Qayrawan in modern Tunisia and Marw in modern Turkmenistan, both in 670 (Hoyland 2014, 125), which were probably intended as bases for future conquests (Map 5.1). The late 7th century also witnessed challenges to Umayyad rule, with the emergence of a rival caliph in Medina, Ibn al-Zubayr (682–92), and ongoing wars with Byzantium which adopted a more aggressive stance under Justinian II (r. 685–96, 705–11) .

The Umayyad response was not just military but also ideological. From the reign of 'Abd al-Malik (685–705), the dynasty resorted to justifying its rule in much more explicitly Islamic terms, and administration underwent a process of Arabisation and centralisation. Greek and Persian were replaced by Arabic as the language of administration, a new coinage unified the previously distinct Sasanian and Byzantine fiscal realms with a common Islamic currency (Treadwell 2009), and the new Arabic language coins proclaimed the ruler to be *khalifat allah* (God's deputy). The use of this title has been interpreted a direct response to both the claims of Ibn al-Zubayr and the Byzantine emperors, who similarly called themselves on occasion God's deputies (Marsham 2018). By the end of the dynasty, we have even more explicit evidence that the Umayyads had started to conceptualise themselves as universal rulers, drawing on the late antique precedents of the Byzantines and Sasanians. Paintings on the Umayyad palace of Qusayr 'Amra in modern Jordan depicted the Visigoth ruler Roderic, the Sasanian ruler, the ruler of Axum and two other Asian rulers (probably those of the Turks, of China or of India) paying homage to the caliph, symbolising Umayyad domination over the entire known earth, while Qur'anic quotations compare the enthroned caliph to Adam, who had dominion over the entire world as God's deputy (Fowden 2004, 197–226; Marsham 2018). Such images were for the private consumption of the Umayyad family and its intimates; but in public monuments such as the al-Aqsa mosque in Jerusalem, constructed in 692, and the Great Mosque of Damascus, completed in 715, imagery suggested a deliberate association between the earthly realm of the Umayyads and paradise (George 2018).

Alongside this universalist rhetoric and the attempts at centralisation, the onset of the 8th century saw new waves of expansion into Spain, into Central Asia, and into India. To what extent, however, these conquests were guided by a deliberate policy is a matter of debate. In 711, for example, the same year as the conquest of Spain under largely Berber armies began, the governor of Iraq al-Hajjaj (d. 714) sent Muhammad b. al-Qasim al-Thaqafi to conquer Sind (Map 5.1). Having achieved his immediate objectives Muhammad b. Qasim wrote to al-Hajjaj asking for permission to advance, receiving the reply 'Advance and you are governor [amir] of whatever you conquer.' The general also wrote to al-Hajjaj's deputy, the governor of Khurasan Qutayba b. Muslim, who responded, 'Whoever gets to China first will be its governor' (Ya'qubi II, 289). In the event, Muhammad spent fifteen years fighting in Sind and India. The anecdote suggests an enduring uncertainty about command structures, objectives and strategy. While later historians are at pains to stress caliphal direction of all three campaigns, in practice the Umayyad writ in these distant frontier regions extended little beyond being able to change sporadically the local Arab governor. The apparently concerted nature of the three-pronged attacks of 711 may be little more than a coincidence: rather than grand strategy, it has been argued that the local initiatives of commanders were responsible for the Arab advance, conquests which were subsequently legitimised by caliphal recognition (Clarke 2018, 308–9). Their motives were doubtless the acquisition of prestige, but more importantly for a commander to reward his followers by providing them with booty, and to discourage the internecine tribal disputes that bedevilled the conquerors. One scholar has recently argued that, 'In a sense, the conquest of Iberia was carried out just to give the Berber rank and file something to do' (Clarke 2018, 309).

Yet the fact that the practice of warfare and expansion was messy does not necessarily negate their being at some level central direction behind it. Al-Hajjaj had been appointed by the Umayyads as viceroy in the east with a mandate to promote conquests, suggesting the importance of expansion, and it has been suggested that the ideological basis of the Umayyad state was jihad, even if the caliphs themselves never personally participated (Bonner 2006, 119–24; Blankinship 1994). Members of the dynasty were, however, appointed to governorships on sensitive frontiers such as Caucasia. Sources depict al-Hajjaj meticulously preparing for campaigns by commissioning maps of areas to be conquered such as Daylam and Bukhara (Pinto 2016, 47), while at the other end of the *dar al-Islam*, there is reason to think that the conquest of Spain constituted a co-ordinated attack supported by the Umayyad fleet in Egypt. If in the long-, and even short-term, Damascus found it difficult to exert its will effectively on the ground in these distant provinces, where local commanders would always have an incentive to put their interests before taxation demands from the centre, that does not mean their conquest was accidental (Moreno 2020). As the evidence from Qusayr 'Amra portraying the suppliant Visigoth ruler suggests, conquests in far-flung areas did resonate in the imperial centre in Syria where they fed into dynastic attempts to portray the caliphs as universal rulers.

Despite their spectacular successes, Muslim armies did meet setbacks. Even under the Rashidun, an attempt to advance beyond Egypt into Nubia was met with strong resistance, and the Muslims were forced to conclude a peace treaty (al-Baladhuri 1987, 331; Hoyland 2014, 76–8). It was not until the 15th century that this region would be definitively incorporated into the *dar al-Islam*. The conquest of North Africa in the second half of the 7th century was a slow and painful process, beset by much local resistance, as was that of Central Asia; in both regions a myriad of local rulers were able to muster resistance and thwart if not ultimately prevent the Arab advance. The 730s represent the high-water mark of Umayyad expansion, when a series of notable military defeats undermined the prestige of the dynasty and drew the borders of the *dar al-Islam*. In Europe, forces from Muslim Spain established a foothold as far north as Narbonne, but their defeat at the Battle of Poitiers (Tours) in 732 ensured that Muslim rule did not extend permanently into France. In Transoxiana, advance was halted by the Türgesh nomadic confederation which inflicted a humiliating defeat on Umayyad forces in 731, pushing the frontier back, while in the Caucasus, the Khazar Empire that dominated the steppe world to the north, was able to advance far into the *dar al-Islam*, sacking the Azerbaijani garrison city (*misr*) of Ardabil (Blankinship 1994, 149–61). From across the conquered territories, the bulk of evidence suggests the Arabs found it easiest to conquer urbanised, centrally ruled areas (such as Syria, Egypt, Spain) and more difficult to take over regions with deep social fragmentation lacking centralised administrative structures (such as North Africa and Transoxiana), or diffuse and decentralised power structures such as the Khazars and Türgesh (Moreno 2020). This perhaps explains the sudden fall of the Sasanian Empire. With its capital at Ctesiphon in Iraq, on the edge of the Arabian deserts, the Sasanians were highly vulnerable to assault. Moreover, the physical geography of Iran, with its large deserts separating provinces, made coordinated resistance hard once the imperial capital had fallen. With no centre left to resist, local communities agreed their own terms with – or fought – the invaders as they saw fit. Although it has been argued that the Sasanian Empire possessed a highly decentralised structure, which facilitated its fall (Pourshariati 2008), in fact, if anything the opposite may be the case (cf. Crone 2012, 1–2).

Rather more explanation is required however of the persistent Arab failure to defeat Byzantium, a centralised, urbanised state that continued to dominate Anatolia and the Balkans despite the loss of the wealthy provinces of Syria and Egypt.[5] It is clear that the conquest and destruction of the Byzantine Empire was a matter of prime strategic importance for the Umayyads, and indeed was a major theme of Muslim apocalyptic literature which saw the defeat or conversion of 'Rum' as presaging the eagerly awaited end of time (Tor 2005, 556–7).

---

[5] On the wealth of Syria and Egypt and their importance to the Byzantine economy see Haldon 2016, 27–9, 240.

Numerous Arab campaigns were launched against Constantinople, the first by Mu'awiya when still governor of Syria in 653. Arab bases were established in northern Syria and southeastern Anatolia from which annual attacks were launched into Byzantium, a pattern that continued until circa 740, although even after this attacks continued. Yet Byzantium proved resilient in its heartland. In part, ecological factors may have hampered a continuous Arab presence in Anatolia. The harsh winters that see most of the peninsula covered in a blanket of snow would have represented a much more inhospitable and unfamiliar environment to the Arabs than the temperate climates of Syria or Egypt; the Abbasid-era author al-Jahiz famously described Anatolia as the 'land where camels die', pointing to the difficulties Arabs might encounter operating in the region (cf. Preisser-Kappeler (Chapter 4, this volume)). In addition, in contrast to Syria or Egypt where towns seem frequently to have surrendered to the Arabs simply because there was no prospect of relief from the imperial armies, settlements in Anatolia were in closer proximity to Constantinople, with which they generally shared the Chalcedonian creed, providing an ideological bond missing in Byzantium's Levantine provinces, and they could at least hope for aid from Byzantine armies. While in Syria, Byzantine armies had been repeatedly trounced on the field of battle by the Arabs, in Anatolia the Byzantines appear to have followed a deliberate strategy of avoiding direct combat that enabled them to preserve sufficient military force to reoccupy and garrison areas temporarily seized by Arab armies during their seasonal raids. Furthermore, a concerted Byzantine effort at creating a border zone in the Tauus mountains to protect from Arab attacks seems to have been effective at preventing a permanent occupation (Haldon 2016, 142–5). Byzantium also seems to have maintained superiority at sea, despite Umayyad investment in the navy (Kennedy 2007, 325–32). Perhaps the most critical achievement of Byzantium, however, was in warding off Arab attacks on Constantinople, in particular a two-year long siege in 667–9, where disease in the Arab camp and the new weapon of Greek fire ensured the Arab defeat. The Byzantine ability to consolidate their defences behind the Taurus Mountains, to maintain control over inner Anatolia and above all to preserve the imperial capital Constantinople constitute the main reasons for its contrasting fortunes compared to the Sasanian Empire.

Initially, many conquered areas, especially the more distant ones, simply paid tribute to the new rulers and maintained a largely autonomous existence, as for example occurred in the Caucasus (Vacca 2017). The conquerors are generally thought to have continued the administrative practices of the areas they conquered, at least at first, yet the case for this may have been overstated. Administrative papyri from Egypt from as early as the 640s reveal Arabic technical terms being adopted into Greek, which remained the administrative language, and formal changes in the ways in which documents were drawn up that bespeak a rather more centralised administrative structure than is sometimes appreciated (Sijpesteijn 2013, 67–70). Indeed, in Egypt at least, the Arabs seem to have introduced a much more centralised administration than had been there in Byzantine times (Donner 1986, 12–13). Similarly, the conquest of Spain was followed rapidly by the institution of a fiscal census and by a new administration that made extensive use of letters, documents and seals, and a new coinage system (Moreno 2020). The empire, at least its central parts, was further linked the postal and road network (*barid*) that the Umayyads had inherited from their Byzantine predecessors and which facilitated the movement of troops. Yet the textual references, as well as the surviving milestones (largely from the reign of 'Abd al-Malik) suggest the limitations of Umayyad rule, or at least its priorities: while Khurasan, and the Hijaz were linked by the *barid* to the imperial centre in Syria, many other parts of the caliphate, such as North Africa, were not (Silversteijn 2007, 60–1).

As the institution of the *barid*, with its Roman roots, indicates, in many places there were continuities of practice; this was true too of policy, as the new regime faced similar problems to its predecessors. Thus in Caucasia, where the Umayyads inherited the Sasanian frontier with Byzantium, local noble families remained the basis of local power (Vacca 2017, 113, 125, 133, 137–40), and just as the Sasanians had sought to consolidate their control over the frontier region by encouraging migration from other parts of their empire, so too did the Umayyad governors promote Arab tribes' settlement in the region (Vacca 2017, 161–2). The conquests also rapidly led to transfer of men between different areas of the Islamic world. On occasion, the Umayyads instituted forced movements of population, and both Mu'awiya and al-Hajjaj are said to have resettled the Zutt people of Sind in Iraq where they formed an important component of the military (al-Baladhuri 1987, 522, 524; Kennedy 2001, 5). Spoils from the conquests prompted men to cross the *dar al-Islam* in search of opportunity. We read in al-Baladhuri of men from Marwarud in Khurasan participating in the conquest of Ifriqiya (al-Baladhuri 1987, 325, 326). Moreover, the governor of North Africa who ordered the conquest of Spain, Musa b. Nusayr, was the son of a Persian convert to Islam (Clarke 2018, 301). Clearly, however, it was the Arabs who made up the bulk (although probably not always the overwhelming majority) of the new set-tlers, except in Spain, where Berbers also played a major role. Initially, Arabs remained largely segregated from the local population in *amsar*, the garrison cities, or else displaced the existing population from parts of conquered cities, as happened in Bukhara. Arab settlement was tribally organised. Yet such settlement was by no means uniform, and it seems clear that initially many areas saw little Arab presence (Pourshariati 1998; Crone 2012, 18). It is only slowly, over the course of nearly a century after the initial conquest, that we can detect the spread of Islam as attested by material culture: the building of mosques, for instance, outside of the main urban centres (Moreno 2011, 125–6).

It was not until the early 11th century, if not later, that Muslims achieved a numerical preponderance over non-Muslims in most regions (Bulliet 1979; Peacock 2017).

5.2   From the Abbasid Revolution to 10th-Century Fragmentation

If the 730s saw Arab expansion halted by a series of reverses on distant frontiers, in the subsequent decade, the *dar al-Islam* started to fracture, firstly with the revolt of the Berbers of North Africa after 739, then in Khurasan, which became the incubator of the Abbasid revolution. In both cases, resentments because of the inferior status (and hence concomitant lack of tax privileges) granted to non-Arab converts (known as *mawali*, or clients, signifying their subordinate status to the Arab tribes) contributed, as feelings of both Berber and Persian identity remained strong. Indeed, unconverted non-Muslims may have played a substantial role in the revolts (Crone 1991; 2012, 7–27). Yet rebels also appealed to aspirations that they would restore a purer and more authentic Islamic state compared to the perceived corruption of the Umayyads. In North Africa this took the form of the idea that the caliph should be the most pious of the Muslims, irrespective of race; in the East, the revolution was based on the idea that a closer relative of the Prophet should hold the position. Both these attitudes had their roots in the religio-political disputes that gave rise to the civil wars that had scarred the Muslim community ninety years earlier, in the wake of which Mu'awiya had seized power, and continued to act as a rallying point for revolt throughout the dynasty's existence. The Umayyad state was also shaken by rebellions in the Hijaz, in Egypt and even in its Syrian heartland, connected to tensions over the legitimate succession to the Umayyad Caliphate and the endemic rivalry between different Arab tribes. By 750, the Khurasani rebels had destroyed the Umayyad Caliphate, massacring leading members of the dynasty, and proclaimed al-Saffah the first Abbasid Caliph, the descendant of an uncle of Muhammad named 'Abbas from which the dynasty took its name.

The Abbasid revolution marked a definitive reconceptualisation of the *dar al-Islam*, and, having come to power on the basis of Khurasani military support, the East played a central role in Abbasid politics. Indeed, reading Abbasid-era historians such as al-Tabari (d. 923), one is struck by how little they have to say even about wealthy provinces such as Egypt compared to Khurasan. For the first half century of Abbasid rule, the dynasty relied on émigré Khurasani soldiers, the so-called *abna' al-dawla*, and these were then replaced by slave-soldiers or mercenaries of Transoxianan origin, who formed the core of the Abbasid military in Baghdad.[6] The Abbasids' commitment to the east was also

---

[6] De La Vassière 2007 argues these troops were led by Soghdian or Turkish aristocrats and were mercenaries; they have been conventionally seen as Turkish slave-soldiers.

symbolised by the despatch of the second caliph al-Mansur's own son, al-Mahdi, as governor to Rayy (outside modern Tehran), which became a major economic centre during the period. For a brief period in the 9th century, under al-Ma'mun, himself born to a Persian mother and who served as governor of Khurasan, the eastern city of Marw became the capital of the caliphate.

More concretely, the Abbasids sought to bind together their reduced if still vast empire with much more intensive centralisation than had been the case under the Umayyads, in particular through a network of intelligence agents (*sahib khabar*) and a road and postal system (*barid*), which was much more extensive than its Umayyad antecedents. There seems to have been an effort to win hearts and minds by reducing the tax burden at least in certain key areas such as Iraq, where support for the claim to the caliphate of the descendants of 'Ali b. Abi Talib remained strong, resulting in several revolts.[7] Yet such attempts at redistribution inevitably created losers too, and in fact the Abbasids were generally perceived to have raised taxes sharply, creating further discontent (Munt 2016, 11). Despite the Abbasids' Khurasani power base, the east remained a hotbed of revolt, with various millenarian and nativist movements threatening Abbasid control locally, even if they never presented an existential threat to the caliphate (Crone 2012). However, Khurasan was far from exceptional: Egypt, the Jazira, Syria and even the Hijaz also witnessed numerous revolts (Munt 2016, 17). As a result, even when the Abbasids did win victories over external forces, such as the Battle of Talas in Central Asia where the Tang armies were defeated in 751, these did not serve as a basis for expansion, as the caliphs were obliged to focus on securing their rule from the centre.

The new dynasty attempted to combat internal threats by legitimising itself through the espousal of titles that suggested millenarian expectations, such as al-Mahdi ('the saviour'), but also through promoting a vision of themselves as pious Muslims in contrast to the worldly kingship of their predecessors. This view needs to be taken with a considerable grain of salt, for as we have seen the Umayyads seem to have espoused an image of themselves as God's deputies and their territories as an earthly reflection of paradise. The most striking and immediate consequence of the new orientation of the Caliphate was the abandonment of Damascus as capital, with Syria losing its political centrality.

---

[7] Supporters of the claim of 'Ali to the Caliphate against the Umayyads came to be known as the *shi'at 'Ali* or 'party of 'Ali' from which the term Shiism derives. In the first century or two of Islam, there were no significant theological differences between Sunni and Shiite, and thus the terms are anachronistic because neither can really be said to exist at this point in a meaningful way. However, if differences of religious doctrine and practice were muted, there were certainly significant groups who believed that 'Ali and his descendants were the rightful caliphs; many of these had supported the Abbasid revolution, whose leaders had maintained a distinct ambiguity as to the identity of the caliphs who would replace the Umayyads, giving the 'Alids hope that a candidate from among 'Ali's descendants would be appointed, hopes that were of course dashed with the Abbasids' accession.

Instead, in 762 al-Mansur built the new capital of Baghdad near the ruins of the Sasanian capital of Ctesiphon, its round plan with the caliphal palace at the centre emulating Sasanian towns, but also representing the disc of the heavens, suggesting Abbasid universalist claims (Lassner 1980, 163–83). Sasanian elements had not been wholly absent from Umayyad literature or art, but they received a new emphasis under the Abbasids (cf. Marsham 2009, 139–42, 185–6, 245–6, 313–14). These eastern influences were doubtless reinforced by the prominent role of bureaucrats of Khurasani origin, such as the Barmakids, a family of secretaries from Balkh in Afghanistan, where their ancestors had probably been Buddhist priests, and who dominated the administration under Harun al-Rashid (r. 786–809). The Abbasids consciously positioned themselves as inheritors of the mantle of the Sasanians, especially under al-Ma'mun (r. 813–33), who sponsored an extensive programme of translation from Pahlavi and Greek that aimed to stake the dynasty's claim to command universal knowledge and hence universal kingship in what has been termed a *translatio imperii* (Gutas 1998). Caliphal ambitions to assert themselves as universal rulers were also supported by the *mihna* (inquisition) by which al-Ma'mun sought to gain the acknowledgement of the religious classes of the caliph's right to determine doctrine – an effort which ultimately failed.

Public emphasis on Islamic piety also led the Abbasids to espouse an ideology (if not the practice) of jihad more conspicuously than the Umayyads. In contrast to their predecessors, Abbasids caliphs such as Harun al-Rashid and al-Ma'mun personally participated in frontier warfare against Byzantium (Kennedy 2001, 105–6), which they resumed after a lull during the Abbasid revolution. Regular frontier campaigns provided a platform for caliphs to display not just their martial prowess but their Islamic piety. A new province was created by Harun al-Rashid along the Syrian–Byzantine border, the *'awasim*, 'protectresses,' which were designed to supply the frontline regions (*thughur*). Yet the rhetoric belied the reality. In practice, the era of expansion was over, and in contrast to Umayyad times, there was no coherent attempt to destroy the Byzantine Empire, despite the regular (sometimes annual) campaigns (Map 5.2). Indeed, the mantle of holy war began to be taken over by private jihadis, known as *mutatawwi'a* or 'volunteers', pious ascetic scholars who from the late 8th century moved to the Byzantine frontier for that purpose, thereby seeking to emulate the example of the Prophet. These *mutatawwi'a* often had little regard for caliphal authority, and their assumption of what had once been one of the key functions of the Islamic state, the waging of war in God's path, in place of the caliph, is indicative of the increasing erosion of caliphal authority that marked the Abbasid period (Bonner 1992, Tor 2005). Even our image of the border regions may reflect the political concerns of the later geographers of the 9th century who were concerned to assert the unity of the *dar al-Islam* in

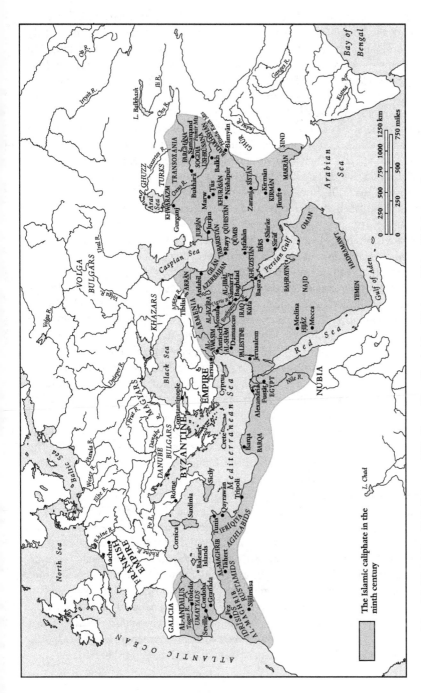

Map 5.2 The Abbasid Caliphate, *c.*800. From *New Cambridge History of Islam* Vol. 1, map 5.

The Islamic caliphate in the ninth century

a period of increasing political fragmentation. 'Like the *'awasim* the description of the *thughur* as fortified border zones filled with *mujahids* [holy warriors] in pitched battle against the enemy, projects a certain unity on Islam by drawing clear and precise lines between the Caliphate and its neighbors' (Vacca 2017, 89, cf. 109). At any rate, it is clear that such clearly delineated border regions were the exception rather than the rule, perhaps testimony to the ideological importance of jihad against Byzantium to Muslim rulers. In most of the Islamic Empire, except Spain where organisation comparable to the Byzantine–Muslim frontier existed, its borders were hazily defined and often simply petered out into desert (Kennedy 2007, 362).

The ending of expansion doubtless had its roots not just in the political collapse of the 740s, but also in the enduring internal political challenges that the Abbasids faced, and the increasing domination of men from the peripheries of the empire, even in its heart (Kennedy 2004). Quite apart from the various 'Alid and nativist revolts, even during what was perceived as the golden age of Harun al-Rashid and al-Ma'mun, provinces were asserting autonomy under effectively independent governors, military strongmen who took advantage of the weaknesses of the state to establish their own de facto dynasties. North Africa, always too distant to be controlled effectively from Baghdad, was from 800 ruled by the general Ibrahim b. Aghlab, founder of the Aghlabid dynasty (800–909), who acknowledged caliphal authority, and remitted tribute. In 821, al-Ma'mun granted the vast province of Khurasan to a Persian general, Tahir b. al-Husayn, who had been a vital support in his power struggle for the succession with his brother al-Amin. Even though Tahir had shown signs of independence before his death, omitting the caliph's name from his coins, al-Ma'mun was obliged to confirm his descendants in place. Further east, in Transoxiana, another dynasty of Persian origins, the Samanids, were in 819 granted the right to rule as hereditary governors, and survived as an effectively independent dynasty until 999. The process was to intensify in the later 9th century, as the caliphs started to lose control even in Iraq. The foundation of a new capital outside Baghdad, Samarra, in 836, aimed both to enhance the prestige of the dynasty with its magnificent palaces and to act as a base for the predominantly eastern, mainly Turkish military, whose relations with the population of Baghdad were poor. Yet the expenditure seems to have virtually bankrupted the caliphs, and left them at the mercy of their soldiers, who from 861 launched regular coups to install favoured candidates as caliph in the hope of extracting cash from them. In this environment of political chaos at the centre, the ground was ripe for the emergence of strongmen in the peripheries who openly challenged caliphal rule, such as the Saffarids, another Persian dynasty of humble origins who seized Sistan (western Afghanistan) from its Tahirid governors, and even marched on Baghdad, before being defeated just outside the city at Dayr al-'Aqul in 876 (Map 5.3).

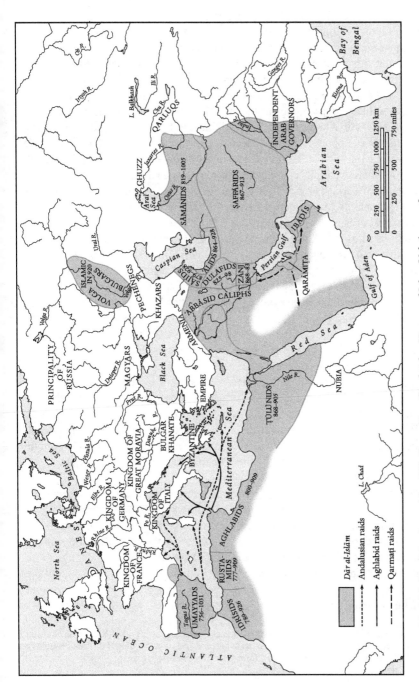

Map 5.3 The Islamic world, *c*.950. From *New Cambridge History of Islam* Vol. 1, map 6.

The process of fragmentation accelerated in the 10th century, with the emergence of rival caliphates. Members of the Umayyad dynasty who had taken refuge in Spain at this point declared themselves to be caliph. This was perhaps of limited significance from the Abbasids' point of view, Spain being a distant periphery they had never effectively controlled, but the emergence of the Ismaili Shiite Fatimids at the beginning of the 10th century presented a much more serious military and ideological threat.[8] The Fatimids, claiming descent from 'Ali b. Abi Talib and his wife Fatima, claimed to be the true legitimate caliphs, and, gaining support from the Berbers, overthrew the Aghlabids and made themselves masters of North Africa in 909. In 969 they occupied Egypt, a region where Abbasid central control had long been delegated to local military governors of Turkish origin. This was only a first step, however, for the Fatimids aimed not merely to dominate the entire Muslim world, but also to convert it to their strand of Ismaili Shiism (Map 5.3). To this end they despatched missionaries (*da 'i*s) across the Abbasid territories, aiming to convert local elites, meeting, it seems, with considerable success in Khurasan (Brett 2017, 116–20). Fatimid hegemony extended loosely into Yemen and even into Sind, but they never succeeded in their aim of taking Baghdad. The Fatimids aimed to assert themselves as leaders in the jihad against Byzantium, fulfilling the traditional function of Caliphs (Brett 2017, 120–4). They clashed with the Byzantines over control of Sicily, and in contrast to the Abbasids they developed a substantial navy to challenge Christian control of Mediterranean waters, but were never able to secure northern Syria, the essential prerequisite for a successful Anatolian campaign. Here, the amir Sayf al-Dawla (d. 967) of the Hamdanid dynasty of Aleppo had made a name for himself fighting Byzantium, exploits which were commemorated by the greatest of Arab poets, al-Mutanabbi, giving his name a lustre it has never lost even if his territorial acquisitions were insignificant. Indeed, faced with a resurgent Byzantium, the Hamdanids ended up as Byzantine tributaries and ultimately a bulwark against the Fatimids (Bianquis 1997; Kaldellis 2017, 24–79).

Even if, as in the case of the Hamdanids, the rhetoric was more impressive than the reality, it was such peripheral dynasties who kept alive the ideology of jihad more effectively than the rival caliphates of the 10th century. In the eastern borders of the Samanid state, volunteers gathered to do battle against the unconverted steppe people – the Turks. These *mutatawwi 'a*, just like those observed earlier on the Byzantine–Syrian frontier, were pious ascetics, but the Samanid state supported these efforts – perhaps less with a view to territorial expansion than because the sale of captured Turks, who were particularly

---

[8] Ismaili Shiism is sometimes also known, not wholly accurately, as 'Sevener' Shiism, recognising seven legitimate successors to Muhammad as imams, leaders of the Muslim community, along with their descendants. It thus differs from 'Twelver' Shiism, recognising twelve imams, the form that prevails in Iran and Azerbaijan today.

valued as military slaves, formed a substantial revenue stream for the Samanids, while the practice of jihad supported the legitimacy of this emergent Persian dynasty (Tor 2009). The gradual incorporation of these steppe peoples into the Islamic world was to have profound consequences and to lead to the second main wave of expansion.

5.3   Turkish Hegemony in the Islamic East, 11th to 12th Centuries

The Samanids recruited Turkish slaves into their own army as well as exporting them, and, as the Abbasids had found, they could constitute a significant and destabilising political force. Exiled from Bukhara for his role in a failed coup that had attempted to put his own candidate on the Samanid throne, in 962 the Turkish slave general Alptegin established himself at Ghazna, south of Kabul, on the far southern periphery of the Samanid state. Although he never formally repudiated Samanid authority, and indeed in due course received a patent of investiture as governor from the Samanids, he and one of his successors, his slave Sebüktegin (d. 997), lay the ground for the emergence of a new Muslim state, the Ghaznavid dynasty (977–1186), who were descended from Sebüktegin. The Ghaznavids, one of the first major Muslim dynasties of slave descent, continued many aspects of Samanid administrative practice, and by the beginning of the 11th century had absorbed large parts of the Samanid realm in Khurasan. Under the greatest Ghaznavid ruler, Mahmud (998–1030), an empire was established that stretched from Sind into Transoxiana, but the capital's location on the fringes of the Hindu Kush mountains gave it a new orientation (Map 5.4). Proclaiming himself to be a holy warrior (*ghazi*), Mahmud launched regular campaigns into India that gained immense wealth for the dynasty, as well as caliphal recognition of his status. The aim of these campaigns was not, it seems, to annex territory so much as to acquire plunder, but the dynasty became increasingly orientated towards India, relocating its capital to Lahore from the mid-12th century after the loss of many of its Khurasani territories. For the first time, India became the base of a significant Muslim state, and the Ghaznavids laid the groundwork for the pattern of the invasion and domination of north India by Muslim armies from Afghanistan and Central Asia that was to continue to the Mughal period (for which see Dale, this volume).

The Ghaznavids had been forced out of Khurasan by the emergence of other Muslim Turkish powers, the Seljuqs (*c.*1030–1194) and the Qarakhanids (*c.*999–1210, also known as the Ilek-Khans). Unlike the Ghaznavids, these were not slaves, although they were also employed as mercenaries in the Samanid forces. They seem to have entered Islam voluntarily (in contrast to the slave-soldiers who were compelled to convert) as a consequence of the broader spread of the faith in the steppe world since the 10th century, albeit a process that was certainly abetted by the Samanid *mutatawwi'a*. As the Samanid dynasty fell

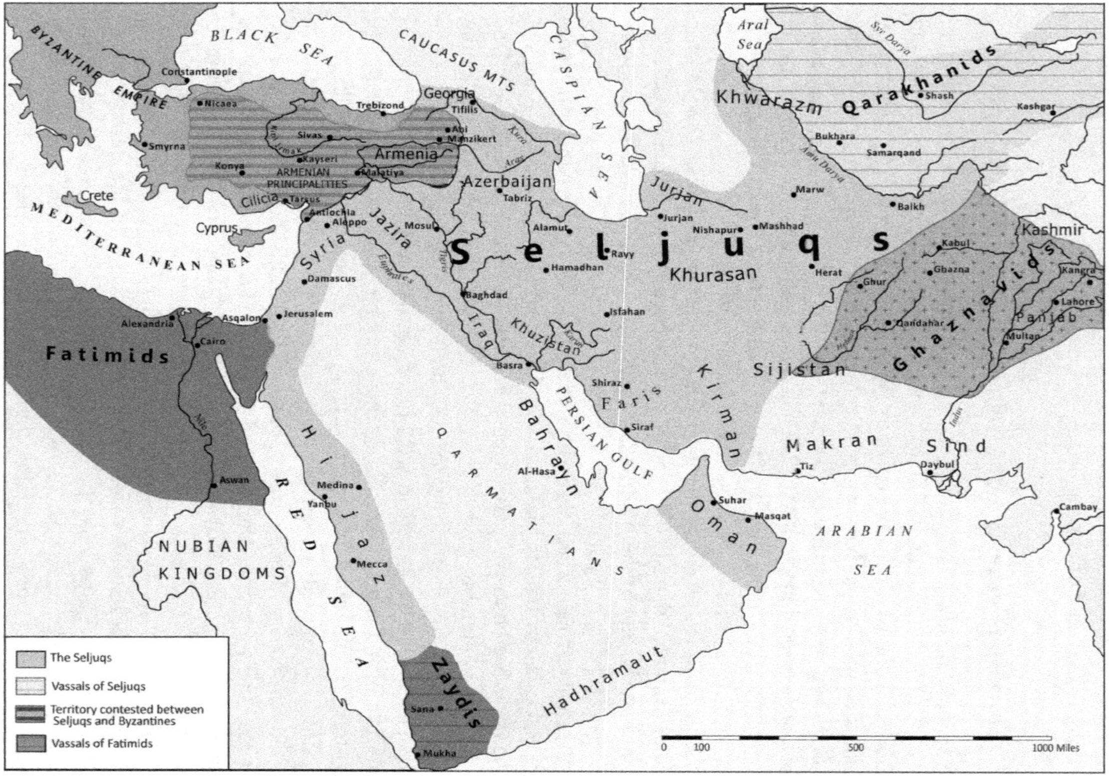

Map 5.4 The Islamic world, c.1050.

Legend:
- The Seljuqs
- Vassals of Seljuqs
- Territory contested between Seljuqs and Byzantines
- Vassals of Fatimids

apart, the Qarakhanids initially divided most of the spoils with the Ghaznavids, making the Samanid heartland of Transoxiana one of the centres of their empire, which spread across a vast extent of Central Asia as far east as Khotan (Golden 1990; Biran 2004). By the 1030s, the Seljuqs emerged as a major force, seizing the Ghaznavids' Khurasani territories and establishing the basis for an empire that its height would stretch from Palestine to Kashgar, incorporating the Qarakhanids as their vassals (Map 5.4). Both the Qarakhanids and the Seljuqs also played a major role in extending the boundaries of the *dar al-Islam*, with the Qarakhanids bringing Islam to much of what is now Xinjiang, while the Seljuqs won the prize that had always eluded the Arabs by securing the definitive conquest of most of Anatolia after their victory over Byzantium at the Battle of Manzikert in 1071. Although celebrated by later Muslim writers as a glorious jihad against Byzantium (contemporaries appear to have paid it little attention (Hillenbrand 2007)), the conquest of Anatolia seems to have come about more by accident than design. Expansion was impelled by ecological requirements, in particular the need for the Seljuqs' nomadic subjects to acquire the pasturelands essential for their lifestyle that were in short supply in much of the arid Middle East, but were abundant in Anatolia and Caucasia (Peacock 2010). As a result of these ecological constraints on the nomads who made up the bulk of their military during the establishment of the empire, Seljuq hegemony never extended over the more arid parts of the Middle East such as Arabia and Egypt, and even to maintain a foothold in Iraq remained a struggle. The limitations of the nomadic army also encouraged the Seljuqs to follow the path of previous Muslim dynasties and employ slave-soldiers.

The Seljuq, and to a degree the Qarakhanid state, about which our sources are much poorer, thus drew on both earlier established Islamic patterns of rule, and their own steppe heritage. The influence of the latter can be seen in the political structures of the two empires. In both, sovereignty was seen as inhering in the ruling family rather than a single individual ruler, and there was no fixed entitlement for any one member of the dynasty to accede to rule (cf. Biran, Chapter 6, this volume). Succession disputes thus often became protracted civil wars as various contenders sought to establish their suitability to rule by fighting for it. Both the Seljuq and Qarakhanid Empires were normally divided into eastern and western parts, with the eastern usually in the hands of the senior member of the ruling family. Such a territorial division between the senior eastern and junior western half can be observed in earlier steppe empires such as the 7th to 8th-century Gök-Türks. In these respects, they differed fundamentally from the Ghaznavids, whose Turkish ancestry was much less decisive in influencing their political structures, which were largely inherited from the Samanids. Yet the steppe influences should not be overestimated either. Like the Ghaznavids, both Qarakhanid and Seljuq realms encompassed major urban centres. In cities such as Bukhara, Samarqand, Isfahan and Baghdad, the Turkish rulers built palaces, becoming at least partially integrated into the Perso-Islamic culture of the lands they conquered, as is suggested by the extensive patronage by both dynasties of Persian literature. Yet such cities probably rarely became permanent bases for rule; rather, at least in the Seljuq case, sultans lived a largely peripatetic existence, perhaps less out of an atavistic nomadism than because only through perpetual itinerancy could power, always closely bound up with the physical presence of the ruler, be effectively asserted. To a large measure then, the Seljuq state lacked a single imperial centre, and the same is probably true of the Qarakhanids too.

The emergence of these three Turkish dynasties in the late 10th to early 11th centuries marks a turning point in the history of the Islamic world. Dynasties of steppe origin would henceforth dominate much of Middle East, Central Asia and India for the next millennium; yet their sudden emergence and rapid expansion defies ready explanation. The early Seljuqs, for example, are depicted in some sources and modern literature as a desperate bunch of half-starving nomads, whose take-over of Khurasan was impelled by the need to escape the ecological collapse of their steppe homeland, where climate change is argued to have made their nomadic lifestyle unviable (e.g. Bulliet 2009; Ellenblum 2012). Recent scholarship (e.g. Paul 2016; Tor 2018) has challenged the idea that climate change occurred in this period; even if it had, there is no reason to assume it would have had such consequences; nomads may often adapt rather than migrate. The success of these Turkish dynasties at establishing their dominion over most of the *dar al-Islam* west of Africa must perhaps, like that of the Arabs in the 7th century, be attributed to serendipity. Existing states such as the Samanids and the Buyids were beset by internal political weaknesses, while the rise of the Fatimids legitimised the emergence of powerful dynasties that explicitly identified themselves as Sunni, although the Seljuqs acted more as the Abbasid caliphs' captors than liberators after their conquest of Baghdad in 1055. Even in the Sunni world of the 11th century, Abbasid authority would not be restored, although with the decline of the Seljuqs in the late 12th century, Caliph al-Nasir li-Din Allah managed briefly to re-establish a limited caliphal government in Iraq, before this attempt too was destroyed by the Mongol invasion and conquest of Baghdad in 1258. The survival of the Abbasid Caliphate long after it had lost any effective power can be attributed to its utility in legitimising the upstart Sunni dynasties of the 10th to 12th centuries through the award of titles and insignia of rulership.

Ideological reasons behind Seljuqs and Qarakhanid expansion should be considered. The Turkish scholar Osman Turan (1955, 2003) argued that the Turks possessed an ideology of 'world domination' which he traced back to the 7th to 8th-century Gök-Türk Empire based in Mongolia. This is earliest Turkish state to have left extensive literary remains in the form of inscriptions attributed to the rulers, which certainly attest the influence of Chinese ideas of the qaghan possessing the 'mandate of heaven' (Biran, this volume). Tracing the trajectory of such views is difficult in the absence of much written evidence for steppe ideology in the subsequent period. Even in the 11th and 12th century, it is hard to discern the ideology of either the Seljuq or the Qarakhanid dynasties themselves as most of our sources were written in Persian or Arabic by bureau-crats from the sedentary peoples that were recruited into the dynasty's service and reflect their own priorities and concerns rather than the conquerors'. The Seljuqs did, however, mark a break with the past by adopting the new title 'sultan', never before employed as part of official titulature. They designated themselves on their coins as 'kings of east and west', perhaps suggesting claims to universal rule, as did their assumption of the ancient Persian title of *shahan-shah*. Signs of authority from the steppe world, such as the *tughra*, or stylised bow and arrow, were also employed on their coins, and the dynasty thus drew on Islamic, Persian and steppe symbols to legitimate itself, reflecting its multiple identities (Peacock 2015, 126–38). Indeed, it seems clear that even if our sources written by outsiders are sometimes none too complimentary about the Turks, they themselves suffered little self-doubt. A Qarakhanid prince, Mahmud al-Kashghari (d. after 1077) who dwelt under Seljuq rule in Baghdad started the Turkish-Arabic dictionary, the *Diwan Lughat al-Turk*, he dedicated to the Caliph al-Muqtadi in 1077 by stating he had written the work because now the time of Turkish domination had come, and it was imperative for others to learn their language:

When I saw that God Most High had caused the Sun of Fortune to rise the Zodiac of the Turks, and set their Kingdom among the spheres of Heaven; that He called them 'Turk,' and gave them Rule, making them kings of the Age, and placing in their hands the reins of temporal authority; appointing them over all mankind, and directing them to the Right; that he strengthened those who are affiliated to them, and those who endeavour on their behalf ... [then I saw that] every man of reason must attach himself to them, or else expose himself to their falling arrows. And there is no better way to approach them than by speaking their own tongue. (al-Kāśyarī 1982, 1: 70)

The idea that the Turks had been appointed by God, in Kashghari's words, 'over all mankind' does indeed seem to reflect claims to universal rulership, although it is harder to say whether these were borrowed from earlier steppe or in fact Abbasid antecedents. Yet as we shall examine below, Kashghari's work does reflect a fundamental shift in how the world was visualised and depicted, and a new conception of Islamic imperial space that puts Central Asia rather than the Middle East at its heart.

5.4   Imagining Islamic Imperial Space, 9th to 11th Centuries

Understanding how the Rashidun and Umayyads conceptualised their world remains a challenge, owing to the paucity of contemporary texts containing geographical information. However, from the 9th century Abbasid patronage sponsored the production of geographical treatises and maps. The earliest of these was the now lost world map by the astronomer and mathematician al-Khwarazmi (d. *c.*850) commissioned by al-Ma'mun as part of his translation project. Al-Khwarazmi's map drew both on Ptolemy's *Geography* and contemporary information from a geodetic survey the caliph ordered. The map, which calculated the earth's circumference with surprising accuracy, aimed to distinguish the *dar al-Islam* from the non-Muslim world, and showed an awareness of locations as distant as China, with which the Abbasids enjoyed extensive trade relations (Park 2012, 59–60). Later 9th and 10th-century geographical treatises were produced by secretaries, who were expected to possess geographical knowledge as part of their duties (Zadeh 2011, 19), and are sometimes referred to as administrative handbooks. While providing information on the routes linking the disparate parts of the Islamic world to Baghdad, they also had an ideological function in promoting a specific vision of the Abbasid Empire, emphasising the centrality of Iraq and Baghdad. Thus Ibn Khurdadhbih, a 9th-century official who was also boon companion to the Caliph al-Mu'tamid (870–92) (Zadeh 2011, 17–18), divides the world up into quarters arranged at compass points radiating out of Baghdad (Antrim 2012, 102–4). Ibn Khurdadhbih starts his geography, the *Kitab al-Masalik wa'l-Mamalik* ('Book of Routes and Realms'), which is essentially aimed at delineating the routes of the *barid*, by saying "I shall start with an account of the Sawad [central Iraq], which the kings of Persia called *dil-i Iranshahr* [lit. the heart of the land of Iran], in other words the heart of Iraq" (Ibn Khurdadhbih 1889, 5). Here, not only is Iraq explicitly identified with the Sasanian heartland, but much of the administrative terminology employed by Ibn Khurdadhbih is drawn from the Persian. Indeed, Ibn Khurdadhbih divides up the regions of the world for administrative purposes according to *tassuj*, or cantons, which he explains as an administrative region deriving from Sasanian practice. He further incorporates Persian legendary history into his conception of the world, describing how the ancient Persian king Faridun divided his lands between his sons, Salm, Tuj and Iran. Alongside these Sasanian antecedents Ibn Khurdadhbih also conceptualises the world in Islamic terms, relating the regions he discusses according to their orientation towards the *qibla* in Mecca, the direction that Muslims are obliged to face when praying. His description of the lands of the *dar al-Islam* strives to associate them with sacred history, such as tales of the Prophet Solomon in Yemen, the events mentioned in the Qur'an, and the life of the

Prophet Muhammad. Persian and Islamic elements are thus integrated in this conception of space, and the Abbasids are identified as the successor to the Sasanians (Zadeh 2011, 25–6; Antrim 2012, 10–4).

The 10th century saw the emergence of a new school of geography, the so-called Balkhi school,[9] of whom the leading representatives were al-Istakhri (d. after 951–2), Ibn Hawqal (d. after 978) and al-Muqaddasi (d. 991). The primary concern of schematic maps such as those in al-Muqaddasi's *Ahsan al-Taqasim fi Ma'rifat al-Aqalim* ('The Best Divisions to Knowledge of the Regions') was to show how the Islamic world was connected through networks of roads (e.g. MS Ayasofya 2971 M[10], which depicts the road network across Arabia (Fig. 5.1)). In contrast to the 9th-century administrative handbooks such as that of Ibn Khurdadhbih, Baghdad is no longer the centre of the Islamic world. Even on the map of Iraq, Baghdad is no more prominent or better connected than the city of Wasit in the south of the country. Rather, these 10th-century maps emphasise regional differences and boundaries, deriving from Abbasid provincial divisions. Several maps in MS Ayasofya 2577 M, a manuscript of Ibn Hawqal's work, underline this point: in that of Sistan province (p. 207) (see Fig. 5.2), the line encompassing the bottom, left and right of the map forms the words *hudud Sijistan*, 'the borders of Sistan', separating the province not just from the *dar al-harb* of India to the south, but equally from other Iranian and Islamic regions to the west, east and north. At the same time the text itself continues to use the old Sasanian administrative terminology such as *kura*; but despite the continuity of terminology, the unity of not just the *dar al-Islam*, but also *Iranshahr* is lost.

We can see the same phenomenon in a Persian translation of al-Istakhri that has come down to us in a 14th-century copy, MS Ayasofya 3156 (Fig. 5.3), which is even more consistent in labelling borders on virtually every map. Its map of Khurasan, for instance (fols. 84b–85a), clearly marks 'the borders of Transoxiana and Bukhara' at the top, in the north, the 'borders of the Indian Ocean in the east (right), the borders of Gurgan and Qumis in the southwest (bottom left) and the deserts dividing Khurasan from other provinces. The desert between Marw and the Oxus also occupies a prominent part of the left side of the map, but the line through its middle indicates it is not impassable. Overall, however, it gives the impression of an Islamic world divided into provinces with clear and recognised borders. If this is doubtless something of a fiction on the part of these writers, as there is no evidence for actual borders in terms of manned border posts between the different regions of the Islamic world, it nonetheless points to a heightened

[9] The school is named after Abu Zayd Ahmad b. Sahl al-Balkhi (d. 934), none of whose geographical works – if indeed he actually wrote any – survive, but whose maps are said to have formed the basis for those of the later three authors. There is however considerable doubt as to accuracy of this attribution of a school of mapping to al-Balkhi, see Pinto 2016, 55–6.
[10] Manuscript copied in 658AH/1260AD.

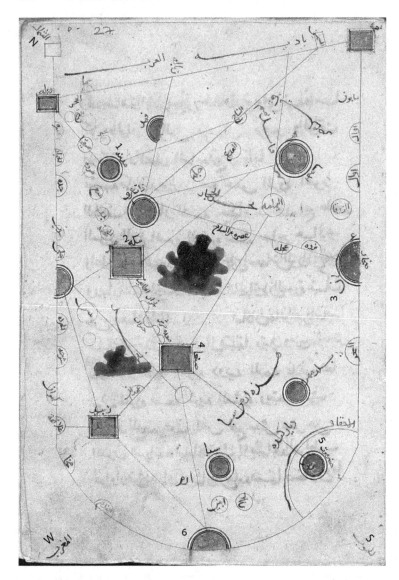

Fig. 5.1 Al-Muqaddasi, *Ahsan al-Taqasim fi Ma'rifat al-Aqalim.* Depiction of the road network of Arabia. Süleymaniye Library, Istanbul, MS Ayasofya 2971M, fol. 50a.
1. Medina; 2. Mecca; 3. Oman; 4. Sana'a; 5. Hadhramaut; 6. Aden

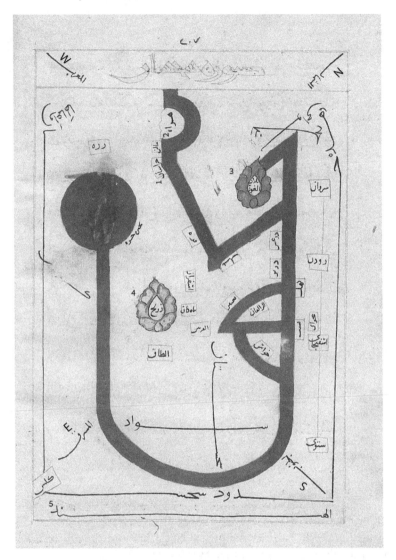

Fig. 5.2 Ibn Hawqal's *Kitab Surat al-Ard*, map of Sistan. Süleymaniye
Library, Istanbul, MS Ayasofya 2577M, p. 207.
1. Khurasan; 2. Herat; 3. Land of Ghur; 4. Zaranj; 5. India (al-Hind)

sense of regional identity, an increasing way in which the province defined
identity. Yet it is striking that maps of the Balkhi school never allude to the
political rulers of these territories (even though the accompanying texts do).

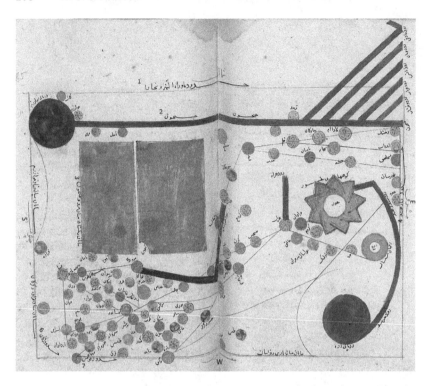

Fig. 5.3 Al-Istakhri, *Kitab al-Masalik wa'l-Mamalik* (Persian translation), map of Khurasan. Süleymaniye Library, Istanbul, MS Ayasofya 3156, fols 84b–85a.
1. Borders of Transoxiana and Bukhara; 2. Oxus (Amu Darya River); 3. Deserts of Turkestan; 4. Borders of the Lands of India; 5. Marw; 6. Borders of Gurgran; 7. Borders of Qumis

There is no indication, for example, that Khurasan is ruled by the Samanids from the map in al-Istakhri. In this way, these maps give voice to regional identities while avoiding explicitly impugning the political unity of the *dar al-Islam*, however theoretical that may have been by this date.

We must remember that these maps – and indeed their accompanying texts – are not precise imitations of the originals which are now lost to us, as no 10th-century copies have survived. Nonetheless, the geographers' written texts do give us a fair indication that these visual representations remain faithful, at least in outline, to the original conception and visual language. Al-Muqaddasi, for example, tells us in his text how he had colour coded his map, using red for roads, yellow for deserts, green for sea, blue for rivers and grey for mountains (cf. Kaplony 2008, 141; Pinto 2016, 46), and precisely such a scheme can be seen in MS Ayasofya 2971-M. Nonetheless, no two manuscripts of the same work contain identical maps, and there is evidence that sometimes alterations could be introduced with a specific political purpose in mind, maps in the same work could be redrawn for different purposes. Ibn Hawqal's *Surat al-Ard*, for example, exists in several versions. One of these (MS Ayasofya 2934) was dedicated to the 10th-century Syrian Hamdanid ruler Sayf al-Dawla, although only a fragment survives, which itself seems to have been updated in the mid-12th century.[11] In its map of the world (fols. 4b–5a, Fig. 5.4), Mecca and Damascus are given centre stage, perhaps reflecting a desire to place the Syrian homeland of the patron at the centre, while playing down the role of Iraq given Sayf al-Dawla's often difficult relations with the Abbasids.[12] However, other versions of Ibn Hawqal's text, which do not mention a specific dedicatee, place Iraq right at the centre of the world map (Ayasofya 2577-M) (Fig. 5.5). It is perhaps significant that in this latter manuscript's map of Iraq, Dayr al-'Aqul, the place where Abbasid forces won a decisive victory over the Saffarids in 876 is prominently marked, perhaps intending to commemorate the enduring independence and prestige of the Caliphate, at least in theory.[13]

In contrast, in Ibn Hawqal's map of Iraq (Fig. 5.6, fol. 44b), Ayasofya 2934 singles out for special attention with red box lines places associated with antiquities – Babel (Babylon), one of the oldest settlements in Iraq, which the text states was the city of the Pharaohs, rebuilt by Mansur b. Mazyad al-Sadi in 470AH, Kawtharba, associated with the Prophet Abraham, and al-Qasr, by which it seems Karbala' is meant.[14] Given the Hamdanids' Shiite tendencies, it is evident that such a reference could have had specific significance for them; yet at the same time it is unclear whether we are dealing with a 10th-century Syrian adaptation of the map, or one of the 12th-century or even later, given the manuscript is 14th century. It is entirely possible that it reflects a variety of influences and interventions, but it is clear that the maps reflect a desire to play down the significance of Baghdad, which could be consistent with either a Hamdanid or later, post-Abbasid agenda.

Political and ideological considerations also seem to have shaped our one surviving complete Fatimid geographical treatise and associated set of maps, the *Kitab Ghara'ib al-Funun* ('Book of Curiosities'), composed in Egypt

[11] The year 550 AH/1155–6 CE is mentioned as the present time, fol. 45b.

[12] Sayf al-Dawla claimed Damascus, though never actually seized it. He was denied the title *amir al-umara'* by the Caliph al-Muttaqi, and was never recognised by the Caliph as ruler of his Syrian territories. See Bianquis 1997.

[13] Ibn Hawqal, *Kitab Surat al-Ard*, Map of Iraq Süleymaniye Library, Istanbul, MS Ayasofya 2577-M, p. 99.

[14] The text states Karbala' is by Qasr Ibn Hubayra; reference to the Mazyadid confirms later intervention in the text.

Fig. 5.4 Ibn Hawqal, *Kitab Surat al-Ard*, map of the world. Süleymaniye Library, Istanbul, MS Ayasofya 2934, fols 4b–5a.

1. Yemen; 2. Mecca; 3. Damascus; 4. Equator

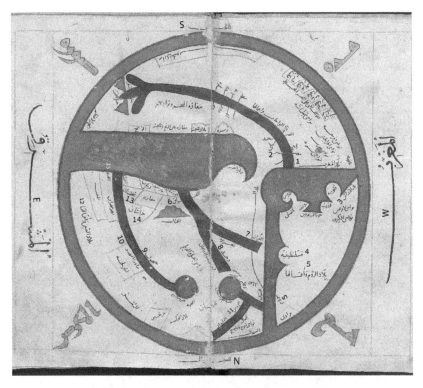

Fig. 5.5 Ibn Hawqal, *Kitab Surat al-Ard*, map of the world. Süleymaniye
Library, Istanbul, MS Ayasofya 2577-M, p. 5.
1. Maghrib; 2. Egypt; 3. Andalus; 4. Constantinople; 5. Rum (two locations);
6. Iraq; 7. Euphrates R.; 8. Tigris R.; 9. Oxus (Amu Darya River); 10.
Transoxiana; 11. Rus'; 12. China; 13. Sijistan; 14. Khurasan; 15. India

*c.*1020–50. Whereas the Abbasid Balkhi tradition had emphasised 'routes and
realms', that is, land-based communication, the *Ghara'ib al-Funun* stresses
seaborne communication across the Indian Ocean and the Mediterranean,
aiming to 'represent the maritime spaces of the entire known world'
(Rapoport and Savage-Smith 2018, 234). In part, this reflects the Fatimids'
own preoccupations, as a major maritime power that sought to dominate the
Mediterranean and enjoyed commercial links far down the African littoral.
The work's depictions of fortifications in major Mediterranean ports such as
Mahdia (in Tunisia) and Palermo may have served a propagandistic purpose,
asserting the impregnability of Fatimid defences, and thus the dynasty's role
in the ongoing jihad against Christianity (Rapoport and Savage-Smith 2018,
173, 179–80). Yet in part the maritime concerns of these maps may also reflect

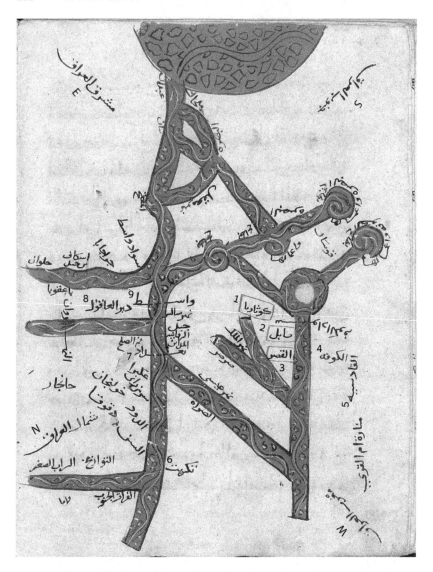

Fig. 5.6 Ibn Hawqal, *Kitab Surat al-Ard*, map of Iraq. Süleymaniye Library, Istanbul, MS Ayasofya 2934, fol. 44b.
1. Kawtharba; 2.Babel; 3. al-Qasr; 4. Kufa; 5. al-Qadisiyah; 6. Tikrit; 7. Baghdad; 8. Dayr al-'Aqul; 9. Wasit

Ismaili ideology, for the *da'wa* (the organisation responsible for Ismaili missionary activity) divided the world into regions called islands (*jaza'ir*), each of which was subject to a regional head of the *da'wa* who reported back to Cairo (Rapoport and Savage-Smith 2018, 234–6).

A similarly politicised conception of space can be found in the map that accompanied Kashghari's *Diwan Lughat al-Turk*, the text cited above that proclaimed that the time of universal Turkish rule had come in the 11th century. The *Diwan Lughat al-Turk* survives in a copy made in Damascus in 1266, and it is clear that the copyist altered and updated the map, given the information in the accompanying text (Kaplony 2008). Kashghari's original had focused on the Turkish tribes of Central Asia, indicated by colour coded dots, who were situated between the two poles of his world – Byzantium and China. In particular, the Qarakhanid heartland around their capital of Balasaghun (in modern Kyrgyzstan) was placed centre stage (Fig. 5.7). This conceptual universe survived in the Damascus 1266 recopying, but the copyist also expanded the map to incorporate territories such as East Africa and Andalus that were probably not originally present. The 1266 copy thus presents an image of the world with Central Asia and Balasaghun at its heart, while Baghdad was marginalised. This representation was in essence faithful to Kashghari's original, but was also pertinent to the circumstances of the *dar al-Islam* shortly after the final destruction of the Abbasid Caliphate by the Mongols in 1258.

Nonetheless, it is remarkable that even Kashghari's map, with its evident political agenda, avoids dividing the *dar al-Islam* into political units. The theme we see running through our various maps' treatment of Islamic imperial space is a desire to obfuscate the reality of political fragmentation and disunity. The maps, then, stand as testimony to the ways in which an ideal of a single imperial polity that encompassed the entire *dar al-Islam*, and ultimately the world, remained potent, even if it had only been fleetingly achieved by the Umayyads, ironically remembered by later generations as the most impious and least Islamic of Muslim dynasties. Nonetheless, throughout early Islamic times, under Umayyads, Abbasids and Turkish rule, we can see evidence too of an ideology of universal rule that drew on late antique precedents. Similarly, the Qur'anically-enjoined ideology of jihad remained a potent ideological tool to which subsequent dynasties such as the Abbasids and Fatimids laid claim; but in reality the political and religious fragmentation of the *dar al-Islam* meant that dynasties tended to prioritise expansion within rather than beyond it after the mid-8th century. It was mainly with the emergence of new Muslim powers on the peripheries of the Islamic world in Central Asia, the Turks, that the process of expansion of the *dar al-Islam* resumed in the 11th century, as well as laying the ground

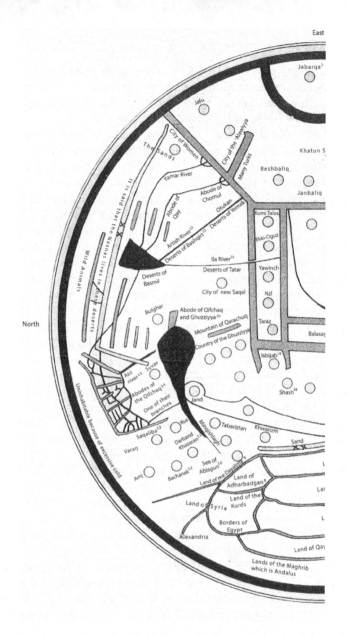

Fig. 5.7 Mahmud Kashghari, *Diwan Lughat al-Turk*, map of the world.
Adapted from al-Kāšyarī, Maḥmūd. 1982. *Compendium of Turkish Dialects*.
Ed. and tr. Robert Dankoff with James Kelly. Cambridge MA: Harvard
University Press, vol. 1, between pp. 82–3.
1. Japan; 2. China; 3. Land of Gog and Magog; 4. Wall of Alexander; 5. Sri
Lanka; 6. Syr Darya River; 7. Black people; 8. Azerbaijan; 9. Dailamites; 10.
Caspian Sea; 11. Khazars; 12. Pechenegs; 13. Slavs; 14. Qipchaks; 15. Volga
River; 16. Kashmir; 17. Amu Darya River; 18. Tashkent; 19. Isfijab; 20.
Qipchaqs and Ghuzz; 21. Ili River; 22. Bashkirs; 23. Irtysh River

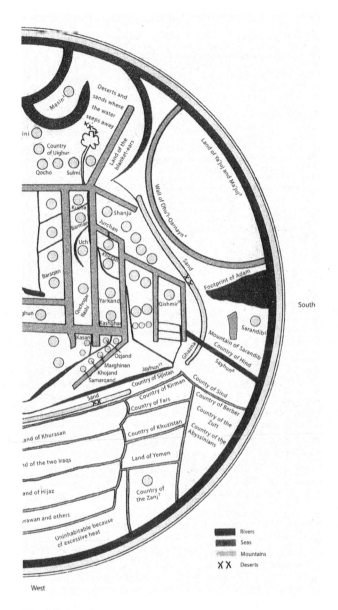

South

West

Rivers
Seas
Mountains
X X Deserts

Masin²
ini
Country
of Uighur
Qocho   Sulmi

Deserts and
sands where
the water
seeps away

Land of the
blanket-ears

Wall of Dhu'l-Qarnayn⁴

Land of Ya'jūj and Ma'jūj³

Kusha
Barman
Uch
Shanju
Jurchan
Khotan
Barsqan
Qochnoga
Balisi
Yarkand
Qishmir¹⁴
Footprint of Adam
yhun
Kasan
Ozjand
Marghinan
Khojand
Samarqand
Kashghar
Jayhun¹³
Sand
Sarandib
Mountain of Sarandib
Country of Hind
Ghazna
Sayhun⁶
Country of Sijistan
Country of Kirman
Country of Sind
Country of Berber
Sand
X X
Country of Fars
Country of Khuzistan
Country of the
Zutt
Country of the
Abyssinians
and of Khurasan
nd of the two Iraqs
Land of Yemen
and of Hijaz
Country of
the Zanj⁷
rrawan and others
Uninhabitable because
of excessive heat

Fig. 5.7 (cont.)

for the subsequent domination of the Muslim world by another steppe people, the Mongols.

Bibliography

Albrecht, Sarah. 2016. 'Dār al-islām wa dār al-ḥarb', *Encyclopedia of Islam, THREE*. Brill Online.

Athamina, Khalil. 1987. '*A'rāb* and *muhājirūn* in the Environment of *amṣār*', *Studia Islamica* 66: 5–25.

Antrim, Zayde. 2012. *Routes and Realms: The Power of Place in the Early Islamic World*. New York: Oxford University Press.

Arberry, Arthur J. 1955. *The Koran Interpreted*, 2 vols. London: Allen & Unwin.

Al-Baladhuri (d. 892). 1987. *Futuh al-buldan*, ed. 'Abdallah Anis al-Tabba' and 'Umar Anis al-Tabba'. Beirut: Mu'assasat al-Ma'arif.

Bianquis, Th. 1997. 'Sayf al-Dawla', *Encyclopedia of Islam*, 2nd edn. Brill Online.

Biran, Michal. 2004. 'Ilek-Khanids', *Encyclopaedia Iranica*, http://www.iranicaonline.org/articles/ilak-khanids

Blankinship, Khalid Yahya. 1994. *The End of the Jihad State: The Reign of Hisham Ibn 'Abd al-Malik and the Collapse of the Umayyads*. Albany, NY: State University of New York Press.

Bonner, Michael. 2006. *Jihad in Islamic History: Doctrines and Practice*. Princeton, NJ: Princeton University Press.

Brett, Michael. 2017. *The Fatimid Empire*. Edinburgh: Edinburgh University Press.

Bulliet, Richard. 1979. *Conversion to Islam in the Medieval Period: An Essay in Quantitative History*. Cambridge, MA: Harvard University Press.

Bulliet, Richard. 2009. *Cotton, Climate, and Camels in Early Islamic Iran. A Moment in World History*. New York: Columbia University Press.

Clarke, Nicola. 2018. 'Caliphs and Conquerors: Images of the Marwanids and Their Agents in Narratives of the Conquest of Iberia'. In *Power, Patronage and Memory in Early Islam: Perspectives on Umayyad Elites*, ed. Alain George and Andrew Marsham, 301–19. Oxford: Oxford University Press.

Crone, Patricia. 1991. 'Mawlā', *Encyclopaedia of Islam*, 2nd edn. Brill Online.

Crone, Patricia. 1994. 'The First-Century Concept of *Hiğra*'. *Arabica* 41: 352–87.

Crone, Patricia. 2012. *The Nativist Prophets of Early Islamic Iran: Rural Revolt and Local Zoroastrianism*. Cambridge: Cambridge University Press.

Daryaee, Touraj. 2002, 'The Collapse of Sasanian Power in Fārs/Persis'. *Name-ye Iran-e Bastan* 2(1): 3–18.

Donner, Fred M. 1981. *The Early Islamic Conquests*. Princeton, NJ: Princeton University Press.

Donner, Fred M. 1986. 'The Formation of the Islamic State'. *Journal of the American Oriental Society* 106: 283–96.

Donner, Fred M. 1995. 'Centralized Authority and Military Autonomy in the Early Islamic Conquests'. In *The Byzantine and Early Islamic Near East, III. States, Resources and Armies*, ed. Averil Cameron, 337–60. Princeton, NJ: Darwin Press.

Donner, Fred M. 2018. 'Talking About Islam's Origins'. *Bulletin of the School of Oriental and African Studies* 81: 1–23.

Dowsett, C.J.F. (trans.). 1961. *The History of the Caucasian Albanians by Movsēs Dasxuranci*. London: Oxford University Press.

Ellenblum, Ronnie. 2012. *Collapse of the Eastern Mediterranean: Climate Change and the Decline of the East, 950–1072*. Cambridge: Cambridge University Press.

Fowden, Garth. 2004. *Qusayr 'Amra: Art and the Umayyad Elite in Late Antique Syria*. Berkeley, CA: University of California Press.

George, Alain. 2018. 'Paradise and Empire'. In *Power, Patronage and Memory in Early Islam: Perspectives on Umayyad Elites*, ed. Alain George and Andrew Marsham, 39–67. Oxford: Oxford University Press.

Golden, Peter B. 1990. 'The Karakhanids and Early Islam'. In *The Cambridge History of Early Inner Asia*, ed. Denis Sinor, 343–70. Cambridge: Cambridge University Press.

Gutas, Dimitri. 1998. *Greek Thought, Arabic Culture. The Graeco-Arabic Translation Movement in Baghdad and Early 'Abbasid Society (2nd–4th / 8th–10th Centuries)*. London: Routledge.

Haldon, John. 2016. *The Empire that Would Not Die: The Paradox of Eastern Roman Survival, 640–740*. Cambridge, MA: Harvard University Press.

Heck, Gene W. 1999. 'Gold Mining in Arabia and the Rise of the Islamic State'. *Journal of the Economic and Social History of the Orient* 42(3): 364–95.

Hillenbrand, Carole. 2007. *Turkish Myth and Muslim Symbol. The Battle of Manzikert*. Edinburgh: Edinburgh University Press.

Hoyland, Robert. 1997. *Seeing Islam as Others Saw It*. Princeton, NJ: Darwin Press.

Hoyland, Robert. 2014. *In God's Path: The Arab Conquests and the Creation of an Islamic Empire*. New York: Oxford University Press.

Ibn Hawqal (d. 988). n.d. *Kitab Surat al-Ard*. Süleymaniye Library, Istanbul, MS Ayasofya 2934 (no date of copying, possibly 13th century); MS Ayasofya 2577M (copied 711AH/1311AD).

Ibn Khurdadhbih (d. 912). 1889. *Kitab al-Masalik wa'l-Mamalik*, ed. M.J. de Goeje. Leiden: Brill.

Al-Istakhri (d. after 951–2). *Kitab al-Masalik wa'l-Mamalik* (Persian translation). Süleymaniye Library, Istanbul, MS Ayasofya 3156 (no date of copying, 14th century).

Kaldellis, Anthony. 2017. *Streams of Gold, Rivers of Blood: The Rise and Fall of Byzantium, 955 A.D. to the First Crusade*. Oxford: Oxford University Press.

Kaplony, Andreas. 2008. 'Comparing al-Kāshgharī's Map with his Text: On the visual language, purpose and transmission of Arabic-Islamic maps'. In: *The Journey of Maps and Images on the Silk Road*, ed. Philippe Forêt and Andreas Kaplony, 137–53. Leiden: Brill.

al-Kāšγarī, Maḥmūd (fl. late 11th century). 1982. *Compendium of Turkish Dialects*, ed. and tr. Robert Dankoff with James Kelly. Cambridge, MA: Harvard University Press.

Kennedy, Hugh. 2001. *The Armies of the Caliphs: Military and Society in the Early Islamic State*. London: Routledge.

Kennedy, Hugh. 2004. 'The Decline and Fall of the First Muslim Empire'. *Der Islam* 81: 3–30.

Kennedy, Hugh. 2007. *The Great Arab Conquests: How the Spread of Islam Changed the World We Live In*. London: Phoenix.

Kristó-Nagy, István. 2016. 'Conflict and Cooperation between Arab Rulers and Persian Administrators in the Formative Period of Islamdom, c.600-c.950'. In *Empires and Bureaucracy in World History: From Late Antiquity to the Twentieth Century*, ed. Peter Crooks and Timothy H. Parsons, 54–80. Cambridge: Cambridge University Press.

Lassner, Jacob. 1980: *The Shaping of 'Abbāsid Rule*. Princeton, NJ: Princeton University Press.

Marsham, Andrew. 2009. *Rituals of Islamic Monarchy: Accession and Succession in the First Muslim Empire*. Edinburgh: Edinburgh University Press.

Marsham, Andrew 2018. '"God's Caliph" Revisited: Umayyad Political Thought in its Late Antique Context'. In *Power, Patronage and Memory in Early Islam: Perspectives on Umayyad Elites*, ed. Alain George and Andrew Marsham, pp. 3–37 Oxford: Oxford University Press.

Moreno, Eduardo Manzano. 2011: *Conquistadores, emires y califas. Los omeyas y la formación de al-Andalus*. Madrid: Editorial Crítica.

Moreno, Eduardo Manzano. 2020. 'Conquest and Settlement: What al-Andalus can tell us about the Arab Expansion at the time of the Umayyad Caliphate'. In *The Umayyad World*, ed. Andrew Marsham. London: Routledge.

Munt, Harry. 2016. 'Caliphal Imperialism and Ḥijāzi Elites in the Second/Eighth Century'. *al-Masāq* 28: 6–21.

Al-Muqaddasi (ca. 945–1000), *Ahsan al-Taqasim fi Ma'rifat al-Aqalim*. Süleymaniye Library, Istanbul, MS Ayasofya 2971M (copied in 658AH/1260AD).

Park, Hyunhee. 2012. *Mapping the Chinese and Islamic Worlds: Cross-Cultural Exchange in Pre-modern Asia*. Cambridge: Cambridge University Press.

Paul, Jürgen. 2016. 'Nomads and Bukhara. A Study in Nomad Migrations, Pasture, and Climate Change (11th century CE)'. *Der Islam* 93(2): 495–531.

Peacock, A. C. S. 2010. *Early Seljuq History: A new interpretation*. London: Routledge.

Peacock, A. C. S. 2015. *The Great Seljuk Empire*. Edinburgh: Edinburgh University Press.

Peacock, A. C. S. (ed.). 2017. *Islamisation: Comparative Perspectives from History*. Edinburgh: Edinburgh University Press.

Pinto, Karen C. 2016. *Medieval Islamic Maps: An Exploration*. Chicago, IL: University of Chicago Press.

Pourshariati, Pervaneh. 2008. *Decline and Fall of the Sasanian Empire*. London: I.B. Tauris.

Pourshariati, Pervaneh. 1998. 'Local Histories of Khurāsān and the Pattern of Arab Settlement'. *Studia Iranica* 27: 41–81.

Preiser-Kappeler, Johannes. 2018. *Jenseits von Rom und Karl dem Grossen: Aspekte der Globale Verflechtung in der langen Spätantike, 300–800 n. Chr.* Vienna: Mandelbaum Verlag.

Rapoport, Yossef and Savage-Smith, Emilie. 2018. *Lost Maps of the Caliphs: Drawing the World in Eleventh Century Cairo*. Oxford: Bodleian Library.

Sijpesteijn, Petra. 2013. *Shaping a Muslim State: The World of a Mid-Eighth-Century Egyptian Official*. Oxford: Oxford University Press.

Tor, Deborah G. 2005 'Privatized Jihad and Public Order in the Pre-Seljuq Period: The Role of the *Mutatawwi'a*.' *Iranian Studies* 38: 555–73.

Tor, Deborah G. 2009, 'The Islamization of Central Asia in the Sāmānid Era and the Reshaping of the Muslim World'. *Bulletin of the School of Oriental and African Studies* 72: 272–99.

Tor, Deborah G. 2018, 'The Eclipse of Khurāsān in the Twelfth Century'. *Bulletin of the School of Oriental and African Studies* 81: 251–76.

Treadwell, Luke. 2009. 'Abd al-Malik's Coinage Reforms. The Role of the Damascus Mint'. *Revue Numismatique* 9: 357–91.

Turan, Osman. 1955. 'The Ideal of World Domination among the Medieval Turks'. *Studia Islamica* 4: 77–90.

Turan, Osman. 2003. *Türk Cihan Hakimiyeti Mefkuresi Tarihi.* Istanbul: Ötüken Neşriyatı.

Vacca, Alison. 2017. *Non-Muslim Provinces under Early Islam: Islamic Rule and Iranian Legitimacy in Armenia and Caucasian Albania.* Cambridge: Cambridge University Press.

De La Vassière, Etienne. 2007. *Samarcande et Samarra. Elites d'Asie centrale dans l'empire abbasside.* Leuven: Peeters.

Al-Waqidi (*c.*747–843). 2004. *Kitab al-Maghazi,* ed. Muhammad 'Abd al-Qadir Ahmad 'Ata. Beirut: Dar al-Kutub al-'Ilmiyya.

Webb, Peter. 2016. *Imagining the Arabs: Arab Identity and the Rise of Islam.* Oxford: Oxford University Press.

Whitby, Michael and Mary Whitby (trans.). 1989. *Chronicon Paschale 284–628 AD.* Liverpool: Liverpool University Press.

Zadeh, Travis. 2011. *Mapping Frontiers across Medieval Islam: Geography, Translation and the 'Abbasid Empire.* London: I.B. Tauris.

6   The Mongol Imperial Space
From Universalism to Glocalization[*]

Michal Biran

The Mongols ruled over a huge imperial space. In the 13th century, Chinggis Khan and his heirs created the largest contiguous empire in world history, an empire that at its height stretched from Korea to Hungary and from Burma and Iraq to Siberia, ruling over two-thirds of the Old World (Map 6.1). Moreover, as the only superpower of that era, the empire also affected regions beyond its control, such as Japan, Southeast Asia, India, the Arab Middle East and Europe, both Eastern and Western, not least due to its contribution to the integration of the Eurasian space.

In imperial terms, the Mongol realm combined together territories that were formerly ruled by various Sinitic, Muslim (and before them Iranian), and steppe empires, as well as territories that were not formerly part of any imperial system, especially in the north. Thus, the Mongols had at their disposal a multifarious imperial tool kit, from which they could – and did – borrow, adding to their own institutions and concepts and thereby creating their own imperial culture.

The empire existed as an ever-expanding unified polity ruled from Mongolia up to 1260 and later dissolved in a process that eventually resulted in the creation of four regional empires seated in China, Iran, Central Asia and the Volga region, each headed by a Chinggisid branch. The state headed by the Great Khan or Qa'an (in Mongolian *Qa'an ulus*),[1] centered in China. It became known as the Yuan dynasty (1271–1368) and enjoyed a nominal, though not uncontested, primacy over the other Chinggisid states. The Ilkhanate (1260–1335, in Mongolian *Ulus Hülegü*) centered in modern Iran and Iraq. The Golden Horde

[*] The research leading to these results has received funding from the European Research Council under the European Union's Seventh Framework Programme (FP/2007–13)/ERC Grant Agreement n. 312397, and from the Humboldt Foundation via my Anneliese Maier Research Award.
[1] *Ulus* in Mongolian originally meant the people subject to a certain lord, and later also became an equivalent of a nation and state (as it still does in modern Mongolian today).

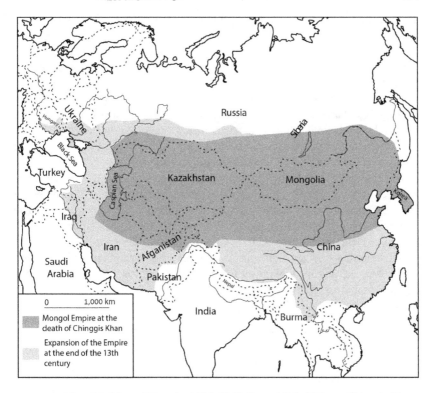

Map 6.1 Mongol Eurasia, 1206–1368. From Michal Biran, *Chinggis Khan*.
Oxford: OneWorld, 2007, pp. 12–13.

(1260–1502, *Ulus Jochi*) centered in the Volga region, and the Chaghadaid
Khanate (1260–1678, *Ulus Chaghadai*) held power in Central Asia.[2] Despite
the many, and often bloody, disputes between the four polities, they retained
a strong sense of Chinggisid unity. In the mid-14th century, all four khanates
became embroiled in political crises that led to the collapse of the Ilkhanate and
the Yuan dynasty, and considerably weakened the two steppe khanates. The fall
of the Qa'an state in 1368 is generally deemed to be the end of the "Mongol
Moment" in world history. For heuristic convenience, I shall differentiate
between two main periods, that of the United Mongol Empire (Mongolian:
Yeke Mongghol Ulus, The Great Mongol Nation 1206–60) and that of the four
successor states (1260–1368). However, as I shall demonstrate below, from the
Mongols' point of view the division between the two eras was not as clear cut as

---

[2] The Mongol name of the three *uluses* derives from the names of their founders, two sons and
a grandson of Chinggis Khan.

it is presented here and in various textbooks (such as Morgan 2007; May 2012; Biran 2015b).

This chapter seeks to explain how the Mongol imperial space was created, organized, and conceived by the Mongols and their subjects in the various realms. I stress the interplay between the Mongols' universal vision, their construction of a "Chinggisid space," and the revival of "glocal" (i.e., local with global characteristic) spatial concepts in Mongol-ruled China and Iran. I start by reviewing Mongol expansion and analyzing the reasons for its unprecedented scale, and conclude in assessing the impact of the Mongol Empire on the shaping of the post-Mongol imperial space.

It is not easy to locate the Mongols' own voice, as most of the sources were penned by their subjects and neighbors, each bounded in the concepts and premises of his own civilization. Yet by using Mongolian sources, such as *The Secret History of the Mongols* (de Rachewiltz 2006), the only indigenous literary source for the rise of Chinggis Khan, together with Mongol letters and inscriptions on seals and coins, by comparing sources from different parts of the empire, and by looking at the Mongols' actions, Mongol indigenous concepts can be traced.

6.1   Creating the Chinggisid Space: World Conquest and Its Aftermath, 1206–60

6.1.1   Expansion: Ideology and Practice

Mongol expansion began due to both practical and ideological reasons, and ideology played a major role in shaping the Mongols' spatial concepts. In 1206, when Temüjin united the tribes of Mongolia after several decades of bitter internecine wars, and was elected as Chinggis Khan (the universal or the fierce ruler), he had no grand design of world conquest. However, the steppe ideology of supra-tribal unity, which he had employed while unifying the Mongolian tribes, included a strong universal component, which became more and more dominant as Chinggis Khan continued to win battles.

In terms of both ideology and military organization, Chinggis Khan owed much to the legacy of former Inner Asian steppe empires,[3] notably the Turkic

---

[3] Steppe empires are often left outside the discussion of Eurasian empires (e.g., Duindam 2016) or described in derogatory terms (Münkler 2007), sometimes called "shadow empires" (Barfield 2001) or, more recently, "formless empires" (Mott 2015, x–xi). Mott defines these empires as "formless" since they did not enforce their religion and language over their subjects. Although this is undeniable, steppe empires did create their own political culture, which displayed an impressive continuity across time and place, even when we see it mainly through the eyes of the empires' sedentary subjects or neighbors, and not from the perspective of the imperial nomads themselves (Biran 2015a; Munkh-Erdene 2018, 30). Steppe empires had their own distinct form that should be understood on its own terms.

empires of the 6th to 8th centuries, but also the Kitan Liao (907–1125) and the Kereyit kingdom in 12th-century Mongolia (Golden 1982, 2006; Munkh-Erdene 2018). The focal point of this ideology was the Mongols' belief that they had received a heavenly mandate to rule over earth. This notion was close to the Chinese Mandate of Heaven (Pines [Chapter 2], this volume), but had its own steppe characteristics: The steppe mandate is conferred by Tengri (Heaven), the supreme sky god of the steppe. Tengri bestows the right to rule on earth and the royal charismatic power (*suu*) upon a single clan, each of whose members (but only they) could theoretically be elevated to the supreme rulership, represented by the title Great Khan (Khaqan/Khaghan in Turkic, Qa'an in Mongolian). This meant not only that succession struggles were endemic, but also that the empire was conceived as the joint property of the whole royal clan, and the Qa'an was therefore expected to share its wealth and territory with his kin. This redistribution in turn contributed both to the dissolution of the empire to various polities and to the ongoing connections among these successor states. Moreover, unlike the Chinese case, Tengri did not bestow his mandate on every generation; in other words, the steppe world was often left without a unifying ruler, sometimes for centuries, as in the period that preceded the rise of the Mongols. However, the notion of the mandate and the ensuing unification remained "an ideology in reserve" (Di Cosmo 1999, 20) even during the periods of disunion, ready to be revived if the creation of a supra-tribal empire were to be attempted again.

Apart from the mandate, Tengri also conferred upon the Qa'an a special good fortune or *suu* that guaranteed his success. This charisma was manifested in battle – not only through victories as such, but also through narrow escapes, last minute warnings, and advantageous changes of weather on the battlefield. The Qa'an's divine knowledge or superhuman intelligence were also seen as manifestations of his unmediated connection to Tengri.[4] Moreover, to augment the Qa'an's personal charisma, additional repositories of *suu* could be found and accumulated among talented people who possessed various kinds of knowledge, among the ancestors if properly honored, and in sacred territories (Allsen 2009). Thus, the Mongol capital, Qaraqorum, was built in the sacred territory of the Orkhon valley in central Mongolia, a region that was sacred also to the Turks and Uighurs (see below 6.2.1). However, the main means for proving the legitimacy of any aspirant Qa'an in terms of both mandate and charisma was success on the battlefield.

---

[4] Chinggis Khan, for example, was enthroned in 1206 by the shaman Teb Tengri, who validated Heaven's choice. When the later intervened in earthly politics, however, Chinggis Khan orchestrated his execution, thereby attesting that the heavenly-ordained Khan's connection to the divine was by far closer than that of any shaman or other religious expert (de Rachewiltz 2006, 1: 168–74; Biran 2015b, 546).

Apart from ideological stimuli there were also practical reasons behind the beginning of Mongol expansion. Mongol and Muslim sources stress the poverty of the Mongols on the eve of Chinggis Khan's accession.[5] Yet the picture of starving nomads erupting from the steppe does not fit the historical reality, as the period of Chinggis Khan's expansion (1211–25) was found to be the wettest era of the last millennium in Mongolia (Pedersen et al. 2014). In other words, the Mongols could have greatly improved their economic situation even if they had stayed in Mongolia in this period. Political factors, however, were more crucial: It took Chinggis Khan longer to unify the tribes of Mongolia than to conquer half of the world. His main interest after 1206 was keeping Mongolia united and securing his position from possible competitors. Military successes abroad served this goal. Besides, some of the steps undertaken by Chinggis Khan to consolidate his new polity became conducive to the future expansion. Here, too, Chinggis Khan was building on the Inner Asian template but molding it to his needs.

A major step for securing his realm – and starting its expansion – was the reorganization of the army. Chinggis Khan retained the typical Inner Asian decimal units (10, 100, 1,000, 10,000), yet he abolished its linkage to the tribal system. The new Mongol units often combined people from different tribes and were led by Chinggis Khan's *nökers* (personal retainers), rather than tribal chiefs. Chosen on the basis of merit and loyalty, this new *nöker* elite provided the Mongols with a highly professional military leadership. Moreover, the khan could confidently assign troops to fight on the extremities of Eurasia without fear of treason. Furthermore, since every Mongol was a soldier (women provided logistical support), this reorganization begat social revolution: the soldiers' loyalty was transferred from tribe to commander and, higher up the chain, to the Chinggisid family. Some tribal connections proved to be more enduring – or more cleverly resurrected – than others, and heads of important tribal lineages were connected to the Chinggisids by marriage to secure their loyalty, but the Chinggisids never faced a serious tribal threat after this reorganization.

The army's allegiance was further buttressed by draconian disciplinary measures, on the one hand, and generous distribution of booty, on the other. The rules governing behavior in these units, together with the growing body of legal precedents that Chinggis Khan had ordered to be registered from 1206 onwards, were probably the basis for the famous *Jasaq* (Turkic: *Yasa*) – the ever-evolving law code ascribed to Chinggis Khan, which remained valid throughout the empire in conjunction with local laws. The Great Khan also appointed judges (*yarghuchis*) who were responsible for the keeping of the new laws and the assignment of booty, captives and appanages.

---

[5] See, e.g., de Rachewiltz 2006, 1: 1–13; Juwayni, 1997, 19–23.

Chinggis Khan also retained the Inner Asian institution of the supra-tribal royal guard (*keshig*). The guard – a combination of crack troops, police force, and personal retinue – became the incubator of the empire's military and administrative elite (Biran 2007, 41–3; 2015b).

The new Mongol army had to be put in action in order to prevent its soldiers turning against each other, provide booty for redistribution, and manifest Chinggis Khan's success. Yet fielding the army did not necessarily mean conquest. Raiding could provide spoils, employment, and legitimacy much more easily than conquest, and it had been the favorite pattern of earlier Inner Asian empires based in Mongolia (Barfield 1989). Indeed, Chinggis Khan's early campaigns were mainly raids motivated by petty grudges or threats to his position in Mongolia (Biran 2007, 47–50). The gradual shift from raids to conquest was determined first by the behavior of Chinggis Khan's rivals and later by his success in the field. In 1205–9, the Mongols raided the Xi Xia (1038–1227, in today's north-west China) and later attacked a harsher rival, the Jin dynasty in north China (1115–1234). Having successfully raided Jin in 1211, Chinggis Khan added the adjective "great" (*yeke*) to the name of his state, thereby creating the *Yeke Mongghol Ulus* (Great Mongol Nation), as it was known ever since. After conquering the Jin capital of Yanjing (current Beijing) in 1215, Chinggis Khan left governors and troops in the newly conquered territories, to prevent the Jin from regaining their losses and as preparation for future confrontations. This, however, was still a tactical move, not a step toward permanent conquest. Conquest became a strategy only later, after Chinggis Khan's campaigns west of Mongolia against the Qara Khitai (1218–19) and the Khwarazm Shah (1219–25) . These campaigns were also ignited by a threat to Chinggis Khan's leadership in Mongolia (in the case of the Qara Khitai, whose throne was usurped by a Mongolian chief who had escaped from Chinggis), or by a severe insult to his authority (in the case of the Khwarazm Shah, whose governor killed a caravan of Chinggis Khan's merchants). Yet the speedy collapse of these vast Central Asian empires, whose leaders were eliminated, obliged Chinggis Khan to station governors and garrisons permanently in the conquered regions, thereby creating an empire (see Map 6.2).

These remarkable victories did not only enlarge considerably the empire's territorial and human resources, including acquisition of many skilled nomadic warriors. They also added another set of imperial precedents, the Islamic one, to Chinggis Khan's toolkit. Chinggis Khan was no longer emulating the northern Chinese model of the Liao and Jin dynasties, which carved out a piece of north China, adding it to their original territory. Instead, he was creating his own model. Moreover, the unprecedented success of his western campaigns convinced both Chinggis Khan and everyone around him that he was indeed destined to rule over the earth (Biran 2007, 47–73). The continued spate of victories by Chinggis Khan's heirs in the following decades – as they

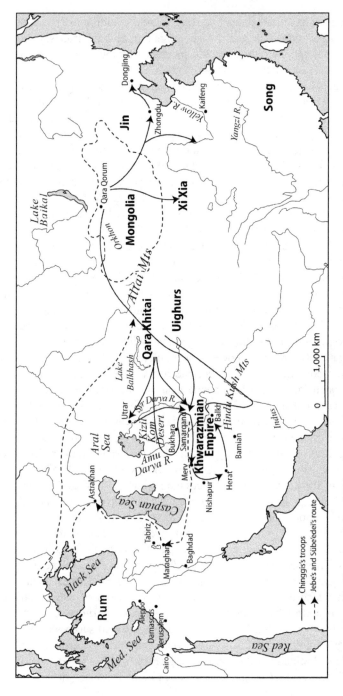

Map 6.2 The campaigns of Chinggis Khan (r. 1206–27). From Michal Biran *Chinggis Khan*, p. 32.

completed the submission of north China under the Jin dynasty (1234), the conquest of the steppe up to the gates of Hungary, wreaking terror across Europe (1237–41), subdued Tibet (1241), Yunnan (1253) and western Sichuan (1259) in south-west China and conquered the Middle East up to Anatolia (1243) and Iraq (1258) – further bolstered the image of the Chinggisids as heavenly-ordained world rulers.

6.1.2   Universal Concepts

This series of victories also led to broadening the scope of the Mongols' heavenly mandate. When Chinggis Khan was enthroned in 1206, his mandate was limited to ruling "the people of the felt walled tents," namely the steppe nomads,[6] just like the mandate of his Turkic predecessors in the steppe, despite their universalistic rhetoric (Golden 1982). Following Chinggis Khan's continuous military successes, however, the mandate was broadened to include the whole world, both steppe and sown. This is made clear in Chinggis Khan's edict: "This is the order of the everlasting God: In heaven there is only one eternal God; on earth there is only one lord, Chinggis Khan."[7] The same idea permeates the titles, seals and letters of Chinggis Khan's heirs. Ögödei, Chinggis Khan's son and first heir (r. 1229–41), is called *dalai-i-qan* (the oceanic or universal khan; glossed in Chinese as *hainei huangdi* [the emperor of all within the seas] or *sihai huangdi* [the emperor of all within the four seas]). The same title appears also on the seal of Ögödei's son and heir, Güyük (r. 1246–8).[8]

The Mongols' universal ideology in its terse Mongolian form (*Möngke Tengri-yin küchün-dür; Qa'an-u suu-dur*, i.e., "By the Might of Eternal Heaven, By the Good Fortune [charisma] of the Qa'an") appeared at the head of their letters, edicts and seals. It was often translated to various other languages and embellished with Quranic verses, references from Confucian classics or even Biblical quotes, according to their prospective audiences.[9] The letter that Chinggis Khan's grandson, Hülegü (d. 1265), sent to Louis IX of France in 1262 illustrates what these full-fledged universal claims sounded like. In this letter, Hülegü quotes the Mongol shaman Teb Tengri, allegedly enthroning Chinggis Khan using the words of the prophet Jeremiah:

---

[6] See de Rachewilz 2006, par 202, 1: 133; par 244, 1:168; cf. Jackson 2005.

[7] William of Rubruck (*c.*1220–1293) cites Möngke's letter to the French king Louis IX, which begins by citing an edict of Chinggis Khan (Rubruck 1990, 248; cf. the discussion in Jackson 2011).

[8] De Rachewiltz 2006, par 280; De Rachewiltz 1983; Cleaves and Mostaert 1952, 485–95; Kim 2015, 285–6.

[9] See, e.g., Vogelin 1940–1[2000]; Rubruck 1990, 248; Mostaert and Cleaves 1952, 485–95; Cai Meibiao 1955, 21, 25, 35, 36, 37, 38, 39, 40; Chavannes 1908, 372, 373, 376, 378, 388, 391; Poppe 1957, 47, 49, 52.

I alone am the Almighty God on high and I have set thee over the nations and over the kingdoms to be king of all the world *to root out and to pull down and to destroy and to throw down to build and to plant* [Jeremiah 1:10, emphasis added]. I tell you to announce my command [mandate] to all the nations, tongues and tribes of the east, the south, the north and the west; to promulgate it in all the regions of the whole world, where emperors, kings and sovereigns rule, where lordship operates, where horses can go, ships sail, envoys reach, letters be heard, so that those who have ears can hear; those who hear can understand and those who understand can believe. Those who do not believe will later learn that punishment will be meted on those who did not believe my commands. (Meyvaert 1980, 252–3, trans. Barber and Bate 2010, 156–7)

This letter represents the scope of the broadened heavenly mandate. The mandate encompasses everything – including the maritime world – and everybody. In terms of space, this means that the Mongols divided the world into two parts: the first, what they had already conquered; and, the second, the part that still need to be subjugated. This is reminiscent of the Muslim concept of the abode of Islam (*dar al-islam*) and the abode of war (*dar al-harb*), or the Chinese concept of All-under-Heaven (*tianxia*), where extension was expected to come not necessarily through war but through the foreigners' recognition of the moral superiority of the Chinese emperor (Albrecht 2016; Pines 2012 and in this volume). Unlike these two concepts, however, the Mongols defined the division not in territorial terms but in terms of people, just as the wealth of a nomadic chief is measured not in territory – quite abundant in the steppe – but in manpower, a much scarcer resource. The Mongols differentiated between people who were pacified or submissive (*il irgen*) and rebellious people (*bulgha irgen*), who would eventually be pacified. The rebellion of the latter was not directed only against Mongol authority but also against Heaven that enabled that authority, and was therefore futile – and punishable – as the Mongols explained in the ultimatums they sent to various rulers.[10] Champions of self-propaganda, the Mongols often supplied foreigners with lengthy catalogues of the rulers they had subdued in order to document their miraculous success.[11]

However, despite the stress on people, Mongol success also had territorial dimensions. The Mongols' typical phrase for describing the universalistic dimensions of their empire was that they rule "from the place where the sun rises till the place where it sets," namely from East to West or the entire world. This idiom, first used in the letter Güyük Qa'an sent to the pope in 1246, if not earlier,[12] was repeated in a variety of Mongolian, Muslim, and Chinese sources

---

[10] Mostaert and Cleaves 1952, 492–3; Rubruck 1990, 172–3; De Rachewiltz 2006, 1: 550–1; Fletcher 1986, 19; Fiaschetti 2014a.

[11] E.g., Barber and Bate 2012, 158–9; Wassaf 1853, 560–1; Juwayni/Qazwini 1912–37, 1: 95; Juwayni 1997, 121–2; Skelton et al. 1995, 85, 104–6.

[12] Juwayni/Qazwini 1912-37, 1:114; Juwayni 1997, 145, mentions a similar phrase, allegedly cited from a copy of an edict (*yarligh*) of Chinggis Khan, which his commanders Jebe and

for describing the empire's realm, both throughout its continuous expansion and after it stopped, when the empire's sheer size was a sufficient proof of its legitimacy.[13]

Another implication of this universalistic concept was that the Mongols hardly differentiated between external and internal territories and policies, since every polity that was not yet taken was a potential conquest target. This universal worldview took the world-conquest mission rather literally, and resulted in a foreign policy that saw conquest by military power as its main aim. The Mongols were willing to accept peaceful submission, but they were not ready to forge any foreign relations based on equality or commit to any sustainable alliances with other polities. They also took great pains to eliminate competing rulers with universal claims, such as the Abbasid Caliph and the Jin and Song emperors. In addition, they refuted calls for conversion (to either Christianity or Islam) by explaining that Heaven was obviously with them already, as proved by their continued military success.[14]

6.1.3   Reasons for the Mongols' Success

Certainly, the empire's unprecedented territorial expansion bolstered its rulers' universal claims, but why were Chinggis Khan and his heirs so successful? That is, why did the Mongol Empire expand more than other contiguous empires before or after? While several objective factors contributed to this phenomenon, most of the credit goes to Chinggis Khan's actions. The political fragmentation of Eurasia in the centuries that preceded the Mongols' rise and the emergence of post-nomadic states along the Eurasian Steppe, in eastern, central, and western Asia, were contributing factors. The climate was also supportive: as mentioned above, tree-ring analysis from Mongolia proves that the years of Chinggis Khan's campaigns (1211–25) were the wettest period of the 2nd millennium CE in Mongolia (Pederson et al. 2014). Thus, the Mongols had ample food to support their main weapon, horses, which they could raise and use in larger numbers. Yet the major explanation of the success should be sought in Chinggis Khan's policies, notably the efficient mobilization of resources – human, material, and spiritual – and the pragmatic willingness to learn from others, in both the military and civil realms (Biran 2007, 69–73).

Chinggis Khan's reorganization of the army has already been discussed. The Mongols' military success derived neither from breakthroughs in military

---

Sübe'edei had given the people of Nishapur in 1220, ordering them to submit. Yet writing around 1260, Juwayni might have inserted a later phrasing into the commanders' message. See also Jackson 2017, 75.

[13] E.g., De Rachewiltz 1971, 213–14 (Güyük's letter); Rubruck 1990, 248 (Latin); Wassaf 1853, 452 (Persian); Ibn al-Fuwati 1995, 3: 319 (Arabic); Wang Shidian 1992, 74 (Chinese).

[14] Mostaert and Cleaves 1952, 450–1; Dawson 1980, 83–6; Rashid al-Din 1999, 2: 488–95.

technology, nor from the use of gunpowder weaponry. In terms of armament and tactics, they mainly continued the traditional form of steppe warfare (May 2012, forthcoming; cf. Haw 2013). Yet it was their better leadership, discipline, and strategic planning that made the difference, enabling them to mobilize the steppe's chief military resource: mounted archers (and later on, also sedentary troops). Another factor was the devastation and massacres on an unprecedented scale that accompanied the conquests, impacting the Mongols' image ever since. This violence, however, should not be interpreted as wanton cruelty. Rather, it was a strategic ploy that went beyond psychological warfare. Destruction was a brutal yet effective means of compensating for the Mongols' numerical inferiority and preventing future resistance. The empire ravaged much more territory than it kept, thereby creating a wide belt of destruction around its borders. This buffer protected its territory from future incursions, facilitated future expansion and increased the available pasture lands. In later stages of the conquest (e.g., southern China in the 1260s–1270s), the devasta-tion was substantially reduced, as by then the conquerors had realized that their subjects were more useful alive. In some areas, the restoration was as potent as the wreckage (Biran 2015b).

Another major reason for the Mongol success was their willingness to learn from others – subjects, neighbors, and visitors – and their skill in doing so. This was particularly apparent in the military field (e.g., the use of siege engineers from both China and the Muslim world, and later the creation of a navy). Yet the Mongols' eye for talent and innovation was conspicuous also in other fields, such as administration, medicine, astronomy, and entertainment, to name only a few. As early as 1204, Chinggis Khan adopted the Uighur script for writing Mongolian, thereby creating a literate staff. Afterwards, the Mongols drew on experienced subjects to administer the conquered territories and operate the various Chinggisid courts. Like in the military case, the efficient mobilization of talent and skills greatly contributed to the Mongols' success. Moreover, the Mongols' policy of religious pluralism and the respect and privileges they conferred upon religious and intellectual elites helped them in co-opting their subjects, while their active promotion of trade secured the support of the merchants, also often useful as imperial administrators.

Last by not least, another factor in the Mongol success was success itself. Thus, Chinggis Khan never suffered a humiliating defeat, and his later victories were easier and quicker than his first attempts at China – nothing stained his unmatched record. Therefore, every victory he achieved further stimulated his soldiers to continue fighting for him and encouraged rivals to submit without a battle. Moreover, it also bolstered his public image as a charismatic ruler, pre-ordained by heaven to conquer the world, a mission, which under his heirs became the collective destiny of the Mongols (Biran 2007, 69–73). The spate of victories continued throughout the era of the United Empire. When the Mongols began to encounter sporadic defeats (e.g., in 1258 in Vietnam or 1260 in Palestine), these were dwarfed by the already immense achievements of the empire.

6.1.4   Administrating the Imperial Space

Administrating such an ever-growing, huge and diverse empire was a particularly challenging task. Regional diversity aside, other factors contributed to the complexity of Mongol administration. First, it had to balance two contradictory concepts of the empire: that of the Qa'an's realm, which meant centralization of rule on a par with sedentary empires; and that of the empire as the joint property of the Chinggisid clan, which meant ongoing decentralization. In addition, the Mongols originally maintained different administrations, for the nomads, mostly included in the army's decimal units, to whom pasturelands were assigned, and for the sedentary populations with their cities and villages. The result – despite obvious cumbersomeness – was a multi-layered system, which included checks and balances. It functioned impressively well for the first fifty years, partly due to its continued accommodation to the empire's growth. Originating in Chinggis Khan's patrimonial administration and the institutions he initiated, it evolved and was systematized under his heirs, notably the Qa'ans Ögödei (r. 1229–41) and Möngke (r. 1251–9).

During the United Empire period, the empire's center remained in Mongolia and from Ögödei's reign especially in the capital Qaraqorum, although in fact the central administration followed the Qa'an's *ordo* (camp, mobile court). At the head of the administration, beneath the Qa'an, stood the Central Secretariat (Chinese: *zhongshusheng*),[15] a sort of Mongol government that evolved out of the *keshig*. The central secretariat was manned mainly by Mongols, in contrast to the bureaucracy's lower echelons, staffed primarily by the subject populations. The secretariat's chief priority was to secure resources for the empire's functioning and continued expansion.

For the most part, and unlike previous nomadic empires, Mongol rule was direct, partly because many of the subjugated elites were eliminated during the conquests. Mongol direct rule was administered by mobile secretariats (Chinese: *xingsheng*), which were replicas of the above-mentioned central secretariat. Such mobile secretariats were established in the early 1230s in northern China, Turkestan, and northern Iran, by then the three main sedentary realms of the empire, and eventually served as the nucleus for the

---

[15] I am using the Chinese terminology as it is the most common and systematic one; Muslim sources use several terms (notably *dīwān*, also used for the mobile secretariat, and see below) but they, like the Mongolian sources, often do not refer to the institution but only to its members. For the *Yuan History* (*Yuanshi*)'s Ming compilers' emphasis on the role of the Secretariat, see Humble 2017, 259–77.

administrations, of Yuan China, Chaghadaid Central Asia and Ilkhanid Iran. Led by experienced administrators, such as the Khwarazmian merchants Mahmud Yalawach and his son Mas'ud Beg or the Kitan Yelü Chucai (but also the Oirat Mongol Arghun Aqa), their main duties were civil. These included census taking and tax collection, operating the postal-relay system (*jam*), which traversed the whole empire, and supervising the restoration of the conquests' damages, which often evolved huge-scale transfer and repopulation. The census, which was adopted from the Chinese, was the key element in the Mongols' efforts to harvest their domains, as it was used to set taxes, recruit troops and labor, and monitor natural and human resources. The Mongols usually retained the existing taxes, but also added the *qubchir* (poll tax), and later the *tamgha*, a commercial tax, and various ad-hoc imposts. The nomads also paid taxes and were rewarded, above all, from the booty that was centrally collected and then redistributed. Below the regional secretariat, there were local governors (Mon. *darughachi*; Chinese *daluhuazhi*; Persian: *shihna*; Turkic *basqaq*), stationed in each city and responsible for carrying on the imperial policies.

Since the empire viewed the administration of all the sedentary lands – whether in China, Turkestan, or Iran – as basically the same (despite local variants), administrative personnel were often transferred from one region to another. Moreover, to prevent administrators from gaining local power bases, the Mongols preferred to rule via strangers, using people from one region to administer a region far from their homeland (e.g., sending Kitans from north China to administer Central Asia and Khwarazmian Muslims to govern north China). To win over the loyalty of these newcomers, the Mongols sought to give them "a taste of home," importing foreign (mostly Muslim) food, medicine, and entertainment to China, and East Asian food, medicine, and entertainment to Western and Central Asia. Such policies obviously accelerated connections and cross-cultural exchanges across the imperial space (Allsen 1994, 1997b; Biran 2004, 2015b).

Whereas direct rule was the norm, in a number of cases, local dynasts were permitted to remain in place and govern with the empire's approval and under the supervision of the same Mongolian-appointed imperial residents known as *darughachi*. This indirect administration was connected not only to the means of submission but mainly to the terrain involved. It existed primarily in regions north of the steppe, most prominently the Rus' principalities, but also among the tribes of northern Manchuria and Siberia, all places that lacked former imperial experience. It was also maintained in various kingdoms on the empire's margins, such as Armenia, Georgia, Anatolia, Tibet and Korea, namely outside of the main steppe belt (see Map 6.3). Although the Mongols allowed their rulers to keep their crowns, these polities were subject to basically similar obligations as the directly administrated regions, in that they had to pay

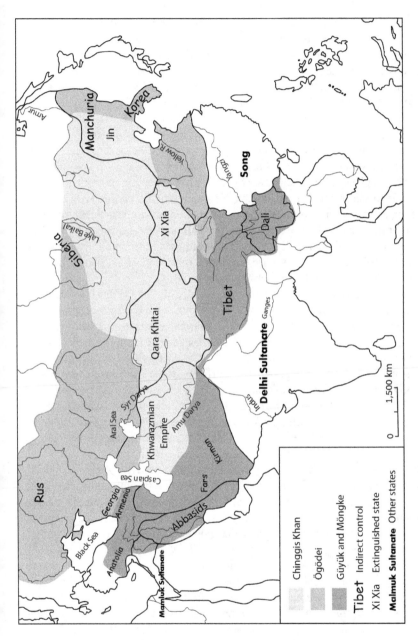

Map 6.3 Conquests of the United Empire, 1206–59.

tribute to the Mongol treasury, participate in the census, provide military units when required, and send their leaders' relatives to the imperial guard (as did princes, generals and high officials in the central administration).

Communication across the imperial space was maintained by the *jam*, the mounted postal courier system. Both directly and indirectly administrated regions had to establish post stations, each of them located roughly a day's journey from the next (about every 40 km), and to provide animals, fodder, and couriers for authorized travelers (those who held the *paiza*, tablet of authority provided by a Mongol khan), who were able to cover about 350–400 km a day. Local variants (dog sleds in Siberia, yaks in Tibet) notwithstanding, the couriers usually used horses, but runners were also part of the system. The stations were often mobile (i.e., located in tents) or located in existing towns, and only in specific places (e.g., Zungaria, Ögödei's private domain in north Xinjiang) were fixed stations built from scratch. Yet supplying the stations with animals, fodder, and food was often a heavy burden on the population, and complaints of unauthorized use of the *jam* were common. This network, however, enabled the Qa'an to transmit his orders efficiently, acquire information from the far reaches of the empire and secure the roads for ambassadors, merchants, and soldiers (Silverstein 2007; Allsen 2011; Hsim 2014).

This centralized administrative system created by the Qa'an, however, was balanced by the nomadic conception of the empire as the common property of all the Chinggisids, whereby the ruler was but *primus inter pares.* Thus, while the *Mongghol Ulus* (the Mongol Nation) established by Chinggis Khan in 1206, known from 1211 as the *Yeke Mongghol Ulus*, replaced all the other tribal *uluses* in Mongolia, already Chinggis Khan began to divide the imperial territory among his kin, creating a structure of nine *uluses*. Four *uluses* of the right (west) were given to his sons, four *uluses* of the left (east) to his brothers, while Chinggis Khan himself held the central *ulus*. The empire's further expansion – mainly westwards – increased the position of the sons' *uluses*. Moreover, succession struggles among the Chinggisids led to several changes in this original structure, such as the division of the *uluses* into secondary and tertiary *uluses*, and the creation of new ones, with various amounts of power and legitimation. Hence the so-called United Empire was actually a conglomerate of multiple *uluses*. Eventually some of these *uluses* dissolved into what we used to call the four khanates, namely four large *uluses* that populated the post-1260 Chinggisid space, often comprising smaller *uluses* (Kim 2019).

Originally, Chinggis Khan's *ulus* allocations referred to pasturelands, not to the sedentary realms, which were subject to the central *ulus* and later administrated by the mobile secretariats. However, from Ögödei's time, the *ulus* heads each had their representatives in the mobile secretariats, with larger representation of the regional khan (i.e., the head of the local *ulus*) in the Central Asian case. The *ulus* leaders (including the Qa'an) headed the military thousands (i.e., the nomadic population), and each was supposed to send troops for the empire's campaigns. Another example of the empire's conceptualization as the Chinggisids' common property was the institution of appanages (*qubi*). During the conquest period, vast territories (almost one-third of north China!) were parceled out to various Chinggisids, including women. Whereas the central government administrated the appanages, their revenues were forwarded directly to their owners. This complex division of space often resulted in overlapping lines of authority: of imperial appointees, generals, princely agents, and local rulers' nominees.

Administrative reforms, resulting in increasing centralization, were usually implemented in tandem with new waves of expansion. One reason for this timing was that the reforms enabled the government to secure funds for new conquests, often accumulated and assigned during the campaigns. Yet further expansion was also used to gain the traditional Mongol elites' consent for increased centralization. The empire's expansion and centralization reached their peak under Möngke (although he failed to abolish the appanages). It is best demonstrated by the campaign led by Möngke's younger brother, Hülegü, who went from Mongolia to conquer the Middle East (1253–60), collecting military personnel, technologies, and supplies mobilized from the entire empire – from China through the Caucasus, to Rus' and Anatolia – as he advanced. This campaign not only manifested Qaraqorum's ability to mobilize resources efficiently, but also the use of the appanage's professional subjects for their ruler's needs, as many of Hülegü's Chinese experts originated in his private domains in north China (Allsen 1987, 1994, 2001b; Biran 2015b; Isahaya 2017). Yet the extraordinary success of the expansion under Möngke's rule was also among the reasons that contributed to the dissolution of the unified empire after his demise in 1259.

6.2   Chinggisid Space Versus Former Imperial Spaces: Post-1260 Concepts

The succession struggle that erupted after Möngke's death led to the empire's dissolution. The process was accelerated by the empire's sheer size that made its management increasingly challenging. Moreover, as the empire expanded beyond the ecological borders of the steppe, it made further expansion – which often served as the glue cohering the various *uluses* – more difficult. Centrifugal processes brought about the consolidation of four big *uluses*, centered in China, Iran, Central Asia, and the Volga region. Nominally the *uluses* remained subject to the Qa'an, who since 1260 had resided in north China, not in Mongolia, but practically they were independent polities, and the relations among them were often sour. Whereas each of these polities continued to voice universal claims and appropriated the Chinggisid achievements, they also started adopting local elements from their subjects, trying to carve out their separate identities. The spatial concepts created at this stage were different and more complex, combining universal and local elements. I call this a glocal world order (Roudometof 2016).

6.2.1   Political History

The four *uluses* were all headed by descendants of Chinggis Khan's sons, but the resulting map did not match the Great Khan's original assignments. The Chaghadaid and Jochid *uluses* retained their original allocations: from Uighuria to the Oxus River, namely Central Asia, for Chaghadai; and from the Irtysh River to "as far west as the hooves of the Mongol horses reach," namely to the Ukraine and the gates of Hungary (much more than the realm ruled by the time of Chinggis Khan's death), in Jochi's case. The two other *uluses* were headed by Möngke's brothers, descendants of Tolui, Chinggis Khan's youngest son and Möngke's father. Qubilai headed the Qa'an's realm, including Mongolia, Tolui's original allocation, but also Manchuria (where most of the eastern *uluses*, those of Chinggis Khan's brothers, were originally located), as well as Korea, Tibet and China (including the territories of the Southern Song dynasty, conquered by Qubilai in 1279). Hülegü ruled over Iran, Iraq, Azerbaijan, and Turkmenistan, as well as significant parts of Afghanistan, Anatolia, and the Caucasus. That Hülegü's realm was not assigned by Chinggis Khan, but only by Qubilai, was marked by his inferior title Ilkhan ("the submissive khan") and tainted his legitimacy. Moreover, the parts of Hülegü's realm that were conquered before his 1250s campaign, mainly Azerbaijan and the Caucasus, as well as Khurasan in north-eastern Iran, were claimed by the Jochids and Chaghadaids, respectively, and these claims were a source of enduring inter-*ulus* conflicts.

The *ulus* of Ögödei, Chinggis Khan's heir whose descendants lost the Qa'anate to the Toluids in 1251, was dissolved by Möngke, and again in 1310, despite the heroic attempts of Ögödei's grandson Qaidu (r. 1271–1301) to revive it. Qaidu's struggle resulted in his taking over the Chaghadaids' realm, and generated repeated anti-Toluid conflicts, which weakened the Qa'an's position, reducing his authority there to purely nominal (Jackson 1978, 1999b; Biran 1997). However, despite the manifold and often bloody disputes among the Mongol successor states, they still saw themselves as brotherly states, parts of a common Chinggisid space, and held on to the ideal of Chinggisid unity. Even at the height of the inter-Mongol conflicts in the last decades of the 13th century, the rival khanates continued to exchange gifts and messengers. They referred to each other in kinship terms (*aqa* and *ini*, older and younger brothers). Even when searching for non-Mongol allies against their own kin, they referred to their conflicts as family feuds, which were never intended to eliminate their rivals (Kim 2009).

In spatial terms, the four polities were connected not only by the postal system that still stretched throughout the Chinggisid realm (Silverstein 2007; Allsen 2011), but also by their appanages, that were often located in the territories of a rival *ulus* (Allsen 2001b). Moreover, they shared other Mongolian institutions, such as the *ordo* (mobile court), the *keshig* (guard), the *yarghuchi* (judges), and the *daruchachi* (local governors). These institutions were applied side by side with local administrative traditions, which at times dictated modifications of a common Chinggisid element (e.g., the abolition of the census in Iraq after 1259). The difficulty of navigating between local and empire-wide institutions brought about quite complex arrangements. In China and Iran, in particular, the Mongols preferred double staffing administrative posts, frequently pairing a home-grown and a foreign official. The idea was to have the two officials keep each other in check. Practically, however, the system often resulted in spiraling administrative costs, inter-official conflicts, and, worse, it could deteriorate to complete administrative standstill (Biran 2015b).

In the post-1260 space, each polity built its own new capitals, often located to the northeast of the region's pre-Mongol capitals, namely closer to the steppe. Thus, in China the capital shifted from Kaifeng and Hangzhou to Daidu (Beijing), and in the eastern Islamic world it moved from Baghdad to Tabriz and Sultaniyya in Azerbaijan. In Russia the capital moved from Kiev, first to old and new Saray (south-east of Kiev but closer to the steppe), and later, after the fall of the Golden Horde, to Moscow (north-east of Kiev). In Central Asia (the least defined case), the capital shifted from Balasaghun, in modern north Kirgizstan to the region of Almaliq, in north Xinjiang (Biran 2004 and see Map 6.4).

Of special importance to the empire's spatial structure was Qubilai Qa'an's transfer of the capital of the Mongol Empire from Qaraqorum to north China, eventually to his newly erected capital at Daidu (Beijing). Qaraqorum, established in the 1230s in the relatively fertile Orkhon valley, was founded on central Mongolia's main trade routes, in a spot allegedly chosen by Chinggis Khan and formerly in the realm of the Kereyit tribe. As mentioned above, it was located in a sacred steppe territory, and we have both Chinese and Muslim evidence that before choosing its site, the Mongols actually looked for remains of former nomadic empires. Excavating steles and checking Chinese history books, they sought for both historical and archaeological evidence as well as folk memories, making the most of them to enhance the charismatic location of their capital.[16] Qaraqorum was founded a few dozen kilometers away from the Turkic and Uighur sites, perhaps both to enjoy the region's repositories of charisma and to stress the uniqueness of the Chinggisid experience.

---

[16] Juwayni/Qazwini 1912-37, 1: 39–46, 191–2; Juwayni 1997, 54–61, 236; Su 1967, 26:1b–2a; Song 1976, 146: 3464–5, 180: 4159; Yelü n.d., 2:7a; Allsen 1996; Atwood 2013.

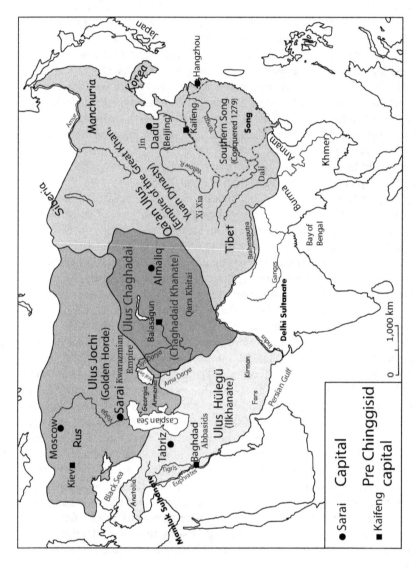

Map 6.4 "The Mongol Commonwealth": the Four Uluses, after 1260.

Qubilai's decision to desert this potent Chinggisid symbol can easily be explained by strategic, political, economic, and now even climatic considerations (Rossabi 1988, 51–75; Di Cosmo 2015): north China was certainly richer, located in Qubilai's original powerbase, and a better starting point for expanding into south China. Moreover, by then the climate in Mongolia had become drier, diminishing the supply of horses and making Mongolia a liability that swallowed external relief rather than an asset (Endicott-West 2005; Pederson et al. 2014). Indeed, the shift entailed the renunciation of Qaraqorum's repositories of charisma. But by 1260, the charisma was so deeply imbedded in the Chinggisid family, by then ruling territories much vaster than the steppe, that such a concession was not a real problem. The shift meant, however, that the empire's center moved from the steppe to the sedentary realm and that Mongolia, the original heart of the empire, was gradually marginalized into a periphery.

The post-1260 Mongol polities still held on to the world conquest ideology, yet after 1260 its implementation via further expansion was much more complicated. This was, first, because the inter-Mongol conflicts prevented the vast mobilization of imperial resources that characterized former campaigns: in fact, these conflicts often even hindered the khanates from concentrating their efforts on expansion, as they had to defend themselves against a rival *ulus*. Second, by 1260 the empire had already reached the ecological border of steppe nomadism on all its fronts. Further expansion therefore demanded organization, warfare techniques, and equipment different from the former light cavalry steppe campaigns. The Mongols managed to break the ecological border in south China – where the gains in terms of both economy and legitimation were by far the greatest – and this was done by mobilizing Chinese and Korean infantry and sailors and with the help of Iranian siege engineers (Rossabi 1988, 76–95; Davis 2009). Yet they were less successful on other fronts: the Ilkhans fought the Mamluks in Syria up to the early decades of the 14th century, but without enduring success, their frequent defeats encouraging the signing of a peace treaty in 1323 (Amitai 2005, 2013, 15–36). The Chaghadaids and the Golden Horde abandoned conquest campaigns altogether and reverted to raids: into north India (Chagadaids) or Eastern Europe (the Golden Horde) (Jackson 1999a, 218–37; Biran 2009; Vasary 2009). In China, beyond the conquest of the Southern Song in 1279, further expansion campaigns met only partial success (in Java, Burma, and Vietnam in the 1290s), or were completely disastrous, as in the case of Japan in 1274 and 1281 (Rossabi 1988, 99–103, 207–20).

The Chinggisids were well aware that their feuds were halting future expansion thereby jeopardizing Chinggis Khan's will. This is best documented in the descriptions of the inter-Mongol negotiations before the signing of the 1304 peace agreement, that was due to end all inter-Mongol enmities, notably the four decades' conflict between the Central Asian Mongols and the Great Qa'an. The Ilkhanid historian Wassaf (Vassaf) paraphrased a message of the

Chaghadaid Khan Du'a (r. 1282–1307) who initiated the peace agreement, in which Du'a suggested that after the peace the Qa'an will turn against the rebellious groups "in the fringes of Khitai (North China) and Manzi (South China)" (i.e. South east Asia and Japan); the Chaghadaids and Ögödeids would expand against "Hind, Sind and Delhi" (i.e., the Indian subcontinent); the Ilkhans to "the lands of the west," namely "Egypt and Syria" (the Mamluk Sultanate), "Rum" (Byzantium) and "the Afranj" (the Franks, i.e., Western Europe); while the Golden Horde rulers would turn against the unspecified "enemies of their family" (Wassaf 1853, 452–3). Thus, the ideal of continuous expansion up to a complete world conquest was still alive by the early 14th century. Moreover, including the Franks among the foes after four decades in which the Ilkhans had tried to forge an alliance with them against their common enemy the Mamluks, suggests that the Mongols saw peaceful coexistence with non-Mongols as temporary at best. They still divided the world into those already conquered and those who had to be conquered.

Despite the impressive rhetoric, however, the Mongol peace did not result in a new expansion wave, partly because the peace agreement merely brought about another decade of warfare in Central Asia with repercussions for the other khanates (Biran 1997, 71–4). Fundamentally, therefore, from the late 1270s the Mongol expansion came to a halt. This remained the situation even after the end of the inter-Mongol warfare in the 1320s, when the three western *uluses* acknowledged the nominal authority of the Yuan Qa'an, creating what we can call "the Mongol Commonwealth."[17]

6.2.2   Universal Concepts

This cessation of military expansion, however, did not mean that the Mongol successor states gave up on their universalist claims. Since all four khanates were vast polities and, moreover, the empire was perceived as a joint patrimony of the Chinggisids, each state could appropriate the achievements of Chinggis Khan and his heirs, and proudly present them to its local audience, for both propaganda against enemies and internal legitimation.[18] In other words, when expansion ceased, the very size of the empire was used as evidence of its continued legitimacy.

The continuing adherence to universal space found expression in Mongol-commissioned historical, geographical, and cartographic works, which flourished after the dissolution of the empire. One important consequence of the

---

[17] The Mamluk historian al-'Umari (d. 1349) compared the other Khanate's submission to the Qa'an to the way in which various Muslim polities acknowledged the Caliph's authority in late Abbasid times, namely nominal submission but membership in "the Islamic commonwealth" (al-'Umari 1968, 26 and see the Introduction to this volume).

[18] Barber and Bate 2010, 158–59; Wassaf 1853, 560–61; Amitai 2007, X: 11–33; Langlois 2009.

empire's dimensions and its world conquest ideology (whether understood as mission accomplished or as work in progress) was the huge increase in the knowledge about the world, in terms of its geography and history, and its visual representation in cartography. Such information was first collected in order to facilitate further military campaigns: Chinggis Khan and his heirs ascribed great importance to gathering good intelligence about their enemies, including spatial information such as the type of the terrain, and possible routes, and made full use of it. The intelligence gathering continued in the period of the successor states, and we find the Mongols collecting and/or preparing maps of border or due-to-be conquered regions such as Java, Burma, Yunnan, Anatolia, and the Mediterranean (Park 2012, 91–160). However, the more ambitious Yuan and Ilkhanid works are explained not just by military needs, but as a cultural outcome of the unprecedented dimensions of the empire:In 1286, Jamal al-Din, a Muslim astronomer in Qubilai's court, who was also responsible for the introduction of the first terrestrial globe to China,[19] asked Qubilai Khan to sponsor the production of a unified geographic treatise that would cover all the lands that the Mongols had conquered and would be accompanied by a map:

The entire land of China was very small in the past. The geographic books of the Khitai [Northern Chinese] had only forty to fifty types. *Now all of the land from the place of sunrise to sunset has become our territory. And therefore, do we not need a more detailed map? How can we understand distant places?* The Islamic maps are at our hands. And therefore, could we combine them [with the Chinese maps] to draw a [world?] map? (Wang 1992, 74; cited in Park 2012, 129–30)

Qubilai approved, and ordered the Palace Library to collect geographic gazetteers and maps from every region of his empire in order to compile the great treatise. Completed in 1303, the *Treatise of the Unified Realm of the Great Yuan (Da Yuan yitongzhi)* contained 1,300 chapters. Although it has not survived, except for part of its introduction, it must have included extensive descriptions of foreign countries. This assumption is reinforced by the available maps. The most impressive map that originated in the Yuan is the *Map of Integrated Regions and Terrains and of Historical Countries and Capitals (Honil gangni yeokdae gukdo jido)*, produced in Korea in 1402 but based on Yuan maps.

---

[19] This terrestrial globe (known as *kurrat al-ard* in Arabic, hence *kulaiyi a'erzi* in Chinese) was one of the western instruments brought by Jamal al-Din to China. "It was made of wood, which is formed into a ball, seven parts of it are water and their color is green, three parts are land, and their color is white. Streams, rivers, lakes and seas are drawn, and they crossed like veins through it. Small squares are drawn and they are used for measuring the circumference and the distance of the routes" (Song 1976, 48: 998–9). This unique object, probably a product of the Ilkhanid astronomical center in Maragha, did not leave its mark on Chinese cartography (this would have to wait for the Jesuits' globes in the 17th century), nor were the longitudes and latitudes implied by the squares adopted there, but the place names might have been helpful for Yuan maps. See Park 2013; Yang 2017.

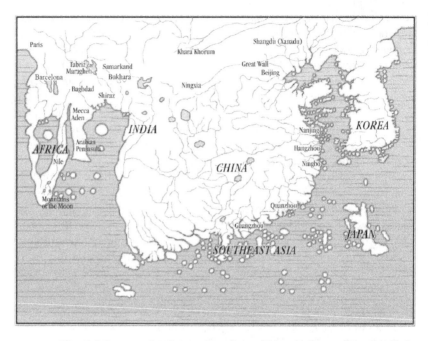

Map 6.5 Integrated regions and terrains and historical countries and capitals, with names. From Park, Hyunhee. 2012. *Mapping the Chinese and Islamic Worlds: Cross-Cultural Exchange in Pre-Modern Asia*. Cambridge: Cambridge University Press, p. 104.

Recently, Kim Hodong, who analyzed its toponyms, suggested that the original place names were written in the Mongolian-Uighur script, and that Jamal al-Din's map was the basis for the Korean map. This map included more than one hundred places in Europe (including Marseille and Seville) and thirty-five in Africa! It makes sense that Muslim works were used to provide such a large amount of new information.[20]

Another famous Yuan map that highlights the Chinggisid space, though acknowledging its internal divisions, was compiled in 1331 and included in the mirror for princes, the *Jingshi dadian* (*Great Compendium for Governing the World*). This map represented the various Mongol *uluses*, called after their 1331 rulers: Özbeg (the khan of the Golden Horde, r. 1313–41); Döre Temür (the Chaghadaid Khan, r. 1331); and the Ilkhan Abu Saʿid (r. 1316–35). It included lines signifying borders between the khanates and between them to

[20] Kim 2014; Park 2012, 103–109; Kauz 2015.

other places, such as Cairo (*Misr*), Damascus, Constantinople, India and Kashmir (Bretschneider 1888, vol. 2; Park 2012, 100–3).

The existing Ilkhanid maps are less impressive, but the Ilkhans' major contribution to the Mongol notion of universality belongs to the field of history rather than cartography. This is the renowned *Compendium of Chronicles* (*Jami ' al-tawarikh*), the first world history, compiled by the Ilkhanid historian and vizier Rashid al-Din (d. 1318). When Ilkhan Öljeitü (r. 1304–16) commissioned the work from Rashid al-Din, he had famously proclaimed:

Until now no one at any time has made a history of all inhabitants of the climes of the world and the various classes and groups of humans, there is no book in this realm that informs about all countries and regions, and no one has delved into the history of the ancient kings. *In these days, when, thank God, all corners of the earth are under our control and that of Chinggis Khan's illustrious family, and philosophers, astronomers, scholars, and historians of all religions and nations – Cathay, Machin, India, Kashmir, Tibet, Uyghur, and other nations of Turks, Arabs, and Franks – are gathered in droves at our glorious court,* each and every one of them possesses copies of the histories, stories, and beliefs of their own people, and they are well informed of some of them. It is our considered opinion that of those detailed histories and stories a compendium that would be perfect should be made in our royal name. (Rashid al-Din 1998–9, 1: 16; Rashid, ed. Rawshan 1994, 1: 8–9; emphasis added)

Rashid al-Din's book was supposed to include also a geographical volume and a map, but neither have survived, and perhaps were never compiled. However, Rashid al-Din's world history which indeed included (apart from that of the Mongols) the histories of the Chinese, the Indians, the Muslims, the Jews, the Turks, and the Franks, contained a huge amount of geographical information, notably on Mongolia and East Asia (Allsen 2001a, 83–114; Akasoy et al. 2013).

In Öljeitü's words, just as in Jamal al-Din's address to Qubilai, it is the space that creates knowledge: it is because we, Mongols, now rule the world that we want to know more about it. Interestingly, both history and map included also regions and people that were not incorporated into the Chinggisid space, i.e., were not politically ruled by the Mongols. Here too Öljeitü's words may be suggestive: in his commission, Öljeitü did not differentiate between people and territories conquered by the Mongols and those that were not, claiming instead that the whole world is under Chinggis Khan's family. Apparently the flocking of these "non-conquered people" (Indians, Franks, Arabs) to his court was taken as their recognition of Chinggisid superiority, in a way similar to the Chinese concept of tribute (see Pines, this volume). By then, even the Great Qa'an in Beijing similarly had to satisfy himself with formal acknowledgment of his superiority from various kingdoms in south and Southeast Asia. The terminology was still one of submission, and the original demands of the tributaries were similar to those made to the submitted rulers, for example, sending people – either as hostages or gifts – to the Yuan court. Yet practically, the Mongols were content with the participation of external rulers in the imperial economic system (Sen 2006; Fiaschetti 2014b). In other words, the Mongols no longer used military power as their main means for world conquest, turning to "soft power" methods, namely using their economic and cultural prestige to maintain the image of universal superiority.

Indeed, after the conquest of south China with its lively ports (1279) the Mongols combined the maritime and continental routes of the Old World into one integrated global system, far larger than the imperial realm (Kuroda 2009; Biran 2015b). Participants in this integrated system could be seen as the new *il irgen* or submitted people, who were taking part in the extensive cross-cultural contacts across the continent. Thus, world conquest was replaced by diplomacy, culture and trade, and expressed in competition for attracting experts from "All-under-Heaven" to the Mongol courts.

The increase in geographical knowledge or the globalization of the Old World was not confined to official compilations, nor even to the empire's realm. Its impact is best manifested in the rich array of travelogues from the Mongol period, the most notable of which were produced by Marco Polo (d. 1324) and Ibn Battuta (d. *c.*1377), natives of Venice and Tangier respectively, both outside the Chinggisid realm.[21] Indeed the huge population movements, which the Mongols initiated and encouraged – of soldiers, administrators, diplomats, merchants, missionaries, adventurers, and experts of various kinds – within the empire's borders and further afield, promoted scientific and cultural exchange throughout Eurasia, and broadened the horizons of the Mongols contemporaries.

6.2.3   Glocal Concepts

Whereas each of the Mongol successor states voiced universal claims and appropriated the Chinggisid achievements, they also adopted a variety of local elements and legitimating concepts. This was perhaps because the legitimating value of Chinggisid soft power was weaker than that of military expansion and it had to be augmented with local elements. Moreover, the localist turn reflects an attempt of each of the four khanates to carve their separate identities within the Chinggisid realm. In addition, the empire's dissolution also brought about closer ties between the Mongols and their subjects in each khanate. These ties evolved both due to practical considerations – such as gaining legitimacy, coopting local elites, or ruling more effectively – and due to the gradual assimilation of the tiny Mongol elite in

---

[21] Another manifestation is the huge encyclopedia of the Mamluk historian Ibn Fadlallah al-'Umarī (d. 1349), *Masalik al-absar fi mamalik al-amsar* ("The Ways of Discernment, with Regard to the Provinces of the Inhabited Areas"), which devoted one of its twenty-five volumes to "the kingdoms of Chinggis Khan's family," namely the four *uluses*. It also covered the whole Old World (al-'Umari 1968, 1–60). See also Allsen 2001a, 103–13.

the huge native populations. One of the clearest manifestation of this adaptation to local cultures was the Mongols' embracing of universal world religions – Tibetan Buddhism in China, Islam in all the other Mongol Khanates – as well as the adoption of local imperial concepts in the khanates with strong native imperial tradition, namely in better-documented China and Iran.[22] In a typical nomadic amalgamation, however, the various legitimation and spatial concepts – Chinggisid, religious, local – coexisted and were not mutually exclusive.

The post-1260 situation therefore led to the revival of local imperial concepts – that of "the Great Unity" (*Dayitong*; and see Pines, this volume) in China and of "the land of Iran" (*Iran-zamin*), namely Iran as a political unit independent of the rest of the Muslim world, in Iran. In the latter case, this meant a revival of the term Iran as a political concept for the first time since the Arab conquest of the 7th century.[23]

Local imperial concepts fitted quite nicely with the borders of the respective khanates: the territory directly under the Qa'an's rule included – after 1279 – both northern and southern China, united by the Mongols after more than 350 years of division. That it also included much broader territory than China proper, for example, Mongolia, Manchuria, Tibet, Yunnan, and Korea, was considered as expanding "All-under-Heaven" and could only add to the Mongols' legitimacy (Pines, this volume). Likewise, the Ilkhanate's territory was reminiscent of the realm of Sassanid Iran (224–651 CE), the last indigenous dynasty before the Arab conquest. In both cases, embracing the local imperial vocabulary was quite easy for the Mongols, as both Chinese and Iranian imperial concepts included a strong universal component and ideological elements similar to the Mongol ones: the Mandate of Heaven in China and the notion of charisma (Persian: *farnah/farrah/khwarnah*) in Iran. Moreover, as highly pragmatic rulers, the Mongols might have realized the advantages of utilizing local imperial ideology as a means for co-opting local elites. The initiative probably came from the Mongols' local advisers, who strove to accommodate their foreign lords into the local tradition. Thus, already

---

[22] In the steppe khanates there were no such developed local imperial concepts to revive. Here, at least in the Chaghadaid case, we can detect an attempt to carve a distinct local spatial image within the Chinggisid space: The Chaghadaids, after their restoration of power under Du'a Khan (r. 1282–1307) referred to themselves as *Dumdadu Monggol Ulus*, the Middle Mongol Ulus, a name attested in Latin as the *Medium Imperium* as well as in Arabic sources (Matsui 2009). The designation, probably playing on the prestige connected with the Chinese concept of the Middle Kingdom, refers to the Chaghadaids' geographical location in the midst of the other Mongol states. The case of Jochids is less clear. In the post-Mongol world, they were known as the Chaghan Khans, namely the White or Western Khans (i.e., the western Chinggisid realm), but I did not find a reference to this in 13th- and 14th-century sources. Mamluk and Ilkhanid sources often refer to the Jochids as "the northern lands" (*bilad al-shimal*), but this may reflect their point of view, not necessarily the Jochid one.

[23] Fragner 1997 and 2006; Krawulsky 2011; Brook 2018. For various other spatial concepts (e.g. Greek ones) which were known in Ilkhanid Iran, see Qazwini 1915–19, 1: 18–21, 2: 20–23.

in 1262, Hülegü received an illustrated copy of the *Shah-Namah*, the Iranian epic *Book of Kings*, in which the Mongols were included as the current Iranian dynasty (Ibn al-Fuwati 1995, 3: 317). As for Qubilai, he was surrounded by Chinese advisers long before he became Qa'an, and their impact on him, for instance in matters of imperial ritual, is undeniable (Rossabi 1988, 14–17, 22–42). For their part, scholars in China and Iran, many of whom were employed or subsidized by the Mongols, were all too happy to promote the revival of native imperial concepts.

Most of the local elites under Mongol rule saw their space in its particular, regional context. See, for example, Song Lian (d. 1381), the would-be compiler of the Yuan official history under the succeeding Ming dynasty, a man who refused to serve the Yuan but certainly acknowledged its mandate. In an introduction to a collection of biographies he compiled in the 1340s or 1350s, Song says:

> Our August Yuan received the bright mandate from Heaven to bring peace to the Sinic world (*xia*); where the heavenly lance pointed, the myriad directions all followed. At the first drum the many [Mongolian] tribes came on board; at the second drum the [Tangut] Xia people sued for peace [in 1227]; at the third drum the [Jurchen imperial] Wanyan clan submitted [in 1234]; and at the fourth drum the Southern Song was pacified [in 1279]. The vast realm was unified under one teaching, all were the emperor's servants. With good plans and judgment, his [the emperor's] every action was victorious. As well, he relied upon capable men and unwaveringly loyal officials; they enabled him to proclaim the power of Heaven, and such was the divine speed with which the deeds were performed and governance was established. (Song 1999, 1; cited in Langlois 2009, 133–4)

Obviously, for Song Lian, the Yuan achievement was the unification of the Chinese world (the Xia and the Jin ruled vast swathes of territory that prior to the 10th century were mostly under Chinese control). Song Lian does not refer to the Mongols' achievements on the other fronts – not even those included in the narrowly defined Yuan realm such as Dali (Yunnan) in southwest China, Korea, or Tibet.[24]

Another major example appears in the introduction of *Nizam al-tawarikh* (*The String of Chronicles*), a Persian work devoted to the history of Iran from the time of Adam to Abaqa (r. 1265–82), Hülegü's son and heir and the reigning Ilkhan. The work was compiled in 1275, that is twenty years before the Ilkhanid Islamization. The author, Qadi Baydawi (d. 1286), a notable Muslim scholar famous for his Quranic commentary, wrote:

> I have collected this book from reliable chronicles and named it "The string of chronicles", for in it I have connected the sequence of governors and kings of Iran – which extends from the Euphrates to the Oxus, or rather from the Arab lands to the borders of Khojand, as will

---

[24] For further examples, see Brook 2018; Humble 2015; and Robinson's Chapter 8, in this volume.

be mentioned – from Adam (peace be on him) to the present day, which is 21 *Muharram* 674 *hijri* [17 July 1275]. (Baydawi 1935, 3, as translated in Melville 2001, 76)

The Mongols appear as the eighth and last dynasty in the book's fourth part, the one devoted to the independent Iranian dynasties (earlier sections are dedicated to the prophets, beginning with Adam; the pre-Islamic Iranian kings; and the Caliphate). Baydawi says:

The eighth group is the Mongols, whose leader and chief is Chinggis Khan. He attacked the Khwarazmians in 617 *hijri* [1220]; he and his sons govern many lands of the Khata [Northern Chinese] and Turk. They conquered the whole of Iran and subjugated its kingdoms and kings. Of his sons, Hülegü Khan[25] was the first who ruled Iran and conquered its territories. His son Abaqa [is] king of *Iran-zamin*, Rum [Anatolia], Iraq and all the [Iranian] kingdoms. He is strongly inclined towards justice and compassion and favors the Muslims entirely. (Baydawi 1935, 94–5, as translated in Melville 2001, 77)

While Baydawi was aware of the Ilkhans' Chinggisid connections, his focus was on their rule of Iran, which he defines once as stretching from the Euphrates to the Oxus, excluding parts of Iraq and Anatolia that were also under Ilkhanid rule.

Did the Mongols also see their space in these terms? Not necessarily. The most striking example of the different concepts is the lack of a Mongolian word for China: The Mongols continued to use Khitai/Kitad for north China and Manzi/Nangiyas[26] for south China, as did their employees, Marco Polo and Rashid al-Din (Kim 2015, 2018). Moreover, in two Sino-Mongolian inscriptions of 1338 and 1362, the Mongols made clear that for them *Da Yuan*, as their dynasty was known in China (Mongolian: *Dai On*) equals *Yeke Mongghol Ulus* (the Great Mongol Nation, i.e., the united Mongol Empire).[27] It seems clear that the *Qa'an ulus*, saw itself as reigning over the whole Chinggisid realm. Namely, for the Mongols "the great unity" refers to the entire Chinggisid space, not to that of China only.

As for the Ikhans, although under Abaqa they built their first palace in Iranian lands on the site of a former Achaemenid and Sasanian site known as *Takht-i Sulayman*, the throne of Solomon, adorning it with tiles bearing citations from the *Shah-Namah* (Huff 2006), their letters, coins and inscriptions hardly mention the name Iran or purely Iranian titles such as the King of Kings (*Shahanshah*). The Chinggisid ideology of world conquest, in contrast, is very much present in these genres (see Hülegü's letter cited above), well into the 14th century. It remained valid even after the Ilkhanate's Islamization in 1295, when Islamic formulas were added (Amitai 2013, 37–62, 102–5).

---

[25] Hülegü was actually a grandson of Chinggis Khan, unlike the leaders of his neighbors, the Jochids and Chaghadaids, called after Chinggis Khan's sons.

[26] *Manzi* in Chinese refers to the southern barbarians, but in Mongolian meant south China; Nangiyas in Mongolian is derived from the Chinese *Nanjia*, southern people.

[27] Cleaves 1951, 53; 1959, 62; Kim 2015.

Apparently, the Mongols felt more at home in the universal world of Islam, the leadership of which they could claim after extinguishing the Caliphate, than in the more limited notion of Iran. In other words, while adopting a more complex, glocal world order favored by their subjects, the Mongols still stressed its universal aspects.

6.3   Shaping Future Imperial Space

Speaking of Mongol legacy, we may conclude that it was the glocal world, rather than the Chinggisid universalism, that had the biggest impact on the shaping of future Eurasian space. In geopolitical terms, united China, independent Iran, and Russia as a Eurasian superpower are still with us. In Inner Asia, in distinction, the Mongol period's main effect was not creating a new imperial entity but rather a major ethnic reconfiguration (namely affecting people rather than territory). The population movements generated by the conquest and post-conquest policies led to the disappearance of various established steppe people, such as the Kitans, Tanguts, Uighurs,[28] and Qipchaqs, and the emergence of new collectivities, such as the Uzbeks, Kazakhs, and Tatars, who became the modern Central Asian Muslim peoples. However, the terms Mongolia and Moghulistan (the eastern Chaghadaid Khanate, roughly equivalent to Kirgizstan, south Kazakhstan and eastern Xinjiang of today) can be considered a certain spatial legacy of the Mongol Empire in the Inner Asian realm.

Moreover, the Mongols left to their followers a host of imperial institutions that continued to be used across Eurasia, contributing not only to the Mongols' direct successor states but also to other regional empires, and facilitating the emergence – especially from the 16th century onward – of a group of regional empires (Mughals, Ottomans, Safavids; Ming and Qing China; Muscovite Russia) that were vaster and more enduring than most of the pre-Mongol polities.[29] Paradoxically, these developments also led to the breaking up of the nomadic world order that gave rise to Chinggis Khan: the division of the steppe between Muslims and Tibetan Buddhists, especially after the Mongols' second conversion to Buddhism in the 16th century, prevented a whole-steppe unification under the standard of Tengri while the Mongol imperial toolkit – proudly adhered to by the Manchus and ostensibly rejected

---

[28] The current Uighur people in Xinjiang are not ethnically related to these 14th-century Uighurs (even though they sometimes appropriate the historical Uighurs' achievements); the name Uighur resurfaced only in the early 20th century, as a common designation to the Muslim Turks in Xingiang's oases, who beforehand had identified themselves merely by the names of their settlements (Kashghari, Turfani, etc).

[29] Biran 2004, 358–61, 2015b; Crossley and Garthwaite, 2016; Neumann and Wigen 2015; Robinson 2019. See also the chapters of Dale (Chapter 7), Robinson (Chapter 8), Mosca (Chapter 9), and Burbank (Chapter 10), in this volume.

by the Russians – could be used against them. This toolkit, in addition to the gunpowder technology that the Mongol Empire had disseminated westwards (and the improved version of which the Jesuits reintroduced to China from Europe in the 16th century), eventually enabled Qing China (1644–1911) and Imperial Russia (1721–1917) to divide the steppe between them in the 18th century, at the expense of the nomads (Allsen 2015).

More indirectly, it can even be argued that the glocal world order established by the Mongols paved the way for the beginning of the early modern period and even for the European expansion. By virtue of the expansion of long-distance commercial and financial exchange, the growing interest in maritime power, the formation of new collectivities, the accelerated rates of diffusion or "connectivity" among different regions, the quantum leap forward in the knowledge of the Old World, which resulted in religious and cultural relativism, as well as the new model of charismatic leadership with direct connection to the divine, the Mongols ushered in the early modern period (Allsen 1997b; Subrahaiman 1997; Kuroda 2009; Brack 2018; Atwood, forthcoming). Moreover, the Mongol legacy was not limited to the continental empires. As Samuel Adshead eloquently argued, "if Europe came to dominate the world, it was because Europe first perceived there was a world to dominate" (Adshead 1993, 77, cited in Biran 2015b, 555). Thus, when Columbus set out on his first voyage in 1492, his principal objective was to find the land of the "Great Khan" that emerges from the *Travels of Marco Polo*, whom he ardently admired. Eventually, the Mongol imperial enterprise contributed, even if indirectly, to the European discovery of the New World.

In conclusion, the Mongols' spatial concepts evolved with the empire. They began with a universal heavenly-ordained mandate to rule over the earth, which led to an unprecedented territorial expansion by military power. This expansion both attested to the holding of the Mandate and brought about its most inclusive interpretation as referring literally to the whole world. In the long run, it also accelerated the empire's dissolution. In the divided, post-1260 Mongol world, the universal concept was gradually replaced by, or at least supplemented with, glocal concepts that combined universal aspirations with local elements and legitimation concepts. In this glocal world order, military power was gradually replaced by economic and cultural prestige as the main channels of claiming universal leadership, while world religions and local pre-Mongol imperial concepts also played a larger role and affected the various Mongol governments. It was this composite glocal phase that had a tremendous impact on the shaping of the future imperial space, both regionally – in China, Iran, Russia, the steppe and across the Muslim world – and globally, not least by ushering in the transition from the medieval to the early modern world and facilitating the discovery of the New World.

Bibliography

Adshead, Samuel A. M. 1993. *Central Asia in World History.* New York: St. Martin Press.

Aigle, Denise. 2007. "The Mongol invasions of Bilād al-Shām by Ghāzān Khān and Ibn Taymīyah's three 'anti-Mongol' fatwas." *Mamluk Studies Review* 11: 89–120.

2014. *The Mongol Empire between Myth and Reality: Studies in Anthropological History.* Leiden: Brill.

Akasoy, Anna, Burnett, Charles, and Yoeli-Tlalim, Ronit, eds. 2013. *Rashīd al-Dīn. Agent and Mediator of Cultural Exchanges in Ilkhanid Iran.* Warburg Institute Colloquia 24. London and Turin: The Warburg Institute.

Albrecht, Sarah. 2016. "Dār al-Islām and dār al-ḥarb." In: *Encyclopaedia of Islam, THREE,* ed. Kate Fleet, Gudrun Krämer, Denis Matringe, John Nawas, Everett Rowson. Online edition.

Allsen, Thomas T. 1987. *Mongol Imperialism: the Policies of the Grand Khan Möngke in China, Russia, and the Islamic Lands, 1251–1259.* Berkeley, CA: University of California Press.

1994. "The Rise of the Mongolian Empire and Mongol Rule in North China." In: *The Cambridge History of China, Volume 6: Alien Regimes and Border States, 907–1368,* ed. Herbert Franke and Dennis Twitchett, 321–413. Cambridge: Cambridge University Press.

1996. "Spiritual Geography and Political Legitimacy in the Eastern Steppe." In: *Ideology and the Formation of the Early State,* ed. Henri J. M. Claessen and Jarich G. Oosten, 116–35. Leiden: Brill.

1997a. *Commodity and Exchange in the Mongol Empire: A Cultural History of Islamic Textiles.* Cambridge: Cambridge University Press.

1997b. "Ever Closer Encounters: The Appropriation of Culture and the Apportionment of Peoples in the Mongol Empire." *Journal of Early Modern History* 1: 2–23.

2001a. *Culture and Conquest in Mongol Eurasia.* Cambridge: Cambridge University Press.

2001b. "Sharing out the Empire: Apportioned Lands under the Mongols." *In:* *Nomads in the Sedentary World,* ed. A.M. Khazanov and A. Wink, 172–90. Richmond: Curson.

2009. "A Note on Mongol Imperial Ideology." In: *The Early Mongols: Language, Culture and History: Studies in Honor of Igor de Rachewiltz on the Occasion of his* 80th *Birthday,* ed. Volker Rybatzki, Alessandra Pozzi, Peter W. Geier and John R. Krueger, 1–9. Bloomington, IN: Indiana University Press.

2011. "Imperial Posts, West, East and North: A Review Article: Adam J. Silverstein, *Postal Systems in the Pre-Modern Islamic World." Archivum Eurasiae Medii Aevi* 17: 237–76.

2015. "Eurasia after the Mongols." In: *The Cambridge History of the World, Vol. 6: The Construction of a Global World, 1400–1800 CE, Part 1: Foundations,* ed. Jerry H. Bentley, Sanjay Subrahmanyam, and Merry E. Wiesner-Hanks, 159–81. Cambridge: Cambridge University Press.

Amitai, Reuven. 2005. "*The Resolution of the Mongol-Mamluk War." In: Mongols, Turks and Others: Eurasian Nomads and the Sedentary World,* ed. *Reuven Amitai* and Michal Biran, 359–90. Leiden: Brill.

2007. *The Mongols in the Islamic Lands: Studies in the History of the Ilkhanate*. Aldershot: Variorum.

2013. *Holy War and Rapprochement. Studies in the Relations between the Mamluk Sultanate and the Mongol Ilkhanate (1260–1335)*. Turnhout: Brespols.

Amitai-Preiss, Reuven. 1995. *Mongols and Mamluks. The Mamluk-Īlkhānid War, 1260–1281*. Cambridge: Cambridge University Press.

1999. "Mongol imperial ideology and the Ilkhanid war against the Mamluks." In: *The Mongol Empire and Its Legacy*, ed. Reuven Amitai-Preiss and David O. Morgan, 57–72. Leiden: Brill. Reprinted in Amitai,

2007. *The Mongols in the Islamic Lands*. Ashgate: Variorum.

Atwood, Christopher P. 2013. "The Uyghur Stone: Archaeological Revelations in the Mongol Empire." In: *The Steppe Lands and the World beyond Them: Studies in Honor of Victor Spinei on his 70th birthday*, ed. Florin Curta and Bogdan-Petru Maleon, 315–43. Iaşi: Editura Universității 'Alexandru Ioan Cuza.

forthcoming. "Mongol Empire and Early Modernity." In: *Asia and the Early Modern*, ed. I. Kaya Şahin and Hendrik Spruyt.

Barber, Malcolm and Keith Bate, trans. 2010. *Letters from the East: Crusaders, Pilgrims and Settlers in the* 12th-13th *Centuries*. Crusade Texts in Translation 18. Fordham: Ashgate.

Barfield, Thomas J. 1989. *The Perilous Frontier: Nomadic Empires and China*. Oxford: Basil Blackwell.

2001. "The S*hadow Empires*: Imperial State Formation along the Chinese–Nomad Frontier." In: *Empires: Perspective from Archaeology and History*, ed. Susan E. Alcock, Terence N. D'Altroy, Kathleen D. Morrison, and Carla M. Sinopoli, 10–41. Cambridge: Cambridge University Press.

Baumann, Brian. 2013. "By the Power of Eternal Heaven: The Meaning of Tenggeri to the Government of the Pre-Buddhist Mongols." *Extrême-Orient Extrême-Occident* 35: 233–84.

Baydawi, Nasir al-Din 'Abdallah (d. 1286). 1935. *Nizam al-tawarikh*, ed. Bahman Karimi. Tehran: Kitabkhana-i 'Ilmi, 1313sh.

Biran, Michal. 1997. *Qaidu and the Rise of the Independent Mongol State in Central Asia*. Richmond: Curzon.

2004. "The Mongol Transformation: From the Steppe to Eurasian Empire." *Medieval Encounters* 10: 339–61.

2007. *Chinggis Khan*. Oxford: OneWorld Publications.

2009. "Central Asia from the Conquest of Chinggis Khan to the Rise of Tamerlane: The Ögodeied and Chaghadaid Realms." In: *The Cambridge History of Inner Asia. Vol. 2. The Chinggisid Age*, ed. Peter B. Golden, Nicola Di Cosmo, and Allan Frank, 46–66. Cambridge: Cambridge University Press.

2013. "Rulers and City Life in Mongol Central Asia (1220–1370)." In: *Turko-Mongol Rulers, Cities and City-life in Iran and the Neighboring Countries*, ed. David Durand-Guédy, 257–83. Leiden: Brill.

2015a. "Introduction: Nomadic Culture." In: *Nomads as Agents of Cultural Change: The Mongols and Their Eurasian Predecessors*, ed. Reuven Amitai and Michal Biran, 1–9. Honolulu, HI: University of Hawaii Press.

2015b. "The Mongol Empire and the Inter-Civilizational Exchange." In: *The Cambridge History of the World. Vol. 5. Expanding Webs of Exchange and*

Conflict, 500CE–1500CE, ed. Benjamin Kedar and Merry Wiesner-Hanks, 534–58. Cambridge: Cambridge University Press.

Brack, Jonathan Z. 2018. "Theologies of Auspicious Kingship: The Islamization of Chinggisid Sacral Kingship in the Islamic World." *Comparative Studies in Society and History* 60: 1,143–71.

Bretschneider, Emily V. 1888. *Mediaeval Researches from Eastern Asiatic Sources*. 2 vols. Toronto: Robats.

Brook, Timothy. 2018. "Chinese Legitimation of the Mongol Regime and the Legacy of Unification." In: *Sacred Mandates: Asian International Relations Since Chinggis Khan*, ed. Timothy Brook, Walt van Praag, M. C. van Miek Boltjes, 49–55. Chicago, IL: University of Chicago Press.

Brose, Michael C. 2006. "Realism and Idealism in the *Yuanshi* Chapters on Foreign Relations." *Asia Major* (Third Series) 19: 327–47.

Burbank, Jane and Frederick Cooper. 2010. *Empires in World History: Power and the Politics of Difference*. Princeton, NJ: Princeton University Press.

Cai Meibiao 蔡美彪, ed. 1955. *Yuandai baihua bei jilu* 元代白話碑集禄. Beijing: Kexue chubanshe.

Chavannes, Edouard. 1908. "Inscriptions et pièces de chancellerie chinoises de époque mongole (2nd series)." *T'oung-pao* 9: 297–448.

Cleaves, Francis W. 1950. "The Sino-Mongolian Inscription of 1335 in Memory of Chang Ying-jui." *Harvard Journal of Asiatic Studies* 13: 1–131.

    1951. "The Sino-Mongolian Inscription of 1338 in Memory of Jigüntei." *Harvard Journal of Asiatic Studies* 14: 1–104.

    1952. "The Sino-Mongolian Inscription of 1346." *Harvard Journal of Asiatic Studies* 15: 1–123.

    1953. "The Mongolian Documents in the Musée de Téhéran." *Harvard Journal of Asiatic Studies* 16: 1–107.

    1959. "The Sino-Mongolian Inscription of 1362 in Memory of Prince Hindu," *Harvard Journal of Asiatic Studies* 22: 1–133.

Crossley, Pamela K. and Gene R. Garthwaite. 2016. "Post-Mongol States and Early Modern Chronology in Iran and China." *Journal of the Royal Asiatic Society* 26: 293–307.

Davis, Richard L. 2009. "The Reign of Tu-tsung (1264–1274) and His Successors to 1279." In: *The Cambridge History of China. Vol. 5, part I. The Sung Dynasty and Its Precursors*, ed. Denis Twitchett and Paul J. Smith, 913–62. Cambridge: Cambridge University Press.

Dawson, Christopher, ed. 1980. *Mission to Asia*. Toronto: University of Toronto Press in association with the Medieval Academy of America.

Di Cosmo, Nicola. 1999. "State Formation and Periodization in Inner Asian History." *Journal of World History* 10: 1–40.

    2015. "Why Qara Qorum? Climate and Geography in the Early Mongol Empire." *Archivum Eurasiae Medii Aevi* 21: 67–78.

Duindam, Jeroen Frans Jozef. 2016. *Dynasties: A Global History of Power, 1300–1800*. Cambridge: Cambridge University Press.

Endicott-West, Elisabeth. 2005. "The Mongols and China: Cultural Contacts and the Changing Nature of Pastoral Nomadism." In: *Mongols, Turks and Others: Eurasian Nomads and the Outside World*, ed. Reuvem Amitai and Michal Biran, 461–82. Leiden: Brill.

Fiaschetti, Francesca. 2014a. "The Borders of Rebellion: The Yuan Dynasty and the Rhetoric of Empire." In: *Political Strategies of Identity Building in non-Han empires in China*, ed. Francesca Fiaschetti and Julia Schneider, 127–45. Wiesbaden: Harrassowitz.

2014b. "Tradition, Innovation and the Construction of Qubilai's Diplomacy." *Mingqing yanjiu* 18: 65–96.

Fletcher, Joseph F. 1986. "The Mongols: Ecological and Social Perspective." *Harvard Journal of Asiatic Studies* 46: 11–50.

Fragner, Bert G. 1997. "Iran under Ilkhanid rule in a World History Perspective." In: *L'Iran face à la domination mongole*, ed. Denis Aigle, 121–31. Tehran: Institut français de recherche en Iran.

2006. "Ilkhanid Rule and its Contributions to Iranian Political Culture." In: *Beyond the Legacy of Genghis Khan*, ed. Linda Komaroff, 68–80. Leiden: Brill.

Golden, Peter B. 1982. "Imperial Ideology and the Sources of Political Unity amongst the Pre-Činggisid Nomads of Western Eurasia." *AEMA* 2: 37–76.

2006. "The Türk Imperial Tradition in the pre-Chinggisid Era." In: *Imperial Statecraft*, ed. David Sneath, 23–61. Bellingham: Western Washington University Press. Reprinted in Golden.

2010. *Turks and Khazars: Origins, Institutions, and Interactions in Pre-Mongol Eurasia*. Farnham, England; Burlington, VT: Ashgate/Variorum.

Haw, Stefan, 2013. "The Mongol Empire: The First Gunpowder Empire?" *Journal of the Royal Asiatic Society* 23: 449–61.

Hsim, Hosung. 2014. "The Postal Roads of the Great Khans in Central Asia under the Mongol-Yuan Empire." *Journal of Song-Yuan Studies* 44: 405–69.

Huff, Dietrich. 2006. "The Ilkhanid Palace at Takht-i Sulayman: Excavation Results." In: *Beyond the Legacy of Genghis Khan*, ed. Linda Komaroff, 94–110. Leiden: Brill.

Humble, Geoffrey F. 2015. "Princely Qualities and Unexpected Coherence: Rhetoric and Representation in 'Juan' 117 of the 'Yuanshi'." *Journal of Song-Yuan Studies* 45: 307–37.

2017. "Biographical Rhetorics: Narrative and Power in *Yuanshi* Biography." PhD dissertation, University of Birmingham.

Ibn al-Fuwati, Kamal al-Din 'Abd al-Razzaq b. Ahmad (1244–1323). 1995. *Majma' al-adab fi mu'jam al-alqab*, ed. Muhammad al-Kazim. 6 vols. Tehran: Mu'assasat al-tiba'a wa-l-nashr, 1416h.

Isahaya, Yoichi. 2017. "Toluid Appanages as Mesoscale Agency in Cross-Cultural Exchange." Paper presented at the workshop "*Networks, Regions and Institutions in Mongol Eurasia: A Meso-Historical Analysis*," The Hebrew University of Jerusalem, May 17–18.

Jackson, Peter. 1978. "The *Dissolution* of the *Mongol Empire*." *Central Asiatic Journal* 32: 186–244.

1999a. *The Delhi Sultanate: A Political and Military History*. Cambridge: Cambridge University Press.

1999b. "*From Ulus to Khanate*: The Making of the Mongol States, c.1220– c.1290." In: *The Mongol Empire and its Legacy*, ed. Reuven Amitai-Preiss and David O. Morgan, 13–28. Leiden: Brill.

2005. *The Mongols and the West: 1221–1410*. Harlow: Pearson Longman.

2011. "World-Conquest and Local Accommodation: Threat and Blandishment in Mongol Diplomacy." In: *History and Historiography of Post-Mongol Central Asia and the Middle East: Studies in Honour of John E. Woods*, ed. Judith Pfeiffer and Sheila A. Quinn in collaboration with Ernest Tucker, 3–22. Wiesbaden: Harrassowitz.

2017. *The Mongols and the Islamic World: From Conquest to Conversion.* New Haven, CT: Yale University Press.

al-Juwayni [Juvaini], ʿAṭa-Malik (1226–1283). 1912–1937. *Taʾrikh-i Jahangusha* Edited Mirza Muhammad Qazwin. 3 vols. London: Luzac.

1997. *Genghis Khan: The History of the World Conqueror*, trans. John A. Boyle. Manchester: Manchester University Press.

Kauz, Ralph, ed. 2015. *"Chinese and Asian Geographical and Cartographical Views on Central Asia and Its Adjacent Regions."* Special Issue, *Journal of Asian History* 49: 1–266.

Kim Hodong. 2009. "The Unity of the Mongol Empire and Continental Exchanges over Eurasia." *Journal of Central Eurasian Studies* 1: 15–42.

2014. "The Compilation of the Gazetteer of the Grand Unification (*Dayitong zhi*) and the Origin of the Mongol World Map." Paper presented at the conference "*Chinese and Asian Geographical and Cartographical Views on Central Asia and its Adjacent Region*," Bonn, January 10–11.

2015. "Was Da Yuan a Chinese Dynasty?" *Journal of Song-Yuan Studies* 45: 279–305.

2018. "Mongol Perceptions of 'China' and the Yuan Dynasty." In: *Sacred Mandates: Asian International Relations Since Chinggis Khan*, ed. Timothy Brook, Walt van Praag, and M. C. van Miek Boltjes, 45–49. Chicago, IL: University of Chicago Press.

2019. "The Formation and Changes of *Uluses* in the Mongol Empire." *Journal of the Economic and Social History of the Orient* 62: 269–317.

Krawulsky, Dorothea. 2011. "The Revival of the Ancient Name Īrān under the Mongol Īlkhāns (r. 656–736/1258–1336)." In: *The Mongol Īlkhāns and their Vizier Rashīd al-Dīn*, ed. Dorothea Krawulsky, 43–52. Frankfurt am Main: Peter Lang.

Kuroda, Akinobu. 2009. "The Eurasian Silver Century, 1276–1359: Commensurability and Multiplicity." *Journal of Global History* 4: 245–69.

Langlois, John M. 2009. "Song Lian and Liu Ji in 1358 on the Eve of Joining Zhu Yuanzhang." *Asia Major* (Third Series) 22: 131–62.

Matsui, Dai. 2009. "'Dumdadu Mongghol Ulus' – 'The Middle Mongolian Empire'". In: *The Early Mongols: Language, Culture and History: Studies in Honor of Igor de Rachewiltz on the Occasion of his 80th Birthday*, ed. Volker Rybatzki, Alessandra Pozzi, Peter W. Geier and John R. Krueger, 112–19. Bloomington, IN: Indiana University Press.

May, Timothy. 2012. *The Mongol Conquest in World History.* London: Reaction-Globalities.

Forthcoming. "The Mongols' Military Machine." In: *The Cambridge History of the Mongol Empire*, vol. 1, ed. Michal Biran and Kim Hodong. Cambridge: Cambridge University Press.

Melville, Charles. 2001. "From Adam to Abaqa: Qāḍī Baiḍāwī's Rearrangement of History." *Studia Iranica* 30: 67–86.

2007. "From *Adam to Abaqa*: Qāḍī Baidāwī's Rearrangement of History (Part 2)." *Studia Iranica* 36: 7–64.

Morgan, David O. 2007. *The Mongols*. 2nd ed. London: Blackwell.

Meyvaert, Paul, 1980. "An Unknown *Letter* of Hulagu, Il-Khan of Persia, to King Louis IX of France." *Viator* 11: 245–59.

Mostaert, Antoine and Francis W. Cleaves. 1952. "Trois documents mongols des archives secrètes vaticanes." *Harvard Journal of Asiatic Studies* 15: 419–506.

1962. *Les lettres de 1289 et 1305 des ilkhan Arγun et Ölǰeitü à Philippe le Bel*. Scripta Mongolica Monograph Series 1. Cambridge, MA: Harvard-Yenching Institute.

Mott, Christopher, 2015. *The Formless Empire: A Short History of Diplomacy and Warfare in Central Asia*. Yardley, PA: Westholme Publishing.

Munkh-Erdene, Lamsuren. 2018. "The Emergence of the Chinggisid State." In: *Sacred Mandates: Asian International Relations Since Chinggis Khan*, ed. Timothy Brook, Walt van Praag, M. C. van Miek Boltjes, 29–33. Chicago, IL: University of Chicago Press.

Münkler, Herfried. 2007. *Empires: The Logic of World Domination from Ancient Rome to the United States*. Cambridge: Polity.

Neumann, Iver B. and Wigen, Einar. 2015. "Remnants of the Mongol Imperial Tradition". In: *Legacies of Empire: Imperial Roots of the Contemporary Global Order*, ed. Sandra Halperin and Ronen Palan, 1–42. Cambridge: Cambridge University Press.

Park, Hyunhee. 2012. *Mapping the Chinese and Islamic Worlds: Cross-Cultural Exchange in Pre-Modern Asia*. Cambridge and New York: Cambridge University Press.

2013. "Cross-Cultural Exchange and Geographic Knowledge of the World in Yuan China." In: *Eurasian Influences on Yuan China*, ed. Morris Rossabi, 125–58. Singapore: Institute of Southeast Asia Studies.

Pederson, Neil, Amy E. Hessl, Nachin Baatarbileg, Kevin. J. Anchukaitis, and Nicola Di Cosmo. 2014. "Pluvials, Droughts, the Mongol Empire, and Modern Mongolia." *Proceedings of the National Academy of Sciences* 111 (12): 4,375–9.

Pines, Yuri. 2012. *The Everlasting Empire: The Political Culture of Ancient China and Its Imperial Legacy*. Princeton, NJ: Princeton University Press.

Poppe, Nicholas. 1957. *The Mongolian Monuments in hPh'ags-pa Script*. Wiesbaden: Otto Harrassowitz.

Qazwini Hamdallah, Mustawfi (1281–1349). 1915–19. *Nuzhat al-qulūb, edited and translated by Guy Le Strange as The Geographical Part of the Nuzhat al-Qulūb* (Gibb Memorial Series 23), 2 vols. Leiden and London: Brill and Luzac.

Rachewiltz, Igor de. 1971. *Papal Envoys to the Great Khans*. Stanford: Stanford University Press.

1973. "Some Remarks on the Ideological Foundations of Chinggis Khan's Empire." *Papers on Far Eastern History* 7: 21–36.

1983. "Qan, Qa'an and the Seal of Güyük." In: *Documenta Barbarorum: Festschrift für Walter Heissig zum 70. Geburstag*, ed. Klaus Sagaster and Michael Weiers, 272–81. Wiesbaden: Otto Harrassowitz.

tr. 2006. *The Secret History of the Mongols: A Mongolian Epic Chronicle of the Thirteenth Century*. 2 vols. Leiden: Brill.

Rashid al-Din, Fadlallah (1247–1318). 1994. *Jami* al-Tawarikh*, ed. Muhammad Rawshan and Mustafa Musawi. 3 vols. Tehran: Nashr-i Alburz.

1998–9. *Jami'ut-tawarikh [sic] Compendium of Chronicles*, trans. Wheeler M. Thackston, 3 vols. Cambridge, MA: Department of Near Eastern Languages and Civilizations, Harvard University.

Robinson, David M. 2008. "The Ming Court and the Legacy of the Yuan Mongols." In: *Culture, Courtiers and Competition: The Ming Court (1368–1644)*, ed. David M. Robinson, 365–421. Cambridge, MA: Harvard University Press.

2019. *In the Shadow of the Mongol Empire: Ming China and Eurasia*. Cambridge: Cambridge University Press.

Rossabi, Morris. 1988. *Khubilai Khan: His Life and Times*. Berkeley, CA: University of California Press.

Roudometof, Victor. 2016. *Glocalization: A Critical Introduction*. Abingdon, Oxon; New York: Routledge.

Rubruck, William of (ca. 1220–1293). 1990. *The Mission of Friar William of Rubruck*. Translated Peter Jackson and edited David Morgan. London: The Haklyut Society.

Sen, Tansen. 2006. "The Formation of Chinese Maritime Networks to Southern Asia, 1200–1450." *Journal of the Economic and Social History of the Orient* 49: 421–53.

Silverstein, Adam. J. 2007. *Postal Systems in the Pre-Modern Islamic World*. Cambridge: Cambridge University Press.

Skelton, R. A. *et al.*, eds. 1995. *The Vinland Map and the Tartar Relation*. New Haven, CT: Yale University Press.

Song Lian宋濂 (1310–1381). 1976. *Yuanshi* 元史. 15 vols. Beijing: Zhonghua shuju.

1999. *Song Lian quan ji* 宋濂全集. 4 vols. Hangzhou: Zhejiang guji chubanshe.

Su Tianjue 蘇天爵 (1294–1352), ed. 1967. *Yuan wenlei*元文類. Taipei: Shijie shuju.

Subrahmanyam, Sanjay. 1997. "Connected Histories: Notes towards a Reconfiguration of Early Modern Eurasia." *Modern Asian Studies* 31: 735–62.

al-ʿUmari, Ibn Fadlallah Shihab al-Din (1301–1349). 1968. *Das Mongolische Weltreich: al-ʿUmarīs Darstellung der mongolischen Reiche in seinem Werk Masālik al-abṣār fī mamālik al-amṣār*, ed. and trans. Klaus Lech. Wiesbaden: Harrassowitz.

Vasary, Istvan, 2009. "The Jochid Realm: The Western Steppe." In: *The Cambridge History of Inner Asia: The Chinggisid Age*, ed. Nicola Di Cosmo, Peter B. Golden, and Allan J. Frank, 67–86. Cambridge: Cambridge University Press.

Vogelin, Eric. 1940–1. "Mongol Orders of Submission to European Powers, 1245–1255." *Byzantion* 15: 378–411.

Wang Shidian 王士點 (d. 1359) and Shang Qiweng 商企翁 (fl. 1341–1367). 1992. *Mishujian zhi* 秘書監志 (Accounts of the Palace Library). Ed. Gao Rongsheng 高榮盛. Hangzhou: Zhejiang guji chubanshe.

Wassaf al-Ḥadrat (Sharaf al-Din ʿAbdallah b. Fadlallah al-Shirazi, fl. 1299–1328). 1853. *Tajziyat al-Amsar wa Tazjiyat al-Aʾṣar* (*Taʾrikh-i Wassaf*). Lithograph. Bombay: Muhammad Mahdi Isfahani.

Yang Qiao. 2017. "From the West to the East, from the Sky to the Earth: A Biography of Jamāl al-Dīn." *Asiatische Studien – Études Asiatiques* 71(4): 1231–45.

Yelü Zhu 耶律鑄 (1221–1285). n.d. *Shuangxi zuiyin ji* 雙溪醉隱集 [Yelü Zhu's Literary Collection]. e-*Siku quanshu* edition.

7 The Territories and Boundaries of Empires
Ottoman, Safavid and Mughal

Stephen F. Dale

The territories and political boundaries of the Mughal, Safavid and Ottoman Empires (Map 7.1) represent particularly intriguing cases of imperial expansion and territorial control. The boundaries of these three, so-called early modern Muslim empires, offer instructive examples of the variant ways in which their dynastic ideologies, geographies, culture, political structures and external relations determined the extent of their dominions. In discussing the topic of imperial dominions, it is logical to begin the discussion of each empire by raising the fundamental question of its original nature and explaining, in so far as sources allow, the identity and ideology of the dynasty's founders. How did these men explain, justify, rationalize – to themselves and others – their conquests and rule and in what ways did successive rulers modify their assertions of legitimacy and alter the initial character of the states they inherited?[1] The problem in this regard is that only Babur, the founder of the Mughal Empire, more accurately termed the Timurid-Mughal Empire, explained exactly why he invaded India. Neither the founders nor early rulers of the Ottoman and Safavid Empires have left similar personal statements of their rationales for conquest and rule.[2] In those two cases historians have to make inferences from fragmentary evidence or from the notoriously unreliable arguments of later court historians.

7.1 Ottomans

7.1.1 Dynastic Ideology

Taking Ottoman origins and ideology first, it is important to emphasize their Turkic lineage, one trait they shared in certain respects with their Safavid and

---

[1] The evolution of these states can only be hinted at in this brief chapter but for a discussion of their changing natures see Dale 2010, 77–81.
[2] Mughal, more accurately Mughûl, is the Persian word for Mongol, but Babur was a patrilineal Turk and a Timurid, although his mother was a Chaghatai Mongol. He would have been appalled to have his empire designated as a Mongol state.

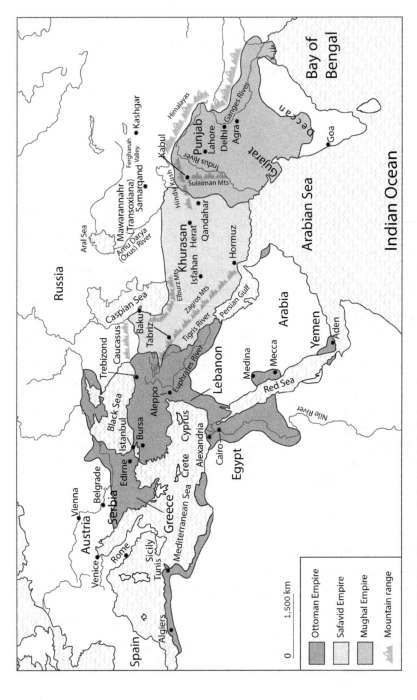

Map 7.1 The Ottoman, Safavid and Mughal Empires.

Timurid contemporaries.[3] The Ottomans, who emerged as a significant dynasty when, led by Osman (d. 1324), they defeated a Byzantine army in western Anatolia at Iznik in 1302, traced their ancestry to the Central Asian Oghuz Turks and more particularly to their legendary leader, Oghuz Khan.[4] Impossibly little is known about their ambitions in early years as leaders of a predatory semi-nomadic Turkic *beğlik* in western Anatolia.[5] In later inscriptions and in the works of dynastic historians, the Central Asian Turkic element seems to have played only a modest, opaque role, representing one, legitimizing strain among several claims to universal kingship.[6] Ottomans continued to use the Turco-Mongol title *khan* (*qan*) in official documents until the end of the dynasty, and by tracing their lineage to Oghuz Khan they implicitly emphasized their descent from an aggressive Turkic tribal formation. While they could not legitimately connect themselves to the Chinggisid assertions of universal authority, in the mid- to late 16th century they did sometimes use the title, *sahib-qiran* the lord of the conjunction of Jupiter and Saturn, a title originating in Mongol Eurasia but later associated primarily with Timur/ Tamerlane and implying the universal rule of an exceptional individual. Yet while their Central Asian Turkic identity did not become a prominent part of their legitimizing identity and expansionist ideology in later times, they ultimately fell back on the Turkic ethnic core of their hitherto multi-ethnic empire as that empire dissolved around them in the early 20th century. It was Mustafa Kemal Atatürk, the "Father of the Turks," who picked up the pieces and formed a Turkish nation-state.

The Ottomans invocation of a Turkic, Central Asian tradition of universal rule was however, overshadowed by their claim that they were leading a *ghazi* or frontier warrior crusade in the Byzantine and European marchlands, known in Ottoman parlance as *uç*, which in modern Turkish connotes an end or terminal point. At least until his aggressive modernizing reforms took hold in 1935 Mustafa Kemal was not only Atatürk but also Atatürk Ghazi. The idea of the *ghaza*, an invasion or attack, was and is not necessarily associated with any faith, including Islam, and for many among the different groups within their territories, including Christians, who sometimes fought with Turks on the Anatolian frontier with Byzantium, it seems to have conveyed only the idea of a border war. Muslim clerics, in contrast, used the term to characterize life in the Byzantine marchlands as a religious confrontation. As ideologues, they did not accept the notion of a permanent frontier with non-Muslim states, normally designated in Arabic, Persian and Turkish by the Arabic *ḥadd (pl. ḥudūd)*. In

---

[3] For an introduction to things Turkish, including early Ottoman and Timurid history see the lavishly illustrated work by Roxburgh 2005.
[4] See Imber 2002, 126–7; Karateke 2005, 13–54; and Barkey 2014, 469–77.
[5] *Beğlik*, the territory of a provincial *bey* or regional ruler.
[6] For a concise discussion of sources of Ottoman legitimacy see Barkey 2008, 98–108.

260 Stephen F. Dale

the minds of clerics the *ghaza* was a continuous struggle that would ultimately result in converting the entire non-Muslim world, the *Dar al-ḥarb*, or abode of war, into the *Dar al-Islam*, the abode of Islam.[7]

Ottoman dynasts' notion of and invocation of the *ghaza*, did not, however, mean that members of the lineage saw themselves, as clerics did, as leaders of a world crusade with an evangelical mission. They appear to have used the *ghaza* ideal as a religious ideal to legitimize predatory expansion in Anatolia and the Balkans as a heroic enterprise, just as Arabs had done earlier in Andalusia – for a far longer period of time – and the Andalusian example should always be taken into account when debating the significance of *ghazi* ideology on the Ottoman–Christian frontiers. In alluding to that earlier Iberian frontier conflict an anonymous Arab poet casually remarked, thinking of the riches in Andalusia, that "God created the Christians to be raided."[8] In both cases Jews and Christians were subjugated but given protected, if second-class, *dhimmi* status, a policy that generated taxes while allowing the armies to move on. Neither *jihad* was conducted as a religious war intended to convert, much eradicate, newly conquered non-Muslim populations, and in fact the Ottomans notably subordinated the *ulama*, the clerical class, to the state, to be patronized but controlled.

Yet the oft-invoked *ghazi* thesis is no longer seen as the holy grail of Ottoman historiography, as it was after Paul Wittek published his brief but influential thesis on the subject in 1938.[9] Apart from the *ghazi* ideal there were still two other aspects Ottoman expansion that led Ottoman rulers to think of or at least to present themselves as leaders and protectors of the Islamic world. The first was the occupation of Constantinople in 1453, a long deferred dream of Arab Muslims, who had twice besieged the city (674–8 and 717–18), which gave the Ottomans enormous prestige in the Muslim world. The second was their defeat of the Mamluks and occupation of Egypt in 1517 and the following extension of their authority to the Hijaz and the holy cities of Mecca and Medina. Even as the Ottoman Empire dissolved after World War I, Muslims in European colonial settings such as British India and Dutch Indonesia still looked to the Ottomans as the legitimate political leaders or protectors of the Muslim world.[10]

Political and imperial prestige represented the third element in the Ottoman combination of universalist ideologies and it is the single most compelling element of their legitimacy. First of all, while in Anatolia, Ottomans claimed to

---

[7] The Arabic term *ḥadd* actually connotes the idea of territorial extent rather than simply a distinct border. See Minorsky 1970, 30. This is a late 10th century Persian geography of the known world. See also Peacock 2009, 1–27.

[8] Rosenthal 1958, 3: 461.

[9] Wittek 1938. Wittek attributed the rise of the Ottoman Empire to *ghazi* ideology and the Empire's collapse to the cessation of *ghazi*-led territorial conquests.

[10] For India see Minault 1982. For Indonesian Muslims among other sources, see Hurgronje 1906.

have inherited the legal authority of the Seljuq Turks. The Seljuq family had led but did not necessarily control Oghuz tribal migrations and invasions of Iran in the 10th and 11th centuries that produced short-lived dynasties in Iran and Anatolia. Early Ottoman rulers initially based their administration on model of the Seljuq Sultanate of Rum.[11] They then transformed their political identity with the conquest of Constantinople. This victory not only conferred enormous religious prestige on the dynasty but it also allowed Mehmet the Conqueror to declare himself not only as the leader of the Muslim world but as the new kaisar, the new caesar. It is difficult to underestimate the degree to which the Ottomans were in their own minds transformed from regional sultans to imperial caesars with the seizure of the city. The territorial ambitions of some early rulers seem to have been unlimited and included Italy itself.

7.1.2 Ottoman Self-Perceptions

A contemporary political theorist described Süleyman Kanuni, who was known to Europeans as Süleyman the Magnificent (r. 1520–66), as one who had created in Constatinople or Istanbul, an Islamic version of the Greek political ideal, the "virtuous city."[12] By Süleyman's time Ottoman dynasts had come to portray themselves as "Chosroes," or Khusrau, claiming the pre-Islamic Sasanid Iranian title as a result of their earlier victory over the Safavids. And in a 1538 inscription Süleyman published the following proclamation, an almost Iranian, Achaemenid-like claim to be the "king of kings," – the king of many lands – as well as the leader of the Muslim World.

I am God's slave and sultan of this world. By the grace of God I am the head of Muhammad's community. God's might and Muhammad's miracles are my companions ... In Baghdad I am the shah, in Byzantium realms the Ceasar, and in Egypt, the sultan who sends his fleets to the seas of Europe, the Maghrib and India. I am the sultan who took the crown and throne of Hungary and granted them to a humble slave.[13]

This proclamation reveals a great deal about early Ottoman self-perceptions and motivations. It reflects the underlying nature of the Ottoman state at this period, which began life as one of many predatory Oghuz tribal elements and then evolved into a sultanate on the model of the Seljuqs of Rum.[14] It was and remained a sultanate and not a caliphate, although Ottomans began invoking this title as early as 1424.[15] Sultanates were the power state of the Islamic world, a type of institution characterized by the Arab historical sociologist, Ibn

---

[11] See among other sources Bosworth 2010. Oghuz Turkic raiders were already tearing Byzantine Anatolia to pieces in the late 10th century, well before the Seljuqs defeated the Byzantines and captured the emperor at the Battle of Manzikert in 1071. See Minorsky 1970, 157.
[12] Tezcan 2001, 119.   [13] Inalcık 2000, 41.   [14] Inalcık 2000, 7.   [15] Imber 2002, 26.

Khaldun (1332–1406) as one whose rulers were motivated primarily by pragmatic self-interest – even while they patronized Islamic institutions and, within reason, tolerated the clerical class.[16] The Ottoman state represented the ultimate and most successful manifestation of the Muslim dynastic sultanate, whose raison d'état was not ideology but power, wealth and perpetuation of the dynasty. Therefore, when discussing Ottoman expansion and the ultimate extent of its territory, the pragmatic nature of this form of state has to be seen as the constant driving factor in its imperial territorial ambitions, with economic and political considerations uppermost in the minds of its rulers and their sycophantic historians, however much members of the dynasty might legitimize their expansion, sometimes before and sometimes after the fact, with professions of faith. Ottoman sultans campaigned to extend their power and enrich themselves by conquering kingdoms. Ottoman charisma and their consequent survival as a dynasty was due, as much as anything, to their successful continued expansion. Lacking a prestigious Chinggisid or Timurid lineage Ottoman sultans nonetheless enjoyed what may be termed the *legitimacy of success*.[17]

7.1.3   Ottoman Conquests

Even understanding the essential nature of its state does not enable students of Ottoman history to identify the immediate cause or goal of each campaign. How did ghazi ideology interact with prospect of economic gain in their Balkan and Hungarian campaigns? Was the conquest of Egypt, the single most important expansion of the Ottoman state, sparked in the first instance merely by territorial disputes of two great powers or were Ottoman rulers intent from the beginning in seizing this wealthy, strategic prize or did they look so far ahead as to grasp the religious value of controlling the Hijaz? Or were all three elements important at various phases of their campaigns?

Then too in examining the full extent of Ottoman dominions there is the question regarding their territories and those of the Byzantine Empire. As Franz Babinger notes in his work *Mehmed the Conqueror and His Time* the borders of the two states were roughly similar.[18] What should historians conclude from this, that Süleyman and his successors consciously sought to replicate

[16] Rosenthal 1958. Ibn Khaldun's realistic portrayal of the pragmatic nature of sultanate regimes is found in scattered comments in various sections of this immense, complex text. He dismisses the *ulama* as an influential force in sultanates, a clerical class that, in his estimation, had long since lost its claim to influence the state.
[17] A phrase suggested by the Iranian historian Said Amir Arjomand when quoting Max Weber's theory of charisma "quintessentially power engenders charisma and ... the continuous exercise of power is self-legitimatory" (Arjomand 1984, 6).
[18] Babinger 1978, 10, 416. See also Gürkan 2010, 125–63 and Colin Heywood's articles on the Ottoman maritime frontier in Heywood 2013.

Byzantine boundaries or that it was "natural" for a state based in Constantinople/Istanbul to seek dominance throughout the Mediterranean Sea? Or was the similarity due to both of these factors? The case of Byzantine conquests in North Africa particularly raises these issues, for apart from Egypt, North Africa was and is an impoverished backwater of the Muslim world, but the region nonetheless had strategic and commercial importance, which would attract any Mediterranean power.

The geography, culture and political structures of Ottoman conquests were also extraordinarily diverse. As was true in all three of these Muslim states, central districts, in the Ottoman case Anatolia and the Balkans, were administered more directly and systematically than frontier regions. The perennially conflicted Ottoman–Safavid frontier is a case in point, where Ottomans allowed Kurds to rule much of eastern Anatolia.[19] The recent publication edited by A. C. S. Peacock, of the British Institute in Ankara, *The Frontiers of the Ottoman World* (2009), gives pause to anyone attempting to simplify how Ottoman frontier districts functioned.[20]

Ottoman military success is a much easier question in the early centuries, given the disciplined Janissary institution and the relative weakness of its opponents, excepting always the Mamluks, who had defeated Ilkhanid Mongol armies at 'Ayn Jālūt in 1260.[21] In the final Ottoman–Mamluk confrontations in 1516 and 1517, however, both Janissaries and sophisticated Ottoman firearms seemed to have prevailed, as they had done only a few years earlier when their armies defeated the Iranian Safavids in 1514. Here also they faced traditional cavalry armies, and forces much less formidable than those of the Mamluks. By this time also Ottomans had developed a navy capable of supplying their armies in Egypt and later contesting the power of Venice and Spain in the Mediterranean. No impassable physical frontiers stood in the way of their expansion, which were initially limited by other factors, such as lines of communication and the financial returns of newly conquered territories.

It is indisputable that the momentum of Ottoman conquests in southeastern Europe and the southern Russian steppe was eventually slowed and then halted by major European powers, principally the Hapsburgs, who twice stymied Ottoman forces before Vienna, and the resurgent Romanovs during and after the rule of Peter the Great (1682–1725). The territorial losses, which Ottomans

---

[19] Ottoman history is blessed or cursed with vast archival collections, and have generated a blizzard of sophisticated modern studies. For surveys see, Faroqhi 2006; Fleet 2009, 2012. For a recent work by an historical sociologist who approaches the subject with comparative analytical questions see Barkey 2008, 82–93 for her discussion of diverse Ottoman frontier policies.

[20] For an interesting, instructive example of how other states managed distant frontier possessions see the discussion of the Chinese Qing by Millward and Newby 2006.

[21] For one of many sources on Ottoman rule in Egypt and other Arab territories see Hathaway and Barbir 2008.

began to suffer in the 19th century, are a more complex matter, involving the changing nature of the Ottoman institutions, including the decline of the Janissary system, as well as its habitual economic problems – inflation, lack of hard currency and others – which led it to cede state control of local resources to tax farmers.[22]

The case of Egypt is one of the most salient examples that illustrate the weakness of the state just as Ottoman rulers began to restructure it in the late 18th and early 19th centuries. By 1798, Egypt had become a semi-autonomous province of the empire when Napoleon invaded. Muhammad Ali (d. 1849), an Albanian Ottoman officer sent in 1801 to restore Ottoman control set about modernizing Egypt, beginning by suppressing its still powerful Mamluk element. After being appointed governor in 1805 he gradually turned the province into an independent power with a formidable modern army and established the dynasty that survived as a tattered remnant until 1953. While he helped the sultan suppress the Greek revolt in 1824, in 1832 he defeated an Ottoman army near Konya, the former capital of the Seljuqs of Rum or Anatolia, and he could have taken Istanbul itself, had it not been for Russian intervention. The loss of Egypt more than any other event signaled the beginning of the end of the empire, a process involving internal weakness, European expansion and the gradual genesis of the idea of a Turkish nation-state with ethnic, not imperial boundaries.

7.2   The Safavids

7.2.1   Origins

If the determinants and nature of the sprawling, diverse Ottoman borderlands cannot be simply summarized, the sultanate's relations with the Safavid state to the east poses a more manageable problem and explains the western boundary of both the Safavid and also the modern Iranian state. This calls in the first instance for a brief account of early Safavid history.[23] If the Ottomans evolved from a predatory tribal confederacy and provincial *beğlik* to an ambitious sultanate with universalist ambitions, what was the nature of the Safavid state? As with the Ottoman case the Safavids arose against a background of Turkic dominance of Ghuzz or Oghuz nomadic and semi-nomadic tribes that had earlier given rise to the Great Seljuq dynasty of Iran (1040–1157). In 1453, when Mehmet the Conqueror entered Constantinople, Iran was divided among a number of Turkic Muslim powers that evolved after the collapse of Ilkhanid Mongol state in 1336 and the ravages of Timur between 1370 and 1405. These

---

[22] For a summary of the complex changes in the Ottoman state as well as the external threats to the regime from the 16th to 19th centuries see Dale, 2010, 270–87.

[23] Regarding the question of whether or not Safavid Iran could be considered an empire see Matthee 2010.

included the descendants of Timur, still fitfully ruling parts of the Iranian plateau from Herat and Samarqand in the late 15th century, and the two Oghuz dynasties that challenged Timurid control of eastern Anatolia and Iran. The latter were first, the Qara Qoyunlu or Black Sheep dynasty (1378–1469) and their tribal competitors, who displaced them, the Aq Qoyunlu or White Sheep (1378–1501), whose leaders allied themselves through marriage with the most influential Sufi order in northwestern Iran at Ardabil.

It is important for an understanding of later relations between the Ottomans and Safavids and their borders that the Aq Qoyunlu, like the Ottomans, began life as a collection of loosely organized band of pastoral nomadic Oghuz raiders in the Diyarbekir region of eastern Anatolia. By the mid-15th century, when the Aq Qoyunlu were evolving into a Perso-Islamic sultanate on the Seljuq model, the dynasty controlled territory in their eastern Anatolian homelands as well as parts of Georgia, Kurdistan and northwestern and central Iran. In the later 15th century the Aq Qoyunlu ruler of the time, Uzun Hasan (r. 1453–78), was eulogized by the Iranian poet Jami (d. 1492) as the "Sultan of ghāzīs" for his successful wars in Christian Georgia. Indeed, rulers of all these three states identified themselves or were accounted by their historians as *ghazi*s at one time or another. By the time of Jami's death, however, the Aq Qoyunlu were losing a struggle with their Sufi allies and maternal relatives, the Safavid family of Ardabil.

From the 14th century, the Ilkhanid Mongol rulers of Iran had patronized the Safavi Sufi shrine at Ardabil in Azerbaijan, encouraging and allowing the order to purchase extensive landed tracts and thereby to expand its economic and religious influence. Not only did the order continue to extend its influence, partly by conducting missionary activities among neighboring Oghuz tribes, but its leaders also became Shi'ahs. By the mid-century Safavi *pir*s or *shaikh*s began transforming the order into a militant, aggrandizing religious-political dynasty. In 1501, Isma'il, one of the surviving sons of the Safavid religious lineage, who earlier had been imprisoned by an apprehensive Aq Qoyunlu leader, seized Tabriz in northwestern Iran from his Aq Qoyunlu relations, and in the following ten years conquered or subdued most of the powers on the Iranian plateau.[24]

7.2.2 Ideology

The Safavids initially constituted an evangelical Shi'i dynasty whose power base was centered primarily in eastern Anatolia and Northwestern Iran, regions where Safavi Shi'i propaganda had succeeded in attracting illiterate Oghuz

---

[24] For an introduction to the bewilderingly complex political situation of Iran during the Ilkhanid and Timurid eras see Manz 1997.

tribesmen and some urban poor to the family's cause. In political terms Isma'il reconstituted the Aq Qoyunlu state and transformed it into a tribal military coalition in the service of a theocratic dynasty committed to the spread of Shi'i Islam. The nature of its ideology is on display in Isma'il's Azeri Turkic poems. Isma'il, who was bi-lingual in Azeri and Persian, legitimized himself with a blizzard of extraordinary religious and political claims, including taking Muhammad's title as the "Seal of the Prophets," as well as proclaiming himself to be the Shi'i Imam, who has returned from eschatological concealment and appeared on earth as mankind's "Perfect Guide."[25] Following his successful campaigns on the Iranian plateau, Isma'il returned to eastern Anatolia, where he, his father and grandfather had proselytized among the Oghuz. His renewed activity in the region, no longer just a Sufi *pir* but now a formidable dynast, attracted Ottoman attention, fearing for the erosion of control among these Turkic tribesmen, who continued to be drawn to the Safavi cause by its Sufi disciples' religious propaganda. In 1514, the Ottoman sultan, Selim (r. 1512–20) marched eastward, carrying a Sunni clerical declaration that Isma'il was a heretic and, using gunpowder weapons and well-disciplined troops, destroyed the pre-gunpowder Safavid tribal army of Oghuz tribesmen at Chaldiran.

7.2.3   Chaldiran and Safavid History

The Safavid loss at Chaldiran shattered Isma'il's charisma as well as his own sense of spiritual invincibility, and he largely withdrew from active military affairs for the remainder of his life. The battle also defined the western boundaries of Safavid territorial control for nearly a century. Even though the borders between the Ottoman and Safavid states fluctuated after that they largely continued to be located in this general region. It is also important to note that quite apart from this particular event, the region of eastern Anatolia, Azerbaijan and Mesopotamia represented a traditional frontier zone between states based in western Anatolia, Constantinople or even Rome, and those ruling Iran, Mawarannahr and Afghanistan. There were major exceptions. In the pre-Islamic Achaemenid (530–330 BCE) and later the Sasanian (224–651 CE) cases, Iranians extended their empires far to the west, the northeast and the east, while Alexander the Great and his Greek descendants subdued territories as far north as Mawarannahr and, like his Achaemenid enemies, east to the Indus. More typically, however, states controlling Anatolia did not penetrate much beyond Mesopotamia, which also represented a kind of marchland for Iranian states. In his history of Iran, the early 19th-century, British East India Company ambassador to Iran, Sir John Malcolm, wrote generally about

---

[25] Minorsky 1942, 1,006a–1,053a.

traditional Iranian borders: "The boundaries of Iran, which Europeans call Persia, have undergone many changes. The limits of this kingdom in its most prosperous periods may however be easily described. The Persian Gulf and the Indian Ocean to the south, the Indus and the Oxus to the east and north, The Caspian and Mount Caucasus to the north and the River Euphrates to the west."[26]

The fate of the ancient city of Dura Europos on the northern border of Syria and Iraq is an early case in point illustrating how control of the region continuously fluctuated between western states and those based on the Iranian plateau. Founded by Alexander the Great's successors, the Seleucid Greeks, in 303 BCE, as a city situated between their eastern and western capitals, it was conquered by the Parthians, an Iranian nomadic people, in 113 BCE. Then in 165 CE the Romans took it, while in 256 the Iranian Sasanids overran the city, leaving it in ruins for posterity and western archeologists.[27] These regions are not so geographically formidable, but with the exception of the immediate riverine districts in Mesopotamia they are desolate, with few resources for marauding armies. Parthians and Sasanids – and later Safavids – did not advance further west, whereas the Romans – and later the Ottomans – much further east.[28]

7.2.4   Ottoman–Safavid Borders

The early focus of Safavid missionary influence and military recruitment in eastern Anatolia was lost to the nascent dynasty after their 1514 defeat at Chaldiran and it was never regained throughout the dynasty's history. Following this loss, the nature of the Safavid state evolved and it increasingly became a dynasty of Iranian monarchs, whose territories resembled the home-lands of pre-Islamic and post Safavid Iranian states. There are two principal reasons for this development. First, the Ottomans never attempted to destroy the Safavid state, although conflicts between the two powers continued for more than a century. The two major foci of Ottoman–Safavid contention were the relatively wealthy regions around Tabriz in the northwest, formerly the Ilkhanid Mongol capital, and Mesopotamia. The Ottomans invaded northwestern Iran in 1546 and 1553 and in 1555 the two powers signed a treaty recognizing Ottoman control of Mesopotamia, including Iraq and Kurdistan. The Ottomans occupied Tabriz, a vital commercial center, in 1585, holding the city until 1603, when the reinvigorated Safavid army under Shah 'Abbas I (r. 1588–1629) recaptured the city. While Ottoman troops attempted to occupy this valuable entrepôt again a little more than ten years later they failed to do so and the city remained in

---

[26] Malcolm 1815, 1: 1–2.

[27] For recent scholarship see Brody and Hoffman 2011 and the exhibit at the Yale University Art Gallery, "Dura-Europos: Excavating Antiquity."

[28] For Parthian and ancient Iranian penetration into South Asia, see especially Gazerani 2016.

Iranian control, as it does today, with its substantial Azeri Turkic speaking population.[29] Ottoman failure to permanently hold the city might be attributed to its distance from major Ottoman population centers, the state's preoccupation with other frontiers and the difficult terrain and cold winter climate of the Azerbaijan region. Moving a large, heavily equipped army to the region from Istanbul, Bursa or the thinly populated areas of eastern Anatolia posed difficult logistical problems.

In retrospect the rise of the Safavids and the Battle of Chaldiran largely settled the Ottoman's eastern frontier, despite the persistent conflicts between the two powers for more than a century.[30] The two events also influenced Safavid identify and territorial ambitions in another way: Chaldiran forced the Safavids back on the Iranian plateau, the historic center of Iranian dynasties, where their Shi'i identity merged with traditional Iranian imperial traditions to produce a new Iranian state for the first time since the fall of the Seljuqs in the twelfth century. These religious and ethnic/cultural strains of Safavid identity were manifest in Shah Isma'il's Azeri verse in which he not only promoted his Sufi and Shi'i identity when appealing to potential Oghuz followers. He also identified himself with the heroes of the Iranian epic, the *Shāh-Nāmah* – "I am Faridun, Khusrau, Jamshid and Zohak ..." Then too when he captured Tabriz in 1501, he proclaimed himself in pre-Islamic terms as the *Pādishāh-i Īrān*. By invoking the Iranian imperial title *pādishāh* and proclaiming his rule over Iran he revived pre-Islamic political terminology and cultural and geographic terminology that had fallen out of use following the Arab Muslim conquest.[31] Ilkhanid Mongols had revived this vocabulary, which the Aq Qoyunlu had also invoked.

7.2.5   Safavids as Iranian Emperors

Isma'il's use of Iranian terms initially does not seem to have meant more than that he thought of himself in political terms as an heir of his relatives the Aq Qoyunlu. Nonetheless, later Safavid monarchs, in particular, Shah 'Abbas, the single dominant figure in this dynasty, gradually but continuously revived elements of pre-Islamic cultural and political identity to legitimize their rule. The Safavids still trumpeted their Shi'i roots and patronized Shi'i Ashura festivals of martyrdom, but they also gradually evolved into an Iranian state

---

[29] For an important description of how Ottomans administered Tabriz, their frontier city and region in Iran, see Murphy 2009.

[30] Ates 2013 prefers to use the term "borderlands" in his careful examination of the factors that led to the modern frontier between the later Ottomans and the Qajar dynasty, based upon a formal treaty that dates to 1639.

[31] Iranian geographers, nonetheless, continued to use terms that designated and celebrated these territories. Al-Iṣṭakhri, for example, in his tenth century work *Masālik al-Mamālik* used the term *Īrānshahr* to include not only his native province of Fārs, but other regions on the plateau as well. It was later formally revived by the Ilkhanid Mongols. See Sabet 2000, 15.

where Persian, not Azeri Turkish, was the language of culture and administration, the pre-Islamic festival of *nauruz* was celebrated and writers characterized Shah 'Abbas as a man who possessed *farr*, the divine essence of Sasanid monarchs and called him "the Shadow of God" and the "Pādishāh of the World." Isfahan, his capital after the 1590s, became known as "Niṣf-i Jahan," "Half the World!"

Despite the latter title, a bit of royal rhetoric and not a reflection of a serious world-conquering ambition, one noticeable aspect of Safavid history after Chaldiran is the disappearance of the dynasty's presumably universalistic religious mission. More to the point of Safavid origins, after Shah Isma'il's brief resumption of missionary efforts in Anatolia, none of his descendants set out to persuade or compel Muslims outside of their Iranian territories to adopt Shi'i beliefs. They largely confined their imposition of Shi'i Islam to the Sunni population of the Iranian plateau. Unlike the earlier aggressively militant Shi'i Fatimids of Cairo (909–1171), they did not establish a systematic policy of dispatching missionaries into Sunni territories, either into Ottoman territories or the other regions on their immediate periphery, Turkistan or western Central Asia and Muslim India.[32] What is most obvious in Safavid relations with these latter regions is that the existence of powerful neighbors there nullified any possibility of Iranian expansion either to the northeast or east. Therefore, in considering the general territorial extent of the Safavid state – and quite apart from issues of its own profound political and economic internal weaknesses throughout most of its history – it was always confined to the general region of the Iranian Plateau. It was an Iranian state in Shi'i dress. After Chaldiran its conquests or campaigns were limited to sections of Georgia, Afghanistan and Mawarannahr.

To the northeast of Khurasan, the wealthy Iranian province that was one of the historic centers of Iranian civilization, the Amu Darya or Oxus River had been the "generally accepted boundary between Iranian and Turanian rulers since the tenth century."[33] It was not and had never been a significant physical frontier, as was reflected in the Achaemenid struggle with the Saka nomads and later the erection of the Parthian–Sasanian wall, which was constructed to keep nomadic tribes at bay.[34] Pre-Islamic Iranian empires had extended their control into this region and Shah Ismai'il himself had defeated and killed the Uzbek Shaibani or Shaibaq Khan in 1510 following Ismai'il's occupation of the important Khurasan city of Herat. By the 16th century Mawarannahr, or Transoxiana, this area "beyond the [Amu Darya] river," had been thoroughly Turcicized.[35] From the 16th century well into modern times in the early 20th

---

[32] For the history of this important dynasty see Canard 2015.
[33] For an excellent introduction to Iranian geography see Barthold 1984.
[34] See "Fortifications," in *Encyclopaedia Iranica* V. X, Fasc. 1, 102–6.   [35] Barthold, 1968, 65.

century, Uzbek Turks not only dominated Mawarannahr or Transoxiana but frequently raided Khurasan. Throughout much of Safavi history, therefore, the country was beset by Ottoman campaigns in the west and Uzbek incursions in the northeast. Only the central part of the Iranian plateau remained relatively untouched by these incursions, which is the immediate reason why Shah 'Abbas moved his capital to Isfahan in the 1590s.

Only in the Afghan marchlands between the Iranian plateau and the South Asian subcontinent, did the Safavids enjoy some room for maneuver. Further east there was an ancient frontier region that historically distinguished Iran from its neighboring powers in South Asia. The Sulaiman Mountains, a southern extension of the Hindu Kush range (see Map 7.1) marks the general borderland region between the two civilizations, while the anonymous author of the *Ḥudūd al-'Ālam* places the western boundary of Hindustan exactly at Gardiz, fifty-five kilometers east of Ghazni and to the west of the Sulaiman Mountains. These mountains represent a far more porous physical barrier than the Himalayas to the north, with the Khyber and Bolan passes being just two of the routes that allow merchants and invaders to traverse the region. Pre-Islamic Iranian empires extended their authority across the mountains to the west bank of the Indus River, which can be seen as at least the symbolic boundary between the Iranian and Indic Aryans.[36] Yet they never appear to have sought to control the entire South Asian subcontinent, or even its wealthy Gangetic heartland. Similarly, whereas powerful Indian states, such as the Mauryan Empire (*c.*323–185 BCE), were able to project power west of the Sulaiman Range and into Central Afghanistan, Indian-based empires do not seem to have attempted to extend their authority beyond the Afghan marchlands onto the Iranian plateau.

Whereas both Iranian and South Asian empires never seem to have attempted to do more than occupy these border regions, both northeastern Iran and northwestern India, experienced successful invasions from Central Asia and Afghanistan over the centuries. In pre-Islamic times the Parthians successfully invaded and ruled Iran while in the Islamic era the Seljuqs began pouring across the Khurasan region in the late 10th century on their way to the Iranian plateau and Anatolia. In South Asia apart from the original Aryan invasions/migrations the most notable early Indian case was the invasion of the Kushanas, a branch of the Central Asian nomadic people, the Yuezhi, who figure so prominently in early Chinese history. They ruled Mawarannahr and northern India from *c.*105–250 CE. Later the Hepthalites, who first invaded Iran, taking Sasanid territory, conquered northwestern India in the 5th century. Muslims, first Arabs in Sind in the late 7th century and later Turks in the persons of Turkic Ghaznavid *ghulams*/*mamluk*s invaded and plundered northwestern India in the late 10th and 11th centuries. If there is a pattern in these few

---

[36] See Brunner 2012.

examples it is that established Iranian and South Asian empires did not extend their frontiers beyond the Afghan borderlands, while Central Asian/Afghan forces repeatedly conquered both civilizational core regions. A minor exception to this pattern was the destructive Indian invasion of the Oghuz Nādir Shāh Afshar, from Iran in 1739, one of many 18th-century events that hastened the disintegration of an already decadent Mughal dynasty. This invasion, however, was little more than a plundering expedition to finance Nādir Shah's campaigns in Iran itself.

7.3   Mughals

7.3.1   The Timurid Background

The Mughals represented yet another Central Asian incursion into North India or Hindustan, then, in the early 16th century, fitfully controlled by the Ludis, an unstable Afghan Muslim tribal oligarchy. While commonly and misleadingly designated as Mughals, their founder, Zahir al-Din Muhammad Babur (1483–1530), was a fifth-generation patrilineal descendant of Temür/ Timur/Tamerlane and justified his invasion of Hindustan as a reassertion of Timurid sovereignty in a territory that Temür had invaded and plundered in 1398. Temür's descendants continued to assert sovereign claims on Hindustan during the first half of the 15th century, but they had relinquished any actual control of the region well before Babur staged probing attacks from Kabul into the Punjab between 1519 and 1526.

Temür "practiced" what might be characterized as a steppe conqueror's limitless sense of boundaries as he ravaged territories through Eurasia, but following his death in 1405 none of his descendants exhibited his grandiose, world-conquering ambitions. They displayed instead a kind of political entropy, ruling as localized, urban-based, territorial monarchs, devoted in varying degrees to the patronage of the dominant Perso-Islamic culture of the region. Temür's immediate successors, his son, Shah Rukh (1377–1447) and grandson Ulugh Beg (1394–1449) ruled from Herat and Samarqand for three decades in the first half of the 15th century, but during these years they did little more than try to maintain Timurid authority over Iran, Mawarannahr and parts of Afghanistan.[37] Under their successors Timurid control of these regions steadily diminished as the two Turkic tribal confederations, the Aq and Qara Qoyunlu, steadily expanded their control of western Iran, while the Chinggisid-led Turkic Uzbeks made increasing inroads into Mawarannahr and northeastern Iran.

---

[37] For Temür see Manz, 1989 and for his successors in Iran and Central Asia Manz, 2007 and Subtelny 2007.

By the time Babur was born in the Ferghanah Valley in 1483 in what is now eastern Uzbekistan, Timurid sovereignty was limited to a few areas in central and northeastern Iran, Mawarannahr and Afghanistan. These included Herat, Samarqand and the Ferghanah Valley, Badakhshan in northern Afghanistan and Kabul and eastern Afghanistan. Herat, under the Timurid Husain Baiqara (d. 1506), controlled much of Khurasan, northeastern Iran's historic cultural region and western Afghanistan, while Babur's paternal uncles Ahmad Mirza (d. 1494), Mahmud Mirza (d. 1495) and Ulugh Beg Kabuli (d. 1502) ruled Samarqand, Badakhshan and Kabul, respectively. Tashkent was held by Babur's maternal or Mongol uncle Yunas Khan (1416–87) the Khan of the Chaghatai Mongols, most of whose clansmen lived in and around Kashgar and the northwestern regions of what is now included in China's Xinjiang Autonomous Region. At this time Timur's descendants and Babur's maternal Mongol relatives constituted a fragmented, contentious group of individuals, who fought among themselves for precedence in these contiguous regions as the Uzbeks, who had been raiding ever deeper into Timurid territories during the latter half of the century, prepared to overrun both Khurasan and Mawarannahr.

Babur inherited his father's Ferghanah Valley appanage in 1494 and was immediately attacked by his paternal and maternal uncles in Mawarannahr as well as by the Mongol ruler of Kashgar in Xinjiang. They all desired to control this well-watered alluvial valley, which was also an important Seidenstrasse or Silk Road route for commerce between China and the West. Babur spent the next decade, first fighting off both Timurid and Mongol relatives, before he attempted to seize Samarqand, Temür's capital and the goal of every ambitious Timurid. He occupied the city on two occasions during these years, before Shaibani Khan Uzbek, who was by then aggressively attacking the Timurid heartlands, defeated him in battle outside Samarqand in 1502. After mounting a failed anti-Uzbek counterattack with his Chinggisid maternal relatives, who joined him from Xinjiang, Babur was forced to abandon his homeland in 1504. He eventually opted to go to Kabul, rather taking refuge in Husain Baiqara's Herat, perhaps because Uzbeks were intent on conquering this last major Timurid city. Kabul was less also exposed to Uzbek forces and Timurids still claimed the city, which until 1502 had been a Timurid political artifact, a territorial relic that Temür bequeathed to his descendants, as he left India following his brief but destructive Indian invasion.

Babur's paternal uncle Ulugh Beg Kabuli, had held the city until his death in 1502 when it was seized by Muqim Arghun, a Mongol or Turco-Mongol whose family had been associated with the Ilkhans, the Mongol rulers of Iran (1256–1335). Babur occupied Kabul in December 1504 and even while still fighting for survival against the Uzbeks and the fractious Pushtun tribes he declared himself *padshah* of the city and surrounding Afghan region a few years later. In his remarkably frank autobiography he describes why he eventually came to invade Hindustan. He writes that he and his men first thought of going across the Indus in 1507, but as refugees, not as invaders. At the time Shaibani Khan Uzbek, having just occupied Herat, seemed ready to attack Babur in Kabul and eliminate this last remaining Timurid political artifact. In a remarkable passage Babur describes how he and his men essentially tossed a coin to decide whether they should flee to Badakhshan in the north or to Hindustan.[38] In a panic they rode out from Kabul toward the Khyber Pass, before hearing that the Uzbek threat had diminished. Initially it seems Babur hoped to use Kabul as a temporary base that would allow him to return north and retake Samarqand, which he did briefly in 1511 with the help of borrowed troops from Safavid Iran. However, after Uzbeks defeated him once again in 1512 and drove him from Mawarannahr a second time, he abandoned his goal of resurrecting a Timurid state based on Samarqand. By 1519, at the latest he decided that the conquest of Hindustan offered him the only opportunity to resurrect Timurid sovereignty, and in December 1525 he left Kabul with his Turco-Mongol army to confront the Afghan Sultan Ibrahim Ludi, whose forces he defeated in April 1526.

7.3.2   Timurids in Hindustan

In contrast to the fragmentary evidence for the motives or ideologies of the early Ottomans and Safavids, scholars seeking to assess the territorial ambitions of the early Mughals are fortunate to have Babur's remarkable literary legacy, which contains a detailed, often intimate account of his life and campaigns. Written in Turki and titled the *Vaqâyi'*, but commonly known as the *Babur-Namah*, this unusually frank – or ingenuous – as well as a self-serving account is one of the few such autobiographical texts ever written by a founder of an empire.[39] Babur is refreshingly open about his motives and ambitions for a new Timurid state in Hindustan, and offers ample evidence for readers to infer what he imagined to be its boundaries at the time. Despite his lineage, which included both Timurid and matrilineal Chinggisid descent, Babur never alluded to the world-conquering ambitions of his ancestors. In this he was consistent with the limited political goals of his father and other late 15th-century Timurids, who confined their aggressive instincts to campaigns against one another as they fought for control of their steadily decreasing Timurid territorial heritage. Like them Babur was a sophisticated urbanite, an observant Hanafi Sunni Muslim, who wanted to establish a sedentary late

---

[38] Mano, 1995, f. 186b.

[39] A superb edition of Babur's Turki autobiography has been published by Mano 1995, with its concordance published in 1996.

Timurid kingdom, distinguished by a flourishing Perso-Islamic culture, which he admired greatly when he visited Herat in 1506, just prior to Shaibani Khan's occupation of the city.

Babur repeatedly reminds readers of his Timurid ancestry but instead of musing in his autobiography about world conquests, he merely asserts that any self-respecting descendant of Temür ought to have what he describes as *mulkgirliq*, "kingdom seizing" or imperial ambitions. Apart from claiming to be legitimately restoring Timurid authority in Hindustan by citing Temür's 1398 invasion, Babur does not offer his Turki audience any ideological rationale for his invasion, but openly reveals his act of conquest to have been a matter of personal survival for him, his immediate family and for a refugee population of displaced Timurid and Chinggisid relatives. He does not invoke Tengri, the Mongol's overarching steppe sky, or Allah to justify his conquest. In his narrative he makes it unmistakably clear that he invaded India because he could not re-establish a Timurid state in Mawarannahr and considered Kabul and its environs to be too poor and politically turbulent to offer an aspiring imperialist the basis for such a state. Hindustan, in contrast, offered the lavish resources for a Timurid renaissance. In north India the Timurids could enjoy, what a Mughal historian, when describing Agra and the 17th-century Taj Mahal complex, would later characterize as "a civilized and comfortable life."[40] Babur's invasion represented simply an old fashioned act of dynastic imperialism.

From the evidence of his *Vaqâyi'* Babur initially conceived of his new Timurid kingdom as one that comprised Kabul and its environs and Hindustan – India's Punjab and its Gangetic Valley. Toward the end of his life he did reveal that he retained a vestige of Temür's expansive territorial ambition, for in November 1528 he wrote to his son Humayun in Afghanistan, whom he chastised for various personal and political failings, saying that he ought to start acting like a Timurid warrior. By that he meant that as a young man he should be campaigning aggressively to seize new territory. Babur told Humayun and also his younger brother Kamran, they ought to conquer any region they could, and he suggested as possibilities Herat, Balkh, Hisar and, most of all, Samarqand. If they were successful Babur told Humayun he could rule from Samarqand and Kamran, his brother, could have Balkh – and if Kamran considered Balkh inadequate his father would try to supplement it with some other territory.[41] Babur, though, never seems to have really pressed his sons to mount serious Iranian or Central Asian campaigns. His descendants retained a revanchist nostalgia for Samarqand, as is revealed in the autobiography of his great-grandson Jahangir (1605–28), who wrote with characteristic insouciance that he planned to re-capture Samarqand.

---

[40] 'Abd al-Hamid Lahori quoted by Koch 2006, 257.   [41] Mano 1995, f. 348b.

As I had made up my exalted mind to the conquest of Mâwarâ'a-n-nahr (Transoxiana), which was the hereditary kingdom of my ancestors ... I desired ... to go myself with a valiant army in due array, with elephants of mountainous dignity and of lightning speed, and taking ample treasure with me, to undertake the conquest of my ancestral dominions.[42]

Jahangir, however, an aesthete and known for his prolonged periods of alcohol- and drug-induced indolence, was merely recording a self-indulgent dreamscape here. He never organized or commanded such an expedition. Apart from what his wistful imagining reveals about Jahangir's personality, the passage contains a brief insight into one of the ways in which the Mughals had become increasingly Indian. No longer composed primarily of swift Central Asian cavalry, their forces had evolved into cumbersome siege armies designed to batter down Rajput stone fortresses. The Mughal military's ineffectiveness in the northern Afghan regions was demonstrated when, in 1645, Jahangir's son, the far more aggressive Shah Jahan (r. 1628–57), dispatched armies to northern Afghanistan with orders to retake Mawarannahr.[43] Whatever the quality of their elephants, the two princely commanders of these forces proved incapable of advancing past Balkh into Mawarannahr. After becoming besieged they had to leave the city to their Uzbek enemies and, like Babur little more than a century earlier, retreat back to Kabul.

Certainly, Mughal rulers, like Ottoman sultans and Safavid shahs, suggested they had world-conquering ambitions, as they projected an exalted, imperial sense of themselves in their titulature. Among his other titles Babur's grandson Akbar (1556–1605), was a *shāhānshāh*, an Iranian king of kings. The full title of the fourth emperor, Jahangir, "the world-seizure" was Nūr al-Dīn [the light of religion] Jahāngīr Pādishāh Ghāzī, in which the assumption of the *ghazi* identity seems almost comic, considering his largely pacific reign, devoted to the aesthetic pleasures of art and the Indian landscape. Jahangir also, like his successor Shah Jahan, the "king of the world," adopted the Timurid title *ṣāḥib-qirān*, the lord of the conjunction – of Jupiter and Saturn, which Ottomans had also deployed to bolster their legitimacy. Otherwise he shared virtually nothing of Temür's world-conquering ambitions. Shah Jahan did take regnal and *sahib-qirân* titles seriously enough to expand his South Asian frontiers within the subcontinent while proclaiming his grandeur with splendid monuments. Despite this royal rhetoric and apart from failed disastrous Samarqand campaign, the Mughals never demonstrated an interest in expanding their empire northward to Mawarannahr or westward beyond Kandahar, the Afghan town that Babur had briefly held and then lost during his Kabul period.

Mughal imperialism became exclusively concerned with expanding territorial control from Hindustan south into the subcontinent – as had been the

[42] Jahângîr 1978, 89.   [43] Dale 2010, 205.

tradition of powerful north Indian states throughout Indian history. From the time of Akbar, who resurrected the Mughal polity, to the last formidable Mughal ruler Aurangzeb (1658–1707), Mughal preoccupation with the Deccan was the single most important sign of the fact that these Timurids had become an Indian dynasty. Babur had never felt himself to be an Indian, as he made clear in his criticism of Hindustani culture, and toward the end of his life when ill he became desperately homesick for Kabul. He felt trapped in India and wanted to return to a life which he had lived for two decades, marked by continuous *suhbat*s or social gatherings in the cool, forested Afghan mountains with his Turco-Mongol companions. However, the idea of ruling Hindustan from Kabul, was never revived by his descendants. Perhaps if Babur had survived to return to Kabul he might have ruled like Mahmud of Ghazna (971–1030), using Indian revenues to fund conquests in Afghanistan, Iran and even Mawarannahr.[44] Instead, the third and fourth Mughal emperors Akbar and Jahangir, became fully acclimatized to India and its culture. Unlike Babur, who disliked Hindustan's geography, culture and society, Jahangir, who was born there of a Rajput mother, took unfeigned delight in the flora and fauna of the country, which he described in appreciative detail as he toured Hindustan, once for more than five years before returning to Agra.

His birth, the product of Akbar's alliance with powerful Rajput lineages, alerts students of the empire to the evolving nature of the state, from one dominated by a small force of Turco-Mongols during Babur's lifetime, to a more complex and ethnically varied elite. According to his daughter, Gul Badan Begim, writing in her own remarkable memoir, Babur commanded only seven thousand Turco-Mongol troops when he destroyed the Ludi Afghan army in 1526.[45] While many Turco-Mongol migrants later entered Hindustan from Mawarannahr and Iran, they did not represent a massive tribal influx that overwhelmed the indigenous Indian population, as the migration/invasion of Oghuz tribesmen had once overwhelmed and Turkicized Iran and Anatolia in the 10th and 11th centuries. That would have been difficult in any event considering the heavily populated subcontinent that may have had a population as much as 100 million by 1600. The sheer size of the non-Muslim Indian population and the vibrancy of its culture meant that the Mughal Empire inevitably became increasingly Indian, even as its last two major emperors Shah Jahan and Aurangzeb also grew noticeably more Islamic.

In consequence of the Indianization of Babur's Turco-Mongol Timurid regime, Mughal's frontier relations were defined by relatively stable boundaries in the west and northwest and aggressive, dynamic expansion within the peninsula. Later Mughal rulers did not attempt to overturn Uzbek control of Mawarannahr or Safavid dominance of western Afghanistan. Boundaries in

---

[44] Bosworth 1963.   [45] Gul-Badan 1901.

those regions fluctuated, but only marginally so. In contrast Mughal rulers from Akbar to the last effective emperor Aurangzeb (r. 1658–1707) continued aggressively to expand control of Muslim states in the Deccan, India's "south," eventually reaching the eastern or Coromandel coast and as far south as Chennai/Madras.

Their principal targets were the wealthy Muslim states that had emerged from the disintegration of the Bahmani Sultanate (1347–1538). It had been formed in the 14th century during the era of the Delhi Sultanate, which ruled Hindustan between 1210 and Temür's invasion in 1398.[46] These later regimes that the Mughals confronted were Ahmadnagar (1490–1636) Bijapur (1490–1686) and Golconda (1512–1687). Mughal conquests of these sultanates have, nonetheless, been generally regarded in Mughal historiography as Pyrrhic victories, both because these territories were never effectively integrated into the Mughal imperial system and because their destruction contributed to the rise of the Marathas. The problems of Mughal conquest in the Deccan have been chronicled and explained with particular care in the case of the Sultanate of Golconda.[47] The Marathas, who emerged as a powerful force as these sultanates were dismembered represented a Hindu confederacy centered in the mountainous regions of western India, whose early raids on Mughal frontiers provoked decades of unsuccessful Mughal campaigns in the late 17th century that altered the Hindustan basis of the empire and fatally weakened it as well. By the early 18th century, Maratha raids became full-scale invasions of the Mughal heartland.[48] Mughal frontier expansion in the Deccan ultimately became the passing bell for Mughal collapse.

At its greatest extent Mughal Empire the controlled territory roughly equivalent to that of the greatest of India's pre-Islamic empires, the Mauryas. Mauryan rulers, most notably Aśoka (r. c.268–232 BCE) , conquered most of the South Asian peninsula and extended their power from their north Indian Gangetic heartland into Afghanistan following the death of Alexander the Great in 323 BCE and the formation of the Greek successor state, the Seleucid Empire.[49] There are two apparent reasons why both of these major Indian empires never sought to expand into Iran and Mawarannahr. Compared with its neighboring territories, India was an extraordinarily wealthy region, whose population and economy dwarfed the economies and combined populations of Iran, Central Asia and Anatolia. There was little to gain in seizing territorial control of these regions.

Second, it was difficult, cold and uncomfortable, and ruinously expensive to dispatch Indian armies westward or to do so northward, and even more

---

[46] For the political history of the Delhi Sultanate see Kumar 2007 and Jackson 1999 and for an introduction to the Deccan Sultanates see Haidar and Sarkar 2015.
[47] Richards 1975.   [48] Gordon 1993.   [49] See especially Thapar 1961.

treacherously problematic to move east into the jungles on the Assam–Burma frontier. Historically the most notable expansion of Indian states beyond the subcontinent had occurred far earlier, when the southeast Indian Chola state extended its territorial control to Southeast Asia between the 9th and the 13th centuries.[50] This followed the centuries of commerce and peaceful Indianization in the region appropriately known as Indo-China, during which Brahmins introduced Vedic and Puranic rituals and theology, which Khmer monarchs eagerly adopted to legitimize their dynasty at Angkor Wat.[51] It is significant when considering political boundaries that Sanskritic culture spread into Southeast Asia while Persian culture retained its prominence in Afghanistan and Mawarannahr.

7.4   Porous Frontiers: The Three Empires Interrelated

In considering the frontiers of these three empires it is important to conclude by stressing that however else they differed – and how much they fought – political and military frontiers did not generally prohibit inter-state commerce or cross-border cultural influence. In that respect the Ottomans, Safavids and Timurid-Mughals resembled European countries, countries that struggled with one another, but belonged to a common civilization. First, rulers or officials in Istanbul, Isfahan and Delhi shared the same general economic ideas and considered inter-state trade a vital aspect of their economies. Bazaar complexes in Istanbul, Isfahan, Agra and Delhi and caravansaries built to service and protect merchants testified to the value monarchs placed on trade. Not only did they try to generate funds by encouraging and protecting merchants but with a brief exception during Shah 'Abbas's reign in Iran, these men also allowed goods and money to flow freely across their borders.

What this ultimately meant in terms of economic relations reflected the reality that Mughal India constituted the commercial superpower of the three, blessed as it was with an enormous agrarian base, a population of perhaps 100 million people, valued manufactures and ruthlessly enterprising merchants. Neither the Ottoman state nor Iran enjoyed these economic advantages as their modest populations suggest. In 1600, Ottoman and Safavid inhabitants together are believed to have totaled little more than 32 million people, with possibly 22 million people in Ottoman territories and eight to 10 million in Iran. India enjoyed a massive balance of payments advantage over the Ottoman and Safavid states – and those in Southeast Asia, generated by a flow of Indian manufactures, principally cloth. A river of currency from Ottoman and Iranian

---

[50]   Of many sources see the early work by Sastri 1984.
[51]   For the Indian–Southeast Asian commerce that had begun in the early Christian era see Wolters 1967 and for Indianization in Cambodia see Zéphir 1997.

dominions disappeared into India's financial black hole. This was supplemented in Iran especially by the presence there of thousands of Indian merchants and financiers, some of whom also operated in Samarqand and other cities within Uzbek dominions in Mawarannahr.[52]

Yet while Iran with its bleak, largely unproductive territory was particularly impoverished, it exerted a powerful and disproportionate cultural influence on both its western and eastern neighbors. Iran had a profound influence in the Middle East and Central Asia in pre-Islamic times, and the Sasanid Empire enjoyed enormous prestige in the Arab Muslim world. Muslim historians such as Ibn Khaldun (1332–1406) and his lesser-known Indian Muslim and near contemporary, Zia al-Din Barani (1285–1357), cited the Sasanids as rulers who administered the model of a non-Muslim pragmatic sultanate-like regime that exemplified how such states should rule.[53] At the rhetorical level Ottoman and especially Timurid-Mughal rulers also invoked Iranian titles from time to time and rulers in both dynasties appreciated – and perhaps saw themselves – in the Iranian imperial epic, the *Shāh Nāmah*. Even more obvious was the continuing influence of Iranian visual and literary culture during the period of these three empires.

Iranian culture constituted the civilized ideal for members of these dynasties. Iranian miniature painting was the artistic precursor of and definitive example for both Ottoman and Mughal ateliers, and was often found in Ottoman translations or Indo-Persian versions of Persian language literary texts such as *Khusrau and Shirin* or the *Shāh Nāmah*. Some Ottoman emperors knew and even wrote verse in Persian, and others appreciated Persian verse. Calligraphic renditions of Persian poems can be found on some Ottoman buildings in Istanbul. This cross-border connection was evident in painting and verse but it was also personified in the Iranians who found employment at the Ottoman and Mughal courts. In India Persian had earlier been the administrative language and literary language of pre-Timurid-Mughal north Indian regimes and during the Timurid-Mughal period India had a cultural relation to Iran somewhat similar to that of the United States to Britain in the 18th and 19th centuries. That is Iranian immigrants and native-born Indian Muslims created a north Indian Persian renaissance, a Perso-Islamic culture, both derivative and then gradually indigenous as well.[54] In art, literature, and for impecunious clerics and literati, no effective boundaries existed between these Muslim states.

The indisputable fact that artists, writers and merchants and the occasional philosopher moved easily and continuously across the geographic boundaries of these empires raises a final question about the sectarian identity of these

---

[52] Dale 2010, 106–34.   [53] Rosenthal 1958, 138–9 and Habib 1961.
[54] See Gulchin-i-Ma'ani's 1990 compendium of hundreds Iranians who composed Persian language verse in India.

states and their populations. The rulers and most of the Muslim populations of the Ottoman and Mughal Empires were Sunnis, who adhered to the Hanafi legal tradition. Ottomans became more aggressively Sunni following the rise of the Safavids, imparting an intense ideological element to their military conflicts. Shi'i clerics would not have received state appointments in Ottoman lands any more than Sunnis would have received such appointments in Iran. Perhaps the most serious religious boundary during the early modern era in these regions was that which existed between the Safavids and very conservative Sunni Uzbeks, who used their sectarian differences to legitimize continuous slave raiding incursions in Iran. In contrast, differences between the Shi'i Safavids and largely Sunni Timurid-Mughals had very little effect, as the Timurid-Mughals took a distinctly laisse faire attitude toward sectarian differences, at least until Aurangzeb fought his way to the throne in 1657. Well-connected Shi'i Iranians commonly found civil and military employment or received patronage in Mughal territories, where Hindus also held high posts in the military and administration. Iranian Shi'i clerics could also find employment in majority Shi'i areas within Mughal territories.

7.5   Conclusion

Perhaps the most notable historical aspect of the territorial boundaries of the Ottoman, Safavid and Mughal Empires is their similarity to the frontiers of earlier states in each of these regions. Ottoman sultans ruled over a Mediterranean state whose possessions replicated the Byzantine territorial map to a considerable degree, while the Safavids, reconstituted an Iranian state in the Achaemenid homelands on the Iranian plateau and the Mughals resurrected Timurid fortunes with a South Asian empire whose final territorial extent resembled the greatest pre-Islamic empire in Indian history. The factors that determined the exact if fluctuating boundaries of these states are almost too numerous to mention and impossible to catalogue in this brief survey, since they included geographic location, agrarian and commercial wealth, political and religious ideologies, international politics and personal ambition. Taking just the case of the relations of these three "Muslim" empires with one another, the vast territorial extent of the Achaemenid Empire stood as evidence that boundaries between them were not an inevitable product of their geography, solely a factor of the wealth of their historic lands, a determinant merely of their political environments or the persuasive power of their cultures. Nonetheless the desiccated, mountainous quality of the Anatolian, Iranian and Afghan borderlands tended to discourage all but the most megalomaniacal individuals from trying to extend their territories beyond their historic core regions: the Mediterranean, the Iranian plateau and the South Asian subcontinent. These three Muslim empires ultimately coexisted with one another, even as Ottoman borderlands were eventually lost to rebellion and European resurgence, while the weak Safavid state had to concede its original Anatolian base and constantly endure Uzbek depredations in Khurasan, and the Mughals expanded their Indian frontiers, but fatally wounding themselves in the process.

Bibliography

Arjomand, Said Amir, 1984. *The Shadow of God and the Hidden Imam*. Chicago, IL: Chicago University Press.

Ates, Sabri. 2013. *The Ottoman-Iranian Borderlands: Making a Boundary*. Cambridge: Cambridge University Press.

Babinger, Franz. 1978. *Mehmed the Conqueror and His Time*. Princeton, NJ: Princeton University Press.

Barkey, Karen. 2008. *Empire of Difference. The Ottomans in Comparative Perspective*. Cambridge: Cambridge University Press.

Barkey, Karen. 2014. "Political Legitimacy and Islam in the Ottoman Empire." *Philosophy and Social Criticism* 40(4–5): 469–77.

Barthold, Wilhelm. 1984. *An Historical Geography of Iran*, trans. Svat Soucek. Princeton, NJ: Princeton University Press.

Barthold, Wilhelm. 1968. *Turkistan Down to the Mongol Invasions*, trans. T. Minorsky and ed. C. E. Bosworth. London: Luzac.

Blake, Stephen P. 2013. *Time in Early Modern Islam*. Cambridge: Cambridge University Press.

Bosworth, Clifford Edmund. 1963. *The Ghaznavids*. Edinburgh. Edinburgh University Press.

Bosworth, Clifford Edmund. 2010. *The History of the Seljuq State*. Oxford: Routledge.

Brody, Lisa R, and Hoffman Gail L. 2011. *Dura Europos*. Boston, MA: McMullen Museum of Art.

Brunner, Christopher J. 2012. "India i. Introduction." *Encyclopaedia Iranica*. Leiden: Brill Online.

Canard, Marius. 2015. "Fatimids." *Encyclopedia of Islam*, ed. P. Bearman, Th. Bianquis, C.E. Bosworth, E. van Donzel, and W.P. Heinrichs, 2nd ed. Leiden: Brill Online.

Dale, Stephen F. 2010. *The Muslim Empires of the Ottomans, Safavids and Mughals*. Cambridge: Cambridge University Press.

Faroqhi, Suraiya, ed. 2006. *The Cambridge History of Turkey*. Volume 3, *The Later Ottoman Empire, 1603–1839*. Cambridge: Cambridge University Press.

Faroqhi, Suraiya and Fleet, Kate eds. 2012. *The Cambridge History of Turkey*. Volume 2, *The Ottoman Empire as a World Power, 1453–1603*. Cambridge: Cambridge University Press.

Fleet, Kate, ed. 2009. *The Cambridge History of Turkey*. Volume 1, *Byzantium to Turkey 1071–1453*. Cambridge: Cambridge University Press.

Gazerani, Saghi. 2016. *The Sistani Cycle of Epics and Iran's National History*. Leiden: Brill.

Gordon, Stewart. 1993. *The Marathas 1600–1818*. Cambridge: Cambridge University Press.

Gul-Badan Begam. 1901. *The History of Humayun*, trans. and ed. Annette Susannah Beveridge. London: Royal Asiatic Society.

Gulchin-i Ma'ani, Ahmad. 1990. *Karvan-i Hind*. Tehran: Intisharat-i quds-i razavi.

Gürkan, Emrah Safa. 2010. "The center and the frontier: Ottoman cooperation with North African corsairs in the sixteenth century." *Turkish Historical Review* 1(2): 125–63.

Habib, Mohammed, 1961. *The Political Theory of the Delhi Sultanate (including a translation of Ziaddin Barani's Fatawa-i Jahandari)*. Alllahabad: Kitab Mahal.

Haidar, Navina Najat and Sardar, Marika. 2015. *Sultans of Deccan India*. New York: Metropolitan Museum of Art.

Haywood, Colin. 2013. *The Ottoman World, the Mediterranean and North Africa*. Farnham: Ashgate.

Hathaway, Jane and Barbir Karl K. Barbir, 2008. *The Arab Lands Under Ottoman Rule*. London: Routledge.

Hurgronje, Snouck C. 1906. *The Achehnese*. Leiden: Brill.

Imber, Colin, 2002. *The Ottoman Empire*. New York: Palgrave Macmillan.

Inalcik, Halil. 2000. *The Ottoman Empire*. London: Phoenix Press.

Jackson, Peter. 1999. *The Delhi Sultanate*. Cambridge: Cambridge University Press.

Jahângîr. 1978. *Tûzuk-I Jahângîrî*, trans. Alexander Rogers, ed. Henry Beveridge, 3rd ed. Delhi: Munshiram Manoharlal.

Karateke, Hakan T. 2005. "Legitimizing the Ottoman Sultanat: a Framework for Historical Analysis." In *Legitimizing the Order: the Ottoman Rhetoric of State Power*, ed. Hakan T. Karateke and Maurus Reinkowski, 13–54. Leiden: Brill.

Koch, Ebba. 2006. *The Complete Taj Mahal*. London: Thames and Hudson.

Kumar, Sunil. 2007. *The Emergence of the Delhi Sultanate*. Delhi: Permanent Black.

Malcolm, (Sir) John. 1815. *The History of Persia*. London: John Murray and Longman, 2 vols.

Mano, Eiji. 1995 (and 1996). *Bâbur- Nâma (Vaqâyi')*, *2 vols*. Kyoto: Syokado.

Manz, Beatrice Forbes. 1997. "Military Manpower in Late Mongol and Timurid Iran." *Cahiers d'Asie central* 3(4): 43–55.

Manz, Beatrice Forbes. 2007. *Power, Politics and Religion in Timurid Iran*. Cambridge: Cambridge University Press.

Manz, Beatrice Forbes. 1989. *The Rise and Rule of Tamerlane*. Cambridge: Cambridge University Press.

Matthee, Rudi. 2010. "Was Safavid Iran an Empire?" *Journal of the Economic and Social History of the Orient* 53: 233–65.

Millward, James and Laura Newby. 2006. "The Qing and Islam on the Western Frontier." In: *Empire at the Margins: Culture, Ethnicity and Frontier in Early Modern China*, ed. Pamela Kyle Crossley, Helen Siu, and Donald Sutton, 113–35. Berkeley, CA: University of California Press.

Minault, Gail. 1982. *The Khilafat Movement*. New York: Columbia University Press.

Minorsky, Vladimir, tr. and ed. 1970. *Hudud al-'Âlam "The regions of the world": A Persian Geography 372 A.H.-982 A.D.*, ed. by Clifford E. Bosworth, 2nd ed. London. Luzac.

Minorsky, Vladimir. 1942. "The Poetry of Shah Isma'il I." *Bulletin of the School of Oriental and African Studies* 10(4): 1,006a–53a.

Murphy, Rhoads. 2009. "The Garrison and its Hinterland in the Ottoman East, 1578–1605." In: *The Frontiers of the Ottoman World*, ed. by A. C. S. Peacock, 354–83. Oxford: Oxford University Press.

Peacock, A. C. S. 2009. "Introduction: the Ottoman Empire and its Frontiers." In: *The Frontiers of the Ottoman World*, ed. A. C.S. Peacock, 1–27. Oxford: Oxford University Press.

Richards, J. F. 1975. *Mughal Administration in Golconda*. Oxford: Clarendon Press.

Rosenthal, Franz, tr. and ed. 1958. *Ibn Khaldûn, The Muqaddimah*. Princeton, NJ: Princeton University Press, 3 vols.

Roxburgh, David, ed. 2005. *Turks, A Journey of a Thousand Years*. London: Royal Academy Books.

Sabet, Firouzeh Kashani. 2000. *Frontier Fictions*. Cambridge: Cambridge University Press.

Sastri, K. A. N. 1984. *The Cholas*. Madras: University of Madras.

Subtelny, Maria E. 2007. *Timurids in Transition*. Cambridge: Cambridge University Press.

Tezcan, Baki. 2001. "Ethics as a Domain to Discuss the Political: Kınalzâde Ali Efendi's *Akhlak-i Alâî*." In: *International Congress on Learning and Education in the Ottoman World*, ed. Ali Çaksu, 109–20. Istanbul: Research Center for Islamic History, Arts and Culture.

Thapar, Romila. 1961. *Ašoka and the Decline of the Mauryas*. Oxford: Oxford University Press.

Wittek, Paul. 1938. *The Rise of the Ottoman Empire*. London: Royal Asiatic Society.

Wolters, O.W. 1967. *Early Indonesian Commerce*. Ithaca, NY: Cornell University Press.

Zéphir, Thierry. 1997. *Khmer, the Lost Empire of Cambodia*. New York: Henry Abrams.

8   Delimiting the Realm Under the Ming Dynasty

David M. Robinson

8.1   Introduction

The Ming dynasty (1368–1644) emerged out the crumbling Mongol Empire and fell during another moment of rapidly expanding global horizons, the early days of West Europe's imperial age and its expansion into Africa, South Asia, East Asia, and the New World. In its formative stages, the fledgling Ming court wrestled with many of the questions that we examined in this volume: Where were borders to be drawn and how were they to be defended? Which peoples were to be incorporated into the realm and how? How were differences among an ethnically diverse population to be articulated and adjudicated? How were relations among the imperial center, the border, and peoples and polities beyond to be conceived and managed? In an age when the memory, institutions, and personnel of the Mongol Empire stood as a legacy to be rejected or embraced, the early Ming court defined itself in relation to the empire of Chinggis Khan and his descendants. At the same time, the Ming emperor and his chief advisers drew selectively on a rich repository of rhetoric, policy, and perspectives developed by previous dynasties (including "classical" polities headed by Chinese elites and later regimes topped by Chinese, Turkic, Kitan, and Jurchen elites) to envision and administer the realm.

The second global moment of the 16th and early 17th centuries posed another set of challenges. Portuguese, Spanish, and Dutch colonial agents (both military and economic) appeared in East Asia. They brought advanced military and navigational technologies. They introduced alien notions of state sovereignty, trade, and foreign relations. Their cartography, social relations, ethics, and religion implicitly raised questions about borders and the realm, the articulation and accommodation of difference, and the basis of rulership and authority. The most consequential responses often appeared at the local level rather than at court, among private subjects rather than office-holders, and as ad hoc measures rather than as systemic imperial reform.

284

The formulation above may raise the hackles of those familiar with the much pilloried Fairbank school of Chinese history that highlighted "outside (read Western) challenge and domestic response" (Cohen 1984). My stress upon alternative models of empire represented by the Mongol Empire and West European countries is intended to highlight the fact that the Ming dynasty was not a self-contained political, military, economic, and intellectual entity that developed in splendid isolation but rather a polity whose multifaceted engagement with Eurasia shaped dynastic objectives and strategies at the same time that more purely domestic concerns influenced its perspectives, resources, and concerns. The "imperial intersections" (Burbank 2012, 14–15), even in attenuated form, were important for the Ming dynasty.

This chapter is organized into five parts. The first briefly considers the ways educated men under Mongol rule in East Asia during the 14th century thought and wrote about the spatial dimensions of the Mongol Empire. The second examines at some length the Ming court's efforts to carve out a place in what was still a Chinggisid-inflected Eurasia. This section explores the Ming court's measures to conquer or coopt Mongol powerholders and their territories, its plans to establish lasting control over those regions and their peoples, and its discursive and administrative strategies to describe and regulate issues of diversity and distance. The third explores the "refounding" of the dynasty in the early 15th century by a usurper who introduced new dynastic ambitions and modes of rulership. The fourth section reviews important changes in the Ming dynasty's geopolitical engagement in eastern Eurasia. It traces the dynasty's loss of territory and influence along the northern and western borders and simultaneously a steady expansion of state institutions into the southwestern frontier. The fifth and final part of the essay touches on developments within the Ming empire during the 16th and 17th centuries, including responses to early Western European agents of empire in East Asia and, more broadly, the expansion of Chinese interest into maritime Asia.

8.2   Conceptions of the Mongol Empire and the Great Yuan

First articulated in the 1240s and further elaborated in both diplomatic correspondence with foreign heads of state and works intended for domestic consumption, Mongolian notions of universal rule have long figured prominently in studies of Mongolian diplomacy, ideology, and identity (Amitai-Preiss 1998). Scholars have also examined in detail how the Mongol Empire contributed to the greatly expanded circulation of geographical knowledge, the rapid dissemination of cartographic techniques, and a greater awareness of distant

lands and peoples.[1] Finally, the work of Thomas Allsen and others has documented how the Mongols' notion of empire – including lands, goods, and
people – as a patrimonial form of wealth to be redistributed among its ruling
family stimulated massive relocations of communities, sending Central Asian
textile artisans to China, Mongolian troops to Cairo, and Tibetan monks to
Persia (Allsen 1997, 2015; Jackson 1999). The resulting empire did not simply
possess unprecedented scale but also integrated contrasting environmental
zones, which had previously stood separate and independent in economic and
political terms, and produced a body of administrative and military personnel
with strikingly diverse backgrounds of language, religion, and culture
(Christian 1994; di Cosmo 1999).

Perception of the realm and its territorial expanse varied by individual.
The founder of the Great Yuan dynasty (as the Mongol Empire was known
in East Asia), Qubilai (r. 1260–94) and those working for him in the
capital embraced a vision of universal rule and all-encompassing territory.
In 1285 Qubilai ordered his officials to assemble maps of all regions in
order to produce a single map that "shows that the breadth of the territory
of the August Yuan dynasty excludes nothing."[2] In response, they first
observed, "Now from the place where sun appears to the place where it
sets, all is ours" and then insisted that Chinese maps were inadequate to
reflect the scale of Qubilai's realm. They needed to combine both Chinese
and Islamic maps.[3] Another Yuan-period writer observed that the Great
Yuan extended in the east to the Korean peninsula, to the south to Dali
(Yunnan), and to the west as far as the Mediterranean Sea, Tibetistan,
Uighuristan, and India.[4] Yet few directly experienced the empire in the
aggregate, and subjugated peoples' notions of empire and territorial units
during the Mongol era deserve closer scrutiny.[5] Although they praised the
unprecedented expanse of the Mongol Empire, Chinese, Korean, Jurchen,
and Turkic observers writing in classical Chinese during the 13th and
especially the 14th centuries generally limited their focus to East Asia,
that is, the Yuan dynasty proper (Zhou 2008). The editor of the 1307 *An
Easy Guide to the Unified Territories of the Great Yuan* observed in his
preface:

[1] Allsen 2001, 103–4; Park 2012. In particular, see the discussion of the Kangnido Map), produced
at the Chosŏn court early in the 15th century on the basis of Mongol-era world maps in Biran
(Chapter 6), this volume.
[2] Anon., *Bi shu jian zhi, juan* 4: 72.
[3] Anon., *Bi shu jian zhi, juan* 4: 74. A leading early Ming official, Song Lian (1310–81), expressed
much the same sentiment. See Song 1999, 1.
[4] See Chen Dezhi 2009, 8. "Tibetistan" (Tubo or Tufan) in this context referred broadly to today's
Qinghai, western Gansu, parts of Sichuan, and most of Tibet (see Dezhi 2009, 12–13).
[5] The Mongol era saw the expansion of first-hand accounts by Chinese writers who traveled
through Central and West Asia as well as through Southeast and South Asia. See Biran's chapter.

Since the time of Tang, Wu, and the Three Dynasties, territory has to the north not exceeded You and to the south has not gone beyond the Ling border.[6] To the east it has reached the sea and to the west it has extended as far as the desert. Within this expanse, many of the lands of Man, Yi, Rong, and Di have not been completely opened.[7] Now all directions are unified. Writing and cart tracks are all the same. This is a realm without precedent in all history. What glory! What splendor! This compilation records in full fashion all mountains, rivers, personages, and historical names of administrative units. Scholars sitting upright at their table by the window who wish to know everything about the realm, writers and painters who wish to know about rivers and mountains, can without any extra effort, have a view of everything. It really is [a work in which] one can read about everything.[8]

Although the editor exclaims that "now all directions are unified," he does not attempt to specify borders or clarify the relationship between the Mongol rule and the Yuan dynasty. The only reference points he provides – You and Ling, Man, Yi, Rong, and Di – are names of regions and peoples with well-established pedigrees in classical Chinese writings.[9] The expression "writing and cart tracks are all the same" is similarly drawn from a moment in Chinese history, the establishment of the Qin dynasty in 221 BCE (Pines [Chapter 2], this volume), when the government mandated the use of an identical written script to facilitate the transmission of imperial orders and the adoption of uniform axle widths to ease dynastic transportation needs. Mongols may have understood the Great Yuan as another name for the Great Mongol Nation, but East Asian authors seem to have had more circumscribed notions.[10]

Yuan-period Sinophone administrative geographies and maps incorporated and naturalized regions recently conquered by the Mongols into the Great Yuan's realm that had not previously been subject to recent or regular Chinese rule – such as Liaodong, Gansu, and Yunnan to the northeast, northwest, and southwest, respectively. First compiled in 1285 and then revised early in the 14th century, the *Treatise on the Unified Realm of the Great Yuan* included the

---

[6] King Tang was the founder of the Shang dynasty (1600–1046 BCE) and King Wu was the founder of the Zhou dynasty (1046–256 BCE). The three dynasties refer to the Xia (*c.*2070–1600 BCE), Shang, and Zhou dynasties. They are often invoked as the ideal standard for all succeeding dynasties in China. You is a classical reference to region around present day Beijing South of Ling is a classical reference to area of present day Guangdong and Guangxi.

[7] Man, Yi, Rong, and Di are classical references for the peoples to the south, east, west, and north of the early Chinese states. The terms may have derogatory connotations. The term "completely opened" is slightly ambiguous. It may refer to agriculture or administration. The two often went hand in hand in Chinese history.

[8] Liu 2003, 1.

[9] In his 1320 preface to his geographical compilation, Zhu Siben (1273–1336?) notes that territories to the distant southwest or northwest regularly submitted tribute to the throne. However, since information regarding these areas was limited and often unreliable, he chose to omit such regions in his treatment. See Zhu 2004, 381–2.

[10] Kim Hodong 2006 and 2009 argues that Mongols not only used the term Great Yuan as the Sinophone equivalent of the Great Mongol Nation but also that they understood the empire as a unified whole well after its famed "dissolution" in 1260. Cf. Chen 2009, 11–13; Bi 2004.

dates of the conquests of Liaodong, Yunnan, and Gansu as well as the administrative structures established there by the Mongols.[11] Later compilations such as the *Great Compendium for Governing the World* and the *An Easy Guide to the Unified Territories of the Great Yuan* too included those regions as the territory of the Great Yuan.[12] Thus, Yuan-period Sinophone works established an important textual and conceptual precedent for the early Ming court. The preface to the *Great Compendium for Governing the World* observes that inclusion of such details "chronicled the expanse of territory and made manifest the reach of kingly transformation. It is great indeed!"[13] The editors explicitly related territory to rulership. This was one element of a wider process of interpreting or translating the Mongol Empire and Mongol rulers into classicizing, educated Chinese and into pre-existing Chinese categories of rulership, dynasty, and governance, whereby Mongol Great Khans (*qaghans*) such as Chinggis Khan and Qubilai Khan were transformed into the Grand Progenitor of the Yuan Dynasty (Yuan Taizu) and the Founding Progenitor of the Yuan Dynasty (Yuan Shizu), respectively.[14]

The Ming court did not assume that it was heir to all Yuan territory. Most of Mongolia, parts of Central and West Asia were included in *An Easy Guide* and the *Great Compendium*, but these regions never became Ming territory – nor is there much evidence that the Ming founder believed that they should. The Ming's footprint in the Tibetan Plateau was far smaller and fainter than that of the Mongols. The same holds true for Jurchen lands in the northeast. The Ming, however, did pay close attention to Mongol territorial precedents, and in areas that remained outside the Ming Empire such as Tibet and the Jurchen lands, it periodically invoked Yuan dynasty's models of interaction when they seemed advantageous. As the discussion below shows, the Ming dynasty's territorial expanse developed in part as a reaction to perceived security threats posed by the Chinggisid polity in the 14th century. Further, the incorporation of recently conquered regions such as Liaodong, Gansu, and Yunnan into Yuan-period Sinophone administrative geographies facilitated the justification of including those areas in the Ming polity.

---

[11] *Treatise of the Great Unified Territory of the Great Yuan* is no longer extant as a complete work, but portions have survived in various collectanea. Liaodong, Gansu, and Yunnan appear in chapters 2, 3, and 4 of the *Treatise* as preserved in *Liaohai congshu* (Jin 1985, 5: 3575, for preface).

[12] See "Map from the King shi ta tien," reproduced in Bretschneider 1967, insert. For detailed discussion of Central and West Asian (i.e., Chaghadaid and Ilkhanid) places names in the *Great Compendium* map (and other sources), see Liu 2006, 576–619.

[13] The *Great Compendium* is no longer extant but prefatory remarks to each chapter are preserved in Zhao Shiyan, "*Jing shi da dian* xu lu," in Su 1993, 498.

[14] Liu 2011, 231.

8.3   The Ming Court's Efforts to Claim a Place in Chinggisid Eurasia

During the first decades of the Ming dynasty, court officials articulated an extensive justification of the founder's armed insurrection against his ostensible ruler, Toghan-Temür (1320–70, r. 1333–70), more widely known as Shundi, "The Obedient Emperor." In their account, the profligate Toghan-Temür ignored matters of state, instead yielding power to grasping and unprincipled subordinates so as to spend his days and nights with nubile female dancers who performed tantric Tibetan ceremonies. The result was moral, social, and political chaos that opened the doors to brutal warlords whose lust for power completely overshadowed concern for the people or the preservation of Chinese culture. In view of such circumstances, Heaven withdrew its mandate from the Chinggisids and selected Zhu Yuanzhang (1328–98, r. 1368–98; below referred to as the Hongwu emperor or founding emperor) as the instrument through which order would be restored to the world. At that point, the fortunes or destiny of the Yuan dynasty drew to a final and irreversible close, a rhetorical turn that freed all men of their previous political loyalties and facilitated (perhaps even obligated) the transfer of allegiance to the new Ming dynasty.[15] If many elements of this critique were customized to fit Toghan-Temür, they also owed much to a millennia old rhetorical tradition of rationalizing dynastic change through castigating last rulers of the preceding dynasty whose moral bankruptcy and political ineptitude doomed their regimes.

Several elements of the early Ming explanation of dynastic change are relevant to our concerns. First, early Ming court writers explicitly linked territorial unification to political legitimacy. Ming officials like Song Lian (1310–81), Liu Ji (1311–75), and others stressed that when effective Yuan rule collapsed in the mid-14th century, China had been "carved up like a melon." This was not an empty claim; close to a dozen major regional polities emerged, several of which oversaw populations of up to several million people. Those regimes declared dynastic names, set up administrative structures, minted coins, and conducted diplomatic negotiations with both nearby neighbors and more distant heads of state, such as the king of Koryŏ (Korea).

Throughout the late 14th and early 15th centuries, senior ministers and court academicians repeatedly invoked the Ming founder's success in restoring territorial integrity as evidence of his military prowess, political legitimacy, and support of Heaven. Depending on the context, Ming court writers highlighted either the founder's personal contributions to the process of reunification or the workings of wider cosmic patterns that unfolded independent of man's control. Such writings were intended for a variety of audiences: these included former Yuan officials (including Mongols, Uighurs, Jurchens, Kitans,

[15] Robinson 2019, chs 4 and 5.

Tibetans, and Chinese), who were now in territory claimed by the Ming dynasty; elite Chinese families that may have felt an obligation to remain loyal to the memory of the Yuan dynasty; members of the Chinggisid ruling elite and their supporters both on the steppe and in strategic regions that the Ming court viewed as essential to its interests; finally neighboring polities and peoples such as Koryŏ, the Jurchens (in today's northeast People's Republic of China and northwest Democratic People's Republic of Korea) to the northeast, and Moghulistan and the Timurid empire to the west (see Map 8.1). Thus, comments about territorial unification are found in imperial edicts intended for domestic consumption, in poems celebrating and justifying the founder's rise, in musical compositions created for the state banquets at the court, and in diplomatic communications to regional leaders and heads of state.

Those claims, despite their volume and variety, remain silent over the specific location of Ming dynastic borders, either at the time or in the future. Although it may have seemed axiomatic that the Ming dynasty, as the latest in a long line of "legitimate" dynasties, would be heir to their territories, yet historically minded, educated elites were fully aware that the borders of individual Chinese dynasties had fluctuated greatly, that the aggregate Chinese borders had varied markedly over the centuries, and that several dynasties, such as the Kitan Liao (907–1125), the Jurchen Jin (1115–1234), and the Mongolian Yuan, ruled territories that extended well into the steppe, into forested Manchuria, and into the deep southwest of Yunnan, much beyond the rule of most native dynasties.

In other words, during the late 14th and early 15th centuries, the Ming dynasty's borders were an open question. The Ming's first priority was consolidating control over regions claimed by earlier Chinese regimes in order to secure the labor and revenue generated through agriculture, manufacturing, and trade. However, security concerns posed by the Chinggisids and their allies in the region almost immediately drew Ming military forces outward. Beginning in the autumn of 1368, the rump Yuan court withdrew northward to a series of walled settlements on the steppe (today's Inner Mongolia and Mongolia). Its allies, which commanded forces that numbered in the several hundreds of thousands, held strong positions in and around the Ordos Loop to the northwest, the mixed topography of Liaodong with its forested mountain, dense riverine system to the northeast, and fertile plains, and finally in semi-tropical Yunnan with its own mix of steep mountains and arable valleys to the southwest.

The Ming court committed great military and economic resources to neutralizing Chinggisid power on its northeastern, northwestern, and southwestern frontiers through repeated military campaigns, nearly constant diplomatic overtures to induce Chinggisid commanders to join the Ming, and finally the punctuated establishment of military garrisons in those territories. Such efforts were largely

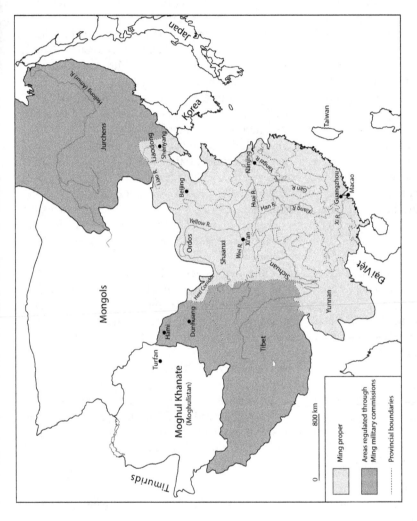

Map 8.1 Ming dynasty, c.1443.

successful; by the late 1380s, the Ming court had conquered, expelled, or coopted major Chinggisid allies in Liaodong, the Hexi (Gansu) Corridor, and Yunnan.

The ruler of Yunnan was a descendant of Qubilai named Vajravarmi, who oversaw a loose confederation of small polities comprised mainly of Tibeto-Burmese speaking peoples in Yunnan.[16] Vajravarmi remained allied to the Yuan dynasty after Toghan-Temür's flight from Daidu (today's Beijing), continuing to mark time by the Yuan calendar, using Yuan reign titles rather those of the Ming court in everything from government orders to inscriptions in Buddhist halls. The Yunnan court periodically traded envoys with the Chinggisids on the steppe. After repeated abortive political overtures, in fall 1381, the Ming sent an army of more than 300,000 against Vajravarmi, who put a reputed 100,000 men into the field. The Ming forces prevailed. Early in 1382, Vajravarmi abandoned his seat, burned his garments of nobility, and committed suicide (with more than two hundred other members of his court) rather than surrender.[17]

The Ming victory over Vajravarmi and the conquest of Yunnan had lasting consequences. Sitting at the intersection of East Asian, South Asian, and Southeast Asia cultural traditions, Yunnan figured prominently in transregional trade. In geopolitical terms, the Mongols had shown Yunnan's potential significance to the security of the Central Plains by using it as a base to attack the Song dynasty (Ueda 2005, 123–6).[18] By the late 13th century, the Mongols had extended administrative-military structures such as a branch secretariat and several pacification commissions into Yunnan, where they operated side-by-side with appanages gifted to influential Mongol nobles and other men who had rendered notable service to the throne. The Mongol state also entrusted important roles in governance to influential local peoples, such as the Baiyi. Thus, the Mongols relied on an interlocking set of administrative structures that integrated traditions of Chinese bureaucratic governance, Mongol patrimonial rule, and local power-holders.

The new territory and peoples of the northeast, northwest, and southwest raised challenges for the Ming court. How was lasting security to be achieved? What form of administration was appropriate? How were the peoples of these newly subjugated regions to be categorized in administrative, juridical, and cultural terms? If the answers' broad outlines soon emerged, fundamental tensions continued for generations. In some ways, they remained unresolved until the dynasty's fall in 1644.

[16] Vajravarmi is also known as Basalawarmi (Chin. Bazalawaermi). He appears in some Qing period sources as Batu (Mong. Batü).

[17] Langlois 1988, 144–6. See also the biographical note on one of the Ming officials sent to Vajravarmi's court, Wang Wei, by A. R. Davis, in *Dictionary of Ming Biography*, 1444–7.

[18] In order to exert pressure on the Song dynasty from the southwest, Qubilai was charged with the conquest of Yunnan, while his brother Möngke pressed the attack the Song dynasty from the northwest. See Rossabi 1988, 22–8.

In Liaodong to the northeast, the Ming court first attempted to win the allegiance of powerful Yuan commanders, regardless of whether they were Mongolian or Chinese. It then expanded control through the establishment of garrisons (from battalions, to guards, and capped by regional military commissions), which oversaw both military and civilian administration. The Ming state used garrisons to organize and mobilize labor. Garrisons first registered local households, then organized a portion of the adult male population into units of imperial soldiers, assigned lands and agricultural quotas to other men, and assessed labor obligations to the state or its local representatives. Located at the crossroads of the Korean peninsula, Manchuria, the Mongolian steppe, and the north China plain, Liaodong's population had long been highly diverse, and Mongol policies of population relocation had only accentuated the region's demographic complexity (Robinson 2009, 23–46). In an effort to win the loyalty of such families, the Ming dynasty created special military and administrative units with such evocative names as Free and Easy Prefecture, which featured fewer compulsory labor obligations to the state and more generous regulations for travel and trade. The Liaodong garrisons not only acted as the first line of Ming military defenses in northeast Asia, they also served as the first point of contact for diplomacy and trade. They were responsible for receiving envoys from the Korean peninsula, Jurchen lands, and from the Mongolian steppe, for organizing border markets to secure livestock goods from the north, for extending Ming influence through economic incentives, and for the initial settlement of Jurchens and Mongols who pledged their allegiance to the Ming throne (Robinson 2015).

Maintenance of Liaodong's multifaceted imperial infrastructure required massive, sustained investment from the Ming state, which committed funds and manpower to maritime and overland transportation infrastructure, supplied annual subsidies in silver to cover rewards and construction costs, established and maintained border markets, and ordered regular delivery of grain from more agriculturally productive regions in the empire.[19] The state also integrated Liaodong into the imperial penal system, sentencing common criminals to lifetime service in military garrisons and exiling educated men to the region's urban centers such as Liaoyang and Shenyang for varying lengths of time. Despite Liaodong's deep ties to the metropole through administrative, military, economic, and penal structures, for many observers Liaodong and its people remained culturally and politically suspect because of its location at the border, its prominent non-Chinese populations, and long stretches of time when non-Chinese polities, including most recently Kitans, Jurchens, and Mongols had ruled the region.

---

[19] Cong Peiyuan 1998, 630–54. For a map of the nearly forty postal-relay stations that ran from the southern coastal tip of the Liaodong peninsula to its northernmost edge, see Yang Zhengtai 1994, 227.

The Ming state also made extensive use of military garrisons to expand its control into a distant, ethnically complex, and strategically vital region, the Hexi Corridor (Gansu), which sat astride key trade routes to Central Asia and formed a buffer zone between the Mongolian steppe and the Tibetan Plateau. For much of the founder's reign, Ming control of the Hexi Corridor was sporadic and sharply contested. The mature Shaanxi Branch Regional Military Commission, which by 1393 oversaw twelve garrisons and three battalions, had been repeatedly established, abolished, reestablished, and relocated in response to local resistance by former and current supporters of the Great Yuan and by the contending demands on the Ming dynasty's economic and military resources.[20] During the early years, Ming armies might through demonstrations of military strength induce Mongol populations to surrender, but the Ming state lacked the labor and logistical wherewithal to station large contingents of imperial regulars in the Hexi Corridor.[21] Some of the early garrisons were established by the Ming state but then manned by Great Yuan personnel who had offered, always on a contingent basis, their allegiance to the Ming throne.[22] Not until 1393, when the Ming court more firmly controlled Liaodong and Yunnan, did the Hongwu emperor possess sufficient energy and resources to implement measures to ensure long-term control. These included opening new agricultural lands, resettling military personnel and their families to farm those lands and man the garrisons, and reducing surrendered Mongols' autonomy.[23]

[20] On the early institutional history of the Shaanxi Branch Military Commission, see Liang 1999; Ma 2008.

[21] The same pattern holds true for the Ordos Loop region, where again Ming control was precarious until the 1390s. For brief discussion and estimates of troop strength in the three main garrisons on the Ordos Loop (86,000 men plus several thousand "local Tatars," who were usually local men who had formerly served in the armies of the Great Yuan but were not necessarily Mongols), see Zhou 2008, 113–29.

[22] The Ming court used garrisons as a way to impose order and some measure of influence on territory and peoples beyond its control. It recognized the approximate territory controlled by a given leader and his followers, created a garrison name for the territory and people, appointed the leaders to nominal posts in the Ming military, granted them access to state-regulated commerce, such as border markets and the privilege of submitting tribute to the throne (which was another opportunity to conduct trade en route to Beijing and receive gifts from the emperor), and on occasion conducted joint military action with such men. The Ming state created a dozen or so such garrisons among the Mongol and Tibetan populations of the northwest frontier and nearly 400 to the northeast among Jurchen and Mongol populations. As one would expect, the size and influence to such communities varied widely. The nature and extent of Ming influence over such garrisons also differed according to time and place with some garrisons subject to significant Ming intervention and others completely autonomous. By the late 16th century, several Jurchen groups with diplomatic and economic ties to the Ming state grew increasingly powerful and unified, eventually undergoing a process of political and military integration and expansion that culminated in the Latter Jin dynasty, the forerunner to the Qing dynasty. For discussion of Ming–Jurchen relations, see Serruys 1955b; Rossabi 1982. Some Chinese scholars refer to such arrangements as "loose-rein garrisons." See Peng 2004.

[23] Serruys 1955a. Historical demography for the Hexi Corridor during the early Ming is challenging. The most recent estimate for the registered population in the Shaanxi Branch Military

Even after incorporation into the Ming polity, the establishment of Ming administrative offices and personnel in key urban sites, and the creation of a series of imperial garrisons, Yunnan remained distant, foreign, and dangerous in the eyes of many educated Ming writers. The editors of the imperially commissioned mid-15th-century administrative geography, *Treatise of the United Realm of the Great Ming*, remark on the extreme diversity of local customs, listing nearly two dozen different local peoples (Li Xian 1990). The Ming state established dozens of postal-relay stations in Yunnan, but they were narrowly concentrated on a few major imperial highways that ran through the center of the province (Yang 1994, 223). Beyond these corridors of imperial power were enormous swathes of territory where influential local families and their clients enjoyed near total autonomy in day-to-day affairs. Such families sought investiture and titles from the Ming state (as they had from the Great Yuan) that confirmed their status and offered access to the imperial court, gifts of expensive, prestigious textiles from the throne, and the opportunity for direct, personal interaction with the emperor. The Ming empire's military and political resources were also potent weapons during periodic struggles among contending members of such local elite families. For its part, the Ming state saw local ruling families as useful tools for ensuring a modicum of regional order, mobilizing military forces to serve in broader imperial campaigns, and confirming the expansive nature of Ming rulership. The dynastic legal code, the *Great Ming Code*, distinguished between the majority population and minority populations, such as those found in Yunnan and elsewhere in the southwest, northeast, and northwest, who were alternately identified as Tatar officers and Tatar soldiers (usually meaning Mongols and Jurchen military personnel and their descendants) or "people beyond the pale" or more literally "those outside the transformation" of Chinese civilization.[24]

To sum up, the borders of the Ming dynasty grew directly from those of the Mongol Empire (Map 8.1).[25] During its early years, the Ming court perceived Chinggisids and Chinggisid allies in neighboring regions to the northeast, northwest, and southwest as acute political and military threats. Through diplomatic accommodation, military pressure, and sustained recruitment efforts, within a few decades the Ming dynasty conquered, expelled, or coopted Mongol and local political actors in such regions. Conceptually, incorporation of such territories, which had been subject to

---

Commissioner is approximately 60,000 households and 160,000 individuals. This figure also includes several thousand Central Asians, who were long-term sojourners. See Ma 2011.

[24] The category "Tatar officer" first appears in Mongol-period Sinophone juridical compilations, a reflection of the Mongol efforts to articulate and adjudicate difference in a multi-ethnic empire. "Beyond the pale" is a Chinese term that first came to prominence in the Tang law code.

[25] Okada 1999, 264–5. Dardess (2003, 111) has also noted that the Ming dynasty succeeded to most of the Great Yuan's territory, with the major exception of the Mongolian steppe.

only sporadic Chinese rule, into the Ming polity was facilitated by Yuan-period administrative geographies and maps that "naturalized" these regions as part of the Great Yuan. Despite repeated military campaigns into the steppe and frequent clashes with groups at what might be described as the eastern edge of Central Asia, the founding Ming emperor did not attempt annexation of these territories in all likelihood for the same reasons that the majority of previous Chinese ruling houses had not – a logistical inability to project military force deep into the steppe and no geopolitical imperative to hold such territory or control such peoples. In addition to establishing the sorts of civilian administrative infrastructure used in the empire's hinterlands, the Ming state leaned heavily on military garrisons both to impose order from the center but also to organize and integrate local political, economic, and military resources. The early Ming state recognized distinctions among segments of its population based on language, culture, and place of residence, distinctions that were then formally articulated and reinforced in legal codes and administrative categories.

8.4   The Yongle Emperor and the Dynastic Refounding

Before his death, the Ming founder selected one of his grandsons, the eldest son of his recently deceased eldest son, to be the next emperor. However, after a bloody civil war, another of the Ming founder's sons, Zhu Di (1360–1424, below referred to as the Yongle emperor), usurped the throne from his nephew in 1402. In one sense the incident was nothing more than a political coup, the seizure of power by one member of the ruling lineage from another, one of innumerable such instances in the history of empire. In other ways, however, the Yongle emperor introduced a new vision of empire, borders, and rulership, leading some scholars to speak of the refounding of the Ming.

Under the Yongle emperor, the Ming dynasty markedly expanded its projec-tion of force and influence abroad. Although campaigns on the steppe had been a regular occurrence during his father's reign, the Yongle emperor broke dynastic precedence by repeatedly leading imperial armies in person against Mongol leaders. Also in the north, he dispatched expeditions along the Amur River to forge alliances deep in Jurchen lands. To the south, he sent his troops into Đại Việt (the northern region of today's Vietnam) and then annexed the territory as the Ming dynasty's 14th province (Lo 1970; Wade 2008). He launched massive naval armadas (often known as Zheng He's voyages) that traveled throughout Southeast and South Asia, where his envoys, military commanders, and troops repeatedly intervened in local and regional political conflicts, often through direct military action and calculated displays of super-ior technology and power (Wade 2005, 2008). To the west, he expanded contacts with religious and secular leaders on the Tibetan Plateau, restoring transportation infrastructure and deepening ties of religious patronage and instruction.

The Yongle emperor's grandson and successor gradually abandoned most such policies, and one can argue that they did not fundamentally change the dynasty's territorial expanse, security concerns, or conceptions of "us and them." Nonetheless, consideration of the Yongle emperor's motives and object-ives, the costs and advantages of his policies, and the way that his court represented his actions reveal something about contending strategic visions, the sustainable limits of Ming sovereignty, and the interplay of personal agency and structural questions of empire.

Scholars have explained the Yongle emperor's dramatic efforts to expand dynastic influence and control as a reflection of his enduring insecurity. Having usurped the throne, betrayed his father's wishes, and killed his nephew, the reigning sovereign, the Yongle emperor, the argument goes, desperately needed to squelch resistance to his rule and to demonstrate his standing as a worthy sovereign. The former objective was achieved in part through the internal security apparatus established by his father and in part through enormous cultural projects such as the *Great Canon of the Yongle Era*, a massive, encyclopedic compilation of all writings of the past that allowed him to simultaneously show his commit-ment to orthodox culture, act as patron to scholar elites, and control the past. The latter objective was to be realized by exceeding his father's accomplishments, particularly in terms of expanding dynastic influence and control abroad.

Even if we accept this line of analysis – an expansive vision of Ming empire and rulership as compensation for political insecurity – it begs the question why the Yongle emperor and his contemporaries considered military prowess, territorial expansion, and a steady stream of tribute missions to the capital as the best way to demonstrate the Yongle emperor's superiority. There were clear alternatives available. The man from whom he had stolen the throne, the Jianwen emperor (r. 1399–1402), had espoused a commitment to civil values, diminution of the military's standing, and a turn away from the harsh punish-ments and sanguinary purges of the founding emperor. The Yongle emperor's immediate successor, the short-lived Hongxi emperor (r. 1425), similarly rejected military expansion and the model of warrior-ruler, instead, assembling a group of like-minded civil officials at his court.

The most proximate model of rulership and territorial expansion for the Yongle emperor was the Mongol Empire. Although writers at the Yongle emperor's court inevitably compared his accomplishments to those of renowned rulers of the distant Chinese past, the Yongle emperor's first and transformative experience, was as the Prince of Yan, when he governed the region surrounding today's Beijing. For nearly two decades from 1380 to 1398, he lived in the palaces of the former Yuan dynasty and occupied a physical and psychic space situated at the confluence of the steppe and the sown. The Ming founder had invested his many sons in key border garrisons and entrusted them with the defense of the dynasty's northern frontier. To that end, he granted them wide-ranging responsibilities over local administrative and military resources.[26] During his years as Prince of Yan, the future Yongle emperor came into regular and direct contact with former Yuan personnel, including large numbers of Mongols who had joined the Ming dynasty and served both in the military units under his direct command and those based in and around the capital, over which he exercised great influence. As part of the early Ming's preemptive defense policy, the future emperor repeatedly led both Chinese and Mongolian soldiers on small-scale, seasonal raids into the steppe and on larger campaigns against Chinggisid commanders. Those same military units would first support him in his civil war against the Jianwen emperor and then accompany him back into the steppe once he had taken the throne.

The Yongle emperor received a first-rate classical Chinese education and assembled a brain trust of Chinese advisers. A firm grasp of classical Chinese models of rulership, however, in no way precluded a keen appreciation of the glories of Chinggisid rulership, especially such celebrated rulers as Qubilai. In addition, the Yongle emperor's first hand experiences on the steppe and intimate contact with Mongolian and Jurchen personnel gave him a fine-grained understanding of the steppe's geography, political dynamics, and people: at least so he thought. He seldom lost an opportunity to display his superior knowledge of topographical features, flora and fauna, hunting sites, language, history, and lifeways of the steppe to his senior civil officials who accompanied on his military campaigns against the Mongols. He owed that familiarity to his previous experiences on the steppe as the Prince of Yan.[27]

That extended exposure to the steppe and its people influenced the Yongle emperor's conception of rulership and borders. When on campaign in the steppe as emperor, the Yongle emperor both attacked Mongol enemies and sought Mongol allies. He once observed that he alone among Chinese emperors since Tang Taizong (in the early 7th century) considered both the Mongols and the Chinese as equally his children. When in 1423, a prominent Mongol leader, Esen-Tügel, pledged his allegiance to the Yongle emperor, court chroniclers recounted the event in detail, allowing the emperor to wax eloquent on his expansive vision of rulership and his superior knowledge of people from afar (Serruys 1959, 228–33). The transfer of allegiance also demonstrated that the Yongle emperor was a better ruler and patron than his Chinggisid counterparts – after all, he had secured Esen-Tügel's loyalty in an

---

[26] During the reign of the founding emperor, Ming princes built fortifications, drilled troops, oversaw border units, possessed the authority to launch small and medium scale campaigns into the steppe without prior imperial approval, and issued orders to provincial authorities. See Xiao 2010, 179–81.

[27] Robinson 2020, chs 1 and 2.

international competition. Finally, although the Yongle emperor made no efforts to annex or occupy the steppe, nor did he consider it completely foreign territory. He renamed mountains and rivers, inscribed prominent stones and cliff-faces with Chinese characters recounting his military triumphs. He used periodic military campaigns into the steppe as a way to prevent Mongol unification, recruit Mongol clients, and maintain a buffer or frontier zone along the northern border.

If the Yongle emperor had expanded (if only temporarily) the empire's size and the emperor's role, his court retained many of the rhetorical positions established during this father's time. As a representative example, one could do worse than the writings of Hu Guang (1370–1418), a senior minister at the Yongle emperor's court who crafted dozens of pieces in praise of his lord and dynasty. In a celebratory prose piece about the reception of a pair of lions submitted from a Central Asian ruler, Hu Guang used the language of universal, encompassing rulership extending as far as the illumination of the sun, moon, and stars reached, as far as wind, rain, frost, and dew touched. The civilizing influence of the ruler brought peace to the Central State (i.e., China) and succor to the barbarians of the four quarters. Ming territory had expanded to an extent without precedent in all antiquity, he gushed.[28] To celebrate the presentation of giraffes at the Ming court by the sovereigns of Bengal and Malindi in 1414 and 1415, Hu Guang wrote that "Imperial benevolence equals Heaven, It embraces the six directions leaving nothing external, Daemonic marvels transform without [leaving] a trace."[29] He highlighted the "sage transformation" and virtue that pervaded the world and touched all.

The language of inclusive rulership and universal submission was on occasion used to highlight the marginality of those few who "remained outside transformation," that is, did not acknowledge the Ming dynasty's claims. In a memorial commemorating the Yongle emperor's ostensible victory over a Chinggisid Great Khan in 1410, Hu Guang observes, "within the four seas all are a single family; subjugating the barbarians brings peace to the Central State; the myriad regions come in submission and being transformed pacifies the men from afar." According to Hu Guang, neighboring countries and peoples had all recognized Ming overlordship – the single exception were "petty caitiffs who live faraway in the desolate wilds" whose recalcitrance and violence spurred the emperor to righteous anger and the mobilization of an imperial army that chastised the Mongols and restored peace.[30] In a poem celebrating a military review in 1410 supervised by the Yongle emperor in preparation for

---

[28] Hu Guang, "Shizi zan," in *Hu Wen mu gong wen ji*, 623.
[29] Hu Guang, "Qilin fu," in *Hu Wen mu gong wen ji*, 624.
[30] Hu Guang, "He ping hu biao," in *Hu Wen mu gong wen ji*, 622.

a campaign against several Mongol leaders, Hu Guang begins with the observation, "All within the four seas is naturally one. The little uglies, however, do not come to court in submission."[31] In this formulation there is a natural unity to the realm, the violation of which leads inevitably to military conflict. The rest of Hu Guang's poem enthuses over the sounds and images of the Ming imperial armies, whose victories powerfully demonstrated the Yongle emperor's status as Eurasia's premier political patron.

The Yongle emperor's successor, the Xuande emperor (r. 1425–35), may have shared his grandfather's vision of rulership and territory, several times leading large military forces along the northern border, but he was unwilling to commit the enormous military, economic, and political resources that such a policy required. He ended Ming annexation of northern Vietnamese territory, curtailed dynastic armadas to South and Southeast Asia, and declined to lead troops into the steppe. As noted above, through charisma and coercion, the Yongle emperor had impelled his ministers to compose celebratory prose and poem accounts of his campaigns, but some senior officials had already begun to voice concern that repeated military campaigns drained dynastic coffers and distracted the emperor from pressing matters of domestic administration without any prospect of permanent security. In the long term, these voices were to determine the Ming's course.

8.5   Developments C 1450–1644

By the mid-15th century, most civil officials had not only concluded that the Yongle emperor's vision was prohibitively expensive and ineffective but were also convinced that it imperiled dynastic interests.[32] Their desire for change had been growing for decades but a single, traumatic event, the Tumu Incident, crystalized many men's fears about the dangers of activist rulership and expanding borders. In 1449, the Yongle emperor's great grandson, the Zhengtong emperor (r. 1436–49), once more led an imperial army into war against a powerful Mongol ruler (Esen), who though not himself a descendant of Chinggis Khan, nonetheless invoked the glories of Chinggisid rule and had raided the Ming's northern frontier. No Ming emperor had led troops into the field since 1434, when the Xuande emperor had patrolled in force along the border. Unlike the Yongle or Xuande emperors, Zhengtong had not been raised as a military commander. He lacked any field experience and, prior to this moment, had demonstrated no interest in military command. When he queried his senior official about his responsibility to defend the dynasty as his

---

[31] Hu Guang, "Shi cong yue wu Mingluan xu," in *Hu Wen mu gong wen ji*, 176.

[32] Highlighting tensions between military- and civilian-oriented rulership, Dreyer 1982 offers insightful treatment of the early Ming and the roads not taken.

forefathers had done, they replied smoothly that the ruler's military prowess certainly equaled that the Yongle and Xuande emperors. The problem, they observed, was that the dynasty lacked the outstanding generals that had made the campaigns of Yongle and Xuande possible. Although such a response was intended to flatter the emperor's ego, one suspects that after fifteen years without a major campaign on the steppe (although Ming forces had been active elsewhere, especially in the southwest) and a marked reduction in military men's status at the court, the Ming military – whether considered in terms of drill, tactical experience, logistical capacity, or generalship, had in fact eroded.

Against much vocal protest, however, the Zhengtong emperor led the army against Esen. Exploiting tactical mistakes, the Mongols inflicted a decisive defeat on the Ming force, captured the Zhengtong emperor at Tumu Fort, raided in the capital's suburbs, and withdrew to the steppe with emperor in tow. Quickly putting another member of the imperial family on the throne, the Ming dynasty was never in serious danger, but the ignominious defeat and resulting political turmoil at court permanently discredited the idea of a Ming emperor as field commander. The entire debacle was blamed on a scheming palace eunuch who inveigled the emperor into a disastrous decision (de Heer 1986; Mote 1974; Wu 1982). With a single exception, early in the 16th century, no Ming emperor would ever lead an army in the field against the Mongols again.[33]

The steppe remained the greatest military problem to the Ming dynasty until the 17th century. Insofar as it is justifiable to speak of Ming's "grand strategy," it consisted of preventing the emergence of a powerful nomadic entity to the north, or at least preventing this entity from threatening Ming's agricultural heartland. But there was no agreement about how to attain this goal. Eventually, the northern border grew increasingly distant from the capital in perceptual terms. Although people and goods continued to move across the northern frontier in both directions, growing numbers of Ming writers cast relations between the Ming and the steppe in terms of an unbridgeable gap between China and the Other.[34] As Arthur Waldron (1990) has detailed, during the remainder of the 15th and 16th centuries, the Ming court alternated among a variety of policy options vis-à-vis power-ful Mongol leaders such as Dayan Khan (1464–1532) and Altan Khan

[33] The sole exception was the Zhengde emperor (r. 1506–21), who most historians past and present have depicted as an absurd young man whose aberrant behavior hastened dynastic decline. For even-handed discussion, see Geiss 1987, 1988a.

[34] Such a conclusion was neither new nor inevitable. Debates over how to understand relations with nomadic horsemen to the north and their place in Chinese polities dated back at least to the 3rd century BCE. See Pines 2005. During the 15th and 16th centuries, educated Ming men sharply debated whether differences with non-Chinese peoples should be ascribed to education and cultural environment or were inherent and inalterable. See Shin 2006b.

(1507–82), experimenting with military strikes, trade embargoes, state-controlled trade, and negotiations, before adopting the expensive and never satisfactory policy of wall-building, which in perceptual and physical terms did much to define the northern border, an unexpected development when considered from the perspective of the early Ming emperors and their conceptions of the border.

Ming officials and other educated men never categorically disavowed military force. In fact, many preferred the strategic, even preemptive, use of military violence and eagerly adopted new military technologies such as firearms, even European models of warships.[35] After the mid-15th century, however, civil officials increasingly voiced their belief that they were best qualified to decide policy, direct military campaigns, and supervise military institutions. They believed the emperor remained essential to governance, but his role was to identify and support men of superior intellect and morality rather than to formulate policy himself. Several emperors during the 16th and 17th centuries chaffed against increasingly restrictive parameters of rulership.[36] They might flout the expectations of the civil bureaucracy by conducting military drill in and near the capital. They might attempt to circumvent civil officials' administrative power by entrusting authority to palace eunuchs, who were thought to be the emperor's men. Finally, they might favor individual military commanders with privileged access to the throne, impressive titles, and gifts of silver (Geiss 1988a: 414–42; Swope 2005). However, unlike heads of earlier and later dynasties, Ming emperors failed to cultivate alternate bases of support to check the power of civil officials and the broader stratum of like-minded men of education and at least modest wealth that constituted the literati.

The Ming has developed an enduring image as a weak dynasty that ignominiously surrendered Chinese territory to neighboring polities during the latter half of the 15th and 16th centuries. The evidence here is mixed. The Ming dynasty did yield several areas along the northern border, but control of a portion of such territory had been sharply contested from the dynasty's outset. The Ming founder had emptied several cities along the border, forcibly relocating his subjects to what he considered more defensible locales, sometimes for decades at a time. Further, it was the Yongle emperor who abandoned several forward bases in the southern reaches of the steppe and resettled their populations to the south, where they might be more easily supported by denser populations, higher agricultural productivity, and better transportation infrastructure.

---

[35] Johnston 1995; Andrade 2016, 124–31, 135–43, 172–81, 199–206.
[36] Huang 1981, 1–41; Geiss 1987; Swope 2008; Robinson 2013, 214–41.

During the late 15th and early 16th centuries, Ming influence along its extreme western border, in such places as today's Turfan, Hami, and Dunhuang, also diminished. Those Inner Asian polities had been part of the Mongol Empire, and Ming observers were aware that local populations had been conditioned to Chinggisid overlordship. During much of the 15th century, through generous patronage and occasional military pressure, the Ming throne exercised considerable influence over local rulers, who were increasingly Islamized and Turkicized.[37] However, by the early 16th century, few at the Ming court felt that maintaining past levels of influence in Hami and Dunhuang were worth the costs, either the short-term expense of a large military campaign or the long-term burden of supporting garrisons, suppressing local insurrection, and placating local elites. More important still were developments within the Moghul khanate, the Ming dynasty's western neighbor. During the late 15th century, the ruling elite of the Moghul khanate, another successor to the Chinggisid empire, expanded eastward. It was driven by its loss of territory to the west by the rising Uzbek polity, an economic desire for control over oasis-cities like Hami that served as key trade and transportation links with the Ming dynasty, and finally a deliberate effort to spread Islam through jihad. By 1513, the Moghul khanate controlled Turfan and Hami, and in the following decades periodically raided cities along the Ming dynasty's northwestern border (Kim 1993).

The most important loss of territory was the Ordos Loop, located along the northwestern border, which Mongol herdsmen came to dominate in the late 15th century. Control of this strategic region, which could support both pastoral and agricultural lifeways, had for centuries shifted back and forth between Chinese polities and those based primarily in the steppe (Waldron 1990, 61–71). How to respond to the loss of the Ordos Loop sparked sustained and heated debate at the Ming court in the late 15th century. Many officials favored a large-scale military expedition to "recover the Ordos Loop," which became a powerful political slogan. The idea appealed to the reigning emperor, again reminding us that neither the ruler nor his ministers opposed military action on principal. However, as the logistical and command difficulties of projecting Ming military power on an ongoing basis into a distant, economically underdeveloped region held by powerful and well-supplied cavalry forces became clear, other proposals gained greater appeal. During the 1470s, plans for constructing a series of fortifications to block further Mongol incursions took form. Such an approach was expensive, labor-intensive, and logistically demanding; further it did not provide the satisfaction of decisive military victory over the enemy. However, the court decided it was the least objectionable option for the moment (Waldron 1990, 91–107). In time, static defense became a central feature of the Ming dynasty's border defenses (Waldron 1990, 108–64) (Map 8.2).

---

[37] Mote 1988, 393–7; Lam 1990; Rossabi 1998, 246–58.

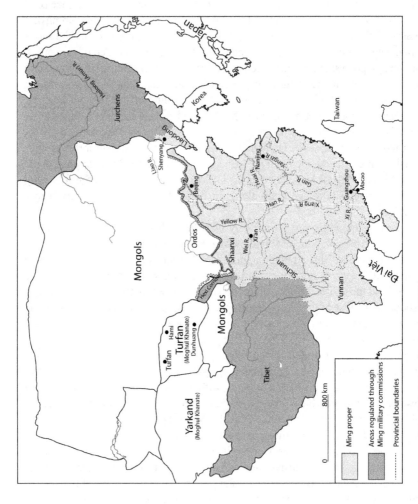

Map 8.2 Ming dynasty, c.1582.

This essay focuses on understanding of territory and its administration by the Ming court, senior officials, and educated men. However, the extent and nature of Ming dynastic territory were conditioned by both local and foreign developments. The most obvious example is the periodic rise of steppe confederations, often under the loose rule of a Chinggisid noble as was the case in the 15th and 16th centuries. When a Mongol leader like Altan Khan gained sufficient power in the mid- and late-16th centuries, he became a more potent military threat to the Ming court and a more attractive patron to a wide variety of actors, including men and women from China, the steppe, and even Tibet.

Less fully appreciated than the loss of territory in the north and west was the expansion of Ming administrative presence into the Southwest. There the Ming dynasty had built on Yuan-era precedents to expand the administrative reach of the central state into more distant parts of borders regions using a series of interlocking administrative structures. The Ming state established Chinese bureaucratic practices (organizing territorial units into prefectures, sub-prefectures, and counties whose governance was overseen by official dispatched by the central government) in areas with larger Chinese populations, much of which had previously been relocated there from the hinterlands by the Ming state. In what some scholars call the outer border zone, the Ming state recognized native leaders who enjoyed hereditary status and exercised high levels of autonomy (Lu and Peng 2013). The large-scale influx of Chinese migrants, many of whom were part of the military garrison population, would in time transform much of the Southwest's social, economic, ethnic, and cultural landscape (Lu 2001; Yu 2010). One result of intensified interaction was a growing interest in demarcation and differentiation, that is, categorizing the diverse populations of the southwest (Shin 2006a).[38] One could likewise argue that similar changes were wrought in Liaodong in the empire's northeastern corner, which only became fully integrated into China in the Ming period.

In addition to the territory it directly governed, the Ming throne maintained an expansive (and expensive) patronage network with greater and lesser leaders from today's Uzbekistan to Japan, from Mongolia to Myanmar. Emphasizing the Son of Heaven's universal rule, unique virtue, and matchless power, imperial rhetoric largely effaces how hard the Ming throne worked to secure neighboring rulers' recognition and loyalty, but those efforts were essential to the Ming dynasty's geopolitical interests. Details in chronicles like the *Ming Veritable Records* reveal that through gift-exchanges, trade privileges, honorary titles, and countless small gestures of royal favor such as dispatching palace physicians, delivering medicine, offering funerary sacrifices, and granting preferential treatment at court banquets, the Ming court sought distant rulers' assistance in protecting envoys, curbing banditry, preventing border raids,

---

[38] Shin focuses on Guizhou but many of his observations hold true for Yunnan.

supplying military and political intelligence, and avoiding alliances inimical to Ming interests. In addition, formal recognition of the Ming emperor's legitimacy through the presentation of gifts to the throne and compliance with dynastic protocol enhanced the Son of Heaven's standing at home and abroad.

8.6   Maritime China and Territoriality

Mongol elites had a keen appreciation for the wealth and information that trade produced. Building on well-established regional trade routes, generations of Mongol rulers across much of Eurasia invested in roads, bridges, and relay stations to facilitate long-distance trade. They actively supported favored merchants through preferential tax policies and political patronage. The result was a significant expansion of both overland and maritime trade networks that linked cities from Gaegyeong (Korea) to Venice. As effective Mongol governance deteriorated in the chaotic mid-14th century, the role of violence in trade grew. Merchants armed themselves against raiders on land and on the seas. Several Chinese warlords along the coast engaged in maritime trade to finance their armies. When the Ming founder came to power, he viewed maritime trade and its lack of clear borders as potentially disruptive. He prohibited private maritime trade and forbade his subject to travel overseas (Li 2010). Maritime prohibitions never fully eliminated private, illicit trade and Chinese emigration to Southeast Asia continued in the early Ming period, but all maritime commerce was legally required to be conducted through a carefully regulated system of state-to-state diplomatic relations, often called the tributary system.

The enormous maritime armadas of the 15th century were also state-centric enterprises. The imperial government organized, funded, and staffed the armadas, which projected Ming dynastic power and prestige throughout Southeast and South Asia. This may be seen as an attempt to revive the sea trade that had boomed under the Mongols but had sharply declined as their empire and its sprawling commercial networks deteriorated in the mid-14th century. Later in the 15th century, the Ming throne halted its support for massive armadas, but the Ming dynasty's maritime borders remained porous. China did not turn inward, although that assertion is repeatedly regularly. Trade, albeit illicit, remained important to Chinese coastal populations throughout the remainder of the 15th and into the 16th centuries. When small numbers of west European traders appeared on Chinese coasts in the early 16th century, they adapted to local conditions and Asian trade networks – rather than immediately transforming those networks as scholars once believed (Clulow and Mostert 2018; Andrade 2018, 239–40).

For the most part, the Ming court handled the appearance of the Portuguese along the southeastern coast in the early 16th century as a local issue. Portuguese envoys were not permitted to present tribute in the capital, that is, they were not incorporated into the Ming state's official diplomatic world order. It was an open secret, however, that Portuguese agents sought to integrate themselves into thriving regional trade networks and that by the mid-16th century local authorities had reached a modus vivendi whereby the Portuguese were allowed to first trade at Guangzhou, where they paid duty on trade goods to Chinese authorities and also offered gifts to several key local officials, and then later to maintain a base in Macau. Thus, the Ming court permitted Portuguese use of a part of its territory without considering such an arrangement as an infraction of imperial sovereignty (Chang 1934; Wills 1998, 335–53).

Such an accommodation was one facet of a broader development that dated back several centuries. Coastal populations participated in international maritime trade that involved Chinese, Japanese, and Portuguese traders, often with the enthusiastic support of local elites (many of whom held posts in the imperial government) and the tacit permission of local government authorities, despite strict prohibitions against unauthorized private overseas trade (Geiss 1988a: 433–34; Wills 1998: 333–53; Elisonas 1991). The mid-16th century saw coastal raiding escalate rapidly in terms of scale and violence. Chinese merchants played the most dominant role, but Japanese and lesser numbers of European were also involved. Military efforts by the Ming imperial government to eradicate illegal maritime trade and its attendant violence were only sporadically effective. In 1567, the Ming court lifted the blanket ban on private overseas trade, permitting foreign ships to conduct commerce in three southeastern ports that were in theory under direct administration of the court in Beijing. Illegal trade and coastal raiding diminished, while the Chinese economy became more deeply integrated into the global economy.

Thus, the Ming state adopted some formal institutional changes in response to new sociopolitical trends that increasingly involved people and rulers beyond Ming borders. However, much of this vibrant and sometimes violent world remained beyond the acknowledgement and thus control of the Ming state. Growing numbers of Ming subjects joined overseas Chinese communities in Japan, Đại Việt, Champa, the Spanish-controlled Philippines, Portuguese-controlled Melaka, Dutch-controlled Batavia, and beyond. Neither the Ming court nor literati in general spent much time considering the status of such people, for instance, their relation to the Ming throne, the Ming state's obligations to overseas subjects, or what such communities meant for the Ming court's relations with the Portuguese or Spanish thrones.

Such unresolved or unaddressed questions are reflected in 17th-century maps produced within the Ming dynasty. By the mid-16th century, a thriving publishing industry produced a wide variety of cartographic and textual descriptions of the Ming polity and its place in the wider world. Many privately compiled and privately published works drew on imperially compiled works. Thus, the majority of Ming-period maps found in privately published encyclopedias, general reference works, collections of maps and travel routes replicated imperial visions of Ming territoriality that were sometimes decades, even centuries old.[39] However, some publishers sought a competitive edge in the commercial market by highlighting new, updated information, including contemporary European cartography and representations of the world.[40] In other cases, privately produced, non-commercial maps such as the so-called Seldon Map represent a mix of old and new (Map 8.3). The representation of the northern border of the Ming dynasty closely follows a long-established imperial vision of a clear border and stark divide with the Mongols and Jurchens. In contrast, the southern half of the map, which was clearly its focus, offers richly detailed information about trade routes and sea currents that extend beyond East Asia into the maritime world of Southeast Asia and beyond.[41] Robert Batchelor argues that this map reflects long-standing, privately compiled trade-maps created by East Asian merchants that the Portuguese used in creating their own maps early in the 16th century. The Seldon Map thus represents the coexistence of a state-approved depiction of the northern borders and an alternate, detailed, and expansive vision of the south that ranged far beyond the empire's borders.

8.7   Conclusion

In the long-term, the maritime world of the south and its ever-expanding ties to the rest of the globe would have ever-greater consequences for China. In the short-term, however, the greatest threat to the Ming court emerged from the northeast, developing out of the complex intersection of the Liaodong garrisons, regional trade, and ambitious Jurchen leaders who exploited access to China's vibrant economy, political culture, and agricultural labor to forge a powerful new polity. In 1644 this new polity occupied the imperial throne in Beijing and in time would create a continent-spanning empire, the Qing dynasty (see Mosca's Chapter 9, this volume).

Like many other instances considered in this volume, the case of the Ming dynasty suggests the difficulty of establishing monocausal explanations for territory and governance of diverse populations. As was true elsewhere in the world,

---

[39] The transmission of information could be extensive. Lukacs 2014 argues that a now privately held map known as *The Provinces of the Great Ming* is a 1691 Japanese copy of a palace map taken from Beijing to Japan when the Ming dynasty fell in 1644. The map measures 13 square meters and shows Mongolia as clearly demarcated from Ming territory. Such territory is noted in cartouches as Tribes of the Northern Di, the Jurchens, and the Tatar Tribes. The map is now held at the Kōbe Municipal Museum in Japan.

[40] Factual accuracy was seldom the primary concern of audiences. Recently revised and widely available texts on the foreign countries and peoples frequently repeated hoary stereotypes and errors. For an insightful case-study, see He 2013, 202–44.

[41] Batchelor 2013 notes that the map's treatment of the Ming's northern border mirrors one found in a popular encyclopedia (1601), *Ershiba xiu fenye huang Ming gesheng di yu zong tu* ("Twenty-eight mansion, field-allocation, imperial Ming, all provinces terrestrial world map"), reproduced in Batchelor 2013, 44, which in turn drew on earlier imperial maps.

Map 8.3 The Seldon Map. MS. Selden Supra 105, Map recto. Bodleian Libraries, University of Oxford. https://bodleianimages.co.uk/en/search/do_q uick_search.html?q=selden%20map&mime_type= Available under Creative Commons Licence CC-BY-NC 4.0.

security concerns, logistical constraints, ideology, domestic politics, and the broader regional environment all shaped the size and contours of the Ming borders. In the formative first century, nearly all these factors were profoundly influenced by the legacy of the Mongol Empire and contemporary Mongol polities on the steppe. In time, however, understanding of the Mongol legacy among educated Chinese men changed as did the nature of the Mongol security threat.

Simultaneously, perceptions about the proper attributes of the emperor and more broadly the status and role of literati underwent important change, which in turn shifted the calculus about the costs of maintaining far-flung parts of the empire.

If the new calculus contributed to the loss of territory in the far west or along the northern border, to the south the Ming period witnessed the steady expansion of private Chinese commercial interests into maritime Asia. If we were to borrow the language of James Scott, the Ming imperial state did not fully "see" that expansion (Scott 1998). Chinese individuals, families, and communities along the Southeastern coast participated in transregional trade in ways that sometimes violated dynasty law, sometimes coopted government agents (both civil and military), and sometimes forced institutional changes, such as when the court reformed trade laws in 1567. In other cases, however, Chinese families moved beyond dynastic borders into an extra-imperial space, sojourning in trade centers in much of Southeast Asia in ways that either rendered them opaque or largely beyond the Ming state's gaze.[42] Those families and communities, however, often retained ties to their ancestral homes. They also worked to adapt the familiar knowledge and artifacts created by the Ming court and by private publishing houses (most especially in Fujian) to new physical and cultural environments (Batchelor 2016). The Ming case suggests that exclusive focus on the state's perspective needlessly narrows and dims our vision of the rich diversity of historical understandings of territory.

Bibliography

Allsen, Thomas. 1997. "Ever Closer Encounters: Appropriation of Culture and the Apportionment of Peoples in the Mongol Empire." *Journal of Early Modern History* 1: 2–23.

Allsen, Thomas. 2001. *Culture and Conquest in Mongol Eurasia.* Cambridge: Cambridge University Press.

Allsen, Thomas. 2015. "Population Movements in Mongol Eurasia." In *Nomads as Agents of Cultural Change: the Mongols and Their Eurasian predecessors*, ed. Reuven Amitai and Michal Biran, 119–51. Honolulu, HI: University of Hawai'i Press.

---

[42] The occasional appearance in Manila of Ming officials and officers sent by provincial authorities (for instance in 1575 and 1603) was the exception that proved the rule. See Wills 1998, 355, 358. Similarly, consider the remarkable *Study of the Eastern and Western Seas*, a wide-ranging account compiled in 1617 that discussed key ports and trade routes in Southeast Asia. The initial impetus of the author Zhang Xie (1574–1640) was a request by a local magistrate in Fujian, who wanted to know more about what the local men got up to when they disappeared from his jurisdiction for months at a time. The book was published by another local official in Fujian. See Zhang 2000, 7. Ming subjects also migrated, sometimes voluntarily and sometimes by coercion, north of the dynastic border, where they were incorporated into Mongolian and later Jurchen polities. The Ming government strenuously objected to such migration, often out of fear that Chinese individuals and communities provided Mongolian and Jurchen leaders not only with valuable intelligence about border defenses and domestic security but also with broader political and military strategies useful in state-building.

Amitai-Preiss, Reuven. 1998. "Mongol Imperial Ideology and the Ilkhanid War Against the Mamluks." In *The Mongol Empire and its Legacy*, ed. Reuven Amitai-Preiss and David Morgan, 57–72. Leiden: Brill.

Andrade, Tonio. 2016. *The Gunpowder Age: China, Military Innovation, and the Rise of the West in World History*. Princeton, NJ: Princeton University Press.

Andrade, Tonio. 2018. "The Dutch East India Company in Global History: A Historiographical Reconnaisance." In *The Dutch and English East India Companies: Diplomacy, Trade and Violence in Early Modern Asia*, ed. Adam Clulow and Tristan Mostert, 239–56. Amsterdam: Amsterdam University Press.

Anonymous (mid-14th century). 1992. *Bi shu jian zhi* 祕書監志. Rpt. Zhejiang Xinhua shudian.

Batchelor, Robert. 2013. "The Selden Map Rediscovered: A Chinese Map of East Asian Shipping Routes, c.1619." *Imago Mundi* 65(1): 37–63.

Batchelor, Robert, 2016. "Maps, Calendars, and Diagrams: Space and Time in Seventeenth-Century Maritime East Asia." In Sea Rovers, Silver, and Samurai: Maritime East Asia in Global History 1550–1700, eds. Tonio Andrade and Xing Hang, 86–113. Honolulu HI: University of Hawai'i Press.

Bi Aonan 畢奧南. 2004. "Menggu hanguo yu Yuanchao guanxi de kaocha" 蒙古汗國與元朝關係的考察 [An Examination of Relations between the Mongol Empire and the Yuan Dynasty]. *Zhongguo bianjiang shidi yanjiu* 中國邊疆史地研究 14 (4): 40–51.

Bretschneider, E. 1967. *Mediaeval Researches from Eastern Asiatic Sources*, Vol. 2. New York: Barnes and Noble, Inc.

Burbank, Jane and Frederick Cooper. 2012. *Empires in World History: Power and the Politics of Difference*. Princeton, NJ: Princeton University Press.

Chang Tien-tse. 1934. *Sino-Portuguese Trade from 1514 to 1644*. Leiden: Brill.

Chen Dezhi 陳得芝. 2009. "Guanyu Yuanchao de guohao, nianhao yu bianjiang wenti" 關於元朝的國號，年號與邊疆問題 [The Yuan Dynasty's Dynastic Title, Reign Titles, and Territory]. *Beifang minzu daxue xuebao* 北方民族大學學報 87: 5–15.

Christian, David. 1994. "Inner Eurasia as a Unit of World History." *Journal of World History* 5(2): 173–211.

Clulow, Adam and Tristant Mostert. 2018. "Introduction: The Companies in Asia." In: *The Dutch and English East India Companies: Diplomacy, Trade and Violence in Early Modern Asia*, ed. Adam Clulow and Tristan Mostert, 13–21. Amsterdam: Amsterdam University Press.

Di Cosmo, Nicola. 1999. "State Formation and Periodization in Inner Asian History." *Journal of World History* 10.1: 1–40.

Cohen, Paul. 1984. *The Discovery of History in China: American Historical Writing on China's Recent Past*. New York: Columbia University Press.

Cong Peiyuan 丛佩遠. 1998. *Mingdai Dongbei bian* 明代東北編 [The Northeast during the Ming Period]. In *Zhongguo Dongbeishi* 中國東北史 [A History of China's Northeast], ed. Tong Dong 佟東, Vol. 3. Changchun: Jilin wenshi chubanshe.

Dardess, John. 2003. "Did the Mongols Matter? – Territory, Power, and Intelligentsia in China from the Northern Song to the Early Ming." In: *The Song-Yuan-Ming Transition in Chinese History*, ed. Paul Smith and Richard von Glahn, 111–34. Cambridge, MA: Harvard University Press Asia Center.

de Heer, Philip. 1986. *The Care-taker Emperor: Aspects of the Imperial Institution in Fifteenth Century China as Reflected in the Political History of the Reign of Chu Ch'i-yü*. Leiden: Brill.

Dictionary of Ming Biography. 1976. Ed. L. Carrington Goodrich and Chaoying Fang. New York: Columbia University Press.

Dreyer, Edward. 1982. *Early Ming China*. Stanford, CA: Stanford University Press.

Elisonas, Jurgis. 1991. "The Inseparable trinity: Japan's relations with China and Korea." In: *The Cambridge History of Japan, Early Modern Japan, volume 4*, ed. John Hall, 235–300. Cambridge: Cambridge University Press.

Geiss, James. 1987. "The Leopard Quarter During the Cheng-te reign." *Ming Studies* 24: 1–38.

Geiss, James. 1988a. "The Cheng-te reign, 1506–1521." In: *The Cambridge History of China*. Volume 7: *The Ming Dynasty, Part One*, ed. Denis Twitchett and Frederick Mote, 403–49. Cambridge: Cambridge University Press.

Geiss, James 1988b. "The Chia-ching Reign, 1522–1566." In *The Cambridge History of China*. Volume 7: *The Ming Dynasty, Part One*, ed. Denis Twitchett and Frederick Mote, 490–505. Cambridge: Cambridge University Press.

He Yuming. 2013. *Home and the World: Editing the "Glorious Ming" in Woodblock-Printed Books of the Sixteenth and Seventeenth Centuries*. Cambridge, MA: Harvard University Asia Center.

Hu Guang 胡廣 (1369–1418). *Hu Wen mu gong wen ji* 胡文穆公文集. Rpt. in *Siku quanshu cunmu congshu* 四庫全書存目叢書, *ji* 集 28.

Huang Ray. 1981. *1587: A Year of No Significance. The Ming Dynasty in Decline*. New Haven, CT: Yale University Press.

Jackson, Peter. 1999. "From Ulus to Khanate: The Making of the Mongol States, c. 1220–1290." In *The Mongol Empire and its Legacy*, ed. Reuven Amitai-Preiss and David Morgan, 12–37. Leiden: Brill.

Jin Yufu 金毓黻, ed. 1985. *Liaohai congshu* 遼海叢書 [A Liaohai Collectionea]. Rpt. Shenyang: Liaoshen shushe.

Johnston, Alastair. 1995. *Cultural Realism: Strategic Culture and Grand Strategy in Chinese History*. Princeton, NJ: Princeton University Press.

Kim Hodong 金浩東. 1993. "Isŭrram seryok ŭi Tongjin kwa Hami wangguk ŭi morrak" 이슬람勢力의 東進과 하미王國의 沒落. *Chindan hakpo* 震檀學報 76: 107–42.

Kim Hodong 金浩東. 2006. "Mong'gol che'guk kwa Tae Wŏn" 몽골帝國과 大元 [The Mongol Empire and the Yuan Dynasty]. *Yŏksa hakpo* 歷史學報 192: 221–253.

Kim Hodong 金浩東. 2009. "The Unity of the Mongol Empire and Continental Exchanges over Eurasia." *Journal of Central Eurasian Studies* 1: 15–42.

Lam Yuan-chu. 1990. "Memoir on the Campaign against Turfan." *Journal of Asian History* 24(2): 105–60.

Langlois, John. 1988. "The Hung-wu Reign." In: *The Cambridge History of China*. Volume 7: *The Ming Dynasty, Part One*, ed. Denis Twitchett and Frederick Mote, 107–81. Cambridge: Cambridge University Press.

Li Kangying 李康英. 2010. *The Ming Maritime Trade Policy in Transition, 1368 to 1567*. Wiesbaden: Harrasowitz Verlag.

Li Xian 李賢 (1409–1467). 1990. "Feng su" 風俗. In *Da Ming yi tong zhi* 大明一統志, 2 vols. Rpt. Xi'an: Sanqin chubanshe, 2: 1311.

Liang Zhisheng 梁志勝. 1999. "Hongwu ershiliunian yiqian de Shanxi xingdusi" 洪武二十六年以前的陝西行都司 [The Provisional Regional Military Commission of Shaanxi prior to 1393]. *Zhongguo lishi dili luncong* 中國歷史地理論叢 3: 165–75.

Liu Ji 劉基 (1311–1375). 2011. "Shanyin xian Kongzi miao bei" 山陰縣孔子廟碑. In *Liu Bowen ji* 劉伯溫集, 4 vols. Rpt. Hangzhou: Zhejiang guji chubanshe.

Liu Yingli 劉應李 (d. 1311), compiler. 2003. "Preface" 題記 *of Da Yuan hun yi fang yu sheng lan* 大元混一方輿勝覽 [An Easy Guide to the Unified Territories of the Great Yuan], 1310 edition. Rpt. Chengdu: Sichuan daxue chubanshe.

Liu Yingsheng 劉迎勝 2006. *Chahatai hanguoshi yanjiu* 察哈台汗國史研究 [A History of the Chaghadaid Qanate]. Shanghai: Shanghai guji chubanshe.

Lo Jung-pang. 1970. "Intervention in Annam: A Case Study of the Foreign Policy of the early Ming Government." *Tsinghua Journal of Chinese Studies* 8. (1–2): 154–82.

Lu Ren 陸韌. 2001. *Bianqian yu jiaorong: Mingdai Yunnan Hanzu yimin yanjiu* 變遷與交融：明代雲南漢族移民研究 [Transformation and Integration: Migration of the Han Ethnicity in Yunnan during the Ming Period]. Kunming: Yunnan jiaoyu chubanshe.

Lu Ren 陸韌 and Peng Hongjun 彭洪俊. 2013. "Lun Mingchao xinan bianjiang de junguan jimi diqu" 論明朝西南邊疆的軍管羈縻地區 [Military Loose Rein Regions of the Southwest Border Region during the Ming Period]. *Zhongguo bianjiang shidi yanjiu* 中國邊疆史地研究 1: 30–9.

Lukacs, Gabor. 2014. "Da Ming sheng guo (sic): An Important Little Known Seventeenth Century Manuscript Map of China." *The British Cartographic Society* 51(1): 52–62.

Ma Shunping 馬順平. 2008. "Mingdai Shanxi xingdusi jiqi weisuo jianzhi kaoshi" 明代陝西行都司及其衛所建置考實 [An Examination of the Establishment of the Provincial Regional Military Commission of Shaanxi and Its Garrisons during the Ming Period]. *Zhongguo lishi dili luncong* 中國歷史地理論叢 23 (2): 109–17.

Ma Shunping 馬順平. 2011. "Mingdai dusi weisuo renkou shue xintan: fangzhizhong liangzu Mingdai Shanxi xingdusi renkou shuju de pingjia" 明代都司衛所人口數額新探：方志中兩組明代陝西行都司人口數據的評價 [A Reexamination of the Population Figures of the Garrisons of Regional Military Commissions of the Ming Period: An Appraisal of Two Sets of Population Data in Local Gazetteers for the Shaanxi Provincial Regional Military Commission during the Ming Period]. *Suzhou keji xueyuan xuebao* 蘇州科技學院學報 (shehui kexue ban 社會科學版) 28(4): 49–54.

Mote, Frederick. 1974. "The T'u-mu Incident." In: *Chinese Ways in Warfare*, ed. Frank Kierman and John Fairbank, 243–72. Cambridge: Harvard University Press.

Mote, Frederick. 1988. "The Ch'eng-hua and Hung-chih reigns, 1465–1505." In: *The Cambridge History of China. Volume 7: The Ming Dynasty, Part One*, ed. Denis Twitchett and Frederick Mote, 343–402. Cambridge: Cambridge University Press.

Okada Hidehiro. 1999. "China as a Successor State to the Mongols." In: *The Mongol Empire and Its Legacy*, ed. Reuven Amitai-Preiss and David Morgan, 260–72. Leiden: Brill.

Park Hyunhee. 2012. *Mapping the Chinese and Islamic Worlds: Cross-Cultural Exchange in Premodern Asia*. Cambridge: Cambridge University Press.

Peng Jianying 彭建英. 2004. "Mingdai jimi weisuo zhidu" 明代羈縻衛所制度述論 [An Overview of the Loose-reign Garrison System of the Ming Period], *Zhongguo bianjiang shidi yanjiu* 中國邊疆史地研究 14(3): 24–36.

Perdue, Peter. 2015. "1557: A Year of Some Significance." In *Asia Inside Out: Changing Times*, ed. Eric Tagliacozzo, Helen Siu, and Peter Perdue, 90–111. Cambridge, MA: Harvard University Press.

Pines, Yuri. 2005. "Beasts or Humans: Pre-Imperial Origins of the 'Sino-Barbarian' Dichotomy." In *Mongols, Turks, and Others*, ed. Reuven Amitai and Michal Biran, 59–102. Leiden: Brill.

Robinson, David. 2009. *Empire's Twilight: Northeast Asia under the Mongols*. Cambridge, MA: Harvard University Asia Center.

Robinson, David. 2013. *Martial Spectacles of the Ming Court*. Cambridge, MA: Harvard University Asia Center.

Robinson, David. 2015. "Chinese Border Garrisons in a Transnational Context: Liaodong under the Early Ming Dynasty." In: *Chinese and Indian Warfare – From the Classical Age to 1870*, ed. Peter Lorge and Kaushik Roy, 57–73. New York: Routledge.

Robinson, David. 2019. *In the Shadow of the Mongol Empire: Ming China and Eurasia*. New York: Cambridge University Press.

Robinson, David. 2020. *Ming China and Their Allies: Imperial Rulership in Eurasia*. New York: Cambridge University Press.

Rossabi, Morris. 1982. *The Jurchens in the Yüan and Ming*. Ithaca, NY: China-Japan Program, Cornell University.

Rossabi, Morris. 1988. *Khubilai Khan*. Berkeley, CA: University of California Press.

Rossabi, Morris. 1998. "The Ming and Inner Asia." In *The Cambridge History of China. Vol. 8, The Ming Dynasty, 1368–1644, part 2*, ed. Denis Twitchett and Frederick Mote, 222–271. Cambridge: Cambridge University Press.

Scott, James. 1998. *Seeing Like a State: How Certain Schemes to Improve Human Condition Have Failed*. New Haven, CT: Yale University Press.

Serruys, Henry. 1955a. "The Mongols of Kansu During the Ming." *Mélanges chinois et bouddhiques* 10: 215–346.

Serruys, Henry. 1955b. *Sino-Jürced Relations during the Yung-lo Period (1403–1424)*. Wiesbaden: Harrassowitz.

Serruys, Henry. 1959. "Mongol Ennobled during the Early Ming." *Harvard Journal of Asiatic Studies* 22: 209–60.

Shin, Leo. 2006a. "The Last Campaigns of Wang Yangming." *T'oung-pao* 92(1–3): 101–28.

Shin Leo. 2006b. *The Making of the Chinese State: Ethnicity and Expansion on the Ming Borderlands*. Cambridge: Cambridge University Press.

Song Lian宋濂 (1310–1381). 1999. "Guo chao ming chen xu song" 國朝名臣序頌, *Qian xi qian ji* 潛溪前集. In *Song Lian quanji* 宋濂全集, 4 vols. Rpt. Hangzhou: Zhejiang guji chubanshe.

Su Tianjue 蘇天爵 (1294–1352), ed. 1993. *Yuan wen lei* 元文類. *Wenyuange Siku quanshu* edition. Shanghai: Shanghai chubanshe, vol. 1367.

Swope, Kenneth. 2005. "A Few Good Men: The Li Family and China's Northern Frontier in the Late Ming." *Ming Studies* 34: 34–81.

Swope, Kenneth. 2008. "Bestowing the Double-Edged Sword: Wanli as Supreme Military Commander." In *Culture, Courtiers, and Competition: The Ming Court (1368–1644)*, ed. David Robinson, 61–115. Cambridge: Harvard University Asia Center.

Ueda Makoto 上田信. 2005. *Umi to teikoku: Min Shin jidai* 海と帝国：明清時代 [The Seas and Empire: The Ming and Qing Periods]. Tokyo: Kōdansha.

Wade, Geoff. 2005. "The Zheng He Voyages: A Reassessment." *Journal of the Malaysian Branch of the Royal Asiatic Society* 78(1): 37–58.

Wade, Geoff. 2008. "Engaging the South: Ming China and Southeast Asia in the Fifteenth Century." *Journal of the Economic & Social History of the Orient* 51 (4): 578–638.

Waldron, Arthur. 1990. *The Great Wall of China*. Cambridge: Cambridge University Press.

Wills, John. 1998. "Relations with Maritime Europeans, 1514–1662." In *The Cambridge History of China. Volume 8, The Ming Dynasty (1368–1644), Part Two*, ed. Denis Twitchett and Frederick Mote, 333–75. Cambridge: Cambridge University Press.

Wu Zhihe 吳智和. 1982. "Mingdai Zhengtong guobian yu Jingtai xingfu" 明代正統國變與景泰興復 [The Zhengtong Incident and the Jingtai Restoration of the Ming Period]. *Shixue huikan* 史學彙刊 8 (1977); rev. version rpt. in *Mingshi yanjiu luncong* 明史研究論叢 [Collected Essays in Ming History], ed. Wu Zhihe, vol. 1: 159–241. Taibei: Dali chubanshe.

Xiao Lijun 肖立軍. 2010. *Mingdai shengzhen yingbingzhi yu difang zhixu* 明代省鎮營兵制與地方秩序 [The Provincial Garrison System of the Ming Period and Local Order]. Tianjin: Tianjin guji chubanshe.

Yang Zhengtai 楊正泰. 1994. *Mingdai yizhan kao* 明代驛站考 [The Postal Relay System of the Ming Period]. Shanghai: Shanghai guji chubanshe.

Yu Xiuqing 于秀情. 2010. *Mingchao jingying Baiyi yanjiu* 明朝經營百夷研究 [The Ming Dynasty's Governance of Baiyi]. Beijing: Zhongyang minzu daxue chubanshe.

Zhang Xie 張燮 (1574–1640). 2000. *Dong xi yang kao* 東西洋考. In *Xi yang chao gong lu jiaozhu: Dong xi yang kao* 西洋朝貢典錄校注：東西洋考. Punctuated by Xie Fang 謝方. Beijing: Zhongguo shuju.

Zhou Shaochuan 周少川. 2008. "Yuanchao de kaifang yishi yu yuwaishi yanjiu" 元朝的開放意識與域外史研究 [The Yuan Dynasty's Sense of Openness and Research into the History of Territories Beyond the Realm]. *Hebei xuekan* 河北學刊 28(5): 78–85.

Zhou Song 周松. 2008. *Mingchu Hetao zhoubian bianzheng yanjiu* 明初河套周邊邊政研究 [Border Policies in the Ordos Region during the Early Ming Period]. Lanzhou: Gansu renmin chubanshe.

Zhu Siben 朱思本 (1273–1336?). 2004. "Yu di tu zi xu" 輿地圖自序. In *Quan Yuan wen* 全元文, Vol. 31, 60 vols. Nanjing: Fenghuang chubanshe, *juan* 1006.

9   The Expansion of the Qing Empire Before 1800

Matthew W. Mosca

Why did the Qing Empire expand to the limits it achieved, and how did it maintain its vast territory? Historians addressing these questions now have access to a richer stock of sources and a wider range of historiographical perspectives than ever before, a development that has shed new light on the empire but also eroded past certainties and raised new questions. Rather than a comprehensive narrative of Qing conquest and rule, or a review of current research trends, this brief essay offers an interpretation of Qing expansion. In particular, it asks why such a contradictory range of understandings of the Qing imperial project have been put forward, and what elements make a historiographical consensus elusive.

The seed that grew into the Qing Empire emerged in 1583, when Nurhaci (1559–1626) inherited control of a lineage within one of several confederations of Jurchens (a people his son Hung Taiji [r. 1626–43] would formally rename Manchu in 1635). When this embryonic power crossed the imperial threshold can be debated, but certainly no later than 1644, when much of northern China was added to Manchuria and Manchu-controlled southern (Inner) Mongolia.[1] Several dates could likewise be advanced for the apex of imperial expansion. Most common is 1759, when the Tarim Basin was incorporated as southern Xinjiang, but some postpone it to the implementation of tighter control over Tibet in 1793. Since Qing expansion lasted for well over a century by even the strictest definition, and over two by looser criteria, it must be studied with sensitivity to its changing character.

In most cases, the Qing expanded by subordinating once-independent leaders (or their more pliable relatives or peers), who acknowledged submission and accepted certain obligations and forms of control.[2] Nominal submission

---

[1] Possible pre-1644 dates for the achievement of imperial status are 1622, when Nurhaci absorbed Liaodong and controlled both a large Chinese agrarian population and some subordinate Mongol allies, and 1636, when his son Hung Taiji made major administrative reforms and changed the regime's name to Qing (Li 2002, 9–72).

[2] For the early stages of this process see Di Cosmo 2002.

316

alone is not a useful criterion for determining the bounds of the empire, however, because the Qing state viewed virtually all rulers with whom it had contact as formal subordinates. Historians have thus tended to distinguish rulers who became actual subjects, their territories incorporated into the realm and their continued tenure in office contingent on imperial consent, from rulers outside the empire who acknowledged very limited forms of Qing suzerainty – often simply participating in the rituals now called the "tributary system" – without substantive Qing oversight of their domestic affairs or foreign relations. Institutions are the surest guide to this distinction: within Qing territory, local conditions were regularly monitored by representatives appointed by the center. For example, while Tibet and Korea both enjoyed almost total autonomy in their internal affairs, Qing officials resided only in Lhasa, not Seoul. Thus, Tibet lay within the Qing Empire, Korea outside it.

9.1   Qing Concepts of Borders

The concept of a border marked by an exact point or line was by no means alien to the Qing state; both posts and fences were erected at various sites, although no standardized system of border marking was shared on all frontiers.[3] Although artificial markers were installed, the limits of Qing territory were most commonly identified by natural landmarks, such as coasts, rivers, mountain peaks, or passes. A gap frequently existed between the boundary of claimed possession and the actual limit of regular patrol by Green Standard army posts in China proper and lines of guard posts (called *karun*) in Inner Asia. Arrangements for such a *cordon sanitaire* varied. In Manchuria, a long Willow Palisade was maintained to keep Qing subjects residing in its more densely settled parts away from the Korean border (and out of lucrative wilderness). In the far west, two separate seasonal borderlines of guard posts were negotiated with the nomadic Kazakhs, both well within the nominal Qing territorial claim marked with posts of wood and stone (Levey 2013, 181–209). In some areas, indigenous inhabitants were responsible for border patrols. There were also instances in which peoples nominally under Qing rule might be simultaneously claimed as subjects of another regime.[4]

The Qing state was well aware that precise borders could be demarcated on maps. However, to my knowledge it did not maintain before 1800 a single master-map that authoritatively recorded the exact limits of all its territories.

[3] The treaties of Nerchinsk (1689) and Kiakhta (1727) made provisions for boundary markers (Mancall 1971, 280–3, 302–10). A stele was erected to clarify the Qing-Chosŏn border on Changbaishan/Paektu-san in 1712, with a fence added later (Schmid 2007).
[4] For instance, Sakhalin was regarded as Qing territory, but also claimed by the Matsumae domain of Tokugawa Japan: (Li and Cribb 2014, 43); similarly, parts of Sipsongpanna accepted both Qing and Burmese jurisdiction (Giersch 2006, 36, 99).

Charts detailing individual frontier zones existed, but whether a comprehensive collection of them was maintained remains to be determined.[5] Information about border zones varied greatly. Some were established through careful negotiation and maintained by regular inspection; elsewhere, particularly in remote areas where no major threat was anticipated, it seems likely that the Qing state was unsure of its precise territorial claims, which were often based on inherited local conventions.

Ideally, a study of the Qing frontier would record how Qing possession was established, maintained, and adjusted, mile by mile.[6] In lieu of such painstaking detail, is it possible to identify an explanatory master-principle guiding Qing expansion? Geography is a tempting candidate, since the Chinese coast and the peaks of the Himalayas and Pamirs mark formidable natural boundaries. Yet if the Qing had not overcome other substantial features, such as the Gobi, the Altai and Tianshan ranges, and the mountains separating central Tibet from Sichuan and Gansu, these might now equally be viewed as the empire's "natural" boundaries. Moreover, to the north with Russia (where the Amur River was rejected as a boundary), to the northwest with the Kazakhs, and to the south and southwest with neighbors like Burma and Vietnam, geographic features served more as a convenient peg on which to hang boundaries than an obstacle commanding them. So varied were Qing territories, which ranged from temperate farmland to desert, from subtropical jungle to Himalayan plateau, that it is difficult to view its expansion as a pursuit of a specific terrain or resource.[7] Climate and topography influenced how closely the Qing could police a particular border area, and the environmental history of Qing expansion is now taking its rightful place as a particular focus of research (Bello 2016; Schlesinger 2017). Still, for all geography's importance, it did not determine the limits of imperial expansion.

Are military or economic factors more compelling? Unlike the Mongol Empire, where famous defeats revealed an appetite for expansion beyond even its unprecedented size, few Qing military reverses permanently thwarted

---

[5] The Kangxi (r. 1661–1721), Yongzheng (r. 1722–35), and Qianlong (r. 1736–95) emperors commissioned excellent survey maps of Qing and foreign territory, but these marked only some borders. World maps drafted in Beijing on European models did mark all Qing boundaries, but there is no evidence that they were used for strategic planning or diplomacy. Maps of individual border zones seem to have been commissioned as necessary, not kept in a comprehensive and routinely updated collection.

[6] One fascinating example of such a micro-study is the "strange case of Dulong" (Wills 2012, 457–64).

[7] J. R. McNeill (1998, 34) has noted that because the Qing state encompassed a range of climatic zones surpassed only by some European maritime empires, its "portfolio of ecological diversity translated into insurance and resilience for the state." However beneficial this ecological diversity was, there is no evidence that its pursuit factored into imperial determinations to expand the empire. No territory added by the Qing to the Ming realm could have substantially alleviated crop or revenue shortfalls elsewhere in the empire.

the acquisition of a region clearly targeted for incorporation.[8] Exceptions could be proposed, but Qing policy was not simply to test its military power to the limit, still less conquer the world. Unlike Russian expansion eastward across Siberia or European expansion westward across North America, Qing state control did not follow in the wake of subjects moving outward in search of resources. When Han Chinese did pursue resources into territory not already under Qing rule, thus escaping imperial control, emperors were inclined to hinder them (by contrast, internal Han Chinese migration into non-Han territory drew a more nuanced cost–benefit analysis). Overseas migration was not encouraged, and while it was known that many Chinese lived in maritime Southeast Asia, no attempt was made to use their presence for territorial expansion.[9] Qing emperors were keenly interested in the finances and revenue potential of their frontier areas, and "cooperation with merchants was part of the Qing imperial program" for extracting revenue and resources in frontier regions (Giersch 2014, 370). Nonetheless, rulers did not expand the empire's external boundaries to promote commerce or capture new revenue streams.[10]

Historical exemplars offer another approach. Virtually all Qing territory had at one time or another been subject to an earlier empire whose capital was located in China proper. Still, no predecessor had simultaneously controlled the exact array of lands conquered by the Qing. Of the three dynasties the Manchu emperors did in some sense claim to succeed, the Jurchen Jin and the Ming were too small to serve as useful guides, and the sprawling Mongol Empire too large. Although the Yuan component of the Mongol realm comes closest as a territorial precursor (Biran [Chapter 6], this volume), and Qing rulers recognized this commonality, there is little evidence that they looked to the Yuan as a specific spatial precedent when considering the optimal boundaries of their own realm. A historical approach is most useful at the local level, as many imperial boundaries were inherited at the time of conquest, and therefore the precise contours of the frontier must often be sought in the political history of a region before the arrival of Qing power. Illuminating in detail, historical precedent does not offer a coherent rationale for the empire's ultimate extent.

[8] Qing armies certainly experienced defeat beyond the empire's frontiers, for instance in Burma and Vietnam, but these were expeditionary forces, not aiming for incorporation.

[9] Qianlong was aware of the 1740 massacre of overseas Chinese in Batavia, and later investigated the role of Chinese in Siam (and the small, independent polity of Ha Tien) during his war with Burma (Masuda 2007). The Ming loyalist roots of many overseas communities darkened Beijing's view of them, but there is no reason to think that they would otherwise have been an instrument of Qing expansion.

[10] Kwangmin Kim (2016) argues that expansion into southern Xinjiang was a "collaborative process" between local begs and the Qing state, underpinned by a mutual interest in commercial development. Although the Qing government was concerned with facilitating commerce and increasing revenue in the region after 1759, there is little evidence that economic factors were decisive in the initial incorporation of these territories.

Perhaps the most persuasive explanation of Qing expansion is to regard it as an imperial project to dominate both China and the Mongols. The latter enterprise expanded over time to include not only the Oirats (regarded by the Qing state as a subgroup among the Mongols), but also non-Mongol territories such as Tibet and the Tarim Basin, both conquered from Oirat control. This interpretation has heuristic value but also pitfalls, notably the fact that while Ming China was a bounded entity occupied by Qing forces within a fairly brief period, the Qing conquest of the Mongols proceeded fitfully over a far longer period, during which the boundaries of the Mongol territories targeted for expansion fluctuated. Still, examining the method by which the Qing state incorporated both China and Inner Asia permits fruitful comparison with the "grand strategies" of other regimes ruling China proper (cf. Pines and Robinson [Chapters 2 and 8], this volume). In this comparative context, what distinguished Qing rule was the duration and intensity of its efforts – surpassing even those of the Tang (618–907) and the Mongol Yuan – to directly integrate Inner Asia as a carefully-regulated and constantly-monitored part of the realm.

In sum, no single geographic, military, strategic, economic, or historical key unlocks the political decisions of Qing emperors and their advisers; each played a guiding but not determining role in imperial expansion, its importance depending on the shifting political context of the moment. Before turning to that context, however, we must consider an ongoing debate over the values and outlook of the Qing leadership.

9.2   The Qing as Empire: Historiographical Perspective

Western scholarship typically divides the Qing Empire into China (or China proper) and Inner Asia, and it has long accepted that Qing expansion and rule combined Chinese and Inner Asian elements. What has come to be disputed is the relative position of the Chinese element in policy-making. Although Nurhaci acknowledged subordination to the Ming early in his career, the statelet he established in the 1580s was not meaningfully Chinese or part of China. By 1911, however, the Qing central government was widely seen as Chinese in its political and cultural norms, even if the Manchu origin of its rulers galled Han revolutionaries.[11] At what point between 1583 and 1911 did an empire that emerged from Inner Asia to conquer China become the vehicle by which China sought to incorporate Inner Asia? A transformation in Qing political identity has been posited at various points: with efforts in the 1630s to partially adopt Ming models of central government, with the transfer of the

---

[11] The 1911 letter in which Khalkha Mongol leaders sought Russian support for their independence complained that, "recently the Han Chinese bureaucrats have grabbed the political power [of the Qing]" (Nakami 1984, 133).

capital to Beijing in 1644, with the reigns of the Shunzhi (r. 1643–61) or Kangxi (r. 1661–1722) emperors, with the 19th century when, in the words of Joseph Fletcher (1978, 35), Inner Asia "commenced being slowly absorbed into an expanding China and began to come under the influence of Han Chinese culture," and with the New Policies of the last decade of dynastic rule. Proposing such a turning-point assumes that one can identify essential criteria of "Chineseness" and "Inner Asian-ness" across centuries, but there is little consensus over how to do so while making due allowance for the internal variety of both and their mutual influence. Nor is there consensus over what gave the empire its identity: the values and orientation of individual emperors, the shifting composition of their trusted advisers, or an evolving balance of power among its constituent regions.

Before the 1990s, historians offered varying conceptions of Qing governance (perhaps most famously John K. Fairbank's concept of Manchu-Han "dyarchy"[12]), but this was not a particular focus of debate. It was widely accepted that the political history of the Qing Empire – then generally termed Qing China or the Qing dynasty – demonstrated progressive Sinicization by adopting the norms of the preceding Ming dynasty. This view took for granted that in aspiring to conquer China, a Jurchen-Manchu leadership (regarded in this interpretation as relatively primitive) recognized the superiority of China's institutions and ideology. It was not denied that Manchu rulers were also concerned with controlling Inner Asians, principally Mongols, but this was regarded as a means to better ensure the conquest of China. To protect its Chinese core, the Qing state followed Chinese precedent and built an Inner Asian security buffer. Moreover, it was widely accepted that while Manchu rulers became sincere admirers of Confucian values, they cynically manipulated Inner Asians by catering to their supposedly more primitive political and religious outlooks. This view, it should be noted, was inherited by 20th-century historians from Confucian observers centuries earlier. Thus, in a formative 1941 study, Fairbank and S. Y. Têng (1941, 135, 158–9) acknowledged that Manchus indeed "modified" Ming foreign relations, but despite these changes Inner Asia was managed "through the forms of the ancient tributary system" inherited from China, with Qing rulers seeking "reverent barbarian submission." A quarter-century later, Ping-ti Ho (1967, 190–1)was more emphatic that even before 1644 Manchu rulers chose "a policy of systematic sinicization" but nonetheless shrewdly developed "a basic long-range policy" to control the Mongols.

Only in retrospect have the unexamined assumptions vitiating the Sinicization model become apparent, most notably vagueness about how the process functioned (Elliott 2011). Because this interpretation of the orientation

---

[12] Fairbank (1953, 40) suggested that the Qing state was a "'synthesis' between the Chinese and their highly Sinicized rulers," amounting to a "sort of dyarchy."

of Qing rulers was based chiefly on their behavior in China proper, it began to be undermined as interest shifted to the Qing Empire as a whole. The first major blow was landed by David M. Farquhar (1968), who pointed out that Qing relations with the Mongols before 1691 owed little to Chinese precedents but conformed closely to Mongolian political ideals. A decade later he sketched out a fuller picture, proposing that emperors tried to "segregate differing policies" toward various imperial peoples, presenting themselves as bodhisattvas to Tibetans and Mongols, but not to Chinese and Manchus. Still, Farquhar (1978, 33) had no doubt that "the Manchu rulers had early decided that their most important economic and political interests lay in China, and that their most visible religio-political image was to be Chinese and Confucian." In the 1990s a more comprehensive challenge to the Sinicization interpretation emerged.[13] As Evelyn Rawski (1996, 833) put it in 1996, "the key to Qing success, at least in terms of empire-building, lay in its ability to use its cultural links with the non-Han peoples of Inner Asia and to differentiate the administration of the non-Han regions from the administration of the former Ming provinces." In other words, it was precisely by *not* looking to Ming institutions that the Manchus incorporated multiple subject groups via flexible policies with no obvious Chinese analogues. This interpretation of the empire stresses that it was composed of distinct zones governed by judicious compromise between the Qing need for centralized oversight and the varied expectations of indigenous leaders. China was only one conquered territory, its scholar-officials only one subordinated local elite. Qing rulers did not identify with any conquered population, nor attempt to homogenize their subjects based on any one civilizational model, but rather maintained internal political and cultural boundaries and adopted different "personae" toward different "constituencies" (Crossley 1999, 44).

This reinterpretation of Qing rule was driven in part by a more extensive use of non-Chinese sources. When Qing policy choices were explained in Chinese, the rhetoric was often similar to that employed by the Ming. Because historians of China took the lead in interpreting Qing governance, these Chinese sources tended to be regarded as the authentic voice of Qing rulers, sufficient on their

---

[13] This development has come to be termed "New Qing History." Studies seen in retrospect to mark the start of this approach began to be published around 1990 and emphasized the importance of the Manchu role in Qing history. The earliest review of the field to identify "new scholarship" tending in this direction was a 1996 essay by Evelyn Rawski. James Millward in his 1998 monograph identified a "new approach" that paid more attention to the "Manchu-ness of the Qing" and did not conflate the Qing and China (Millward 1998, 14–15). The term "New Qing History" appeared with Joanna Waley-Cohen's (2004) review of monographs published between 1997 and 2001. Although now a loose label for studies stressing ethnicity, imperialism, and colonialism, especially with regard to the Manchus and Inner Asia, relatively few authors have explicitly designated their work "New Qing History," and some have disavowed the term. The Sinicization thesis, now a minority perspective in American and European scholarship, still has its proponents (Huang 2011).

own to explain the imperial outlook. Scholars of Inner Asian history have long been familiar with Mongolian, Manchu, and Tibetan sources, in which non-Han ideologies were more prominent. They, however, tended to be regional specialists who rarely ventured a conceptualization of the Qing state as a whole (Farquhar being an exception). Only recently has the large-scale availability of Manchu sources, coupled with new attention to evidence in other languages, led to a focus on facets of Qing rule obscured in Chinese sources. Though they remain crucial, materials in Chinese can no longer be used alone to interpret the Qing Empire.

Because the political identities imputed to Qing emperors by historians have greatly influenced understandings of the motivations behind imperial expansion, the current moment of conceptual fluidity suggests that new interpretations will continue to emerge. It is now untenable to view the Qing Empire, at least between 1600 and 1800, as simply a Chinese political project inherited and furthered by Manchu emperors. Yet understanding the empire as a solar system of isolated politico-cultural planets brought into the orbit of the imperial sun leaves many unanswered questions about the inter-action of different parts of the empire. One emerging approach emphasizes "Qing Cosmopolitanism," arguing that both rulers and subjects blended multiple political and cultural frameworks into new formulations that were not simply Chinese or Inner Asian, but Qing.[14] This approach does not preclude the finding that some cultural commonalities could emerge from Chinese political concepts influencing Inner Asia (Atwood 2000). Another approach concentrates on administration, suggesting that while the Qing state neither promoted Sinicization in Inner Asia nor viewed Chinese norms as superior, it did seek increasingly centralized and standardized control, inject-ing into Inner Asian governance "an expert and efficient bureaucratic appar-atus" (Di Cosmo 2009, 361). Since such centralized control was achieved primarily by employing Chinese administrative precedents and bureaucratic technologies (notably the extensive use of documents and multiple layers of review), even a culturally neutral search for greater control in effect promoted Chinese political norms.[15] Finally, some historians are beginning to ask how the Inner Asian and Chinese frontiers functioned in coordination, with

---

[14] Johan Elverskog (2011, 245) has argued that, "rather than generating ethnic cantons as often imagined, Qing rule actually fostered the crossing of boundaries, a mixing and fusion, and ultimately the creation of new forms that defined a distinctive Qing culture."

[15] Dorothea Heuschert (1998) argues that while the Qing did not have a "civilizing mission" in regard to the Mongols, efforts to enforce centralized, bureaucratic control nonetheless led Chinese legal norms to be increasingly imposed on Mongolia. In her study of Qing imperial institutions, Evelyn Rawski (1998) has also emphasized the progressive bureaucratization of the imperial household and the Eight Banners. Max Oidtmann (2018) has studied the application of a Chinese bureaucratic procedure, drawing lots from an urn, to determine succession in Tibetan Buddhist incarnation lineages.

reference to foreign policy, intelligence gathering, and scholarship, and how the Qing operated as an integrated empire in the face of large-scale threats and crises (Mosca 2013, 2014; Herman 2014). In short, historians continue to grapple with the relationship between empire-wide commonalities and obvious regional specificity. If scholarship over the past decades has tended to accentuate the latter by concentrating on the differences among the political and ideological tethers linking elites to the imperial court, there appears to be a growing interest in examining how China and Inner Asia, during and after the period of expansion, were shaped by common trends within an integrated imperial entity.

9.3   The Process of Qing Expansion

Although the division of Qing territory into China (or China proper) and Inner Asia commonly used by historians approximates the empire's main administrative division, it does not reflect Qing political terms and concepts. Administratively, China proper corresponds to the *junxian* mode of administration, a hierarchy of nested territorial units, the largest of which were provinces (*zhisheng*), overseen by centrally appointed officials routinely transferred between positions. These territories were China in that their boundaries were, with a few exceptions, those of Ming China; and the vast majority of officials and inhabitants within this system identified with Chinese (*Hua, Huaxia*) cultural traditions. By contrast, Inner Asia, a term wholly alien to Qing-era usage that includes Manchuria, Mongolia, Tibet, Qinghai (Köke-naghur), and Xinjiang (Map 9.1), had no single administrative system. Aside from Manchuria, these regions did share a common relationship to one Beijing-based agency, the Lifanyuan, which mediated between them and the throne.[16] However, the local elites supervised by this agency followed a diversity of procedures for judicial matters, taxation, and administration (Di Cosmo 2009).

The majority of Inner Asian territory was governed by some permutation of the *jasagh*-banner system, with the significant exceptions of central Tibet, the Turkic Muslim settlements of the Tarim Basin, most of Manchuria, and the fraction of Inner Mongolia kept under direct central control. First implemented in 1635, this *jasagh*-banner administrative structure warrants special attention as the earliest and most widespread form of Qing territorial

---

[16] The original name of the Lifanyuan, which dates back at least to 1634, and possibly earlier, was the *Monggo yamun* ("Mongol Office"); this link was maintained in the Mongolian name for the agency, *ghadaghadu mongghol-un törö-yi jasaqu yabudal-un yamun* (translated by Nicola Di Cosmo as "Court of Administration of the Autonomous Mongolian States"), but not in its Manchu or Chinese equivalents. Di Cosmo discusses the complexities of translating the name Lifanyuan, which he and others now tend to leave untranslated (Di Cosmo 2009, 343).

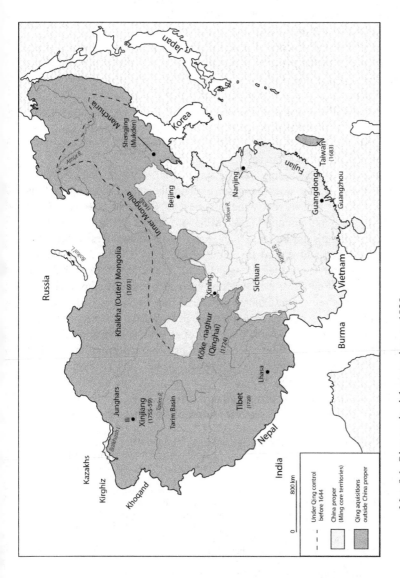

Map 9.1 Qing territorial expansion, to 1820.

jurisdiction in Inner Asia. At its height, it covered, with adjustments for local circumstances, Inner and Khalkha (Outer) Mongolia, and Oirats in Qinghai and northern Xinjiang. Significantly, when in 1697 Kangxi first extended direct rule over local leaders in what would later become eastern Xinjiang, he chose to incorporate them into *jasagh*-banners as well.[17] Only after 1720 did the Qing first attempt to control a major part of Inner Asia, central Tibet, without recourse to the *jasagh*-banner institution. Given its chronological precedence and geographic predominance, the *jasagh*-banner can be regarded as the primary mode of administration in Inner Asia, comparable to the *junxian* system of China proper. The fact that both the Lifanyuan and *jasagh*-banner system were created to govern the Mongols buttresses the view, supported by very early evidence, that the Qing Empire was originally divided into Mongol and Chinese territorial spheres.[18]

Understanding the emerging Qing Empire as an effort to dominate both China and the Mongols does much to explain the logic and limits of its expansion. Once it embarked on the conquest of China in 1644, the Qing state quickly set about conquering all Ming provinces; by the end of 1646 troops had entered distant Fujian, Guangdong, and Sichuan. Resistance from multiple foes ebbed and flowed for almost four decades before all of Ming territory was securely controlled. Despite the enormous, almost overwhelming effort this conquest entailed, the Qing government seems never to have considered conquering only some Chinese provinces and allowing a rival regime to coexist in others. This had an obvious strategic rationale: the persistence of rival regimes would preclude stable control over the Qing portion of China. Dorgon himself made this point in 1644, doubtless influenced by the ideal of a "Great Unity" inherited from earlier Chinese dynasties (an ideal elucidated by Yuri Pines in chapter 2, this volume).[19] The suppression of all organized opposition within the *junxian* provinces after the defeat of the Three Feudatories rebellion (1681) and the surrender of the Zheng regime on

---

[17] In 1697 Kangxi introduced the *jasagh*-banner system to Hami, and in 1733 Emin Khwāja was put in charge of a *jasagh*-banner after leading a group of refugees from Turfan into Gansu. Only after 1755 did the Qing abandon the *jasagh*-banner system in the settled Turkic oasis cities of Xinjiang (Brophy 2008).

[18] Nurhaci, in a 1622 entry in the *Old Manchu Archives* (*Manwen laodang*), stated that his power had united the Jurchens, Chinese, and Mongols (see Fitzgerald, 2016). A lingering indication of the centrality of the original Mongol *jasagh*-banner territories in Qing Inner Asia is the fact that the first gazetteer of the realm (*Da Qing yitong zhi*, preface 1744) lists the "51 banners of the *waifan* Mongols," that is, Inner Mongolia, and then lists all other parts of Qing territory in Inner Asia, such as the Khalkha, Qinghai, Tibet, Hami, and Turfan, as "Mongol dependencies" (*Menggu shuguo*).

[19] Already in 1644, Dorgon aimed at the "unification" of all Ming territory (Wakeman 1985, 402–9). The initial decision to cede considerable autonomy to the Three Feudatories in southern and western China as "almost independent regional strongholds" was an acceptance that Eight Banner forces could not secure all of China immediately after 1644. However, these territories were always considered part of China under direct Qing control (Oxnam 1975, 141–5).

Taiwan (1683) did indeed eliminate large-scale challenges to Qing rule in China proper for over a century.[20] Moreover, positing that Qing forces had the limited aim of conquering only the *junxian* provinces of Ming China rather than the general aim of expanding wherever possible helps to explain the decision not to attempt to exert direct Qing control over mainland Southeast Asia even when a Qing army pushed deep into Burma in pursuit of a Ming pretender to the throne (1661–2).[21] The only augmentation of Ming China effected during the Qing conquest was the expansion of direct control over the plains of western Taiwan, but since this territory was taken from the ethnically-Chinese, nominally Ming-loyalist Zheng regime it could be viewed as already in some sense part of China. Indeed, the Qing rejected Zheng attempts to have Taiwan recognized as a foreign country along the lines of Korea precisely because of these Chinese origins (Cheng 2013, 230, 242).

Expansion in Inner Asia was not an exact analogy to the effort to secure all of China. Whereas the *junxian* system had given China a clear administrative identity before 1644, Inner Asia had none. Compared to the conquest of China, that of Inner Asia was slow and fitful. By 1620 a rivalry had developed between the Qing and the Chakhar Mongol leader Ligdan Khan, ending in 1634 with Qing domination over Inner Mongolia. Almost immediately, Hung Taiji asserted his right to rule the Khalkha, the closest and most obviously Mongol bloc outside of his direct control. Indeed, the next major Qing expansion was their absorption in 1691, after more than a half century of diplomatic overtures, tension, and sometimes open conflict. Given that Qing control over Inner Mongolia accelerated during Ligdan Khan's competing effort to unify it, and that the proximate cause of incorporating Khalkha territories was their invasion by the Junghars under Galdan (1644–1697), expansion could be seen not as a long-held strategy but as an *ad hoc* response to external threats. It would be desirable to know more about the perspective of Qing opponents: How far were the loose and short-lived Khalkha-Oirat alliance of 1640 and Galdan's subsequent invasion motivated by fear that the Qing intended to expand beyond Inner Mongolia (Lhamsuren 2010)? Did Galdan himself aspire to someday unify the Oirats, Khalkha, and Inner Mongols? At the very least, it is certain that the political ambitions of the Qing and their Inner Asian rivals evolved in relation to each other.

The question of intentionality thus distinguishes the Qing conquests of China and Inner Asia. By 1644, there was little doubt that Qing leaders knew the

---

[20] Before the turbulence of the period after 1795, the largest rebellions in China occurred on its fringes, notably the Zhu Yigui (1721) and Lin Shuangwen (1786–8) rebellions on Taiwan and Muslim rebellions in Gansu (1781 and 1784). The few rebellions that took place within China's core territories, for instance the Wang Lun rebellion of 1774, were less militarily formidable (Naquin 1981).

[21] Qing forces were more restrained in Southeast Asia than those of the Yuan and Ming, the latter of which attempted to make Annam a Chinese province (1407–27).

boundaries of China and wished to seize as much of it as possible. Their intentions toward Inner Asia were murkier, and often shifted within individual reigns. Mongolia south of the Gobi had been under Manchu rule for over fifty years before Kangxi defeated Galdan and gained the submission of the Khalkha. He made peace with Galdan's successor Tsewang Rabtan (d. 1727), only later to war with him and (again in response to a Junghar invasion) extend Qing control to Tibet. His son Yongzheng (r. 1723–35) extended direct rule over the Qoshud in Qinghai shortly after taking the throne, and then planned a massive, failed campaign to capture the Junghar homeland. Qianlong (r. 1736–95), who became emperor in the wake of this defeat, began with retrenchment, going so far as to negotiate a boundary with the Junghars in the Altai and permit them trade. Only later did internal strife give him the opportunity to launch a final conquest.

Nicola Di Cosmo (2009, 339) rightly cautions against imagining Qing expansion in Mongolia to be "manifest destiny." Still, there is reason to see it as something more than a series of defensive campaigns and opportunistic windfalls. Inner Asia was not taken in a fit of absence of mind, and even if the scope of Qing ambitions at any given time remain hard to know with certainty, certain trends and tendencies suggest that the ultimate absorption of the Oirats may have been imagined much earlier than 1755. One is the history of *jasagh*-banner administration. After his conquest of the Khalkha, Kangxi began on a tiny scale to create Oirat banners as well, beginning in 1697.[22] Yongzheng expanded their scope to include the conquered Qinghai Qoshud. In 1730, just before his campaign against them, Yongzheng demanded that the Junghars accept incorporation into a Khalkha-style *jasagh*-banner system (Shibuya 2011, 604). A severe defeat in this campaign forced Yongzheng, and later Qianlong, to deal with the Junghars as an independent power, but Qianlong ultimately did impose this administrative system on them.

Parallels with China are also illuminating. No rival Chinese regime was permitted to survive, but Qing forces were remarkably cautious about pushing beyond the Ming provinces: Korea was twice invaded by the early Jurchen-Manchu state, but not ruled directly; by 1800 expeditions had reached far into Burma, Annam, and Nepal, but no attempt was made to absorb them. Similarly, the Qing state did not attempt to apply the *jasagh*-banner system to non-Mongol and non-Oirat nomads such as the Kazakhs or Kirghiz. Aside from the lands due north of the Manchu homeland, all Qing conquests of non-Mongol and non-Oirat lands in Inner Asia, notably central Tibet and the Tarim Basin, were direct

---

[22] The first Oirat *jasagh*-banner was that created for the Qoshud Baghatur Erke Jinong in Alashan in 1697 (Qi Guang 2013, 81–90). I am indebted to Onuma Takahiro for this reference. Another was created for Danjin-Rabtan, a surrendered follower of Galdan, in 1703. I am indebted to Tsongol B. Natsagdorj for this information.

consequences of wars against the Junghars. A convincing interpretation of this is Peter Perdue's observation that "... the Qing could not tolerate a rival *Mongolian* Central Eurasian state. In this sense, Qing definitions of geopolitical strategy were cultural and even ethnic. All Mongolians had to be encompassed by the universal empire; but other peoples need not be" (Perdue 2005, 406). And indeed, just as control over all of China led to political stability, so did the conquest of the Junghars end major uprisings among Mongols and Oirats.[23]

Even if it is accepted that the absorption of the Oirats into the *jasagh*-banner system ended the impetus for expansion in Inner Asia, just as the conquest of the *junxian* provinces ended if further south, many issues require further research. One is why in 1757 Qianlong asserted his claim to the Tarim Basin on the grounds that he had inherited all Junghar lands, but seemingly had no interest in using the same argument to absorb Central Asian and Pamir territories once under nominal Junghar overlordship. Whether this is because such claims were nearly forgotten in 1757, or because Qianlong realized that his realm was at its infrastructural and financial limits, is a matter for future research. It is noteworthy that Xinjiang was not only the last major Qing conquest, but also the most controversial among Han literati, generating open fears of imperial overstretch and unprecedented opposition (Millward 1998, 38–43).

This final conquest of the Junghars did not complete Qing control over the Mongol world. Although the territory of the Russian-dominated Torghuts (Kalmyks) on the Volga was too remote to contemplate ruling directly, the migration of a large segment of them to Qing territory in 1771 was celebrated as a culminating step in gathering the Mongols under Qing rule. North of the Qing frontier, the Buriats constituted another fringe of the Mongol and Tibetan Buddhist world. Qianlong was aware of this, and at least considered an attempt to incorporate them, but judged the idea infeasible (Afinogenov 2016, 172). The Uriyangkhai living on the western edge of the northern border, although they spoke a Turkic language and lived a distinctive lifestyle in forested territories, were characterized as Mongols and organized into banners (Schlesinger 2012, 276–8). By contrast, although the Qing state was aware that the steppe-dwelling Kazakhs claimed Chinggisid heritage, they seem never to have regarded them as Mongols, and Qianlong from the beginning of his relations with them explicitly ruled out a *jasagh*-banner arrangement (Onuma

---

[23] These uprisings had at first been relatively frequent. In 1646 Tenggis of the Sönid Mongols renounced submission to the Qing and fled to the Khalkha; in 1675 Burni of the Chakhar rebelled after the Three Feudatories rebellion broke out in China. In the eighteenth century, the instigators of Mongol or Oirat rebellions and defections were in contact with the Junghars, expected their aid, or escaped to them, the most famous examples being Lobzang Danjin (1723–4); Lamajab (1732); and Chinggunjab (1756). After the Junghar conquest, Qing rule in Mongolia faced no major armed opposition.

2014, 157–84).[24] As these examples show, it means little to argue that the Qing aimed to control the Mongols or Mongolia, unless close attention is given to how the use of these labels shifted with time and circumstance (Crossley 2006).

Alternatively, Qing expansion in Inner Asia could be understood as an attempt to dominate not the Mongols and Oirats, but the Tibetan Buddhist oecumene. From the early 17th century onward, it is difficult to disentangle clashes among Mongol and Oirat rulers from the context of sectarian conflict in Tibet. As Peter Schwieger (2014, 75) has recently pointed out, not only were the Oirats much firmer supporters of the Gelukpa sect than were the Khalkhas or Manchus, but it is possible to see the Dalai Lama's conferral of the title Boshughtu Khan on Galdan in 1678 as an effort to give him "a leading position among the Mongols as a whole, a measure that ultimately brought Galdan into conflict with both the Qalqas [Khalkhas] and the Qing emperor."[25] The Qing were well aware of this, and Kangxi even suggested in 1696 that it was not Galdan who was most "responsible for the war in Inner Asia," but the Dalai Lama's regent (and de-facto successor), Sangs rgyas rgya mtsho (Sangye Gyatso) (Schwieger 2014, 95). From this perspective, then, the Qing-Oirat clash could be viewed as part of a larger civil war within the Tibetan Buddhist world. The balance of piety and political calculation in the interactions between the Qing state and the Tibetan Buddhist church is a particularly vexing problem for historians, because attempts to dominate the Mongol-Oirat world and to dominate the Tibetan Buddhist world were inseparable sides of the same process.

The *junxian* and *jasagh*-banner systems were not the totality of Qing administration. The Eight Banner system incorporated the Manchus and descendants of their earliest Chinese and Mongol allies into a distinct socio-political structure. It was not designed to exercise territorial jurisdiction, although banners and the Imperial Household Department owned vast agricultural and pastoral lands in China and Inner Asia, and some groups, notably the Chakhars, belonged to administrative units blending features of Eight and *jasagh*-banners. Rather, bannermen in Beijing and throughout the realm lived apart, subject primarily to the jurisdiction of their commanding officers (Elliott 2001, 197–200).

---

[24] Onuma (2014, 228–39) notes that between 1761 and 1778 Qing policy allowed small groups of Kazakhs to request resettlement within its territory. In 1778, a single independent Kazakh company (*niru*) was created, on the model of an Eight Banner company. No Kazakh *jasagh*-banner was created.

[25] From the Mongol perspective, legitimate khanship was normally restricted to descendants of the family of Chinggis Khan (the "Chinggisid principle"), excluding Oirat rulers. The Dalai Lama's decision to grant Galdan the title of Boshughtu Khan (variously translated as "King of Heavenly Destiny" or "Khan with the Mandate") in acknowledgment of his resolute defense of Tibetan Buddhism therefore represented both an alternative, religious form of political legitimation and a decision by the Dalai Lama to assist Galdan's political ambitions. Miyawaki Junko (1999) has however argued that Galdan's maternal links to the Qoshud, the only Oirat ruling family of Mongol origin, may have made it easier for him to legitimately hold the title of khan. His successors held the lower title of *khong tayiji*.

Like Manchu bannermen, Tibetan Buddhist clergy lived in many parts of the empire, but also outside the regular administration of those territories. In Tibet, Qinghai, and Mongolia, high-ranking reincarnate clergy or powerful monasteries controlled large territorial estates where they exercised secular authority, most prominently the vast estate or Great Shabi of the Jebtsundampa Khutughtu, the primate of the Khalkha. Unlike bannermen, Tibetan Buddhist clergy were not subject to one centralized hierarchy. The Lifanyuan was invested with the power to establish regulations for clergy, but how far its writ ran in practice has yet to be established.

Finding a suitable administrative formula for ruling central Tibet proved singularly difficult. It effectively remained a state-within-a-state, bound to the larger Qing polity primarily by religious ties and the oversight of Qing *ambans* ("residents") stationed in Lhasa.[26] Control was even looser in Khams, nominally split between central Tibet and Sichuan, but in reality dominated by local power-holders (Dai 2009, 124–35). Outside of central Tibet, many Tibetan-speaking peoples fell under the jurisdiction of either Oirat *jasagh*-banners, particularly in Qinghai, or the *junxian* system, notably in Sichuan, but also in Gansu and Yunnan (Oidtmann 2016).

Manchuria and Xinjiang were areas of particular administrative complexity. From the 1650s, Manchuria was effectively divided into a northern sphere (ruled in its mature form by two military governors supported by banner garrisons) and a southern sphere administered by a combination of military governor, the apparatus of the auxiliary capital at Shengjing, and the staff of a *junxian*-style prefecture. Some groups in Manchuria lived in administrative units that combined features of both Eight and *jasagh*-banners (Lee 1970; Kim 2019). The administration of Xinjiang was dominated in the north by *jasagh*-banners and large Eight Banner garrisons, and in the south by indigenous officials called *begs* who had jurisdiction over Muslim inhabitants. To some extent *beg* rule resembled the autonomy granted to central Tibet, since *begs* had great latitude in the everyday governance of Turkic Muslims, but since each was assigned to an individual settlement with no provision for conciliar *beg* jurisdiction over all of southern Xinjiang, and since the network of centrally-appointed officials was much denser there, it cannot be regarded as a state-within-a-state.

Compared to Inner Asia, the *junxian*-style provinces were far more administratively homogeneous. Apart from special measures taken in and around

---

[26] Qing rule in Tibet is notoriously controversial. In Petech's (1972, 19) balanced view, the dispatch by Kangxi of an official to aid the secular ruler of Tibet, Lajang Khan (1705–17), was "a first attempt to establish a sort of protectorate in Tibet," but one that ended with the official's return to Beijing in 1711. The mature form of Qing rule via *ambans* emerged in 1728 (Petech 1972, 156). Although the Qing state determined the structure of government in Tibet, changing it several times between 1720 and 1793, the effectiveness of its day-to-day oversight is hotly debated.

Beijing itself, the main administrative anomaly was the *tusi* system, which in some provinces operated in parallel to the regular bureaucracy. In the words of John Herman (2007, 105–6), "*tusi* offices were located along China's geopolitical periphery, *tusi* offices were filled almost exclusively by non-Han. . .and *tusi* offices were responsible primarily for governing an alien, non-Han population." This system, already in place at the time of Qing conquest, allowed indigenous leaders to maintain their authority even after their lands were nominally absorbed into provinces.

The administrative division between China and Inner Asia was never absolute, but since its evolution is not directly related to imperial expansion, only a few facets of it will be raised here. The largest transfer of territory between the two zones before 1800 occurred in Khams. Before central Tibet came under Qing control, its border with Sichuan lay at Dajianlu (Tibetan, Dar rtse mdo). To secure communication between China and Lhasa, the Qing state took the unusual step of bestowing *tusi* offices on local leaders who lay outside of a *junxian* province. In 1727, Yongzheng decided to transfer these *tusi* territories from the jurisdiction of Lhasa to that of Sichuan (Herman 2014, 81–92). The *tusi* instrument allowed for similar but less dramatic transfers of jurisdiction, which effectively augmented the provinces of Gansu and Yunnan (Ma 2008). A slightly different dynamic prevailed along the China–Mongolia frontier, where the in-migration of Chinese settlers was much more pronounced. There, the Qing dealt with the presence of Chinese subjects moving into *jasagh*-banner territory by establishing a *ting* (sub-prefecture) with jurisdiction only over Chinese migrants, thus establishing two forms of administration in a zone hitherto subject only to a *jasagh*-banner. This process began at the intersection of Mongolia and China in 1723, with the creation of Rehe *ting* and Guihuacheng *ting*, and continued into the 19th century (Hu 2014, 101–3). In extreme cases, jurisdiction over Han Chinese in parts of Inner Asia could be virtually attached to the legal jurisdiction of a *junxian* province some distance away. Generally speaking, the architects of the Qing Empire built their administration on the assumption that discrete territorial units could contain different peoples and accommodate their political cultures. Over time, as internal migration proved uncontrollable, it built overlapping structures to administer different peoples sharing the same territory.

9.4   Universality and the Qing Imperial Mission

Ideologically, the Qing Empire was universal: emperors acknowledged other rulers only as their subjects. Russian tsars alone won grudging diplomatic equality, and even then only in documents passing between the two sides (and sometimes only after forceful Russian protest) (Yanigasawa 2005, 73–6). Opponents were "rebels" and "bandits," whether or not they had ever been under Qing control. Still, emperors were acutely aware of the actual limits of their authority, and the language of *noblesse oblige* could use arrogant assertions to cover pragmatic concessions. Tributary status was rarely forced on foreign monarchs. Indeed, Kangxi's 1684 reform allowing maritime trade without tribute removed a major inducement for seeking it. Britain's East India Company, for instance, traded in China for over a century without political relations, before voluntarily choosing to dispatch the famous Macartney embassy in the hope that access to the emperor and high ministers might allow substantive negotiations. Tribute was rarely a way-station to absorption, especially outside of Inner Asia; to the contrary, some tributaries slid into the orbit of other empires, even before 1800, without particular Qing concern.

Ideologically, emperors proclaimed the ability to transcend the supposedly parochial views of their subjects and discern commonalities beneath the surface diversity of different groups. They professed to work for the benefit of all, regardless of background. They were more restricted, however, in the personae they adopted, representing themselves primarily as custodians of Manchu traditions, sagely practitioners of Confucian teachings, pious Tibetan Buddhists, and indirect heirs of the Chinggisid great khans. Although Kangxi made gestures in support of Beijing's Christian churches, and Qianlong funded a mosque in that city, they never presented themselves as Muslim or Catholic rulers.[27] Just as Qing emperors made rhetorical claims to universal authority without aiming for universal expansion, so too did they profess tolerance of various cultures while practicing only a few.

Making due allowance for long periods of conciliar rule and regency before 1667, emperors were the political nucleus of the empire. The great triumvirate of Kangxi, Yongzheng, and Qianlong were conscientious and detail-oriented stewards of their realm. By comparison to other empires, Qing frontier officials operated under close oversight, with relatively little discretion to act on their own authority. Sub-imperialism via military expeditions launched on the initiative of frontier officials and only later approved by the imperial center played virtually no role in Qing expansion. Still, the talents and loyalties of subordinates were crucial to the empire's success. As a heuristic device, Qing elites can be divided into two categories: imperial, eligible to hold positions of authority throughout the realm; and local, with power and influence circumscribed to one part of it. Imperial elites were relatively few in number; almost all emerged from the Eight Banners, with Manchu and Mongol bannermen being particularly prominent in empire-wide administration. These men owed their wealth and status wholly to the imperial

---

[27] Qianlong in 1763 sponsored the construction of a mosque in Beijing for surrendered Turkic Muslims, an act he likened to his sponsorship of Tibetan Buddhist temples and attributed to his support for the customs of different peoples. However, he had no systematic policy of patronizing Islam throughout the empire (Onuma 2008).

infrastructure, flourishing as it flourished. By contrast, members of local elites might have divided loyalties, gaining income and authority from the Qing system, but not necessarily standing to lose everything if it collapsed. For obvious reasons, then, the Qing state delegated everyday administration to local elites – Chinese literati officials, Mongol *jasagh*s, Turkic *beg*s, and others – but kept them under the watchful oversight of carefully placed bannermen of unquestionable fidelity. Before 1800 very few local elites rose to empire-wide influence. Non-Eight Banner Inner Asians never administered Chinese territories. Han Chinese officials, particularly the vast majority from non-banner backgrounds, played a somewhat more prominent but still very constrained role in Inner Asia. Han soldiers from the Green Standard forces were sometimes sent there, typically on commissariat duty or in agricultural colonies. Few Han Chinese held important military commands in Inner Asian warfare. Apart from exiles undertaking minor, usually clerical, duties, Han Chinese bureaucrats did not help administer Inner Asian populations. In Beijing emperors certainly had close advisers from Han literati backgrounds. Such men sometimes led the empire's highest policy-making bureau, the Grand Council, but their influence on Inner Asian warfare and high politics seems to have been limited.

As a mechanism for gathering political and economic power, then, the Qing Empire was designed to serve emperors and their households, high bannerman grandees, and even ordinary bannermen, who gained more modest economic and legal privileges from Qing rule. Many other groups prospered under the Qing order, for instance aristocrats in *jasagh*-banners and Han literati, but for them the balance of gains and losses was more equivocal. We know much less about what subjects thought of Qing rule, an intrinsically difficult topic because few wrote fully and frankly of their views on it. In the decades after 1644 and before 1911, many Chinese lamented alien rule, but how widely this was true between 1700 and 1850 is far from clear. There was certainly covert dissent, but also evidence that literati took proprietary pride in the empire's size and glory (Mosca 2011). Attitudes in Inner Asia have been even less studied. Some Mongols despised Qing rule, others identified with "our great Qing" (Elverskog 2006). A particular desideratum is to clarify how far Inner Asian subjects understood their rulers to be Chinese or specifically Manchu, and what this distinction meant for them (Shim 2018).

9.5   Conclusion: The Culture of Qing Expansion

What order did the Qing Empire aspire to create? One approach to this question is through the different policies applied to China and Inner Asia. In China proper, the Qing state asserted Chinese political and cultural norms, in some respects more thoroughly and forcefully than their Ming predecessors had done. From Taiwan to Yunnan, Han settlers continuously migrated into the southern frontier, displaced indigenous inhabitants, and eked a living from local resources. These economic and social developments (and the cultural attitudes toward indigenes they engendered) have reminded Western historians of European colonialism in the New World.[28] Beginning in the early 18th century, *tusi* administrative units under indigenous leadership were abolished on a large scale, replaced with standard units under centrally appointed officials. The children of local leaders were encouraged to study the Confucian classics. Manchu officials were no less supportive of these policies than their Han Chinese counterparts, and indeed a Manchu, Ortai, was perhaps their most aggressive proponent. Stevan Harrell (1994, 18–20) finds that in southwest China the Qing inherited and furthered a "civilizing project" based on Confucian norms aimed at the "transformation from raw and untutored to fully civilized." William Rowe (1994, 446) concludes of a drive to expand educational infrastructure in Yunnan in the 1730s, "Genuinely committed to overcoming exploitation of non-Han peoples and to equality of opportunity for all imperial subjects regardless of ethnic background, it nevertheless presupposed the fundamental error of non-Chinese life-styles and social mores ... it sought to acculturate natives of the southwest into a rigidly patriarchal, deferential, and puritanical social system ...." Elsewhere, campaigns were periodically launched to extirpate Christianity as a dangerous heterodoxy, and in the northwest Jonathan Lipman (1997, 100–1) has found that the Qing state came to single out Muslims for harsher treatment, which "helped to create an atmosphere within the government ranks that militated against the impartiality proclaimed by the emperors."

These policies were, in most respects, repudiated in Inner Asia. There, the in-migration of Chinese agricultural settlers was generally forbidden, to be combated or tightly regulated when the state discovered it. Far from attempting to suppress indigenous leadership, the Qing state worked to uphold the viability of the *jasagh*-banner system. These *jasaghs* enjoyed more autonomy than their *tusi* counterparts, reporting not to Han Chinese superiors but to the Lifanyuan. In the rare cases when *jasagh*-banners deemed unreliable were abolished, their territories were not incorporated into provinces but placed under Eight Banner appointees. Far from attempting to change local culture, the Qing state made no efforts to promote Chinese-language, Confucian education, whereas the active sponsorship of Tibetan Buddhism was a central justification for its rule.[29]

---

[28] For example, Laura Hostetler (2001, 30) highlights "similarities between the methods, technologies, and ideologies that the Qing employed ... and those used by European colonial powers during the same period." See also Teng 1998.

[29] In 1728 Yongzheng ordered the Confucian Five Books and Four Classics translated into Mongolian (Xiao 2009, 109). However, I have found no evidence that this project was completed.

Indeed, when it came to the Manchus or Inner Asia more generally, emperors were averse to any imputation that Chinese culture was more worthy or more developed. This different treatment of *jasagh*-banners and *tusi* territories, despite their typological similarity, suggests that the Qing imperial order was committed to maintaining China and Inner Asia as two distinct and autonomous halves of the realm, consonant with the view that the Qing Empire emerged as two simultaneous but separate projects to dominate China and Mongolia.

Even before 1800, however, this distinction was far from absolute. Certain policies and administrative principles that proved successful in one area could be implemented throughout the empire. As Peter Perdue (2005, 335) has put it, "Although no single policy was applied all over the empire, the issues were the same everywhere." In China proper, emperors sometimes tried to shield indigenous peoples from Han Chinese migration, albeit far less consistently than their protection of Inner Asia. Some cultural accommodation was offered by provincial officials to *tusi* leaders, albeit in a more limited and fragile form than that found in Inner Asia (Giersch 2006, 87–91). In parts of Inner Asia, especially in Mongolia and Xinjiang, Beijing knew that Chinese merchants were indispensable to the local economy, and to the financing and logistics of Qing rule. Emperors even realized that Han farmers and foragers could not be completely eliminated and had to be managed and regulated. As Qing law tried to settle disputes between Mongols and Chinese, each governed by their own legal codes, it increasingly inclined toward Chinese legal norms. Thus, although the China and Inner Asia divide was recognized and upheld, it was not absolute, and certain administrative dynamics transcended it. Still, where policy in Inner Asia resembled that in *tusi* regions, this seems to have arisen not from an active project to "normalize" Inner Asia on a Chinese template, but in response to the movement of Han Chinese migrants into both places. Put another way, change in China proper was at least partly engineered from the top-down, that in Inner Asia was from the bottom-up.

This reminds us that Qing policies were not always in harmony with certain realities that they were powerless to adjust, most notably that China proper was economically and demographically the empire's center of gravity. No firm statistics are available, but its population was perhaps thirty times greater than all of Inner Asia combined.[30] Given that this population diligently farmed the empire's most fertile territories and favorable climates, its ratio of economic productivity must have been greater still. Many Chinese migrated into Inner Asia before 1800, whereas vanishingly few Inner Asians migrated into *junxian* provinces. Chinese merchants dominated parts of Inner Asia, and were present

---

[30] China's population around 1800 is usually estimated at around 300 million; Fletcher (1978) estimates that Manchuria in that year had a million inhabitants, including many Han Chinese (p. 39); he pegs the population of all Mongolian speakers at 3.5 million (p. 48), the Turkic population of Xinjiang at 300,000 (p. 69), and all Tibetan speakers (presumably also some Himalayan populations outside of Qing rule) at about six million (p. 91).

almost everywhere; Inner Asian and non-Qing merchants traded on the edges of China, but played no comparable role within it (Millward 1998). Fiscally, China was the foundation of the central government. Although Inner Asians undertook services for the Qing state and provided local products and livestock, it was the *junxian* provinces of China that provided the cash and grain permitting the conquest and governance of Inner Asia. "The eighteenth-century economy" – that is, the Chinese economy – "was the base of imperial control" (Perdue 2005, 336). It is surely no coincidence that the majority of Qing expansion in Inner Asia occurred only after 1683, when control of China and its revenues was firmly established. More open to debate is how far China's predominance extended into other spheres, for instance material culture, administrative techniques, and the realm of political ideology. Still, China's massive gravitational pull was unquestionably felt in the most distant corners of the empire.

Here, perhaps, is what makes the Qing Empire so enigmatic when approached as a single entity, especially before 1800. It is not simply that China's core economic and demographic position was in tension with its political status as merely one among several conquered territories, but rather that this very political order relied heavily on China's resources. Without China's productivity, Qing expansion throughout Inner Asia would not have succeeded, but this successful expansion provided an internal counterweight to the centrality that China might otherwise claim. In other words, keeping the Qing Empire from becoming entirely China-centered, maintaining a semblance of China–Inner Asia balance, was an artificial equilibrium that required the massive expenditure of resources to shore up Qing power in Inner Asia, resources mostly drawn from China. This central paradox provoked a number of subordinate paradoxes: the Qing state was simultaneously the main force keeping Chinese merchants and settlers out of Inner Asia and, by its logistical and revenue needs, and the chronic indebtedness of Inner Asian aristocrats, also the principal architect of the order facilitating their commercial and agricultural penetration. In a state committed to keeping various administrative orders separate, Chinese technologies of bureaucratic, centralized rule, adapted and applied in Inner Asia, brought non-Chinese administrative structures increasingly in line with Chinese norms. Culturally, the Qing state endeavored to maintain and even accentuate boundaries between the two zones of the empire, while at the same time fostering the connections that increasingly broke them down. Before 1800, the Qing Empire was not China, but without China, it could not have existed.

Bibliography

Afinogenov, Gregory. 2016. "The Eye of the Tsar: Intelligence-Gathering and Geopolitics in Eighteenth-Century Eurasia." Doctoral dissertation, Harvard University.

Atwood, Christopher. 2000. "'Worshipping Grace': The Language of Loyalty in Qing Mongolia." *Late Imperial China* 21(2): 86–139.

Bello, David A. 2016. *Across Forest, Steppe and Mountain: Environment, Identity and Empire in Qing China's Borderlands.* New York: Cambridge University Press.

Brophy, David. 2008. "The Kings of Xinjiang: Muslim Elites and the Qing Empire." *Études Orientales* 25: 69–90.

Cheng, Wei-chung. 2013. *War, Trade and Piracy in the China Seas, 1622–1683.* Leiden: Brill.

Crossley, Pamela K. 1999. *A Translucent Mirror: History and Identity in Qing Imperial Ideology.* Berkeley, CA: University of California Press.

Crossley, Pamela K. 2006. "Making Mongols." In: *Empire at the Margins: Culture, Ethnicity, and Frontier in Early Modern China*, ed. Pamela K. Crossley, Helen F. Siu, and Donald S. Sutton, 58–82. Berkeley, CA: University of California Press.

Dai, Yingcong. 2009. *The Sichuan Frontier and Tibet: Imperial Strategy in the Early Qing.* Seattle, WA: University of Washington Press.

Di Cosmo, Nicola. 2002. "Military Aspects of the Manchu Wars against the Čaqars." In *Warfare in Inner Asian History: 500–1800*, ed. Nicola Di Cosmo, 337–67. Leiden: Brill.

Di Cosmo, Nicola. 2009. "The Qing and Inner Asia: 1636–1800." In *The Cambridge History of Inner Asia: The Chinggisid Age*, ed. Nicola Di Cosmo, Allan J. Frank, and Peter B. Golden, 333–62. Cambridge: Cambridge University Press.

Elliott, Mark C. 2011. "Pei Huang, *Reorienting the Manchus: A Study of Sinicization, 1583–1795*" (Review). *Journal of the Economic and Social History of the Orient* 54: 584–8.

Elliott, Mark C. 2001. *The Manchu Way: The Eight Banners and Ethnic Identity in Late Imperial China.* Stanford, CA: Stanford University Press.

Elverskog, Johan. 2006. *Our Great Qing: The Mongols, Buddhism and the State in Late Imperial China.* Honolulu, HI: University of Hawai'i Press.

Elverskog, Johan. 2011. "Wutai Shan, Qing Cosmopolitanism, and the Mongols." *Journal of the International Association of Tibetan Studies* 6: 243–74.

Fairbank, John K. 1953. *Trade and Diplomacy on the China Coast: The Opening of the Treaty Ports, 1842–1854.* Cambridge, MA: Harvard University Press.

Fairbank, John K. and S.Y. Têng. 1941. "On the Ch'ing Tributary System." *Harvard Journal of Asiatic Studies* 6(2): 135–246.

Farquhar, David M. 1968. "The Origins of the Manchus' Mongolian Policy." In: *The Chinese World Order: Traditional China's Foreign Relations*, ed. John K. Fairbank, 198–205. Cambridge, MA: Harvard University Press.

Fitzgerald, Devin. 2016. "Discussing 'The Making of "China" out of "Zhongguo."'" *Journal of Asian History* 50(2): 299–305.

Fletcher, Joseph. 1978. "Ch'ing Inner Asia c. 1800." In *The Cambridge History of China,* Volume 10, Part 1: *Late Ch'ing, 1800–1911*, ed. John K. Fairbank, 35–106. Cambridge: Cambridge University Press.

Giersch, C. Patterson. 2014. "Commerce and Empire in the Borderlands: How do Merchants and Trade Fit into Qing Frontier History?" *Frontiers of History in China* 9(3): 361–83.

Giersch, C. Patterson. 2006. *Asian Borderlands: The Transformation of Qing China's Yunnan Frontier.* Cambridge, MA: Harvard University Press.

Harrell, Stevan. 1994. "Introduction: Civilizing Projects and the Reaction to Them." In *Cultural Encounters on China's Ethnic Frontiers*, ed. Stevan Harrell, 3–36. Seattle, WA: University of Washington Press.

Herman, John E. 2014. "Collaboration and Resistance on the Southwest Frontier: Early Eighteenth-Century Qing Expansion on Two Fronts." *Late Imperial China* 35(1): 77–112.

Herman, John E. 2007. *Amid the Clouds and Mist: China's Colonization of Guizhou, 1200–1700*. Cambridge, MA: Harvard University Asia Center.

Heuschert, Dorothea. 1998. "Legal Pluralism in the Qing Empire: Manchu Legislation for the Mongols." *The International History Review* 20(2): 310–324.

Ho, Ping-ti. 1967. "The Significance of the Ch'ing Period in Chinese History." *The Journal of Asian Studies* 26(2): 189–95.

Hostetler, Laura. 2001. *Qing Colonial Enterprise: Ethnography and Cartography in Early Modern China*. Chicago, IL: University of Chicago Press.

Hu, Ying. 2014. "Justice on the Steppe: Legal Institutions and Practice in Qing Mongolia." Doctoral dissertation, Stanford University.

Huang, Pei. 2011. *Reorienting the Manchus: A Study of Sinicization, 1583–1795*. Ithaca, NY: East Asia Program, Cornell University.

Kim, Kwangmin. 2016. *Borderland Capitalism: Turkestan Produce, Qing Silver, and the Birth of an Eastern Market*. Stanford, CA: Stanford University Press.

Kim, Loretta E. 2019. *Ethnic Chrysalis: China's Orochen People and the Legacy of Qing Borderland Administration*. Cambridge, MA: Harvard University Press.

Lee, Robert H.G. 1970. *The Manchurian Frontier in Ch'ing History*. Cambridge, MA: Harvard University Press.

Levey, Benjamin S. 2013. "Jungar Refugees and the Making of Empire on Qing China's Kazakh Frontier, 1759–1773." Doctoral Dissertation, Harvard University.

Lhamsuren, Munkh-Erdene. 2010. "The 1640 Great Code: An Inner Asian Parallel to the Treaty of Westphalia." *Central Asian Survey* 29(3): 269–88.

Li, Gertraude Roth. 2002. "State Building Before 1644." In *The Cambridge History of China* Vol. 9, Part 1: *The Ch'ing Empire to 1800*, ed. Denis Twitchett and John K. Fairbank, 9–72. Cambridge: Cambridge University Press.

Li Narangoa and Robert Cribb. 2014. *Historical Atlas of Northeast Asia, 1590–2010*. New York: Columbia University Press.

Lipman, Jonathan. 1997. *Familiar Strangers: A History of Muslims in Northwest China*. Seattle, WA, University of Washington Press.

Ma, Haiyun. 2008. "Fanhui or Huifan? Hanhui or Huimin? Salar Ethnic Identification and Qing Administrative Transformation in Eighteenth-Century Gansu." *Late Imperial China* 29(2): 1–36.

Mancall, Mark. 1971. *Russia and China: Their Diplomatic Relations to 1728*. Cambridge, MA: Harvard University Press.

Masuda, Erika. 2007. "The Fall of Ayutthaya and Siam's Disrupted Order of Tribute to China (1767–1782)." *Taiwan Journal of Southeast Asian Studies* 4(2): 75–128.

McNeill, J. R. 1998. "China's Environmental History in World Perspective." In *Sediments of Time: Environment and Society in Chinese History*, ed. Mark Elvin and Liu Ts'ui-jung, 31–49. Cambridge: Cambridge University Press.

Millward, James. 1998. *Beyond the Pass: Economy, Ethnicity, and Empire in Qing Central Asia, 1759–1864*. Stanford, CA: Stanford University Press.

Miyawaki, Junko. 1999. "The Legitimacy of Khanship among the Oyirad (Kalmyk) Tribes in Relation to the Chinggisid Principle." In *The Mongol Empire and Its Legacy*, ed. Reuven Amitai-Preiss and David O. Morgan, 319–31. Leiden: Brill.

Mosca, Matthew W. 2011. "The Literati Rewriting of China in the Qianlong-Jiaqing Transition." *Late Imperial China* 32(2): 89–132.

Mosca, Matthew W. 2013. *From Frontier Policy to Foreign Policy: The Question of India and the Transformation of Geopolitics in Qing China*. Stanford, CA: Stanford University Press.

Mosca, Matthew W. 2014. "The Qing State and Its Awareness of Eurasian Interconnections, 1789–1806." *Eighteenth-Century Studies* 47(2): 103–16.

Nakami, Tatsuo. 1984. "A Protest Against the Concept of the 'Middle Kingdom': The Mongols and the 1911 Revolution." In *The 1911 Revolution in China: Interpretive Essays*, ed. Etō Shinkichi and Harold Z. Schiffrin, 129–49. Tokyo: University of Tokyo Press.

Naquin, Susan. 1981. *Shantung Rebellion: The Wang Lun Uprising of 1774*. New Haven, CT: Yale University Press.

Oidtmann, Max. 2016. "Overlapping Empires: Religion, Politics, and Ethnicity in Nineteenth-Century Qinghai." *Late Imperial China* 37(2): 41–91.

Oidtmann, Max. 2018. *Forging the Golden Urn: The Qing Empire and the Politics of Reincarnation in Tibet*. New York: Columbia University Press.

Onuma, Takahiro. 2008. *250 Years History of the Turkic-Muslim Camp in Beijing*. Tokyo: Department of Islamic Area Studies, University of Tokyo.

Onuma Takahiro 小沼孝博. 2014. *Shin to Chūō Ajia sōgen: yūbokumin no sekai kara teikoku no henkyō e* 清と中央アジア草原：遊牧民の世界から帝国の辺境へ [The Qing and the Central Asian Steppe: From the Nomads Arena to the Imperial Frontier]. Tokyo: University of Tokyo Press.

Oxnam, Robert B. 1975. *Ruling from Horseback: Manchu Politics in the Oboi Regency, 1661–1669*. Chicago, IL: University of Chicago Press.

Perdue, Peter C. 2005. *China Marches West: The Qing Conquest of Central Eurasia*. Cambridge, MA: Harvard University Press.

Petech, Luciano. 1972. *China and Tibet in the Early XVIIIth Century: History of the Establishment of Chinese Protectorate in Tibet*, 2nd ed. Leiden: Brill.

Qi Guang 齊光. 2013. *Da Qing diguo shiqi Menggu de zhengzhi yu shehui: yi Alashan Heshuote bu yanjiu wei zhongxin* 大清帝國時期蒙古的政治與社會：以阿拉善和碩特部研究為中心 [Mongol Government and Society in the Period of the Qing Empire: Research Centered on the Alashan Qoshud]. Shanghai: Fudan daxue chubanshe.

Rawski, Evelyn S. 1998. *The Last Emperors: A Social History of Qing Imperial Institutions*. Berkeley, CA: University of California Press.

Rawski, Evelyn S. 1996. "Reenvisioning the Qing: The Significance of the Qing Period in Chinese History." *Journal of Asian Studies* 55(4): 829–50.

Rowe, William T. 1994. "Education and Empire in Southwest China: Ch'en Hung-mou in Yunnan, 1733–38." In: *Education and Society in Late Imperial China,*

1600–1900, ed. Benjamin A. Elman and Alexander Woodside, 417–57. Berkeley, CA: University of California Press.

Schlesinger, Jonathan. 2012. "The Qing Invention of Nature: Environment and Identity in Northeast China and Mongolia, 1750–1850." Doctoral dissertation, Harvard University.

Schlesinger, Jonathan. 2017. *A World Trimmed with Fur: Wild Things, Pristine Places, and the Natural Fringes of Qing Rule*. Stanford, CA: Stanford University Press.

Schmid, Andre. 2007. "Tributary Relations and the Qing-Chosŏn Frontier on Mount Paektu." In: *The Chinese State at the Borders*, ed. Diana Lary, 126–50. Vancouver: University of British Columbia Press.

Schwieger, Peter. 2014. *The Dalai Lama and the Emperor of China: A Political History of the Tibetan Institution of Reincarnation*. New York: Columbia University Press.

Shibuya Kōichi 渋谷浩一. 2011. "1734–40-nen no Shin to Jūn-garu no kōwa kōshō ni tsuite: Kyafuta jōyaku teiketsu go no Chūō Yūrashia no kokusai kankei" 1734-40 年の清とジューン・ガルの講和交渉について：キャフタ条約締結後の中央ユーラシアの国際関係 [Peace Negotiations between the Qing and the Junghars, 1734–1740: Central Eurasian International Relations after the Conclusion of the Treaty of Kiakhta]. *Tōyōshi kenkyū* 東洋史研究 70(3): 608–572.

Shim, Hosung. 2018. "Oyirad Terms for the Manchus." *Saksaha: A Journal of Manchu Studies* 15: 113–36.

Teng, Emma Jinhua. 1998. "An Island of Women: The Discourse of Gender in Qing Travel Writing about Taiwan." *The International History Review* 20(2): 353–70.

Wakeman, Jr., Frederic. 1985. *The Great Enterprise: The Manchu Reconstruction of Imperial Order in Seventeenth-Century China*. Berkeley, CA: University of California Press.

Waley-Cohen, Joanna. 2004. "The New Qing History." *Radical History Review* 88: 193–206.

Wills, Jr., John E. 2012. "Functional, Not Fossilized: Qing Tribute Relations with Đại Việt (Vietnam) and Siam (Thailand), 1700–1820." *T'oung Pao* 98: 439–78.

Xiao Minru 蕭敏如. 2009. *Cong 'Hua-Yi' dao 'Zhong-Xi': Qingdai 'Chunqiu' xue Hua-Yi guan yanjiu* 從'華夷'到'中西'：清代'春秋'學華夷觀研究 [From "Chinese and Barbarians" to "China and the West": Research on the Chinese-Barbarian Perspective in Qing-era Scholarship on the *Chunqiu*]. Taipei: Huamulan wenhua chubanshe.

Yanagisawa, Akira. 2005. "Some Remarks on the 'Addendum to the Treaty of Kiakhta' in 1768." *Memoirs of the Toyo Bunko* 63: 65–88.

10 All Under the Tsar
Russia's Eurasian Trajectory

Jane Burbank

10.1 Space for Empire: The Advantage of Disadvantage

For Russia, space was everything. The princes of Moscow, holed up in a backwater town in western Eurasia, got their chance at empire because they lived in an undesirable place. Who wanted their bend in the river? From time immemorial well into the 15th century CE, no one with power and wealth on the mind would choose this location for an imperial start-up.[1]

Other areas of western Eurasia had attracted attention before Moscow appeared on the earth. (The first record mentioning Moscow refers to the year 1147.)[2] The Volga River route from the Baltic Sea and the northern forests to the empires of the Mediterranean and the far East plus the enticing places in between was pioneered more than once. In the 9th century, a gang of long-distance raiders and traders, the Rus', anchored themselves in Kiev on the Dnieper River – a shorter, but treacherous run toward Byzantium and its attractions. The Rus' spread their control outward over the spaces of what we now call central Russia. Riurikid princes – descendants of Riurik, founder of the Rus' dynasty – put themselves in charge of the region's towns. Kiev with its nodes of control and collection and Novgorod with its ties to the Baltic trade were far more active and wealthy than mingy Moscow (Map 10.1).

In the 13th century the Mongols defeated Kievan Rus' as they swept into western Eurasia, but the Mongols had little interest in swamplands and forests. They left their westernmost conquests, including the small town of Moscow, for their new clients – surviving and duly subordinated Riurikid princes – to exploit and manage.

---

[1] I wish to thank the editors for organizing a fascinating conference and especially Yuri Pines for his comments on this chapter.

[2] For the story of the founding of Moscow from an official present-day source, see the website of the Moscow mayor's office: https://www.mos.ru/en/city/about/.

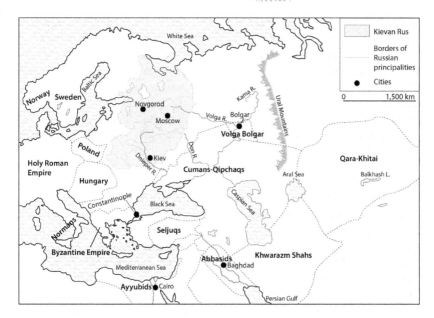

Map 10.1 Kievan Rus', around 1200.

In hindsight, we can see that Moscow's untempting space was an asset in the formative years of the young polity (13th to 16th centuries). Its leaders could gradually reach out from their city, overcome rival Riurikids and learn to control scattered populations without having to confront head-on the major powers of their times – the declining Byzantines, the assertive Ottomans, the Mongol khanates, China under Yuan and Ming dynasties. A certain distance (not just in absolute space, but in connectivity) from the overwhelming cultural and military power of established empires was an asset for empire-builders.

This point about space can be applied to republican Rome and to Mecca in Muhammad's time. Both cities were far enough away from the dominant powers of the eastern Mediterranean to enjoy, if that is the word, a longish spell of learning to do empire their way, before having to compete in the big time. One possible implication of getting off to one's own start, before greater powers took notice, is that each of these empires – Rome, the Islamic Caliphate, Russia – came up with a particular way of rule, based on both home schooling and distance learning. A marginal situation (whose margins is the obvious question) implies both awareness of and separation from power centers. On-the-fringe locations offered connections – economic, cultural, military – to the dominant powers and opportunities for selective adaptation of others' techniques, strategies, and attitudes. At the same time, distance and undesirability meant that these choices could be worked out in new ways and become familiar to rulers and subjects before the tests of competition with other powers began in earnest.

In Moscow's case, the contact with great power was close, but fortunately – from the Russian perspective – not crushing. It was the Mongols who gave Moscow a chance to reconstruct Riurikid power after Kiev's decline and defeat. The decision of Batu Khan, Chinggis Khan's grandson and the triumphant leader of the Mongols' western campaign, to return to Mongolia in 1241 rather than advance further into Europe opened a crucial chapter in the spatial story of the Russian Empire. (And not just of Russia: the shape of the political world might have been quite different if Batu had not felt compelled to stop his drive to the west.)[3] In the event, what mattered most for Russia was the subsequent configuration of the Mongols' power in the multiple regions of their conquest.

The Mongols established their western empire, known as the Golden Horde, with a capital at Sarai on the southern Volga River. This new imperial center was, like the older ones, at a politically usable distance from Moscow and other towns led by Riurikids. The Mongols were content to have others do the work of tribute collection for them in the forest zones, and the Moscovite princes understood where their interests lay. With time these small-town princes transformed themselves into imperial intermediaries who became very rich from their expansive tax and tribute collecting activities.

My spatial argument now takes another turn. Space meant everything to Russia, first, because Moscow was far enough away (distant and undesirable) from imperial power and contestation to have time to extend the range of its leaders' authority, and second, because when Muscovites began to expand from their city, they did it under the guidance of particular imperial overlords – Mongols – whose statecraft derived from human mastery of a specific kind of terrain. The encounters – initially destructive, later interactive – between Riurikid princes and Mongol overlords took place in a distinctive geophysical region – the western edge of the Eurasian plain. The Mongols were one of many empire-makers who partook of a transmitted imperial tradition adjusted to the demands of survival in the Eurasian steppe.[4]

Riurikid princes shared Mongol notions about how power should be organized – in the hands (armed) of loyal subordinates who served a superior leader, himself a member of a ruling dynasty. After dramatic demonstrations of the Mongol khan's power to choose a principal leader (the grand prince) from

---

[3] On Batu's about-face, see the classic article by Joseph Fletcher 1986, 45–7.

[4] I use Eurasian here in its restrictive sense relating to the great expanse of steppe and forest that extends between what is now Ukraine and China. This is the location of the "silk" and other transcontinental trading routes and the habitat of multiple nomadic peoples and animals. The term "Eurasian" used in the rest of this chapter refers to the political cultures produced in this region by nomadic peoples in their intersection with settled and other polities on the edges of this region.

among Rus' competitors and to destroy (kill) insubordinates, ambitious members of the Riurikid clan and their followers worked the new system to their own advantage. In so doing, they acquired expertise in the management of a sparsely populated space – regulatory mechanisms, including census-taking, surveying systems, record keeping.[5] A single paramount sovereign empowered by personal charisma and dynastic legitimacy, delegation of authority to intermediaries, taxation or other exactions from subjected populations by these empowered authorities, and a certain amount of protection of the lowly through legal procedures – all these were part of both Mongol and Riurikid repertoires that derived, directly or indirectly, from political cultures that had been evolved, enforced, and transmitted by Eurasian nomads.[6]

There was a third spatial dimension to Moscow's eventual success as an imperial polity. This derived from the cultural contacts of the Riurikids' earlier empire in Kiev. Kiev's wealth came primarily from its successful commercial and military relations with Byzantium, during one of that empire's magnificent comebacks (see Preiser-Kapeller [Chapter 4], this volume). However, the Rus' brought home to Kiev more than booty; they adopted the Byzantines' religion and acquired an alphabet, clerical services, artists, architects, artisans – in short, a high culture. Among Moscow's assets as an aspirant to empire were retentions from Kiev's imperial episode – the dismembered, but recognized, Rus' dynasty – and a high culture that could enforce and bulk up the surviving princes' legitimacy.

The argument thus far: space in an uncoveted region, marginal to great powers, turned out to advantage Moscow in three ways. The unpromising physical environment offered time to grow without being absorbed; the one-time conquerors (the Mongols) arrived with a political culture adapted to long-distance, transcontinental rule; and an imperial predecessor (Kiev) had already acquired transmittable cultural assets from a great neighbor (Byzantium) at Eurasia's western edge.

Putting the Russian imperial novice in a wider frame: other empires had already found or would find their limits quite far from Moscow. This meant that Moscow had room to combat and eventually absorb minor competitors and vulnerable scattered populations in its expanding neighborhood. It was only after the Riurikid princes had significantly extended their political reach that Moscow ran up against the might – technological and cultural – of forceful empires and discovered its own limits. At the start, distance from great powers gave Moscow time to run over smaller ones, but eventually extension outward into contact with multiple and unlike imperial formations would be critical to what Moscovites learned as they transformed their polity.

---

[5] On Mongol–Muscovite interactions and technologies, see Grinberg 2011.
[6] For the concept of imperial repertoire, see Burbank and Cooper 2010, 3–4.

10.2   Location and Political Possibility

Let us step back in time before the Mongol conquest to look at other players – other beginners at empire – in the neighborhood (the space) of the Muscovites' eventual primacy. One early candidate for imperial growth was the Bulgar Khanate, which enjoyed a promising location on the Volga trade route. Promising, however, meant vulnerable to the attentions of more powerful states. The Bulgar Khanate (9th to 13th centuries) and the Kazan Khanate that eventually emerged in roughly the same area (15th to 16th centuries) offer examples of how a desirable location can inhibit a polity's chance to survive on its own (Map 10.2). Both khanates disappeared as political units, while Moscow survived. But note that while too close contact with greater powers inhibited the formation of a lasting empire based along the profitable Volga River route, this same setting was conducive to the local development of political strategies and imaginaries useful for survival, and even well-being, inside someone else's empire.

The Volga Bulgars were a group of Eurasian origin who migrated into the middle Volga region in the 7th century. They displaced or subordinated Finno-Ugric populations, the ancestors of the present-day Mari people who now have

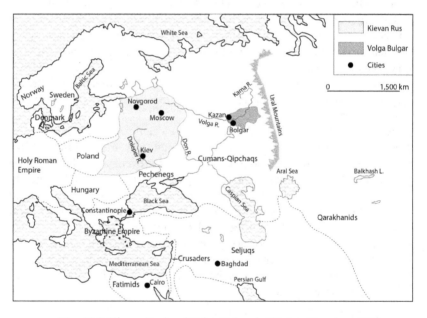

Map 10.2 Kievan Rus' and Volga Bulgar in Western Eurasia, *c.*1100.

their own republic inside the Russian Federation.[7] The Bulgars contended with rival Turkic tribes and provided defensive services as well as problems to the Byzantines. The capital of the budding empire was Bolgar, located near the confluence of the Volga and Kama rivers, 130 kilometers south of today's Kazan. The city of Bolgar became rich from its advantageous situation, which linked northern Europe and waterways west of the Urals to the Mediterranean, Central Asia and beyond. The city's wealth attracted the attention of other polities – the multi-faith Khazars and the dynamic Muslim dynasties. For long periods, Bulgar khans were subject to the overlordship of the great Khazar Empire that dominated the northern Caucasus, the lower Volga, and coastal regions of the Caspian and Black Seas from the mid-7th to mid-10th centuries.[8]

In 921, having received a request for advice and enlightened instruction in Islamic law from the Bulgar ruler Almysh, the Abbasid Caliph sent the indefatigable traveler Ibn Fadlan from Baghdad to Bolgar. Upon arriving in Bolgar the next year, the Caliph's delegation was met by the Bulgar leader and his entourage. Ibn Fadlan's account credits Almysh with knowledge of Islam and claims that visitors to Bolgar encountered 5,000 men and women who professed the Muslim faith. One way or another, the Bulgars had become Muslims around this time (Bariev 2005, 83).[9]

On another (northwestern) edge of the Pontic steppe, some six decades later, the Riurikid ruler in Kiev, Grand Prince Vladimir, also converted to a monotheistic faith, in his case Christianity. Conversion to Christianity or Islam in the 10th century brought cultural and economic assets to rulers: connections to the old, distinguished Byzantines or to the young, sophisticated Caliphate. Kievan princes went one way; Bulgar khans the other. In both cases, the leaders brusquely converted the denizens of their cities along with royal families. These choices became part of political repertoires and cultural assets of descendant polities – in Bolgar's case, the Kazan Khanate that eventually took its place and for Kiev, its successor state the Grand Princedom of Moscovy. The two confessions inflect discourses of sovereignty in these areas to this day. Viewed from an anachronistically territorialized concept of the state, Islam came to lands that would later become part of "Russia" a good sixty years before the iconic date (988) of Grand Prince Vladimir's conversion in Kiev.[10]

---

[7] On the Maris (also known as Cheremis) in the late Romanov empire, see Werth 2002 and Geraci 2001.
[8] On the history of Bulgars, including discussion of sources, see Bariev 2005. The Bulgar origins story comes in many variants; Soviet and post-Soviet versions are not easy to disentangle; see Graney 2009, 2–4.
[9] A Russian-language version of Ibn Fadlan's account, based on a 1939 publication, packaged with a description of the Baghdad Caliph's mission to the Bulgar "tsar" can be found in *Puteshestvie* 1992.
[10] On Vladimir's conversion in its imperial context, see Burbank and Cooper 2010, 186–8. On the historiographically tortuous relationship between "Russian" history and Kazan, see Keenan 1967.

Contests for power over the open terrain of the Pontic steppe enforced structural, conceptual, and spatial elements of Eurasian politics. First, borders, if they existed at all in any one's imagination, were fungible. In the steppe region, what was desired was not demarcated territory, but control over trade routes, city centers with their cultural and artisanal production, and laboring populations who could supply agricultural, forest, and other products.[11] Bulgars, Khazars, Riurikid princes, and other warrior clans extended their power by securing positions as superior rulers who could collect from the populations they conquered. People and resources were at issue, not frontiers.

Second, establishing political command in these conditions usually meant conquest, but maintenance of control depended on sustaining the cooperation of local intermediaries. Islam and Christianity were useful in at least two respects: their ritual practices could enhance the rule of an earthly sovereign, and their clerics (monks, priests, teachers, spiritual guides, etc.) were informed managers of the region's populations. Toiling people, whether farmers or horsemen, were expected to follow their leaders, including religious ones. The art of imperial rule was in creating or absorbing effective power brokers and keeping them loyal.[12]

Third, retaining superior authority required savvy approaches to dangers posed by outsiders to the polity. Wealth depended on trade routes that had to be secured; nodal cities were targets for take over. Asserting power over rivals who had the skills to manage long-distance trade and to organize migrations of people and herds was no mean feat. But the game was worth the candle, and there were multiple contenders for the position of ultimate ruler.

The technical means of competition was armed warfare, or the threat of armed warfare, mostly on horseback;[13] the political instrument was personal allegiance connecting commanders of troops. This meant that contenders changed not just horses but loyalties all the time. There were no fixed "sides" to this game of empowerment steppe-style; instead the players could re-group at any moment and take the ball with them to places they found propitious. Ethnicity and religion were not determining or even recognized factors, as warriors followed their leaders' shifting alliances. In the conflicts internal to the Golden Horde, Mongols and Russians were frequently allies – against other Mongols and Russians.

A long-term view of this contracting and contesting field of power relations reveals intersecting factors that really did make a difference: geographic and

---

[11] On the notion of an administrative center for the collection of taxes and as a node of trade for the Rus', see the discussion of the word *pogost* (settlement) in Kaiser 1980, 181–3. Kaiser notes (p. 180), "the idea of territoriality is developed very weakly in the *Russkaia Pravda* [Russian Truth (early law code)]."

[12] On the critical relationship of local elites to a leader's hold on power, see Grinberg 2013, 895–921.

[13] On the horse and steppe warfare, see Stanziani 2012, 26–8.

technical conditions. When rivers established the major lines of commercial transport, the ball would be chased to some place along them. Bolgar, Kazan, Kiev, and Astrakhan are cases in point; their situations on waterways with enriching connections inspired competitors' ambitions. Centuries later, the invention of railroads and airplanes would change the spatial contours of the game.

In the decades when the Bulgars were migrating west and setting themselves up in the Balkans and on the Volga, Constantinople located at the junction of major land and sea routes, had the best site of all.[14] This made the Byzantine Empire a target for greater and lesser powers in the region. By the 8th century, Bulgars were threatening contenders for a share of Byzantium's riches (Threadgold 2002, 137–42), but never strong enough to take over the empire's capital. Instead, Bulgar leaders managed to consolidate authority in the middle Volga area – a propitious, but less opulent place. There, though, they had to fend off their own rivals for control of Byzantine hinterlands. The city of Kazan emerged out of these multiple contests, probably at the juncture of the 10th and 11th centuries.[15] A displaced Bulgar prince named Khasan may be responsible for the city's name.[16] Located north of the junction between the Volga and Kama rivers, Kazan was more defendable than Bolgar, which was repeatedly attacked by Rus' princes (Bariev 2005, 55–84).

Bulgar and Kievan princes, and everyone else in the way, met more than their match during the Mongols' great campaigns (1236–42) through Central Asia, the Caucasus, the Pontic steppes, along the Volga and Dnieper rivers, and into the heart of central Europe (Morgan 1990, 61–73, 136–45). After the Mongol victories, Bolgar and Kazan, like Moscow, were absorbed into the new Mongol polity, the Golden Horde. The Horde, also known as the Qipchak Khanate and the Ulus of Jochi, was a product of the division of Mongol conquests among Chinggis Khan's children (Biran [Chapter 6], this volume). This westernmost Mongol realm had originally been designated for Chinggis Khan's eldest son Jochi; it was ruled by Jochi's son Batu Khan from 1227 to his death in 1255 and by Jochi's descendants for the next century.[17]

---

[14] This chapter concerns the Bulgars who settled on the Volga and not those who established themselves in the region of today's Bulgaria.

[15] In 2005, Kazan, with the approval of Russian authorities, celebrated its millennium. The date was a political issue, and a victory for Tatarstan, but scholars know that it is more than approximate. On the millennium and its meaning, see Graney 2009, 140–5.

[16] For a judicious summary of scholarship on the emergence and name of the city, see Ilya Zaytsev n.d. I thank Ilya Zaytsev for his counsel on the early history of Kazan.

[17] For versions of the defeat and subordination of Bolgar, on the issue of whether the Mongols ever made Bolgar a major site of rule, and on Bolgar's flourishing economy as a Golden Horde client, see Bariev 2005, 153–84. On the Qipchak Khanate, see Morgan 1990, 141–5. The controversy over the name is a minor skirmish in scholars' ongoing war over the relationship of the Mongols to Russian state formation. See Ostrowski 1998 for a strong position.

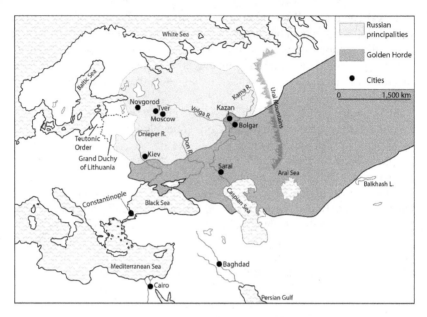

Map 10.3 The Golden Horde and Russian principalities, 14th century.

The region of the former Bulgar Khanate on the Volga route was of far greater interest to the Mongols than was Moscow (Map 10.3). Kazan became a nexus of trade, tribute, and culture under Mongol rule, and later a place of refuge and a target of contention during struggles for control in Bolgar. As the Ulus of Jochi disaggregated in strife beginning in the mid-14th century, one of the descendant polities was a new khanate, centered in Kazan, and ruled by the heirs of Chinggis the conqueror.[18]

Looking back at the Golden Horde and its multiple progeny, we might ask why Moscow and not Kazan or another Mongol khanate proved capable of building a durable empire, one that lasts to our own time. Did space have something to do with the result?

I suggest that it did, in three ways. First, as argued above, Moscow's locational disadvantage, in terms of economic resources, kept it off the radar long enough (13th to 15th century) for the local princes to expand their own area of control, impelled by the essential and enriching duty of collecting the goods for their Mongol overlords and of course for themselves. Second, the larger space of contestation and potential empire-making (roughly the Pontic

[18] The Kazan Khanate, like Muscovy, was a "Juchisid state," a descendant of the ulus of Juchi. See the term "Juchidskie gosudarstva" (Juchisid states) used by a Russian specialist on this area: Zaitsev 2010, 194. For almost all of its history, the Khanate was ruled by a Chinggisid, see Zaytsev n.d.

steppe and the Volga watershed) was one in which combatants shared notions of sovereignty and politics. This shared Eurasian political culture[19] established the conditions for empire over the whole space. A very sparsely populated area could be subordinated to an overlord ruler without too much trouble because political elites were used to the politics of parceling out authority and resources and because populations were used to being ruled by outsider overlords. Third, the spaces that Moscovy (and not Kazan) acquired or eventually encompassed intersected with at least three quite distinct imperial civilizations: the Eastern Roman empire with its pragmatic and spectacular tradition of Christian rulership; the Turkic-Mongol empires with their Eurasian-style sovereignty; and several variants of European Christian polities – initially Catholic, militant, and learned, later Protestant and technically dynamic. Possibly a fourth, underestimated world that affected Moscow's imperial possibilities was that of the dispersed animist cultivators and forest peoples – Finns, Slavs, and many others – who provided the labor and the products for whatever power overwhelmed them on this terrain.

The Muscovites, led first by the Riurikid dynasts and later by Romanovs, thus had a triple spatial advantage. At the beginning, they were far enough away from other imperial powers; then, they expanded and consolidated their authority in a sparsely populated area where the rules of overlord-style politics were widely shared; third, their statecraft developed in encounters with several distinctive imperial traditions, each one challenging yet also exploitable.

These spatial conditions could be applied to another question, specific to Russian debates – why Moscow and not Novgorod? Novgorod's fortunes were connected, primarily, to a different geographical context – the Baltic. One might argue, along the above lines, that Novgorod was too close to bigger powers at the start, that it was not as entangled as Moscow with Eurasian political culture, and that Novgorod's leaders were not the favored subordinates of the Mongol overlords. Nothing in my interpretation, however, would preclude the possibilities of other towns ruled by Riurikids and located roughly in the same area as Moscow, to have emerged as budding imperial centers. (Tver, which rivaled Moscow for supremacy, might have succeeded had the historical cards fallen differently.) The personal qualities of Moscow's princes, their choices of where to reside, their success at subduing competitors – all these and other human factors contributed to Moscow's predominance over other towns in the region.

10.3   Moscow Moves East

Moscow's conquest of the Khanate of Kazan in 1552 is usually regarded as the beginning of Russian Empire.[20] This version of what makes an empire assumes

---

[19] See note 4 for the definition of "Eurasian" as used here.
[20] For an example, see Andreas Kappeler's authoritative study, Kapeller 2001, 14.

that incorporating people of a different faith – in this case, Muslim Tatars – into the grand princedom was somehow a break with Moscow's earlier status, presumed to be uniformly Slavic and Christian. Setting aside this misleading notion of Muscovy, which from the beginning expanded by incorporating unlike cities, tribes, villages, leaders, and followers – many of them pagan in one way or another – let us look at what made it possible for the budding Russian Empire to overpower the Kazan Khanate and to hold onto this valuable center of Tatar culture and power.

A first point is that Kazan and Moscow were both players in a larger game for control in the same space (Map 10.4). The Khanate of Kazan was only one by-product of intra-dynastic struggles for leadership within and around the fission-prone Golden Horde. Mongol unity was brief, and the khanates themselves became objects of contentious ambition. For a short time at the end of the 14th century, the great warrior Timur managed to reconnect much of the terrain that the Mongols had conquered and to devastate cities in Syria and India. Timur died on his way toward China in 1405, after having defeated the khan of the Golden Horde and destroying its capital at Sarai (Manz 1989, 72). Subsequent contests for power in the unruly lands north of the Black Sea produced other new or reconfigured powers, among them the Khanate of Astrakhan further south along the Volga River and the Khanate of Crimea. In the southern steppe

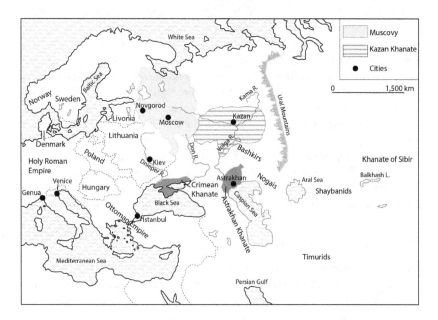

Map 10.4 Moscow and Kazan, around 1500.

and along the lower Volga, confederations of nomadic tribes – Nogais and Bashkirs – profited from the vulnerabilities of trade routes and jockeyed for beneficial alliances with other powers. Ambitious empire-builders loomed outside this turbulent middle ground – the Grand Duchy of Lithuania to the west and the aggressive Ottomans to the south. The distant location of these greater powers left room for smaller entities to compete for resources and, if successful, to expand.

Moscow's Riurikid princes were aggressive upstarts in the region. Like the khans in Kazan, they had learned, by necessity, lessons in politics from the Golden Horde. Effective cultivation of the Mongol khans' good will earned Muscovites the upper hand over other Riurikids in their often violent intra-family struggles. The Grand Princes of Moscow continued to pay tribute to Mongol khans until late in the 15th century, all the while expanding the principality's control over what would become known as central and northern Russia.[21] Alliances between Riurikid princes or would-be grand princes, and Chinggisid khans or would-be khans were frequent in the multiple contests over resources and lands that had earlier been united by the Mongols into a huge Eurasian economic space.[22]

In this volatile context Moscow made its great move east and ultimately into sovereignty in Kazan. Beginning in the 1480s, Moscow tried both assault and clientage. After an attack on Kazan in 1487, Moscow tried to put a compliant khan into power in the khanate. This worked off and on. Kazan with Nogai allies struck back effectively against the Russians in the early 1500s. Collaboration in managing trade routes was another option; peace was sworn more than once (Zaytsev, n.d.). For a time, a separate Mongol-led polity, the Khanate of Kasimov, was set up under Moscow's supervision on the Oka river, part way to Kazan.[23] In the first half of the 16th century, Moscow projected its lines of fortresses further east. The multi-ethnic and sparsely populated region nominally under Kazan's control offered a perfect context for peeling off the khanate's discontented subjects (Davis 2007, 26–79; Stevens 2007, 40–55, 71–85).

This move by Moscow made the Mongol rulers of Crimea, who were both contenders for and allies of the Kazan Khanate, nervous. The close, if abrasive, relations between the Crimean and Kazan khanates (Zaytsev, n.d.) in turn threatened Moscow and may have been a factor in the decision of Ivan IV (the Terrible) to renounce the politics of clientage and attempt to take over Kazan militarily. It took more than one try. In 1551 the Russian forces built a fort on the Volga upstream from Kazan, from which they could block supply routes, attract support from local people, and potentially attack the city.

[21] On Moscow's expansion and its rivals, see Stanziani 2012, 95–101.
[22] On the earlier Mongol-run Eurasian connections, see Allsen 2001; Biran 2004; Biran, this volume.
[23] Romaniello 2012, 28. On the Kasimov khanate, see Rakhimzianov 2009 and Ostrowski 1998, 54. The nature and even existence of this khanate are contentious subjects to this day.

354   *Jane Burbank*

Efforts to elicit peaceful submission from Kazan's elites and Crimean delegates failed. In early October 1552, after a month-long siege, the city fell to the Moscovite army.[24]

10.4   Eurasian Rules

Conquest was one thing, but what made it possible for Moscow to retain its hold on huge spaces to the east (the khanates of Kazan and Astrakhan, and the enormous Siberian expanse; Map 10.5)? The "conquest of Kazan" was just that – the capture of a city; it did not signal a securely demarcated territory or a united populace. Kazan's new overlords would have to work hard to bring the surrounding peoples under their command and their systems of exploitation.[25]

To make the transition from conquerors to rulers, Moscovites relied on practices of sovereignty that they shared with the khanate's former rulers and surviving elites. At the apex of power was the ultimate leader: the Russian tsar replaced the khan.[26] His military commanders – of many origins – were delegated considerable powers in the first decades of Russian rule, as troops managed to extend lines of defense with or against Nogais, Bashkirs, and other groups (Davies 2007; Khodarkovsky 2004; Stevens 1995, 2007, 78–85). Gradually, Russian officials set up administrative and judicial institutions. The establishment of imperial authority over the multiple peoples of the area proceeded with the usual combination of tactics – the stick of violence and the carrot of protection by an imperial overlord.

There was one, big, difference for people in Kazan. Now the religion of the rulers was Russian Christianity, not Islam. Earlier, Muslim clergy had played substantial roles in Kazan's governance; now the Orthodox church became a major ideological and institutional support for Russian power. An archbishop was established for the area; he promptly set off on a four-month procession from Moscow to Kazan, blessing each town along the way. In Kazan, the archbishop sprinkled the walls and gates of Kazan's Kremlin (fortress) with holy water, turning the commanding height of the city into a Christian space. The city's Tatar inhabitants, considered infidels by the church, were pushed out of the center into a special Tatar quarter. Churchmen

---

[24] For an account of the conquest, see Tagirov 2008, 140–53. For the date, from a recent authoritative source, see "Kazanskoe vziatie" (The Seizure of Kazan), *Tatarskii entsiklopedicheskii slovar'*, 1999, 150.
[25] Matthew P. Romaniello (2012, 19) notes that it took until the 1570s for the Russians to subdue populations outside the city of Kazan.
[26] On the adoption of the title "tsar" and its complex relationship to "caesar/tsesar," "Kaiser," khan and khagan, see Ostrowski 1998, 177–186.

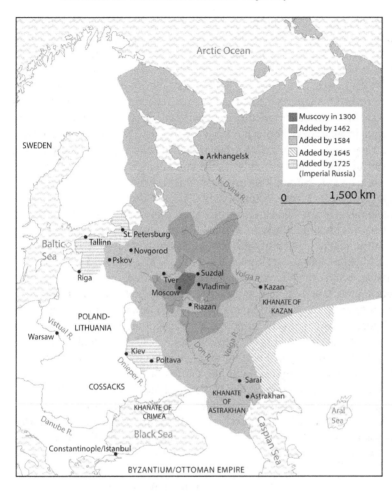

Map 10.5 Expansion of Moscow, 1300–25. From Jane Burbank and
Frederick Cooper, *Empires in World History: Power and the Politics of
Difference*. Princeton: Princeton University Press, 2010, map 7.2, p. 192.

were aggressive constructors of fortified monasteries that extended Moscow's
control outward in the area (Romaniello 2012, 31–5, 40–2).

The representation of Russia's Christian conquest played out spectacu-
larly back in Moscow: the famous St. Basil's Cathedral outside the Moscow
Kremlin was built to commemorate the victory over Kazan. But as Matthew
Romaniello points out, the tsar's policies were much more cautious than
such dramatic gestures suggest. Moscow's success in the middle Volga

region brought the prospect of conflict with greater powers to the south. In an ambiguous gesture, the tsar informed the Ottoman sultan that he, the tsar, would protect his new Muslim subjects (Romaniello 2012, 37).

An immediate concern was the tsar's need for troops to subordinate multiple tribes in the region. Conveniently, both Tatars and Nogais were interested in gains to be had by helping the new rulers out. Tatar nobles were able to make their way into Moscow's good graces as loyal servitors. This openness to absorbing local leaders into state service was a handy tool in the Eurasian political package. The Orthodox Church had its own interests to look after, however, and these could conflict with the military imperative. By Russian law Christian peasants, but not Muslims or animists, could be granted as dependents to military servitors. Consequently, monasteries that relied on non-Christian villagers for labor shared with their dependents an interest in keeping Tatar peasants Muslim. While defending the superiority of their state-supported religion, clerics could put profit above conversion and disregard the confession of their Muslim labor force (Romaniello 2012, 6, 37, 72–82, 153–5).

Russian rulers thus took a characteristically pragmatic and Eurasian approach to the task of governing new populations and faiths. The recognition of diversity came naturally to them – it had been essential to their expansion and formation as a polity. The normality of incorporating elites with their followers into armies, and of ruling over peasants with a multitude of customs prevailed after Muscovy had become strong enough to defeat a Muslim khanate. Orthodox Christianity, unlike Islam, did not provide a legal apparatus for governing people of other faiths, and Christian churchmen could be inconveniently aggressive in their universalistic quests. But Orthodoxy was the only high culture available to the Russian tsars in the 16th century. They took from it what worked, and later, gradually, acquired other languages of legitimation.

The conquest of Kazan occurred shortly before the most threatening period for Russia's survival as a state, the crisis called the Time of Troubles, 1584–1613. When Ivan IV's only surviving heir, the weak-minded Fedor, died, the Riurikid dynasty came to an end. This disastrous event for a polity where peace rested on the hard-earned rule of a single clan led to a lengthy struggle for the throne, involving not just pretenders from Muscovy, but also the forces of powerful neighbors – Sweden and Poland-Lithuania. By this time, after four centuries of unremarked adolescence, Moscow had become a desirable conquest.

Countering the usual assumptions about imperial power, Russia's new subjects in Kazan did not try to break away in this turbulent time. Instead, local elites and military men took part in many episodes of the struggle for control over Moscow's realm, including efforts to place a dynastically legitimated person on the throne. Some from Kazan fought for the "false Dmitri," who posed as a surviving Riurikid to be supported against the Russian nobleman (Prince Shuiskii) who had been proclaimed tsar; at a later date, people from the region helped drive out Poland's troops.[27] Within a few decades of the 1552 assault, Russian rule in Kazan had been turned into a fact of life, and one worth protecting.

Why did people in the Kazan region act for, not against, the authority of their recent conquerors? At stake were offices vulnerable to the multiple contests over power as well as something that some of Kazan's denizens seemed to see as essential to order, well-being, or just survival – a legitimate ruler at the head of state with a clear chain of command to local authorities. Revival of Moscow's control would bring back the distributive practices and imperial oversight fundamental to Eurasian sovereignty.

10.5   Russia Moves West

The re-anchoring of Russian power in Kazan under the new Romanov dynasty (1613–1917) turned out to have long-lasting consequences: the area would remain part of Russia's several empires for the next four centuries, and still counting. The tricky business of managing a large Muslim population produced several shifts in strategy. Institutions of governance in the Volga region were altered multiple times, as they were throughout the realm. As the empire stretched out over Siberia, Kazan became less a border region and a more a center of imperial management for areas to its east and south. Activists in Kazan would be influential in at least two more near crashes of the Russian state, in 1917 and 1991. But, as in the 17th-century crisis, Kazan and its hinterlands remained within Russia's imperial domains – in communist and post-communist variants.

Summing up my argument about the significance of space for the Russian Empire in formation and expansion, I make three observations. In the beginning, the Eurasian steppe created the ecological conditions where only certain kinds of sovereignty could succeed. Exercising long-term and long-distance control in this region privileged peoples with certain technical and political skills. The political culture of legitimate one-man command over allies and subordinates who could in turn command armies of horse-mounted warriors had been honed by Eurasian nomads for centuries; this way of organizing power had sustained multiple federations of clan-based tribes in the past. The Bolgars, the Mongols, the Riurikids and the Tatars in Kazan all shared fundamental expectations about how power worked or should work. The states that took shape on the Volga watershed built on these established imaginaries, consolidating their control over populations and resources, and, when possible, pushing outward and expanding their reach. That is, making space into place.

[27] See the excellent account in Romaniello 2012, 46–50.

But in addition to setting environmental conditions for social organization, the Eurasian area offered a particular advantage to ambitious empire-builders. After all, other great steppe and tundra regions around the globe might seem to offer the same conditions for political claims to widely separated nodes of settlement and resources. The North American continent is a case in point: the great plains, forests, tundra, and arctic coasts resemble the situation of what became Russian Siberia. Indeed, a 20th-century Russian Eurasianist, P. N. Savitskii made this connection in his theory of cultural migration from south to north over time. (He postulated that Canada and Russia would do well in the 3rd millennium, replacing Europe.)[28] But if it was climate and geography that counted for civilizational creations, why did the Mongols and later the Moscovites create a huge polity in their transcontinental space, while North American Indians did not do the same?

The answer requires us to think about the edges of steppelands and continents, about the seas beyond those edges, and about the human achievements that made it worthwhile for nomads to conduct long-distance commerce. North American Indians did make federations and empires, but these only became rich when the land-and-sea empires of the Europeans raised the economic stakes. As Pekka Hämäläinen has shown, Comanchee warriors could construct a powerful empire once there was largesse to fight for (Hämäläinen 2008). The obstacle to making a successful and expansive empire earlier was not techno-logical – Native Americans rapidly absorbed new military technologies (guns, especially) introduced by the European invasions – but rather the absence of a "China" – a rich, productive, organized state capable of concentrating wealth and re-allocating it when threatened.

Thus, a second critical spatial factor for the formation of Russian Empire was the existence of rich civilizations at the edges of the Eurasian steppe. These polities in the past constituted the "pull" for making empire in Eurasia, as nomads strove to raid, buy, or blast their way into a higher living standard. Intersections of settled and mobile cultures in war and in peace enriched nomadic federations, whose leaders acquired expertise as they conquered or struggled with their wealth-producing neighbors. The Mongols as late-comers to Eurasian empire profited from both their direct contact with China and their absorption of earlier and more experienced Eurasian groups. For example, the Mongols acquired an alphabet from Uighurs, whose polity had been subordinated to the khan of Qara Khitai; that khanate, which itself had acquired many bureaucratic skills, was in turn conquered by Chinggis Khan in 1218 (Biran 2004, 344–5). Moscow, allowed to grow up in its backwater location, could piggy-back onto a millennium of accumulated statecraft when it came under Mongol rule.

---

[28] On Savitskii, see Burbank 1986, 215–17. For Savitskii, it was temperature that counted: he traced culture along a declining gradient, from ancient Mesopotamia and Egypt, through Greece and Rome, to Europe, and so on to the north. Typically of Russian intellectuals, he ignored the southern hemisphere altogether.

For the empire that Moscow's rulers successfully built, there turned out to be more than one edge and more than one civilization to learn from. If the existence of China on the edge of the steppe inspired the formation of Eurasian empires, the eventual spread of the Russian Empire out from Moscow in all directions gave it an advantage that powers and would-be powers to Russia's east lacked. The third way in which space mattered to Russian Empire was through the polity's location in an area that permitted outreach and, at times overreach, toward the north, west, and south, as well as the east (Map 10.6). From the 16th century, when the dynamics of world power shifted and the world economy became literally global, Moscow's position on the western side of Eurasia became a cultural asset. This geographical attribute meant that Russia's rulers could blend "European" ways into their ways of rule.

Space – geography – thus reentered the story of Russia's political possibilities, enriching them. The Romanovs, taking over from the Riurikids as rulers of the expanding Russian Empire, proved adept at using their already diversified tool kit, but found themselves up against powers to their west that were beginning to get the upper hand in commerce, production, and technology. Challenged on their moving borders, Romanov and subsequently communist and post-communist rulers were inspired to mix in, selectively, resources from the "west" during its three centuries of hegemonic power. Moscow was lucky in location, luckier as it turned out than Kazan, although no one would have thought so in the 12th century.

10.6   Spatial Mix-ins and Mix-ups

Let us review the implements in the Romanovs' imperial tool kit, with an eye on the consequences of their multi-sided encounters with other imperial powers. Romanov command relied, as did that of empires generally, on the use of intermediaries who could in principle manage dispersed and disparate populations. Like their Riurikid predecessors and in accord with the Eurasian approach, the Romanovs attracted elites from a variety of groups into imperial management. Tatar and other high-status individuals could attain places in the "Russian" nobility, and earn rewards for their service.[29] At a time when Russian interests and aspirations intersected with those of European empires, the Romanovs could draw upon military and other experts from the "west" as well. Peter the Great's great mission to learn from Dutch and other European powers was only the most visible of Russian efforts to acquire knowledge from outside the polity – both from non-Russians, such as Baltic nobles who ended up inside the empire, and from servitors who came from afar to join the host of "foreign" experts in many fields.[30]

[29] See Romaniello 2012, 213, on how this history of elite service has been distorted by recent nationalizing historians.

[30] For an example of such service in the early 20th century, see the astonishing story of Baron von Ungern-Sternberg: Sunderland 2014, esp. 25–123.

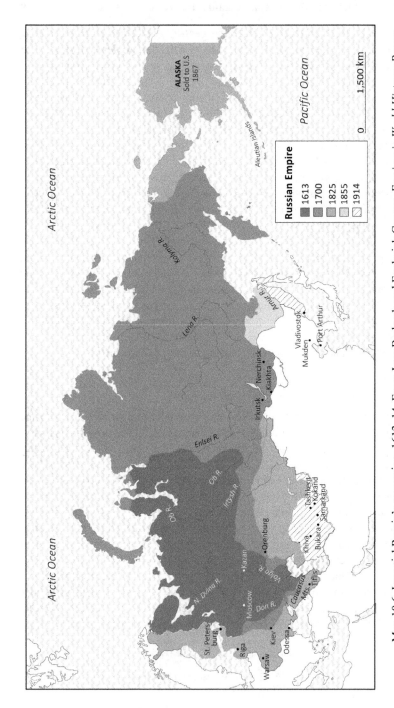

Map 10.6 Imperial Russia's expansion, 1613–14. From Jane Burbank and Frederick Cooper, *Empires in World History: Power and the Politics of Difference*, map 9.2, p. 253.

One kind of recompense for elite service was the land grant, and often the labor to go with it. Like the Mongol khans earlier, Russian tsars asserted their right to control the land of the realm, which meant, generally, assigning it to noble servitors, of many ethnic and national origins.[31] A particularity of Russia's labor regime was that the vast expanses of the empire made holding onto workers problematic. Gradually the rulers introduced legislation to attach peasants to the lands they worked for their noble masters.[32]

Ruling through law was a practice of Russian governance well before the accession of the first Romanov to the throne in 1613. Like a Eurasian khan or a Riurikid prince, the tsar was expected to issue laws and to provide access to judicial procedures. This obligation was one expression of the rulers' duty to protect his subjects, often from harm caused by the same intermediaries on whom the tsar depended.[33] The tsar managed his various peoples collectively: laws defined the rights of different groups in the population. Through this regime of allocated rights, subjects received legally protected possibilities to engage in particular kinds of commerce, take on defined tasks, exploit resources, and construct family and other social relations.[34] As Russia tried to make itself a member of the European club of great powers, law was an area of both interest and tension. Through the great codification of law in the 19th century, advisers sought ways to apply and publicize Russia's legal traditions (Borisova 2008). A more disruptive innovation was the mix-in of "western" legal procedures in the 1860s, when a bar, the jury trial and adversarial justice were introduced.

As these innovations suggest, a prominent characteristic of Romanov rule was its flexibility. With the tsar as the sole source of law, the legal regime could be manipulated and adjusted to fit new circumstances. The tsar (from 1721 re-titled emperor) was a critical actor in the imperial regime of rights, but so too were the high-ranking servitors, court and other intimates, and top administrators who could influence the making and remaking of the laws. To participate in the highest politics of the realm, one had to be part of the inner circles of top advisers, companions, and selected members of the imperial family. The politics of personal allegiance and of shifting alliances had moved from the open field of military competition and into the capitals of Romanov power, first Moscow, then St. Petersburg.

As for religion, the Romanovs had inherited an official faith and imperial ideology from their predecessors. The Riurikids had buttressed their authority with Eastern Christianity, enhanced and transformed as the Russian church acquired its metropolitan and later its patriarch, headquartered in Moscow. The

---

[31] See Pravilova 2014 for an extended and revisionist discussion of the allocation of property to servitors by the tsar. On land donation as an imperial prerogative, see Pravilova 2011.

[32] On Russian labor law, see Stanziani 2008.

[33] On the ethic of imperial protection in Muscovy, see Kollmann 1999.

[34] On the regime of allocated rights, see Burbank 2006.

first Romanov was the son of the patriarch of the Russian church. Over the course of the next two centuries, the Romanovs got the upper hand over their clerical advisers, constricted and controlled church and monastic resources, and turned Orthodoxy into a well disciplined partner of the commanding emperor.

This politics of subordinating Russian Christian authorities to secular control had significant consequences for Muslims and people of other non-Christian confessions. Although Orthodox hierarchs routinely pushed for a politics of conversion, the state could back off from extreme measures when these proved inconvenient.[35] Catherine the Great's 1773 law, "On the tolerance of all confessions and on the forbidding of hierarchs to interfere in matters concerning the other [*inovernye*] confessions and concerning the building according to their law of prayer houses, and the transfer of all these [matters] to the secular authorities,"[36] expressed in enlightened fashion the Eurasian politics of confessional pluralism.

Oversight by the "secular authorities" took different routes, for different religions. One track – modeled on the empire's taming of the Christian hierarchy – was official control over the religious leaders. Islam, in its multiple interpretations, everywhere presented severe challenges to imperial rulers, including and perhaps especially Muslim ones, but Russian officials tried with some success to institutionalize surveillance of Muslim clerics. In 1789, the state opened the Orenburg Muslim Spiritual Assembly to train Islamic clerics under imperial oversight. In the 19th century, the conquests of the Caucasus and Central Asia complicated this strategy of consolidated control.[37]

The partitions of Poland in the late 18th century brought a large Jewish population into the Romanovs' domains. Divisions among Jewish elites, most prominently between modernizers and conservatives, presented obstacles to the strategy of relying on officially recognized and surveilled intermediaries to manage Jewish subjects. With regard to this confession, the Romanovs relied primarily on a different, but also Eurasian, approach – the application of distinctive regulations to each legally defined group. In 1786 Catherine the Great required that all the new Jewish subjects be registered as members of the "merchant" estate, but pressure from Russian merchants led the administration to use its regulatory capacity to restrict areas of Jewish residence and to define Jews' possibilities in education, civic activities and work.[38]

The issuing of distinctive rules for Jews was in itself not exceptional. Imperial law and administrative practice was built on the principle of differentiated rules

---

[35] For an example of such an episode, see Geraci 1997.

[36] Catherine the Great's law on tolerance was issued as an *ukaz* by the Holy Synod on June 17, 1773: *Polnoe sobranie zakonov Rossiiskoi imperii*, 1 series, t. 19, no. 13.996, s. 775–776.

[37] On imperial legislation in the 18th century on religion in the Kazan region, see Nogmanov 2002, 100–32. On the Muslim Spiritual Assembly, see Crews 2006, 52–91 and Geraci 2001, 22. On imperial control of "other" religions in the 19th and early 20th centuries, see Werth 2014.

[38] On regulation of Jews in the empire, see Stanislawski 1983; Nathans 2002; Freeze 2002; and Avrutin 2010.

for the many groups – defined by status, location, religion, function, etc. – in the empire. This multi-cultural approach was explicit in imperial law. Russian statutes described distinctive marital regimes that would be applied to people of different faiths; most family matters would be settled by religious institutions to which subjects belonged (Burbank 2006). The variability of legislation was an irritant to those who wanted more general rules, while others used it to plead for better adjustment to particular needs. The empire's multiplex approach thus made both particularity and generalization into handy arguments for revising the rules.

Modernizers of various faiths and allegiances took heart as imperial politics loosened up in the early 20th century. Party politics, the latest import from the "west," was interpreted in Russia's own way by both officials and activists. The language of ethnic belonging was mobilized by some delegates to the empire's short-lived parliament (the Duma, 1906–17). Reformers and critics mobilized around multiple claims, not restricted to those of ethnicity and not oriented toward making new nation-based states. On its part, the administration tinkered with the electoral regulations between sessions of the Duma (Tsiunchuk 2007). Imperial scenarios retained their useful ambiguities about the relationship of Russians and Orthodoxy to other peoples and faiths. Great displays of multi-culturalism decorated both the opening of the Duma in 1906 and the Romanovs' tercentenary celebrations in 1913. Remaking the rules engaged the empire's elites, both in the Duma and outside it.

The many shifts in administrative structure under the Romanovs expressed, rather than challenged, the basic components of a long-lasting Eurasian sovereignty regime: dynastic rule, reformable regulatory practices emanating from contingently empowered elites dependent on the emperor, a legal umbrella sheltering multiple ethnic and confessional cultural norms, a network of officials operating at the provincial and lower levels. The experiment in representational politics at the beginning of the 20th century highlighted the fungibility of formal institutions. Politics was about recalibration of who controlled what, expressed in the decade-long dance of disdain between Duma and emperor. This tension was resolved later in the Bolshevik revitalization of one-man rule in a one-party guise, only to reemerge in the 1990s with the repeated adjustments of democratic rules to sovereign practices in the Russian Federation and its "near abroad."[39]

10.7   Space and Empire, Russian-Style

My account of the trajectories of Russian Empire calls into question some categories that have been conventionally used to analyze empires. First, our chronological typologies are usually Eurocentric. While time is of course an

---

[39] This term was coined in the 1990s to refer to areas that had been part of the USSR before they became independent states.

inevitable component of how empires are configured and how they develop, a period (medieval, early modern etc.) that has been used to describe the history of western Europe does not delineate a globally relevant kind of sovereignty. The variety of imperial practices at any point in history should be revealed and respected, without privileging a particular condition as "typical" for a particular time. In this volume, the neutral, but still time-conscious concept of "waves" of Eurasian empires provides a useful and intriguing organizational principle and provokes questions about the ebb and flow of political structures.

Second, "continental" is a deceptive category when applied to empires. As the introduction to this volume indicates, most of the so-called "land" empires – Russia, Ottoman, Habsburg, China at various times – had sea coasts or wanted them. These empires relied on water routes and exploited long-distance trading lines that, even if terrestrial, were similar in their demands, limits, and potentials to the maritime connections of the so-called "overseas" empires. Russia's goals and achievements included waterways, ports, and sea routes. Islands in the straits between Asia and America were overrun by Russian fur-hunters in the 18th century (Jones 2014). For a time, Russia possessed territories on both sides of the Pacific – the Californian forts and Alaska most notably – as well as outposts in Hawaii. Roman and Chinese empires were both terrestrial and seaborne. The distinction between "continental" and "overseas" empires ignores geographic realities, let alone the aspirations, of many empires.

Like the categories "ancient" and "modern," the distinction between land and sea empires derives from and seems to validate a world history configured by representations of 19th-century western Europe empires. Time and space are tied together in the convention that western European empires were distinctive because of their "overseas" dimension. But let us remember that these "western" empires all had landed dimensions utterly critical to their being. Leaders and would-be leaders of France, Spain, Great Britain, the Netherlands, and Portugal struggled over centuries to enforce their imperial command inside Europe as well as overseas, trying to draw disparate peoples and locales into a more uniform cultural and political sphere. Empire had to be conquered and/or cultivated both "at home" and abroad by the Habsburgs, the Bourbons, the British crown and parliament, not to speak of Napoleon.[40] The most volatile and insecure of the territories acquired by western European empires were the "overseas" ones. The North American colonies rebelled and escaped from Great Britain in the 18th century; most colonies established in Asia and Africa in the 19th century exited empire less than one hundred years later. Are we to count Ireland as "land" or "overseas"? In any case, the struggle over that element in British empire is still ongoing. The decisive factor is not land or water.

[40] For the most ambitious effort before Hitler's, see Woolf 1991.

Third and returning to the Russian case, we should also challenge the oft-used vocabulary of core and periphery. Russian leaders did not develop, even ideologically, firm distinctions between a single core and its periphery, nor a fundamental bifurcation between inner and outer regions. The space of the empire was always up for redesign and re-division. For one thing, the potential periphery was enormous and enormously variegated. It was inconceivable to treat Ukraine, the Baltic regions, Siberia, the Caucasus, Central Asia with uniformly "outsider" status. Each cultural arena, each group of people, each confessional arrangement presented its own opportunities and challenges to imperial leaders. From a physical standpoint, multiple regions were always in play and keeping them that way was part of the imperial repertoire.[41]

But there was also no agreement on what might have constituted a "core." Was it what came to be known as "European Russia"? But that would have put Poland in the core, which hardly worked. Was it Russian ethnicity? This too was problematic, in that "Russian" heartland areas were filled with people of non-Slavic, non-Orthodox backgrounds and Russian ethnics were dispersed all over the imperial territories. Could a core be defined in a political/cultural way? Not so easy as it turned out. In the early 19th century, writers had no clear idea about where the boundaries of "Russia" in a spatial sense lay. Did the whole empire revolve around only one city – Moscow – or were Novgorod and Kiev also capitals of distinctive cultural areas, as the travel writer Vadim Passek (1808–42) suggested in 1834?[42]

The capital itself, while fundamentally important to Russian power, was not fixed. Moscow was a spreading node, not a center, of "Russian" empire. Eventually, under the Romanovs, the capital was moved to St. Petersburg (renamed three times in the 20th century). In 1918, the Bolsheviks transferred the center of government back to Moscow, and a return to St. Petersburg is rumored in today's Russian Federation. The moving and renaming of principal cities could be seen as a Eurasian trait. In 1991, the leader of independent Kazakhstan first renamed the capital city of the former Soviet republic, and then moved the government to a new site, renamed Astana in 1998. Kazakhstan's second president gave Astana another name, Nur-Sultan, in 2019 to honor his predecessor.[43]

Russia's ongoing mélange of political practices from diverse sources, combined with its leaders' international deployment of well targeted and also

---

[41] On the manipulation of internal borders (regionalization), see Burbank and von Hagen 2007.

[42] It is of relevance that Passek did not consider St. Petersburg, the empire's capital, as the primary node: Gorizontov 2007, 71.

[43] Nur-Sultan boasts a presidential palace that according to Kazakhstan's official website "reflects a steppe civilization in the mirror of the European culture, a synthesis of arts of the planet's largest continent – Eurasia." For the official description of the capital, see Republic of Kazakhstan 2019.

diverse political discourses, gives scholars and politicians headaches, but from a spatial perspective who can deny the success of Russian Empire? Even cut back from Soviet scale (Map 10.7), the Russian Federation covers a large portion of the globe – one-eighth of its land mass. The country stretches across what we think of as two continents and nine time zones (recently reduced from eleven). Russia is the ninth most populous state in the world, inhabited by 143 million people of 193 ethnicities, according to the categories of the 2010 census (Federal'naia sluzhba gosudarstvennoi statistiki 2013; see Map 10.8 below).

Do we know where this state begins and ends? Returning to questions of territory, borders, and the spatial dimensions of imperial power, did the spatial dynamic – the intersection of power and place that I have described – come to a stop? Were there limits to Russia's imperial expanse and if so, what were these constraints?

My account of Moscow's "rise" – actually a spread – from a small town with a kremlin to the capital of a recognized and authoritative empire suggests that limits were reached only in competition with other empires and when disparities in technologies of warfare and diplomacy forced Russia to draw back from further expansion. Space/place mattered in that limits were set differently in unlike regions and at different times.

From the earliest Muscovite years into the 18th century, extension of state power over the vast areas of Siberia where widely scattered populations did not expect to rule themselves was not significantly obstructed. Rebellions were put down, and deals were cut with nomadic and other powers. By the late 18th century, the last nomadic challengers (the Zhungars/Jungars) had been destroyed, and the remaining nomads extruded or restrained (Burbank and Cooper 2010, 213–18). In this direction, even the sea was no limit; Russian Empire crossed the Pacific and only retreated in North America when the Romanovs' priorities made it desirable to do so (Vinkovetsky 2011).

As described above, expansion to the west and south became difficult as Muscovite rulers reached toward the areas controlled by other competitive and often greater powers. The Romanovs nonetheless continued to push both borders and outposts as far as they could. To the west, Russia made gains as a partner on one side or another of European wars; the prizes included partitions of Poland and annexations from Sweden (Finland). To the south, as the Ottoman Empire weakened, Russia was able to expand its land and sea power. The Romanovs used both diplomacy and war to reach across the Black Sea and into the imperial competition over control of the Mediterranean. Crimea was annexed by Catherine the Great in 1783, putting an end to the last semi-independent Mongol Khanate. Russian leaders made every effort to expand their claims to authority inside Ottoman domains in southern Europe and the Middle East. Military conquest brought in much of Central Asia, but in Afghanistan limits

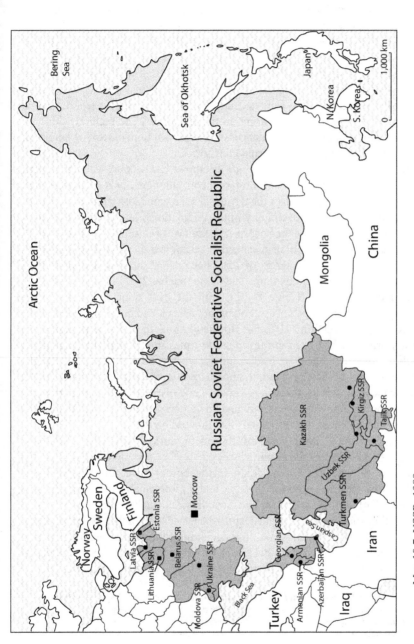

Map 10.7 USSR, 1989.

were set – for a while – by the ambitions of another imperial power, the British. The edges of Romanov empire were never fixed; borders were re-drawn multiple times.[44] The decisive factor in each case was the particular moment of imperial competition, but this meant that no boundary was final.

After 1917, the Soviet Union's commanders fought hard to bring as many of the Romanov territories back into their control as they could, at a time when their imperial competitors were themselves exhausted militarily. In the aftermath of World War II, when Stalin had the strength to insist, the USSR reached beyond the regions he had divvied up with Hitler in 1939, extending Soviet control further into central Europe. In the late 1980s, competition with great powers and technological imbalances once again set limits to Soviet empire, in both its directly and indirectly ruled territories.

In Russia's case, the great space of its empire has become well anchored in its political discourse, at least for internal consumption, but is this space stable today? Has the legal fiction of the territorial state with fixed boundaries, treated as a unit of legitimate sovereignty in the international law of our times, come true? Do we know where the borders of Ukraine or Moldova, or for that matter, Estonia, are? Does the Russian leadership accept that these borders and its own are now fixed?[45] In the terms of this chapter, has the spatial expansion of Russian Empire reached its limits and come to a halt?

A recent study by Sabine Dullin, with the marvelous title, *La frontière épaisse*, examines the perspective on borders developed in the first two decades of Soviet power (Dullin 2014). The Bolsheviks took the place of the Romanovs in a world that had been cut up multiple times into states with boundaries. Dullin shows that the Soviet leaders did not want a line – in the sand, in the dirt, in the water – at all. For them, the border was a zone. It was a space for the simultaneous exercise of sovereign control and disruptive revolutionary initiatives. The frontier zone was not pinned down permanently to a particular place on the map: it could be "thickened" and it could be moved.

In the realm of discourse, Soviet leaders worked with what seem from conventional perspectives on statehood to be completely contradictory accounts of what they were doing in the border zone. But for Bolshevik authorities, this was a normal, useful, and unproblematic way of conducting their kind of political business. The most dramatic dualism was that of making revolution, that is, attempting to destroy the foundation of their neighbor states' sovereignty, while at the same time declaiming the Soviet Union's rights as a state protected by international law. A Soviet poster from 1921 reproduced in Dullin's book declares, "We destroy the boundaries between countries." But at

---

[44] Willard Sunderland notes that borders with Poland, the Ottoman Empire and the Crimean Khanate were altered six times between 1772 and 1795 alone: Sunderland 2007, 52.

[45] In late 2016, Vladimir Putin joked that "Russia's border does not end anywhere." See the BBC report http://www.bbc.com/news/world-europe-38093468 (accessed April 5, 2018).

that very moment, Soviet diplomats were trying to get agreements with Poland, Finland, and the new Baltic states on the creation of a border – with a zone on both sides – that would protect the USSR from hostile powers.

In both Ukraine and in Moldova today we see phenomena very similar to what happened in the 1920s, when the USSR was trying to recover imperial terrain. The border politics in Moldova in the 21st century replicate the frontier zone strategies of Soviet times – a joint control commission, a demilitarized zone, regulation of commerce across borders, the highlighting of national minority rights, and the contested and thoroughly ambiguous political status of the Pridnestrovian Moldavian Republic. In Moldova, in Ukraine, and in the "new" republics of South Ossetia and Abkhazia, the frontier has already thickened (Map 10.8).

Within two decades after the Bolshevik revolution of 1917, the communist leaders of the USSR recognized and appealed to Peter the Great's territorial gains as a foundation of Soviet power. Now, almost three decades after 1991, are we seeing yet another revival of Russian Empire, based once again on multiple, inconsistent, yet functionally effective claims and practices, nurtured by the long-term politics of contracting and contesting expansion, delegation of military and administrative tasks to willing intermediaries, and indifference to fixity in space? And as before, will the limits be set by competitions among great powers and by critical disparities in technologies of warfare and diplomacy?

10.8   Space, Politics, Place and back to Space?

A strong convention of modern state theory is "territoriality." States are supposed to have defined borders, to control strictly movement across these absolute boundaries, and to govern the space inside these lines. But as we have seen, even at present, Russian leaders are comfortable with, indeed cultivate, ambiguity about where their state begins and ends. We do not see in Russia's history the emergence of a sharp divide between center and periphery. Rather, political, cultural, and even geographical space has been imagined differently over time and in shifting configurations of imperial competitions.

Before Russia appeared as a polity, steppe-based economies inspired Eurasian peoples to create expansionist and workable imperial arrangements and to exploit such conditions. The interplay of humans in a region whose inhabitants shared a political culture set limits on the outcomes of power struggles. Space in this sense of physical environment impacted political culture and thus set limits on and possibilities for the type of empire that could survive in a particular place on the globe. It is hard for contenders who do not share the political imaginary of the occupants of a particular space or cannot adapt to their practices to maintain control over that region.

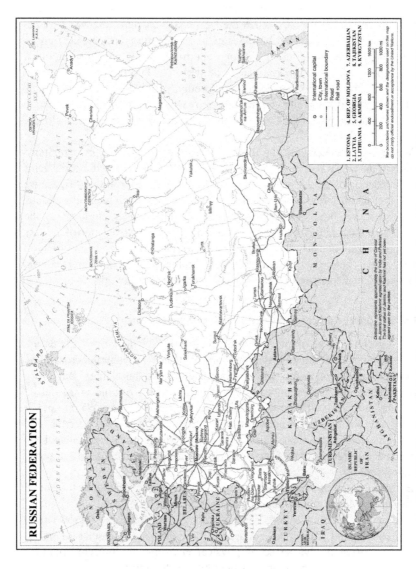

Map 10.8 The Russian Federation and its neighbors. From https://en.m.wikipedia.org/wiki/File:Un-russia.png.

Victorious powers on a particular terrain, though, may reach as far as they can, enhancing resources, wealth, well-being for some as they go. In so doing they create opportunities coveted by others. They then come to intersect with contenders for power in a less predictable, unstable dynamic. Over the long term, both the demands of governing particular areas and the exigencies of competition with unlike or like competitors will transform the repertoires of imperial rule, including the reconfiguration of space itself.

The actions of empires – redirecting and pioneering trade routes on land and/ or sea, improving technologies of connection (long-distance communications and transport), conducting war, making peace, developing production, and resource extraction – have transforming effects on both conceptions and physical qualities of space. Power contests among empires can produce both secured places and fractious spaces. To take a contemporary example from Russia's undefined southern regions, a shift from empire to warlordism and from "our native peoples" to families and individuals in flight can wipe states or parts of them off the map and reopen the space for politics and eventual place-making. Another way to put this is: empires have the capacity to transform space into place, or in the case of failed imperial projects, to turn place back into space, open for more contestation.

To sum up my argument, my first point is that the spatial possibilities for empire depend on what other empires have set in place or ignored. This prior configuration of possibilities derives from political economies – from ideas about resources and the means to get at them – configured in specific geographical-ecological regions. Moscow emerged as a bud of imperial power in roughly the 14th century, after the collapse of Kievan empire and the Mongol conquest, when the Rus' princely clan had settled in small towns in what we know now as central Russia. This was possible because at first, no great power was interested in this backwater. Like other cities/towns that eventually expanded into empires, Moscow enjoyed a distance from the super states of its times. Its leaders had a chance to expand and learn how to govern before other powers took notice. A poor resource environment can be of help.

Second, Moscow's princes then had the good fortune of rubbing up against multiple imperial powers during their history. Their dynasty, the Rus', integrated Viking and Eurasian-style family practices on the way to power in Kiev. Kiev in turn through its contacts with Byzantium left Muscovites a distinctly imperial state religion – Byzantine-style Christianity with its linguistic tolerance, writing systems, resplendent art. When the Mongols established their western empire in the lands of the Rus', the Muscovites acquired more administrative techniques and were compelled into expansion to retain their hold as first rank subordinates. The subsequent dynasty and the later communist and post-communist leaders continued the practices of expansion and the concomitant integration of disparate military, economic, and cultural skills.

These two arguments about space and political culture are related to each other. It is ecology – the perceived resource environment – as well as proximity to established imperial powers with their cultural/political attributes that counts in my analysis. Moscow expanded its wealth as a good client of the Mongols, but the very paucity of the region's resources as perceived by the most powerful and proximate powers let the Russians do their expansion on their own. By the time European empires – Swedish and Polish in the first place – came to see their huge neighbor as a threat – it was too late. Russia had created a vast space of resources and the tools to keep it theirs – or expand it. Russia's leaders would keep learning from imperial competitors – the Habsburgs, the Prussians, the British, and the rest of what became known as the "west" – over the next centuries and into the present. The recent turn by the Putin regime toward Asia may bring with it new technologies to mix into Russia's porous and mutable politics, as space continues to shape empires and empires continue to redefine place.

Bibliography

Allsen, Thomas T. 2001. *Culture and Conquest in Mongol Eurasia*. New York: Cambridge University Press.

"Astana." 2017. *Geograficheskaia entsiklopediia* (Geographical Encyclopedia). http://dic.academic.ru/dic.nsf/enc_geo/617. Accessed June 1, 2019.

Avrutin, Eugene M. 2010. *Jews and the Imperial State: Identification Politics in Tsarist Russia*. Ithaca, NY: Cornell University Press.

Bariev, Riza Kh. 2005. *Volzhskie bulgary: Istoriia i kul'tura* (Volga Bulgars: History and Culture). Saint Petersburg: Agat.

Biran, Michal. 2004. "The Mongol Transformation: from the Steppe to Eurasian Empire." *Medieval Encounters* 10(1–3): 339–51.

Borisova, Tatiana. 2008. "Russian National Legal Tradition: Svod versus Ulozhenie in Nineteenth-century Russia." *Review of Central and East European Law* 33(3): 295–341.

Brower, Daniel R. and Edward J. Lazzerini, eds. 1997. *Russia's Orient: Imperial Borderlands and Peoples, 1700–1917*. Bloomington, IN: Indiana University Press.

Burbank, Jane. 1986. Intelligentsia and Revolution: Russian Views of Bolshevism, 1917–1922. New York: Oxford University Press.

Burbank, Jane. 2006. "An Imperial Rights Regime: Law and Citizenship in the Russian Empire." *Kritika: Explorations in Russian and Eurasian History* 7(3): 397–431.

Burbank, Jane and Frederick Cooper. 2010. *Empires in World History: Power and the Politics of Difference*. Princeton, NJ: Princeton University Press.

Burbank, Jane and Mark von Hagen. 2007. "Coming into the Territory: Uncertainty and Empire." In *Russian Empire: Space, People, Power, 1700–1930*, ed. Jane Burbank, Mark von Hagen, and Anatolyi Remnev, 3–29. Bloomington, IN: Indiana University Press.

Burbank, Jane, Mark von Hagen, and Anatolyi Remnev, eds. 2007. *Russian Empire: Space, People, Power, 1700–1930*. Bloomington, IN: Indiana University Press.

Crews, Robert D. 2006. *For Prophet and Tsar : Islam and Empire in Russia and Central Asia*. Cambridge, MA: Harvard University Press.

Davies, Brian L. 2007. *Warfare, State and Society on the Black Sea Steppe, 1500–1700*. New York: Routledge.

Dullin, Sabine. 2014. *La frontière épaisse: Aux origines des politiques soviétiques (1920–1940)*. Paris: Editions de l'EHESS.

Federal'naia sluzhba gosudarstvennoi statistiki. 2013. *Vserossiiskaia perepis' naseleniia 2010 goda* (2010 Census of Russia). http://www.gks.ru/free_doc/new_site/p erepis2010/croc/perepis_itogi1612.htm. Accessed June 1, 2019.

Fletcher, Joseph. 1986. "The Mongols: Social and Ecological Perspectives." *Harvard Journal of Asiatic Studies* 46(1): 11–50.

Freeze, ChaeRan Y. 2002. *Jewish Marriage and Divorce in Imperial Russia*. Hannover: Brandeis University Press.

Geraci, Robert P. 1997. "Russian Orientalism at an Impasse: Tsarist Educational Policy and the 1910 Conference on Islam." In *Russia's Orient: Imperial Borderlands and Peoples, 1700–1917*, ed. Daniel R. Brower and Edward J. Lazzerini, 138–61. Bloomington, IN: Indiana University Press.

Geraci, Robert P. 2001. *Window on the East: National and Imperial Identities in Late Tsarist Russia*. Ithaca, NY: Cornell University Press.

Gorizontov, Leonid. 2007. "Representations of 'Internal Russia' from the First Half of the Nineteenth Century." In *Russian Empire: Space, People, Power, 1700–1930*, ed. Jane Burbank, Mark von Hagen, and Anatolyi Remnev, 67–93. Bloomington, IN: Indiana University Press.

Graney, Katherine E. 2009. *Of Khans and Kremlins: Tatarstan and the Future of Ethno-Federalism in Russia*. Lanham, MD: Lexington Books.

Grinberg, Lyuba. 2011. "From Mongol Prince to a Russian Saint: A Neglected Fifteenth-century Russian Source on Mongolian Land Consecration Ritual." *Kritika: Explorations in Russian and Eurasian History* 12(3): 647–73.

Grinberg, Lyuba. 2013. "'Is this city yours or mine?' Political Sovereignty and Eurasian Urban Centers in the Ninth through Twelfth Centuries." *Comparative Studies in Society and History* 55(4): 895–921.

Hämäläinen, Pekka. 2008. *The Comanchee Empire*. New Haven, CT: Yale University Press.

Jones, Ryan. 2014. *Empire of Extinction: Russians and the North Pacific's Strange Beasts of the Sea, 1741–1867*. New York: Oxford University Press.

Kappeler, Andreas. 2001. *The Russian Empire: A Multiethnic History*. Harlow: Longman.

Kaiser, Daniel. 1980. *The Growth of Law in Medieval Russia*. Princeton, NJ: Princeton University Press.

Keenan, Edward L. 1967. "Muscovy and Kazan´: Some Introductory Remarks on the Patterns of Steppe Diplomacy." *Slavic Review* 26(4): 548–58.

Khodarkovsky, Michael. 2004. *Russia's Steppe Frontier: The Making of a Colonial Empire, 1500–1800*. Bloomington, IN: Indiana University Press.

Kollmann, Nancy Shields. 1999. *By Honor Bound: State and Society in Early Modern Russia*. Ithaca, NY: Cornell University Press.

Manz, Beatrice Forbes. 1989. *The Rise and Rule of Tamerlane*. Cambridge: Cambridge University Press.

Mayor of Moscow Official Portal. 2019. https://www.mos.ru/en/city/about/. Accessed June 2, 2019.

Morgan, David. 1990. *The Mongols*. Malden: Blackwell.

Nathans, Benjamin. 2002. *Beyond the Pale: The Jewish Encounter with Late Imperial Russia*. Berkeley, CA: University of California Press.

Nogmanov, Aidar. 2002. *Tatary srednego povolzh'ia i priural'ia v Rossiiskom zakonodatel'stve vtoroi poloviny XVI-XVIII vv.* (Tatars of the Middle Volga and Urals in Russian Legislation from the Second Half of the 16th to the 18th centuries). Kazan: Fen.

Ostrowski, Donald. 1998. *Muscovy and the Mongols: Cross-Cultural Influences on the Steppe Frontier, 1304–1589*. Cambridge: Cambridge University Press.

Polnoe sobranie zakonov Rossiiskoi imperii (Complete Collection of the Laws of the Russian Empire). 1 series, t. 19, no. 13,996, s. 775–6.

Pravilova, Ekaterina. 2011. "The Property of Empire: Islamic Law and Russian Agrarian Policy in Transcaucasia and Turkestan." *Kritika: Explorations in Russian and Eurasian History* 12(2): 353–86.

Pravilova, Ekaterina. 2014. *A Public Empire: Property and the Quest for the Common Good in Imperial Russia*. Princeton, NJ: Princeton University Press.

Puteshestvie Akhmeda Ibn-Fadlana na reku Itil' i priniatie v Bulgarii islama. Drevnii tekst pereskazal Sultan Shamsi (The Journey of Akhmed Ibn-Fadlan to the Volga River and the Adoption of Islam in Bulgaria. The Ancient Text Retold by Sultan Shamsi). 1992. Kazan: Mifi-Servis.

Rakhimzianov, Bulat. 2009. *Kasimovskoe khanstvo (1445–1552 gg.) Ocherki istorii* (The Kazimov Khanate (1445–1552) Outlines of a History). Kazan: Tatarskoe knizhnoe izdatel'stvo.

Republic of Kazakhstan. 2019. http://www.akorda.kz/en/republic_of_kazakhstan/akorda. Accessed June 1, 2019.

Romaniello, Matthew P. 2012. *The Elusive Empire: Kazan and the Creation of Russia 1552–1671*. Madison, WI: University of Wisconsin Press.

Stanislawski, Michael. 1983. *Tsar Nicholas and the Jews: The Transformation of Jewish Society in Russia, 1825–1855*. Philadelphia, PA: Jewish Publication Society of America.

Stanziani, Alessandro. 2008. "Serfs, slaves, or wage earners? The legal status of labour in Russia from a comparative perspective, from the sixteenth to the nineteenth century." *Journal of Global History* 3: 183–202.

Stanziani, Alessandro. 2012. *Bâtisseurs d'empires: Russie, Chine et Inde à la croisée des mondes, XVe – XIXe siècle*. Paris: Raisons d'agir éditions.

Stevens, Carol B. 1995. *Soldiers on the Steppe: Army Reform and Social Change in Early Modern Russia*. DeKalb, IL: Northern Illinois University Press.

Stevens, Carol B. 2007. *Russia's Wars of Emergence 1460–1730*. Harlow: Longman.

Sunderland, Willard. 2007. "Imperial Space: Territorial Thought and Practice in the Eighteenth Century." In *Russian Empire: Space, People, Power, 1700–1930*, ed. Jane Burbank, Mark von Hagen, and Anatolyi Remnev, 33–66. Bloomington, IN: Indiana University Press.

Sunderland, Willard. 2004. *Taming the Wild Field: Colonization and Empire on the Russian Steppe*. Ithaca, NY: Cornell University Press.

Sunderland, Willard. 2014. *The Baron's Cloak: A History of the Russian Empire in War and Revolution*. Ithaca, NY: Cornell University Press.

Tagirov, Indus R. 2008. *Istoriia natsional'noi gosudarstvennosti Tatarskogo naroda i Tatarstana* (History of National Stateness and the Tatar People and Tatarstan). Kazan: Tatarskoe knizhnoe izdatel'stvo.

Tatarskii entsiklopedicheskii slovar' (Tatar Encyclopedia). 1999. Kazan: Institut tatarskoi entsiklopediii AN RT.

Threadgold, Warren. 2002. "The Struggle for Survival (641–780)." In *The Oxford History of Byzantium*, ed. Cyril Mango, 129–52. Oxford: Oxford University Press.

Tsiunchuk, Rustem. 2007. "Peoples, Regions, and Electoral Politics: The State Dumas and the Constitution of New National Elites." In *Russian Empire: Space, People, Power, 1700–1930*, ed. Jane Burbank, Mark von Hagen, and Anatolyi Remnev, 366–397. Bloomington, IN: Indiana University Press.

Vinkovetsky, Ilya. 2011. *Russian America: An Overseas Colony of a Continental Empire, 1804–1867*. New York: Oxford University Press.

Werth, Paul W. 2002. *At the Margins of Orthodoxy: Mission, Governance, and Confessional Politics in Russia's Volga-Kama Region, 1827–1905*. Ithaca, NY: Cornell University Press.

Werth, Paul W. 2014. *The Tsar's Foreign Faiths: Toleration and the Fate of Religious Freedom in Imperial Russia*. Oxford: Oxford University Press.

Woolf, Stuart. 1991. *Napoleon's Integration of Europe*. London: Routledge.

Zaitsev, Ilya V. 2010. "Novye knigi ob islame v Vostochnoi Evropy" (New Books on Islam in Eastern Europe). *Pax islamica* 1(4): 192–202.

Zaitsev, Ilya V. n.d. *Kazanskoe khanstvo. Zapadnaia gruppa bashkir v sostave Kazanskogo khanstva* (Khanate of Kazan). The Western Group of Bashkirs in the Khanate of Kazan MS.

Index

Abaqa, Ilkhan (r. 1265–82), 246, 247
Abbasids, Abbasid Caliphate (750–1258), 23,
    162, 167, 180, 192–9, 204, 205,
    209, 213
'Abd al-Malik, Umayyad Caliph (r. 685–705),
    162, 187, 191
Abkhazia, 369
abode of Islam. *See dār al-Islām*
abode of war. *See dār al-harb*
Abū Bakr, Caliph (r. 632–634), 183
Abū Sa'īd (Ilkhan, r. 1316–35), 242
Achaemenid Empire, 9, 15, 19, 20, 21, 29, 34,
    70, 137, 247, 261, 266, 269, 280
    communications in, 30, 63–7
    court, mobile in, 56–9
    downfall of, 69–72
    maritime power of, 67–9
    perceptions of, 49–53
    spatial dimensions of, 53–6
    territorial control in, 59–63
administration, 25, 33, 39, 59
    Achaemenid, 51, 59, 66, 67, 68, 72
    Byzantine, 149, 151
    in Caliphate, 187, 191, 194
    in China, 80, 105
        Han, 101
        Ming, 292, 293, 300, 305, 307, 322
        Qin, 34, 94
        Qing, 323, 324, 326, 328, 330, 331, 332,
           333, 334
        Warring States period, 84, 85
    in Mongol Empire, 230, 231, 232, 234,
        235
    Mughal, 280
    Roman, 118, 119, 126, 128, 132, 134
    Russian, 362, 363
    Safavid, 269
    See also bureaucracy
Adriatic Sea, 142
Aegean Sea, 119, 151, 153
Aelius Aristides (117–81), 113
Aeneas, 111

Afghanistan, 52, 194, 196, 199, 236, 266, 269,
    270, 271, 272, 274, 275, 276, 277,
    278, 366
Africa, 2, 155, 211, 242, 284, 364
    Roman province, 119
    See also North Africa
Aghlabids (800–909), 196, 198
Ahmadnagar Sultanate, 277
Ahura Mazda, 21, 56, 57
Akbar, Mughal ruler (r. 1556–1605), 275,
    276, 277
Akkad (2334–2193 BCE), 15
Alans, 147
Alaska, 364
Albania, Caucasian, 155, 264
Alemanni, 130
Aleppo, 198
Alexander the Great (356–323 BCE), 6, 9,
    19, 20, 49, 63, 71, 119, 137, 266,
    267, 277
Alexandria, 134, 144, 146, 154
Alexios I Komnenos (r. 1081–1118), 142
'Ali b. Abi Ṭalib, Caliph (r. 656–661), 183,
    193, 198
All-under-Heaven (*tianxia* 天下), 10, 17, 18,
    19, 20, 34, 79, 82, 86–94, 104, 105, 106,
    228, 244, 245
Almaliq, 237
Almysh, Volga Bulgar ruler (d. 925), 347
Alps, 118
Altan Khan (1507–82), 305
Amarna Letters, 147
ambans, 331
Ambrones, 122
amīr al-mu'minīn ('Commander of the
    Believers'), 182
    See also caliphs
'Amr b. al-'Āṣ, military commander (d. 664),
    186
Amu Darya River (Oxus), 205, 236, 246, 247,
    267, 269
Amur River, 296

376

Anatolia, 24, 70, 149, 153, 154, 161, 181, 189, 190, 198, 201, 227, 232, 235, 236, 241, 247, 259, 260, 261, 263, 264, 265, 266, 267, 268, 269, 270, 276, 277, 280, 281
Anchises, 111
Andalusia, 260
Ando, Clifford, 33
"Angevin empire" (1154–1204), 7
Angkor Wat, 278
animals (pack animals), 60, 64, 154, 161, 234, 344
   See also camels
Ankara, 127, 263
Anna Komnene (1083–1153), 142
Annam. *See* Vietnam
Antioch, 146
Antium, 116
Antonius Pius (r. 138–61 CE), 128
Antonius, Marcus (Mark Antony, 83–30 BCE), 125
Apennine, 117
apocalypse, 164, 189
appanages (*qubi*), 224, 235, 237
Appian (*c.* 95–165), 31
Aq Qoyunlu/White Sheep Dynasty (1378–1501), 265, 266, 268
   See also Oghuz
Ara Pacis (Altar of Augustan Peace), 126
   See also peace: Rome
Arabia, 128, 182, 183, 201, 205
Arabic language, 187
Arabs, 24, 151, 154, 155, 157, 162, 182, 189, 190, 191, 201, 202, 243, 260, 270
   See also Caliphate
Arachosia, 54, 64
Aral Sea, 68
Aramaic, 52, 55, 65, 66, 68, 72
Arausio, 122
Ardabil, 265
Arghun Aqa (d. 1278), 232
Arghun, Muqim (fl. 1500), 272
aristocrats. *See* nobles, nobility
Armenia, 62, 123, 147, 148, 153, 154, 155, 160, 161, 162, 165, 232
armies, 24, 25
   Achaemenid, 55, 57, 71
   Afghan, 199, 276
   Berber, 187
   Byzantine, 151, 153, 154, 161, 164, 185, 190, 259
   Caliphate, 161, 162, 180, 183, 186, 189, 190, 201
   China
      Han, 99
      Ming, 292, 294, 296, 299, 300, 301

   pre-imperial, 84
   Qin, 93, 96
   Qing, 317, 319, 327
   Tang, 24, 193
   warlords, post-Yuan, 306
   Macedonian, 51, 60, 66, 67, 71, 72
   Mongol, 19, 224, 225, 229, 263, 294
   Mughal, 273, 275, 277
   Ottoman, 260, 263, 264, 268
   Roman, 31, 114, 116, 118, 121, 122, 126, 127, 130, 132, 136
   Russian, 356, 357
   Safavid, 266, 267
   Samanid, 199
   Sasanian, 185
   See also decimal system; Eight Banners; Green Standard army; *keshig*; legions; logistics; military
Arnason Johann, 3, 5
Arrian, historian (2nd c. CE), 55, 58, 60, 62, 69
Artaxata, 160
Artaxerxes II (r. 404–358 BCE), 57, 62, 63, 70
Artaxerxes III (r. 358–338 BCE), 70
Arthaśāstra, 34
Ashura ('Āshūrā') festival, 268
Asia, 364
   Western, 229
   See also: Central Asia, East Asia, Inner Asia, Middle East; South Asia, Southeast Asia
Asia Minor, 38, 49, 55, 59, 62, 65, 68, 69, 70, 119, 121, 122, 134, 142, 144, 149, 151, 153, 154, 161
   See also: Anatolia; Rum
Aśoka (r. *c.* 268–232 BCE), 12, 22, 277
Aššur, 21
Assyria, Assyrian Empire, 9, 17, 19, 24, 29, 35, 67
Astana, 365
Astrakhan, 349, 352, 354
astronomy, astronomers, 1, 230, 243
Aswan, 71
Atatürk, Mustafa Kemal (1881–1938), 259
Athens, 1, 6, 68, 113, 134
Augustus (63 BCE–14 CE), 18, 31, 111, 119, 123–30, 135, 137
Aurangzeb, Mughal ruler (r. 1659–1707), 276, 277, 280
Austria-Hungary, 2
Avars, 185
Axum, 155, 187
'Ayn Jālūt, Battle of (1260), 263
'Ayn Manāwir, 52
Azerbaijan, 189, 198, 236, 237, 265, 266, 268
al-'Azīz, Fatimid Caliph (r. 975–996), 165

Babinger, Franz (1891–1967), 262
Bābur, Zāhir al-Dīn (1483–1530), 26, 257,
    271–6
Bābur-Nāmah (*Vaqâyi'*), 273
Babylon, 34, 35, 49, 53, 57–70, 209
Bactria, 52, 54, 55, 56, 57, 63, 64, 66, 72
Badakhshān, 272, 273
Baghdad, 162, 163, 164, 165, 166, 180,
    192–209, 213, 237, 261, 347
Bahmani Sultanate (1347–1538), 277
Bahrain, 19, 186
al-Baladhuri (d. 892), 182, 191
Balāsāghūn, 213, 237
Balkans, 144, 148, 149, 154, 161, 189, 260,
    263, 349
Balkh, 194, 274, 275
Balkhi school of cartography, 205, 207, 211
Baltic (Sea and region), 342, 351, 359,
    365, 369
Ban Gu 班固 (32–92 CE), 103, 104, 105
Bang, Peter Fibiger, 7
Baranī, Ziā' al-Dīn (1285–1357), 279
"barbarians"
    and Byzantine Empire, 144
    and China, 82, 89, 91, 92, 99, 247, 299
    and Greeks, 55
    and Rome, 31
barid (postal system), 191, 193, 204
Barkey, Karen, 36
Bashkirs, 353, 354
Batavia, 307, 319
Batu Khan, 344, 349
Baydawī, Qāḍī (d. 1286), 247
Bayly, Christopher A., 7
bazaar, 278
beğlik, 259, 264
begs, 319, 331, 334
Behistun inscription, 68
Beijing 北京, 225, 237, 243, 287, 292, 294,
    297, 307, 308, 318, 319, 321, 324, 330,
    331, 332, 333, 334
    See also: Daidu
Belgium, 2
bellum iustum (just war), 27
Berbers, 186, 188, 191, 192, 198
Bijapur Sultanate, 277
biome, 24, 25
bishop, bishopric, 146, 147
Bithynia, 133, 151
Black Sea, 68, 144, 153, 347, 352, 366
Bolan pass, 270
Bolgar, 347, 349, 350
Book of Kings. See *Shāh-Nāmah*
borders and boundaries, 5, 278, 279, 280,
    284, 369

Achaemenid, 51, 56, 58, 59–63, 68,
    69, 72
Byzantine, 141–4, 147, 149, 154, 155, 160,
    162, 167, 263
Caliphate's, 189, 196, 201, 205
    internal, 205
China's, 105, 106, 284, 290, 310, 328
    maritime, 306
    Ming, 285, 290, 295, 307, 308, 309
    pre-imperial, 87
    Qing, 317–20, 324, 337
    cultural, 279, 322
    in the steppe, 348
Iran's, 267
Moldova's, 368
Mughal, 257, 271, 273, 276, 278, 280
natural, 23–6, 144, 154, 280
of macro-regions, 8
of Mongol Empire, 230, 235, 242, 245, 287
Ottoman, 29, 257, 262, 264, 265, 266,
    278, 280
Roman, 28, 29, 112, 128, 130
Russian, 359, 365, 366, 368
Safavid, 257, 265, 266, 267–8, 278, 280
Samanid, 198
Ukraine's, 368
See also: frontiers
Bourbons, 364
Brahmins, 278
Britain, 2, 4, 8, 15, 29, 279, 333, 364
    as Roman province, 19, 31, 127, 128, 137
British India, 260
Budapest, 154
Buddhism, 22, 248
    Tibetan, 245, 323, 330, 331, 333, 335
Bulgar Khanate, 346, 347, 349, 350
Bulgaria, Bulgarians, 144, 147, 148, 157,
    158, 349
Burbank, Jane, 5
bureaucracy, 34
    in Caliphate, 194, 203
    in China, 34, 36, 84, 149, 292, 302, 305, 323,
        332, 334, 337
    in Mongol Empire, 231, 358
    Ottoman, 36
    in Rome, 35, 132
Burma, 220, 239, 241, 278, 317, 318, 319,
    327, 328
Bursa, 268
Byzantine Empire, 12, 21, 131, 141–68, 180,
    189, 194, 213, 280, 343, 345, 349, 351
    armies of, 185
    and the Caliphate, 161–6, 167
    as commonwealth, 155–8
    elites in, 149–51

hierarchical organization of, 146–8
in Islamic demonology, 164
logistics in, 151–4
mental maps of, 144–6
and Sasanian Iran, 158–61, 167
spatial dimensions of, 141–4, 262

Cadusians, 62
Caere, 116
Caesar, C. Julius (d. 42 BCE), 19, 111, 119, 122, 123, 125, 126
Cairo, 165, 180, 213, 243, 269, 286
cakravartin (universal king), 22
California, 364
Caliphate, 9, 12, 15, 18, 21, 23, 144, 162, 163, 165, 167, 247, 248, 261, 343, 347
Abbasid, 14, 21, 33, 38, 158, 164, 165, 192–9, 213
communications in, 30, 191
fragmented, 198
political nature of, 181–2
under Righteous Caliphs, 161, 182–6
space of, imagined, 204–16
terrritorial extent of, 180–1
under Turkish domination, 199–203
Umayyad, 162, 186–91
caliphs, 14, 28, 163, 181, 182, 187, 188, 193, 194, 196, 198, 202, 209, 229, 261
authority of challenged, 196
military role of, 188, 194
Righteous (Rashīdūn) (632–60), 23, 183, 189, 204
See also Abbasids; Fatimids; Umayyads
Cambyses, 49, 67
camels, 30, 161, 190
Campania, 118
Canada, 358
Cannae, 118
Canon of Documents (Shu jing 書經), 89
Capdetrey, Laurent, 58
capital(s)
and Achaemenids, 58
of Bulgar Khanate, 347
of Byzantium, 131, 153, 165, 190, 349
of Caliphate, 165, 180, 193, 196
and Carolingians, 58
of Ghaznavids, 199
of the Golden Horde, 344, 352
of Jin, 225
of Kazakhstan, 365
of Ming, 297, 298, 301, 306
of Mongols, 223, 231, 237, 267, 286
of Qing, 319, 321, 331
of Roman Empire, 113, 117, 126, 133, 141
of Russia, 237, 361, 365, 366

of Safavids, 270
of Sasanians, 189, 194, 269
of Seleucids, 267
of Seljuqs, 264
of Timurids, 272
Capua, 118
caput mundi (Rome as the Capital of the world), 113, 127, 137
caravansarai, 278
Carolingians (800–88), 12, 14, 58
Carpathian Mountains, 127
Carrhae, 123
Carthage, 1, 115, 118, 119
cartography, 145, 241, 243, 284, 308
Caspian Sea, 68
Catherine the Great, Russian Empress (r. 1762–96), 362, 366
Cato the Elder (234–149), 119
Caucasus, 52, 147, 149, 155, 161, 162, 189, 190, 235, 236, 267, 347, 349, 362, 365
cavalry, 114, 117, 239, 263, 275, 303
Celts, 116, 119
census, 94, 191, 232, 234, 237, 345, 366
Central African Empire (1976–79), 2
Central Asia, 52, 56, 62, 99, 105, 161, 180, 181, 186, 187, 189, 193, 199, 201, 202, 203, 213, 220, 221, 225, 232, 234, 235, 236, 237, 239, 240, 248, 271, 277, 286
centralization
under Achaemenids, 51, 67
in Caliphate, 193
in China, 34, 35, 84, 93, 94, 104, 322, 323, 331, 337
in Mongol Empire, 231, 234, 235
ceremonies
Achaemenid, 62
Byzantine, 147, 153, 162, 163
Tibetan, 289
Chaghadai (Chagatai, d. 1242), 236
Chaghadaid Khanate (1260–1687), Chaghadaids, 221, 232, 236, 239, 240, 242, 245, 247, 248, 288
Chaghatai Mongols, 257, 272
See also Chaghadaids; Moghulistan
Chakhar Mongols, 327
Chalcedon. Council of (451), 185
Chaldiran, Battle of, 266, 267, 268, 269
chanyu 單于, Xiongnu leader, 97, 102
charisma, 223, 227, 230, 239, 245, 249, 262, 266, 300, 345
Charlemagne (742–814), 58, 158, 164
Charles V (1500–58), 7
Cheremis, 347
China, 2, 3, 24, 25, 32, 37, 79, 163, 181, 187, 188, 204, 213, 220, 222, 225, 230, 231,

232, 235, 237, 239, 241, 245, 246, 249, 272
core territories of, 32, 36, 37, 104
political culture of, 79
polycentric view of, 80
territoriality of, 29
See also All-under-Heaven; Han; Ming; Northern Wei; Qin; Qing; Shang; Song; Sui; Tang; Warring States period; Yuan; Zhou
Chinggis Khan (d. 1227), 19, 27, 28, 32, 220–41, 243, 244, 247, 248, 284, 288, 300, 330, 333, 344, 349, 358
Chinggisids, Chinggisid family, 220, 221, 224, 227, 230, 231, 234–47, 259, 262, 271, 272, 273, 274, 285, 288, 289, 290, 292, 295, 298, 299, 300, 303, 305, 329, 333, 353
Chola state, 278
Chorasmia (Khwārazm), 54
Christian oecumene, 155, 158, 163, 166
Christianity, 22, 23, 185, 211, 229, 335, 347, 348, 351
  Catholic, 18, 333, 351
  Orthodox, 21, 347, 354, 356, 361, 371
  Protestant, 351
Christians, 164, 165, 260
  under Byzantine Empire, 155, 157
  under the Caliphate, 182
  under the Ottomans, 259, 260
Chu 楚, state of (to 223 BCE), 82, 88
church, 18, 23, 146, 155, 158, 165, 166, 185, 330, 333, 354, 356, 361, 362
Cicero, M. Tullius (106–43 BC), 111, 112, 121
Cilicia, 162, 163
Cimbri, 122
cities
  under Achaemenids, 55, 58, 59
  in Byzantine Empire, 145, 146
  in Caliphate, 183, 191, 202, 260
  and empire-building, 347, 348, 352, 365, 371
  in Roman Empire, 116, 121, 131, 132, 133
  in Transoxania, 279
citizenship, Roman, 26, 111, 116, 117, 122, 126, 131, 132, 133
civil wars
  in Caliphate, 192, 201
  in China, 97
  in Rome, 111, 123, 125, 130, 131, 136
  in Tibet, 330
Claudius (r. 41–54 CE), 127
Cleopatra VII (69–30 BCE), 125
clerics, 259, 260, 279, 280, 348, 356, 362
  See also 'ulamā
clients, clientelism, 122, 149, 192, 295, 299, 342, 353

climate, 8, 23, 25, 26, 185, 190, 202, 229, 239, 318
coasts, 116, 306, 317, 358, 364
Colbert, Jean-Baptiste (1619–83), 67
colonialism, modern, 7, 8, 23, 260, 284, 335, 364
colonies
  agricultural, China, 99, 102, 334
  Roman, 31, 116, 117, 118, 119, 131, 132, 136
Columbus, Christopher (1451–1506), 249
Comanchee, 7, 358
commerce, 69, 278, 294, 306, 307, 319, 358, 359, 361, 369
  See also merchants, trade
Commodus (r. 180–92), 130
commonwealth, 14
  Byzantine, 22, 155, 157, 158, 167
  Christian, 157
  Latin, 23
  Mongolian, 240
  Muslim, 14, 23, 163, 240
communications, 24, 29, 30
  under Achaemenids, 51, 63–7
  in Byzantine Empire, 151
  in Caliphate, 211
  in China, 287, 293, 297, 302, 303
  in Mongol Empire, 234
  in Ottoman Empire, 263
  in Russia, 371
  See also postal system; roads
Compendium of Chronicles (Jāmi' al-tawārīkh), 243
confessions, 347, 362
Confucius (Kongzi 孔子, 551–479 BCE), 87
conscription, 67, 85
Constantine I, the Great (r. 306–37), 22, 145, 155
Constantine VII Porphyrogennetos (r. 913–59), 147, 148, 153
Constantine VIII (r. 1025–8), 165
Constantinople, 111, 131, 141, 146–66, 185, 190, 243, 260, 261, 263, 264, 266, 349
  See also Istanbul
consuls, Roman, 115, 119, 121, 123, 126
continental empires, 12, 15, 25, 39, 249
conversion, 22, 23, 183, 186, 189, 191, 229, 248, 347, 356, 362
Cooper, Frederick, 5
core and periphery, 365
Corinth, 119
Corsica, 118
Cossaeans, 60, 62, 69
court, courtiers
  Achaemenid, 57, 58, 59, 60, 65
  Byzantine, 146, 147
  in China, 28, 36, 86

Ming, 284–310
  pre-imperial, 87
  Qin-Han, 93, 94, 99, 102, 103, 104
  Qing, 324
  Yuan, 243, 290
Fatimid, 165
Korean, 286
Mongol, 230, 231, 241, 243, 244, 292
Mughal, 279
Ottoman, 279
  in Rome, 128
Russian, 361
See also: *ordo*
craftsmen, 133, 162
Crassus, M. Licinius (*c*. 115–53 BCE), 123
Cremera, 114
Crete, 153
Crimea, Khanate of, 352, 353, 366
Croatia, Croatians, 144, 148
crusades, crusaders, 141, 158, 165, 259, 260
Ctesiphon, 128, 189, 194
cult, imperial (Rome), 126, 134, 135
customs, local, 53, 87, 128, 147, 295, 333, 356
Cyprus, 19, 162, 163
Cyropolis, 55
Cyrus the Great (r. 550–530 BCE), 49
Cyrus the Younger (d. 401 BCE), 63, 70

da'wa (Ismaili mission), 198, 213
Dacia, 127, 128, 131
Đại Việt. *See* Vietnam
Daidu 大都, 237, 292
  See also *Beijing*
Dalai Lama, 330
Dali 大理, 246, 286
Dalmatia, 144
Damascus, 65, 187, 188, 193, 209, 213, 243
Daniel, prophet, 123
Danube, 54, 127, 128, 130, 131, 142, 144
dār al-ḥarb (*dar al-harb*) (abode of war), 18, 19, 181, 228
dār al-Islām (*dar al-Islam*) (abode of Islam), 18, 19, 181, 182, 186, 188, 189, 191, 192, 194, 201, 202, 204, 205, 208, 213, 228, 260
Darius III (r. 336–330 BCE), 20, 57, 63, 71, 72
Darius the Great (r. 522–486 BCE), 19, 49, 52, 53, 54, 55, 56, 57, 64, 65, 67, 68, 69, 70
darughachi (*shiḥna*, *basqaq*), 232
Daskyleion, 62
Dayan Khan (1464–1532), 301
Dayr al-'Aqul, 196, 209
Deccan, 277
decentralization, 231
decimal system, Mongols, 224, 231

Delhi, Delhi Sultanate (1206–1526), 240, 277, 278
deserts, 8, 71, 94, 189, 205, 208
destruction
  and Caliphate, 165, 189, 213
  and Mongols, 230
  and Mughals, 277
  and Romans, 115, 116, 119
dharma (religious law), 22
dhimmī, 260
Diadochi, 49
dictator, Roman, 118, 122, 125
Diocletian (r. 284–305), 131, 145
diplomacy
  Byzantine, 148, 155, 162
  Caliphate, 162
  China, 104
    early empires, 97
    Han, 102
    Ming, 289, 290, 293, 294, 295, 306
    pre-imperial, 83, 87
    Qing, 318, 332
  Mongol, 244, 285
  Russian, 366
diversity, 54, 231, 285, 295, 310, 318, 324, 333, 356
Diyarbekir, 265
Dnieper, 342, 349
Dölger, Franz, 147
Domitian (r. 81–96 CE), 127
Dorgon (d. 1650), 326
Drusus (38 BCE–9 CE), 127
Du'a, Chaghadaid Khan, (r. 1282–1307), 240, 245
Dullin, Sabine, 368
Duma, 363
Dunhuang 敦煌, 303
Dura Europos, 267
Dürrenmatt, Friedrich (1921–90), 1, 40
Dutch. *See* Holland

East Asia, 8, 10, 12, 14, 20, 24, 32, 34, 101, 167, 232, 243, 284, 285, 286, 287, 292, 308
Easy Guide to the Unified Territories of the Great Yuan (Da Yuan hun yi fang yu sheng lan 大元混一方輿勝覽), 286, 288
Ecbatana, 49, 57, 58, 59, 60, 63, 64, 65, 69
  See also Hamadān
ecology, 1, 8, 23–6, 32, 39, 232
  and Achaemenid Empire, 54
  and Arabs, 161, 190
  and Byzantine, 151, 167
  and China, 80, 103, 104, 105, 239, 318

ecology (cont.)
  and Russia, 357, 371
  and Seljuqs, 201, 202
  and the steppe, 235, 239
  See also biome
economy, 1, 24, 249
  and Achaemenids, 62
  and Byzantine Empire, 146, 151, 155, 166,
    167, 185, 189
  and Caliphate, 193, 196
  and China, 80, 82, 83, 84, 86, 96, 104,
    105, 239
    Han, 101
    Ming, 285, 290, 293, 294, 296, 300,
      307, 308
    Qing, 28, 320, 322, 334, 335, 336, 337
  of empire-building, 29–32
  of Ḥijāz, pre-Islamic, 185
  and Mongols, 224, 239, 244, 286, 349
  and Mughals, 277, 278
  and Ottomans, 262, 264, 265, 278
  and Rome, 27, 111, 112, 113, 115, 117, 127,
    128, 130, 133, 136, 137
  and Russia, 350, 353, 358, 359, 371
  and Safavids, 269, 278
Egypt, 34, 240
  and Achaemenids, 35, 52, 54, 56, 65, 66, 68,
    69, 70, 71
  ancient, 17, 49, 358
  and Byzantine Empire, 144, 148, 151, 154,
    155, 161, 164, 189
  and Caliphate, 165, 180, 183, 185, 186, 188,
    189, 190, 191, 192, 193, 198, 201, 209
  coveted by, 29
  and Macedonians, 55
  and Ottomans, 260, 261, 262, 263, 264
  and Romans, 119, 125, 128, 130
Eight Banners, 323, 328, 333
Eisenstadt, Shmuel N. (1923–2010), 3
Elamite tablets, 52, 64
Elbe, 127
Elephantine, 55, 56
elites
  in Achaemenid Empire, 35
  under Byzantine empire, 149, 151, 158,
    166, 167
  in Caliphate, 198
  in China, 92, 284
    Han, 101, 103, 104
    Ming, 290, 295, 297
    pre-imperial, 36, 79, 80, 84, 85, 87
    Qing, 324, 333
  intellectual, 230
  Jewish, 362

  local, 198, 244, 245, 246, 295, 303, 307, 324,
    334, 356
  Moghul, 303
  in Mongol Empire, 224, 225, 231, 235, 244,
    290, 306
  in Rome, 35, 112, 115, 121, 125, 126,
    130, 134
  in Russia, 351, 354, 356, 359, 361, 363
Emperor Taizong of Tang 唐太宗
    (r. 626–49), 298
Emperor Wen of Sui 隋文帝 (r. 581–604), 22
Emperor Wu of Han 漢武帝 (r. 141–87 BCE),
    98, 99, 101, 104
Emperor Xuan of Han 漢宣帝 (r. 74–49
    BCE), 102
emperors, 2, 22, 39
  Byzantine, 21, 147, 158, 160, 187
  of China, 19, 28, 92, 98, 105, 229, 298, 302,
    318, 319, 320, 321, 322, 323, 332, 333,
    334, 335, 336
    military functions of, 297, 300, 301
    universal power of, 17, 20, 106
  Mughal, 275
  Roman, 19, 31, 35, 121, 126, 127, 130, 131,
    133, 134, 135, 136, 147, 148
  of Russia, 361, 362, 363
  See also caliphs; Great Kings; khans, Qa'an;
    Sons of Heaven; sultans; tsars
empires
  attitudes toward, 2, 3, 4
  definitions of, 5–8
  first wave, 9–12, 15
  post-nomadic, 15
  second wave, 12–14, 15
  third wave, 14–15
  See also ideology, imperial; military and
    empires; religion and empires;
    universalism
Engels, Donald, 71
entertainment, 230, 232
Epirus, 117
eschatology, 266
Esen, Oirat leader (d. 1455), 300, 301
Esen-Tügel (fl. 1420s), 298
Estonia, 368
Ethiopia, 2, 155
  See also Axum
ethnicity, ethnic, 4, 23, 37, 56, 89, 92, 99, 112,
    149, 151, 248, 259, 264, 268, 295, 305,
    322, 323, 329, 335, 348, 353, 361, 363,
    365, 366
Etruria, 117
eunuchs, 301, 302
Euphrates River, 69, 137, 142, 246, 247, 267

Eurasia, 1, 4, 5, 8–15, 18, 19, 22, 24, 144, 220, 222, 229, 244, 248, 249, 259, 271, 285, 300, 306, 342, 344, 345, 353, 365
Eurasian political culture, 7, 344, 348–68, 369, 371
  See also Inner Asia: political culture of
Europe, 7, 8, 12, 134, 227, 242, 249, 261, 344, 364
  Central, 158, 161, 349, 368
  Eastern, 157, 239
  Northern, 347
  Southeastern, 151, 263
  Southern, 366
  Western, 12, 240, 285, 364
Eusebius (260–339), 22
experts, 235, 244, 359

Fabius Maximus Cunctator, Q. (c. 280–203 BCE), 118
Fairbank, John K. (1907–91), 321
false Dmitri (contender for Russian throne), 356
"family of kings," 147
Farīdūn, 204, 268
farr (divine essence), 269
  See also charisma
Fatimids (909–1171), 165, 166, 167, 180, 198, 202, 211, 213, 269
Fedor, Russian Tsar (r. 1584–98), 356
Ferghanah Valley, 272
Festus (governor, fl. 50–60 CE), 132
Finland, Finns, 351, 366, 369
firearms, 263, 302
First Emperor of Qin 秦始皇 (emp. 221–210 BCE), 19, 94, 95, 96, 106
Five (or Nine) Zones (*wu fu* 五服 or *jiu fu* 九服) (Chinese terrestrial concept), 90, 94, 102
Flavius Josephus (37–100) , 160
Fletcher, Joseph, 228, 321, 336
food, 59, 64, 71, 131, 133, 229, 232, 234
forest, 25, 85, 344, 348, 351, 358
Fowden, Garth, 22, 23, 155, 157
fragmentation
  in Byzantine Empire, 141
  in Caliphate, 163, 166, 181, 196, 198, 213
  in China, 7, 14, 20, 86, 88
  of Eurasia, 229
France, 2, 29, 37, 189, 227, 364
Franks (Afranj), 158, 240, 243
frontiers, 167
  Achaemenid, 54, 56
  Byzantine, 141, 144, 149, 155, 161, 167
  Caliphate's, 186, 188, 191, 192, 194, 198
  China's, 104, 105, 161

Ming, 290
Qing, 323
Mughal, 271, 275, 277, 278, 280
Ottoman, 259, 260, 263, 268, 278, 280
Roman, 113
Safavid, 278, 280
  See also: borders and boundaries
Furius Camillus, M. (*c.* 446–365 BCE), 116

Galdan (1644–97), 327, 328, 330
Gandhara, 56, 64
Ganges, River and its valley, 270, 274, 277
Gansu 甘肅 , 29, 99, 105, 286, 287, 288, 292, 318, 326, 327, 331, 332
  See also Hexi Corridor
Gao Xianzhi 高仙芝 (d. 756), 24
garrisons, 59, 63, 225, 290, 293, 294, 295, 296, 298, 303, 308, 331
Gaugamela, Battle of (331 BCE), 49, 71
Gaul, 122, 123, 127, 131
geographers, 1, 194, 208, 268
geographic knowledge
  in China, 92
  in Mongol Empire, 244, 285
  in Rome, 19
geography, administrative, 287, 288, 295, 296
geopolitics, 49, 99, 166, 167, 180, 248, 285, 292, 296, 305, 329
Georgia, 155, 232, 265, 269
  Eastern (Iberia), 160, 162
  Western (Lazika), 160
Germanic tribes, 122, 127, 130
Germany, Germania, 2, 127
Ghana, 7
ghaza (invasion, attack), 199, 259, 260, 262, 265, 275
Ghazna, 199
Ghaznavid Dynasty, 199, 201, 270
ghulāms (military slaves), 270
Gibbon, Edward (1737–94), 141
Gibraltar, 128
gifts, 54, 58, 62, 97, 236, 243, 294, 295, 302, 306, 307
  See also: tribute
Gilgit, 24
glocal, glocalization, 222, 236, 248, 249
Gök-Türks, 201, 203
  See also: Turkic Khaganate
Golconda Sultanate, 277
gold, 54, 118, 155, 167, 185
Golden Horde (1260–1502, Ulus Jochi), 221, 237, 239, 240, 242, 344, 348, 349, 350, 352, 353
Goldstone, Jack A., 6

Gongyang zhuan 公羊傳 (Commentary on the *Springs-and-Autumns Annals*), 91, 92, 99
Gracchus, Gaius Sempronius (d. 121 BCE), 121
Gracchus, Tiberius Sempronius (d. 133 BCE), 121
Grand Council, Qing (*junjichu* 軍機處), 334
Grand Duchy of Lithuania, 353
Grand Duchy of Poland-Lithuania, 356
   See also Poland
Grand Princedom of Moscovy, 347, 351
   See also Moscow; Muscovy; Russia
Great Canon of the Yongle Era (*Yongle dadian* 永樂大典), 297
Great Compendium for Governing the World (*Jingshi dadian* 經世大典), 242, 288
Great Khan, 220, 223, 224, 236, 249, 288
   See also Qa'an
Great Kings, Persian, 20, 38, 49, 52, 53–63, 68, 69, 70, 71, 147, 160, 163, 203, 247, 261, 275
Great Ming Code (*Da Ming lü* 大明律), 295
Great Unity ideal (*da yitong* 大一統), 80, 245, 247, 326
   See also: unity, political: of China
Great Wall (*changcheng* 長城). *See* walls:in China
Greece, Greeks, 54
   and the Achaemenids, 34, 53, 55, 58, 62, 63, 66, 68
   under the Byzantines, 151, 153
   under the Ottomans, 264
   under the Romans, 113, 114, 117, 119, 122, 134
   See also Hellenistic empires
Green Standard forces, 334
Guangdong 廣東, 96, 287, 326
Guangxi 廣西, 96, 287
Güchülüg (d. 1218), 27
gunpowder, 230, 249, 266
Gupta Empire (fourth-sixth centuries), 12
Gurkha, 24
Güyük Qa'an (r. 1246–8), 227, 228

Hadrian (r. 117–38), 128, 136, 137
Hainan 海南, 99, 101
al-Hajjāj, governor of Iraq (d. 714), 188, 191
al-Hākim, Fatimid Caliph (r. 996–1021), 165
Haldon, John, 6, 154
Hallock, Richard, 63, 66
Hamadān, 49
Hämäläinen, Pekka, 358
Hamdānid dynasty, Hamdānids (890–1004), 198, 209
Hami, 303, 326

Han 漢 dynasty (206/202 BCE–220 CE), 10, 12, 14, 15, 25, 28, 37, 80, 97–104, 137
   communications in, 30
   elites in, 27, 32
   expansion of, 32, 36
   Latter Han (25–220 CE), 103, 104
   princedoms in, 37, 102
   tribute system, 102
   and Xiongnu, 97, 101
Han Fei 韓非 (d. 233 BCE), 96
Han 漢 River, 80
Hanafi school (of Sunni Islam), 181
Hangzhou 杭州, 237
Hannibal (247-*c*. 181 BCE), 118
Hapsburgs, 263, 364
"harmony of the kin" (*heqin* 和親), 97
Hārūn al-Rashīd, Abbasid Caliph (r. 786–809), 194, 196
Hawaii, 364
Heaven (*tian* 天, highest God, China), 21, 81, 92, 246, 289, 299
   See also mandate of Heaven; Tengri
Hellenistic empires, 10, 20
   See also Ptolemaic empire; Seleucid empire
Hepthalites, 270
Herāt, 265, 269, 271, 272, 273, 274
Herder, Johann Gottfried von (1744–1803), 2
Herodotus (*c.* 480–425 BCE), 30, 54, 56, 63, 66
Hexi (Gansu) Corridor 河西走廊, 294
hierarchy, 5, 146, 324, 331, 362
Hierokles (6th century), 145
Hijāz, 185, 186, 187, 191, 192, 193, 260, 262
hijra, 180, 183
Himalaya Mts., 24, 270, 318
Hindu Kush, 199, 270
hinterlands, 132, 296, 305, 349, 357
Hisar, 274
Hitler, Adolph (1889–1945), 364, 368
Holland, 2, 37, 284, 307, 359, 364
Holy Roman Empire, 12, 157, 158, 163
holy war, 19, 165, 183, 194
   See also crusade, *ghaza*, *jihād*
Hongwu 洪武 Emperor (r. 1368–98), 289, 294
Hongxi 洪熙 Emperor (r. 1425), 297
Horace (65 BCE–8 BCE), 127
household registration, 293
Hu Guang 胡廣 (1370–1418), 299, 300
Huai 淮 River, 80
Huet, Pierre Daniel (1630–1721), 67
Hülegü (Ilkhan, r. 1260–5), 227, 235, 236, 246, 247
Humayun (1508–66), 274
Hundred Schools of Thought, China (5th–3rd centuries BCE), 86

Hung Taiji, Latter Jin/Qing emperor (r. 1626–43), 316
Hungary, 220, 227, 236, 261
Husain Baiqara (r. 1469–1506), 272
Hyphasis River, 56

Iberia, 118, 119, 188, 260
See also Spain
Ibn al-Zubayr, contender for Caliphate (682–92), 187
Ibn Baṭṭūṭa (d. c. 1377), 244
Ibn Faḍlān, Aḥmad (d. 960), 347
Ibn Ḥawqal, geographer (d. after 978), 205, 209
Ibn Khaldūn (1332–1406), 262, 279
Ibn Khurdādhbih, geographer (d. 912), 204, 205
Ibrāhīm Lūdī (d. 1526), 273
identities, local, 23, 87
ideology, imperial, 17, 18, 19, 21, 23, 24, 29, 31, 202, 257
  and Alexander the Great, 20
  in Byzantine Empire, 21, 147, 148, 149, 157, 167, 190
  in Caliphate, 19, 181, 185, 187, 188, 194, 196, 198, 213, 266
  in China, 80, 86, 88, 89, 99, 104, 105, 245, 323, 335
  in Mongol Empire, 222, 223, 224, 227, 241, 245, 247
  in Ottoman Empire, 257, 259, 260, 262, 273
  in Rome, 126, 135, 142
  in Russia, 354, 361
  Sasanian, 245
  and Seljuqs, 202, 203
  in the steppe, 203, 222, 223
  See also religion and empire; unity, political; universalism
Ilkhanate (Ulus Hülegü, 1260–1335), 220, 221, 232, 239, 240, 243, 245, 247, 263, 264, 265, 268, 272, 288
  historiography in, 243, 246, 247
Illyria, 118, 127
imperialism, 26, 112, 322, 333
  in China, 99
  modern, 2, 3, 4, 36, 112
  Mughal, 274, 275
  Roman, 112, 113, 136
India, 12, 21, 24, 32, 54, 63, 64, 70, 127, 163, 167, 180, 181, 187, 188, 199, 202, 205, 220, 243, 257, 260, 261, 269–80, 281, 286, 352
  See also British India, Maurya Empire, Mughals
Indian Ocean, 19, 205, 211, 267
Indian subcontinent, 8, 9, 12, 22, 32, 240, 275

See also South Asia
indirect rule, 33, 34, 35, 36, 103, 122, 132
Indonesia, 260
See also Java
Indus, 54, 56, 69, 71, 266, 267, 270, 273
Inner Asia, 8, 14, 303, 326
  empires in, 10, 222, 225, 351
  Mongol impact on, 248
  political culture of, 224, 225, 320, 321
  and Qing, 317–37
Inner Mongolia, 290, 326, 327
integration, political (and/or cultural), 32–8
  in Achaemenid Empire, 62
  in Byzantine, 151
  in China, 84, 85
  in Mongol Empire, 220
  in Rome, 112
  in Russia, 371
international law, 368
Iran, 24, 37, 69, 154, 180, 186, 187, 189, 198, 220, 222, 232, 235, 236, 237, 245–9, 261, 264–79, 280
  See also Achaemenid Empire, Ilkhanate, Sasanian Empire, Safavids
Īrān zamīn, 245
Iranian culture. See Persian culture
Iranian plateau, 24, 49, 70, 265, 266, 267, 268, 269, 270, 280
Iranians. See Persians
Iranshahr, 204, 205, 268
Iraq, 148, 182, 183, 187, 189, 191, 193, 196, 201, 202, 204, 205, 209, 220, 227, 236, 237, 247, 267
Ireland, 364
Irtysh River, 236
Isfahan, 202, 269, 270, 278
Islam, 22, 23, 165, 182, 183, 186, 187, 191, 192, 196, 199, 201, 229, 245, 248, 259, 260, 276, 303, 333, 347, 348, 354, 356, 362
  See also dar al-harb; dar al-Islam; Hanafis; Ismailis; Shi'ites; Sunnis
Ismā'īl I, Safavid ruler (1487–1524), 266
Ismailis, Ismailism, 165, 198, 213
  See also Shi'ites
Issos, Battle of (333 BCE), 71
al-Istakhrī, geographer (d. after 951–2), 205, 208
Istanbul, 154, 261, 263, 264, 268, 278, 279
  See also Constantinople
Italy, 2, 114, 116, 117, 118, 119, 122, 125, 130, 131, 133, 134, 135, 136, 157, 158, 166, 167, 261
Ivan IV, the Terrible, Russian Tsar (r. 1547–84), 353, 356
Iznik, 259

Jahāngir (Mughal ruler, r. 1605–27), 17, 274, 275, 276
al-Jāḥiẓ, Amr b. Baḥr (d. 868), 161
jam (*yam*; Mongol postal-relay system), 232, 234
Jamāl al-Dīn (Muslim astronomer, d. *c.* 1289), 241, 242, 243
Jāmī, Iranian poet (d. 1492), 265
Jamshīd, 268
Janissaries, 263, 264
Japan, 2, 20, 220, 239, 240, 305, 307, 308, 317
jasagh-banner, 324, 326, 328, 329, 330, 331, 332, 334, 335, 336
Jasaq (*Yasa*) (Mongol law), 224
Java, 19, 239, 241
Jebtsundampa Khutughtu, 331
Jerusalem, 146, 164, 165, 187
Jews, 165, 182, 243, 260, 362
Jia Yi 賈誼 (200–168 BCE), 97, 98
Jianwen 建文 Emperor (r. 1399–1402), 297, 298
jihād, 19, 181, 183, 188, 194, 196, 198, 199, 201, 211, 213, 260, 303
Jin 晉, state of (disintegrated in 403 BCE), 83, 84
Jin 金 dynasty (1115–1234), 27, 28, 225, 227, 229, 246, 290, 319
   See also Jurchens
Jochi (d. 1227), Jochids, 236, 245, 247
   See also Golden Horde
Judea, 35
Junghars (Zhungars), 327, 328, 329
junxian system, 326, 327, 331
Jupiter, 21, 135, 259, 275
Jurchens, 105, 284, 288, 289, 290, 293, 308, 316, 326
   See also Jin 金 dynasty
Justin (c. 2nd century CE), 123
Justinian I (527–65), 145, 154, 157, 166
Justinian II (r. 685–96, 705–11), 162, 187
Juvenal (late 1st-early 2nd century CE), 133

Kabul, 199, 271, 272, 273, 274, 275, 276
Kaifeng 開封, 237
Kaisar or Caesar, 261
Kallinikon, 161
Kama river, 347, 349
Kāmrān (1509–57), 274
Kandahār, 52, 64, 66, 275
Kangxi 康熙 Emperor (r. 1661–1722), 106, 318, 321, 326, 328, 330, 331, 333
Karbalā', 209
Kāshgar, 201, 272
al-Kāshgharī, Mahmud (d. after 1077), 203, 213

Kashmir, 243
Kasimov, Khanate of, 353
Katmandu, 24
Kazakhs, Kazakshtan, 248, 317, 318, 328, 329, 330, 365
Kazan (city), 347, 349, 350, 351, 352, 353, 354, 355, 356, 357, 359, 362
Kazan Khanate, 27, 346, 347, 350, 351, 352, 353
Kelly, Thomas, 67
Kereyit, Mongol tribe, 223, 237
keshig (royal guard), 225, 231, 234, 237
Khalkha (Outer Mongolia), 320, 326, 327, 328, 329, 330, 331
Khams, 331, 332
khans, 224, 227, 344, 347
Khazars, 185, 189, 347, 348
Khmer, 278
Khurāsān, 180, 188, 191, 192, 193, 196, 198, 199, 201, 202, 205, 208, 236, 269, 270, 272, 281
Khusrau and Shirin, 279
Khwarāzm Shāhs (1097–1231), 225
al-Khwārazmī (d. c. 850), 204
Khyber Pass, 273
Kiakhta, Treaty of (1727), 317
Kiev, Kievan Empire, 237, 342, 344, 345, 347, 349, 365, 371
   See also Rus'
Kim Hodong, 242, 287
King of kings. *See* Great Kings, Persian
kinship, 81, 133, 147, 163, 236
   fictitious, 147
   spiritual, 149
Kirgizstan, 237, 248
Kitan, Kitans, 223, 232, 248, 284, 289, 290, 293
   See also Liao Empire, Qara Khitai
Korea, 2, 37, 99, 220, 232, 236, 239, 241, 242, 245, 246, 286, 289, 293, 306, 317, 327, 328
Koryŏ. *See* Korea
kremlin, 354, 355, 366
Kurds, Kurdistan, 263, 265, 267
Kush, 54, 55
   See also Nubia
Kushanas (Yuezhi 月氏), 270

Lamos River, 162
landowners
   in Rome, 121, 133, 134
Laozi 老子 (*c.* 4th century BCE), 87
Last Judgement, 164
Latin League, 115, 117
law

Islamic, 162, 181, 347
Mongol, 224
in Qing, 336
Roman, 114, 132, 133
in Russia, 348, 356, 361, 362, 368
in Tang, 295
See also *Jasaq*
legions, Roman, 121, 126, 127, 128, 133, 136
legitimation
in Byzantine Empire, 163, 166
in Caliphate, 188, 193, 198, 199, 202
in China, 14, 79, 81, 87, 98, 105, 239, 289, 306
of Khmer monarchs, 278
in Moghul Empire, 274, 275
in Mongol Empire, 229, 234, 236, 240, 244, 245, 249, 330
in Ottoman Empire, 259, 260, 262
in Rome, 111
in Russia, 157, 356
in Saffavid Empire, 266
of Seljuqs, 203
in the steppe, 26, 223, 225, 345
Leo III, Pope (d. 816), 158
Lepidus, M. Aemilius (c. 89–13 BCE), 125
Li Hongzhang 李鴻章 (1823–1901), 29
Liao 遼 Empire (907–1125), 223, 225, 290
See also Kitan, Kitans, Qara Khitai
Liaodong 遼東 peninsula, 92, 287, 288, 290, 292, 293, 294, 305, 308, 316
Lifanyuan 理藩院 , 324, 326, 331, 335
Ligdan Khan (d. 1634), 327
limes, 40, 130, 131
Liu Bang 劉邦 (d. 195 BCE), emperor Gao of Han 漢高帝 (r. 206/202–195 BCE), 97, 99
Liu Ji 劉基 (1311–75), 289
Liutprand of Cremona (c. 920–72), 148
Livy (64 or 59 BCE–12 or 17 CE), 112, 114, 127, 133
logistics, 67, 71, 151, 153, 161, 268, 336
See also armies
Lombards, 157
Louis IX, king of France (r. 1226–70), 227
Lu Jia 陸賈 (d. 178 BCE), 97
Lucullus, L. Licinius (118–57 BCE), 123
Luttwak, Edward, 27, 28, 136, 154
Lycia, 68
Lydia, Lydian Kingdom, 49, 54, 55

Macedon, Macedonians, 29, 119
See also Alexander the Great
MacedonianWars, 119
Magdalino, Paul, 148, 151, 164
magistrates, Roman, 27, 114, 115, 126, 136

Mahdia, 211
Maḥmūd of Ghazna (971–1030), 276
Maḥmūd Yalawach (d. 1254), 232
Malcolm, (Sir) John (1769–1833), 266
Mamertines, 118
Mamlūks, Mamlūk Sultanate (1250–1517), 239, 240, 260, 263
al-Ma'mūn, Abbasid Caliph (r. 813–833), 193, 194, 196, 204
Manchuria, 232, 236, 245, 290, 293, 316, 317, 324, 331, 336
Manchus, 248, 321, 322, 328, 330, 336
See also Qing dynasty
mandate of heaven
in China (*tian ming* 天命), 223, 245
in the steppe, 203, 223, 227
Mongol, 223, 227, 228, 246, 249, 289
Manila, 310
Manuel I Komnenos (1118–80), 166
Manzikert, Battle of (1071), 142, 151, 201, 261
Map of Integrated Regions and Terrains and of Historical Countries and Capitals (*Honil gangni yeokdae gukdo jido* 混一疆理歷代國都之圖); aka Kangnido Map, 241, 286
maps
in Caliphate, 188, 204–16
mental, 144
in Ming, 307, 308
and Mongol Empire, 241, 243, 286, 287, 296
in Qing, 317
See also cartography; geographic knowledge
Marathas, 277
marchlands, 259, 270
Marco Polo (d. 1324), 244, 247, 249
Marcomanni, 130
Marcus Aurelius (r. 161–80), 130
Margiana, 123
marginal location, 36, 345
Mari, 346, 347
Maritza, 144
Marius, Gaius (157–86 BCE), 121, 122
Marseille, 242
Marw, 187, 193, 205
Marxism, 2, 112
Masinissa (d. 148 BCE), 119
Mas'ūd Beg (d. 1289), 232
Mauretania, 128
Maurikios (r. 582–602), 160
Maurya Empire, 10, 12, 34, 277
communications in, 30
Mawarannahr. See Transoxiana
McKitterick, Rosamond, 58
Mecca, 164, 180, 183, 204, 209, 260, 343

Media, 49, 53, 54, 57, 62, 64, 65, 66, 68, 70
medicine, 230, 232, 305
Medina, 180, 183, 186, 187, 260
Mediterranean Sea, 8, 19, 24, 55, 67, 68, 71,
    112, 114, 119, 133, 148, 151, 166, 198,
    211, 241, 263, 280, 286, 342, 343,
    347, 366
Mehmet the Conqueror (Ottoman Sultan)
    (r. 1444–6 and 1451–81), 261, 264
Melaka, 307
Melkites, 155
Memphis, 57
Mengzi 孟子 (aka Mencius, *c.* 380–304
    BCE), 88
mercenaries, 118, 153, 192, 199
merchants, 121, 133, 225, 230, 232, 234, 244,
    270, 278, 279, 306, 307, 308, 319, 336,
    337, 362
Mesopotamia, 9, 18, 21, 49, 123, 128, 161, 163,
    266, 267
    See also Iraq
Middle East, 8, 68, 180, 181, 185, 201, 202,
    203, 220, 227, 235, 279, 366
migration, 57, 65, 121, 183, 191, 261, 270, 276,
    310, 319, 329, 332, 335, 336, 348, 358
miḥna, 194
Milan, 118
military
    and Achaemenids, 56, 57, 62, 63, 69, 71
    and Byzantine, 146, 148, 149, 153, 155, 167
    and Caliphate, 185, 186, 187, 190, 191, 192,
        196, 198, 199, 201
    and China, 79, 80, 81, 82, 83, 84, 85, 86, 90,
        104, 105
        Han, 101, 102, 103, 104, 105
        Ming, 285, 289–307, 310
        Qin, 97, 104
        Qing, 318, 319, 320, 331, 333, 334
    and empires, 1, 26–9, 33, 36, 39, 343
    and Macedonians, 55, 66, 71
    and Mongols, 222, 224, 225, 227, 229, 230,
        234, 235, 240, 241, 244, 249, 286, 292
    and Mughals, 275, 280
    and nomads, 25, 97
    and Ottomans, 36, 154, 263
    and Rome, 26, 31, 111, 112, 113, 114, 115,
        116, 117, 121, 122, 123, 125, 126, 127,
        130, 132, 133, 134, 135, 136, 137
    and Russia, 345, 354, 356, 358, 359, 361,
        366, 369, 371
    and Safavids, 266, 267
    See also armies; garrisons; legions; logistics;
        strategy
Ming 明 dynasty (1368–44), 15, 21, 27, 28, 32,
    37, 104, 248, 284–310, 343

contraction after 1450, 300–6
expansion of, 297, 305, 310
foreign ties of, 303
under Hongwu Emperor, 288–96
ideology of, 309
maritime aspects of, 306–8
and Mongol legacy, 295, 288–96, 298, 305
overview, 284–5
territorial extent of, 105, 288, 289, 290, 295,
    302, 303, 305, 306, 307, 308
under Yongle Emperor, 296–300
Misenum, 130
Mithridatic Wars, 122
Moghulistan, 248, 290
Moldova, 368, 369
Mommsen, Theodor (1817–1903), 112, 113
monasteries, 331, 355, 356
Möngke Qa'an (r. 1251–9), 227, 231, 235,
    236, 292
Mongol Empire, 9, 27, 220–49, 297, 342
    administration of, 230–5
    as commonwealth, 240
    communications in, 30, 232, 234
    expansion of, 26, 220–9, 239–40
    ideology of, 222–4, 227–9, 241, 245,
        247, 248
    mobilization of resources, 229, 230, 235,
        239, 244
    political culture of, 222
    spatial legacy of, 248–9
    strategy of, 225
    success of explained, 229–31
    See also Chaghadaid Khanate; Golden
        Horde; Ilkhanate; *Yeke Monggol Ulus*;
        Yuan dynasty
"Mongol Moment," 221
Mongolia, 15, 203, 220, 222, 223, 224, 225,
    229, 231, 234, 235, 236, 239, 243, 245,
    248, 288, 290, 305, 316, 324, 326, 328,
    329, 330, 331, 332, 344
    See also: Chahar; Inner Mongolia; Khalkha;
        Mongols
Mongolian language, 335
Mongols, 14, 15, 21, 22, 27, 28, 213, 216,
    220–49, 276, 286, 287, 288, 289,
    292–302, 306, 308, 320, 321–30, 334,
    336, 342, 344, 345, 348, 349, 350, 352,
    353, 357, 358, 371, 372
monotheism, 22, 166
Montesquieu (1689–1755), 67
Moorey, Roger, 51
Moscow, 1, 157, 237, 342, 343, 344, 345, 346,
    349, 350, 351, 352, 353, 354, 355, 356,
    357, 358, 359, 361, 365, 366, 371, 372
mosques, 165, 166, 191

Mozi 墨子 (c. 460–390 BCE), 87, 91
Muʿāwiya, Umayyad Caliph (r. 661–80), 186, 190, 191, 192
al-Muʿīzz, Fatimid Caliph (r. 953–75), 165
al-Muʿtamid, Abbasid caliph (r. 870–892), 204
Mughals, empire of, 15, 26, 31, 167, 199, 248, 257, 271–81
    early history of, 271–3
    expansion of, 276–8
    ideology of, 273–6
    Indianization of, 275, 276, 278
    See also Timurids
Muḥammad ʿAlī of Egypt (1769–1849), 264
Muḥammad b. al-Qasim al-Thaqafī (d. 715), 188
Muḥammad, Prophet (d. 632), 164, 165, 180, 182, 183, 185, 186, 192, 205, 261, 266, 343
mulkgirliq ("kingdom seizing"), 274
Mummius, Lucius (2nd century BCE), 119
al-Muqaddasī, geographer (d. 991), 205, 208
al-Muqtadī, Abbasid Caliph (r. 1075–94), 203
al-Muqtadir, Abbasid Caliph (r. 908–32), 163
Muscovy, Muscovite Russia, 350, 352, 356, 361
    See also Russia
al-Mutanabbī, poet (d. 965), 198
Mutina, 116
Mycale, battle of (479 BCE), 67

Nabataean kingdom, 128
Nāder Shāh Afshār (r. 1736–47), 271
Naimans, 27
Nan Yue 南越 kingdom (c. 204–113 BCE), 97
Naples, 158
Napoleon Bonaparte (1769–1821), 7, 264, 364
Naram-Sin, king of Akkad (r. c. 2211–2175 BCE), 15
Narbonne, 189
al-Nāṣir li-Dīn Allāh, Abbasid Caliph (r. 1180–1225), 202
nation-state, 2, 4, 5, 86
nauruz festival, 269
navigation, 68
navy, 68, 190, 230, 263
    Achaemenid, 71
    Arab, 165
    Byzantine, 165
    Fatimid, 198
Nebuchadnezzar, 1, 123
Neo-Babylonian Empire (609–539 BCE), 9, 49, 62
Nerchinsk, Treaty of (1697), 317

Nero (r. 54–68 CE), 134
Netherlands. See Holland
New Qing History, 322
Nikephoros II Phokas (r. 963–9), 148, 164, 165
Nikolaos I Mystikos (852–925), 163
Nile, 70
Nine Provinces (jiu zhou 九州) (Chinese terrestrial concept), 89, 90
Nisibis, 161
Niẓām al-tawārīkh (The String of Chronicles), 246
nobles, nobility
    in Caliphate, 191
    in China, 82, 83, 84, 85, 334, 337
    in Mongol Empire, 292, 305
    Persian, 57, 71, 72
    in Rome, 114, 115, 117, 121, 122, 123, 126, 160
    in Russia, 356, 359, 361
Nogais, 353, 354, 356
nökers (personal retainers), 224
nomads, nomadism, 8, 25, 26, 27, 28, 32, 60, 93, 96, 97, 105, 201, 202, 222, 224, 227, 231, 232, 239, 249, 269, 328, 345, 357, 358, 366
Noreia, 122
North Africa, 8, 117, 118, 122, 130, 151, 157, 165, 180, 181, 186, 189, 191, 192, 196, 198, 263
North America, 319, 364, 366
Northern Wei dynasty 北魏 (386–534), 12
Notitia Dignitatum, 145, 146
Novgorod, 342, 351, 365
Nubia, 54, 55, 155, 189
    See also Kush
Nurhaci (1559–1626), 316, 320, 326

Obolensky, Dimiter, 155, 157
Ocean, 19, 24, 68, 136
Odoacer (d. 493), 157
Oghuz Khan, 259
Oghuz Turks, 259, 261, 264, 265, 266, 268, 271, 276
    See also Aq Qoyunlu; Ottomans; Qara Qoyunlu; Seljuqs
Ögödei Qaʾan (r. 1229–41), 227, 231, 234, 236
Ögödeids, 240
Oirats, 232, 320, 326, 327, 328, 329, 330, 331
Olivelle, Patrick, 22
Öljeitü, Ilkhan (r. 1304–16), 243
ordo, mobile court, 231, 237
Ordos, 95, 99, 290, 294, 303

Orenburg Muslim Spiritual Assembly, 362
Orkhon River, 223, 237
Osman, Ottoman dynastic founder
    (d. 1324), 259
Otto I (936/962–73), 148
Ottomans, Ottoman Empire, 2, 15, 29, 36, 51,
    167, 248, 257–64, 267, 280, 343,
    353, 366
  borders of, 36, 144, 263, 265, 267,
    268, 368
  conquests of, 131, 157, 260, 262–4, 267
  disintegration of, 36, 260, 263
  early history, 260, 261, 264, 273
  ideology of, 151, 257–61, 273, 275
  self-perception of, 261–2
Ovid (43 BCE–17/18 CE), 127
Oxus. *See* Amu Darya River
Özbeg, Khan of Golden Horde
    (r. 1313–41), 242

Pacific Ocean, 364, 366
padishah/padshah, 272
pagan, 352
Palermo, 211
Palestine, 144, 161, 201, 231
Palmyra, 131
Pamir Mts., 24, 180, 318, 329
Papacy, 157, 158
  See also Pope
Paphlagonia, 62, 151
parliament, 363, 364
Parma, 116
Parthians, Parthian Empire, 123, 127, 128, 130,
    137, 158, 267, 270
party politics, 363
Pasargadae, 49, 57, 58, 69
Passek, Vadim (1808–42), 365
patriarch, patriarchate, 146, 157, 163,
    361, 362
patrimonialism, patrimonial administration,
    231, 286, 292
patronage, patrons, 86, 117, 126, 132, 147,
    149, 202, 204, 271, 280, 297, 303,
    305, 306
Paul, apostle, 132
Pax Romana, 112, 113
  See also peace: and Rome
peace, peace agreements/treaties
  and Achaemenids, 53, 62
  in Byzantine Empire, 160, 165
  in Caliphate, 165, 185, 189
  and China, 10, 20, 83, 87, 88, 96, 99, 104,
    299, 328
  in Islamic law, 162
  in Mongol Empire, 239, 240, 246, 247

  and Rome, 111, 114, 115, 118, 119, 126, 127,
    130, 160
  and Russia, 353, 356, 358
Peacock, A.C.S., 263
peasants, 85, 114, 121, 356, 361
Pergamum, 119, 121
Persepolis, 49–69, 72, 77
Perseus, King of Macedon (d. 166 BCE), 119
Persia. *See* Iran
Persian culture, 53, 57, 202, 204, 205, 246,
    278, 279
Persian Gulf, 19, 55, 66, 68, 69, 128, 267
Persian language, 205, 269, 279
Persians, 56, 57, 62, 67, 68, 69, 70, 191,
    192, 193
Peter the Great, Russian Tsar (1682–1725),
    263, 359, 369
Petronius, 1st century CE, 134
Petros Patrikios (6th century), 160
Philip V of Macedon (r. 221–179 BCE), 119
Philippines, 307
Phoenicians, 68
Phraates, King of Parthia (r. 37–2 BCE), 123
piracy, pirates, 69, 134
Pisa, 142
Plato (d. 348 BCE), 49
plebeians, Rome, 114, 121
Pliny the Elder (23–79 CE), 123
Pliny the Younger (d. 113), 133
Poitiers, Battle of, 189
Poland, 365
Pollock, Sheldon, 6
Polybius (*c.* 208–125 BCE), 112, 115, 118,
    119, 134
Pompey (Gnaeus Pompeius Magnus)
    (106–48 BCE), 122, 123, 125
Pope, 158, 228
  See also Papacy
population, 277, 294, 316, 336, 354
  in Byzantine Empire, 151
  in Caliphate, 180, 191
  in China, 85, 94, 289, 296, 302, 305, 336
  in Ḥijāz, 185
  Indian, 276
  in Middle East, 185
  in Mongol Empire, 245, 248, 293
  Mughal, 278
  Ottoman, 278
  Russian, 343, 351, 357
  Safavid, 278
  in the steppe, 32
Portugal, Portuguese, 2, 284, 306, 307,
    308, 364
postal system
  Achaemenid, 30

in Caliphate, 193
in China
  Qin and Han, 30
in Mongol Empire, 30, 234, 237
See also *barid; jam*
prefect, Roman, 125, 130
Pridnestrovian Moldavian Republic, 369
principate, Roman, 27, 28, 33, 35
  as military monarchy, 111, 112, 125, 126, 136
proconsul, Roman, 121, 123
provinces, 53
  in Byzantium, 145, 146, 151, 153, 154, 155, 161, 190
  in Caliphate, 33, 180, 188, 189, 192, 196, 205
  in China, 89, 308, 322, 324, 326, 327, 328, 329, 331, 332, 335, 336, 337
  in Mongol Empire, 244
  in Persia, 53
  in Rome, 31, 35, 118, 119, 126, 127, 128, 130, 133, 135, 142
Prussians, Prussia, 372
Ptolemaic Empire, 119
Punic Wars, 35, 113, 118, 119
Punjab, 56, 271, 274
Puranas, 278
Pushtuns, 272
Putin, Vladimir V., 368, 372
Puyi 溥儀 (China's emperor, abdicated 1912), 93
Pyrenees, 123
Pyrrhus, 117, 118, 133

Qa'an (Great Khan), 220, 221, 223, 227, 231, 234, 235, 236, 239, 240, 243, 245, 246, 247
Qaidu Khan (r. 1271–1301), 236
Qajar dynasty, 268
Qara Khitai Empire, 225, 358
Qara Qoyunlu/Black Sheep Dynasty (1374–1468), 265, 271
  See also Oghuz
Qarakhanids, 181, 199, 201, 202
Qaraqorum, 223, 231, 235, 237, 239
Qayrawān, 187
Qiang 羌, 99, 103
Qianling County 遷陵縣, 93, 94
Qianlong 乾隆 Emperor (r. 1736–95), 106, 328, 329, 333
Qin 秦, state (*c.* 800–221 BCE) and imperial dynasty (221–207 BCE), 6, 10, 15, 26, 27, 28, 29, 32, 34, 35, 36, 80, 85, 86, 93–9, 101, 102, 104, 106, 287
  communications in, 30

Qing 清 dynasty (1636/1644–1912), 15, 21, 24, 25, 28, 31, 37, 106, 248, 249, 263, 292, 294, 308, 316–37
  administration of, 316, 323, 324–32
  borders of, 317–20
  cultural policies of, 323, 334–7
  expansion of, 106, 316, 319, 324–32
  ideology of, 332–4
  imperial nature of, debated, 320–4
  See also Manchus
Qinghai 青海, 37, 286, 324, 326, 328, 331
Qipchaqs, Qipchak Khanate, 248, 349
Qubilai Qa'an (r. 1260–94), 19, 236, 237, 239, 241, 243, 286, 288, 292, 298
Qur'an, 183, 187, 204
Quraysh, 186
Qutayba b. Muslim (d. 715), 188

Radner, Karen, 29
Raeti, 127
raids, 27, 55, 130, 162, 190, 225, 239, 277, 298, 305
Rajputs, 276
Rashīd al-Dīn (1247–1318), 243, 247
Ravenna, 130, 158
Rayy, 193
rebellions
  in Caliphate, 192
  in China, 14, 34, 80, 327
  in Mongol Empire, 228, 329
  in Ottoman Empire, 281
  in Russia, 366
Red Sea, 68
redistribution, 193, 223, 225
religion and empire, 21–3, 151, 348
  in Byzantine Empire, 22, 23, 145, 146, 151, 167
  in Caliphate, 19, 23, 181, 182, 183, 194, 213
  in early China, 81, 86
  and Ming, 296
  in Mongol Empire, 223, 230, 245, 249
  and Ottomans, 23, 259, 260, 261, 262
  and Qing, 321, 331
  in Roman Empire, 115, 135, 137
  in Russian Empire, 362, 363
  and Safavids, 265, 266, 268, 269, 280
  See also Buddhism; Christianity; cult, imperial; Islam
res publica Romana (Roman republic), 33, 111, 113, 114, 115, 119, 122, 123, 138
Revere, Robert B., 67
rhetoric, 14, 67, 79, 187, 194, 198, 227, 240, 269, 275, 284, 305, 322
Rhine, 29, 123, 127, 128, 130
rights, 62, 116, 131, 361, 368, 369

Rites of Zhou (*Zhouli* 周禮), 90
Riurikids, 342, 343, 344, 345, 351, 353, 357, 359, 361
roads, 30, 53
    Achaemenid, 60–6, 72
    under Caliphate, 205, 208
    in Mongol Empire, 234, 306
    Roman, 126, 130
    See also communications
Roderic, king of the Visigoths (d. 711 or 712), 187
Roman Empire, 3, 9, 10, 12, 15, 21, 27, 29, 31, 62, 111–37, 141, 163, 166, 167, 180, 267, 343
    achievements of, 111–12
    administration of, 34, 35, 119–21
    and Christianity, 22
    in Christian theology, 164
    communications in, 30
    crisis and decline of, 130–1
    as cultural entity, 135
    expansion of explained, 135–7
    ideology of, 17, 18, 126, 135, 142, 181
    imperialism of, debated, 112–13
    as military monarchy (principate), 125–31
    during Republican period, 26, 113–25
    socioeconomic structure of, 131–4
    successors of, 12
Romanos II (r. 959–63), 148
Romanovs, Romanov dynasty (1613–1917), 263, 351, 357, 359, 361, 362, 363, 365, 366, 368
Rome, city, 27, 29, 31, 35, 111–37, 147, 157, 158, 164, 266, 343
Romulus, 111, 113, 135
Rong Cheng shi 容成氏 (*Mr. Rong Cheng*), 91
Rouran 柔然 Khaganate (402–555), 12
Rum, 189, 240, 247, 261, 264
Rus', 235, 237, 342, 345, 349
    See also Russia
Rus' principalities (in the Mongol Empire), 232
Russia, 2, 15, 27, 36, 248, 249, 319, 342–72
    early history, 346–51
    as Eurasian polity, 248, 249, 354–7, 359–63
    as New Rome, 157
    and the Ottomans, 263, 264
    and Qing, 318, 332
    the rise of Moscow, 351–4
    under Romanovs, 357–63
    spatial dimensions of, 342–5, 363–72
    See also Muscovy; Rus'; Russian Federation; Soviet Union
Russian Federation, 347, 363, 365, 366
Rwanda, 4

Safavids, Safavid Empire, 15, 18, 248, 264–71, 278, 280
    ideology of, 265, 273
    imperial nature of questioned, 264
    origins of, 264
    and the Ottomans, 36, 261, 263, 265, 267–8
al-Saffāḥ, Abbasid Caliph (d. 754), 192
Ṣaffārids, Ṣaffārid dynasty (861–1003), 180, 196, 209
ṣāḥib-qirān (the lord of the conjunction of Jupiter and Saturn), 259
Saka, 54, 55, 68, 269
Salamine, battle of (480 BCE), 67
Salt and Iron Debates, 81 BCE, 101
Sāmānids, Sāmānid dynasty (819–999), 180, 196, 199, 201, 202, 208
Samarqand, 31, 202, 265, 271, 272, 273, 274, 275, 279
Sāmārra, 196
Samnites, 117
Sancisi-Weerdenburg, Heleen, 51
Sanskrit, 278
Sarai, 344, 352
Sardinia, 118
Sardis, 54, 55, 56, 57, 63, 64, 65, 66, 67, 71
Sargon of Akkad, 15, 19
Sarmates, 130
Sasanian Empire (224–651), 12, 21, 130, 160, 161, 162, 163, 167, 180, 183, 185, 187, 189, 190, 205, 245, 247, 266, 267
satraps, 35, 38, 52, 59, 68, 70
Savitskii, P.N., 358
Sayf al-Dawla, Ḥamdānid emir (d. 969), 198, 209
Scheidel, Walter, 154
Scipio Africanus, P. (236–183 BCE), 118
Scythia, Scythians, 19, 55, 56, 62, 127
Sea of Marmara, 68
Sebüktegin (d. 997), 199
The Secret History of the Mongols, 222
secretariats, mobile, Mongol, 231, 234
    See also Mongol empire: administration
Seldon Map, 308
Seleucid empire, 119, 123, 267, 277
Selim I, Ottoman sultan (r. 1512–20), 266
Seljūqs, 166, 181, 199, 201, 202, 203, 261, 264, 268, 270
    See also Oghuz
senate, Roman, 115, 121, 122, 125, 126, 131, 132, 134
Serbia, Serbs, 148
Sertorius, Quintus (d. 72 BCE), 122
Servile War (73–71 BCE), 123
Seville, 242

Shāh 'Abbās I, Safavid ruler (r. 1588–
1629), 267
Shāh Jahān, Moghul ruler (r. 1628–1658)
Shāh Rukh, Timurid ruler (1377–1447), 271
Shāhanshāh. *See* Great Kings, Persian
Shāh-Nāmah, The Book of Kings, 246, 247,
279
Shaibani (Shaibaq) Khan, Uzbek khan (1451–
1510), 269, 272, 273, 274
Shang 商 dynasty (1600–1046 BCE), 10, 80,
81, 82, 287
Shang Yang 商鞅 (d. 338 BCE) and the *Book of
Lord Shang* (*Shangjunshu* 商君書),
85, 88
Shapur I, Sasanian ruler (r. 240–70), 131
Shenyang 瀋陽, 293
shi 士 ("men of service" or "intellectuals,"
China), 84, 87
Shi'ah, Shi'ites, 165, 193, 198, 209, 265, 266,
268, 269, 280
See also Islam; Ismailis
Shuiskii, Prince, contender for Russian throne
(d. 1612), 356
Shulgi, Sumerian king (*c.* 2029–1982 BCE), 15
Shunzhi 順治 Emperor (r. 1643–61), 321
Siberia, 220, 232, 234, 319, 354, 357, 358,
365, 366
Sichuan 四川, 24, 92, 227, 286, 318, 326,
331, 332
Sicily, 118, 121, 151, 158, 165, 198
silk, 155, 344
Silk Road, 99, 272
Sind, 188, 191, 198, 199, 240, 270
Sinicization, 321, 322, 323
Sistan, 196, 205
Skaff, Jonathan Karam, 149
Slavs, 157, 351, 352, 365
Social War (Rome, 91–88 BCE), 122, 131
soft power
Byzantine, 155, 157
Mongol, 244
Sogdiana, 52, 54, 55, 56
Soghdians, 192
Song 宋 dynasty (960–1279), 14, 18, 104, 149,
229, 236, 292
Southern Song (1127–1279), 25, 239
Song Lian 宋濂 (1310–81), 246, 286, 289
Sons of Heaven (*tianzi* 天子), 81, 82, 83, 88,
89, 90, 91, 93, 98, 99, 102, 105,
305, 306
See also emperors: China
South Asia, 15, 24, 267, 270, 271, 275, 277,
280, 284, 286, 292, 296, 306
See also India, Indian subcontinent
South Ossetia, 369

Southeast Asia, 8, 18, 21, 220, 240, 243, 278,
286, 292, 296, 300, 306, 308, 310,
319, 327
sovereignty, 4, 36, 59, 62, 112, 181, 201, 271,
272, 284, 297, 307, 347, 351, 353, 354,
357, 363, 364, 368
Soviet Union, 368, 369
space, imperial, 5, 17, 18, 20, 26, 28, 29, 30, 34,
37, 38, 39, 222, 249
of Achaemenid Empire, 38, 51, 54, 58, 63,
66, 69, 72
in Byzantine Empire, 141, 145, 146
in Caliphate, 181, 203, 213
in China, 18, 37, 80
and Mongols, 220, 222, 232, 236, 245, 249,
288, 319
and Romans, 27
and Russian Empire, 344, 345, 351, 358,
365, 366, 368, 371
Spain, 2, 118, 119, 122, 127, 157, 180, 181,
186, 187, 188, 189, 191, 196, 198,
263, 364
Spartacus (d. 71 BCE), 123
Spirit of Laws (by Montesquieu), 67
Springs-and-Autumns Annals (*Chunqiu* 春
秋), 91
Springs-and-Autumns period, China (Chunqiu
春秋, 770–453 BCE), 83, 85,
89, 92
St Basil's cathedral, 355
St. Petersburg, 361, 365
Stalin, Joseph (1879–1953), 368
steppe belt, 8, 10, 25, 232, 348
and Byzantine Empire, 185
and Caliphate, 189
and China, 25, 28, 93, 96, 97, 99, 102, 103,
104, 105, 249, 290, 292, 293, 296, 298,
299, 300, 301, 303, 305, 309
ecology of, 8, 25, 32, 202, 224
Islam's spread into, 199
manpower deficit in, 228
and Mongols, 28, 221, 227, 229, 237, 239,
248, 249, 344, 349
and Ottomans, 263
and Russia, 27, 249, 347, 357
and Samanids, 198
warfare in, 230, 239
See also: Inner Asia
steppe empires, 8, 12, 14, 25, 201, 220, 222,
223, 237, 358, 359, 369
research of, 222
tribute extraction by, 32
See also: Inner Asia: empires
Strabo, geographer (*c.* 64 BCE–24 CE), 55,
69

strategy, imperial, 24
  Byzantine, 190
  Caliphate, 161, 186, 187, 188
  China, 28
    Han, 99, 103
    Ming, 285, 301, 302, 310
    Qing, 320, 329
  Mongol Empire, 225, 327
  Roman, 27, 112, 136
  Russian, 346, 362, 369
  See also Luttwak, Edward
succession struggles
  in Caliphate, 183, 196, 201
  and Mongols, 223, 234, 235
  in the steppe, 28
Suez Canal, 68
Sufis, 23, 265, 266, 268
Sui 隋 dynasty (581–618), 12
Sulaiman Mts., 24, 270
Süleyman Kanuni, the Magnificent, Ottoman
    sultan (r. 1520–66), 261, 262
Sulla, L. Cornelius (*c.* 138–78 BCE), 122, 125
sultanates, 261, 262, 277, 279
Sulṭāniyya, 237
sultans, 181, 202, 203, 261, 262, 275, 280, 356
Sunni Islam, Sunnites, 165, 193, 202, 266, 269,
    273, 280
Susa, 49, 54, 57, 58, 59, 60, 63, 64, 65
suzerainty, 36, 160, 317
Sweden, Swedes, 356, 366, 372
Syr-Darya (Jaxartes), 55
Syria, 69, 123, 130, 144, 148, 151, 155, 161,
    162, 163, 164, 165, 183, 185, 186, 187,
    188, 189, 190, 191, 192, 193, 198, 209,
    239, 240, 267
Syriac language, 164

Tabriz, 29, 154, 237, 265, 267, 268
Tabula Peutingeriana, 145
Tacitus (58–120), 158
Ṭāhirids (821–73), 180, 196
Taiwan 臺灣, 327, 335
Tāj Mahal, 274
Takht-i Sulayman, the throne of Solomon, 247
Tamukkan, 66, 69
Tang 唐 dynasty (618–907), 12, 14, 24, 105,
    193, 295, 320
Tangier, 244
Tanguts, 248
  See also Xi Xia
Tarentum, 117
Tarim Basin, 29, 316, 320, 324, 328, 329
Tashkent, 272
Tatars, Tatarstan, 248, 294, 349, 352, 356, 357
Taurus Mts., 24, 144, 161, 162, 190

taxation, taxes, 34, 53
  Achaemenid, 58, 67
  in Byzantium, 149
  in Caliphate, 188, 193
  in China, 85, 324
  in Mongol Empire, 232, 345
  in Ottoman Empire, 260
  in Rome, 118, 132
  in Russia, 348
Teb Tengri, 223, 227
technologies, technology, 15
  military, 84, 134, 230, 235, 249, 302, 335
  navigational, 284
Temüjin. *See* Chinggis Khan
Temür (Timur or Tamerlane, 1336–1405), 26,
    242, 271, 272, 274, 275, 277, 352
Tengri (Heaven, Sky God), 21, 223, 227,
    248, 274
  See also Heaven
territoriality, 369
  Ming, 308
  Russia, 348
  See also space, imperial
Tetrarchy, Rome (284–305), 131
Teutoburg Forest, 127
Teutones, 122
textiles, 295
Theophylaktos Simokattes (7th cent.), 160
Three Feudatories (*san fan* 三藩) Rebellion
    (1673–81), 326, 329
thughur (frontline regions), 194, 196
  See also: frontiers
Tiber, 111, 113, 125
Tibet, 14, 24, 25, 28, 31, 37, 106, 227, 232, 234,
    236, 243, 245, 246, 286, 288, 290, 305,
    316, 317, 318, 320, 324, 326, 328, 330,
    331, 332
Tibull (*c.* 55–19 BCE), 111
Tiglath-pileser I (1114–1076 BCE), 19
Tigris River, 69
Time of Troubles, Russia (1598–1613), 356
Timurids, empire of, 15, 31, 257, 259, 262, 265,
    271, 272, 273, 274, 275, 276, 278, 279,
    280, 290
Titus Quinctius Flaminius (*c.* 229–174 BCE),
    119
Toghan-Temür (1320–70, r. 1333–70), (a.k.a.
    Shundi 順帝 "The Obedient Emperor"),
    289, 292
tolerance, 333, 362, 371
Tolui (d.1232), Toluids, 236
topography, 8, 18, 23, 24, 25, 30, 39, 71, 96,
    241, 268, 290, 318, 344, 348, 351, 352,
    369, 371
Torghuts (Kalmyks), 329

trade, 32
  Byzantine, 160
  Caliphate, 204
  China, 204
    Han, 99, 102
    Ming, 284, 290, 292, 293, 294, 302, 303,
      305, 306, 307, 308, 310
    Qing, 328, 333, 337
  European in Asia, 306, 307
  maritime, 306, 307, 333
  Mongol Empire, 230, 244, 306, 350
  Mughal, 278
  Ottoman, 278
  Roman, 117, 118, 133, 134
  routes, 29, 116, 237, 294, 306, 308, 346, 348,
    353, 371
  Russian, 342
  Safavid, 278
  See also: commerce, merchants, Silk Road
Trajan (r. 98–117), 31, 127, 128
Transoxiana, 189, 192, 196, 199, 201, 205, 266,
  269, 270, 271, 272, 273, 274, 275, 276,
  277, 278, 279
travelogues, 39, 244
Treatise of the Unified Realm of the Great Yuan
  (Da Yuan yitongzhi大元一統志),
  241, 287
Treatise of the United Realm of the Great Ming
  (Da Ming yitongzhi 大明一統志), 295
tribe, tribal, 28, 31, 117, 119, 128, 188,
  191, 192, 213, 222, 223, 224, 228,
  232, 234, 246, 259, 261, 264, 265,
  266, 269, 271, 276, 347, 352, 353,
  356, 357
tribute, tribute system
  in Achaemenid Empire, 54, 56, 68
  under Alexander the Great, 60
  in Byzantine Empire, 162
  in Caliphate, 162, 190, 196
  in China, 90, 91, 103, 105, 243, 287
    Han, 37, 102
    Ming, 294, 297, 306
    Qing, 317, 321, 333
  in Mongol Empire, 234, 344, 350, 353
  in the steppe, 32
Trimalchio, 134
triumphs, Rome, 116, 127, 136
Trogus, Pompeius (1st century BCE), 123
tsars, 332, 347, 354, 355, 356, 361
Tsewang Rabtan (d. 1727), 328
Tumu 土木 Incident (1449), 300
tundra, 358
Turan, 269
Turfan, 303, 326
Türgesh, 189

Turkestan, 231, 232
Turkic Khaganate, 12, 21, 33, 163, 222
  See also Gök-Türks
Turkmenistan, 187, 236
Turks, 161, 185, 187, 192, 198, 202, 203, 213,
  223, 243, 248, 259, 270
  See also Oghuz Turks; Ottomans; Seljuqs;
    Turkic Khaganate
tusi 土司 (indigenous leaders, Chinese empire),
  37, 332, 335, 336
Tyre, 19

Uighur Khaganate (744–840), 14
Uighur script, 230
Uighuristan, 286
Uighurs, 223, 248, 289, 358
Ukraine, 236, 344, 365, 368, 369
'ulamā, Muslim scholars, 260
  See also clerics
Ulugh Beg Kābulī (d. 1502), 272
Ulugh Beg Samarqandī (1394–1449), 271
ulus (Mongolian: nation, state), 220, 221, 234,
  235, 236, 237, 239, 240, 242, 244,
  245, 350
'Umar, Caliph (d. 634–644), 183, 186
al-'Umari, (d. 1349), 240
Umayyad Caliphate (660–750), 19, 21, 23, 26,
  167, 180–93, 194, 204, 213
Umayyad Caliphate, in Spain, 198
United States of America, 2, 3, 4, 279
unity, political, 17
  of the Achaemenid realm, 54
  of China, 20, 79, 80, 82, 83, 87, 88, 89, 91,
    96, 104, 106, 300
  Chinggisid, 221, 236
  of dar al-Islam, 194, 205, 208
  of Iranian world (Iranshahr), 205
  of the Mongol Empire, 352
  in the steppe, 21, 222
  See also Great Unity ideal
universalism, universal rule, 7–8, 9, 14, 15–21,
  38, 39, 79, 168, 259
  and Achaemenids, 54
  and Byzantine Empire, 144, 148, 166
  and Caliphate, 187, 188, 194, 213
  in China, 37, 80, 87, 90, 91, 96, 106, 305
    Han, 97, 99
    Ming, 299
    Qin, 93–6
    Qing, 329, 334
    Western Zhou, 82
  in Mongol Empire, 222, 227–9, 235, 240–4,
    248, 249, 259, 285, 286
  and Ottomans, 259
  and Romans, 127, 128, 130, 135, 137, 148

universalism, universal rule (cont.)
   and Safavids, 264
   and Turks, 202, 203, 213, 259
Urals, 347
Uriyangkhai, 329
'Uthmān, Caliph (r. 644–656), 183, 186
Uxians, 60, 62, 69
Uzbekistan, Uzbeks, 37, 248, 269, 270, 271,
      272, 273, 275, 276, 279, 280, 281, 305
Uzun Ḥasan (r. 1453–78), 265

Vajravarmi (d. 1381), 292
Vasilij (Vasily) I of Moscow
      (r. 1389–1425), 157
Vedas, 278
Veii, 114, 115, 116
Venice, 158, 244, 263, 306
Verres (*c*. 120–43 BCE), 121
Vienna, 141, 263
Vietnam, 2, 25, 37, 96, 105, 231, 239, 296, 300,
      307, 318, 319, 327, 328
Vikings, 371
violence, 80, 230, 299, 302, 306, 307, 354
Virgil (70–19 BCE), 111, 127, 148
Visigoths, 187
Vladimir, Grand Prince of Kievan Rus'
      (r. 980–1015), 347
Volga River, 220, 221, 235, 329, 342, 344, 346,
      347, 349, 350, 351, 352, 353, 355, 357

walls
   in Byzantine Empire, 144
   in China, 28, 85, 96, 98, 103, 104, 105,
      106, 302
   Parthian-Sasanian, 269
   in Roman empire, 128, 137
war, warfare, 1, 25, 26, 161, 348
   of Achaemenids, 49, 69
   of Byzantine Empire, 151, 154, 161, 162,
      185, 187
   of Caliphate, 165, 188, 194
   in China, 83, 86
      Han, 99
      Qin, 97
      Qing, 334
      Warring States, 86
   of Mongols, 27, 222, 230, 239, 240,
      265, 329
   in Rome, 27, 112, 127, 130, 136, 142
      republican, 114, 115, 117, 119, 121, 122
   in Russia, 366
   See also armies; civil wars; *dar al-harb*;
      ghaza; holy war; *jihād*; military
Warring States period, China (Zhanguo 戰國
      453–221 BCE), 20, 86, 87, 88, 89, 92

Wāsit, 205
Waṣṣāf (Vassaf) (d. after 1329), 228,
      229, 239
Wei 渭 River, 80
Wittek, Paul, 260
world conquest, 127, 222, 239, 241, 244,
      247, 274
   See also universalism
World War I (1914–18), 2, 260
World War II (1939–45), 2, 368
Wu 吳, state of (till 473 BCE), 92

Xanthos, 53
Xenophon (*c*. 440–355 BCE), 30, 49, 54, 62,
      63, 66, 71
Xerxes I (4. 486–65 BCE), 70
Xi Xia 西夏 (1038–227), 225, 246
   See also Tanguts
Xinjiang 新疆, 28, 29, 31, 37, 99, 102, 201,
      234, 237, 248, 272, 316, 319, 324, 326,
      329, 331, 336
Xiongnu 匈奴 empire, 10, 12, 14, 21, 96, 97,
      98, 99, 101, 102, 103
Xuande 宣德 Emperor (r. 1425–35), 300, 301
Xunzi 荀子 (died after 238 BCE), 91
Xusrō (Chosro/Khusrau) II (r. 590–628), 160

Yangzi (Changjiang 長江), 80, 92
yarghuchi (Mongol judge), 224, 237
Yeke Monggol Ulus (The Great Mongol
      Nation), 221, 225, 234, 247
Yellow River (Huanghe 黃河), 80, 82, 85,
      95, 105
Yelü Chucai 耶律楚材 (1189–1243), 232
Yemen, 164, 180, 198, 204
Yongle Emperor 永樂 (r. 1402–24), 296, 297,
      298, 299, 300, 301, 302
   as Prince of Yan 燕王, 297, 298
Yongzheng 雍正 Emperor (r. 1723–35), 106,
      318, 328, 332, 333, 335
Yu 禹, demiurge, 89, 91
Yuan 元 dynasty (1271–1368), 25, 27, 106,
      220, 221, 240–7, 286–92, 294, 295,
      297, 305, 319, 320, 343
   See also Mongols
Yue 越, state of (till *c*. 300 BCE), 92, 96
Yugoslavia, 4
Yunas Khan (1416–87), 272
Yunnan 雲南, 99, 105, 227, 241, 245, 246, 286,
      287, 288, 290, 292, 294, 295, 305, 331,
      332, 335

Zagros Mts., 24, 38, 60, 62
al-Ẓāhir, Fatimid Caliph (r. 1021–35), 165
Zama, 118

Zheng He 鄭和 (d. 1433), 296
Zhengde 正德 Emperor (r. 1506–21), 301
Zhengtong 正統 Emperor (r. 1436–49), 300, 301
Zhongshan 中山, state of (till 296 BCE), 92
Zhou 周 dynasty (c. 1046–255 BCE), 10, 18, 83, 85, 89, 92, 93, 287
  ritual culture of, 85
  sage kings of, 87, 91

Western Zhou period (c. 1046–771 BCE), 80–3, 90, 94, 104
Zhu Di 朱棣 (1360–1424). See Yongle Emperor (r. 1402–24)
Zhu Siben 朱思本 (1273–1336?), 287
Zhu Yuanzhang 朱元璋 (1328–98). See Hongwu Emperor
Zohak, 268
Zungaria, 234
  See also Junghars

CPSIA information can be obtained
at www.ICGtesting.com
Printed in the USA
LVHW081740140321
681516LV00003B/22